The Definitive Guide to SUSE Linux Enterprise Server

Sander van Vugt

The Definitive Guide to SUSE Linux Enterprise Server

Copyright © 2007 by Sander van Vugt

Softcover reprint of the hardcover 1st edition 2007

ISBN 978-1-4302-1167-9

Lead Editors: Jason Gilmore and Keir Thomas
Technical Reviewer: Rob Bastiaansen
Editorial Board: Steve Anglin, Ewan Buckingham, Gary Cornell, Jason Gilmore, Jonathan Gennick, Jonathan Hassell, James Huddleston, Chris Mills, Matthew Moodie, Dominic Shakeshaft, Jim Sumser, Keir Thomas, Matt Wade
Project Manager: Denise Santoro Lincoln
Copy Edit Manager: Nicole Flores
Copy Editor: Kim Wimpsett
Assistant Production Director: Kari Brooks-Copony
Production Editor: Ellie Fountain
Compositor: Linda Weidemann, Wolf Creek Press
Proofreader: Elizabeth Berry
Indexer: Julie Grady
Artist: Kinetic Publishing Services, LLC
Cover Designer: Kurt Krames
Manufacturing Director: Tom Debolski

Distributed to the book trade worldwide by Springer-Verlag New York, Inc., 233 Spring Street, 6th Floor, New York, NY 10013. Phone 1-800-SPRINGER, fax 201-348-4505, e-mail orders-ny@springer-sbm.com, or visit http://www.springeronline.com.

For information on translations, please contact Apress directly at 2560 Ninth Street, Suite 219, Berkeley, CA 94710. Phone 510-549-5930, fax 510-549-5939, e-mail info@apress.com, or visit http://www.apress.com.

This book is dedicated to my oldest son, Franck.
Alex, the next one will be yours.

Contents at a Glance

PART 1 ▪ ▪ ▪ Getting Familiar with SUSE Linux Enterprise Server

PART 2 ▪ ▪ ▪ Administering SUSE Linux Enterprise Server

PART 3 ■ ■ ■ Networking SUSE Linux Enterprise Server

PART 4 ■ ■ ■ Advanced SUSE Linux Enterprise Server Configuration

Contents

PART 1 ■■■ Getting Familiar with SUSE Linux Enterprise Server

PART 2 ▪▪▪ Administering SUSE Linux Enterprise Server

PART 3 ■ ■ ■ Networking SUSE Linux Enterprise Server

PART 4 ▪▪▪ Advanced SUSE Linux Enterprise Server Configuration

About the Author

 SANDER VAN VUGT performed his first Linux installation in 1992. Since then, he has been an enthusiastic Linux user, working with it on a professional basis since 1995. Sander is an independent trainer and consultant living in the Netherlands. He has worked professionally everywhere from Singapore to San Francisco (and is willing to cover the rest of the planet as well). Sander is a Novell-certified trainer for the SUSE Linux Advanced Technical Trainer program and is authorized to teach most other Novell technical courses as well. In addition to being a trainer, he is an author, having written more than 30 books and hundreds of technical articles. Sander is also working as a volunteer for the LPI organization, contributing topics for the LPIC-3 certification. Most important of all, Sander is the father of Alex and Franck and the loving husband of Florence. You can reach Sander via his website at http://www.sandervanvugt.com or via e-mail at mail@sandervanvugt.nl.

About the Technical Reviewer

 **ROB BASTIAANSEN** is an independent consultant, trainer, and author. Rob has a strong focus on Linux and NetWare, clustering services, eDirectory, and ZENworks. He delivers advanced technical training for Novell in EMEA regarding these topics. Rob is also a technical writer; he writes for several IT magazines in the Netherlands, where he lives. VMware is another area in which Rob works as a consultant and trainer. In 2004, Rob wrote and published his first book, *Rob's Guide to Using VMware* (Books4brains, 2004), and a second edition was published in 2005. In 2005, he published *The NetWare Toolbox* (Books4brains, 2005). He is a master-certified Novell instructor; he has all the major Novell certifications, including Certified Linux Professional; and he is LPI level 1 certified.

Acknowledgments

Although my name is the only one printed on the cover of this book, this book is the result of some fine teamwork, and I would like to thank everyone who was part of that team for all their efforts. First I'd like to thank Jason Gilmore, who had enough trust to start this project. Then I'd like to thank Keir Thomas for taking over the role of responsible editor while at the halfway point of this project. The work of both of them has definitely made this a much better book. Next, I'd like to thank my technical editor and friend Rob Bastiaansen for some very valuable tips and comments that helped improve this book. Next, I want to thank Denise Santoro Lincoln, the project manager, who with patience and kindness helped me complete this book in a timely manner. Next I'd like to thank Kim Wimpsett, who had the—I hope not too difficult—task of transforming my manuscript into easy-to-read English prose. Last but not least, I'd like to thank Florence, Franck, and Alex for their support. Even if they didn't modify a word in this book, without their help I wouldn't have been able to complete it.

Introduction

This book is about SUSE Linux Enterprise Server 10. With SUSE Linux Enterprise Server 10, Novell launched the best professional Linux server operating system ever, based on work that started more than 10 years ago by the people from SUSE in Germany. With this software, Novell has managed to create an easy-to-manage yet very complete, robust, and versatile operating system that can perform a broad range of tasks everywhere within a company.

This book is meant as a complete work, helping people who have never worked with Linux before to set up a functional server while also helping advanced administrators of SUSE Linux by providing some details about new functionality and about some of the most complex parts of SUSE Linux.

Who This Book Is For

This book was written for new as well as experienced administrators of SUSE Linux Enterprise Server. The first part of the book contains some introduction-level material that new administrators will like, and the last part of the book contains some advanced information aimed at experienced Linux administrators. Everything in between was written to help the reader set up all the important services on SUSE Linux Enterprise Server. Because of its broad approach, this book is an indispensable reference guide for everyone administrating SUSE Linux Enterprise Server.

How This Book Is Structured

This book is divided into four parts, with a total of no less than 35 chapters.

Part 1: Getting Familiar with SUSE Linux Enterprise Server

As the name suggests, this part is for people who are new to SUSE Linux Enterprise Server and even for people who haven't worked with Linux before. In this part, you'll learn how to install SUSE Linux Enterprise Server and understand the way it is structured. This part includes information about working from the GNOME graphical user interface, working with the file system, and working with the management utility YaST.

Part 2: Administering SUSE Linux Enterprise Server

In this part, you'll get in-depth information about generic SUSE Linux administration tasks. This part starts with a discussion of Linux users and groups management. This is followed by a chapter about working with file and directory permissions. Next, two chapters cover all the important tasks related to managing the file system. Then you'll learn how to manage software. Next, I'll cover system initialization, process management, and system logging.

Part 3: Networking SUSE Linux Enterprise Server

In this part, you'll get detailed information about the most important network services and how to set them up in a SUSE Linux Enterprise Server environment. At the start of this part, you'll learn how to configure the network interface. This part covers popular services such as Apache, DNS, DHCP, Postfix, and Squid, as well as some essential network functionality such as remote access. In addition, this part covers setting up an LDAP server and managing cryptography. Finally, I'll discuss the topics of remote access, NTP time synchronization, and the CUPS print server.

Part 4: Advanced SUSE Linux Enterprise Server Configuration

After reading the first three parts of this book, you'll be able to install and manage a completely functional SUSE Linux Enterprise Server. In this part of this book, I'll discuss some of the more advanced tasks. The chapters in this part cover tasks that are not essential but that make your SUSE Linux Enterprise Server a lot more useful. You will find chapters about tasks that will make you a better system administrator, such as kernel and hardware management, shell scripting, optimization, troubleshooting, and firewall configuration. Also, I'll cover some new technologies such as Heartbeat clustering, AppArmor application security, and Xen virtualization. Finally, I'll cover some useful techniques such as creating an installation server and working with the Service Location Protocol.

Prerequisites

To get the most out of this book, you should have a copy of SUSE Linux Enterprise Server at hand. You can download this for free from http://www.novell.com/download.

Contacting the Author

You can reach the author of this book by e-mail at mail@sandervanvugt.nl or on the Web at http://www.sandervanvugt.com.

PART 1

■ ■ ■

Getting Familiar with SUSE Linux Enterprise Server

This book is divided into four parts. This first part is for people who are new to Linux in general or SUSE Linux Enterprise Server in particular. The first chapter describes how to install SUSE Linux Enterprise Server. After that, Chapters 2 through 4 show you how to navigate the SUSE Linux Enterprise Server interface. These chapters will be especially interesting to users not only new to SUSE Linux but also new to Linux, since this part covers many Linux basics.

■ ■ ■

## CHAPTER 1

Installing SUSE Linux Enterprise Server

This chapter teaches you everything you need to know to properly install SUSE Linux Enterprise Server 10.

Meeting the Installation Requirements

Before you can start installing SUSE Linux Enterprise Server 10, you need a computer that meets the minimal requirements. The following are the minimal system requirements:

- A CPU that runs at 1GHz or better
- 256MB RAM
- A network card
- A CD drive
- 4GB of available disk space

Although such a configuration would be fine in a test lab, you may think it is rather minimal. Indeed, if you're planning on running SUSE in an even mildly critical environment, you should greatly improve upon these minimum specifications. As for the CPU, it doesn't need to be an Intel i386 CPU. SUSE Linux Enterprise Server runs on almost all hardware platforms, from i386 to the IBM Z series. In this book, however, I will assume you are installing on i386 architecture or compatible (such as AMD).

Starting the Installation

In the "old days" to install a server, you needed to insert a CD in the CD drive and boot from the CD. For SUSE Linux Enterprise Server, this is not the only option. In addition to installing it from a CD, you can start the installation from a boot image delivered by an installation server.

Using a bootable CD is the most common installation method. If you need to install many servers, you may be able to use an installation server. Chapter 35 covers this subject in detail.

After booting from the installation device, you will see the installation welcome screen, as shown in Figure 1-1. Note that on this screen, the option Boot from Hard Disk is selected by default; this prevents you from starting a new installation by accident if you forget to remove the installation medium from the drive after adding some packages.

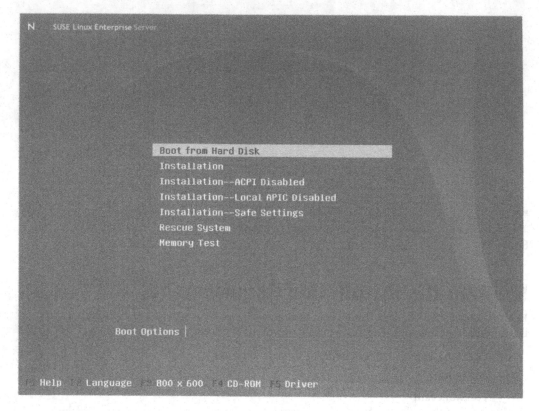

Figure 1-1. *In the installation menu, the option Boot from Hard Disk is selected by default.*

The menu offers four installation options; under normal circumstances, you should select the Installation option. If that doesn't work, you can try one of the safe options; the Installation—Safe Settings option is the simplest way of booting your installation system. You cannot use the Rescue System option for installation; it is for troubleshooting a server that has already been installed. You can use the last option—Memory Test—to diagnose the RAM chips in your server and exclude faulty RAM chips from usage.

In addition to the options in the installation menu, the welcome screen offers some other options. In particular, an important element is the Boot Options prompt. Using this prompt you can enter any option you want to pass to the kernel when starting the installation. Usually this is the work of an expert; in other words, don't use it if you don't know exactly what you're doing.

Tip Having problems starting the graphical installation? Use the option x11i=fbdev at the Boot Options prompt. This starts a generic driver for your graphics hardware known as the *frame buffer device*. This allows the graphical installation to start in almost all cases.

On the bottom of the welcome screen, you see the five function keys you can use to tune the installation:

F1: Press this key to display help about the installation procedure.

F2: Press this key to change the language of the installation program.

F3: Press this key if you need to change the resolution of the installation program. Usually the installer selects the best resolution for your hardware automatically. If that doesn't work, from this menu you can select any supported resolution. If you are having problems with the graphical installation, select Text Mode. This runs the installation in text mode without the graphical interface. Note that this is the same installation as the one used in graphical mode; it just looks different.

F4: Press this key to select the installation source. Currently, six different sources are supported:

- *CD-ROM*: This option installs from either a CD or a DVD.

- *SLP*: This option uses the Service Location Protocol (check Chapter 33 for more details) to locate an installation server automatically and use it.

- *FTP*: Select this option if you want to use an FTP server for installation.

- *HTTP*: This option allows you to install from an HTTP server.

- *NFS*: If your network has an NFS server offering the installation files, use this option to start the installation from it.

- *SMB/CIFS*: Use this option if the installation files are on a share on a Samba or Windows server.

F5: This option opens a prompt where you can load an additional driver. Use this option if you need a specific driver to support the device on which you want to install.

After selecting the way you want to install, press Enter. This will load the installation kernel and bring you to the next phase of the installation procedure. While loading the kernel, you will see a blue screen with the text *SUSE Linux Enterprise Server* on it. This isn't very helpful if you want to know exactly what is happening. To close this screen, press the Escape key. You'll then see information about what is happening, as shown in Figure 1-2. If something goes wrong, you'll see information about what part of the installation went wrong.

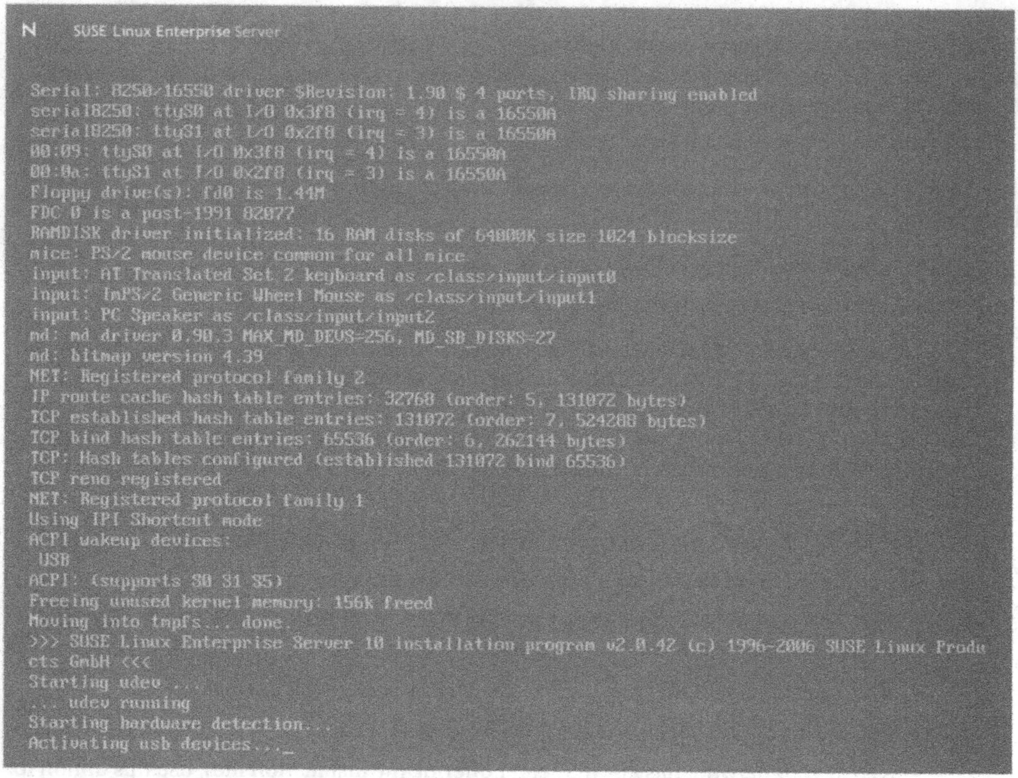

Figure 1-2. *Hit the Escape key when the kernel is loading to see more details.*

Preparing the Installation

When the installation kernel has loaded, the preliminary phase of the installation process begins. As the first step of this phase, you need to select the language you want to work with (see Figure 1-3). For support reasons, I recommend using English (US) or German, but if so required, you can choose another local language. In that case, you should be aware that although much is translated into a local language, not everything is localized, so you will still see some elements in English. After selecting the language you want to use, click Next to continue.

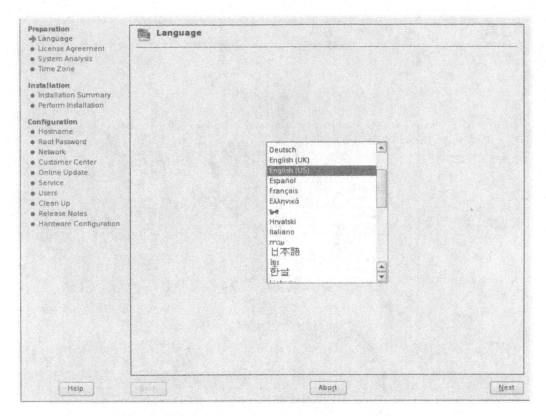

Figure 1-3. *For support reasons, it is best to install your server in English (US).*

Note Since Novell's support system is internationalized, it supports only English (US) and German. (After all, SUSE has German roots.) If you really need to run it in another language, check with your local Novell contact to learn more about the possibilities.

After selecting the language, read and accept the license agreement, as shown in Figure 1-4.

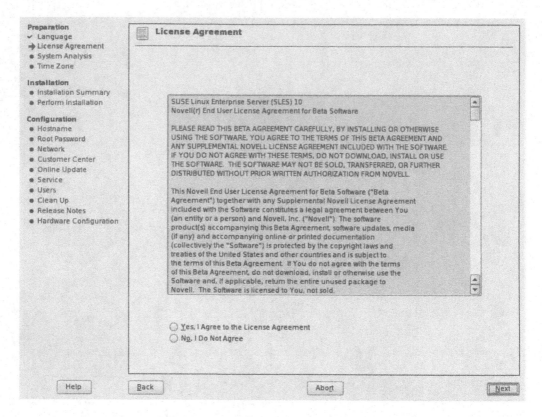

Figure 1-4. *You must accept the license agreement to proceed with the installation.*

As shown in Figure 1-5, now you can indicate the preferred installation mode. If nothing is installed on your server's hard drive, you must select New Installation. On an installed server that contains a previous version of SUSE Linux Enterprise Server, you can select the Update option. This option will install new versions of existing packages on your server. If you have add-on products you want to install during the installation procedure, select the Include Add-On Products from Separate Media option. Also, clicking the Other button will present some useful options, including Repair an Installed System. This option allows you to start an automatic troubleshooting module that helps you find any existing problems on your server and repair them automatically. You'll learn more about this in Chapter 34. In this chapter, I'll assume you want to perform a new installation; therefore, select New Installation, and then click Next to proceed.

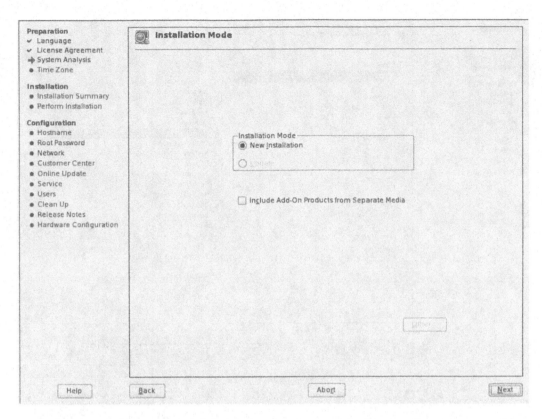

Figure 1-5. *In addition to a new installation, you can update an existing server that contains an older version of SUSE Linux Enterprise Server.*

Now, to finish preparing the installation, you can specify the region and time zone you are in (see Figure 1-6). After doing this, you need to set the hardware clock of your server. Linux servers often are set to UTC so that all clocks on servers—no matter where on Earth they are—can communicate the same time. If for whatever reason you don't want that, you can use local time on the hardware clock. You should be aware that no matter what clock setting you specify, the software clock you'll see on your server will always indicate local time. Based on the Region and Time Zone settings, local time is calculated as an offset to UTC. After selecting the clock type you want to use, you can also change the current time setting. Be sure to do this only after setting the hardware clock to local time or UTC; otherwise, you might get confused about the type of time currently in use on your server. After specifying the time settings you want to use, click Next to continue.

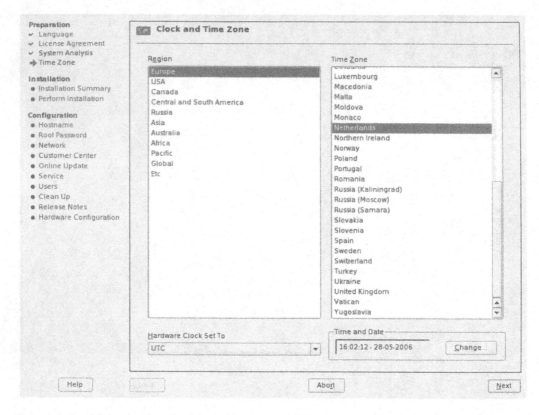

Figure 1-6. *In addition to selecting the proper time zone, you also need to set what time you use on the hardware clock of your server.*

Selecting What to Install

After preparing for the installation, the real part of the installation begins. At this time, you specify the settings you want to use. As you can see in Figure 1-7, this part of the installation offers you two tabs. The Overview tab contains the most commonly used options. The Expert tab contains all options that you can tune during the installation.

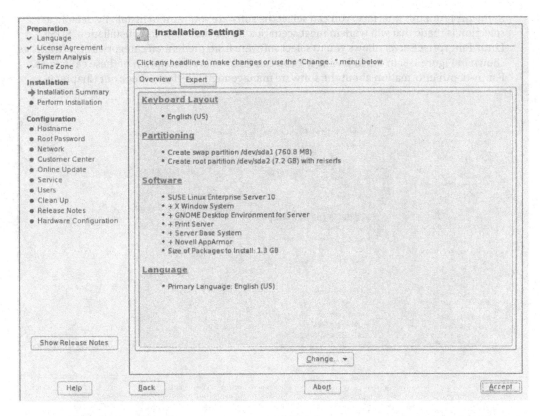

Figure 1-7. *To make installing the server as easy as possible, the most commonly used settings are available on the Overview tab.*

The following installation settings are available:

System (Expert tab): Under this option, you can see all system settings that were detected automatically. Normally, the probe module that finds this information is accurate. If you do find an error, check the functioning of the hardware in your computer.

Keyboard Layout: Use this option to define the layout of the keyboard that is used on your server.

Partitioning: Use this option to define something other than the default partitioning scheme. By default, one root partition is created as a traditional partition. The size of this partition is all the available disk space minus the amount of disk space needed for the swap partition. By default, a swap partition of 1.5 times the amount of physical RAM present in your server is created, with a maximum of 1GB. This is because anything more than 1GB of swap can't be used anyway, so it doesn't make sense to create a bigger swap partition. SUSE Linux Enterprise Server 10 can work with logical volumes managed by LVM and EVMS as well. In Chapter 8 you can read how to create these partitions.

Add-On Products (Expert tab): Use this option to select any add-on products you want to install while installing your server.

Software: From this interface, you can select the software you want to install. By default, a selection is made that will work in most scenarios. To facilitate software installation, SUSE Linux Enterprise Server allows you to select software from predefined categories of software, as shown in Figure 1-8. In the following list you can find a short description of these categories. For in-depth information about the software management interface, check out Chapter 9.

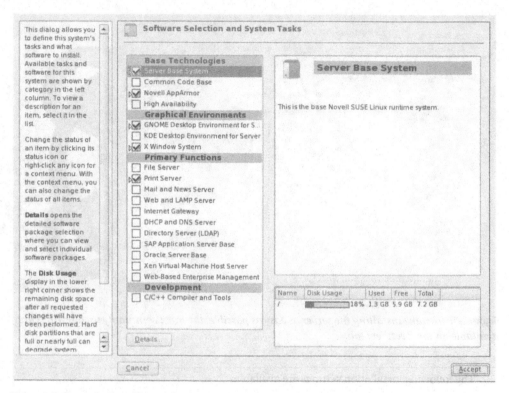

Figure 1-8. *To make installing software easy, the installation program allows you to select from some predefined categories of software.*

- *Server Base System:* You always need this; it contains the base packages of your server.

- *Common Code Base:* SUSE Linux is compliant to Linux Standard Base (LSB) 3.0. If this compliancy is important for you, make sure to select this option.

Note The LSB project is an ongoing effort to standardize the structure of Linux operating systems so that a method that works on one distribution can be used on other distributions as well. Check http://www.linuxbase.org for more details about this project.

- *Novell AppArmor:* AppArmor is a Novell application security solution that helps you prevent unauthorized use of applications. This software category is selected by default. In Chapter 32 you'll learn more about AppArmor.

- *High Availability*: SUSE Linux Enterprise Server includes the Linux Heartbeat 2 software, which allows you to make a fail-over cluster. In Chapter 29 you can read more about the configuration of this cluster.

- *GNOME Desktop Environment for Server*: SUSE Linux Enterprise Server uses the GNOME desktop environment as the default graphical desktop. As an alternative, you can use the KDE desktop. See Chapter 2 for more details about the graphical desktop.

- *KDE Desktop Environment for Server*: On SUSE Linux Enterprise Server, you can choose for yourself what graphical environment you want to use. By default, only the GNOME desktop environment is installed. If you want to work with tools from both graphical environments, select this option. If you just want the KDE graphical interface, select KDE Desktop Environment for Server, and make sure the GNOME Desktop Environment for Server option is deselected.

- *X Window System*: No matter what graphical environment you want to use, you'll always need the X Window System. This is the graphical engine that sits under the graphical desktop environment. I recommend you always install it; you will also need it if you don't want to run a graphical interface by default. If for whatever reason you need to run some graphical utilities later on your server, you need the X-server because it is the motor underneath all graphical screens.

- *File Server*: Select this option if you want to use your server to offer shared files to users. This option selects popular file servers such as Samba and NFS.

- *Print Server*: On SUSE Linux Enterprise Server, CUPS is used as the default print system. Select this option to make your server a print server that can share printers with clients.

- *Mail and News Server*: This option selects the Postfix mail server, and everything related to it, and the news server that allows you to set up your server to create news groups.

- *Web and LAMP Server*: Use this if you need Apache, MySQL, and PHP to offer web-based services to users.

- *Internet Gateway*: If you want to replace your Cisco router with a Linux server, select this option. It will install the Squid proxy and the iptables-based firewall, and it allows your server to function as a VPN server.

- *DHCP and DNS Server*: Select this service if you need DNS and DHCP on your network.

- *Directory Server (LDAP)*: OpenLDAP is the default directory server for SUSE Linux. This option, which is selected by default, makes sure the OpenLDAP LDAP server is installed. I recommend leaving it selected, because many services depend on it.

- *SAP Application Server Base*: You can use SUSE Linux Enterprise Server as an application server running SAP. If you plan to install SAP on your server, the software in the category makes sure everything needed to run SAP is present.

- *Oracle Server Base*: SAP is not the only commercial application you can run on SUSE Linux Enterprise Server. Novell offers some predefined profiles to allow you to run Oracle. Select this category if you plan on installing Oracle later.

- *Xen Virtual Machine Host Server*: Virtualization is one of the major trends in the data center. For that purpose, SUSE Linux Enterprise Server comes with all software that can make your server a host for other virtual servers running on top of it and using the Xen virtualization software. Enable this option, and review Chapter 31 if you plan on using Xen.

- *Web-Based Enterprise Management*: In SUSE Linux Enterprise Server, the Cimom standard allows for web-based enterprise management. Cimom is not a tool itself; it is a standard that can be used by the tools you plan to use to manage your server. Since it is becoming important as a standard, it is a good idea to install this software category as well.

- *C/C++ Compiler and Tools*: Usually, you shouldn't use a server as a development platform. This is because the tools needed to develop software decrease the security level of your server. If, however, you need the ability to compile software or modify some kernel modules based on the kernel sources, make sure this option is selected.

Booting: SUSE Linux Enterprise Server uses the GRUB boot loader to start an operating system on your server. By default, this boot loader is selected in the master boot record of your server. See Chapter 10 if you want to tune the way your server boots.

Time Zone: Earlier, you entered everything required for the time configuration of your server. If you made a mistake, you can correct it by using this option.

Language: Select this option if you need to change the server language you selected earlier.

Default Runlevel: By default, SUSE Linux Enterprise Server starts in its complete graphical mode, the so-called runlevel 5. If you don't need this, use this option to start the nongraphical runlevel 3 as the default. From this runlevel, you can always start a graphical environment later (if the required software is installed) by using the startx command.

After selecting all the settings you want to use for installation, click Next. You will see a pop-up window in which you have to confirm you really want to start the installation. Up to this moment, nothing has changed on your server, and you can still back out. If you click Install on this screen, your server's hard drive will be formatted, and the installation will start. From that moment on, there is no return.

After clicking the Install button, the software packages will be installed to your server. If your installation media requires it, you will be prompted to change media. When all files are copied, your server will restart, and you can configure the server you've just installed.

Tip Usually, the installation runs smoothly. If, however, you encounter problems, it is good to know you can open a virtual console while running the installation. Do this by pressing Ctrl+Alt, followed by a function key. Any function key from F1 to F6 will give you access to a virtual console where you can tune what happens and troubleshoot the installation if necessary.

Configuring the Server

When all software has been copied to your server, it's time to configure. The steps required to do this start automatically. As you can see in Figure 1-9, you first need to enter the host name and DNS domain name. By default, a random host name is used, and "site" is used for the DNS domain. This is because the default value also specifies that DHCP changes the host name automatically, if you have a DHCP server available that is set up to do this for you. You should definitely enter a real host name and DNS domain name here, especially since quite a lot of other services you will install later depend on these names. After specifying the host and domain name, click Next to continue.

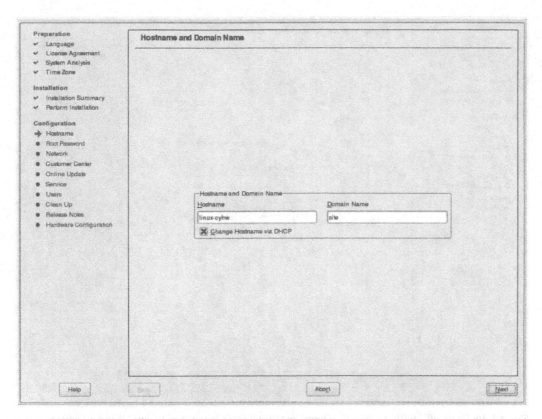

Figure 1-9. *If you don't specify something else to happen, the name of your server is generated randomly.*

As you can see in Figure 1-10, you next need to enter the password you want to use for the user root. Since root is the almighty administrator of your server, you should be serious about this password and choose something complicated. A complex password is at least six characters and has a mix of uppercase and lowercase letters and digits. If so required, you can select options on the Expert tab that allow you to choose between three password encryption algorithms. By default, the Blowfish algorithm is selected. This is the most secure algorithm, and it allows you to work with strong passwords that are longer than eight characters. If for any reason you can't use these strong passwords (for example because one of the applications used on your server cannot handle them), you can select DES or MD5 as an alternative. After specifying the password you want to use, click Next to continue.

■Caution If after clicking Next you get a warning that the password is too simple, think twice before you click Yes. A weak password for the user root compromises your system's security severely, so change it to something safe now.

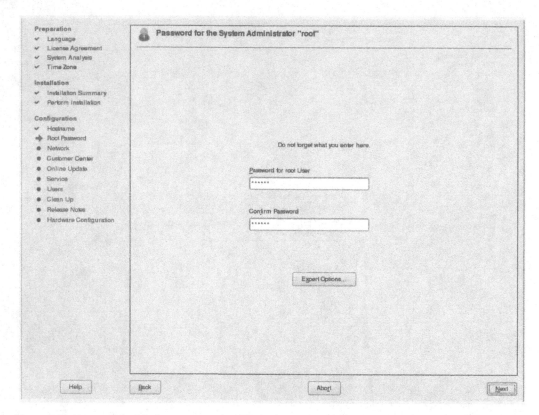

Figure 1-10. *Be careful with the root password because it gives you access to everything on your server.*

The next step in the setup procedure is important. In this step you will configure the network. On the screen shown in Figure 1-11, several options are available.

Tip You can tune all the options available from the Network Configuration screen later with the YaST management program as well. (YaST stands for *yet another setup tool.*) Since most services store the IP address of your server somewhere in their configuration files, however, you should set the communications settings now and keep them that way.

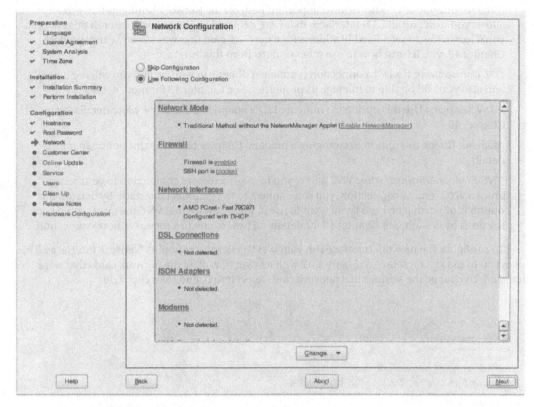

Figure 1-11. *The configuration of the network interface is one of the most important parts of your server's configuration.*

The following are your options:

Network Mode: This option specifies whether you want to use the NetworkManager applet. This applet sits in the taskbar of your server and allows you to turn the network configuration on and off easily. Although this is useful for a desktop computer running SUSE Linux Enterprise Desktop that needs to switch between a wired network and a wireless network often; for most servers, this is not an important feature. Therefore, the NetworkManager applet is off by default.

Firewall: By default the firewall on your server is enabled and blocks access to all services offered by your server. If you don't like that, you can change it here by clicking the Enabled link. In this book, I'll assume your firewall is disabled by default. In Chapter 30, you'll learn how to work with the firewall.

Network Interfaces: This is the most important item on the Network Configuration screen: it allows you to set up all LAN interfaces that were detected on your server. Later in this chapter, you'll learn how to set a fixed IP address for a network card that was already discovered. In Chapter 13, you'll learn how to use other options from this interface.

DSL Connections: If a DSL connection is attached directly to your server, you will see it here, and also you will be able to manage its properties. See Chapter 13 for more details.

ISDN Adapters: Use this option to configure ISDN adapters if available. More details are in Chapter 13.

Modems: Check this option to configure a modem. Chapter 13 covers this option in more detail.

VNC Remote Administration: VNC allows you to make a remote connection to your server. From a VNC remote connection, you can connect to the graphical interface. By default, this option is off; turn it on here if you want to use it, but be aware that VNC uses unsecured connections by default. See Chapter 18 for details on how to create a secure remote connection.

To configure the network interfaces on your server, click the hyperlink Network Interfaces. This takes you to the screen shown in Figure 1-12 with an overview of all the network cards that were detected. To change the settings of a network card, select it first, and then click Edit.

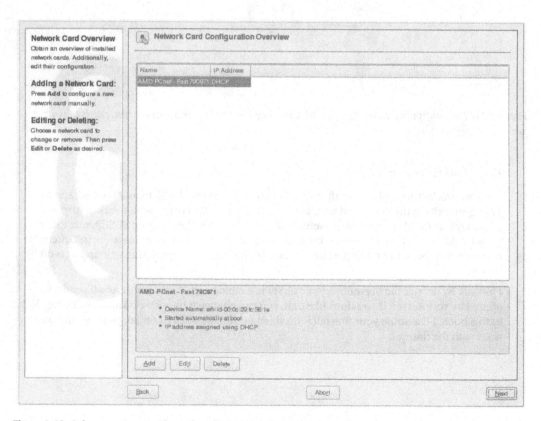

Figure 1-12. *Select your network card, and click Edit to modify its settings.*

You now see the Network Address Setup screen, as shown in Figure 1-13. On this screen, make sure the Address tab is selected. Next, to specify a fixed IP address, select the Static Address Setup option. Then enter the IP address you want to use and the appropriate subnet mask. Be aware that the utility doesn't calculate any subnet mask for the address you have entered, so make sure you enter the correct address.

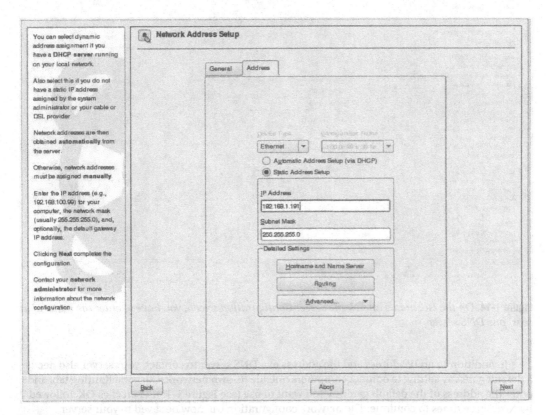

Figure 1-13. *Make sure you don't only enter the IP address but also the subnet mask you want to use because it isn't calculated automatically.*

After entering the IP address and subnet mask, click the Hostname and Name Server button. On the Hostname and Name Server Configuration screen, you can change the name of your computer, which probably isn't necessary because you just set the name, and you can enter the IP address of the DNS server you want to use. Use at least one IP address of a DNS server and two if possible. Your server will contact only the second DNS server if the first server is unavailable; therefore, entering a second IP address for a DNS server adds some redundancy. If you want your server to search in a list of default domains for incomplete host names, enter the domains you want it to search in the Domain Search box. See Figure 1-14 for an example.

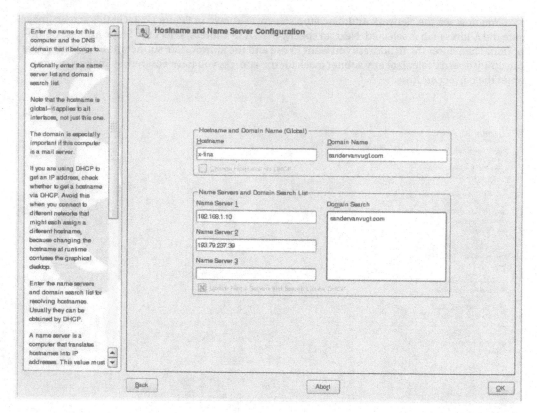

Figure 1-14. *On the Hostname and Name Server Configuration screen, you have to enter the name of at least one DNS server.*

In addition to an IP address and the address of a DNS server to contact, your server also needs a default gateway setting to contact computers outside its own network. Click the Routing tab, and enter the address of the default gateway you want to use (see Figure 1-15). Then click OK, followed by Next three times to continue. The network configuration will now be saved to your server.

To make sure your server is safe, it should always be up-to-date with patches. For that reason, you will now see the Test Internet Connection screen. On this screen, you can test Internet connectivity and, if that works, download and install patches. Chapter 9 covers how to install patches. By default, the first network card that is listed on your system is used to test the connection to the Internet. If you want to use another network card, click the Change button, and select the card you want to use. Then click Next to continue.

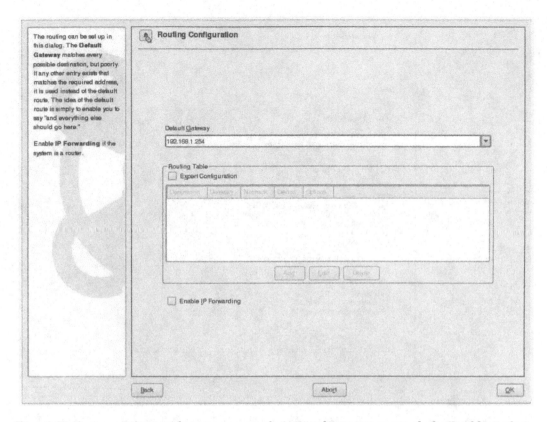

Figure 1-15. *To communicate with computers on other networks, your server needs the IP address of the default gateway it should use.*

Next, you can configure the certificate authority and the OpenLDAP server that will be used on your server. A certificate is created automatically using the settings you entered in the initial phase of the installation procedure. Click the CA Management link (shown in Figure 1-16) if you want to change the properties of the default certificate server and certificate. An OpenLDAP server is created automatically as well. You can change its settings by clicking the OpenLDAP Server link. You can change both options from the Change drop-down list. For more details about how to configure OpenLDAP, refer to Chapter 17, and for more about the certificate server, see Chapter 21.

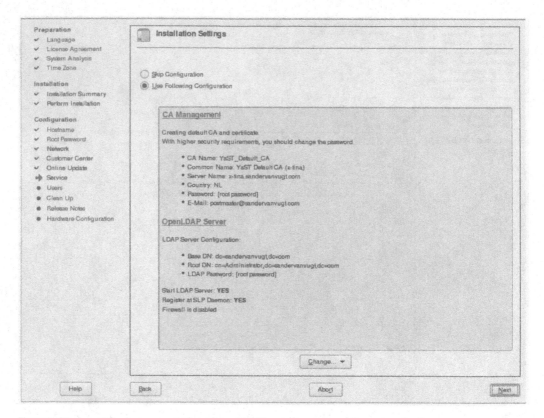

Figure 1-16. *A certificate server and an OpenLDAP server are created automatically.*

After creating the OpenLDAP and the certificate server, you have to configure the user environment. First, you need to check where you want users to be authenticated. By default, they will authenticate on the OpenLDAP server (see Figure 1-17); if you don't like that, you can change it so users authenticate on an NIS domain, on a Windows domain, or just locally on the /etc/passwd file. Because many services integrate with OpenLDAP well, it is a good idea to let users authenticate on that server; however, if you don't have any experience with OpenLDAP and you want to be able to tune what is happening, it is a good idea to specify that users should authenticate on the /etc/passwd file first and change that setting later. See Chapter 5 and Chapter 17 for details on how to do that. After specifying the way you want users to authenticate, click Next to proceed.

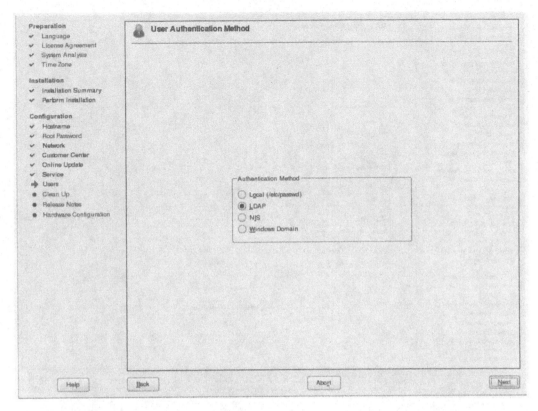

Figure 1-17. *By default, users will authenticate on the OpenLDAP server that you configured on the preceding screen.*

If you have selected that the OpenLDAP server should be used for user authentication, next you have to configure what server your server should connect to in order to get the LDAP data (see Figure 1-18). By default, your server is the OpenLDAP server and client at the same time. If you don't like that, specify the server that should be contacted in the LDAP Client box. You should always check the LDAP TLS/SLL box if the LDAP server is somewhere else: it makes sure passwords are not sent in clear text. If your applications need LDAP version 2 compatibility, check the LDAP Version 2 box as well. It is better not to check this option by default, though, since LDAP version 2 is less secure. The Start Automounter option makes sure users can connect to home directories that are offered by some other server by means of a network protocol such as NFS. In Chapter 15, you can read more about that option. Chapter 17 deals with the advanced configuration options in detail.

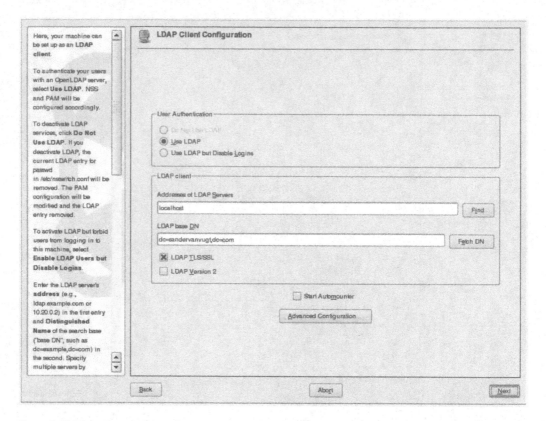

Figure 1-18. *If you want users to log on to an LDAP server, you need to specify how to contact that server.*

After clicking OK on the LDAP Client Configuration screen, you will see a message indicating that changes are applied only after restarting the LDAP server or rebooting the complete server. At this moment, you can just finalize the installation and reboot your server later. Now you will see the screen where you can create a new user. The screen is called New LDAP User if you have specified that an LDAP server should be used and is called New User if you are creating the user in the local password file. On this screen, as shown in Figure 1-19, enter the first name, last name, username, and password you want to use for that user. If this is the user account you will be using as the administrative user, you can select the Receive System Mail option to make sure this user will receive all messages sent to the user root. Never use the automatic login feature; it will log in this user automatically, which is a very bad security practice. To do some more user management, click the User Management button. Refer to Chapter 5 for more details on this. Click Next to create your user. If you get warnings about the password not being secure enough, reconsider whether you want to change the password and apply all the necessary settings.

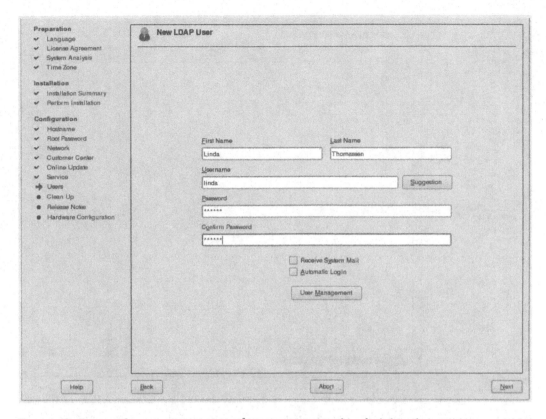

Figure 1-19. *Create at least one user account that you can use as the administrative user.*

After creating the user account, all settings are written to your server. This can take a minute or two, and during that time, you will see the screen shown in Figure 1-20. Be patient here, because this is an important phase in the installation procedure that makes sure you end up with a usable system.

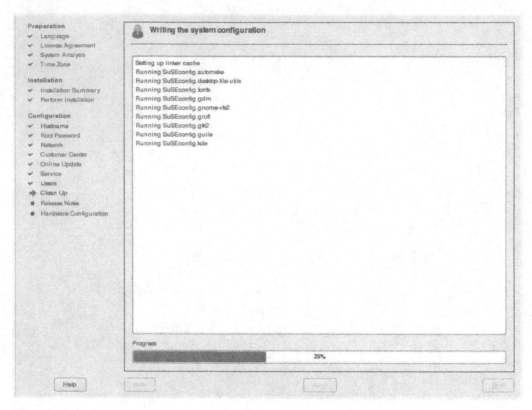

Figure 1-20. *It takes a minute or two to write all the settings to your server.*

The installation is almost complete now. On the next screen (see Figure 1-21), you can read the release notes. It is highly recommended that you read them; they may contain important information about the services on your server. Then click Next to continue.

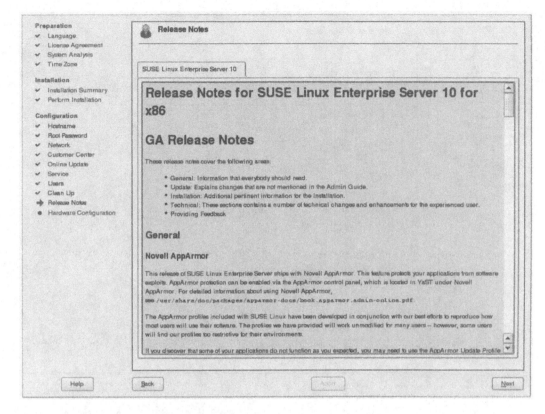

Figure 1-21. *In the release notes, you can find important information about the use of the services included in SUSE Linux Enterprise Server 10.*

In the last step of the configuration procedure, you have the opportunity to configure hardware settings of your server. On the Hardware Configuration screen, you can, for example, change the resolution of the graphical display or configure printers and sound cards (see Figure 1-22). You do not need to do such configuration now, because you can also do it later when the installation has finished. In Chapter 3 of this book, you'll find more information about these tasks.

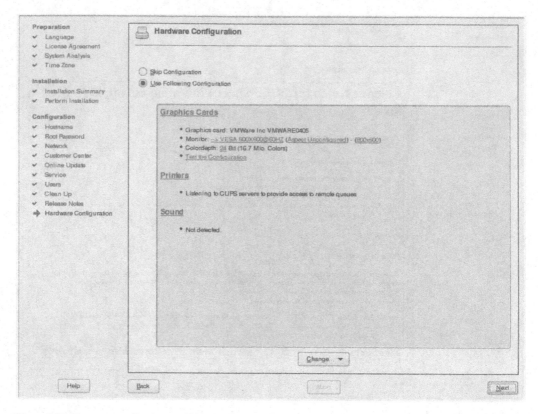

Figure 1-22. *You can configure graphics cards, printers, and sound on the Hardware Configuration screen. You can also configure them later.*

After you click Next on the Hardware Configuration screen, you will see the Installation Completed screen. On this screen, you will be informed about the status of the installation; it tells you whether the installation was successful. By default, the installation will be cloned as well. This means the installation settings you have used are written to an XML file that you can use with AutoYaST to perform an automatic installation; see Chapter 35 for more details on that. For now, you can click Finish. This will finalize the installation and start the installed system with a login prompt. In the next chapter, you can read what to do with that.

Summary

In this chapter, you learned how to install SUSE Linux Enterprise Server. Congratulations, you now have a server up and running. Read the next chapter for more information about what to do with it.

CHAPTER 2

■ ■ ■

Exploring SUSE Linux Enterprise Server

In the first chapter of this book, you learned how to install SUSE Linux Enterprise Server. Assuming that this is your first time on Linux, this chapter will help you get familiar with the Linux operating system. I'll teach you the most essential skills to allow you to manage a SUSE server. Specifically, in this chapter you'll take a tour of the server desktop from a graphical perspective, and you will learn how to work from the GNOME graphical environment that is installed by default. Also, you will learn what default directories are installed on SUSE Linux Enterprise Server. Basically, I'll introduce many topics in this chapter to get you going as fast as possible in the SUSE Linux Enterprise Server desktop. Already know how it is organized? In that case, you can safely skip this chapter.

Logging In

Linux is a multiuser operating system. This means several users are defined on it, and several users can be logged in to it at the same time. So, before you can work on a Linux box, you must tell the system what user account you want to use for logging in. Therefore, the first screen you will see after your server has successfully booted after installation is a graphical login prompt. At this prompt, you will specify who you are, and if you like, you can also choose the graphical environment from which you want to work. In this chapter, I won't make it any more difficult than necessary, so I'll show just how to work with the GNOME environment, which is loaded by default.

■ **Tip** Don't like the graphical login? No problem, you can change your server so it will boot with a text interface by default. Check Chapter 10 for more details on how to do that.

Exploring the Linux User Accounts

To log in to your system, you need a valid user account. Although you are the administrator of your server, it is not too sensible to make a habit of logging in with the account of the user root, the administrator for your server. The most important reason for this is to protect you from making mistakes. This is because in most situations your Linux operating system will not ask you whether you are sure you want to perform a certain action. If you give a command and hit the Enter key, your Linux operating system will just do as asked. Linux assumes you know what you're doing. Therefore, to protect yourself, it is a good idea to log in as a regular user and become the administrative user root only if you really need to do so.

Working with Virtual Consoles

After booting your server, you'll see a graphical login screen. But what if something is wrong with your graphical environment and you can't log in from there? In that case, it is nice to know you can work from six virtual consoles as well. These are like physical monitors connected to your server that are hidden under some key sequences. You can open these consoles by pressing the Ctrl+Alt+F1 to F6 keys. (In the nongraphical environment, you would access them with the Alt key only.) From there, you can work from a text-based environment, which can help you if your graphical environment is broken or if you want to experiment while being logged in as another user on your server. You'll learn more about this in Chapter 4.

You can activate the text-based virtual consoles whenever you want. You can do it when you see the graphical login screen, but you can also activate them after you have logged in to the system. If you want to leave the text-based virtual console and return to your graphical environment, you can press Ctrl+Alt+F7.

When you are working with more than one virtual console, it's easy to get confused about the console you are actually using. If this is the case, there are some means to find your way back. The first help is the login prompt you see when activating the virtual console; it will say which console you are working with by means of something like (tty2), as shown in Figure 2-1. Specifically, tty2 means that this is the second terminal (virtual console) attached to your computer. You have activated it with the Ctrl+Alt+F2 key combination.

Figure 2-1. *When you activate a virtual console, you see the* tty *number of the virtual console.*

You can also find out which console is active while you are working. Whenever you get confused about your identity, you can open the GNOME terminal from the GNOME menu (click Computer in the lower-left part of the screen) and from there enter the command who am i (basically if you do that, you use the command who followed by the options am and i, which in fact is a clever trick to refer to the option -m for who). This command will always show you the console you are using. Don't confuse who am i with whoami; the latter will just show you your login name and nothing else.

Getting Administrative Access

As I said before, it is good practice *not* to log in as an administrative user to your server but as a normal user. However, what if you need administrative access to perform some task? In that case, you can use the command su from a text-based console or a GNOME terminal. When you enter the command su, you will be prompted for a password. The server expects you to enter the password of the user root now. Once finished, you are temporarily root, and you can perform any task you like with the privileges of this system administrator account. Done with your work as root? Then you can use exit to return to the environment in which you started.

It might sound cool to become root from a text-based console, but this is not the only way you can work. Another option is to work from the graphical environment. Sometimes when you start a tool that usually needs root access, such as the configuration utility YaST, you will be prompted for root's password, although this works only for programs that have been programmed to do this. Once you have entered the password for user root, you will have root privileges for that program only; in other programs, you will have the permissions only of your regular user account.

One of the characteristics when working with su is that it doesn't overwrite the environment variables of the original user who was logged in before you used su to become root. This could lead to problems, especially when you try to start a graphical program from your su console window in a graphical session. To prevent these problems, on SUSE Linux you can use sux - instead. This command is typical for SUSE and doesn't work on other Linux distributions. If you use sux -, all the environment variables will be set correctly. The result is that this prevents you from getting error messages when you are trying, for example, to start graphical programs from a console window.

If you want to start an administrative program such as the overall SUSE configuration tool YaST, you don't have to think hard how to do that. If you start YaST as a normal user, it will prompt you to enter the root password (see Figure 2-2).

Note Ever heard about KDE? KDE is one of the graphical interfaces you can use on any kind of SUSE Linux. In earlier releases of SUSE Linux Enterprise Server, KDE was the default interface. Since Novell has a lot of knowledge about the GNOME desktop because of its acquisition of Ximian in 2001, SUSE Linux Enterprise Server defaults to the GNOME desktop. If you really want, you can select KDE to be your default desktop environment when performing an installation; however, for the topics discussed in this book, it doesn't really make a difference. The key components to administer SUSE Linux Enterprise Server are YaST and the command line, and these are always the same, no matter what graphical environment you are using. When I'm discussing the graphical desktop in this book, it will be the GNOME desktop environment since it's the default.

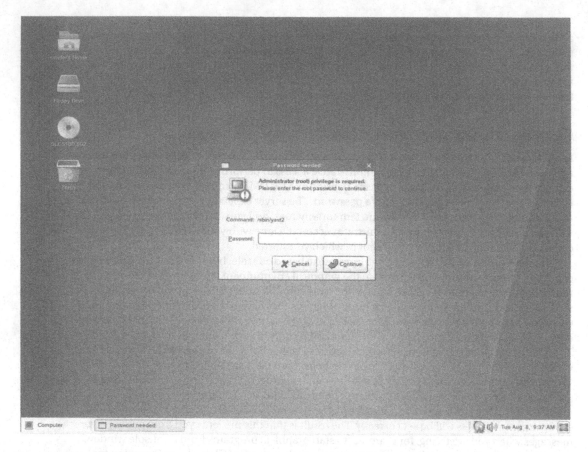

Figure 2-2. *When you start YaST as a user other than* root, *you are prompted for the password of the user* root.

Finding Your Way in the File System

Now that you know how to log in to your server, it is time to get more familiar with the structure used in the file system on your server. Even nowadays, it is still important you know your way around the file system; this is because Linux is still a file system–centric operating system. Even if you want to work from only the graphical environment, you must know where you can find all the important files on your server. If you know how to handle the files on your server, you know half of what you need to know to manage your Linux server. On Linux, everything is a file. Even devices that are connected to your server are managed as files. Therefore, knowing how the file system works and is organized is of the highest importance.

Exploring the Default Directories

If this is your first introduction to Linux, you might be surprised by the way the file system is organized. In this section, you'll read about the default directories that are used by almost all Linux systems.

First, if you want to grasp the way a Linux file system is organized, you must understand that in the Linux file system structure, a clear distinction is made between files that are accessible to ordinary users and files that are accessible to the system administrator. If these are program files, you will find the former in a directory called bin (binary) and the latter in a directory called sbin (system binaries). You will find these directories at different levels in the file system.

Second, you need to understand that on a Linux server it is quite usual to work with more than one partition. This is because your server is hosting a multitude of files for the services that it offers. Linux also has different file systems that all have their own advantages; for example, you could use a different file system for the volume where your mail server stores its files than for the volume where your company database is stored. In Chapter 8 you will learn more about the organization of your server in different partitions.

No matter how many partitions you use, the start of the file system structure on any Linux system is the root partition. This is the partition on which you will find the root directory, and it is referred to with a slash (/).

Tip Don't confuse the root directory with the directory /root. The root directory (/) is the starting point of your file system under which you'll find all other directories. The directory /root is one of these directories. /root is the home directory for the user root, the administrator of your system.

As I said before, it is possible to separate the contents from different directories from this root partition and split off other partitions or volumes. (Chapter 8 covers the difference between these two.) The reason why you want to do this is obvious: if you have separated, for example, the directory /home in which you will find user home directories from the rest of the directory structure, it is impossible for a user who has no limitations set to fill up the entire file system. Also, different types of files need different types of file systems than you've just read about.

Now, it is good to work with more than one partition, but it also implies a certain risk. It could, for example, happen that one of these partitions is damaged and impossible to mount when you start your server. For this reason, you will find program files on many levels. Most essential utilities that are needed to maintain and repair your system are directly in the root partition. You will find, however, less critical programs and utilities one level lower, under /usr, for example. This /usr directory also has the subdirectories bin and sbin (and some others), and you can find them under the root of the file system.

On SUSE Linux Enterprise Server, you'll find the following default directories:

/bin: This is the location where you'll find binaries accessible to all users. These are essential binaries that must be available at all times, even if other partitions on your system have a problem. For that reason, the directory /bin is always on the root partition. In it you will find essential utilities and commands such as /bin/bash (the shell), cp (used to copy files), and many more. Some of the more complicated items, however, are elsewhere on your system.

/sbin: In this directory you will find binaries for system administration. These are critical binaries that must be available at all times in case you need to repair your system. You will also find commands and utilities you'd rather not see in the hands of your users, such as the launcher for the general system management tool yast2 or the partitioning tool fdisk.

/boot: The directory /boot contains your secondary boot loader. A boot loader consists of two parts. The first part of it is installed in the master boot record and—depending on your configuration—in the boot sector of an active partition. The second part, the so-called secondary boot loader, is in the directory /boot. For more details on its contents, read Chapter 10. The directory /boot is critical for booting your system, so don't touch it. Under normal circumstances, there is absolutely no need to modify anything in this directory.

/dev: On a Linux system, all the hardware you work with corresponds to a file on your system. If you want to address the hardware, you have to address the corresponding file. You can find these device files in the directory /dev. You will find, for example, a device called /dev/fd0 that refers to a floppy drive, if that is present in your system. On SUSE Linux you will have the device file only if the device is really present on your server. Amongst the properties of these device files are the so-called major and minor numbers. You will find them if you look at the properties of the file by using the command `ls -l` (see Figure 2-3). These major and minor numbers indicate to the kernel what device it actually is. Apart from the major and minor numbers, all devices are of a certain type. The most common types are block and character devices. Whether a device is a block or a character device is indicated with a `b` or a `c` in the properties of the device file. You can see these properties by using the command `ls -l`.

■ Tip One of the nice features of Linux is its flexibility. I once lost my device /dev/hdc, which I needed to address my CD drive. I did, however, find out from another Linux system that the associated major and minor numbers were 22 and 0. If you have this information, you can use the command `mknod` to create your own devices. In this case, I used `mknod /dev/hdc b 22 0` to restore access to my CD drive. You can even use `mknod` to create entirely new devices.

```
File  Edit  View  Terminal  Tabs  Help
crw-rw-rw-  1 root tty      3,  49 Aug  8  2006 ttys1
crw-rw-rw-  1 root tty      3,  50 Aug  8  2006 ttys2
crw-rw-rw-  1 root tty      3,  51 Aug  8  2006 ttys3
crw-rw-rw-  1 root tty      3,  52 Aug  8  2006 ttys4
crw-rw-rw-  1 root tty      3,  53 Aug  8  2006 ttys5
crw-rw-rw-  1 root tty      3,  54 Aug  8  2006 ttys6
crw-rw-rw-  1 root tty      3,  55 Aug  8  2006 ttys7
crw-rw-rw-  1 root tty      3,  56 Aug  8  2006 ttys8
crw-rw-rw-  1 root tty      3,  57 Aug  8  2006 ttys9
crw-rw-rw-  1 root tty      3,  58 Aug  8  2006 ttysa
crw-rw-rw-  1 root tty      3,  59 Aug  8  2006 ttysb
crw-rw-rw-  1 root tty      3,  60 Aug  8  2006 ttysc
crw-rw-rw-  1 root tty      3,  61 Aug  8  2006 ttysd
crw-rw-rw-  1 root tty      3,  62 Aug  8  2006 ttyse
crw-rw-rw-  1 root tty      3,  63 Aug  8  2006 ttysf
crw-r--r--  1 root root     1,   9 Aug  8 09:34 urandom
crw--w----  1 root tty      7,   0 Aug  8  2006 vcs
crw-rw----  1 root tty      7,   1 Aug  8  2006 vcs1
crw--w----  1 root tty      7,  10 Aug  8 09:36 vcs10
crw--w----  1 root tty      7,   2 Aug  8 09:34 vcs2
crw--w----  1 root tty      7,   3 Aug  8 09:34 vcs3
crw--w----  1 root tty      7,   4 Aug  8 09:34 vcs4
crw--w----  1 root tty      7,   5 Aug  8 09:34 vcs5
crw--w----  1 root tty      7,   6 Aug  8 09:34 vcs6
crw--w----  1 root tty      7,   7 Aug  8 09:36 vcs7
crw--w----  1 root tty      7, 128 Aug  8  2006 vcsa
crw-rw----  1 root tty      7, 129 Aug  8  2006 vcsa1
crw--w----  1 root tty      7, 138 Aug  8 09:36 vcsa10
crw--w----  1 root tty      7, 130 Aug  8 09:34 vcsa2
crw--w----  1 root tty      7, 131 Aug  8 09:34 vcsa3
crw--w----  1 root tty      7, 132 Aug  8 09:34 vcsa4
crw--w----  1 root tty      7, 133 Aug  8 09:34 vcsa5
crw--w----  1 root tty      7, 134 Aug  8 09:34 vcsa6
crw--w----  1 root tty      7, 135 Aug  8 09:36 vcsa7
crw-------  1 root root    10, 130 Jun 16 15:07 watchdog
pr--------  1 root tty           0 Aug  8 09:38
crw-rw-rw-  1 root root     1,   5 Jun 16 15:07 zero
BTN:/dev #
```

Figure 2-3. *A device has some special properties that help the kernel understand what the device's purpose is.*

/etc: Most services running on Linux use an ASCII text file to store all necessary configuration information (although more services have started using XML also). These text files are kept in the directory /etc. In this directory, you will find some important configuration files such as /etc/passwd, which contains the database of local Linux users (see Figure 2-4). You will also find configuration files for all other important services such as dhcpd.conf, which stores the configuration of your DHCP server. In /etc you will find a lot of subdirectories. If a service uses more than one configuration file, it will usually create a subdirectory in which all these files are stored. For example, the Apache 2 web server configuration is in the subdirectory /etc/apache2/.

Figure 2-4. *Important configuration files such as the user database* /etc/passwd *are stored in* /etc *or one of its subdirectories.*

/home: Every server must have a place for the user home directories. On Unix, the directory /home is used for this purpose. To prevent a user from filling up the entire file system by accident, in most cases a separate partition is created for this directory.

/lib: Many programs that are used in a Linux environment share some of their code. This shared code is stored in different library files. All the libraries needed by binaries that are in a subdirectory of your file system root are in the directory /lib. You will also find some other important modules in this directory, such as the driver modules that are used by the kernel of your server.

Tip You want to know which modules are used by a certain binary? Use `ldd`. For example, you can find out exactly which libraries are used by /bin/bash by typing `ldd /bin/bash`. This will show you that all the libraries it uses are in /lib (see Figure 2-5).

```
Terminal                                                    _ □ ×
File  Edit  View  Terminal  Tabs  Help
BTN:/etc # ldd /bin/bash
        linux-gate.so.1 =>   (0xffffe000)
        libreadline.so.5 => /lib/libreadline.so.5 (0xb7f7b000)
        libhistory.so.5 => /lib/libhistory.so.5 (0xb7f74000)
        libncurses.so.5 => /lib/libncurses.so.5 (0xb7f2d000)
        libdl.so.2 => /lib/libdl.so.2 (0xb7f29000)
        libc.so.6 => /lib/libc.so.6 (0xb7e08000)
        /lib/ld-linux.so.2 (0xb7fc0000)
BTN:/etc #
```

Figure 2-5. *With* `ldd` *you can find out exactly which libraries are used by a certain command.*

/media: On a Linux system, to access files that are not on the hard disk of your computer, you need to mount the media they are on. When you mount, for example, a CD, you connect it to a directory on your file system. This must be a directory that exists before you start mounting anything. The default directory that is used for regular mounts is /media. In this directory, a subdirectory is created automatically when a new removable device is detected. CDs, DVDs, and USB sticks will appear here (and on the graphical desktop) once they are mounted with the label of the device used as the name of the directory where the device is mounted. Check Chapter 4 for more information about mounting devices.

/mnt: On older Linux systems, /mnt was the default directory for mounting devices. On more recent systems, this has been replaced by the /media directory. However, /mnt still has a purpose: it is used for mounts that don't occur often, such as a mount to a server that has to be accessed only once.

/usr: The directory /usr is probably the largest directory on your system. In it you'll find almost all the user-accessible files. Because so many files appear in this directory, you will find an entire structure of subdirectories in this directory. There is, for example, /usr/bin, where most programs are stored; /usr/X11R6, where your graphical user environment resides; and /usr/src, where you can put the source files of the open source programs and kernel you use. Because there are so many files in /usr, it is usual to put /usr on its own partition.

Tip Have you always wanted to find out how much space a directory occupies on your hard disk? Use du -hs from a console environment. It will show you the disk usage of a specified directory. The normal output of this command is in blocks; the parameter -h presents the output in a human-readable form, and the parameter -s summarizes a directory's totals instead of showing individual subdirectory entries. Use, for example, du -h /usr to find out exactly how much space /usr occupies.

/opt: In /usr you will find a lot of binaries. Many of these are small software packages. Usually large software installations, such as office suites, are stored in /opt. On SUSE Linux Enterprise Server, you will find, for example, the GNOME graphical interface and the Oracle database (if installed) as subdirectories of this directory.

/proc: The directory /proc is a strange directory. This is because it doesn't really exist on the hard disk of your computer. /proc is an interface to the memory of your server; consider it the location where the operating system gives information about how it works to the user. An advanced administrator can use it to tune how the server works and get information about its current status. You can find a lot of information about your server in the files in this directory. Try, for example, the command cat /proc/cpuinfo to show the contents of the text file /proc/cpuinfo (you must be root to do this). This command will show you a lot of information about the processors in your server (see Figure 2-6).

/root: Ordinary users have their home directories in /home. A system administrator is not a normal user; in a Unix environment, a system administrator is therefore respectfully called the *superuser*. Since this user may have some important tools in the home directory, this directory is not in /home with those of the other users. Instead, the user root uses /root as the home directory. This is for good reason: on many servers, the directory /home is on a separate partition. If, for any reason, you cannot access this partition anymore, at least user root has still access to the home directory, which probably contains some important files.

/srv: You will find all the files from some important services in this directory. This directory is, for example, used to store your entire web server and FTP server file structures. If you want to configure your server as an installation server, /srv is the place to put the installation files needed by this server.

/sys: You can use the directory /sys to store information about the state of your system. Its use is like the use of /proc, with the difference that the information in /sys is kept on the hard disk of your server, so it is still available after you have rebooted it. The information in /sys is more directly related to the hardware you are using on your server, whereas /proc is used to store information about the current state of the kernel.

/tmp: As the name suggests, /tmp is used for temporary files. This is the only directory on the entire system that every user can write to. This is a bad idea, however, because the content of this directory can be wiped automatically by any process or root without any warning being issued before that happens.

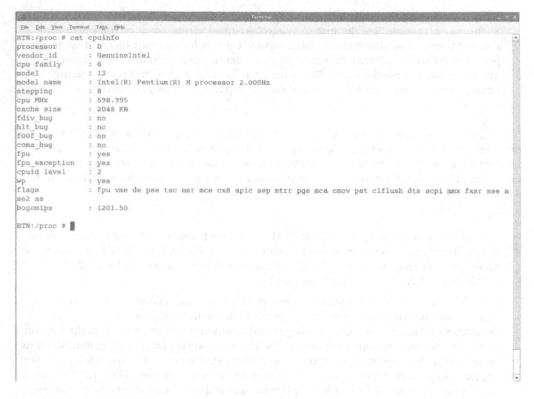

Figure 2-6. *You can get a lot of information about your system from the files in* /proc.

/var: The last directory you will find on any Linux server is /var. This directory contains mostly files that are created by your server and whose content can grow very fast; think of the mail folders of users when the server is used as a mail server. Because /var is so dynamic, it is a good idea to keep /var on a separate partition. The exact contents of /var depend on what you have installed on your system. In most cases, you will find a directory called /var/spool in which print jobs are spooled before they are processed by your server. Another important subdirectory of /var is the directory /log in which you will find several log files, such as the main system log file in /var/log/messages.

Performing Essential Tasks in the File System

Now that you know which directories are important on your server, the next step is to find out how to manage the files in these directories. The easiest way to do this is by means of a graphical file manager such as GNOME's Nautilus. You don't need a book to learn how to work with it; just click the icon of your home folder on the desktop, and it will start, displaying the contents of your home folder to you. As an alternative, you can also select the Computer menu (from now on, I'll call it the GNOME menu) and then select More Applications ➤ Browse ➤ File Manager ➤ Nautilus, which will also open the file manager for you, as shown in Figure 2-7. An alternative file manager is KDE's Konqueror, which you can start from the same menu, if you have chosen to install the KDE software on your server.

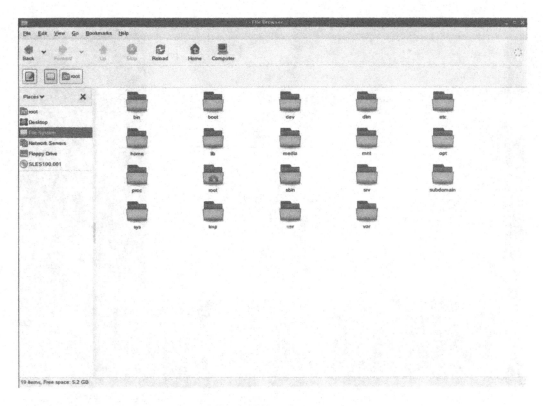

Figure 2-7. *In GNOME, you can use Nautilus for file management.*

After starting the Nautilus file manager, you have three ways of working with your files. First, you can right-click items displayed by the file manager. This will open a quick menu (see Figure 2-8). This menu gives you access to the most common options for that particular item, as well as the properties of the item. By selecting Sharing Options, for example, it is easy to share the file across the network. Next, you can use the buttons in the button bar, although they are not as useful as the other options. Last, you can work from the Nautilus menus, where all options that are available for the selected item are offered as well. In these menus, you will find options to copy or move files, as well as options to make a connection to other servers in your network.

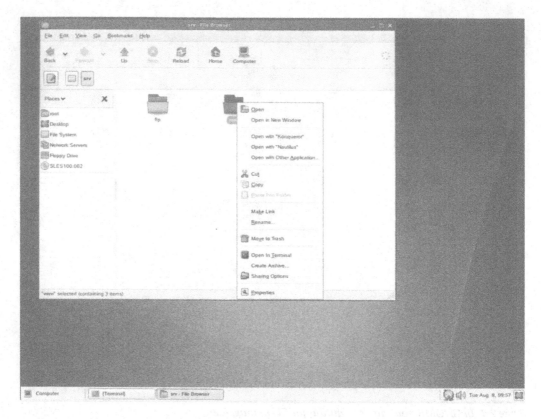

Figure 2-8. *You can access the most relevant file management options by right-clicking the file or directory.*

Working with the GNOME Interface

On the GNOME desktop, a few application icons give you access to some important utilities, such as the home folder and the trash bin. You'll also see the GNOME menu in the lower-left part of the screen. This menu gives you access to most applications that are installed on your server.

Using the GNOME Menu

On SUSE Linux Enterprise Server, Novell provides a completely redesigned menu that allows you to access graphical applications. Its new layout, which you can see in Figure 2-9, allows you to find the information you need as fast as possible. On top, you'll see the Show drop-down list. This list gives you access to your Favorite Applications list. Immediately after installation, these are Firefox, YaST, the GNOME terminal, and the Home Folder application. A list of all available applications appears after clicking the More Applications button; you'll learn how to install these applications in the section.

Also available from the Show drop-down list are the options Recently Used Applications and Recently Used Documents. These give you access to applications and documents that you've accessed recently from the GNOME menu.

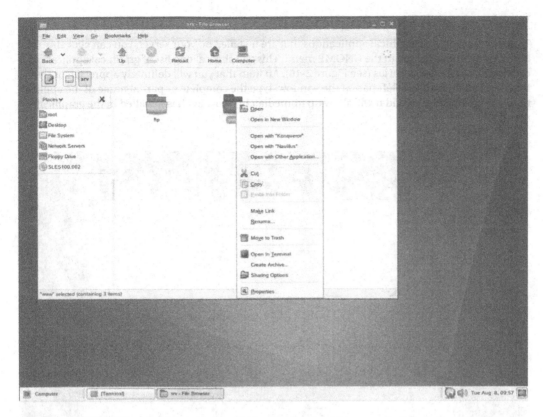

Figure 2-9. *In SUSE Linux Enterprise Server 10, you can work with a completely redesigned graphical menu.*

In the upper-right part of the GNOME menu, you'll find some system items. The following items are available:

Help: This gives you access to the Help interface. Click it for help on many features.

Control Center: Use this to start the GNOME Control Center. From there, you can tune almost all the GNOME settings.

Install Software: Use this to start the interface from which you can install software. Check Chapter 9 for more details on that.

Lock Screen: Use this to lock your screen. You can unlock it by providing the password of the user who is currently logged in.

Log Out: This logs you out from the graphical interface. It will return you to the login screen from where you can log in again or shut down or restart your server.

In the lower-right part of the GNOME menu, you see a quick status overview. From this overview, you can see how you currently are connected to the network and how much disk space still is available on your hard drive. You can click both icons for more details and management options.

Working with More Applications

To get access to most graphical applications that are installed on your server, you can click the More Applications button in the GNOME menu. This will show a long list of graphical applications, divided into several categories (see Figure 2-10). An item that you will definitely appreciate is the Filter option in the upper-left part of the window; type the complete or partial name of the application you are looking for, and it will show up immediately (provided it is installed in the graphical menu).

Figure 2-10. *The More Applications button gives you access to all the graphical applications installed on your server.*

All sorts of applications appear here; some of them are used for useful things such as administering your server, and others are a bit less relevant, such as the group Audio & Video that offers, in addition to some useful utilities, a utility to manage the volume of the sound system in your server. Next, you will find a short description of the submenus of the Applications menu and their contents.

Audio & Video

In the Audio & Video submenu, you find some useful programs. Most important is the GNOME CD/DVD Creator (a plug-in to Nautilus) that you can use to burn CDs and DVDs on your system. You'll also find the recording tool Sound Recorder, which helps you record audio streams on your server, and the Volume Control program, which helps you control the sound volume of your server, provided your server has a speaker.

Browse

The Browse submenu gives you access to the Nautilus file manager and a file search utility. You'll also find a shortcut to the Mozilla browser that you can use to browse the Internet. For help in your work as a system administrator, you may find the File Manager – Super User Mode useful. After starting it, enter the password of the root user to manage all the files on your server.

Communicate

In the Communicate submenu, you'll find several items after installation. From KDE (if installed) come some useful programs such as a newsreader, mail client, and Internet dial-up program. If KDE is not installed, you'll see only the Akregator RSS reader and a GUI front end to the Mutt mail client.

Images

In the Images menu, you won't find much. The Eye of GNOME item is an image viewer you can use to locate and display graphical images on your system.

Office

You won't find any OpenOffice item in the Office submenu. You'll just find a dictionary and the Envince document viewer, which allows you to look at the content of documents such as PDF files. If installed, the KDE address book KAddressBook and the contact manager Kontact appear on this menu.

System

The System submenu is what you will like most as an administrator. You'll find SUSE's YaST utility, as well as a whole lot of other utilities that you can use for system management. For example, the GNOME terminal and the X terminal both give you access to a console on your server, you can use the Configuration subsection to configure the GNOME desktop completely the way you need it, and you can use the GNOME System Monitor to monitor current process activity and the general system status (see Figure 2-11).

In the System submenu, you'll find the most important application that is available on your SUSE Linux Enterprise Server: the terminal. From the terminal window (also referred to as the *console*), you get fast access to a command-line environment. From the command line, you will be able to unleash the complete power of Linux. In later chapters in this book, you will learn about most important tasks that you can perform from the command line.

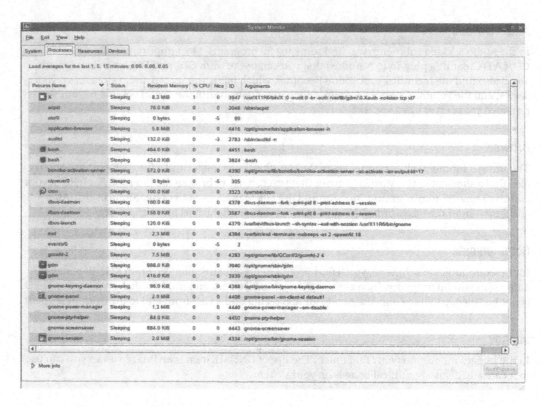

Figure 2-11. *The GNOME System Monitor helps you monitor all the important aspects of your server's performance.*

Tools

The Tools subsection is the last section in the administration menu. In it you'll find useful tools such as the archiving utility, the GNOME Calculator, and the editor gedit, which you will probably use often when tuning configuration files on your server (see Figure 2-12). Also in this menu, the Printing application helps you print all different kinds of documents and set up new printers on your server.

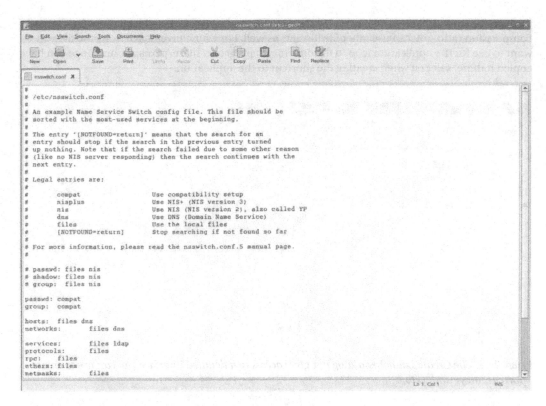

Figure 2-12. *If you are new to Linux, you will probably use the editor gedit a lot to create and modify all kinds of configuration files.*

Modifying the GNOME Desktop

Like any other computer desktop, GNOME offers some options to modify the look of the desktop. For example, you can add new items to the desktop, the desktop menus, and the panel (which is the toolbar you see on the bottom of the screen). Other options are available as well, such as the option to change the background of your graphical desktop. The following sections describe some of the most common tasks.

Adding Items to the Desktop

Adding items to the desktop can be easy enough: select the item you want to add from the Nautilus browser, and drag and drop it on the graphical desktop. This automatically creates a shortcut if you have all the necessary rights to the desktop and the item you want to put on the desktop. You can also right-click somewhere on the desktop, and from the pop-up menu select Create Folder, Create Launcher, or Create Document. In the window that pops up (see Figure 2-13), enter all the information that is required to create the item. If, for example, you want to create a shortcut to an application, select Create Launcher, browse to the application you want to add, and click OK to create it. You now have a shortcut to your application. If needed, you can also click the Icon button to change the icon for your application. Most buttons are created in the PNG format, because it offers a good compression ratio. You can use other file formats as well. For your convenience, copy the file you want to use for the application icon to the directory /opt/gnome/share/pixmaps/, and once you have copied it there, select it when creating the shortcut to the application.

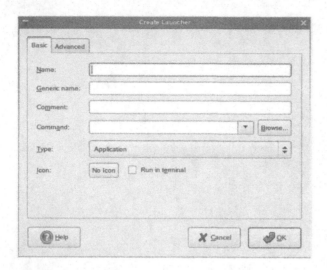

Figure 2-13. *The Create Launcher dialog box gives access to a detailed interface you can use to create shortcuts on your desktop.*

Changing the Menu

Novell spent a lot of time making a menu that is easy to use. You do have, however, some options to modify it. Most important, you can add one or more applications to the list of favorite applications. This is easy to do; first click More Applications to browse to the application you want to add. Then right-click it. This opens a small menu from which you can select the Add to Favorites option. The next time you open the GNOME menu, you will see that your application is listed amongst your other favorites.

Modifying Other Desktop Items

I could write an entire book about configuring the desktop, but that's not what I want to do here. To finish this short introduction to the GNOME desktop, let's look at the GNOME Control Center utility (see Figure 2-14). With it, you can change all aspects of the GNOME desktop. For example, from the Hardware section, it is easy to change the keyboard settings or screen resolution, and the Look and Feel options allow you to change the look of the desktop quickly. Some personalization options are available from the Personal section. For example, you can change your default language or password here or create shortcuts to start programs you need often. Last, the System section helps you set generic system settings, such as setting the date and time you want to use, setting the Power Management options, or setting up access to the desktop of your server by means of a Remote Desktop Protocol.

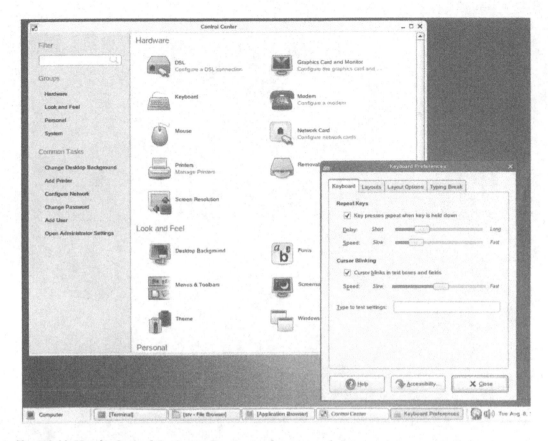

Figure 2-14. *Use the Control Center application to change any desktop setting you want.*

Summary

In this chapter, you were introduced to working with the Linux graphical desktop. It was by far not a complete overview of all the items offered by the GNOME desktop, which is used as the default desktop on SUSE Linux Enterprise server; it should, however, be enough to get you started. Also, you learned how to find your way in the file system from the discussion of the directories that are created on a SUSE Linux server by default. In the next chapter, you will learn how to manage your server from the YaST graphical management utility.

■ ■ ■

## CHAPTER 3

Managing SUSE Linux Enterprise Server with YaST

You can manage a SUSE Linux Enterprise Server 10 server in two ways: from the command line or from YaST. YaST is the management utility that is used on all versions of SUSE Linux. Using YaST, you can perform most common system administration tasks. However, you should be aware that you can perform certain advanced system administration tasks only from the command line. Chapter 4 introduces how to work from the command line. In this chapter, you will learn how to work with the YaST administration tool.

In this chapter, I'll cover the following topics:

- *YaST options*: You'll learn about the options offered from the YaST interface.

- *YaST and its configuration files*: When making a modification in YaST, some information is written to its configuration files. This section describes how that works.

- *YaST modularity*: YaST is modular. You'll learn how to work with YaST modules.

Exploring YaST Options

To start the YaST administration tool, from the graphical interface of your server you can press Alt+F2 to open the Run Application dialog box. From there, issue the command yast to start the YaST management utility. If you are logged in as an ordinary user, next you have to provide the root user's password for complete access to all the possibilities. This is not a necessity, but it is recommended that you do it anyway, or else you won't be able to modify most of the settings. If you were already logged in as root, you don't need to supply an additional password. Next, you will see the main screen of the YaST management utility, as shown in Figure 3-1.

Note You may have heard of YaST2 instead of YaST. Both refer to the same management utility. If from a console window on the graphical desktop you use the yast command, the text-based version of YaST starts. This interface offers the same options as the graphical interface and is an excellent choice if you want to use YaST from a nongraphical environment. In this chapter, I'll use *YaST* to refer to both YaST and YaST2.

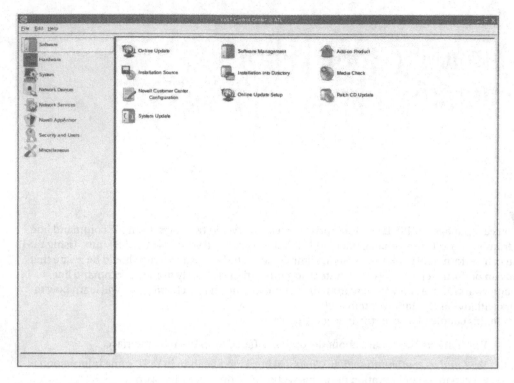

Figure 3-1. *The YaST management utility offers easy access to all the important administration tasks.*

In the YaST management interface, on the left you can see all the categories of management utilities. In this book, I will refer to them as YaST *menu options.* These give you access to the management utilities, which appear on the right side when you select a menu option. The following menu options are available:

- Software
- Hardware
- System
- Network Devices
- Network Services
- Novell AppArmor
- Security and Users
- Miscellaneous

The following sections describe the most important tasks you will find in these menus.

The Software Menu

In the YaST Software menu, you can find everything needed to install and update software on your computer. One of the most important utilities found in this menu is the Software Management utility, offering an extensive interface that allows you to install, remove, and update individual software packages. You can learn more about the Software Management utility in Chapter 9.

The Hardware Menu

You can access the YaST Hardware menu for initializing and configuring hardware devices on your computer. Here you'll find several utilities for hardware management. I describe these utilities in the following sections.

Disk Controller

On the Disk Controller Configuration screen (see Figure 3-2), you get access to the configuration of the different disk controllers on your server. Usually, each of these disk controllers has a corresponding kernel module that allows the operating system to address the kernel in the right way. In the Module to Use drop-down box, you can choose what specific module you want to use for a given controller, and you can enter specific parameters for that module. Last, when you select the Load Module in Initrd option, the module for the disk controller is available from the first stage of the boot procedure. This is a requirement if you want to be able to boot from the selected disk controller.

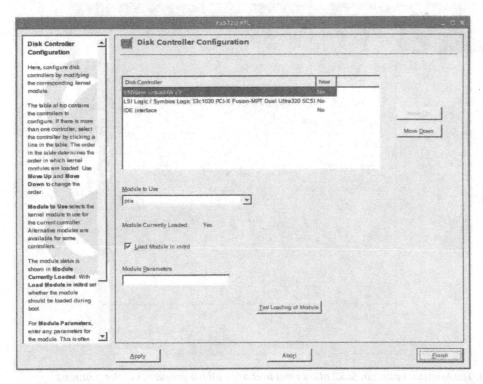

Figure 3-2. *On the Disk Controller Configuration screen, a disk controller is matched to the right driver module.*

Graphics Card and Monitor

Included with all versions of SUSE Linux is the SUSE Automatic X version 2 (SaX2) configuration utility. You can use this tool to tune the properties of the graphical display hardware on your server. You can run this utility from the YaST interface, but you can also run it as a stand-alone utility by entering the sax2 command in the console. The latter can be useful after changing the graphical hardware components in your server. In that case, you can open a console window and, from there, use the sax2 -r command. This will automatically detect relevant changes and write them to the relevant configuration files.

Upon starting, SaX2 will suggest ideal settings to use for your system. You can click OK on this screen or click Change Configuration to make any additional modifications. On the SaX2 configuration screen, you have several options:

Monitor. This option allows you to change monitor settings. A tab is available for every monitor that has been detected. In Figure 3-3 you can see that just one monitor is detected. On this screen, you can modify four properties. First, if the wrong video card was detected or if you have a better driver available for the video card in your server, click the Card option's Options button to change its settings. Next, the Monitor option's Change button allows you to select a different monitor. This is typically what you would want to do if the system detected the wrong monitor and you want to select a better one. Finally, you can use the drop-down boxes to select the best available resolution and the best colors for your monitor.

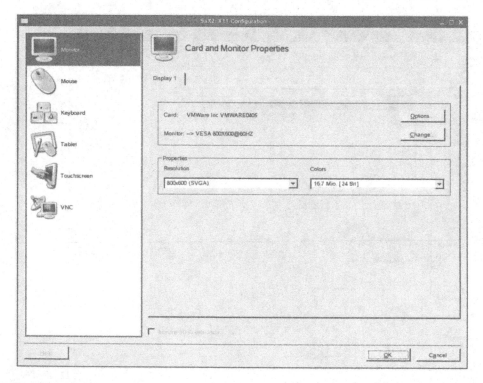

Figure 3-3. *The Monitor option in SaX2 allows you to change all the properties of the monitors connected to your server.*

Mouse. This button allows you to change all the properties of the mouse that is connected to your server. You can click the Change button to change the type of mouse that was detected, and other options such as Activate 3-Button Emulation and Activate Mouse Wheel are available.

Keyboard: Here you can change the properties of the keyboard connected to your server. On the Layout tab, you can select the proper keyboard layout. If the selected layout has variants, you can select the appropriate variant as well. You can also set some keyboard options. For example, you can define what should happen when you press the Caps Lock key. You'll rarely use most of these options.

Tablet: Since SUSE Linux Enterprise Server 10 is based on the same code as the SUSE Linux desktop products, you'll rarely use some options. One of them is the Tablet interface, which allows you to set all the properties for the tablet if you are using a tablet PC.

Touchsceen: This option is used rarely on a server; you can use it to set the properties of a touch screen connected to your computer.

VNC: One option that is important for configuring and managing most servers is the VNC option. This option allows you to switch on or off VNC access to the server (see Figure 3-4). If switched on, you can use VNC to access the graphical display on your server from another computer, which is useful when accessing a server remotely. If you want to switch this option on, select the Allow Access to Display Using VNC Protocol check box. Next, you can specify some VNC options. An option you should always use is the Activate Password Protection option. After selecting this option, specify the password you want to use twice before a remote connection can be established. If you need VNC access to the server from more than one computer at the same time, check the Allow Multiple VNC Connections box. Use Activate HTTP Access to enable VNC access from a browser using HTTP. If you do so, you should also select the HTTP port you want to use for VNC access from the browser. By default, port 5800 will be used. You should be aware that this port is not opened automatically in the SUSE firewall; refer to Chapter 30 for more details on that.

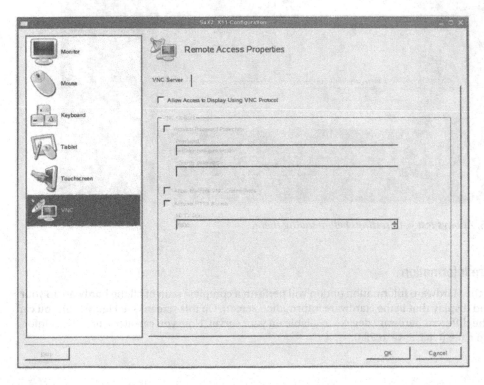

Figure 3-4. *One of the options for managing your server remotely is to enable VNC.*

Note VNC is not the only option to enable remote access to a server, and it is not the most secure option. In Chapter 18, you can read how to enable secure remote access to your server by using the Secure Shell (SSH).

After making modifications in SaX2, you can click the OK button. This will show a Message window where you can select what to do next. I recommend always clicking Test so you can make sure the new settings work. A new window will pop up in which you can make some final adjustments to your selections (see Figure 3-5). After tuning your settings (if necessary), click Save to store the new settings on your computer. Be aware that the settings are applied only the next time the graphical environment on your computer restarts. If you have used SaX2 from a graphical environment, you can restart the graphical environment by using the menu or by using the Ctrl+Alt+Backspace shortcut.

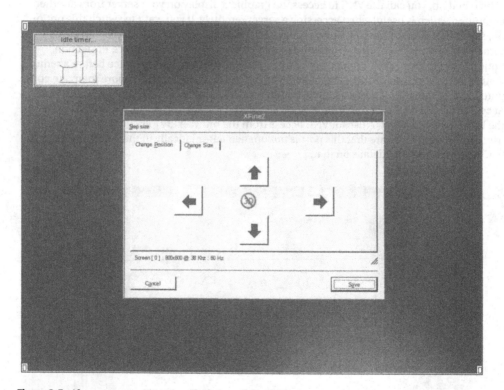

Figure 3-5. *Always test your settings before saving them.*

Hardware Information

Clicking the Hardware Information option will perform a complete scan of all the hardware in your server and display that in the Hardware Information screen. On this screen (see Figure 3-6), you can peruse the different hardware devices available on your server. Note you can also save all this information to a file (click Save to File).

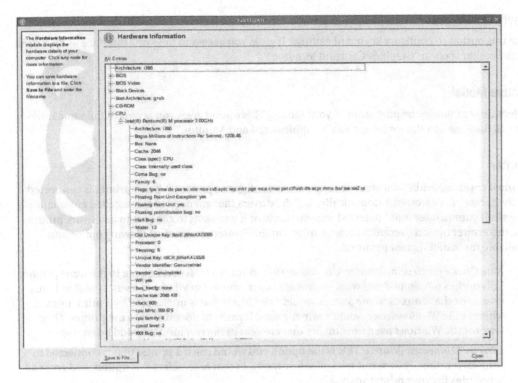

Figure 3-6. *On the Hardware Information screen, you get an overview of all the hardware that is in your server.*

IDE DMA Mode

If your computer uses IDE devices such as a hard drive or a CD drive, enabling DMA access will greatly enhance the access times for the selected devices. By default, the option DMA On is set for all IDE devices. In case this doesn't work well, select any of the other options that are available, and make sure this gives a better performance for the selected IDE device. Check Chapter 31 for more information about tuning and optimizing SUSE Linux Enterprise Server. Usually, however, no changes are required to the DMA mode of your IDE devices, because in most cases SUSE Linux Enterprise Server 10 will detect and apply the appropriate settings automatically.

Infrared Device

This option allows you to configure an infrared device. Since these are not typically used on servers, I won't discuss this option in this book.

Joystick

This option allows you to configure a joystick. Since these devices are typically not used on servers, I won't discuss this option.

Keyboard Layout

Use this option to configure keyboard settings. It gives you access to the same interface as discussed in the earlier section "Graphics Card and Monitor."

Mouse Model

Select this to change the properties of your mouse. This option gives you access to the same interface as discussed in the earlier section "Graphics Card and Monitor."

Printer

In most cases, no additional steps are required to configure a printer. When a printer is connected to the server, it is detected automatically, and the drivers that are needed are installed automatically as well. If your printer is not detected automatically or if you want to connect to a network printer, use the Printer option to configure the printer. On the Printer screen, the following options are available for installing new printers:

> *New Queue for Existing Printer:* Use this option to connect a second queue to the same printer. This option is helpful if you want to provide Linux printers to Windows users as well as Linux users. For the Linux user, the printer would need input that is interpreted by a printer driver, whereas the Windows user would normally send formatted documents to the printer. Therefore, for the Windows user, documents that are sent in the raw format would be enough.

> *Directly Connected Printers:* This is the option you would use if a printer that is connected to your server directly were not recognized properly. In that case, select this option, and enter all properties for your printer manually.

> *Network Printers:* Use this option to connect to a network printer that is somewhere on the network.

> You can find more in-depth information about printer configuration in Chapter 14.

Sound

Even on a server, it can be useful to configure a sound card. In YaST, you do that on the Sound screen. On this screen, you will normally see the current configuration of the sound card in your server—if a sound card is present (see Figure 3-7). If your sound card is not detected automatically, click the Add button on this screen to configure it manually. This requires access to the right kernel module (driver), which you can select from a list.

To modify the properties of an existing sound card, select the sound card, and click Edit. This displays advanced options for the server's sound card. For example, if a joystick port is present on the sound card, you can set its properties here. Usually, you shouldn't need to use this option often on a server.

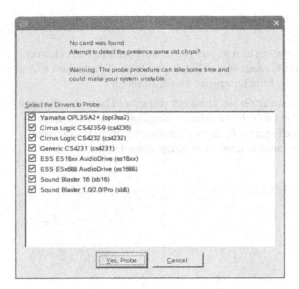

Figure 3-7. *If a sound card is present in your server, you can configure it with YaST.*

The System Menu

The System menu contains many options you can use to configure system settings on your server. I discuss most of these menu options in other chapters in this book. The following briefly describes each option:

/etc/sysconfig *Editor:* The /etc/sysconfig editor gives you access to configuration files that are in the directory /etc/sysconfig. As you'll learn in the section "YaST and Its Configuration Files" later in this chapter, many of these files are modified automatically when using different YaST settings. You can modify all these files manually as well. This requires good knowledge of when to use a particular file. If the file is tuned manually, you have two options to do so, either using YaST or using an editor such as vi.

Boot Loader: The Boot Loader option specifies how your server should boot. You'll learn more about this in Chapter 10.

Boot or Rescue Floppy: If a floppy drive is available in your server, you can create boot and rescue floppies to ensure that you will be able to boot your server in the case of problems. Since this functionality is available from the first installation CD or the installation DVD, I won't discuss it here.

Date and Time: Click this option to change the current date, time, and time zone. An easy-to-use interface helps you make these changes as required. Basically, you have three options. First, you can select the region and time zone you are in. Next, you can set the time and date on your server. The last option is an important one; use Hardware Clock Set To to set your server's hardware clock. Most common for servers is to set the hardware clock to UTC, which is related to Greenwich mean time. Setting this time allows your servers to communicate with the same time. Local time is then calculated by taking an offset for local time while also considering daylight saving time. This happens automatically.

High Availability: The High Availability option configures Linux heartbeat clustering. You'll learn more about this in Chapter 32.

LVM: Logical Volume Manager (LVM) is a system that allows you to work with logical volumes as opposed to physical allocated partitions on your server. In Chapter 8, you'll learn how to create and manage logical volumes on a SUSE Linux Enterprise Server 10 server.

Languages: Dozens of different languages are available, although you should be aware that you cannot apply all languages everywhere. You can select a primary language as well as a secondary language on the Languages screen (see Figure 3-8). After changing the primary language, you need to restart your graphical environment to apply the change completely.

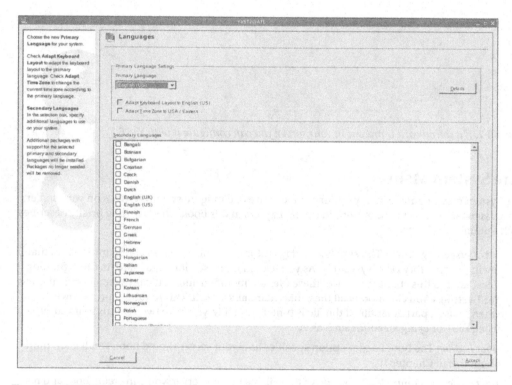

Figure 3-8. *SUSE Linux can work with a primary language as well as secondary languages.*

PCI Device Drivers: You can use the PCI ID Setup option to tune PCI drivers on your server. These are expert settings; you should not use them if you don't know exactly what you are doing.

Partitioner: The Partitioner utility helps you create partitions and volumes on your server. You can find an in-depth discussion of this in Chapter 8.

Power Management: If you are using a laptop, you can use the Power Management settings to create energy-saving schemes. On a server that is always AC powered, it does not make sense to use this option. You would always want it set to the Performance scheme, which makes sure your server is performing in the most optimal way. In the Other Settings drop-down list, one option, however, is useful for servers: the ACPU Buttons option. This option allows you to set the default behavior when a certain button is clicked on your server. For servers, only the Power Button option makes sense; by default, clicking the power button on the server will shut down the server gracefully. Other options are available as well, as shown in Figure 3-9; you may want to consider setting the default action for clicking the power button on your server to something less interrupting than shutting down the complete system. For example, it is a good choice just to have your server ignore the power button being pressed or have it start the screen saver when it's pressed. By doing so, you can minimize the risk that someone shuts down your server by accident.

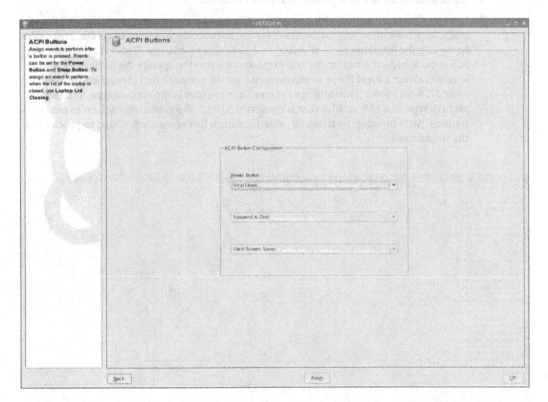

Figure 3-9. *To prevent an unscheduled shutdown of your server, I recommend switching the ACPI Button Configuration options, which are under the Power Management option.*

Powertweak: The Powertweak utility helps you tune and optimize your SUSE Linux Enterprise 10 server from a graphical interface. Since I discuss tuning and optimizing in Chapter 31, I haven't included information about the Powertweak utility here.

Profile Manager: The Systems Configuration Profile Management (SCPM) option helps you in creating hardware profiles. This is useful for laptops that are switched from a docking station to stand-alone mode from time to time; however, it doesn't make sense to use this option on a server. Therefore, I recommend leaving the status of this option to its default, which is Disabled, and not to do anything with it.

System Backup: You can use the System Backup tool to create a backup of the most important files and settings on your server. The utility was developed to make a backup of system settings, not to make a backup of data on your server. Before you can make a system backup, you must create a backup profile. Therefore, every backup should start by using the Profile Management option. The following procedure describes how to create a backup profile:

1. From the System Backup utility, select the Profile Management drop-down list, and select Add to create a new profile.

2. Enter a name for the new profile, and then click OK.

3. Next, as shown in Figure 3-10, a window pops up where you can specify the archive settings. In this window, enter a filename for the backup file you want to create. Make sure to specify the filename as an absolute path; in other words, use /tmp/mybackup and not just mybackup. As the next mandatory option, you need to specify the backup location, which is either a local file or a remote server on the network that is reached by means of an NFS file server. The third option you have to enter is the archive type. The default archive type of a TAR archive that is compressed with the gzip utility will do in most situations. After making the required selections from this screen, click Next to proceed to the next screen.

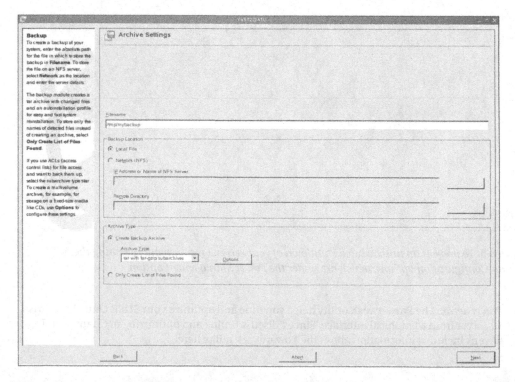

Figure 3-10. *The System Backup utility provides an easy-to-use interface to create a backup of the most important files on your server.*

4. The purpose of this backup utility is to make a system backup. Such a backup should include all configuration files on your server that have changes since the installation of the server. If such a backup is available, it is so much easier to restore your server to its current operational state later. To create such a backup, all the options selected in the Backup Options screen by default will do fine. Therefore, on this screen, just click Next to proceed.

5. Now you can create a list of items that can be excluded from the search and the files that should be included (see Figure 3-11). The default list of items to be excluded will do fine in most situations. If you need to add any directory or file system type to this list, click Add to do so. Also, you can remove directories or file systems from the exclusion list (which will actually include them) by selecting the item and then clicking the Delete button. After making your selection, click OK to finish creating the backup profile.

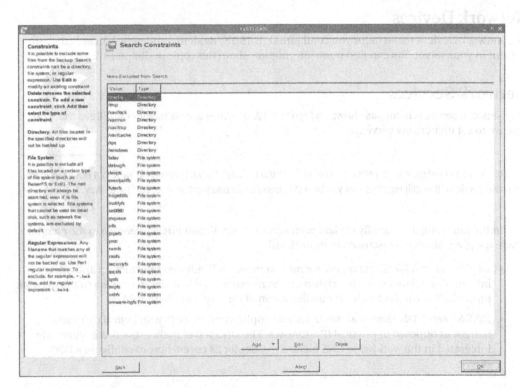

Figure 3-11. *You should use a list of items that should never be searched for changed files in the backup profile.*

6. You are now back at the System Backup screen. On this screen, select Create Backup to start creating the backup. Then click Close to close the System Backup screen and continue what you were doing.

System Restoration: You can restore a backup that was created by the System Backup option, as discussed before, by using the System Restoration option. This screen lets you select the file from which you want to restore the backup. Then it allows access to an interface where you can specify what exactly you want to restore from the backup file. Once that is done, the system restore can start. You should, however, always be careful when using this option. If you're not paying attention, it is easy to overwrite files that shouldn't be overwritten!

System Services (Runlevel): The System Services screen is an important one; it helps you select all processes that should start automatically when booting your server. You can find an in-depth discussion of the options that are available from this interface in Chapter 10 of this book.

Virtual Machine Management (Xen): Use this option to configure a Xen virtual machine. Check Chapter 34 for more information about working with Xen.

Network Devices

The Network Devices menu helps you configure DSL, ISDN, modems, and network cards that are present in your server. You can find more information about this topic in Chapter 13.

Network Services

The Network Services menu, as shown in Figure 3-12, provides access to a lot of utilities that you can use to set up network services.

Note You can configure most network services from the Network Services screen in YaST, but not all of them. For some services, it is still required that you tune the associated configuration files the "hard" way.

In the following list, I briefly explain each service. You will also find a reference to the chapter where the given service is discussed in more detail.

- *DHCP Server:* A DHCP server is a server that provides IP address information and other information related to IP that clients on the network need in order to connect to the network properly. You can find an in-depth discussion of this topic in Chapter 24.

- *DNS Server:* A DNS server allows users and applications to work with logical computer names, as opposed to physical IP addresses. The DNS server makes sure these names are integrated in the worldwide DNS hierarchy. Chapter 23 covers how to configure a DNS server.

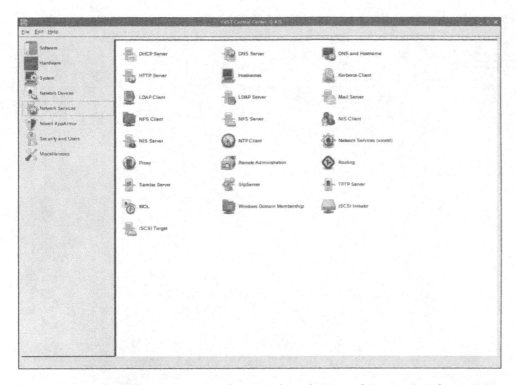

Figure 3-12. *You can configure most network services from the Network Services interface in YaST.*

- *DNS and Hostname*: Every server in the network must have a unique name. As a minimal requirement, all servers need a host name, because some services rely on that. In most situations, it is also most useful for servers to have a DNS name as well. Usually you configure these names when configuring the network interface on your server, as discussed in Chapter 13. If you need to change just the name of this computer, use this interface instead.

- *HTTP Server*: One of the most popular uses of Linux is as an HTTP server. This is a server serving web documents that can be read from a browser. For this purpose, SUSE Linux Enterprise Server includes the Apache 2 web server. You can configure the web server from this interface. You can find more details about web server configuration in Chapter 22.

- *Hostnames*: Usually, you will use a DNS server to address servers by their host names. As an alternative, you can store host names and their IP addresses in the ASCII text configuration file /etc/hosts. Of course, you can manage this file just by modifying its contents with an editor such as vi. As an alternative, you can use the Host Configuration screen shown in Figure 3-13 to enter the names of computers and their IP addresses on the network.

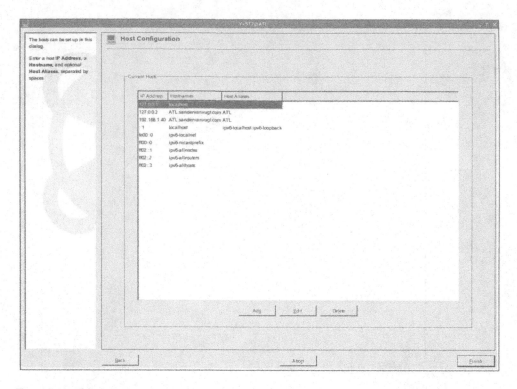

Figure 3-13. *The YaST Hostnames screen provides an easy way to tune the contents of the /etc/hosts file on your server.*

- *Kerberos Client:* Kerberos is a protocol that is used to connect to network services in a secure, encrypted manner. In Chapter 21 you can read how to configure Kerberos.

- *LDAP Client:* In the past, every service had its own configuration file, which was fine when all these servers were more or less stand-alone services. However, if you need to manage the network services centrally, a centralized repository such as the LDAP server proves to be useful. If an LDAP server is configured on the network, then you can use the LDAP Client option to connect to such a server. You can find more about the configuration of both the LDAP client and the LDAP server in Chapter 17.

- *LDAP Server:* The LDAP Server option helps you configure a central database that can be used for different purposes on the network. You can learn more about this in Chapter 17.

- *Mail Server:* SUSE Linux Enterprise Server comes with the Postfix mail transfer agent (MTA). This option provides an interface to modify the Postfix mail server's settings. Read Chapter 16 for more details about this subject.

- *NFS Client:* SUSE Linux Enterprise Server offers many options for sharing files on the network. One of these is NFS, the traditional way of offering shared files on a Unix network. In Chapter 15 you will learn how to use SUSE Linux Enterprise Server both as an NFS server and as an NFS client.

- *NFS Server:* This option allows you to set up SUSE Linux Enterprise Server 10 as an NFS file server. You'll read more about this in Chapter 15.

- *NIS Client*: NIS is a legacy service to share information across the network. In particular, it is used to share information about users, networks, hosts, and more. However legacy, in environments where Unix is still operational, this service is often still required. Use the NIS Client option to configure your server so it can get its NIS-related information from some server in the network.

- *NIS Server*: You can use even a modern Linux distribution such as SUSE Linux Enterprise Server 10 as an NIS server.

- *NTP Client*: On modern networks, having the right time on your servers has become really important. This module allows you to set up SUSE Linux Enterprise Server 10 as an NTP client. For more information about the configuration of SUSE Linux Enterprise Server 10 both as an NTP server as well as an NTP client, read Chapter 20.

- *Network Services (xinetd)*: Many services are started with their own daemon process that is simply listening all the time for incoming requests. For a busy Samba server or web server, there is no problem with that. If, however, a network service is needed only occasionally, it doesn't make sense to have it active and waiting all the time. This is where the xinetd daemon comes in. This is a service that is configured to listen on ports for other services. If, for example, an FTP request comes in on the FTP port and xinetd is monitoring that port, it will wake up the FTP server. If no requests come in on the FTP port, the FTP server can keep sleeping and that way doesn't waste any system resources. You'll learn more about xinetd in Chapter 19.

- *Proxy*: SUSE Linux Enterprise Server includes Squid, a powerful proxy server. In Chapter 28 you can read in detail how to configure that service. From YaST, use the Proxy module to configure it from a graphical interface.

- *Remote Administration*: SUSE Linux Enterprise Server offers many options for remote administration. One of them is the VNC service that was discussed shortly earlier in this chapter. The Remote Administration interface also gives you the option of enabling remote administration using VNC on SUSE Linux Enterprise Server 10. You can find more information about remote administration in Chapter 18.

- *Routing*: Most companies use dedicated hardware to route IP packets where they need to go. If, however, a small workgroup needs a router, any Linux distribution will do just fine.

- *Samba Server*: One of the best services on Linux is the Samba service. This is an open source implementation of the Windows SMB protocol that is used for file sharing across the network. The best part of it is that Samba does its work much faster than Windows itself! Everything you need to know about setting up SUSE Linux Enterprise Server 10 as a Samba file server is in Chapter 15.

- *SLP Server*: Service Location Protocol (SLP) is a service you can use for easily finding services on the network. Use this button to configure an SLP server, and check Chapter 33 for more details on it.

- *TFTP Server*: If in your network there are many Linux machines and you want to set up these machines automatically, you can use a TFTP server. This server can deliver a boot image to all the clients requesting it, no matter whether they are just booting from a floppy and making contact with the server or whether they are doing a PXE boot.

- *WOL*: Wake on Lan (WOL) is a management standard that you can use to wake up a PC by simply sending it a packet over the network. Use this interface to add machines that you want to wake up automatically.

- *Windows Domain Membership:* If you use SUSE Linux for file sharing on the network but you have a Windows Active Directory or domain that is used for user authentication, you can make your Linux server a member of the domain. You use the winbind process, which is part of the Samba server, to make that connection.

- *iSCSI Initiator:* The iSCSI initiator is a software component that is needed to connect to a SAN or server that offers shared storage by means of an iSCSI target. Check Chapter 32 for more details on that.

- *iSCSI Target:* You can use the iSCSI target to offer shared storage over the network. You can configure SUSE Linux Enterprise Server 10 as an iSCSI target. Check Chapter 29 for more details.

Novell AppArmor

You can use the Novell AppArmor service as an application-level firewall. It makes sure an application can do only the things it is allowed to do and nothing else. To protect an application with AppArmor, you must create an AppArmor profile. In Chapter 32 you can read how this works.

Security and Users

This menu has programs to secure your server. In it, you will find six applications:

- *CA Management:* The CA Management program allows you to configure a certificate authority (CA). This software makes it possible for you to grant PKI certificates on the network. These certificates are used for securing communications between clients and network services such as the web server. In Chapter 21 you can learn how to set up a certificate authority for your network.

- *Common Server Certificate:* Every server needs a certificate to secure applications that are offered by the server. You can find more information about tuning the server certificate in Chapter 21.

- *Firewall:* Every Linux distribution has the netfilter firewall that you can use to tune which packets are allowed to come in and go out through a given server. On SUSE Linux Enterprise Server 10, the kernel-level functionality of the netfilter firewall is integrated into the easy-to-use interface of the SUSE firewall. In Chapter 30, you can read how to configure this firewall.

- *Group Management:* Since Linux is a multiuser system, you need groups and users on your server. In Chapter 5, you can read how to configure users and groups on SUSE Linux Enterprise Server 10.

- *Local Security:* The Local Security option provides a wizard that walks you through some options to secure your server quickly. In the next section, you will learn how to use this wizard.

- *User Management:* You can use this program (see Figure 3-14) for user management on your server. See Chapter 5 for more details.

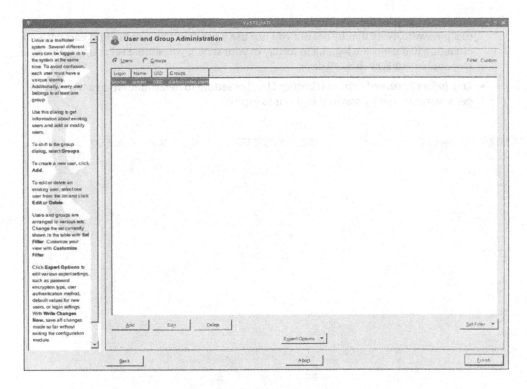

Figure 3-14. *YaST provides an easy interface for user and group management.*

The YaST Local Security Configuration program allows you to set up a secure server easily. After starting the program, you can choose from four settings: Home Workstation, Networked Workstation, Network Server, and Custom Settings. You will now learn how to apply some custom settings:

1. On the Security Settings screen, select Custom Settings, and then click Next.

2. You'll see the Password Settings screen (see Figure 3-15). On this screen, enter all required properties for new passwords that are created on the server. After making required changes, click Next to continue. The following properties are available:

   - *Check New Passwords*: Use this option if you want new passwords to be checked against a dictionary in order to make sure no weak passwords are used.

   - *Test for Complicated passwords*: This option will require passwords to be a mix of letters and numbers.

   - *Password Encryption Method*: You can choose between Blowfish, MD5, and DES. Choose Blowfish for optimal security, and use DES or MD5 if you need compatibility.

   - *Minimum Acceptable Password Length*: You can this option to specify the minimal length for new passwords. By default, a password must be five characters or more. Be aware that only the Blowfish encryption algorithm allows you to use passwords longer than eight characters.

- *Password Age*: Use the Minimum and Maximum settings to determine the maximal use of a password. Note that by default you can use a password for almost 300 years without changing it! If users are logging in locally to your server, you should set this to a more reasonable value, such as 40 days.

- *Day before Password Expires Warning*: Use this setting to determine when a user should get a warning that a password is about to expire.

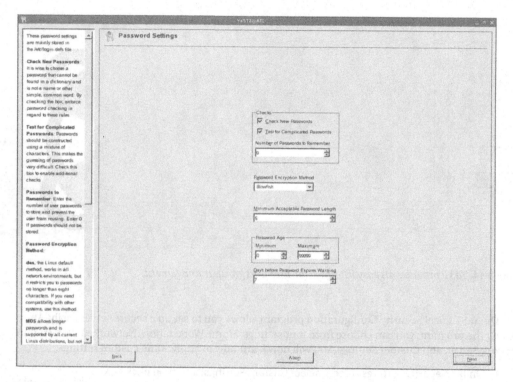

Figure 3-15. *On the Password Settings screen, you can set policies for new passwords that are created on your server.*

3. Now you can enter some default boot settings. If no changes are made, the Ctrl+Alt+Del shortcut will reboot the server. I recommend changing this to prevent you from rebooting your server by accident. kdm's shutdown behavior is relevant only if the KDE graphical desktop is used (kdm is the program used to log in and out of a KDE environment). The default setting makes sure that only the user root is allowed to shut down the server from a KDE graphical session. After making the required modifications, click Next to proceed to the next step.

4. Now you'll see the Login Settings screen, which has three options, all related to logging in to your system. The first option specifies that a delay (one minute by default) should occur after three incorrect login attempts by default. Next, the Record Successful Login Attempts option makes sure that successful logins are also logged to the generic system log file /var/log/messages. Last, make sure the option Allow Remote Graphical Login is selected if you want to be able to make a VNC remote connection to this server. Then click Next to proceed.

5. Now you enter a window where you can set the minimum and maximum user and group IDs (see Chapter 5). In almost all cases, the defaults are fine.

6. On the Miscellaneous Settings screen (see Figure 3-16), you can set some miscellaneous stuff. First, the File Permissions setting is set to the Easy profile, which will be fine in most cases. On a server where users log in frequently, use the Secure setting for more security. Usually, you will never use the Paranoid setting because it will disable most services until you enable them again manually. The other two important settings here are Current Directory in Root's Path and Current Directory in Path of Regular Users. For security reasons, you should never enable these two, because they make you more vulnerable to viruses. After selecting the required options, click Finish to complete the wizard and store your settings.

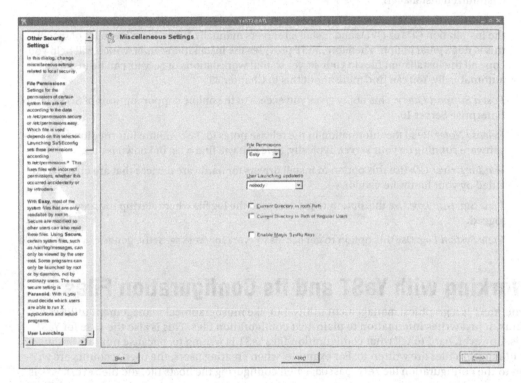

Figure 3-16. *The Miscellaneous Settings screen allows you to set file permissions for important files by selecting the appropriate profile.*

Tip It's not necessary to sit behind your server to run YaST. Using SSH, you can also run it remotely. To run the graphical interface over the network on your workstation, just initialize an SSH session using the `ssh -X` command, and from SSH, start YaST. You can learn more about configuring SSH in Chapter 18.

Miscellaneous Options

Everything that doesn't really belong to one of the other menu items in YaST appears under the Miscellaneous options. These are the Miscellaneous options:

Autoinstallation: Use this option to create an AutoYaST installation file. This file contains all the settings you want to be configured automatically on servers you are installing in your network. You can find more details in Chapter 35.

CD Creator: When working with AutoYaST to install other servers running SUSE Linux Enterprise Server 10 in your network, you have the option to burn all the settings to an installation CD. If you want to do that, use the CD Creator utility to make CDs that you can use start the customized installation.

Installation Server: When installing a new server (or workstations) in your network, you can use the installation CDs or DVDs and install all servers manually. When installing a lot of machines, this is not a great option. Therefore, YaST provides the installation server, which will help you copy all the installation files to your server so that workstations or servers can be installed automatically. You can find more about this in Chapter 35.

Post a Support Query: This utility gives you access to the online support options of SUSE Linux Enterprise Server 10.

Release Notes: Read the information in the release notes for last-minute information about the software running on your server. Typically, here you will find a list of known issues.

Vendor Driver CD: Use this option to install drivers for hardware devices that are on a CD provided by your hardware vendor.

View Start-up Log: Use this option to get access to the log file where startup messages are logged.

View System Log: Use this option to get access to /var/log/messages, the generic system log file.

Working with YaST and Its Configuration Files

True, YaST is a graphical management utility, but like most graphical management utilities on Linux, it just writes information to plain-text configuration files. This is also the case for YaST. It is, however, hard to tell what configuration files YaST is writing to, because not one but many configuration files are written to. For example, when creating users, the user accounts are written to the configuration file /etc/passwd; when configuring the hosts file, the file /etc/hosts is written; and so on.

When you are planning on modifying configuration files manually by using an editor such as vi, you should be aware that YaST sometimes doesn't like that. This is because YaST in some cases puts a checksum on the configuration file so it can detect when changes have been made. If a change is detected, different things can happen: YaST can refuse to modify the configuration file, YaST will store its own configuration to the file and therewith overwrite the current information in the file, or YaST will write its settings to a separate file. In many cases, a clever system is used where YaST writes its configuration to variables in files stored in the directory /etc/sysconfig. However, if you want to make sure nothing goes wrong, don't mix YaST and other management utilities.

Many settings from YaST are reflected in configuration files in the directory /etc/sysconfig. For example, the settings related to the clock on your system are written to the file /etc/sysconfig/clock. Figure 3-17 shows an example of this file.

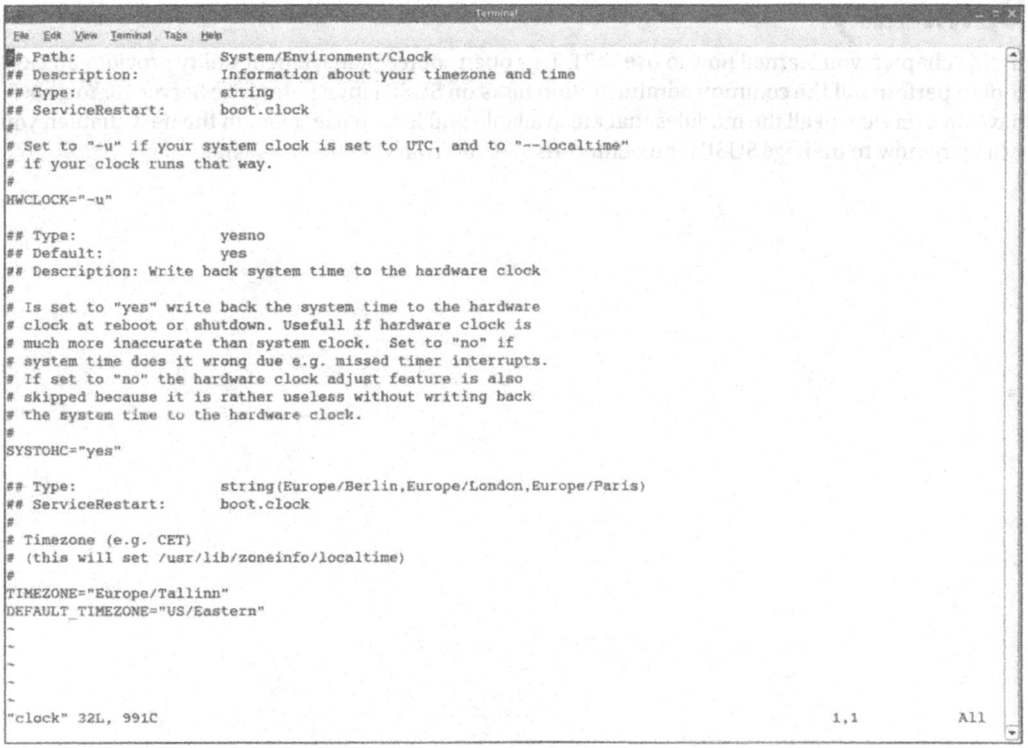

```
File Edit View Terminal Tabs Help
## Path:               System/Environment/Clock
## Description:        Information about your timezone and time
## Type:               string
## ServiceRestart:     boot.clock
#
# Set to "-u" if your system clock is set to UTC, and to "--localtime"
# if your clock runs that way.
#
HWCLOCK="-u"

## Type:               yesno
## Default:            yes
## Description: Write back system time to the hardware clock
#
# Is set to "yes" write back the system time to the hardware
# clock at reboot or shutdown. Usefull if hardware clock is
# much more inaccurate than system clock.  Set to "no" if
# system time does it wrong due e.g. missed timer interrupts.
# If set to "no" the hardware clock adjust feature is also
# skipped because it is rather useless without writing back
# the system time to the hardware clock.
#
SYSTOHC="yes"

## Type:               string(Europe/Berlin,Europe/London,Europe/Paris)
## ServiceRestart:     boot.clock
#
# Timezone (e.g. CET)
# (this will set /usr/lib/zoneinfo/localtime)
#
TIMEZONE="Europe/Tallinn"
DEFAULT_TIMEZONE="US/Eastern"
~
~
~
~
"clock" 32L, 991C                                        1,1          All
```

Figure 3-17. *Changes made to the clock setting from YaST are written to the configuration file* /etc/sysconfig/clock.

Working with YaST Modules

YaST is a modular utility. You can start all the programs you access from the YaST interface from the command line as well. These programs are called the YaST *modules*. You can list the existing YaST modules with the yast -l or YaST -l command. You can start each of these modules as an argument to the yast command. For example, if you want to start the YaST module for user management, issue the command yast users from the command line. This will just start the required module and therefore be faster than when first starting YaST and selecting the module you want to use in the graphical interface.

Because it is possible to run YaST as a command from a console environment, some other interesting options are available as well. For example, it is possible to use YaST to install a software package that is in the RPM format by issuing the command YaST -i somepackage.rpm. Another option that is useful is the option --log logfile. This option allows you to write to a log file what YaST is doing when you start it; this may help you when troubleshooting any apparent YaST problems.

Tip Having problems starting YaST from the menu? In that case, just open a console window, and from there, use the YaST command. The advantage is that YaST will write to the console what it is doing. If YaST cannot start properly, you will see the reason in the console window.

Summary

In this chapter, you learned how to use YaST. This open source management utility provides an easy tool to perform all the common administration tasks on SUSE Linux Enterprise Server 10. You now have an overview of all the modules that are available and how to use them. In the next chapter, you will learn how to manage SUSE Linux Enterprise Server from the command line.

CHAPTER 4

■■■

Finding Your Way on the Command Line

Although SUSE Linux Enterprise Server 10 comes with a full graphical environment and offers YaST as the graphical management application, as a Linux administrator you will occasionally need to work from the command line. Even nowadays the most advanced management tasks are executed from there. Therefore, this chapter introduces you to the basic skills needed to work from the command line.

Working with the Bash Shell

To communicate commands to the operating system kernel, you need an interface that sits between the kernel and the user and issues these commands. This interface is known as the *shell*. On Linux, several shells are available, with Bash (short for the Bourne Again Shell) being the most commonplace. The reason for this is that Bash is an enhanced version of sh, a common shell that has been around since 1977. You should, however, be aware that Bash is not the only shell you can use. You can also use other shells:

tcsh: A shell with a scripting language that works like the C programming language. This is rather popular with C programmers.

zsh: A shell that is compatible with Bash but offers even more features.

sash: The stand-alone shell. This is a minimal shell that runs in almost all environments. Therefore, it is well suited for system troubleshooting.

Making the Most of Bash

Basically, in a Bash environment an administrator is working with commands. An example of such a command is ls, which you can use to display a list of files in a given directory. To make working with these commands as easy as possible, Bash has some useful features to offer. Some of the most used Bash features are automatic completion and the history mechanism.

Some shells offer the option to complete a command automatically. Bash also has this feature but goes beyond the option to just complete commands. Bash can complete almost everything—not just commands but also filenames and shell variables.

Note A *variable* is a common value, stored with a given name, that is used often by the shell and by the commands working from the shell. An example of such a variable is PATH, which stores a list of directories that should be searched when a user enters a command. To refer to the contents of a variable, prepend a $ sign before the name of the variable. For example, the command echo $PATH would display the content of the current search path Bash is using.

To use the completion feature, press the Tab key. The following is an example of how this works. In this example, the cat command displays the contents of an ASCII text file. The name of this file, which is in the current directory, is this_is_a_file. To open this file, the user can type cat thi and next press the Tab key. If just one file starts with the letters *thi*, Bash will automatically complete the name of the file. If there are more options, Bash will complete the name of the file as far as possible. This happens, for example, when the current directory contains files with the names this_is_a_text_file and thisAlsoIsAFile. Since both files start with this, Bash will complete only up to this and not go beyond that. To display a list of possibilities, you can then hit the Tab key again. This allows you to manually enter more information. Of course, you can then pressing the Tab key again to use the completion feature once more.

Knowing the Important Key Sequences

Sometimes you will enter a command from the Bash command line and nothing will happen or something totally unexpected will happen. If that happens, it is good to know that some key sequences are available to perform basic Bash management tasks. The following is a short list of the most useful key sequences:

Ctrl+C: Use this key sequence to quit a command that is not responding (or simply takes too long to complete). This key sequence works in most scenarios where the command is operational and producing output to the screen.

Ctrl+D: This key sequence is used to send the end-of-file (EOF) signal to a command. Use this when the command is waiting for more input. It will indicate this by displaying the secondary prompt, >.

Ctrl+R: This is the reversed search feature. When used, it will open the "reversed I-search" prompt. This prompt helps you locate commands you have used previously. The feature is especially useful when working with longer commands. Type the first characters of the command, and you will see immediately the last command you used that started with the same characters.

Ctrl+Z: Some people use Ctrl+Z to stop a command. In fact, it does stop your command, but it does not terminate it. A command that is interrupted with Ctrl+Z is just momentarily halted and can be restarted using the fg command. You can continue running the command in the background by issuing the bg command with the job number as the parameter. Use the jobs command to find the command's job number in your shell environment.

Working with the Bash History

Bash's history mechanism helps you remember the last commands you used. By default, Bash remembers the last 1,000 commands for any user. You can see an overview of these commands when using the history command from the Bash command line. This command shows a list of all the recently used commands. From this list, you can restart a command as well. If, for example, in the list of commands you see command number 51, you can easily run this command again by using its number preceded by an exclamation mark; so in the case of this example, you would use !51 for that purpose, as shown in Figure 4-1.

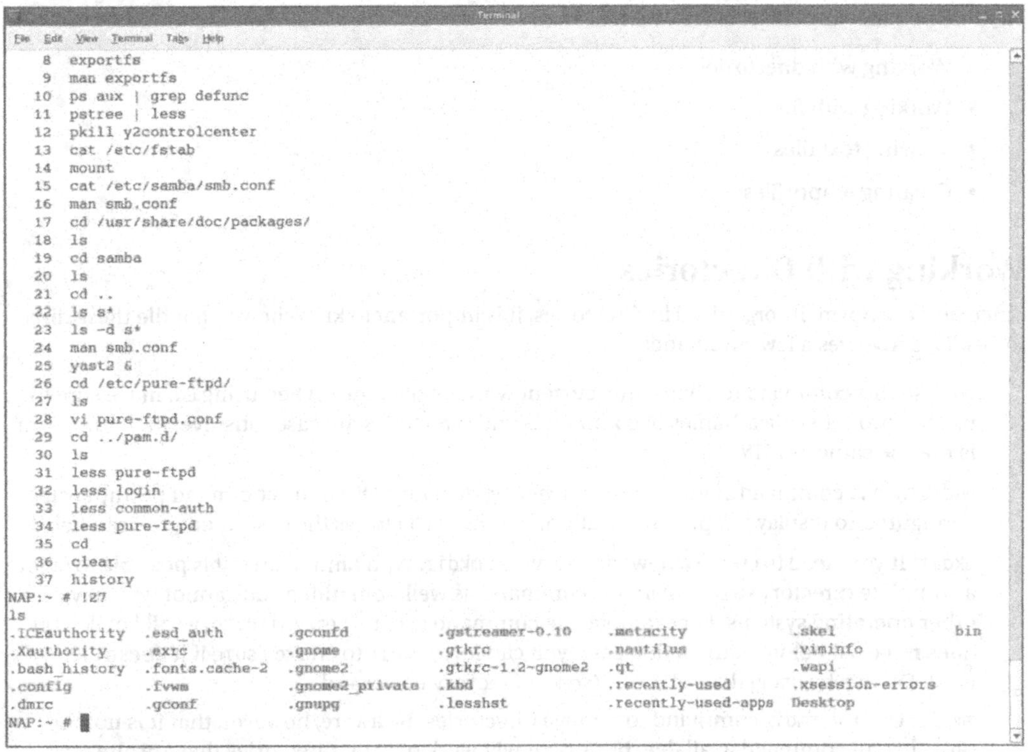

```
                                          Terminal                                        _ □ ×
 File  Edit  View  Terminal  Tabs  Help
      8   exportfs
      9   man exportfs
     10   ps aux | grep defunc
     11   pstree | less
     12   pkill y2controlcenter
     13   cat /etc/fstab
     14   mount
     15   cat /etc/samba/smb.conf
     16   man smb.conf
     17   cd /usr/share/doc/packages/
     18   ls
     19   cd samba
     20   ls
     21   cd ..
     22   ls s*
     23   ls -d s*
     24   man smb.conf
     25   yast2 &
     26   cd /etc/pure-ftpd/
     27   ls
     28   vi pure-ftpd.conf
     29   cd ../pam.d/
     30   ls
     31   less pure-ftpd
     32   less login
     33   less common-auth
     34   less pure-ftpd
     35   cd
     36   clear
     37   history
NAP:~ # !27
ls
.ICEauthority  .esd_auth    .gconfd         .gstreamer-0.10   .metacity          .skel            bin
.Xauthority    .exrc        .gnome          .gtkrc            .nautilus          .viminfo
.bash_history  .fonts.cache-2  .gnome2      .gtkrc-1.2-gnome2 .qt                .wapi
.config        .fvwm        .gnome2_private .kbd              .recently-used     .xsession-errors
.dmrc          .gconf       .gnupg          .lesshst          .recently-used-apps Desktop
NAP:~ # ▮
```

Figure 4-1. *The Bash history mechanism helps you easily execute a command again.*

As an administrator, you sometimes need to manage the commands that are in the history list. You have two ways of doing this. First, you can manage the file .bash_history where all commands you have used before are stored. Every user has such a file that is stored in the home directory. If, for example, you want to delete this file for user joyce, just remove it with the command rm /home/joyce/.bash_history. Notice that you must be root or joyce to do this. Also note that joyce normally won't see the file. This is because the name of the file begins with a dot, it is a hidden file, and normal users cannot see hidden files.

A second way of administering history files, which even regular users can deploy, is by using the history command. The most important option offered by this Bash internal command is c; this will clear the history list for the user who uses the command. So, use history -c to make sure your history is cleared. In that case, however, you cannot use the up arrow key any longer to access commands used previously.

■ **Caution** In the command history, everything you enter from the command line is saved. So, passwords you type in plain text are saved in the command history. For that reason, never type a plain-text password on the command line, because someone else might be able to see it.

Performing Basic File System Management Tasks

Everything on your SUSE Linux Enterprise Server is a file. Therefore, working with files is an important task when administering Linux. In this section, you will learn about file system management basics. The following subjects are covered:

- Working with directories
- Working with files
- Viewing text files
- Creating empty files

Working with Directories

Since files are normally organized in directories, it is important to know how to handle these directories. This involves a few commands:

cd: Use this command to change the current working directory. When using cd, make sure to use the proper syntax. Names of commands and directories are case sensitive; therefore, /bin is not the same as /BIN.

pwd: The pwd command stands for *print working directory*. Often the command prompt will be configured to display the present location, but this isn't always the case. If not, pwd can help.

mkdir: If you need to create a new directory, use mkdir. With Linux mkdir, it is possible to create a complete directory structure in one command as well, something you cannot typically do on other operating systems. For example, the command mkdir /some/directory will fail if /some does not exist beforehand. In that case, you can force mkdir to create /some if it doesn't already exist. Do this by using the mkdir -p /some/directory command.

rmdir: Use the rmdir command to remove directories. Be aware, however, that it is not the most useful command available, because it will work only on directories that are already empty. If the directory still has files and/or subdirectories in it, use rm -r instead.

Working with Files

An important task from the command line is managing the files in the directories. Four important commands are used for this purpose:

- ls lists files.
- rm removes files.
- cp copies files.
- mv moves files.

Using ls to List Files

To manage files on your server, you must first know what files are available. For this purpose, you can use the ls command. If you just use ls to show the contents of a given directory, it will display a list of files. These files, however, have properties as well. For example, every file has a user who is the owner of the file, some permissions, a size that is stored in the file system, and more. To see this information, use ls -l.

Apart from -l, ls has many other useful options, such as -d. For example, when working with the ls command, you can use wildcards; ls * will list all the files in the current directory, ls /etc/*a.*

will list all the files in the directory /etc that have an a followed by a . somewhere in the filename, and ls [abc]* will list all the files with names that start with either a, b, or c in the current directory. Now without the option -d, something strange will happen. If a directory matches the wildcard pattern, the entire contents of that directory are displayed as well. This isn't very useful, and for that reason, you should always use the -d option with the ls command when using wildcards.

One last thing you should be aware of when using ls is that it will work differently depending on who you are. If you are logged in as root, you will see all files, including hidden files. If, however, you are working as a normal user, hidden files are not displayed by default. As a normal user, you should specifically use the -a option to show them.

■ **Note** A *hidden file* is a file with a name that starts with a dot. Most configuration files that are stored in user home directories are created as hidden files; this prevents the user from deleting the file by accident.

Removing Files with rm

A task that needs to be performed on a regular basis is cleaning up the file system. For this purpose, you can use the rm command. For example, use rm /tmp/somefile to remove somefile from the /tmp directory. If you are root and have all the proper permissions on the file, you will succeed without any problems. (See Chapter 6 for more about permissions.) Since removing files can be delicate (imagine removing the wrong files), it may be necessary to push the rm command a little. You can do this by using the -f (force) switch. For example, use rm -f somefile if the command complains that somefile cannot be removed.

You can use the rm command to wipe entire directory structures as well; in this case, you have to use the -r option. If you combine this option with the -f option, the command will become very powerful. For example, use rm -rf /somedir to clear out the entire content of /somedir. You should be careful when using rm this way, especially since a small typing mistake can have serious consequences. Imagine, for example, that you type rm -rf / somedir (with a space between / and somedir) instead of rm -rf /somedir. As a result, the rm command will first remove everything in / and, once finished, will remove somedir as well. You should understand that the second part of the command is no longer required once the first part of the command has completed.

Copying Files with cp

If you need to copy files from one location on the file system to another, use the cp command. This command is easy to use; for example, use cp ~/* /tmp to copy all the files from your home directory to the directory /tmp. If subdirectories and their contents need to be included in the copy command as well, use the option -r. You should, however, be aware that cp normally does not copy hidden files with names that start with a dot. If you need to copy hidden files, make sure to use a pattern that starts with a dot; for example, use cp ~/.* /tmp to copy all the files that start with a dot from your home directory to the directory /tmp.

Moving Files with mv

It's also possible to move files. For example, use mv ~/somefile /tmp/otherfile to move the file somefile to /tmp. The interesting part of this command is that it is not possible to predict exactly what will happen when using this command. If a subdirectory with the name otherfile exists in /tmp, somefile will be created in this subdirectory. If, however, no directory with this name exists in /tmp, the command will save the contents of the original file somefile under the new name otherfile in the directory /tmp. To prevent this behavior, use the -i option. This option causes mv to prompt you if a file of the same name exists in the target directory.

You can use mv to rename directories, regardless of whether those directories contain any files. If, for example, you need to rename the directory /somedir to /somethingelse, use mv /somedir /somethingelse.

Viewing the Content of Text Files

When administering your SUSE Linux Enterprise Server, you will find that often you are modifying configuration files, which are all ASCII text files. Therefore, the ability to browse the content of these files is important. Different methods exist to perform this task:

cat: Displays the contents of a file

tac: Does the same but prints the result backward

tail: Shows just the last lines of a text file

head: Displays the first lines of a file

less: Opens an advanced file viewer

more: Is like less but not as advanced

The cat command just dumps the content of a file on the screen. This can be useful, however; if the content of the file does not fit on the screen, you will see some text scrolling by, and as the final result you will see only the last lines of the file being displayed on the screen. As an alternative for using cat, you can use tac as well. This command will dump the content of a file to the screen but with the last line first and the first line last.

Another useful command is tail. If no options are passed, this command will display the last ten lines of a text file. You can also modify the command to show any number of lines on the bottom of a file; for example, tail 2 /etc/passwd will show you the last two lines of the configuration file where usernames are stored. Also useful for monitoring what happens on your system is the option to keep tail open on a given log file. For example, executing tail -f /var/log/messages will immediately output any new line written to the bottom of that file. To display the top lines of a text file, use head.

less and more are two other common commands used to learn more about the contents of text files. The most important thing you need to remember about them is that you can do more with less. The less command is basically an improved version of more. Both commands will open your configuration file in a viewer. In this viewer, you can browse down in the file by pressing the Page Down key or the spacebar. Only less offers the option to browse up as well. Also, both commands have a search facility. If the less utility is open and displays the content of your file, use /sometext from within the less viewer to locate sometext in the file. Enter n to forward to the next entry in the file that matches the search request. To quit both utilities, use the q command.

Creating Empty Files

The last file management task I'll mention is the option for creating empty files. This can be useful for testing purposes. To do this, use the touch command. For example, touch somefile will create a zero-byte file with the name somefile in the current directory.

However, the main purpose of creating touch was never to create empty files; it was to open a file so that the last-access date/time of the file that is displayed with ls is modified to the current time. For example, touch * will set this time stamp to the current time on all the files in the current directory. If, however, touch is used with the name of a file that doesn't exist as its argument, it will create this file as an empty file.

Using Piping and Redirection

One of the most powerful features of the Linux command line is the option to use piping and redirection. *Piping* is the system used to send the result of a command to another command, and *redirection* sends the output of a command not to another command but to a file. This file doesn't necessarily need to be a regular file, but it can also be a device file, as you will see in the following examples.

Using Piping

The goal of piping is to execute a command and send the output of that command to the next command so this next command can do something with it. For instance, if the output of a command doesn't fit on the screen, the command can be piped to less, which allows you to browse the output of the first command screen by screen. This is, for example, useful when working with ls -lR. This command normally displays a list of files where all properties of the file are displayed and files in all subdirectories of the current directory are displayed. You would use ls -lR | less to send the output from the first command to the second command.

Another useful command you can use in a pipe construction is grep. You can use this command as a filter to filter out information that you want to see. Imagine, for example, that you want to check whether a user with the name julie exists in the user database /etc/passwd.

One solution is to open the file with a viewer such as cat or less and next browse the content of the file to check whether the string you are looking for is present in the file. That is a lot of work, however; a much easier solution is to pipe the content of the file to the filter grep that would filter out all lines that contain the string that is mentioned as an argument of grep. This command would look like cat /etc/passwd | grep julie: the first part of the pipe dumps the complete content of /etc/passwd on the screen, and the second part of the command filters out only those lines where the text julie is present. Notice that grep julie /etc/passwd would do the same thing.

Using Redirection

Where piping is the system used to send the result of a command to another command, redirection sends the result of a command to a file. This file can be a text file, but it can also be a special file like a device file. An easy example of redirection appears in the command ls -l > list_of_files. In this command, the > sign will make sure to cause the output of ls to be redirected to the file list_of_files. Now the interesting part of this command is what will happen when list_of_files already exists. In that case, the Bash shell just overwrites the existing file with the new content.

If you don't want to overwrite the content of existing files, you shouldn't use the single redirector sign (>); you should use a double redirector sign (>>) instead. For example, who > myfile will put the result of the who command (which displays a list of users currently logged in) in the file myfile. If next you want to append the result of the free command (which shows information about memory usage on your system) to the same file myfile, then use free >> myfile.

Apart from redirecting the output of commands to files, the inverse is also possible when using redirection. In that case, you are redirecting the content of a text file to a command that will use that content as its input. For example, use mail root < somefile to send the content of somefile to the user root by mail.

When using redirection, you should be aware that you can do more than just redirect output (technically referred to as STDOUT). Commands can produce error output as well. This error output is technically referred to as STDERR. To redirect this STDERR, use the 2> construction to indicate you are interested only in redirecting error output. For example, the command grep root * 2> somefile would perform the grep command. You can use this command to find the text root in all files in the current directory. Now the redirector 2> somefile will make sure all the error output is redirected to the file somefile that will be created for this purpose. It is possible to redirect both STDOUT as STDERR in one command as well. This would happen if you use the command grep root * 2> somefile > someotherfile.

One of the interesting features of redirection is that not only is it possible to redirect to regular files, but you can also redirect output to device files. One of the nice features of a Linux system is that any device that is connected to your system can be addressed by addressing a file. Before seeing how that works, next you'll see a short list of some important device files that you can use:

/dev/null: The null device; use this device to redirect to nothing.

/dev/zero: Use this device to return zeroes (used with the dd command).

/dev/ttyS0: The first serial port.

/dev/lp0: The first legacy LPT printer port.

/dev/hda: The master IDE device on IDE interface 0 (typically your hard drive).

/dev/hdb: The slave IDE device on IDE interface 0 (not always in use).

/dev/hdc: The master device on IDE interface 1 (typically your optical drive).

/dev/sda: The first SCSI or serial ATA device in your computer.

/dev/sdb: The second SCSI or serial ATA device in your computer.

/dev/sda1: The first partition on the first SCSI or serial ATA device in your computer.

/dev/tty1: The name of the first text-based console that is active on your computer. These TTYs are available from tty1 up to tty12.

/dev/fd0: The floppy disk drive in your PC.

One way of using redirection together with a device name is by redirecting error output of a given command to the null device. You would modify the previous command like this: grep root * 2> /dev/null. Of course, you run the risk that some serious issue is preventing your command from working well. In that case, use the command grep root * 2> /dev/tty12, which would log all error output to tty12, which can be activated with the key sequence Ctrl+F12 (use Ctrl+Alt+F12 if you are working from a graphical environment).

Another cool feature you can use with redirection is redirecting the output from one device to another device. To understand what happens, let's first look at what happens when you are using cat on a device, such as in cat /dev/sda. As you can see in Figure 4-2, this would display the complete content of the sda device on the standard output (notice that you should be root to do this).

The interesting part of displaying the contents of a storage device like this is that you can redirect it. Imagine a situation where you have a /dev/sdb as well and this sdb device is at least as large as /dev/sda. In that case, you can clone the disk just by using cat /dev/sda > /dev/sdb! This redirecting to devices can also be very dangerous. Imagine what would happen if you used the command cat /etc/passwd > /dev/sda; it would just dump the content of the passwd file to the beginning of the /dev/sda device. And since you are working on the raw device here, no file system information is used, so this command would overwrite all important administrative information that is stored at the beginning of the device that is mentioned. You would never be able to boot the device again! In Chapter 8, you will learn about the dd command that can be used to copy data from one device to another device in a way that is much more secure.

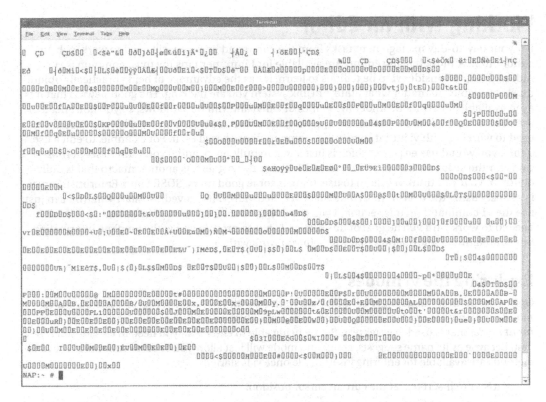

Figure 4-2. *When* cat *is used on a device like* /dev/sda, *it just shows the binary content of the device on the screen.*

Finding Files

Another useful task you should be able to perform on your server is finding files. Of course, you can use the facility that is available to do just that from the graphical interface, but when you are working on the command line, you probably don't just want to start a graphical environment to find some files. In that scenario, use the find command instead. This is a powerful command that helps you find files based upon any property the file can have. For example, you can find files by their names; the access, creation, or modification date; the user who created them; the permissions set on the file; and much more. If, for example, you want to find all the files with names that start with hosts, use find / -name "hosts*". I recommend always putting the string of the thing you are looking for between quotes; this makes sure that find knows where the argument starts and where it stops.

You can also find files based on the user who created them. For example, find / -user "britney" will locate all files created by user britney.

You can also execute a command on the result of the find command by using the -exec option. If, for example, you want to copy all files of user britney to the directory /files, use find / -user "britney" -exec cp {} files \;. In such a construction, you should pay attention to two specific elements used in the command. First there is the {} construction, which is used to refer to the result of the foregoing find command. Next, there is the \; element, which is used to tell find that this is the end of the part of the command that began with -exec.

Working with an Editor

For your day-to-day management tasks from the command line, you will need to work with an editor often. Although many editors are available for Linux, perhaps the most common is vi. Although some consider vi to be tedious to learn, it has the advantage of being practically ubiquitously available, no matter what Linux or Unix system you are hacking. The good news is that it is even available for Windows under the names of winvi and vim for Windows, so you don't need to use the Notepad editor in that operating system. Another important reason why you should get used to working with vi is that some other commands are based on it. For example, to edit a user's quota, you would use edquota, which is just a macro built on vi, and if you want to set permissions for the sudo command, use visudo, which as you can guess, is another macro that is built on top of vi. If you think vi is hard to use, there is some good news. SUSE Linux Enterprise Server is actually using the user-friendly version of vi called vim (vi improved). To start vim, you can just use the vi command. In this section, I will provide the bare minimum of information that is needed to work with vi. The goal of this section is not to provide you with complete information but with minimal information that will help you work with vi.

Exploring the vi modes

One of the hardest things to get used to when working with vi is its modal nature. There is the *command mode* that is used to enter new commands, and there is the *insert mode* (also referred to as *input mode*) that is used to enter text. Before being able to enter text, you need to enter insert mode first, because as its name suggests, command mode will just allow you to enter commands. Several methods are available for entering insert mode once vi is started:

- Use i to insert text at the current cursor position.
- Use a to append text after the current position of the cursor.
- Use o to open a new line under the current position of the cursor (my favorite option).
- Use 0 to open a new line above the current position of the cursor.

After entering insert mode, you can enter text, and vi will work just like any other editor. Now if you want to save your work, you should next return to command mode and use the appropriate commands to save your work. To return to command mode, press the Esc key.

Tip When starting vi, always give as an argument the name of the file you want to create with vi or the name of an existing file you would like to modify. If you don't do that, vi will display help text, and you will have to find out how to get out of this help text. Of course, you can always just read the entire help information to find out how that works.

Saving and Quitting

After activating command mode, you can use commands to save your work. The most common way to do so is by using the :wq! command. With this command, several tasks take place at once. First, a colon is used, just because it is part of the command. Then, w is used to save the text you have typed so far. Because no filename followed w, the text will be saved under the same filename that was used when opening the file. If you want to save it under a new filename, just enter the new name after the w command. Next in the :wq! command is q, which will cause the editor to quit after saving the file. Last, the exclamation mark is used to tell vi that it shouldn't complain but just do its work. Since vi has a tendency to be smart with remarks like "A file with this name already exists," you are probably going to like the exclamation mark.

As you have just learned, you can use :wq! to write and quit vi. You can, however, also use just parts of this command. For example, use :w if you just want to write the changes while working on a file without quitting it, or use :q! to quit the file without writing changes. The latter option is a nice panic key if something has happened that you absolutely don't want to store on your system. This is useful because vi will sometimes do magic to the content of your file when you have hit the wrong keys by accident. However, an alternative exists; use the u command to undo the last changes you made to the file.

Cutting, Copying, and Pasting

If you think you need a graphical interface to use cut, copy, and paste features, you're wrong. vi could already do that back in the 1970s. You have two ways of executing the cut, copy, and paste commands: the easy way and the hard way. If you want to do it the easy way, you can use the v command, which enters visual mode. In visual mode, you can select a block of text by using the arrow keys. After selecting the block, you can cut, copy, and paste it:

- Use d to cut the selection. This will remove the selection and place it in a buffer in memory.

- Use y to copy the selection to the designated area reserved for that purpose in your server's memory.

- Use p to paste the selection. This will copy the selection you have just placed in the reserved area of your server's memory back into your document. For this purpose, it will always use the current position of your cursor at that particular moment.

Deleting Text

Another task you will probably use often when working with vi is deleting text. You can use many methods to delete text from vi. The easiest of them is from insert mode; just use the Delete and Backspace keys to delete any text you like. This works the same way you would do it from, for example, a word processor. Then, some options are available from vi command mode as well:

- Use x to delete a single character. This has the same effect as using the Delete key while in insert mode.

- Use dw to delete the rest of the word. That is, dw will delete anything from the current position of the cursor to the end of the word.

- Use dd to delete a complete line. This is a useful option that you will probably like a lot.

Getting Help

Linux offers many ways to get help. Let's start with a short overview:

- The man command offers documentation for most commands that are available on your system.

- Almost all commands listen to the --help argument as well. This will display a short overview of available options that can be used with the command.

- For Bash internal commands, you can use the help command with the name of the Bash internal command that you want to know more about. For example, use help for to get more information about the Bash internal command for.

Note An *internal command* is a command that is a part of the shell and does not exist as a program file on disk. To get an overview of all internal commands that are available, just type help on the command line.

- For almost all programs that are installed on your server, extensive documentation is available in the directory /usr/share/doc/packages.

Using man to Get Help

The most important source of information for using commands that are available on your Linux system is man. man is short for the system programmer's *manual*. In the past, these were books in which all parts of the Unix operating system were documented. This structure of different books (nowadays called *sections*) is still present in the man command; therefore, you will now find a list of the available sections and the type of help you can find in these sections:

0: Section 0 contains information about header files. These are files that are typically in /usr/include and contain generic code that can be used by your programs.

1: Executable programs or shell commands. For the user, this is the most important section. Usually, all commands that can be used by end users are documented here.

2: System calls. As an administrator, you will not use this section frequently. The system calls are functions that are provided by the kernel. This is interesting if you are a kernel debugger; normal administrators, however, don't need this information.

3: Library calls. A *library* is a piece of shared code that can be used by several different programs. Typically, you don't need the information here to do your work as a system administrator.

4: Special files. In here, the device files in the directory /dev are documented. It can be useful to use this section to find out more about how specific devices work.

5: Configuration files. Here you'll find the proper format you can use for most configuration files on your server. If, for example, you want to know more about the way /etc/passwd is organized, use the entry for passwd in this section by issuing the command man 5 passwd.

6: Games. On a modern Linux system, this section contains hardly any information.

7: Miscellaneous. Contains some information on macro packages used on your server.

8: System administration commands. This section does contain important information about the commands you will use frequently as a system administrator.

9: Kernel routines. This is documentation that isn't even installed standard and optionally contains information about kernel routines.

So, the information that is important for you as a system administrator is in sections 1, 5, and 8. Most of the time you don't need to know anything about these different sections, but sometimes an entry can exist in more than one section. For example, there is information on passwd in section 1, but also in section 5. If you would just use man passwd, man would show the content of the first entry it finds. If you want to make sure that all the information you need is displayed, use man -a <yourcommand>, which makes sure man browses all sections to see whether it can find anything about <yourcommand>. If you know beforehand what section to look in, specify the section number as well, as in man 5 passwd, which will open the passwd item from section 5 directly.

The basic structure for using man is to type man followed by the command you want information about. For example, type man passwd to get more information about the passwd item. This will show a man page, as shown in Figure 4-3.

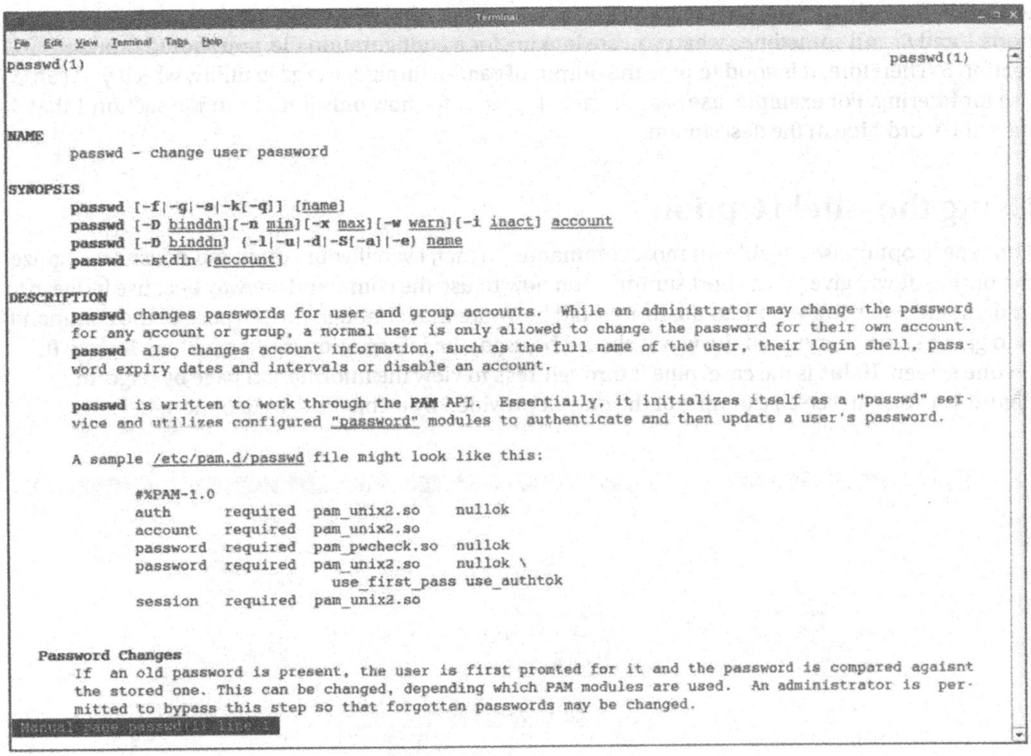

```
                                           Terminal                                          _ □ ×
File   Edit   View   Terminal   Tabs   Help
passwd(1)                                                                        passwd(1)


NAME
       passwd - change user password

SYNOPSIS
       passwd [-f|-g|-s|-k[-q]] [name]
       passwd [-D binddn][-n min][-x max][-w warn][-i inact] account
       passwd [-D binddn] {-l|-u|-d|-S[-a]|-e} name
       passwd --stdin [account]

DESCRIPTION
       passwd changes passwords for user and group accounts.  While an administrator may change the password
       for any account or group, a normal user is only allowed to change the password for their own account.
       passwd  also changes account information, such as the full name of the user, their login shell, pass-
       word expiry dates and intervals or disable an account.

       passwd is written to work through the PAM API.  Essentially, it initializes itself as a "passwd" ser-
       vice and utilizes configured "password" modules to authenticate and then update a user's password.

       A sample /etc/pam.d/passwd file might look like this:

            #%PAM-1.0
            auth       required    pam_unix2.so      nullok
            account    required    pam_unix2.so
            password   required    pam_pwcheck.so  nullok
            password   required    pam_unix2.so      nullok \
                                   use_first_pass use_authtok
            session    required    pam_unix2.so

  Password Changes
       If  an old password is present, the user is first promted for it and the password is compared agaisnt
       the stored one. This can be changed, depending which PAM modules are used.  An administrator is  per-
       mitted to bypass this step so that forgotten passwords may be changed.

Manual page passwd(1) line 1
```

Figure 4-3. *All* man *pages are structured in the same way.*

Each man page consists of the following elements:

Name: This is the name of the command. It describes in one or two lines what the command is used for.

Synopsis: Here you can find short usage information about the command. It will show all available options and indicate whether an option is optional (it will be between square brackets) or mandatory (it will not be between brackets).

Description: The description gives the long description of what the command is doing. Read it to get a complete picture of the purpose of the command.

Options: This is a complete list of all options that are available. It documents how to use all of them.

Files: This section provides a brief list of the files, if any, that are related to the command you want more information about.

See also: A list of related commands.

Author: The author and also the mail address of the person who wrote the man page.

Now man is a useful system to get more information about how to use a given command. So far, it is useful only if you know what the name of the command is that you want to have more information about. If you don't have that information and need to locate the proper command, you will like man -k. The -k option allows you to locate the command you need by looking at keywords. This will often show a long list of commands from all sections of the man pages. In most cases, you don't need to see all that information; the commands that are relevant for the system administrator are in sections 1 and 8, and sometimes when you are looking for a configuration file, you should browse section 5. Therefore, it is good to pipe the output of man -k through the grep utility, which you can use for filtering. For example, use man -k time | grep 1 to show only lines from man section 1 that have the word time in the description.

Using the --help Option

The --help option is available for most commands. In fact, even if your command doesn't recognize the option, it will give you a short summary on how to use the command anyway because it doesn't understand what you want it to do. You should be aware that although the purpose of the command is to give a short overview of the way it should be used, the information is often still too long to fit on one screen. If this is the case, pipe it through less to view the information page by page. In Figure 4-4 you can see an example of the output provided by using the --help option.

```
File  Edit  View  Terminal  Tabs  Help
NAP:~ # ifconfig --help
Usage:
  ifconfig [-a] [-i] [-v] [-s] <interface> [[<AF>] <address>]
  [add <address>[/<prefixlen>]]
  [del <address>[/<prefixlen>]]
  [[-]broadcast [<address>]]  [[-]pointopoint [<address>]]
  [netmask <address>]  [dstaddr <address>]  [tunnel <address>]
  [outfill <NN>] [keepalive <NN>]
  [hw <HW> <address>]  [metric <NN>]  [mtu <NN>]
  [[-]trailers]  [[-]arp]  [[-]allmulti]
  [multicast]  [[-]promisc]
  [mem_start <NN>]  [io_addr <NN>]  [irq <NN>]  [media <type>]
  [txqueuelen <NN>]
  [[-]dynamic]
  [up|down] ...

  <HW>=Hardware Type.
  List of possible hardware types:
    loop (Local Loopback) slip (Serial Line IP) cslip (VJ Serial Line IP)
    slip6 (6-bit Serial Line IP) cslip6 (VJ 6-bit Serial Line IP) adaptive (Adaptive Serial Line IP)
    strip (Metricom Starmode IP) ether (Ethernet) tr (16/4 Mbps Token Ring)
    tr (16/4 Mbps Token Ring (New)) ax25 (AMPR AX.25) netrom (AMPR NET/ROM)
    tunnel (IPIP Tunnel) ppp (Point-to-Point Protocol) arcnet (ARCnet)
    dlci (Frame Relay DLCI) frad (Frame Relay Access Device) sit (IPv6-in-IPv4)
    fddi (Fiber Distributed Data Interface) hippi (HIPPI) irda (IrLAP)
    x25 (generic X.25)
  <AF>=Address family. Default: inet
  List of possible address families:
    unix (UNIX Domain) inet (DARPA Internet) inet6 (IPv6)
    ax25 (AMPR AX.25) netrom (AMPR NET/ROM) ipx (Novell IPX)
    ddp (Appletalk DDP) x25 (CCITT X.25)
NAP:~ #
```

Figure 4-4. *The --help option provides a short summary on how to use a command.*

Learning More About Installed Packages

Another often neglected help option is the documentation that is installed for most software packages in the directory /usr/share/doc/packages. In this directory, you will find a long list of subdirectories that all contain some level of usage information. In some cases, the information is really short; in other cases, extensive information is available. Often this information is available in ASCII text format and can be viewed with less or any other utility that is capable of handling clear text. In other situations, the information is in HTML format and can be displayed properly only with a browser. If this is the case, it is good to know that you don't necessarily need to start a graphical environment to see the contents of the HTML file; SUSE Linux Enterprise Server comes with the w3m browser, which is a browser that is developed especially to run from a nongraphical environment (see Figure 4-5 for a snapshot on that). In w3m you can use the arrow keys to browse between hyperlinks. To quit the w3m utility, use the q command.

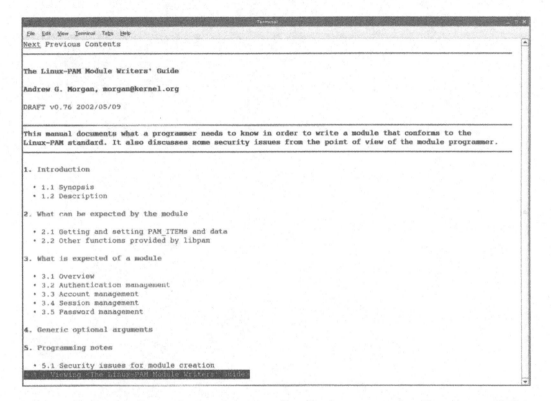

Figure 4-5. *You can use the w3m browser from a text-based environment to show the contents of HTML help files from a nongraphical environment.*

Summary

This chapter has prepared you for the work you will be doing from the command line. Because even a modern Linux distribution such as SUSE Linux Enterprise Server still relies heavily on its configuration file, this is important information. In the next chapter, I will give you more information about how to manage the user environment. To help you get used to the command-line environment, the next chapter will focus heavily on the management tasks that you can perform from the command line.

PART 2

■ ■ ■

Administering SUSE Linux Enterprise Server

In the first part of this book, you learned the basic skills needed to find your way in SUSE Linux Enterprise Server. In this part, you'll start the real work; you'll learn everything you need to know to perform your day-to-day SUSE Linux administration tasks. Specifically, Chapters 5 through 12 cover how to administer a stand-alone SUSE Linux Enterprise Server, including working with users and groups, managing the file system, managing processes, and more.

■ ■ ■

## CHAPTER 5

Managing Users and Groups

Like any other multiuser operating system, managing users and groups is one of the key tasks of a Linux administrator. In this chapter, you will learn how to perform these tasks. To make you really understand what happens, I will focus on the way users and groups are stored in configuration files on the Linux server. This chapter will discuss local users only; I won't discuss systems to centralize the storage of users on a SUSE Linux Enterprise Server. For more on that, see Chapter 17 for more information about the OpenLDAP directory server.

Managing Users

To create users from the command-line environment, you can take two different approaches. You can use the useradd command to add users; alternatively, it is possible to add users to the relevant configuration files manually. The latter can be useful in an environment where users are added from a custom-made shell script, but usually this is not recommended because an error in the main user configuration files might disable login for all users on your server. In the following sections, I will discuss how to add users from the command line using useradd, how to modify the relevant configuration files for the users, and finally how to add users using YaST.

Using Commands for User Management

If you want to add users from the command line, useradd is the command to use. Some other commands are available as well. The following are the most important commands used to manage the user environment:

- useradd: Use this for adding users to the local authentication system.
- usermod: Use this to modify properties for existing users.
- userdel: Use this to delete users properly from a system.

Using useradd is simple. In its basic form, useradd just takes the name of a user as its argument; for example, useradd jocelyn will create a user called jocelyn on the system. However, you'll want to use the option -m as well, because if you don't, the user will be created without a home directory. Normally it is useful for users to have a home directory, because this is the environment where a user can store files. Unfortunately, if you have created a user without a home directory, there is no easy way to correct this problem later. So, to create user mike and his home directory at the same time, use useradd -m mike.

Tip Did you forget to create a home directory, and you want to create it afterward? To create a home directory for user `jocelyn` after creating the user, first use `mkdir /home/jocelyn` to create the directory. Then use `cd /etc/skel` to activate the directory that contains all the files that normally need to be present in a user's home directory. Now use `tar cv . | tar xvC /home/jocelyn` to copy all the files, including hidden files, from this directory to the user's home directory. Next, use `chown -R jocelyn.users /home/jocelyn` to set the proper file ownership for the user `jocelyn`, for the group `users` for the home directory, and for all the files and directories in it. You have now created a home directory properly.

In addition to -m, useradd offers several options. If you don't specify an option, useradd will read its configuration file in /etc/default/useradd; in this configuration file, it finds some default values. These specify what groups the user should become a member of, where to create the user's home directory, and more. For a complete list of available options, execute man useradd.

The following are the most common options:

c comment: Use this option to enter a comment field to the user. You can request this information, set this way, with the finger command.

e date: This option sets the expiration date for the user. Use this option to disable the user account automatically on the date specified. You must specify the date as the number of days since January 1, 1970, that you want the user to expire, but you can also set it in the YYYY-MM-DD format where the system will calculate the number of days automatically. You probably prefer the former way of doing it. The number of days to expire is stored in the /etc/shadow file in the second-to-last column.

G groups: Use this option to make the user a member of some additional groups. By default, the user will become a member only of the groups listed in /etc/defaults/useradd.

g gid: This one is used for the primary group of a user (see the next section for more details).

m: This will create a home directory automatically.

Assigning Users to Groups

In any Unix environment, a user can be a member of two different kinds of groups: the primary group and all others. Every user must be a member of a primary group. If one user on your system does not have a primary group setting, no one will be able to log in anymore, so membership in a primary group is vital. By default, on a SUSE Linux system, all users are added to the group users. Users can be a member of more than just the primary group and will automatically have access to the rights granted to these other groups. The most important difference between a primary group and the other groups is that the primary group will automatically become a group owner of a new file a user creates. In Chapter 6, I will discuss file permissions and ownership in detail, but just to give you a short idea of how it works, I'll offer an example here.

Imagine a user has the group users set as his primary group and is also a member of the group sales. Now the user wants to create a file to which only members of the group sales have access. If he creates just a file, the default group users will become the group owner of the file, and all users who are members of this group will have access to the file. Therefore, the user needs to deploy the newgrp command to set his primary group to sales on a temporary basis. If the user creates the file after executing newgrp sales, the group sales will be the owner of that file and of all the other files the user creates until he executes newgrp users to switch the primary group setting back to users.

As you can see, group membership in a stand-alone Linux file system environment is way less sophisticated than it is in a Novell or Microsoft network environment. This sounds primitive but hardly ever causes any problems because permissions are just set at another level, such as when the user is accessing the server through a Samba share (see Chapter 15 for more on that).

You now know the relation between the primary group and the other groups of which a user is a member. In the "Managing Groups" section, you will learn how to apply this knowledge.

Managing the UID

Another major type of information used when creating a user is the user ID (UID). For your server, this is the only way to identify a user; usernames are just a convenience for humans who in general can't remember numbers too well. Basically, all users need a unique UID. SUSE Linux Enterprise Server 10 starts generating local UIDs at 500, and 16 bits are available for creating UIDs. This means the highest available UID is 65535, and this is also the maximum amount of local users supported on your server. Typically, UIDs less than 500 are reserved for system accounts, which are needed to start services. The UID 0 is also a special one; the user who has it has complete administrative permissions to the server. UID 0 is typically reserved for the user root.

You might want to give the same user ID to more than one user to create a backup root user. If you want to do that with useradd, execute useradd with the options -o and -u 0. For example, to make user stacey a backup root user, execute the following:

```
useradd -o -u 0 stacey
```

Setting a Default Shell

A user requires a shell in order to log in to your server. The shell will enable interpretation of commands the user enters from the console. The default shell in Linux is /bin/bash, but several other shells are available as well (see Figure 5-1). One of the common alternative shells is /bin/tcsh, which is a shell that has a scripting language like the C programming language. This makes tcsh the perfect shell for C programmers. You should, however, be aware that not all users need shells. A user with a shell is allowed to log in locally to your system and access any files and directories stored on that system. If you are using your system as a mail server where users need to access their mailboxes only with POP, it makes no sense to give them a login shell. Therefore, you could choose to specify an alternative command to be used as the shell. For example, you can use /bin/false if you don't want to allow the user to interact with your system locally. Any other command will do as well. If, for example, you want Midnight Commander, a clone of the Norton Commander program that was popular in the 1990s, to start automatically when a user logs in to your system, make sure /usr/bin/mc is specified as the shell for that user, or use /bin/passwd as the user shell if you want to allow your user to change his password only.

Tip You must make sure to include the complete path to the command you want to execute as the shell environment for a user. Don't have a clue about the complete path for your favorite command? Use the command whereis. For example, whereis mc will give a line showing where the program file you are looking for is located.

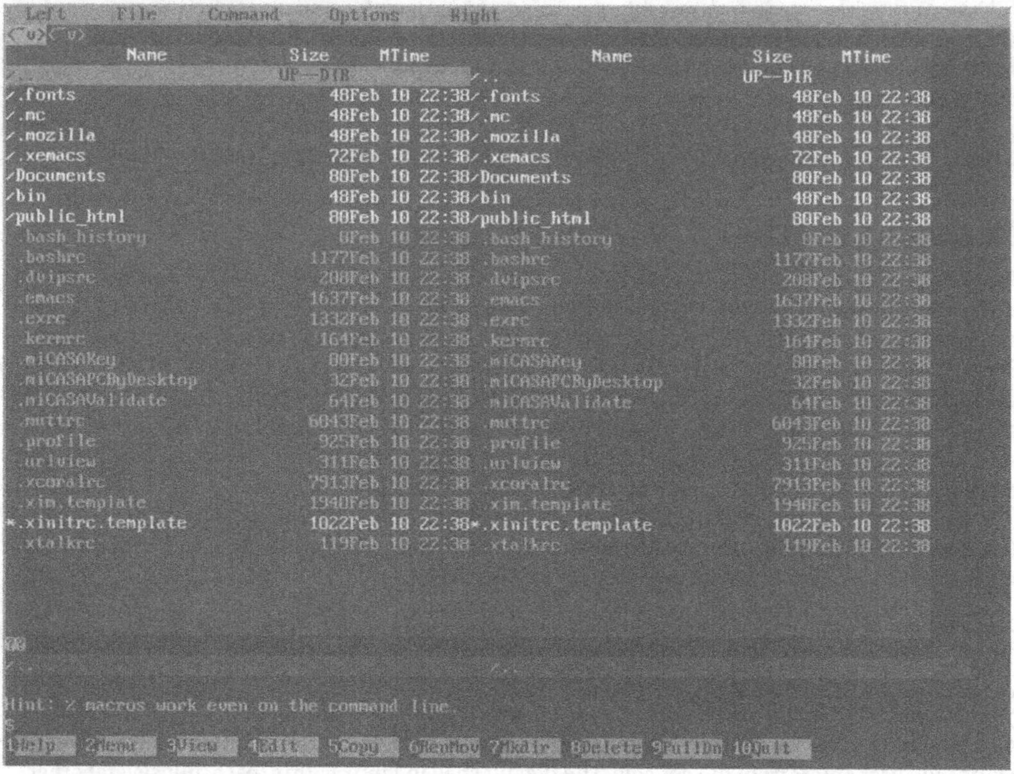

Figure 5-1. *Any program will do as a default shell for a user.*

Managing Passwords

By default, newly created users are denied the ability to log in, and no password is supplied. Accordingly, these users will be unable to perform any tasks. To grant a user permission to do so, use the passwd command. This command is simple and can be used in two ways. First, a user can use passwd to change a password. In that case, the passwd command will prompt for the old password first and then will prompt for the new password. In doing so, the user will have to meet some complexity requirements; you will learn how that works in the "Managing Authentication: PAM" section. For the root user, it is possible to change people's passwords as well. Only root can add the name of the user to change a password as an argument to the passwd command. For example, root can use passwd linda to change the password for user linda, a useful capability should she forget her password.

In addition to using the passwd command for password maintenance, you can also use it to set password expiry information, which specifies that a password will expire at a given day. Lastly, you can use the passwd command for account maintenance. An administrator, for example, can use passwd to lock a user's account so that login is disabled temporarily. If, for example, you want to lock the account for user rob, use passwd -l rob.

Performing Account Maintenance with passwd

In an environment where many users are using the same server, it is important to perform some basic account maintenance tasks. These include locking accounts when they are unneeded for a longer time, unlocking an account, and reporting the password status. Also, an administrator can force a user to change his password on the first occasion. To perform these tasks, the passwd command has several options available:

-l: This enables an administrator to lock an account; for example, passwd -l jeroen will lock the account for user jeroen.

-u: This unlocks an account that has been locked before.

-S: This reports the status of the password for a given account.

-e: This forces the user to change her password on her next login.

Managing Password Expiry with passwd

Another nice feature that not many people are aware of is the password expiry feature. This feature allows you to manage the maximum amount of days that a user can use the same password. The passwd command has four options to manage password expiry:

-n min: You can use this rarely used option to set the minimum amount of days that a user must use a password. If this option is not used, a user can change the password at anytime.

-x max: You can use this option to set the maximum amount of days that the user can use a password without changing it.

-c warn: When a password is about to expire, you can use this option to send a warning to the user. The argument of this option specifies the number of days before expiry of the password that the user will get the warning.

-i inact: Use this option to expire an account automatically when it hasn't been used for a given period. The argument of this option specifies the exact duration of this period.

Caution By default, no password expiry options are set. So if you do nothing, a user can use a password forever without changing it.

Modifying and Deleting User Accounts

If you know how to create a user, modifying an existing user account is no big deal. The usermod command, which is used for this purpose, has a lot of options that are the same as the options used with useradd. For example, execute the following command to set the new primary group of user linda to the group with the unique ID 101:

```
usermod -g 101 linda
```

The usermod command has many other options; for a complete overview, consult the appropriate man page.

Another command you will need occasionally is userdel. Use this command to delete accounts from your server. Basically, userdel is a simple command; for example, userdel lynette will delete user `lynette` from your system. However, if used this way, `userdel` will leave the home directory of your user untouched. This may be necessary to ensure that your company still has access to the work a user has done, but it may also be necessary to delete the user's home directory as well. For this purpose, you can use the option `-r`; for example, `userdel -r lynette` will delete the home directory of user `lynette` as well. However, if this home directory contains files that are not owned by user `lynette`, `userdel` can't remove the home directory. If this is the case, use the option `-f`; this will make sure all files from the home directory are removed, even if they are not owned by the given user. So finally, to make sure user `lynette` is removed, including all the files in her home directory, execute `userdel -rf lynette`.

You now know how to remove a user including the user's home directory. But what about other files the user may have created in other directories on your system? They will not be removed automatically when using `userdel`. If you want to make sure these other files are removed as well, you may find the `find` command useful. With `find`, you can search for all the files owned by a given user and remove them automatically. For example, to locate all files on your system that are created by `lynette` and remove them automatically, you can execute the following:

```
find / -user "lynette" -exec rm {} \;
```

This may, however, lead to problems on your server. Imagine an environment where `lynette` is an active user of the group `sales` and has created a lot of files in the directory `/home/sales`; they will all be removed as well, and that may lead to serious problems. Therefore, I don't recommend using the `-exec` option to remove files immediately; instead, copy them to a safe place. If after a couple of months no one has complained, you can remove them. To move all files owned by `lynette` to a directory called `/trash/lynette` (which must have been created beforehand), execute the following:

```
find / -user lynette -exec mv {} /trash/lynette \;
```

Going Behind the Commands: Configuration Files

In the previous section, you learned all the commands required to manage users from a console environment. These commands will put all user-related information in some configuration files. A configuration file is also used for default settings that are applied when managing the user environment. The aim of the following sections is to give you some insight into these files. I'll discuss the following files:

- `/etc/passwd`
- `/etc/shadow`
- `/etc/login.defs`

/etc/passwd

The first and probably most important user-related configuration file is `/etc/passwd`. This file is the primary database where user information is stored: everything except the user password is stored in this file. In Listing 5-1, you can get an impression of what the fields in this file look like.

Listing 5-1. *Contents of the User Database* /etc/passwd

```
dhcpd:x:102:65534:DHCP server daemon:/var/lib/dhcp:/bin/false
radiusd:x:103:103:Radius daemon:/var/lib/radiusd:/bin/false
privoxy:x:104:104:Daemon user for privoxy:/var/lib/privoxy:/bin/false
vdr:x:105:33:Video Disk Recorder:/var/spool/video:/bin/false
quagga:x:106:106:Quagga routing daemon:/var/run/quagga:/bin/false
nobody:x:65534:65533:nobody:/var/lib/nobody:/bin/bash
sander:x:1000:100:sander:/home/sander:/bin/bash
linda:x:1001:100:Linda Thomassen:/home/linda:/bin/bash
kluser:x:1002:1000::/var/db/kav:/sbin/nologin
jgoldman:x:1003:100::/home/jgoldman:/bin/bash
```

In /etc/passwd, you'll see the following fields, separated with a colon:

Loginname: In the first field in /etc/passwd, the user's login name is stored. In older Unix versions, there was a maximum length limitation on login names; they could be eight characters maximum. In SUSE Linux Enterprise Server, this limitation doesn't exist.

Password: In older Unix versions, the encrypted passwords were stored in this file. However, one major issue existed when passwords were stored here, even if encryption was used: everyone was allowed to read /etc/passwd. Therefore, an intruder would be able to read the encrypted passwords as well. Since this poses a security risk, nowadays passwords are stored in the configuration file /etc/shadow, which is discussed in the next section. When passwords are stored in the shadow file, this field will contain only the character x.

UID: As you have already learned, every user has a unique UID. SUSE Linux Enterprise Server starts numbering local UIDs at 1,000, and typically the highest number that should be used is 65,550 (the highest numbers are reserved for special-purpose accounts).

■ **Note** SUSE starts numbering user accounts automatically at UID 1,000. Want to change that? Check the file /etc/login.defs where you can set a parameter to tune this.

GID: As discussed in the previous section, every user has a primary group. The group ID (GID) of this primary group is listed here. For ordinary users, by default the GID 100, which belongs to the group users, is used.

GECOS: The General Electric Comprehensive Operating System (GECOS) field includes some comments about the user. This makes identifying a user easier for an administrator. The GECOS field, however, is optional, and often you will see that it is not used at all.

Home directory: This is a reference to the directory used for the user's home directory. Note that it is only a reference and has nothing to do with the real directory; so the fact that you see something here doesn't mean the directory that is listed here also really exists.

Shell: The latest field in /etc/passwd refers to the program that should be started automatically when a user logs in. Most often, this will be /bin/bash, but as discussed in the preceding section, every binary program can be referred to here, as long as the complete path name is used.

For an administrator, it is perfectly possible to edit /etc/passwd and the related file /etc/shadow manually. If you make an error, however, the consequences can be serious; it can even lead to a system where logging in is no longer possible. Therefore, if you make manual changes to any of these files, you should check the integrity of these files. To do this, use the pwck command. You can run this command without any options, and it will tell whether any serious problems need fixing.

/etc/shadow

In /etc/shadow, the encrypted user passwords are stored. Also, information regarding password expiry is kept in this file. Listing 5-2 shows an example of its contents.

Listing 5-2. /etc/shadowpostfix:!:13126:0:99999:7:::

```
privoxy:!:13126:0:99999:7:::
quagga:!:13126:0:99999:7:::
radiusd:!:13126:0:99999:7:::
root:$2a$10$CxoodF.y9vTQb.ijl56r2u/.neljvXzL8jVt/66:13180:::::::
sshd:!:13126:0:99999:7:::
uucp:*:13126::::::
vdr:!:13126:0:99999:7:::
wwwrun:*:13126::::::
sander:$2a$05$hkHdB2UOjR7J.dLMNDhwOu7ZZd609BPz88W:13126:0:99999:7:::
alexander:!:13127:0:99999:7:::
kluser:!:13132:0:99999:7:::
jgoldman:novell:13133:0:99999:7:::
```

Like /etc/passwd, the lines in /etc/shadow are divided in different fields. For an average administrator, only the first two fields matter. The first field stores the name of the user, and the second field stores the encrypted password. Note that in the encrypted password field, you can use an ! and an * as well. If an ! is used, the login is currently disabled. If an * is used, it is a system account that can be used to start services, but that is not allowed for interactive shell login. Also note that by default an encrypted password is stored here, but it is perfectly possible to store a nonencrypted password as well. The following is an enumeration of fields used in the lines in /etc/shadow:

- Login name
- Encrypted password
- Days since Jan 1, 1970, that password was last changed
- Days before the password can be changed
- Days after which the password must be changed
- Days before the password is to expire that user is warned
- Days after the password expires that the account is disabled
- Days since Jan 1, 1970, that the account is disabled
- Reserved field

/etc/login.defs

A configuration file that relates to the user environment but is used completely in the background is /etc/login.defs. In this configuration file, some generic settings are defined. These settings determine all kinds of things relating to user login. This file is a readable configuration file that contains variables relating to logging in or to the way certain commands are used. On every system, this file must exist, because otherwise you will see unexpected behavior. Some of the most interesting variables you can use in this file are as follows. For a complete overview, consult man 5 login.defs.

CHARACTER_CLASS: This variable defines what characters you can use in a username or group name. By default, this includes all alphanumeric characters.

DEFAULT_HOME: By default, a user will be allowed to log in, even if his home directory does not exist. If you don't want that, modify the default value of 1 for this parameter to the boolean value 0.

ENV_PATH: This variable contains the default search path that is applied for all users who do not have UID 0.

ENV_ROOTPATH: This is the same as the previous variable but for root.

FAIL_DELAY: After a login failure, it will take a few seconds before a new login prompt is generated. This variable, which is set to 3 by default, specifies exactly how long it will take.

GID_MAX and GID_MIN: Specifies the minimal and maximal GID used by groupadd (see the "Using Commands for Group Management" section).

LASTLOG_ENAB: If enabled by setting the boolean value 1, this setting specifies that all successful logins must be logged to the file /var/log/lastlog. This works only if the lastlog file also exists.

UID_MAX and UID_MIN: This is the minimum and maximum UID used when adding users with useradd. Use this parameter if you want to change the first UID that is assigned when working with useradd.

/etc/default/passwd

When setting user passwords, some default values are applied. Some of these values are read from the configuration file /etc/default/passwd. This file works the same way as the login.defs file: variables are used to set defaults for given parameters. Only one variable is of interest, but it is an important variable because it specifies the encryption algorithm that should be used. The CRYPT variable is used for this purpose. The default value is des. As an alternative, you can use md5 and blowfish. The advantage of des is its compatibility. For more options, use blowfish. This is, for example, the only algorithm that allows you to use passwords longer than eight characters. The md5 algorithm should be used only as a last resort, because it is rather unsecure.

Managing Users with YaST

In the previous sections, you learned how to add users from the command line. I also discussed what files are modified when doing so. You have some other options as well, and the best of these is of course SUSE's all-round configuration tool YaST. The following steps show how to create a user with YaST:

1. From YaST, select the Security and Users option, and next select User Management. This will list all users who currently exist on your system.

2. To create a new user, select the Add option. You will now see a menu where you can enter the user's full name (which will be applied to the GECOS field in /etc/passwd), the user's login name, and the password. To create a user using all default options, click Accept, and the user will be added.

3. Click the Details button to specify more information for the user you are creating. On this screen, you can browse to a location where you want to create the user home directory and complete all the other relevant information for your user (see Figure 5-2). You also have the option to select all the groups of which you want the make the user a member.

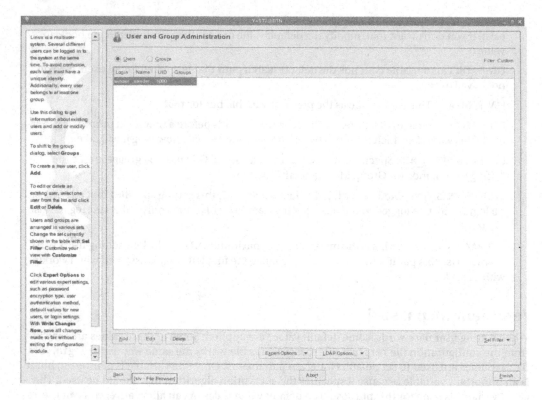

Figure 5-2. *YaST allows you to easily set all the options required for creating a user.*

4. To specify password settings for your user, click the Password Settings option. You will now see a screen where you can configure all the required password expiration options.

5. Click Accept to create the user. Your user will now be added to your system.

6. In the User and Group Administration screen, click Expert Options to get access to advanced options. From these options, you can modify defaults for new users, set the password encryption algorithm you want to use, and specify login settings that can help you, such as logging in automatically on your server (which is a bad idea, of course). You can also use the option Authentication and User Data Sources to specify an external service such as NIS, LDAP, Kerberos, or even a Windows server used for user authentication.

7. When finished, close YaST. You now have created the new user account.

Managing Groups

As you have already learned, all users require group membership. You have read about the differences between the primary group and the other groups; you just have not read yet how to create these groups. Of course, you can use YaST for this purpose, but in the following sections I will not explain how to use YaST for group management, since it is similar to creating users with YaST. Instead, I'll discuss the commands you can run from the shell and its related configuration files.

Using Commands for Group Management

Basically, you can use three commands to manage the groups in your environment:

- groupadd: Use this to add new groups to the /etc/group file.
- groupdel: Use this to remove a group from your system.
- groupmod: Use this to change properties of an existing group.

So as you can see, group management follows the same patterns as user management. There is also some overlap. For example, you can use usermod as well as groupmod to make a user a member of some group. The basic structure for using the groupadd command is simple: groupadd somegroup, where somegroup, of course, is the name of the group you want to create. Also, the options are mainly self-explanatory; for example, it probably doesn't surprise you that you can use the option -g gid to specify the unique GID you want to use for this group. Probably just one option is difficult to understand, and that's the option -p for password. Because what on Earth would you ever need a group password for?

In the preceding section, you learned the difference between the primary group of a user and the other groups a user can be a member of. By default, a user takes advantage of all the permissions of all the groups he is a member of, but when creating a new file, the primary group will automatically become the group owner of that file (see the next chapter in this book for much more information about ownership). Now what if the user wants to create a new file but doesn't want the default primary group users to become its owner? In that case, the user can use the newgrp command to set the primary group to some other group on a temporary basis. For newgrp to work, the user needs some permissions to the group to which he wants to change. Most of the time, the user can do it, because he is listed as a member of the given group in the group configuration file /etc/group. If the user is not a member of the group, the newgroup command will prompt for a password, and that's what you might need a group password for.

The funny thing about group passwords is that you don't use groupadd -p to add this password. This is because this old option requires a password string that is already encrypted. Instead, use passwd -g groupname to add a password to a group.

Going Behind the Commands: /etc/group

When you create a group with either groupadd or YaST, you need to store the information entered somewhere. The location for that is the file /etc/group. As shown in Listing 5-3, this is a rather simple file that has just three fields for each group definition.

Listing 5-3. *Contents of* /etc/group

```
xok:x:41:
trusted:x:42:
modem:x:43:
named:!:44:
ftp:x:49:
postfix:!:51:
maildrop:!:59:
man:x:62:
sshd:!:65:
ldap:!:70:
ntadmin:!:71:
messagebus:!:101:
```

```
haldaemon:!:102:
radiusd:!:103:
privoxy:!:104:
mysql:!:105:
quagga:!:106:
nobody:x:65533:
nogroup:x:65534:nobody
users:x:100:jgoldman
klusers:!:1000:
```

The first field in /etc/group is reserved for the name of the group. Then in the second field the password for the group is stored, or an exclamation mark appears, which signifies that no password is allowed for this group. You can see that some groups have an x in the password field; this is a remainder of the old days when there still was an /etc/gshadow to store encrypted group passwords. Nowadays this file is used no longer for the simple reason that no one uses group passwords anymore. In the third field of /etc/group, a unique group ID is provided, and finally in the last field, the names of the members of the group are present. These names are required only for users for whom this is not the primary group; primary group membership is managed from the /etc/passwd configuration file.

Managing Authentication: PAM

Usually, on a user login on a Linux workstation, the local user database in the Linux files /etc/passwd and /etc/shadow is checked. In a network environment, however, the login program must often fetch the required information from somewhere else, for example in an LDAP directory service such as OpenLDAP or Novell eDirectory. But how are you going to tell the login program? That's where the Pluggable Authentication Modules (PAM) feature comes in. PAM makes the login procedure on your workstation flexible. With PAM, you can redirect any application that is related to authentication. You can use PAM, for example, if you want to authenticate with your private key that is stored on a USB stick. Also, you can use PAM when enabling password requirements, when disallowing the root user to establish a telnet session, and more.

The main advantage of PAM is its modularity. In a PAM infrastructure, you can use any type of authentication, as long as there is a PAM module for it. So if you want to implement some kind of strong authentication, ask your supplier for a PAM module, and it will work. PAM modules are stored in the directory /lib/security, and the configuration files specifying how these PAM modules must be used by the procedures are in /etc/pam.d. An example of such a configuration file is in Listing 5-4, where the login procedure learns it first has to contact Novell eDirectory before trying any local login. You can specify that it has to contact eDirectory first by referring to the pam_nam.so module.

Listing 5-4. *Sample PAM Configuration File*

```
auth        sufficient      /lib/security/pam_nam.so
account     sufficient      /lib/security/pam_nam.so
password    sufficient      /lib/security/pam_nam.so
session     optional        /lib/security/pam_nam.so
auth        requisite       pam_unix2.so
auth        required        pam_securetty.so
auth        required        pam_nologin.so
#auth       required        pam_homecheck.so
auth        required        pam_env.so
```

```
auth            required            pam_mail.so
account         required            pam_unix2.so
password        required            pam_pwcheck.so      nullok
password        required            pam_unix2.so nullok use_first_pass use_authok
session         required            pam_unix2.so
session         required            pam_limits.so
```

The authentication process has four different instances, and these are reflected by the previous example. In the first instance, authentication is handled. These are the lines that start with the keyword auth. After that, the validity of the account and other account-related parameters are checked (think of things such as login time restrictions). This happens in the lines that start with account. Then, all settings relating to the password are verified. This happens in the lines that start with password. Last, settings relating to the establishment of a session with a network resources are defined. This happens in the lines that start with session.

The procedure that will be followed after the completion of these four instances is defined by calling the different PAM modules. This happens in the last column of the example configuration file. For example, you can use the module pam_securetty to verify that the user root is not logging in via an insecure terminal to a Linux computer. You use the keywords sufficient, optional, required, and requisite to define the importance that the conditions in a certain module are met. Except for the first four lines (which are added to the default PAM configuration file by the SUSE installer), conditions defined in all modules must be met; they are all requisite or required. Without going into the details, this means authentication will fail if one of the conditions implied by the specified module is not met.

When enabling a server for login on Novell eDirectory, four lines are added to the default PAM configuration file in /etc/pam.d/login. In the example, these are the first four lines. These four lines offer an alternative for valid authentication by using the module pam_nam.so. Passing the conditions imposed by these first four modules is sufficient to authenticate successfully but is not required. sufficient in this context says that if the instance auth, for example, will pass all conditions defined in pam_nam.so, this is enough for local authentication to the Linux workstation; the local Linux authentication mechanism will no longer be used, since the user can authenticate against eDirectory in this case. For this to work, you need a valid user account that has all the required Linux properties in eDirectory, of course. You can read how to create such a user account later in this section.

The nice thing about this example PAM configuration file is that it will first check whether eDirectory can be used to authenticate to the network. If this doesn't work, the default Linux login mechanism is used. The workings of this default mechanism are defined from the fifth line in the example configuration file.

By default, many services on SUSE Linux Enterprise Server are PAM enabled. You can learn this from a simple ls from the directory /etc/pam.d, which will show you that there is a PAM file for login, for su, for sudo, and for many other files. I won't cover them all here, but I'll cover them where relevant later. The true flexibility of PAM is in its modules that you can find in /lib/security. Each of these modules has a specific function. You can find an overview of all modules and the way you can use them in /usr/share/doc/packages/pam/pam.txt. In the following sections, I'll discuss some of the more interesting of them. But before you dive into that, you will learn how to set a secure default policy.

Creating a Default Policy for Security

In a PAM environment, every service should have its own configuration for PAM. However, the world is not perfect, and it may happen that a given service does not have a PAM configuration. In that case, I recommend creating the PAM configuration file /etc/pam.d/other. In this file, you can deal with all the PAM applications that don't have their own configuration files. If you really want to know whether your system is secure, give it the contents shown in Listing 5-5.

Listing 5-5. *Configuring PAM for Security in* /etc/pam.d/other

```
auth       required      pam_warn.so
auth       required      pam_deny.so
account    required      pam_warn.so
account    required      pam_deny.so
password   required      pam_warn.so
password   required      pam_deny.so
session    required      pam_warn.so
session    required      pam_deny.so
```

For all of the four phases in the authentication process, two modules are called. The first is the module pam_warn: it will generate a warning and write that to your log environment (/var/log/messages by default). Next, for all of these instances, the module pam_deny is called. This simple module will just deny everything. The results? All modules will handle authentication properly, as defined in their own configuration file, but when that is absent, this generic configuration will make sure no trouble is happening.

Tip Want to know whether a program is PAM enabled? Use `ldd programname`, such as `ldd /usr/bin/passwd`, to find out the library files used by this command. If the modules `libpam_misc` and `libpam` are listed, the module is PAM enabled. In that case, it should have its own configuration file.

Discovering PAM Modules

PAM offers a number of interesting capabilities through modules. Some of these modules are still under development; others are pretty mature and can be used to configure a Linux system. For a complete overview, see Section 6 of the PAM documentation file pam.txt, which is in /usr/share/doc/packages/pam; I discuss some of the most important modules and how to use them.

Tip Would you rather see HTML instead of plain text? Use w3m on the HTML files, and open `index.html`. w3m is an excellent, easy-to-use text-based browser.

---

cracklib

The cracklib module is amongst the most used of all PAM modules. This module is used with the password option in a PAM configuration script to determine whether secure passwords are being deployed. The module works with a password dictionary in /usr/lib/cracklib_dict and checks to see whether the password being used is safe. The cracklib module performs other checks as well, such as, is the new password similar to the old password, is it too simple, and is it already being used? In these cases, the password will be denied if issued by a normal user. The user root, however, has the right to set simple passwords for users on a system, so cracklib determined that the user will get a warning only when a simple password is used.

pam_deny

As shown in Listing 5-5, you can use the pam_deny module to deny all access. This is helpful if used as a default policy where access to the system is denied as a default system policy.

pam_env

The module pam_env creates a default environment for users when logging in. In this default environment, several system variables are set to determine what the environment looks like that a user is working in. For example, there is a definition of a PATH variable in which some directories are included that must be in the search path of the user. To create these variables, pam_env uses a configuration file in /etc/security/pam_env.conf.

pam_limits

In some situations, you need an environment where limits are set to the system resources a user can use. For these environments, the pam_limits module was developed. This module reads its configuration from the configuration file /etc/security/limits.conf to determine which limitations should be applied. In this file, you can set limits for individual users as well as groups. You can apply the limits to different items, including the following:

- fsize: Maximum file size
- nofile: Maximum number of open files
- cpu: Maximum CPU time in minutes
- nproc: Maximum number of processes
- maxlogins: Maximum amount of times this user can login

Listing 5-6 shows two examples of how you can apply these limitations.

Listing 5-6. *Applying Limitations to Resources*

```
ftp             hard      nproc          0
@student        -         maxlogins      4
```

When applying these limitations, you should be aware of the difference between hard and soft limits. A *hard limit* is absolute; a user cannot move above it. A *soft limit* can be passed, within the settings the administrator has applied for these soft limits. If you want to set the hard limit to the same as the soft limit, use -, as shown in Listing 5-6 for the group @student.

pam_mail

This is a useful module that looks at the user's mail directory and indicates whether there is any new mail in it. It is typically applied when a user logs in to the system with the following line in the relevant PAM configuration file:

```
login     session     optional     pam_mail.conf
```

pam_mkhomedir

If a user authenticates to a machine for the first time and doesn't yet have a home directory, you can apply the pam_mkhomedir module to create the home directory automatically. This module will also make sure the skeleton /etc/skel is copied to the new home directory. This module is useful in particular in a network environment where users authenticate through NIS or LDAP. It is recommended in such situations, however, to centralize users' home directories on an NFS server so that no matter where a user logs in to a server, a home directory will always be present. The disadvantage of pam_mkhomedir is that, in the end, a user may have home directories on lots of machines in your network.

pam_nologin

If the administrator needs to do system maintenance such as installing new hardware and the server must be brought down for a few moments, the pam_nologin module may prove useful. This module, which is applied on SUSE Linux Enterprise Server 10 by default, makes sure no users can log in when the file /etc/nologin exists. The user root will always be allowed to log in to the system, though.

pam_permit

pam_permit is by far the most insecure PAM service available. It does only one thing; it always grants access, no matter who tries to log in. All security mechanisms will be completely bypassed. However, it is recommended that you log in with existing usernames only, or the user will have no permissions to local files. The only sensible use of pam_permit is to test the PAM awareness of a certain module or to disable account management on a workstation completely.

pam_rootok

This module grants access to the user, without any need to enter a password. It is, for example, used by the su utility to make sure the user root can su to any account, without needing to enter a password for that user account.

pam_securetty

In the "old days" when telnet connections were still common, it was important for the user root never to use a telnet session for login, since telnet sends passwords in clear text over the network. For this purpose, the securetty mechanism was created. It creates the file /etc/securetty, which lists all the TTYs from which root can log in. By default, these include only local TTYs tty1 to tty6. On SUSE Linux Enterprise Server, this module is still used by default.

pam_tally

You can apply this useful module to maintain a count of attempted access to the system. It also allows the administrator to deny access if too many attempts fail. pam_tally works with the application pam_tally, which you can use to set the maximum amount of failed logins that are allowed. All attempts are logged by default in the /var/log/faillog file. If this module is called from a configuration file, the options deny=n and lock_time are the minimal options to use. The former determines the maximum number of login attempts a user can make, and the latter determines how long an account must be locked after the number of login attempts that is specified with deny=n has been reached. The value given to lock_time is expressed in seconds by default.

pam_time

Based upon the configuration file /etc/security/time.conf, the pam_time module limits the times users can log in to the system. Using this module, you can limit access for certain users to specific times of the day. Also, you can limit the access to services and specific TTYs from which the user logs in. In the configuration file time.conf, the lines have the following form:

```
services;ttys;users;times
```

The following is an example of a configuration line from time.conf where all users except root are denied access (the exclamation mark in front of the times disallows any access) to the system from any TTY. This might be a perfect solution to prevent users from breaking in to a system where normal users shouldn't log in anyway.

```
login ; tty* ; !root ; !Al0000-2400
```

pam_unix

This is probably the most important of all modules; it is used to redirect authentication requests through the /etc/passwd and /etc/shadow files. You can use the module with several arguments, such as nullok and try_first_pass. The former allows a user with an empty password to connect to a service, and the latter will always try the password a user has already used if a password is asked for again.

pam_warn

The pam_warn module is useful in regard to log errors; its primary purpose is to enable logging information about proposed authentication or password modification. You can use it in conjunction with the pam_deny module to log information about users trying to connect to your system.

Managing the User's Shell Environment

As a system administrator, you do not only need to create users and make them a member of the appropriate groups. It is necessary to create the necessary login environment as well. Without going into details about specific shell commands, I'll now provide an overview of what you need for that. First I will explain the files you can use as login scripts for the user, and then you will read about files used to display messages for users logging in to your system.

Creating Shell Login Scripts

When a user logs in to a system, the configuration file /etc/profile is used. In this generic shell script, which can be considered a login script, environment settings for users are issued. Also, you can include commands that need to be issued when the user first logs in to a server. The file /etc/profile is a generic file processed by all users logging in to the system. It also has a user-specific version that can be created in the home directory of the user. The name of this user-specific version is either ~/.bash_profile, ~/.bash_login, or ~/.profile; all three names will work. The user-specific version of the Bash login script is executed last, so if there is a conflict in settings between the two files, the user-specific settings will always be used. In general, it is not a good idea to configure many individual login files for users but rather to work it all out in /etc/profile.

Now, /etc/profile is not the only file that can be processed when starting a shell. If, from a current environment a user starts a subshell, such as by executing a command or by using the command /bin/bash again, a configuration file can be processed again. The name of this configuration file is /etc/bashrc. This file also has a user-specific version in ~/.bashrc. Although some distributions use this file to manage the user environment, it is not used by default on SUSE Linux Enterprise Server 10.

Displaying Messages to Users Logging In

As an administrator, it is sometimes necessary to display messages to users logging in to your server. You can use two files for that purpose. First, the /etc/issue text file has content that is displayed to users before they are logging in. To process this file, the getty program that is responsible for creating login terminals will read it and display its content. You can, for example, use it to display a message about how users should log in to your system or include a message if login has been disabled on a temporary basis. Second, related to this file is /etc/motd, which displays messages to users after they have logged in. Typically, you can use this file to display messages related to day-to-day system maintenance.

Summary

In this chapter, you learned how to create users and groups. You saw that PAM performs an important role in the way the user logs in to the system. Also, you learned which files you can use to create a working environment for your users. In the next chapter, you will learn how to use permissions in a Linux environment to secure access to files.

CHAPTER 6

■ ■ ■

Managing Linux Permissions

At first sight, it seems easy to manage permissions in a Linux environment; after all, you have just three permissions to grant instead of the many permissions some other operating systems have! With a closer look, however, you will see that the system that was invented in the 1970s is only the foundation for a system that can be pretty complex. In this chapter, you'll get an overview of all the subjects relevant to permission management:

- Granting read, write, and execute
- Understanding the concept of ownership
- Working with advanced Linux permissions
- Setting permissions
- Working with access control lists for granular permission control
- Applying attributes to files and directories

Granting Read, Write, and Execute: The Three Basic Linux Permissions

The foundations of working with permissions in a Linux system are the three elementary permissions: read (r), write (w), and execute (x). Using these permissions is not hard: *read* allows a user to read the file or the contents of the directory to which the permission is applied, *write* allows the user to change an existing file if applied to a file and to create or remove files in a directory to which it is applied. Finally, *execute* on files allows a file to execute executable code. If applied to a directory, it allows a user to activate that directory. Therefore, the execute permission is applied as a default permission to all directories on a Linux system. Table 6-1 summarizes the behavior of the three basic permissions.

Table 6-1. *Overview of Linux Basic Permissions*

Permission	Applied to Files	Applied to Directories
Read	Reads contents of a file	Lists files in a directory with the ls command
Write	Modifies existing files and their properties	Creates or deletes files from a directory
Execute	Executes files that contain executable code	Activates a subdirectory with the cd command

Understanding Permissions and the Concept of Ownership

To determine the permissions a given user has on a file or directory, you must understand the Linux operating system concept of ownership. Ownership is set on every file and directory; therefore, there is no such thing as inheritance.

Note In fact, on Linux you can apply inheritance when working with the SGID permissions and access control lists (ACLs). I'll cover these subjects later in this chapter.

Linux works with three entities that can be set as the owner of a file or directory: owner, group owner, and others. By default, the user who creates a file will also become the *owner* of that file, but an administrator can change ownership later using the chown command. Also by default, the primary group of the user who is the owner of a file will become the *group owner* of that file.

Note When I refer to a *file* in this section, I'm also referring to a directory, unless stated otherwise. From a file system point of view, a directory is just a special kind of file.

Finally, the *others* entity typically refers to the rest of the world: permissions granted to the others entity are permissions that apply to everyone who is able to access the given file. You can see the ownership of files and the permissions that are set for the three file owners by using the ls -l command, as shown in the following code line. See also Figure 6-1 for a schematic overview.

```
-rw-rw-r--  1  linda users  145906 2006-03-08 09:21 somefile
```

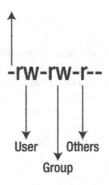

Figure 6-1. *Meaning of permissions as displayed with* ls -l

In the previous output of the command ls, the name of the file is somefile. The first ten positions of the ls output are reserved for information about permissions that are applied. The first character refers to the type of file. In this case, it is just an ordinary file; therefore, a - is displayed. Next, three groups of three characters refer to the permissions applied to the user, group, and others, respectively. As you can see, the user has read as well as write permission, the group has read as well as write permission, and the others entity has just read permission. The next important pieces of data are the names linda and users; these refer to the user linda who is the owner and the group users that is the group owner. Note that in the basic Linux permission scheme, just one user and just one group can be assigned as the owner of a file.

With regard to Linux rights, ownership is the only thing that really matters. For example, imagine the home directory of user linda. Typically, the permissions on a home directory are set as in the following output line of the ls command:

```
-rwxr-xr-x  1 linda users 1024   2006-03-08 09:28 linda
```

Now imagine that in that user's home directory the user root creates a file that has the name rootsfile and sets the permissions on this file as follows:

```
-r--r-----  1  root root 1 537   2006-03-08 10:15 rootsfile
```

So, what can user linda do to this file? The answer to that question is simple, but a caveat exists. Since linda is not the owner of the file and also is not the member of the group that owns the file, she has no permissions at all to this file. The fact that it is in her home directory doesn't change a lot about that either, because on Linux permission inheritance does not exist. However, linda has permission to write within her home directory, and therefore she can remove the file from her home directory. This is not inheritance; this is simply because the write permission in a directory applies to the things a user can do to files in that directory.

Changing File Ownership

To change the ownership of a file, you can use the chown command. The structure of this command is as follows:

```
chown {user|.group} file
```

For example, to make linda the owner of user root's file in the previous example, you must use the command chown linda rootsfile. To change the group owner of somefile to the group sales, you can use the command chown .sales somefile. It is also possible to change the ownership of a user and a group with one command, separating the user and group with a dot or colon. Note that for changing group ownership, you can use the command chgrp. Therefore, chown .sales somefile will do the same thing as chgrp sales somefile. Note that when using chgrp, you do not need to precede the name of the group with a dot.

Note If you are using chown to change group ownership, make sure you precede the name of the group with a dot or a colon. Otherwise, the chown command will think it is a user. You could, of course, use chgrp instead.

By default, chown and chgrp apply only to the file or directory on which they are used. You can, however, use the commands to work recursively as well; for example, chown -R linda somedir will make user linda the owner of all the files in somedir and all the subdirectories of somedir.

Understanding Group Ownership

When working with group ownership, you should be aware of the way Linux handles group ownership. By default, the primary group of the user who creates a new file will become the group owner of that file. If, however, the user is a member of more than one group, you can manipulate this default setting. When a user uses the newgrp command, the user can change the primary group setting on a temporary basis. The following steps show what happens:

1. Log in as some normal user on your computer. Then from a console window, use the groups command to get an overview of all the groups of which you are currently a member. As root you can also use it on another user to see what groups that user is a member of (see Listing 6-1). The primary group is listed first in this overview. If you haven't modified anything for this user, it will be set to the group users.

   Listing 6-1. *The* groups *Command*

   ```
   BOS~ # groups linda
   linda : users dialout video
   ```

2. Now from the console window, issue the touch newfile command. This will create a new file with the name newfile. Use ls -l newfile to display the ownership information for this file. You will see that users is set as the owner of the file.

3. Next, use su to become root. Then use groupadd to create a new group; for example, use groupadd -g 101 sales to create a group with the name sales and a group ID of 101. Next, as root, use usermod -g 101 linda to set root's group as the primary group for user linda. After changing this group information, execute exit to close the su session and become the regular user account again.

4. As the regular user, use groups again to get an overview of all the groups of which you are currently a member. The new group should be listed now.

5. As the regular user, use newgrp sales. This will set the primary group to your new group on a temporary basis. You can use the groups command to check this; the new group should be listed first now. You will also see that if you create a new file (use touch somenewfile), the new group will be the group owner of the new file.

In the previous procedure, you saw one method you can use to set a group that you are member of as the primary group on a temporary basis. You can also use group passwords, which allow you to set the group to your temporary primary group, even if you are not a member of that group. If a user is not listed as a member of a group but tries to use the newgrp command anyway to set its primary group, the user will be prompted for the group password. By default, groups don't have a password, but you can use the passwd -g command to set a password for a group.

Working with Advanced Linux Permissions

Thus far, I've discussed at length the three basic Linux permissions: read, write, and execute. But you can also use a set of advanced permissions. This section describes how these permissions work. Before diving into the details, the following list gives a short overview of the advanced permissions and the way you use them:

SUID: This permission is also known as *set user ID*. If applied to an executable file, the user who executes the file will have the permissions of the owner of the file while executing it.

SGID: This permission is also known as the *set group ID* permission. You can apply the permission in two ways. First, if you apply it to executable files, the user executing the file will do so under the guise of the permissions of the file's group owner. Second, you can use the permission to set the default group owner of files created in a given directory. If applied on a directory, all files and directories created in this directory, and even in its subdirectories, will get the group owner of the directory as its group owner. Imagine that all members of the group sales normally save the files they create in /data/salesfiles. In that case, you would want all the files created in that directory to be owned by the group sales. You can do this by setting sales as the group owner for salesfiles and next applying the SGID permission bit to this directory.

Sticky bit: If you use the sticky bit, users can remove files only if one of the following conditions is met:

- The user has write permissions on the file.
- The file is in a directory of which the user is the owner.
- The user is the owner of the file.

The sticky bit permission is especially useful in a shared data directory. Imagine that user linda creates a file in the directory /data/sales. She wouldn't want her co-workers from the sales group who also have write permissions in that directory to remove her file by accident, because normally they can since they have the write permission on the directory. If you apply the sticky bit, however, other users can remove the file if only one of the previous conditions has been met.

You should realize the dangers of the SUID and SGID permissions if applied improperly. Imagine, for example, that an application owned by user root has a security issue that allows users with the right knowledge to access a shell environment. This shell environment would be owned by user root, giving the attacker carte blanche to do what he pleases! Therefore, you should be extremely cautious in applying SUID or SGID to files. On the other hand, you may notice that some files have SUID set by default. For example, the program file /usr/bin/passwd cannot work without it. This is because a user who changes her password needs to write information to the file /etc/shadow. On this file, only the user root can write data, and normal users cannot even read its contents. The operating system solves the problem by applying the SUID permission that grants users root permission, just on a temporary basis to change their passwords.

■**Tip** Someone using a backdoor to get access to your server may use SUID on some obscure file to get access when returning. As an administrator, you should regularly check your server for the occurrence of the SUID permission on unexpected files. You can do that by running find / -perm +4000; this will display all the files that have the SUID permissions set.

If applied the wrong way, the SGID permission can be a dangerous permission; however, the SGID permission is useful. For instance, you can apply this permission on directories where members of some user group need to share data with each other. The advantage of this permission, if it is applied to a directory, is that all the files created in that directory will get the same group owner, allowing all members of that group to read the file. If you make the group sales the owner of the directory /data/sales and apply the SGID permission to that, all files in that directory get the group sales as the owner of the file, so the file will always be accessible for all members of the group. This allows users to work together in a shared group data directory in an efficient way.

The SGID permission is one way of ensuring that members of the same group can work together efficiently. However, in the scenario you just read about, you can still encounter a problem; if the group has write permissions on the shared directory (which is typical for a shared data directory), one user can remove the files created by another user who is a member of the same group. Both have write permissions in the directory, and that's enough to remove files. You can prevent this by applying the sticky bit. When this permission is set, users cannot remove a file if they have only write permissions to the directory the file is in without being the owner of the file.

Setting Permissions

That's enough about how you can use permissions; it is time to set them now. Of course, you can set permissions from the file browser on your server. Although convenient, this utility isn't half as powerful as the utilities that are available from the command line. Therefore, in the following sections, you will learn how to use chmod and umask to set permissions.

Using chmod to Change Permissions

You can use the chmod command to set permissions on existing files. You can use this command by the user root or the owner of a file to change permissions of files or directories. You can use the chmod command in two ways: an absolute way or a relative way. When using chmod in a relative way, you specify the entity that permissions are granted to (user, group, or others), followed by the +, -, or = operator and then followed by the permissions you want to apply. In absolute mode, a numeric value grants the permissions.

Using chmod in Relative Mode

When working in relative mode, you have to use the following values for the permissions that are available:

Read: r

Write: w

Execute: x

SUID: u+s

SGID: g+s

Sticky bit: t

The relative mode is useful when changing permissions that apply to everyone. For example, you can easily make a script file executable by using chmod +x myscript. Because u, g, or o are not used in this command to refer to the entity the permissions are applied to, the file will be made executable for everyone. You can, however, be more specific; for example, just remove the write permission for the others entity by using chmod o-w somefile.

SUID is set with u+s, and SGID is set with g+s. In the output of the ls -l command, however, there is no reserved permission to display this permission alone. As the result, you will see the SUID permission at the position of the x for users and the SGID permission at the position of the x for groups. You can see this in Listing 6-2 where the first file has SUID applied and the second file has

SGID applied. Both permissions really make sense only in combination with the execute permission; therefore, I won't discuss the hypothetical situation of a file having SUID applied but not execute for the owner or having SGID but not execute for the group.

Listing 6-2. *Displaying SUID and SGID with* ls -l

```
-rwsr-xr-x  2  root root 48782 2006-03-09 11:47 somefile
-rwxr-sr-x  2  root root 21763 2006-03-09 11:48 someotherfile
```

Using chmod in Absolute Mode

Although chmod's relative mode is easy to work with if you just want to set or change one permission, it can get complicated if you need to change more than that. In that case, the absolute mode is more useful. In the absolute mode, you work with numeric values to determine the permissions you need. For example, you can use chmod 1764 somefile to change the permissions on a given file. Of these four numbers, the first refers to the special permissions SUID, SGID, and sticky bit; the second indicates permissions for the user; the third is for the group permissions; and the last is for the permissions for others. Of these four digits, you can omit the first. In that case, no special permissions are set for this file. When working with chmod in absolute mode, the permissions you are working with have the following values:

Read: 4

Write: 2

Execute: 1

SUID: 4

SGID: 2

Sticky bit: 1

For example, to set permissions to read, write, and execute for others, to read and execute for group, and to nothing for others, you can use chmod 750 somefile. As an alternative, you can use chmod 0750 somefile as well; however, it makes no sense to use the initial 0 because no special permissions are used in this case.

Using the Graphical Interface to Set Permissions

Although you should absolutely know how to handle permission management from the command line, it is possible to set permissions from the graphical interface as well:

1. From the Applications menu on the GNOME desktop, select Browse ➤ File Manager ➤ Nautilus.

2. Right-click any folder in the graphical desktop, and then select Properties.

3. Now click the Permissions tab (see Figure 6-2). Here you will see all permission-related properties discussed so far. From this interface, you can set the file owner and file group as well as all the available permissions.

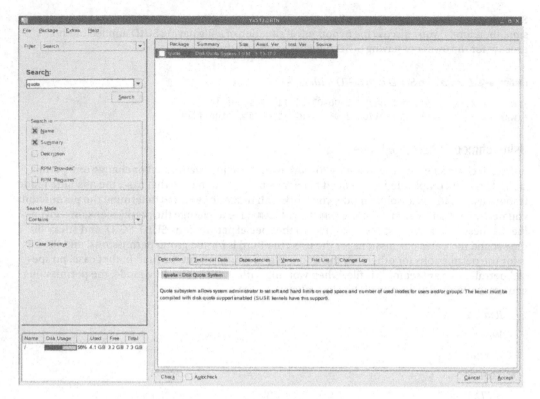

Figure 6-2. *The Nautilus file browser makes it easy to set permissions.*

Using umask to Set Default Permissions

You probably noticed that when creating a new file, some default permissions are set. These permissions are determined by the umask setting. This is a shell setting that is set for all users when logging in to the system. In the umask setting, a numeric value is used that is subtracted from the maximum permissions that can be set automatically to a file; the maximum setting for files is 666 and for directories is 777. However, some exceptions to this rule exist; therefore, you can find a complete overview of umask settings in Table 6-2. Of the digits used in the umask, such as with the numeric arguments for the chmod command, the first digit refers to user permissions, the second digit refers to the group permissions, and the last refers to default permissions set for others. The default umask setting of 022 gives 644 for all new files and 755 for all new directories that are created on your server.

Table 6-2. umask *Values and Their Results*

Value	Applied to Files	Applied to Directories
0	Read and write	Everything
1	Read and write	Read and write
2	Read	Read and execute
3	Read	Read
4	Write	Write and execute
5	Write	Write
6	Nothing	Execute
7	Nothing	Nothing

You have two ways to change the umask setting: for all users and for individual users. If you want to set the umask for all users, you must make sure the umask setting is entered in the configuration file /etc/profile.local. The configuration file /etc/profile is a generic configuration file that is processed by all users logging in to the system. Since, however, YaST doesn't like modifications to be made directly to this file, you must make all modifications you want to apply in /etc/profile.local. If the umask is changed in this file, it applies to all users logging in to your server.

An alternative to setting the umask in /etc/profile.local, where it is applied to all users logging in to the system, is to change the umask settings in a file with the name .profile, which is created in the home directory of an individual user. Settings applied in this file are applied for the user who owns the home directory only; therefore, this is a nice method to create an exception for one user only. You could, for example, create a .profile file in the home directory of user root and there apply the umask setting of 027, whereas the generic umask setting for ordinary users is set to 022 in /etc/profile.local.

Working with Access Control Lists

Up to now, you have read about the basic model to apply permissions on a generic Linux system. When you use an advanced file system such as ReiserFS, it is possible to add some options to the default model of working with permissions in the Linux environment by using the ACL mechanism. In the following sections, you will learn how you can apply this technique to allow for a more flexible security mechanism.

The main reason for the development of the Linux ACL system was to compensate for the shortcomings of the default Linux permissions. Basically, this system has two problems:

- Default Linux permissions do not allow you to set more than one entity as the user or group owner of a file.

- In a default Linux permissions scheme, you can't set default permissions on a per-file or per-directory basis.

The ACL system is an optional system that you can use to compensate for these shortcomings. In the following sections, you will learn how to apply this system.

Using ACLs to Grant Permissions to More Than One Object

When mounting a device, there is normally no space to store ACL information. Therefore, you must specify, for all devices where you want to use ACLs, that ACLs have to be enabled for that device; only then can you set ACLs. If you want to use them, you must check in the configuration file /etc/fstab, which is used for the automatic mounting of all the file systems on your server, that ACL support is enabled. For instance, if ACL support for the device /dev/sda1 is enabled, you will find a line like the first line in Listing 6-3 of the /etc/fstab file. In this example, you can see that acl is specified as an option. By default, SUSE Linux Enterprise Server 10 will enable ACLs for all devices where it is supported.

Listing 6-3. *Enabling ACL Support in* /etc/fstab

```
/dev/hda1     /               reiserfs   acl,user_xattr    1 1
/dev/hda2     swap            swap       defaults          0 0
proc          /proc           proc       defaults          0 0
sysfs         /sys            sysfs      noauto            0 0
usbfs         /proc/bus/usb   usbfs      noauto            0 0
devpts        /dev/pts        devpts     mode=0620,gid=5   0 0
```

If ACLs are enabled for a given device, you can use the setfacl command to set them. Using this command is not too hard; for example, you can add setfacl -m u:linda,rwx somefile to add user linda as a trustee who has rights on the file somefile. This command does not change file ownership; it just adds a second user in the ACL that also has rights to the file. The normal output of the ls -l command does not show all users who have rights by means of an ACL; however, ls puts a + sign behind the permissions list on that file. To get an overview of all the ACLs currently set to a given file, you can use the getfacl command. The following steps give you an opportunity to try how it works:

1. Make sure you are root, and then create a file somewhere in the file system. You can use the touch command to create an empty file; for example, use touch somefile to create a file.

2. Now use getfacl somefile to monitor the permissions that are set for this file (see Listing 6-4 for an example). You will see an overview like in Listing 6-4, indicating only the default permissions that are granted to the users, group, and others.

Listing 6-4. getfacl *Displaying Normal User, Group, and Others Information*

```
myserver:~# touch somefile
myserver:~# getfacl somefile
# file: somefile
# owner: root
# group: root
user::rw-
group::r--
other::r--
```

3. Now use the command setfacl -m g:account:rw somefile (you must have a group with the name account for this to work). The group will now be added as a trustee to the file, which you can see when you use getfacl on the same command again, as shown in Listing 6-5.

Listing 6-5. getfacl *After Adding Another Trustee*

```
myserver:~# touch somefile
myserver:~# getfacl somefile
# file: somefile
# owner: root
# group: root
user::rw-
group::r--
group:account:rw-
mask::rw-
other::r--
```

Working with ACL Masks

In Listing 6-3, you can see what happens when you create a simple ACL. Not only is a new entity added as the trustee of the object, but also a mask setting is added. The mask is the summary of the maximum of permissions an entity can have on the file. This mask is not important because it is modified automatically when new permissions are set with the ACL. You can use the mask, however, to reduce the permissions of all trustees to a common denominator. Since it is set automatically when working with ACLs, I recommend just ignoring the ACL masks. It complicates things if you try to modify them in a useful way.

Using Default ACLs

On a directory, you can apply a default ACL. When using a default ACL, you can specify the permissions that new files and directories will get when they are created in a given directory. Therefore, you can consider the default ACLs to be a umask setting that is applied on a directory only. If a directory has a default ACL, all files will get the permissions specified in the default ACL. Also, subdirectories will get the permissions from the default ACL, and these permissions will be set as their own permissions as well. If a default ACL exists for a directory, the umask setting for that directory is ignored.

To set a default ACL, you must use the setfacl command with the -d option. For the remainder, you can use it with parameters as you saw before. The following example will apply a default ACL to somedir:

```
setfacl -d -m group:account:rwx somedir
```

Since in this command the option -d is used, a default ACL is set for all entities that currently are listed as trustees of the directory. You can see that in Listing 6-6, where the command getfacl is used to display the permissions currently applied to the directory somedir.

Listing 6-6. *Displaying the Default ACL for a Directory*

```
myserver:~# getfacl somedir
# file: somedir
# owner: root
# group: root
user::rwx
group::r-x
other::r-x
default:user::rwx
default:group::r-x
default:group:account:rw-
default:mask::rwx
default:other::r-x
```

The nice feature of working with default ACLs is that the rights that are granted in a default ACL are automatically added for all new files and directories created in that directory. However, you should be aware that files and directories that currently exist under the directory where a default ACL is applied are not touched by the default ACL. If you want to change permission settings in ACLs for existing files and directories, you can use the setfacl command with the option -R (recursive).

Understanding ACL Limitations

You should be aware of some limitations that exist when working with ACLs. The first limitation is that ACLs are not cumulative. This means that user and group permissions are not added to each other. Let's imagine a situation where stacey is the owner of a file and has only the read permission. She is also a member of the group sales, which is a trustee of the same file and has read write permission. As a result when the permissions for this user are calculated, she will not have both read and write. When determining the effective permission, the operating system will check whether she is the owner of the file. Since she is the owner, the operating system will look no further, and the permissions for the owner are applied. Therefore, the permissions for the group are ignored.

Note ACLs are not cumulative, and normal permissions aren't either. You can see this when you try to give a user who is an owner no permissions at all to a file and you give some permissions (for example, rw) to the group that is the owner of the file. Next, make sure your user is a member of that group and see what he can do. You'll notice that read or write access is denied for that user. The file system checks to see whether that user is the owner, and if that's the case, it looks no further.

The problem of nonaccumulation even gets more complex if a file or directory belongs to more than one group. When determining group rights, the group it will get its rights from will be selected randomly.

Another problem when working with ACLs is that a lot of applications still lack support for ACLs. For example, most backup applications cannot handle it, and probably your company database doesn't either. However, some changes are coming, and some applications are starting to support ACLs. One of them is the Samba file server (check Chapter 15 for coverage of this server), and that makes an interesting combination for rights management. Also, some of the basic Linux utilities such as cp, mv, and ls support it currently. However, it still is not possible to manage ACLs from graphical file manager utilities. For example, when you copy files with the KDE file manager Konqueror, you will lose the ACL settings.

Applying File Attributes

When working with permissions, there is always a combination between a user or group object and the permissions these user or group objects have on a file or directory. An alternative method of securing files on a Linux system is by working with attributes. Attributes do their work, regardless of the user who accesses the file. Of course, there is a difference: the owner of a file can set file attributes, whereas other users (except for root) cannot do that.

For file attributes as well, an option must be provided in /etc/fstab before they can be used. This is the user_xattr option you can see in the fstab example in Listing 6-1 earlier in this chapter. The following are the most useful attributes you can apply:

A: This attribute ensures that the file access time of the file is not modified. Normally, every time a file is opened, the file access time must be written to the file's metadata. This affects performance in a negative way; therefore, on files that are accessed on a regular basis, you can use the A attribute to disable this feature.

Tip What if you don't like the access time being modified at all? In that case, use the noatime option in /etc/fstab to specify this feature must be disabled for all files on a volume. You'll learn more about this in Chapter 8, which is about Linux file system management.

---

a: This attribute allows a file to be added to but not to be removed.

c: If you are using a file system where volume-level compression is supported, this file attribute makes sure the file is compressed the first time the compression engine gets active.

D: This attribute makes sure changes to files are written to disk immediately and not to cache first. This is a useful attribute on important database files to make sure they don't get lost between the file cache and hard disk.

d: This attribute makes sure the file is not backed up in backups where the dump utility is used.

I: This attribute enables indexing for the directory where it is enabled. This allows for faster file access for primitive file systems such as ext3 that don't use a B-tree database for fast access to files.

j: This attribute ensures that on an ext3 file system the file is first written to the journal and only after that to the data blocks on the hard disk.

s: This overwrites the blocks where the file was stored with zeros after the file has been deleted. This makes sure the recovery of the file is not possible after it has been deleted.

u: This attribute saves undelete information. This allows a utility to be developed that works with that information to salvage deleted files.

Note Although you can use quite a few attributes, you should be aware that most attributes are rather experimental and are of use only if an application is used that can work with the given attribute. For example, it doesn't make sense to apply the u attribute as long as no application has been developed that can use this attribute to recover deleted files.

If you want to apply attributes, you can use the chattr command. For example, use chattr +s somefile to apply the attribute s to somefile. Need to remove the attribute again? Then use chattr -s somefile, and it will be removed. To get an overview of all attributes that are currently applied, use the lsattr command.

Apply Quota to Allow a Maximum Amount of Files

A completely different way to apply restrictions to the way users can create files and directories is to use a user *quota*, a system to limit the amount of available storage space. Configuring user quotas is a five-step procedure:

1. Install the quota software.

2. Prepare the file system where you want to use the quota.

3. Initialize the quota system.

4. Apply the quota to users and groups.

5. Start the quota service.

Before starting to apply the quota, you should realize how it must be applied. Quotas are always user or group related and apply to a complete volume or partition. That is, if you have one disk in your server with one partition on it that makes your complete root file system and you apply a quota of 100MB for user alex, this user can create no more than 100MB, no matter where on your server.

When working with quotas, you need to apply a hard limit, a soft limit, and a grace period. The *soft limit* is a limit that cannot be surpassed on a permanent basis. That is, a user *can* create more files than the quota allows on a temporary basis. The period for which this is allowed is defined by the *grace period*. There is also a *hard limit*, which is an absolute limit. When this limit is reached, it is impossible for the user to create new files.

Working with soft and hard limits is confusing at first but has some advantages. If a user has more data than the soft limit allows, the user still can create new files and isn't stopped from working immediately. The user will, however, get a warning about needing to clean up files, because when the hard limit is reached, no more new files can be created whatsoever.

Installing the Quota Software

To work with quotas, you must install the quota software. The following procedure describes how you can use YaST to do this:

1. Start YaST, and provide the password of your root user when requested.

2. Select Software ➤ Software Management to open the interface used for installing and removing software.

3. In the drop-down list in the upper-left corner of the screen, make sure the Search option is selected, and then in the search bar, enter **quota**. Then click Search. This will show the quota package.

4. Now click Accept to start installing the quota software, and insert all the media the installer requests. After completing the installation, you can continue with the next step.

Preparing the File System for the Quota

Before you can use the quota software, you must add an option to /etc/fstab for all the file systems where quotas must be supported. The next steps describe how:

1. Open /etc/fstab with an editor.

2. Select the column with options. Add the option usrquota if you want to apply a quota to users and grpquota to add a quota for groups. Repeat this procedure for all file systems where you want to use quotas.

3. Remount all the partitions where quotas have been applied (or restart your server). For example, to remount the root partition so that new settings are applied, use mount -o remount /.

Initializing the Quota

Now that you have taken all the preliminary measures, you need to initialize the quota system. The purpose of this procedure is that all file systems have to be searched on files that are already created. The reason why this has to be done may be obvious: existing files count for the quota of users as well. The report that is generated by this quota initializing is saved in two files. The file aquota.user is created to register user quota, and aquota.group is created for group quota.

To initialize a file system for the use of quota, you need to use the quotacheck command. You can use this command with some options; the most important options are as follows:

-a: This option makes sure all file systems are searched when initializing the quota system.

-u: This option makes sure user information is searched for. This information will be written to the file aquota.user.

-g: This option ensures that group information is searched for as well. This information is written to the file aquota.group.

-m: Use this option to make sure no problems will occur on file systems that are currently mounted.

-v: This option ensures the command will work in verbose mode, and it will show what it is doing.

So, the best way to initialize the quota system is by using the quotacheck -augmv command. As the result of this command, after some time the files aquota.user and aquota.group are created to list all quota information for current users.

Setting the Quota for Users and Groups

Now that the quota databases have been created, it is time to start the real work. You can now apply the quota for all users and groups on your system. To do this, you use the edquota command. This command will use the editor vi to create a temporary file. In this file, you can create the soft limit and the hard limit you want to apply for your users and groups. If you want to apply a soft limit of 100,000 blocks for a user called florence and a hard limit of 110,000 blocks, you have to follow these steps:

1. Issue the command edquota -u florence.

2. The editor will now open. In the editor screen, six numbers specify the quota for all file systems on your computer. The first of these numbers shows the amount of blocks your user has in use currently. The second and third numbers are important. The second number is the soft limit for the number of blocks in kilobytes; the third number is the hard limit on blocks in kilobytes. The fifth and sixth numbers do the same for inodes, which roughly represent the number of files you can create on your file system (see Chapter 8 for more information on that). The first and fourth numbers are used to record the number of blocks and inodes that are currently in use for this user.

3. In the editor, first press the Escape key, and then use the command :wq! to write changes to the quota system.

In the previous procedure, you read that you can apply quota for the number of inodes and for blocks. If you use quota on inodes, these specify a maximum number of files that can be created. Most administrators think it doesn't make sense to work that way and therefore set the values for these to 0. A value of 0 indicates there is currently no limitation for this item.

After setting the quota, if the soft limit and hard limit are not set to the same value, you need to use the edquota -t command to set the grace time. This will open another temporary file in which you can specify the grace time you want to use, either in hours or in days. The grace time is set per file system. Therefore, there is no option to specify different grace time settings for different users.

Once you have set the quota for one user, you may want to apply it to other users as well. Instead of following the previous procedure for all users on your system, you can use the edquota -p command. For example, edquota -p florence alex will copy the quota currently applied for florence to alex.

Caution To set quota, the user you are setting quota for must be known to the quota system. This is not done automatically; to make sure that new users are known to the quota system, you must initialize the quota system again after creating new users. I recommend making a cron job (see Chapter 11) to automatically run the quotacheck command at a reasonable interval.

When all quota have been set the way you like it, you can monitor the current quota settings for your users. Use the repquota command to do this. The command repquota -aug shows current quota settings for all users and groups on all volumes.

Starting the Quota Service

Now that you have set all the quota you want to work with, you just have to start the quota service and make sure it restarts when your computer reboots. To do this, use the insserv quota command. This command makes sure the quota system initializes after rebooting your server. To start the quota service manually, use the rcquota start command.

Summary

In this chapter, you learned how to secure files and directories on your SUSE Linux Enterprise Server. First you read about the basic Linux permissions and the way they are applied. Next you read about all the extensions that have been made to the Linux permission system by means of the SUID, SGID, and sticky bit but also by means of ACLs and attributes. Finally, you learned how to apply a quota to your server to prevent users from filling up the file system completely. In the next chapter, you will learn about file system management.

CHAPTER 7

■ ■ ■

Performing Daily File System Management Tasks

In Chapter 4, you learned how to perform basic management tasks related to the file system of your server. In this chapter, you will learn about some more elementary tasks related to file system management. I'll discuss device mounting, and you will learn how to perform mounts automatically by using the /etc/fstab configuration file. Also, you will learn about the purpose of hard and symbolic links and how you can create them. Finally, I'll discuss some basic tools for making file system backups.

Mounting Devices

If you work from the graphical interface, all you have to do to access an external storage medium such as a DVD or USB stick is insert it in the drive, and it will load automatically. However, if you work from the console or you work with drives that are not recognized automatically, the devices will not be activated automatically. In that case, you need to use the mount command to make sure you are able to access the device. In the next sections, you will learn everything you need to work with this command.

Using the Mount Command

To mount devices by hand, you have to use the mount command. The structure of this command is easy to understand: mount /what /where. For the what part of the option, you must specify a device name, and for the where part, you use a directory. Basically, you can use any directory, but it doesn't make sense to mount a device, for example, on /usr; it can even be dangerous because it will temporarily make all the other files in that directory unavailable. Therefore, on SUSE Linux Enterprise Server 10, two directories are created as default mount points. The first of these directories is the directory /mnt. This is typically the directory you would use for a mount that happens only occasionally. The second is the directory /media. In there, you would mount devices that are connected on a more regular basis. You would, for example, mount a CD, DVD, or USB stick in that directory with the command mount /dev/cdrom /media/cdrom.

The mount command makes it possible not only to mount devices such as CDs and DVDs but also network shares. If you want to do that, you must be a little bit more specific, however. For example, if you want to mount a share with the name myshare on your Windows computer that has the name mira, you would use the following command:

```
mount -t smbfs -o username=yourname //mira/myshare /mnt
```

This command has some extra information. First, it mentions the file system that needs to be used. The mount command is perfectly capable of determining the file system for local devices; however, if you are using a network device, you need to specify it. In this case, since you want to make a mount to a Windows file system, you use the smbfs file system type. (Table 7-1 later in this chapter lists other commonly used file system types.) Next, you specify the name of the user who performs the mount. This must be the name of a valid user account on the other system. Then you specify the name of the share. The previous example used a computer name (mira); if your system has problems resolving that, you can use an IP address. Follow the computer name with the name of the share. As the final part, you specify the name of the directory where the mount has to be created. In this example, I've mounted it on /mnt, since this typically is a mount that you would make only occasionally (consider working with subdirectories if you plan on having simultaneous mounts in this directory). If it would be a mount you were using on a regular basis, you would create a subdirectory under /media (/media/mira would make sense here) and create the mount in that subdirectory.

Using the mount Command Options

The mount command offers many options. Some of these are rather advanced. For example, to perform the mount using the backup of file administration in the superblock that ordinarily sits on block 8193, you can use the following command:

```
mount -o sb=8193 /dev/somefilesystem /somedirectory
```

These, however, are options you would use only in the case of an emergency. Some other more advanced options are really useful; for example, when troubleshooting your server, you can boot it with a read-only file system (you can find out more about boot modes in Chapter 10). When the system is mounted read-only, you cannot change anything; therefore, after successfully starting in read-only mode, you would want to mount read-write mode as soon as possible. To do that, use the command mount -o remount,rw /; this would make your root file system read-writable without actually disconnecting the device first.

One of the most important options for the mount command is the -t option. This option specifies the file system type you want to use. Usually, your server will detect what file system to use all by itself. Sometimes, however, you need to help it if the file system self-check isn't working properly. Table 7-1 lists the most commonly used file system types.

Table 7-1. *Linux File System Types*

Type	Description
minix	This is the mother of all Linux file systems. It was used in the earliest Linux version. Since it has some serious limitations, such as the inability to work with partitions greater than 32MB, it isn't used often anymore. Occasionally, you'll still see it on small media, such as boot disks.
ext2	This has been the default Linux file system for a long time. It was first developed in the early 1990s. The ext2 file system is a completely POSIX-compliant file system, which means it allows you to work with all the properties that are typical for a Unix environment. It has, however, one serious drawback: it doesn't support journaling, and therefore it has been replaced with journaling file systems such as ext3 and ReiserFS.
ext3	Basically, ext3 is ext2 with a journal added. The major advantage of ext3 is that it is completely backward compatible with ext2. The major disadvantage is that it is based on the ext2 file system, which is a rather old file system that was not developed for a world where partitions of several hundred gigabytes are used.

Type	Description
reiserfs	ReiserFS also is a journaling file system. It was developed by Hans Reiser as a completely new file system in the late 1990s. Because it is a feature-rich file system, SUSE Linux Enterprise Server 10 uses it as its default file system.
msdos	If, for example, you need to read a floppy disk with files on it that were created on a computer using MS-DOS, you can mount it with the msdos file system type. This is, however, somewhat of a legacy file system that has been replaced with VFAT.
vfat	The VFAT file system is used for all Windows and DOS file systems that are using a FAT file system, regardless of which one is used. Use it if accessing files from a Windows-formatted disk or from optical media.
ntfs	On Windows systems, NTFS nowadays is the default file system. In Linux, there is no stable open source solution to write to NTFS file systems. However, it is possible to read from an NTFS file system. To do this, mount the media with the NTFS file system type.
iso9660	This is the file system that is used to mount CDs. Normally, you don't need to specify that you want to use this file system because it will be detected automatically when inserting a CD.
smbfs	When working on a network, the smbfs file system type is important. This file system allows you to make a connection over the network to a share that is offered by a Windows server, as shown in the previous example.
nfs	NFS is the Network File System. This file system is used to make connections between two Unix computers. You can find more about this file system in Chapter 17.

The mount command has many other options, which can be specified by using the -o option. These options are file system dependent; therefore, I won't provide a list of them here.

■**Tip** You can mount more than just partitions and external media. It is, for example, also possible to mount an ISO file. To do this, use the command mount -t iso9660 -o loop nameofyouriso.iso /mnt. This will mount the ISO file on the directory /mnt, which allows you to work on it like you work on real optical media.

Getting an Overview of Mounted Devices

Every device that is mounted is recorded in the configuration file /etc/mtab. You can browse the content of this file with a utility such as cat or less; it is also possible to get an overview of file systems that are currently mounted by using the mount command. If you use this command without any other parameters, you'll see a list of all mounted file systems and the options they were mounted with; see Listing 7-1 for an example.

Listing 7-1. *An Overview of All File Systems Currently Mounted*

```
SFO:~ # mount
/dev/hda2 on / type ext3 (rw,acl,user_xattr)
proc on /proc type proc (rw)
sysfs on /sys type sysfs (rw)
debugfs on /sys/kernel/debug type debugfs (rw)
udev on /dev type tmpfs (rw)
devpts on /dev/pts type devpts (rw,mode=0620,gid=5)
/dev/hda3 on /data type xfs (rw)
securityfs on /sys/kernel/security type securityfs (rw)
```

Unmounting Devices

On a Linux system, a device not only has to be mounted, but when you want to disconnect the device from your computer, you have to dismount it as well. For this purpose, you can use the umount command. This command can work with two arguments: either the name of the device or the name of the directory where the device is mounted. So, umount /dev/cdrom and umount /media/cdrom will both work.

When using the umount command, you may encounter the message "Device is busy" and end up with a failing dismount. When files on the device are open or someone currently has the directory as the current prompt, the mount command does not allow you to disconnect the device. You first have to make sure no more open files are present on the device. The solution is sometimes simple: if you want to dismount a CD but your current directory is set to /media/cdrom, it is not possible to disconnect the device. You first browse to another directory because if you are in the directory where the mount is on, the umount will fail. Sometimes, however, the situation can be more complex. In that case, you need to find out first which processes are currently using the device.

To do this, you can use the fuser command. This command displays the IDs of processes (these are called PIDs) using specified files or file systems. For example, fuser -m /var lists all the processes that currently have open files in /var. The fuser command also offers you the ability to kill these open files automatically. To do this for open files on /var, use fuser -km /var. After using fuser with the -k switch that kills active processes, you should always make sure the process is really terminated by using fuser -m /var again.

Another way of forcing the umount command to do its work is to use the -f option. The umount -f /somemount command will force the unmount to occur. This option is made in particular for use on an NFS network mount that has become unreachable and does not work on other file systems that are busy. Another nice option, especially if you don't like to hurry, is the -l option. You can use this option to do a *lazy unmount*; it will detach the file system from the file system hierarchy and clean up all references to the file system as soon as it is not busy anymore. Using this option allows you to do an unmount now, even if the file system is busy.

Tip An easy way to dismount and eject optical media is to use the eject command. This command will open the CD or DVD drive for you and eject the optical media that is currently in the drive. All you have to do is take it out.

Automating Mounts with /etc/fstab

When starting your server, you need to issue some mounts automatically. For this purpose, SUSE Linux Enterprise Server uses the /etc/fstab file to specify how these file systems must be mounted. This file lists all the mounts that have to occur on a regular basis. In /etc/fstab, you can state per mount if it has to happen automatically when your system starts. From this file, some system devices are mounted automatically. For example, the proc file system that gives access to running kernel processes is mounted here, like other important system file systems. Listing 7-2 shows an overview of the content of this file.

Note /etc/fstab is used at system boot time. You can also use it from the command line. Just use the mount -a command to mount all the file systems in /etc/fstab that are currently not mounted and have the option set that mounts them automatically.

Listing 7-2. /etc/fstab

```
SFO:~ # cat /etc/fstab
/dev/hda2          /                    ext3       acl,user_xattr    1 1
/dev/hda3          /data                xfs        defaults          1 2
/dev/hda1          swap                 swap       defaults          0 0
proc               /proc                proc       defaults          0 0
sysfs              /sys                 sysfs      noauto            0 0
debugfs            /sys/kernel/debug    debugfs    noauto            0 0
usbfs              /proc/bus/usb        usbfs      noauto            0 0
devpts             /dev/pts             devpts     mode=0620,gid=5   0 0
```

In fstab, each file system is described on a separate line. The fields in these lines are separated by tabs or spaces. The following fields are always present:

fs_spec: This is the first field. It describes the device or the remote file system to be mounted. Typically, you will see names like /dev/sda1 or server:/mount on this line.

___

Tip When using ext2 or a compatible file system on the device, you can replace the device name with a label, such as ROOT. You can create these labels with the e2label command on an ext2 file system or with xfs_admin on an XFS file system. Using labels makes the system more robust and will prevent a situation where adding a SCSI disk will add all device names. Labels are static and do not automatically when a disk is added or a LUN on the SAN changes.

___

fs_file: The second field describes the mount point for the file system. This is usually a directory on which the file system must be mounted. Some file systems (such as the swap file system) don't work with a specific directory as their mount point. In the case of swap, just swap is used as the mount point instead.

fs_vfstype: The third field specifies the file system type you can use. As shown earlier and explained in more depth in Chapter 8, many file systems are available for use on Linux. No specific kernel configuration is needed, because most file systems can be activated as a kernel module that is loaded automatically when needed. Instead of the name of a file system, you can also use the word ignore in this field. This is useful to show a disk partition that is currently not in use. In /etc/fstab, never use the option auto on fixed disk devices, because this may lead to a failure in mounting the device.

fs_mntops: The fourth field specifies the options that should be used when mounting the file system. Many options are available. For most file systems, the option default is used, which makes sure the file system is mounted automatically when the server boots and makes sure regular users are not allowed to disconnect the mount. Also, the options rw, suid, dev, exec, and async are common. Some of the most often used options are as follows:

- async: This does not write to the file system synchronously but by using the write cache mechanism. This ensures that file writes are performed in the most efficient way.
- dev: This treats block and character devices on the file system as devices and not as regular files.
- exec: This permits the execution of binary files.
- hotplug: This does not report errors for this device if it does not exist. This makes sense for hot-pluggable devices such as USB media.
- noatime: This does not update the access times on this file system every time a file is opened. This makes your file system somewhat faster.

- noauto: The file system will not be mounted automatically when the system boots, or a user uses the mount -a command to mount everything in /etc/fstab automatically.

- mode=: This sets a permission mode (see Chapter 6) for new files that are created on the file system.

- remount: This remounts a file system that is already mounted. It makes sense to use this option only from the command line.

- user: This allows a user to mount the file system. Usually this option is used only for removable devices such as disks and CDs.

- sync: This makes sure the content of the file system is synchronized to the medium first before the device is dismounted.

fs_freq: This field is for using the dump command, a primitive way of making backups of your file system. It determines which file systems need to be dumped when the dump command is called. If the value of this field is set to 0, it will not be dumped; if it is set to 1, it will be dumped when dump is invoked.

fs_passno: This last field in fstab is to determine how a file system needs to be checked with the fsck command. This command is started automatically at boot time. The root file system always must be checked first and therefore has the value 1. Other file systems should have 2. If the file systems are on the same device, they will be checked sequentially; if they are on different drives, they can be checked in parallel. If the value is set to 0, no automatic check will occur.

Checking File System Integrity

When a system crashes unexpectedly, the file systems that were open can get damaged. If that happens, you need to check the consistency of these file systems. For this purpose, you can use the fsck command. You can start this command with the name of the device you want to check as its argument; for example, use fsck /dev/hda1 to check files on /dev/hda1. If you run the command without any options, fsck will check the file systems in /etc/fstab serially. Usually, this will always happen when booting your system.

Nowadays, a system administrator does not have to use fsck regularly, since most modern file systems are journaling file systems. If a journaling file system gets damaged, the journal is checked, and from the journal, you can easily roll back all the incomplete transactions.

Tip On a nonjournaling file system, fsck really can take a long time to complete. In that case, you can use the -C option. This option displays a progress bar; therefore, you'll know how much longer you still have to wait. Currently, the -C option is supported only on the ext2 and ext3 file systems.

Working with Links

A link is a useful option that is not often understood. You can compare a link to a shortcut—basically, a *link* is a pointer to another file. Linux (like any Unix system) supports two kinds of links: hard links and symbolic links.

Understanding Why You Want to Use Links

Basically, the purpose of a link is to make it easier to find files you need. You can create links for the operating system and for the program files that are used on that operating system, and they can make life easier for users as well. Imagine that some users are members of the group account, and you want them to create files in the directory /home/groups/account that are readable by all the other group members. To do this, you can ask the users to change to the proper directory every time they want to save a file. As an alternative, you can create a link for each user in the user's home directory. Such a link can have the name account and can exist in the home directory of all the users who need to save work in the shared directory for the group account; this makes it a lot easier for the users to save their files at the proper location.

Another example of why links can be useful comes from the FHS standard, which describes in what directory a Linux system should store files of a particular kind. In the "old days," the X Window System had all its binaries installed in the directory /usr/X11. Later, the name of the directory where the X Window System stored its configuration files changed to /usr/X11R6. Now imagine what would happen if an application made a hard call to the directory /usr/X11 after the change; it would fail because the directory no longer exists. A link is the solution; if the administrator just creates a link with the name /usr/X11 that points to the directory /usr/X11R6, all the applications that still refer to /usr/X11 can be used.

On a common Linux system, links are everywhere. The default SUSE Linux Enterprise Server installation comes with several existing links; and as an administrator, you're free to add others. To do so, you should, however, understand the difference between a symbolic link and a hard link.

Working with Symbolic Links

A *symbolic link* is a link that refers to the name of a file. The most important advantage is that you can use it to refer to a file that is anywhere. Even if the file is on a server at the other side of the world, the symbolic link will still work. The most important disadvantage is that the symbolic link depends on the original file. If the original file is removed, the symbolic link will no longer work.

To create a symbolic link, use the ln command with the option -s. When using the ln command, make sure you first refer to the name of the original file and then to the name of the link you want to create. If, for example, you want to create a symbolic link with the name computers in your home directory that refers to the file /etc/hosts, use the command ln -s /etc/hosts ~/computers. As a result, in your home directory a shortcut with the name ~/computers will be created. This shortcut refers to /etc/hosts. Therefore, any time you open the ~/computers file, you really are working in the /etc/hosts file.

When comparing the symbolic link and the original file, you will notice a clear difference between the two of them (see Listing 7-3). First, the link and the original file do not share the same inode, which is where all the administration of the file is stored. In the inode you can also find a list of all the blocks that are read when the file is opened. As you can see in Listing 7-3, the symbolic link and the original file have different inodes; the original file is just a name that is connected directly to the inode, and the symbolic link refers to the name. You can see the latter in the ls -il (-i displays the inode number) output: after the name of the symbolic link, an arrow indicates the file on which you are really working. Also, you can see that the size of the symbolic link is significantly different from the size of the real file. The size of the symbolic link is as large as the number of bytes in the name of the file it refers to, because no other information is available in the symbolic link. Also, you can see that the permissions on the symbolic link are completely open. This is because the permissions are not managed here but in the original file. Finally, you can see that the file type of the symbolic link is set to l, which indicates it is a symbolic link.

Listing 7-3. *The Difference Between a File and a Link*

```
SFO:~ # ln /etc/hosts computers
SFO:~ # ln -s /etc/hosts symcomputers
SFO:~ # ls -il computers symcomputers
4056764 -rw-r--r-- 2 root root 689 Jun 27 20:29 computers
3013477 lrwxrwxrwx 1 root root  10 Aug 20 20:45 symcomputers -> /etc/hosts
```

You may ask, what happens to the symbolic link when the original file is removed? Well, that isn't hard to predict. The symbolic link will fail. SUSE Linux Enterprise Server will show this when displaying file properties with the ls command, and it will give a "File not found" error message when you try to open it.

Working with Hard Links

Every file on a Linux system has an inode. This inode keeps the complete administration of the file. This includes a list of all the blocks that have to be read when the file is opened and other relevant administrative information, such as the permissions set to the file, the user and group owner, and the access time, creation time, and modification time that are set on all the files on your system. In fact, your computer works with inodes; filenames are only a convenience for humans, who tend not to be too strong in working with numbers. Every name that is connected to an inode can be considered a *hard link*. Basically, when you create a hard link for a file, all you really do is add a new name to an inode. To do so, use the ln command without any options; ln /etc/hosts ~/computers will create such a hard link.

The interesting fact about hard links is that no difference exists between the original and the link. They are just two names connected to the same inode. The disadvantage is that hard links must exist on the same device. Therefore, you are rather limited in your attempts to create hard links. However, if it is possible, always create a hard link instead of a symbolic link because hard links are faster.

Creating Backups

You can go in two different directions when creating backups on Linux. You can use tar, the mother of all backup programs. The tar (which stands for *tape archiver*) utility is an old but flexible solution originally developed to write file system backups to tape. Its major disadvantage is that it is a stand-alone utility. Therefore, to make backups in a network environment, you may prefer using a commercial backup solution. In the following sections, you will learn how to use tar as a backup solution. You will also learn how to work with tape devices in a Linux environment.

Using tar to Create and Restore Backups

tar is a flexible utility that you can use to write backups to files or devices. To make a backup of a directory, you would use a command like tar -cvf /mybackup.tar /home. This command is using three options. The first option (-c) tells tar that it has to create a backup. Then the -v option, which is not mandatory but is useful, tells tar to be verbose so you can see what it is doing. Then the option -f, which is followed immediately by a filename, tells tar where it has to create the backup. In this example, it will create a file with the name mybackup.tar in the root of your file system. Then as the final argument, you specify the directory you want to back up.

Mastering tar Basics

In the previous example, tar was used to write a backup to a file. If you are running a server, you'll probably prefer to write your backup to a tape device instead. To do so, replace the name of the file with the name of the tape device you want to work with; for example, `tar -cvf /dev/st0 /home` does the job.

If you know how to create a backup with `tar`, it isn't hard to extract the backup. All you have to do is replace the c with an x. For example, `tar -xvf /home.tar` extracts the contents of `/home.tar` to the current directory.

> **Tip** When extracting files from a `tar` archive, you refer to the backup file's current location in your file system. If the file is on a tape device, make sure it is mounted in your file system first.

When writing backups, absolute paths are always made relative by default. This means a filename like `/home/joyce/somefile` is written to the backup medium as `home/joyce/somefile`. This is no problem if the file is extracted to the same directory as the directory where the backup was made from. It can, however, be a problem if you are extracting to a different directory. This situation would happen if you wanted to copy the entire content of the `/usr` directory to some other directory by using the `tar` utility.

> **Note** `tar` is more flexible than `cp`. The most significant difference between the two is that by default `tar` will back up all files, including hidden files, stale files (files with a size of 0 bytes), and file rights. Therefore, it makes sense to use `tar` instead of `cp` if you want to copy a complete directory and want to make sure everything really is included.

Imagine, for example, that an administrator uses `tar -cvf usr.tar /usr` to create a backup of the `/usr` directory, then activates the directory `/newusr` where he wants to move the entire contents to, and from there extracts the tar archive with `tar -xvf /usr.tar ..` As a result, in `newusr` a subdirectory with the name `usr` would be created, and in that subdirectory, the files from the original `/usr` would be placed. Probably this is not what the administrator intended to do, so you should be aware of this feature.

To prevent problems like this, one solution is to activate the directory you want to back up (`cd /somedirectory`) and then start the tar command like `tar -cvf /usr.tar ..` This would make the content of the archive file relative to the current directory. So in that case, if you want to put the content of `/usr.tar` in `/newusr`, first activate `/newusr`, and from there use `tar -xvf /usr.tar`. In this example, cd first activates the directory you want to create a backup of and then activates the directory where you want to create the backup. You can do that with a tar option as well; for example, `tar -cvf /usr.tar -C /usr` would create the backup file and use `/usr` as its current directory (because the option -C tells it to set its working directory), and `tar -xvf /usr.tar -C /newusr` would extract the contents of `usr.tar` to the directory `/newusr`.

If you want to use `tar` to copy the content of one directory to another directory, you have to use a faster method. In the example just discussed, first an archive file was created and then the archive file was extracted. This is double work, and besides, you also need a lot of free disk space to store the archive file. As an alternative, you can use `tar -cvC /usr | tar -xvC /newusr ...` The first part of this piped command would write an archive of the `/usr` directory. Because, however, the destination file is not specified, `tar` would write the archive to the STDOUT. Ordinarily this is not useful, but since on the STDOUT the pipe is waiting to redirect the output directly to the `tar -xvC /newusr` command, it becomes useful indeed. The part after the pipe makes sure every bit that is written to the `tar` archive with the first part of the command is written immediately to the `/newusr` directory.

When working with `tar`, it is also useful to look at the contents of a tar archive. You can do this with the -t option. For example, use the `tar -tvf /usr.tar` command to see what's inside. This is helpful if you want to determine whether complete filenames or filenames relative to a given directory are in the archive.

Using tar As a Backup Utility

When using tar as a backup utility, you need to do a few things with it. One option that is useful is to extract just one file. You can do this by specifying the name of the file as the argument to the -C option. For example, use tar -xvf /home.tar -C /home/hilary/noise.doc to extract only the noise.doc file from the tar archive.

Also useful is the option to exclude files from a backup. You can use tar to do that if you create an exclude file with the names of all the files you want to exclude in it. The content of the exclude file is just a plain list of files, and you can use any name you want for the exclude files. Listing 7-4 shows an example of an exclude file.

Listing 7-4. *An Exclude File*

```
/boot/*
/home/hilary/.hidden.doc
/var/*
```

In this file, two directories and one specific file are excluded. To include the name of this file in the tar command when making the backup, use the -X option, for example: tar -cvf /dev/st0 / -X excludefile.

Like any other decent backup utility, you can use tar to make incremental backups as well. In an incremental backup, only files that have changed since the last backup will be backed up. To do this with tar, you first need to create a snapshot file. This snapshot file is created when creating the full backup with tar, and it basically lists all the files that have been backed up. To create the snapshot, you can use the -g option, for example: tar -cvg /backup/snapshotfile -f /backup/complete.tar /. This would make a complete backup of / and write that to the file /backup/complete.tar. A list of everything backed up is written to /backup/snapshotfile. To create an incremental backup the next day, you can use the same command: tar -cvg /backup/snapshotfile -f /backup/complete.tar /. Because the snapshot file exists at that time, tar will not create it but use its contents to create an incremental backup. So when making a full backup with a snapshot file, make sure the name of the snapshot file does not exist already and always use a unique filename for it.

Compressing the Archive

The tar utility is a great utility for creating backups. However, by default it will not compress the backup. If you want to compress the backups you make with tar, you can choose from three options:

   -z: This compresses the backup with the gzip utility. This utility offers a great balance between speed and compression ratio.

   -Z: This uses the zip utility. Speed is good, but the compression ratio is not optimal.

   -j: This uses the bzip2 utility. This utility compresses about 10 percent more than gzip but takes considerably longer to complete.

You can use all of these compression utilities from the tar command line. As an alternative, it is possible to use them as separate commands. Therefore, you have two ways to create a compressed archive with tar; tar -czvf /usr.tar.gz /usr will make a complete archive of the /usr directory and compress that with gzip. Alternatively, first use tar -cvf /usr.tar /usr and then compress the resulting archive with gzip.

Using gzip isn't hard; just call the utility followed by the name of the file you want to compress. For example, use gzip somefile. Uncompressing a file that is compressed with gzip isn't hard either; for that purpose you can use the gunzip utility. For example, gunzip somefile will uncompress the file you have just compressed by using gzip. Instead of gzip and gunzip, you can also use bzip2 and bunzip2. They work the same as gzip and gunzip, but the name of the command is different.

Working with Magnetic Tapes

When writing files to a tape, you should be aware of some tape drive–specific information on Linux. The issue is that ordinarily tape drives can be rewound. On Linux, you can use two devices to communicate with a tape device:

/dev/st0: This device communicates with the first tape drive.

/dev/nst0: This is a particular instance of the tape drive; it addresses the same tape device as /dev/st0, with the difference being that you cannot rewind an nst0 device.

To work with a tape drive, you can use the mt command. For example, you can query the status of a tape by using the mt -f /dev/st0 status command. The most important information that you can get from this command is the file number and the block number. If both are set to 0, the tape is positioned at the beginning of the first file. It is possible to forward the tape to another position as well; for example, the command mt -f /dev/nst0 fsf 5 will forward the tape by the specified number of files (5 in this example). You can see this when using the mt -f /dev/st0 status command again; the file number will now be set to 5. As you can see from the example, a nonrewinding device was used for tape repositioning. In general, you should always use nonrewinding devices for repositioning a tape. If, after the reading or writing process, you want to rewind the tape, use mt -f /dev/nst0 rewind. If, after working with the tape, you want to eject it, use the mt -f /dev/nst0 offline command. This will eject the tape from its drive.

Using dd to Make a Backup

Another useful command that is related to file system backups is the dd command. The abbreviation stands for *convert and copy* (*cc*), but because cc was already some other command (the C compiler), the name of the utility became dd. The purpose of dd is to convert and copy files byte by byte. The command is written to get its input from the STDIN and write its output to the STDOUT, but by using the arguments if (input file) and of (output file), you can use it to copy files from and to anywhere. The dd command distinguishes itself from other commands such as copy in that it can work bytewise. With dd it is possible to specify exactly what bytes you want to copy, but you can use it as well to copy complete files. For example, dd if=/etc/hosts of=/root/computers would just copy the /etc/hosts command to a new name. Of course, you wouldn't use dd for that, because cp can also do it and can do it in a much easier way. However, something that cp can't do is dd if=/dev/sda of= /dev/sdb, which would make a byte-by-byte image of /dev/sda and copy that to /dev/sdb.

If you want to use dd to make a backup, that's possible as well. It works especially well to create a backup of an entire device or a part of the device. For example, use dd if=/dev/sda1 of=/media/ someserver/sda1.bakup to make a backup of a complete partition. Also useful is the option to write a backup of an important area on your hard disk. For example, use dd if=/dev/sda of=/boot/mbr. backup bs=512 count=1 to make a backup of the master boot record of your first SCSI hard drive; this backup needs to be one block of 512 bytes only, because the master boot record is no bigger than that. Another thing dd can do is write an image of a CD to a file: dd if=/dev/cdrom of=/cdrom. iso. Once this image is created, you can even mount it with mount -t iso9660 -o loop /cdrom.ido /mnt and work with it like you are used to working with a regular CD.

Using rsync to Synchronize Files

Where dd is useful to create a backup of a complete device and tar is useful to create backups based on file system information, the rsync command is useful if you want to synchronize two directories. The main advantage of rsync is that it looks only at files that have changes since the last time that rsync was active, and it thus copies just them. A simple example of how you can do that is to use rsync /etc /temp; this will first copy the complete contents of /etc to /temp, and the next time the same command is used, it will copy only the content that has changed since the last time you ran rsync.

The nice thing about rsync is the r in the name of the command, which stands for *remote*. The purpose of rsync is to synchronize files with a remote server. If rsync is installed on both computers, the command rsync -av /home root@server:/home will synchronize the contents of the directory /home with the directory /home on the computer with the name server. On the remote server, the command is executed as the root user. Before executing the command, you need to enter the password of the user account you want to use. Running rsync this way has one disadvantage, though; no security is applied when sending the password over the network. To solve this problem, you can use the -e option to specify that you should use some other command as the shell to establish the connection. Secure Shell (SSH) is the most appropriate choice for that. If you use rsync -ave ssh /home root@server:/home, you will establish a secure shell session, and the password will be unreadable while transferred over the network. You can find more about SSH in Chapter 18.

When using rsync, lots of options are available for the best possible performance. Next you will find a short list of the most important options you can use with this command:

-a: This enables archive mode. In this mode, symbolic links, permissions, and all other file attributes are preserved in the transfer.

-v: This option enables verbose mode; this mode makes sure that rsync shows exactly what it is doing.

-z: When transferring files across the network, you want to make sure the files are compressed. Use -z to compress files before they are transferred over the network (and decompress them when they arrive at the other side).

-e: This specifies the remote shell to be used. SSH is a popular remote shell that can be used for this purpose, especially because of the security it adds to an rsync session.

--delete: This removes files from the target if they don't exist on the source. By using this option, you can make sure that file deletions are synchronized as well.

Automating Backups with cron

The tar and rsync utilities are useful for creating backups. If you want to apply them in a useful way, you have to make sure they are executed on a regular basis. A good solution to make sure that happens is to use cron for that purpose. *Cron* comes from the Greek word for time (*chronos*) and on your server is a process that makes sure that jobs are executed at regular intervals.

cron consists of two distinguished parts: a cron daemon with the name crond and some related cron configuration files. The main configuration file has the name /etc/crontab, but this configuration file is not used often nowadays. On a SUSE Linux Enterprise Server 10, you will find the jobs that are actually executed in the directories /etc/cron.hourly, /etc/cron.daily, /etc/cron.weekly, and /etc/cron.monthly. By putting a script in one of these directories, you can make sure the command is executed on a regular basis. From the generic /etc/crontab file, the script /usr/lib/cron/run-crons is activated automatically. This script makes sure all the scripts from the /etc/cron.hourly, and so on, directories are executed at the proper time. If, for example, you want tar to make a complete backup of your server on a daily basis, use the following steps to make sure that happens:

1. Use an editor to create a script file. This can be a simple script that just executes the tar command. The following three lines do just that:

```
#!/bin/bash
tar xvf /dev/st0 /
exit 0
```

2. Save the script in the directory /etc/cron.daily; this will ensure it is executed on a daily basis.

3. You don't need to do anything else. The cron daemon crond will start the script every day. If anything goes wrong, the user root will receive an e-mail about that.

■**Tip** Want to make sure that a script scheduled with cron has been executed properly? Look in /var/spool/cron/lastrun; this directory contains information about the last time a script was run.

Another way of working with scheduled jobs managed by cron is to give users their own crontab files. These files are stored in the directory /var/spool/cron/tabs and have the name of the user whose account is used to execute the jobs in that crontab file. For example, if you want to create a crontab file for the user root, use crontab -u root (or log in as root and use crontab -e), and next give the file its proper contents.

When manually creating crontab files for users, you should make sure the proper syntax is used. Next you can see an example:

```
15 23 * * * tar -cvf /dev/st0 /
```

The first five positions of this line are used as indicators for the time when the file needs to be executed. The first position refers to minutes, the second position indicates the hour, the third position specifies the day of the month, the fourth position indicates the month, and the fifth position tells on what day of the week the command has to be executed. So in the previous line, the command is executed every day of the week, every day of the month, and every month at 15 minutes after the 23rd hour, which is 11:15 p.m.

Another example of the time specification in the crontab files is as follows:

```
* 11 * * 5 tar -cvf /dev/st0 /
```

This line provides a not-so-great example; the major problem is that the minute is not specified here. And an asterisk (*) at a given position in the crontab file is just equal to "every." So in this configuration, every minute from 11:00 a.m. to 11:59 a.m., with no regard to the day of the month and the month but on Friday only, a backup is created.

A third method to use the crontab mechanism is to just add the script you want to execute automatically to the /etc/crontab file. This method is not recommended; if you have a lot of cron jobs that you want to schedule, it is easy to lose track of them, but it will work if you put your jobs in there. If you do, make sure that after the time specification, you include the name of the user with whose permissions you want to run the script. So if, after a long working week on Friday at 5 p.m., you want to bring down your server and not wake it up before next Monday, include the following line in /etc/crontab:

```
0 17 * * 5 root shutdown -h now
```

You don't have to do anything else; the crond process, which is activated by default, scans every minute to see whether any changes have occurred in the cron files, and if this is the case, it will make sure these changes are activated automatically.

Summary

In this chapter, you became familiar with some of the most important file system management tasks. First, you learned how to mount devices and how to automate the mounting of devices by using the configuration file /etc/fstab. Then you read how to use the fsck command to check the consistency of file systems on your server. After that, you learned how to create links to make your file system more flexible. Next, I discussed some options that can help you make backups of your server. You learned how to use the tar command for that purpose, and you saw how you can use some other utilities such as dd and rsync. At the end of this chapter, you read how you can use crond to make sure your backup is scheduled to be executed at regular intervals.

CHAPTER 8

■ ■ ■

Configuring Storage

In the previous chapter, you learned how to perform daily file system management tasks. There is, however, more to managing storage on your server. In this chapter, you will learn about the more advanced file system management tasks involved with managing storage devices. First, I'll discuss differences between file system types. Then you will learn about creating file systems, which involves creating and formatting partitions and logical volumes. Finally, you'll read about how to set up a software RAID solution.

Comparing File Systems

An important goal of this chapter is to teach you about setting up the best file store for your server. Setting up file storage space is one of the most important tasks on a Linux server, because everything on Linux is available as a file. This goes for programs and regular text files but also for more advanced things such as devices. Your server is probably going to host lots of different applications that all create their own files. Some will create a few huge files, and others will require the fastest possible access no matter what files exist. And you may have a mail server, which creates thousands of small files.

SUSE Linux Enterprise Server offers you the ability to choose the best file system for all these different needs, and it supports many file systems out of the box. Before covering how to create the partitions that host the different file systems, I'll compare the most important file systems SUSE Linux Enterprise Server has to offer. In the following sections, you will learn about the file systems that are supported as default installation options from YaST. I won't discuss every file system that can be loaded as a module by the kernel, because most of them are not tuned for use in a SUSE Linux Enterprise Server environment. Specifically, I'll cover the following file systems:

- ext2
- ext3
- ReiserFS
- FAT
- XFS

Using ext2

The extended file system version 2 has long been the de facto standard for Linux. It was the first stable file system that offered all the elements of a POSIX file system. However, these days a feature known as *journaling* has become an important option, which ext2 doesn't offer.

> **Note** POSIX stands for *portable operating system interface for Unix*. If any element running on Linux or any other Unix version is POSIX compliant, this means it will run without problems on any flavor of Unix.

In a journal, you can track all transactions with regard to open files. The advantage to this is that if anything goes wrong while working with a system, the only thing that is required to repair damage to a file system is to do a rollback based upon the information in the journal. Because ext2 doesn't have a journal, it is not a good choice for large volumes: larger volumes will always take longer to check if no journal is present. However, if a small (less than 500MB) volume is created, ext2 is still a good choice. The first reason is mainly that it doesn't make sense to create a journal on a small file system because the journal itself will occupy space; an average journal can be about 40MB in size. Other good reasons to use ext2 are that it is a mature file system, everyone knows how it works, it works on many distributions, and many utilities are available for managing an ext2 file system. Some advanced utilities are available for tuning and troubleshooting ext2 file systems as well:

e2fsck: This is the utility that is run automatically when an administrator activates the fsck command. This utility has some options that are specific to an ext2 file system. One of them is the -b option, which allows you to repair the file system in case the first sectors are damaged. In an ext2 file system, the critical information about the file system is written to the superblock. A backup superblock is always present; its exact location depends on the block size that is used. If 1KB blocks are used, the backup superblock is in block 8,193. If 2KB blocks are used, it is in 16,384. If 4KB blocks are used, you can find it in 32,768. For example, by running e2fsck -s 8193, you may be able to repair a file system that cannot be mounted anymore. Running e2fsck -D will cause e2fsck to optimize directories. It can do this by indexing them, compressing them, or using other optimization techniques.

tune2fs: The ext2 file system has some tunable parameters. For example, by using the maximum mount count option (set using the -c option), you can force the program e2fsck to run automatically every once in a while by forcing an integrity check. This option may sound good, but on a server where a file system is sometimes rarely remounted, it can make more sense to use the -i option to set an interval defined as a time period. For example, tune2fs -i 2m will force an e2fsck on your ext2 file systems every two months. The options to check the consistency of your ext2 file system automatically are not the only options you can use with tune2fs. The option -l will list all information from the file system's superblock. Another interesting option is the -L *label* option, which allows you to set a volume label. This can be useful if device names on your system change on a regular basis; by using volume names, you can use the name of the volume when mounting the file system in /etc/fstab instead of the name of the device on which the file system is created. The last interesting option is -m; you can use this option to set a percentage of reserved blocks for your ext2 file system. By default, the last 5 percent of available disk space is always reserved for the user root to prevent users from filling up the file system completely by accident. Use e2fsck -m 2 to decrease the amount of reserved disk space, for example.

dumpe2fs: Every file system maintains a lot of administrative information. ext2 does this in the file system superblock. This is an item in many file systems designed specifically to store administrative data. Also, block groups are used as groups of data files that ext2 can administer as one entity. If you need to see the information about this file system administration, use dumpe2fs followed by the name for which you want to dump the administrative information, as shown in Figure 8-1.

Note When using a tool such as dumpe2fs, you will see information about available inodes. Every file on every POSIX-compliant file system needs an inode to store its administrative information. On ext2 and ext3, inodes are created only when you are creating the file system. Normally one inode is created for about every four data blocks. However, if you create many small files, you can run into a situation where free disk blocks are still available but there are no more available inodes. This will make it impossible to create new files. As an administrator, you can use dumpe2fs to get an overview of the available inodes on your ext2 file system.

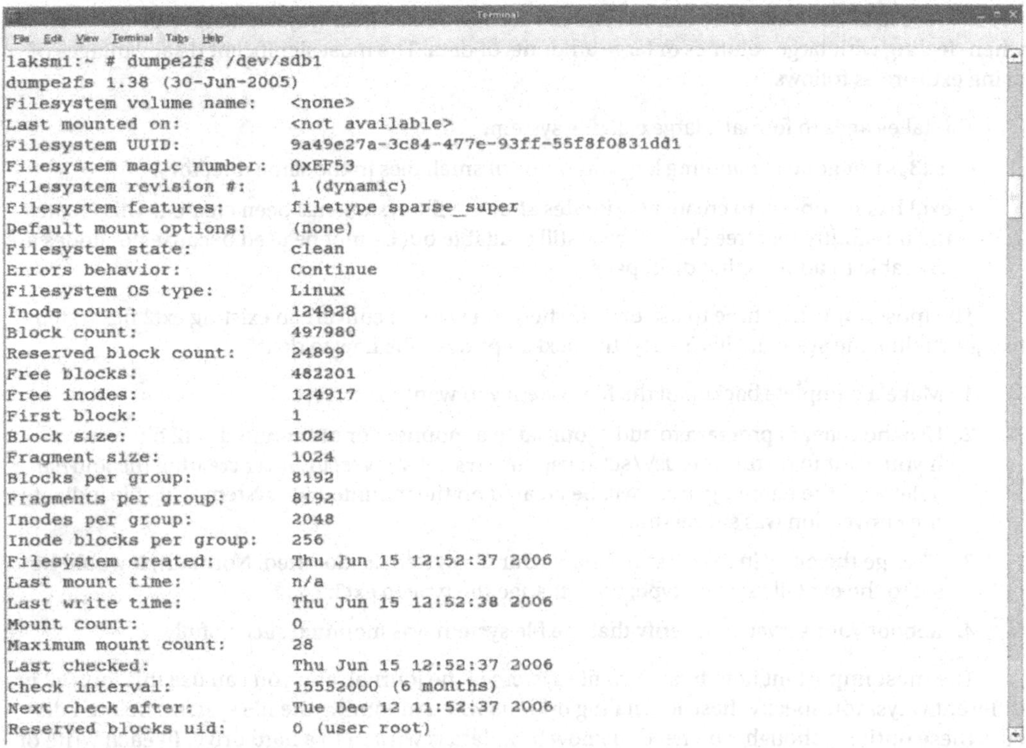

```
laksmi:~ # dumpe2fs /dev/sdb1
dumpe2fs 1.38 (30-Jun-2005)
Filesystem volume name:    <none>
Last mounted on:           <not available>
Filesystem UUID:           9a49e27a-3c84-477e-93ff-55f8f0831dd1
Filesystem magic number:   0xEF53
Filesystem revision #:     1 (dynamic)
Filesystem features:       filetype sparse_super
Default mount options:     (none)
Filesystem state:          clean
Errors behavior:           Continue
Filesystem OS type:        Linux
Inode count:               124928
Block count:               497980
Reserved block count:      24899
Free blocks:               482201
Free inodes:               124917
First block:               1
Block size:                1024
Fragment size:             1024
Blocks per group:          8192
Fragments per group:       8192
Inodes per group:          2048
Inode blocks per group:    256
Filesystem created:        Thu Jun 15 12:52:37 2006
Last mount time:           n/a
Last write time:           Thu Jun 15 13:52:38 2006
Mount count:               0
Maximum mount count:       28
Last checked:              Thu Jun 15 12:52:37 2006
Check interval:            15552000 (6 months)
Next check after:          Tue Dec 12 11:52:37 2006
Reserved blocks uid:       0 (user root)
```

Figure 8-1. *Use* dumpe2fs *to dump administrative information about your ext2 file system on the screen.*

debugfs: The debugfs utility allows you to open the ext2 file system debugger. From this debugger, you can perform powerful tasks. To do this, some internal commands are available from the file system debugger. One of them is the lsdel command, which will list files that were recently deleted from your file system. After finding the inodes of these recently deleted files, you can use the dump command, followed by the number of the inode. For example, use dump <17468> /somefile to dump everything the inode refers to in the file /somefile that is created automatically. You must be aware, however, that this works only if you are acting quickly. When a file is removed on a Linux file system, the inode and blocks that were used by the file are flagged as available, and the next time data is written to the volume, they can be overwritten. Also, you should be aware of on disadvantage of the debugfs method—it doesn't know anything about file or directory names. Therefore, you can see the inode number of a deleted file but not its name, and that can make recovery rather difficult.

To summarize, ext2 offers both advantages and disadvantages. It's advantageous when used for small volumes. However, if the size of a volume grows up to several gigabytes, ext2 is not recommended, because it can take ages to complete a file system check.

Using ext3

Put simply, the ext3 file system is just ext2 with the journaling feature added to it. Therefore, ext3 is completely compatible with ext2. As compared to other journaling file systems, however, using ext3 has some important disadvantages. Most of them are because ext3 uses tables for storing information about the files, not a B-tree database, which is the case in ReiserFS and XFS file systems. Because these tables have to be created and are accessed in a linear way, working with ext3 is slow when dealing with large volumes or large amounts of data. The most significant disadvantages of using ext3 are as follows:

- It takes ages to format a large ext3 file system.

- ext3 is not good at handling large amounts of small files in the same directory.

- ext3 has no option to create new inodes after the file system has been created. This creates the possibility that free disk space is still available but cannot be used because no inodes are available to address that disk space.

The most important time to use ext3 is when you want to convert an existing ext2 file system to a journaling file system. This is easy; the next steps describe how to do it:

1. Make a complete backup of the file system you want to convert.

2. Use the tune2fs program to add a journal to a mounted or unmounted ext2 file system. If you want to do this on /dev/sdb1, use tune2fs -j /dev/sdb1. After creating the journal, a file with the name .journal will be created on the mounted file system. This file indicates the conversion was successful.

3. Change the entry in /etc/fstab where your file system is mounted. Normally, it would be set to the ext2 file system type; now, change the type to ext3.

4. Reboot your server, and verify that the file system was mounted successfully.

The most important item in an ext3 file system is the journal, and you can use this journal in different ways. You specify these journaling options when mounting the file system. Before I discuss these options, though, you need to know how data is written to a hard drive. In each write of files, two different kinds of information need to be written: first the data blocks and then the metadata of a file. The metadata includes all the administrative information about the file; basically, you can think of the information that is displayed when using ls -l (but some more information is added as well). When tuning an ext3 journal, you can specify whether both metadata and blocks need to be journaled or whether just the metadata needs to be written to the journal.

The following options are available; you can activate them by using mount -t ext3 -o data=xxxx /yourdevice /yourmountpoint:

data=journal: With this option, both the data and the metadata of the file that is written are written to the journal. This is the safest but also the slowest option.

data=ordered: With this option, only the file's metadata is journaled. However, before updating the metadata with information about the changed file, a data write is forced. This ensures file system consistency with minimal performance impact.

data=writeback: Only metadata is written to the journal, and nothing happens to the data blocks. This is a rather insecure option where you have a serious risk of corruption of the file system.

In short, ext3 is not the best file system you can use. This is basically because it is built upon a file system that dates from a period where a 120MB hard disk was considered huge. ext3 is not able to handle the needs of current large files and file systems efficiently. Therefore, I recommend not using it and using ReiserFS or XFS instead.

Using ReiserFS

The ReiserFS file system was developed in the late 1990s by Hans Reiser. It was developed as a completely new file system that was no longer based on file system tables but on a balanced-tree database structure. Using this database makes locating files very fast compared to old file systems such as ext2 and ext3. ReiserFS offers other advantages as well. One of them is that it has better disk utilization. This is because ReiserFS is capable of using *disk suballocation*. In disk suballocation, it is not necessary to use a complete block when writing a small file. More than one small file can be written to the same disk block using one leaf node in the B-tree database. Therefore, ReiserFS is more efficient in writing many small files. Also, ReiserFS is more flexible. This is because it allows for dynamic inode allocation: if a file system runs out of available inodes, new inodes can be created dynamically. Because small files are stored with their metadata in the same database record, ReiserFS is fast when handling small files.

It has some disadvantages as well: ReiserFS is relatively slow in heavy write environments, and it also gets slow if it is more than 90 percent full.

Like ext2 and ext3, ReiserFS also has some management utilities:

reiserfsck: The reiserfsck tool checks the consistency of a ReiserFS file system. It has some powerful repair options. One of them is --rebuild-sb, which stands for *rebuild superblock*. Use this option when you get the error "Read super_block: can't find a ReiserFS file system." Another option is the --rebuild-tree option, which I hope you will not see too frequently. This option is required when reiserfsck isn't able to repair the file system automatically because it found some serious tree inconsistencies. Basically, the --rebuild-tree option will rebuild the complete B-tree database. Before using this option, always make a backup of the complete partition on which you are running it, and never interrupt the command, because it will definitely leave you with a file system that is inaccessible.

reiserfstune: You can use the reiserfstune command for several purposes. Basically, you use it to tune options with regard to the ReiserFS journal, but you can also use it to set a universal unique identifier (UUID) and a label. Some interesting options are available with this command. One of them is the -j option, which allows you to specify the journal device you want to use. This option makes it possible to separate the ReiserFS journal from the actual file system; it is a useful option if you want to avoid a situation where a single point of failure can make your system inaccessible. Another interesting option that you can use with reiserfstune is the option -l; this allows you to specify a label for the file system. You can use this label when mounting the file system, and thus it makes working on the file system much more flexible.

resize_reiserfs: As its name suggests, the resize_reiserfs utility resizes a ReiserFS file system. You should be aware that resizing a file system involves two steps. First you need to resize the device the file system is created on, and only then can you resize the file system. You'll learn more resizing devices throughout this chapter. Using resize_reiserfs is rather simple; for example, use resize_reiserfs -s /dev/sdb2 to resize the ReiserFS file system on sdb2 in a manner that it fills this device completely. Alternatively, you can specify the size to resize it with in kilobytes (K), megabytes (M), or gigabytes (G). For example, if you want to shrink a file system by 500MB, use resize_reiserfs -M 500 /dev/sdb2.

debugreiserfs: The debugreiserfs command allows you to dive into the ReiserFS administrative information to see whether it's all set according to your expectations. If you run it without options, it will just give an overview of the superblock. Several options are available to tune its workings. For example, debugreiserfs -j /dev/sdb2 would print the contents of the journal. It is also possible to dive into specific blocks when using the -1 option. This option takes as its argument the block whose contents you want to see. Using this option can be useful if you want to do a block-by-block reconstruction of a file that was destroyed by accident.

In summary, ReiserFS is a robust file system that offers many advantages. This is also the reason why SUSE Linux Enterprise Server 10 uses it as its default file system. However, it has limitations, especially when the ReiserFS partition becomes more than 90 percent full; if that happens, the file system becomes rather slow.

Using XFS

For very large environments, the XFS file system that was developed by SGI for use on super-computers is probably the best choice. Like ReiserFS, it is a full 64-bit file system, and its major benefit is that it works well on very large files. XFS uses *allocation groups*; an allocation group is like a file system in a file system. The advantage of using these allocation groups is that the kernel can address more than one group at the same time; in addition, each group has its own administration of inodes and free disk space. Of course, XFS is capable of creating new inodes dynamically when this is needed.

The XFS file system consists of three parts: the data section, the log section, and the real-time section. In the data section, user data and metadata are written. The log section contains the journaling information for XFS, and the real-time section stores the real-time files. These are files that are updated immediately. Each XFS file system is identified by a UUID. This UUID is stored in the header of each allocation group and helps you distinguish one XFS file system from the other. For this reason, never use a block-copying program such as dd to copy data from one XFS volume to another XFS volume; use xfsdump and xfsrestore instead to make copies of XFS file systems.

A unique feature of XFS is the delayed allocation feature. This feature makes sure that a pending write is not written to the hard disk immediately but to RAM first. The decision to write is delayed to the last minute. The advantage is that when it is not needed to write the file after all, it is not written. In this way, XFS reduces file system fragmentation, and at the same time it increases write performance. Another great feature of XFS is preallocation. This makes sure that space is reserved before the data blocks are actually written. This increases the chances that a complete file can be written to a series of consecutive blocks and thus avoids fragmentation. When creating an XFS volume on SUSE Linux Enterprise Server, some specific options are available as well, as shown in Figure 8-2:

Block Size in Bytes: This option allows you to set the block size you want to use. By default, it is set to 4,096 bytes, but alternatively you can set it to 512 bytes, 1,024 bytes, or 2,048 bytes.

Inode Size: Use this option to specify the size of inodes you want to create on the file system. You need this option only if you need to perform specific tasks on your file system, such as working with files that have lots of extended attributes.

Percentage of Inode Space: If so required, you can limit the percentage of the file system that can be used for storing inodes. By default, there is no maximum setting.

Inode Aligned: Make sure this option is always set to yes, because it will ensure that no fragmentation occurs in the inode table.

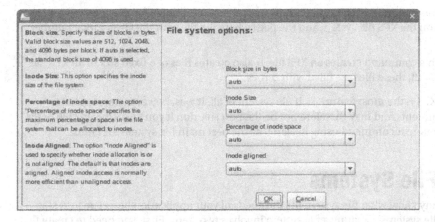

Figure 8-2. *XFS has some specific options that you can set from YaST when creating an XFS file system.*

Like all other file systems, XFS has its own management tools. Since it is a rather complex file system, many utilities exist:

xfs_admin: This command changes the parameters of an XFS file system.

xfs_logprint: This command prints the log (journal) of an XFS file system.

xfs_db: This command is the XFS file system debugger.

xfs_growfs: This command expands the XFS file system.

xfs_repair: This command repairs an XFS file system.

xfs_copy: This command copies the content of an XFS file system while preserving all of its attributes. The main advantage of using xfs_copy instead of the normal cp is that it will copy data in parallel and thus work much faster than a normal copy command.

xfs_info: This command shows generic administrative information about XFS.

xfs_rtcp: This real-time copy command was designed specially for use on XFS. Files copied with this command are put on the real-time section of the XFS file system, which makes sure they will be updated immediately.

xfs_check: This command checks the consistency of an XFS file system.

xfs_quota: This command allows you to work with quotas on an XFS file system.

xfs_io: This command debugs the I/O path of an XFS file system.

xfs_bmap: This command prints block mapping for an XFS file system. The command allows you to see exactly what extents are used by a file.

■ **Note** An *extent* is a group of blocks. Working with extents makes administrating and file handling a lot faster on file systems that work with large files.

---

xfs_ncheck: This command generates path names for inode numbers for XFS. Basically, it lists all the inodes on the XFS file system and the path where the file with the given inode number is stored.

xfs_mkfile: This command creates an XFS file. It also creates files of a fixed size to an XFS file system. By default, these files are filled with zeroes.

In summary, XFS is the most feature-rich file system of all. It was, however, developed for mainframe environments and may therefore not be the best solution if you are using an i386 or i64 architecture. I therefore recommend using ReiserFS as the best main file system for Linux.

Creating File Systems

You probably already know what file system fits the needs of your application best. The next step is to create these file systems. Creating a file system involves two steps. First, you need to create the device where you want to store the files. This can be a partition, but it can also be an LVM or EVMS logical volume. After creating the device, you can use mkfs or YaST to create the file system of your choice. The following sections cover how to create the devices where you want to store your files. First you will learn about the design of a partition layout, and then you will learn how to create traditional partitions or logical volumes.

Designing a Partition Layout

If you are performing a default installation, YaST will create one partition and mount that as the root of your server. On that partition, all files will be stored. It will also create a swap partition that is used for swap purposes. Although this solution works well for general needs, it is not the best solution available. Storing all files on the same device has some disadvantages:

- A service that goes mad could fill the entire device by accident, thus disabling critical services by accident.
- The file system that is the best for one purpose can be lousy for other purposes.
- For some situations, it is more secure to store the files on a dedicated partition.

If you want to work with more than one partition on your server, consider putting the following directories on their own partitions. After creating the partition (see the next section) and putting the right file system on it, make sure to include an entry in /etc/fstab that will mount the partition automatically when rebooting your system.

/boot: The files in the boot partition have some specific needs. Therefore, to avoid problems, you can put them on their own partition; 50MB is large enough for such a partition, and since this will be a very small partition, use ext2 as its file system.

/var: In the /var directory, many things can happen. If you are running a mail server, it is most likely that this mail server will store all incoming and outgoing mail in the /var directory. Many other servers also store their files in this directory. For a general-purpose file server, 5GB formatted as ReiserFS is good enough. However, if you are going to use your server as a mail server, make it much bigger. The exact size depends on the number of users your server will be handling. If it will be a really heavily used server, use XFS as its file system; otherwise, ReiserFS will do fine as well.

/home: If you are using your server as a file server, the user home directories typically are in /home. Depending on the number of users you are hosting, this can be a rather huge partition; you may even want to put it on its own storage device (disk or RAID array). ReiserFS or XFS are the best choices for the file system if it will be relatively small. (Smaller than about 500GB, ReiserFS will do fine; if hundreds of users are working on it actively and it will be a huge volume, use XFS instead.)

/srv: If you are hosting a server that stores its data files in /srv (web and FTP servers by default), put this directory on its own partition and format it as ReiserFS. But if it is a dynamic and large partition, you can consider using XFS instead.

/: All the rest can be in the root partition of your server. Some directories (/etc, /root, /bin, /sbin, and /tmp, for example) must be in this partition and can never be on their own volume; for others such as /usr and /opt, you can use a separate volume if you have a good reason for that.

Creating Traditional Partitions

On SUSE Linux Enterprise Server, you can use two tools to create traditional partitions. In the following sections, you will first learn how to use YaST, and then you will learn how to use fdisk to create partitions from the command line.

Creating Partitions with YaST

YaST is a convenient tool to create partitions and assign file systems to them. The next steps show how to do this:

1. Start YaST. From the System menu, select Partitioner. This starts the module you can use to manage partitions and volumes on the storage devices of your server.

2. On the warning dialog box that pops up, click Yes to continue.

3. As shown in Figure 8-3, the Expert Partitioner opens. It will give an overview of all the devices that already exist. In the Expert Partitioner, the following columns provide information about the device you are managing:

   - *Device*: This is the name of the storage device as it exists in the /dev directory.

   - *Size*: This column mentions the size of the device in megabytes or gigabytes.

   - *F*: This indicates whether the device is currently marked to be formatted. If so, it will be formatted when you click the Apply button.

   - *Type*: If the device is a hard drive, this column indicates what type of hard drive it is. If it is a partition, it will show the partition type currently used.

   - *Mount*: Here you can see the default mount point for the device.

   - *Mount By*: This indicates the name that is used when mounting the device. The default value is to mount the device by its device name, such as /dev/sdb2. This is indicated by a K in this column. As an alternative, a device can be mounted by its label (L), its UUID (U), or the device path (P).

   - *Start*: This column indicates the first cylinder used by the device.

   - *End*: This indicates the last cylinder occupied by the device.

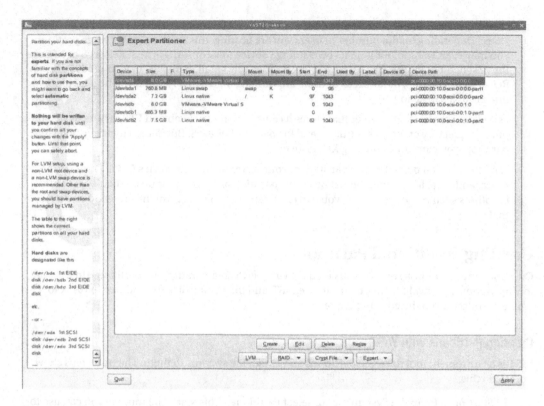

Figure 8-3. *The Expert Partitioner gives an overview of all the devices that already exist on your server.*

4. To create a new traditional partition, click Create. If more than one storage device is available in your server, you now have to select the device where you want to create the partition.

5. Now select the type of partition you want to create. Since the amount of space reserved in the partition table for creating partitions is rather limited, you can't create more than four partitions. To overcome this limitation, you can work with extended partitions. Within an extended partition, you can create a virtually unlimited amount of logical partitions. If you want to create more than four partitions on a disk, you must create one extended partition (more is not possible), and in that extended partition you can create logical partitions.

6. Next, you see the screen where you can enter all the properties of the partition you want to create, as shown in Figure 8-4. In the format box you can select the file system type you want to use on the partition; if options are available for this file system, you can set them by clicking the Options button. Next, in the Size box, specify the size for the partition. You can enter this size by selecting the start and end cylinder. As an alternative, you can select the start cylinder and next enter the end boundary for the partition by specifying a size in megabytes or gigabytes. To indicate that this is a size in megabytes or gigabytes, use +10G to make it a 10GB partition, for example, or use +100M to create a 100MB partition. Then click the Fstab Options button to select file system–specific options. Finally, in the Mount Point box, enter the name of the directory where you want to mount the partition. After specifying all the required options, click OK.

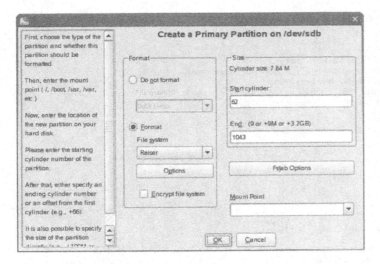

Figure 8-4. *On the Create a Primary Partition screen, you can enter all the properties for the partitions you want to create.*

7. You are now back on the Expert Partitioner screen. Click Apply to start creating the partitions. Then you will see a pop-up window where all changes you have requested are summarized. On this pop-up window, click Finish to apply the requested changes. When YaST has finished all the tasks you have requested, the partition is ready for use immediately.

Creating Partitions with fdisk

YaST works well in creating partitions, but it is not the only method you can use. As an alternative, you can create partitions from the command line with fdisk, cfdisk, or any other tool that is made for this purpose. Sometimes this is even the recommended way, because the command-line utilities give access to many more options than YaST. If you choose to create partitions this way, you should know that after creating the partition, you need to make a file system on it. The next steps outline how to create a ReiserFS partition in this way:

1. Working as root, execute the fdisk command followed by the name of the device where you want to create the partition. For example, if you want to create a partition on /dev/sdb, use fdisk /dev/sdb to open fdisk.

2. The fdisk utility will now open its prompt. It is possible that it will complain about a number of cylinders greater than 1,024. This dates from a time where many boot loaders were not able to handle hard drives with more than 1,024 cylinders. You can ignore this message. Enter m (for *menu*) to tell fdisk to show a menu with all the available options (see Figure 8-5).

```
laksmi:~ # fdisk /dev/sdb

The number of cylinders for this disk is set to 1044.
There is nothing wrong with that, but this is larger than 1024,
and could in certain setups cause problems with:
1) software that runs at boot time (e.g., old versions of LILO)
2) booting and partitioning software from other OSs
   (e.g., DOS FDISK, OS/2 FDISK)

Command (m for help): m
Command action
   a   toggle a bootable flag
   b   edit bsd disklabel
   c   toggle the dos compatibility flag
   d   delete a partition
   l   list known partition types
   m   print this menu
   n   add a new partition
   o   create a new empty DOS partition table
   p   print the partition table
   q   quit without saving changes
   s   create a new empty Sun disklabel
   t   change a partition's system id
   u   change display/entry units
   v   verify the partition table
   w   write table to disk and exit
   x   extra functionality (experts only)

Command (m for help):
```

Figure 8-5. *All* fdisk *commands are in the menu, which you can display by entering* m.

3. Next, enter p to print the current partition table. This will give you an overview of the size of your disk in cylinders, the size of a cylinder, and all the partitions that already exist on that disk. Then fdisk asks again what you want to do. Enter n to create a new partition.

4. After entering n to create a new partition, fdisk will ask what kind of partition you want to create. In this example, I will show you how to create an extended partition, so enter e to start the interface that helps you create an extended partition.

5. The utility now asks what partition number you want to use, and it will also show the numbers you can use. Make sure you enter a partition number that is not already in use.

6. Now you have to enter the first cylinder. By default, fdisk offers you the first cylinder that is still available. It is often a good idea to accept that offer by hitting Enter.

7. Next fdisk asks for the last cylinder. Instead of entering a cylinder number, you can also enter a size in megabytes or gigabytes. Since, however, this is an extended partition that serves only as a repository where logical partitions are created, you can hit Enter to accept the default value, which will use all the available disk space to create the partition.

8. The extended partition is now created. Use the n command again to create a logical partition in the extended partition. The partition number of any logical partition is always 5 or greater, no matter whether smaller partition numbers are already in use. When finished, enter p to print the partition table you have created so far.

Note When creating a partition with Linux `fdisk`, it will flag the partition as a Linux partition with ID 83 automatically. If you are planning on doing something else with it, you can use the `t` key to change the partition ID of your partition. A list of all available partition types appears when you enter `l` from the `fdisk` menu.

---

9. Until now, nothing has been written to the partition table. If you want to back out, you can still do that by entering `q`. If you are sure you are happy with what you have done, enter `w` to write the changes to the partition table to disk, and then exit `fdisk`. Before the changes are really activated, you have to reboot your server.

When the server has rebooted, you can use your new partitions. The next step is to create a file system on it. This is not too hard. If you know what file system you want to create, you just have to make the file system with the proper utility. `mkfs` is a perfect wrapper utility you can use to create any type of file system; just use the option `-t` to specify the type of file system you want to create with it.

Working with Logical Volumes

Working with fixed-size partitions has one major disadvantage. Imagine a situation where on a system with multiple partitions, you are running out of available disk space on one partition but more than enough disk space is still available on another partition. When using fixed-size partitions, you can't really do anything. However, if you use logical volumes, you can easily resize the logical volumes and the file systems that sit on them to make some more space. Therefore, for a flexible environment, it is recommended you work with logical volumes.

In a system where logical volumes are used, all available disk space is assigned to a volume group (the exact terminology may be different on specific volume managers). This volume group is a pool from which volumes can be created. The advantage of working with volume groups is that a volume group can include several storage devices and is therefore not limited to one physical device. From the volume group, the logical volumes themselves are created.

Currently, two systems are available for working with logical volumes. The first is Logical Volume Manager (LVM). This is a volume manager that has been around for some time and can be considered mature technology. The other option you can use is Enterprise Volume Manager System (EVMS), a volume manager that was created by IBM and open sourced by that company. Although LVM is the more mature volume manager, EVMS does one task better: since volumes can be marked as shareable, it is the perfect volume manager system for using in a cluster environment where volumes have to swap over from one node to another. In the next sections, you can read how both of them are created.

Creating LVM Volumes

Like all file system management tasks in SUSE Linux Enterprise Server, you can use YaST to create LVM volumes, but as an alternative, some command-line utilities are available as well. In the next section, you can read how to accomplish this task from YaST; in the section after that, you will learn how to do it with the command-line utilities. Then, you can read about some advanced LVM features.

Creating LVM Volumes with YaST

The easiest way to create logical volumes is to use YaST. In the next steps, you will learn how to accomplish this task from the generic SUSE Linux management utility:

1. Start YaST, and enter the root password if prompted. Then from the Expert Partitioner, click LVM.

Tip YaST is modular, and each single module you work with from YaST can be called individually. To start the module to create LVM volumes from YaST, enter yast lvm_config from the command line and start working.

---

2. Since no logical volumes exist yet, the LVM Configuration utility prompts you to create a volume group first (see Figure 8-6). It suggests you use the volume group name system, which is fine, and also it needs to know the physical extent size you want to use. The physical extent is like a group of blocks that can be addressed by the LVM as one logical entity. The default value for the physical extent size is 4MB, which is fine. If you need to add logical volumes from a pre–SUSE Linux Enterprise Server 10 environment, check the option to use the old LVM1-compatible metadata format. Then click OK to create the volume group and continue.

Figure 8-6. *To start volume creation, create a volume group first.*

3. After creating the container to create the logical volumes in, you need to add physical volumes to it. By default, after creating the volume group, you will see a list of physical volumes that are available for that. These are typically hard disks and unused partitions. To mark a physical volume to be added to a volume group, click the physical volume, and then click Add Volume to add it to the volume group. By doing this, you will see the amount mentioned for the physical volume size increase to the total of all the physical devices. Also you will see that under Logical Volumes, the available size is indicated. You can see all this in Figure 8-7.

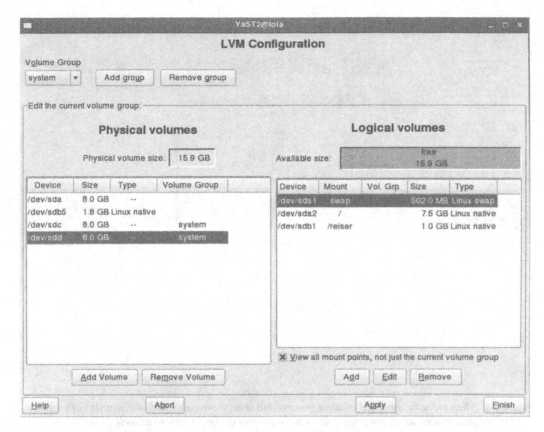

Figure 8-7. *After creating the volume group, you need to add physical devices to it.*

4. Now in the right pane, you can create the logical volumes in the volume group. Click Add to start the interface that helps you with that. The Create Logical Volume dialog box will appear (see Figure 8-8). This dialog box is pretty similar to the one used to create partitions. Some options are available that haven't been discussed so far:

   - *Logical Volume Name:* This is the device name given to the logical volume. The name of the device in /dev will be /dev/*volumegroupname/volumename*, such as /dev/system/ datavol.

   - *Stripes:* This is the number of stripes that are written simultaneously. If a volume consists of three disks, it makes sense to load balance writes to these three disks simultaneously. You can do this by selecting three stripes. The maximum number of stripes that LVM supports is eight, and it is never possible to use more stripes than the number of hard drives physically present in your server.

   - *Stripe Size:* This refers to the size of the stripe. By default, a stripe is 64KB, which works well with most controllers of modern hard drives. Leave it at 64, unless you are sure your hard drives controller can do better.

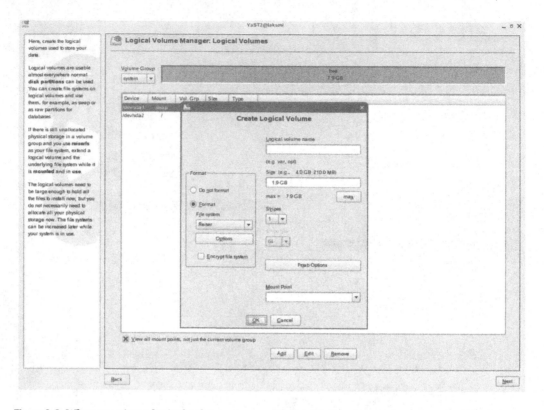

Figure 8-8. *When creating a logical volume, you need to specify the volume name, number of stripes, and stripe size, as well as all the properties you would specify for partitions as well.*

5. After creating the logical volume, you will return to the LVM configuration screen. From there, create more logical volumes as needed, or click Apply to apply all the changes and write them to disk.

Creating LVM Volumes from the Command Line

You have just read how to create logical volumes from YaST. As an alternative, you can create them from the command line. Basically, this is a simple three-step procedure:

1. Use pvcreate to assign the physical volumes you want to add to the volume group. For example, use pvcreate /dev/sd{b,c,d} to assign the devices sdb, sdc, and sdd to be used by LVM.

2. Next create the volume group. If you have used pvcreate before to assign the physical volumes, now you can use vgcreate to create the volume group. For example, use vgcreate somegroup /dev/sd{b,c,d} to create the volume group. Note that in this name, somegroup is the name of the volume group that is created. When making volumes from the volume group, you have to refer to this volume group name.

3. Now use lvcreate to create the logical volumes. For example, lvcreate -n somevol -L150M somegroup would create the volume somevol as a new volume with a size of 150MB from the logical volume group somegroup.

Tip If you want to include a complete hard disk in a volume group, it is important that no partition table is present on that hard disk. To wipe an existing partition table, use dd if=/dev/zero of=/dev/sdx; after that, the hard disk will be ready for use by LVM. This is something you need to do when working from the command line. If you are using YaST, it will happen automatically.

After creating logical volumes this way, some commands are available to manage them. For example, you can add new devices to the volume group after the device has been installed in your computer. For this purpose, use vgextend somegroup /dev/sde, which will add the device /dev/sde to the volume group somegroup.

As long as the media is not in use, you can remove it from the volume group by using the vgreduce command. For example, vgreduce somegroup /dev/sde would remove sde from the volume group again. Another important task is to monitor the status of the volume group or the volume. Use vgdisplay somegroup to display the properties of the volume group; if you want to show properties of a logical volume, use lvdisplay somevol instead. (somegroup is the name of the volume group you want to monitor properties for, and somevol is the name of the volume you want to inspect.)

Using Advanced LVM Features

One of the cool features of logical volumes is that some advanced options are available. For example, you can resize the volume, and it is possible to work with snapshots as well. In the next two sections, you will learn how to accomplish these tasks.

Resizing Logical Volumes

When resizing logical volumes, you should be aware that it always is a two-step procedure. The volume and the file system that is used on the volume both need to be resized. You should also be aware that not all file systems can be resized without problems. Both ReiserFS and ext3 support resizing. Of course, you can resize volumes from YaST as well as from the command line. Resizing from YaST is simple and self-explanatory; therefore, I will discuss in this section how to do it from the command line.

The following steps show how to first bring the volume offline and then resize the file system that sits on the volume. I'm assuming that the volume you want to shrink is called data and is mounted on the directory /data.

1. Use umount /data to unmount the volume from the directory /data.

2. Before shrinking the volume, you must shrink the file system used on it. Use resize_reiserfs -s -1G /dev/system/data to make it 1GB smaller.

3. Now you have to resize the volume itself; use lvreduce -L -1G /dev/system/data.

4. Finally, you can mount the volume again. To do this, use mount -t reiserfs /dev/system/data /data.

In the previous steps, you learned how to shrink a volume. It is also possible to increase its size. When increasing a volume, you have to invert the order of the steps. First you need to extend the size of the volume, and only when that has been done can you increase the size of the file system. After dismounting the volume, this is a two-step procedure:

1. Use `lvextend -L+10G /dev/system/data` to add 10GB of available disk space from the volume group to the volume.

2. Next use `resize_reiserfs -f /dev/system/data`. This command will increase the ReiserFS file system that is sitting in the volume to the maximum amount of available disk space automatically.

You now know how to resize a volume with a ReiserFS file system in it. Of course, you can resize ext3 as well. Since ext3 basically is no different from ext2, it should work even with ext2. However, it is not supported in that environment, so do it at your own risk! To increase the size of an ext3 file system, you would use `e2fsadm -L+10G /dev/system/data`.

Creating LVM Snapshots

One of the best features of LVM is the ability to make snapshots. A *snapshot* is a new block device that functions as a complete copy of the original volume. This works, however, without a complete copy being made; only changes are written to the snapshot, and therefore a snapshot can be disk-space efficient. When making a snapshot, the block bitmap that provides an overview of all the blocks on a device that are occupied or free is copied to the snapshot volume. Since no data is copied when the snapshot is created, all reads to the snapshot device are redirected to the original device. When writing anything to the original device, a backup of the old data is written to the snapshot device. Therefore, the snapshot volume will contain the original status whereas the original volume will always include the changed status.

Using snapshot technology can also be convenient for making backups of volumes that cannot be closed. Imagine, for example, the data volume of a mail server: you cannot take the mail server down for a couple of hours to make a backup. The solution, therefore, is to make a snapshot of the original volume; back up the snapshot volume, which contains the frozen state of the logical volume at the moment the snapshot was made; and when finished making the backup, remove the snapshot again.

The good part about using a snapshot is that it doesn't take nearly the same amount of disk space as used by the original volume. Normally, it would take about 10 percent of the total amount of disk space that is used by the original volume. Of course, this amount of disk space increases if the snapshot is online for a longer period.

The following steps show how to use a snapshot volume in a backup procedure:

1. In the first step, you are using the `lvcreate` command to make a snapshot. The snapshot gets the name `databackup`. Since the original volume is in the system volume group, the snapshot will be created there as well. Do this by using `lvcreate -L500M -s -n databackup /dev/system/data`. In this command, the option `-L500M` makes the snapshot 500MB, `-s` makes it a snapshotted volume, and `-n` specifies the name `databackup`. Finally, `/dev/system/data` refers to the original volume that needs to be snapshotted.

Tip Problems creating the snapshot volume? Make sure that the kernel module `dm_snapshot` is loaded! Check this with the `lsmod` command, and if it is not loaded, load it manually with `modprobe dm_snapshot`.

---

2. If next you want to create a snapshot of the volume, first mount it. Do this the same way you would mount any other volume, such as with `mount /dev/system/databackup /somewhere`.

3. To create a backup from the snapshot volume, use your regular backup, such as `tar`. To write a backup to a rewindable tape device, you would use `tar -cvf /dev/rmt0 /somewhere`.

4. Finished making the backup? Then you can remove the snapshot with `lvremove /dev/system/databackup`. Of course, this will work only after you have first unmounted the snapshot device.

Creating EVMS Volumes

LVM is one way of creating logical volumes. Another method is available as well: the Enterprise Volume Manager System (EVMS). EVMS is the correct choice if you want to use logical volumes in a cluster environment. This volume manager is completely cluster aware, and it sits as a shell above other techniques such as LVM and has the option to create software RAID devices (see "Setting Up Software RAID" later in this chapter). Therefore, EVMS is the way to go if you need to combine several techniques on the same storage devices. Using EVMS has some limitations, though. Don't use it on the drive from which you are booting. You can make it work when installing EVMS on the drive you are booting from, but it is not supported and may lead to severe trouble such as losing all your data. You don't want that, so don't do it.

The following steps show how to create EVMS volumes on a drive other than the first drive in your server. To keep the work easy, you can use YaST for this purpose:

1. Start YaST, and enter the password of the root user if so required.

2. From the YaST main window, select System ➤ Partitioner. When the warning appears, click Yes to continue.

3. Now the Expert Partitioner utility appears. From this utility, click EVMS to enter the EVMS management utility, as shown in Figure 8-9. In this utility, you can see two different parts. The upper part of the utility gives you the ability to create EVMS containers. Once the container is created, in the lower part of the utility you can click Add to configure EVMS devices. Before you start, however, you need to click Create Container to start creating your EVMS environment.

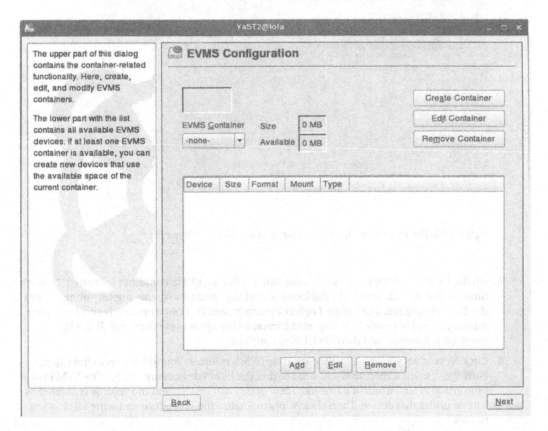

Figure 8-9. *To configure EVMS, you first have to create an EVMS container.*

4. On the Create EVMS Container screen (see Figure 8-10), you must specify several options to be able to create the EVMS container. First, you need to specify the container type. Linux LVM2 is the better choice, but if you need to be backward compatible, you can select Linux LVM as well. Next, you need to specify the name of the container you want to create. Then you need to select a physical extent size; 4MB does well in most cases. However, if you want to create single volumes with a size greater than 256GB, you need to increase the physical extent size. Doubling the physical extent size means you can double the maximum size of any EVMS volume as well. After providing these basic options, you need to add physical volumes to the EVMS container. You can use both unused hard disks as empty partitions for this purpose. To add a volume, select the volume, and then click the Add Volume button. After adding all physical devices you want to use to the EVMS volume, click OK to return to the main screen.

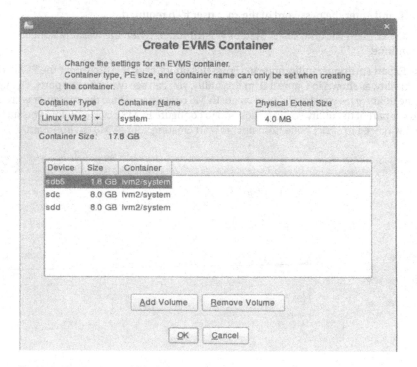

Figure 8-10. *You must add physical volumes to the EVMS volume first.*

5. On the EVMS Configuration screen, you can see that an EVMS container is created. Now it's time to click the Add button in the lower part of the window to create logical volumes from the EVMS container. The Create Logical Volume screen that pops up now is similar to the screen you use to create LVM logical volumes; all the options are the same. Enter the required properties, and then click OK to continue.

6. Click Next when you have finished creating EVMS volumes. You will return to the Expert Partitioner main screen, and you can see that the EVMS devices are added. The EVMS volume group is added with a name like /dev/evms/lvm2/system, and the volume is created as a node under that device. Then click Apply to finalize the procedure and write all changes to disk.

Monitoring Your EVMS Environment

With EVMS, a powerful management utility is available: the EVMS Administration Utility, as shown in Figure 8-11. You can start this utility with the evmsgui command. This tool provides a graphical overview of the complete EMVS configuration, shown from different perspectives such as the volumes, the containers, the segments, and the disks that exist on your server. On this screen, you can add and remove devices easily. For example, if you need to bring down the device sdc that is a part of the EVMS container on your server, browse to it, and just remove the check box in the active column; it will be deactivated.

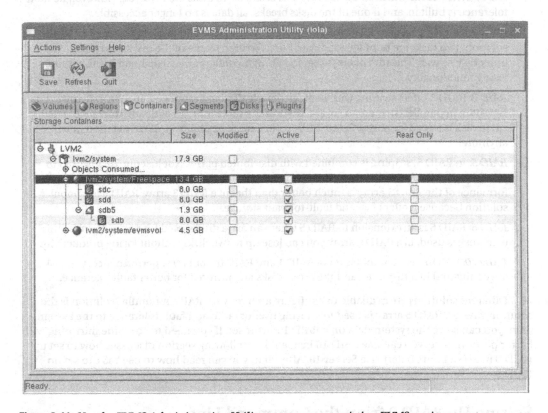

Figure 8-11. *Use the EVMS Administration Utility to manage an existing EVMS environment.*

Setting Up a Software RAID

Most people don't consider software RAID to be a serious option because it is not implemented in hardware. However, since Linux RAID is implemented in the kernel of the operating system, it is almost as good as any hardware solution. And the advantage is that it is free. You don't need an expensive RAID controller, and you can configure and manage the software RAID by using nothing but Linux routines and commands. In the following sections, you will learn how to create a software RAID 0 configuration by tuning the /etc/raidtab file, learn how to set up a RAID 5 array with YaST, and learn how to manage a RAID device on your server.

Understanding Your RAID Options

Before setting up a software RAID, it is useful to refresh the options a little. In RAID, hard drives are bundles to offer better speed and fault tolerance. The following RAID options are available in SUSE Linux Enterprise Server 10:

RAID 0: In RAID 0, which is also referred to as *disk striping*, different hard disks are working together to offer better performance. In RAID 0 two disks are bundled so that data can be written synchronously on both hard disks. This dramatically increases the speed on a system where lots of writes occur and increases reads as well, since two disks are involved. However, no fault tolerance is built in, and if one of the disks breaks, all data is no longer accessible.

RAID 1: Where the goal of RAID 0 is speed, RAID 1 is built to offer fault tolerance. In a RAID 1 solution, two disks are bundled, and data that is written to one of the disks is written to the other disk as well. The advantage is that in a RAID 1 configuration a disk can break without losing functionality.

RAID 3: RAID 3 offers striping with dedicated parity. To increase speed, in a RAID 3 array, data is written in parallel (striped) to several disks at the same time. To add fault tolerance, a dedicated disk is added for parity. Since RAID 5 offers more flexibility, RAID 3 isn't used much anymore.

RAID 5: In RAID 5, striping is combined with distributed parity. Not just one disk is used to store the parity information, but parity is stored on each disk in the array. That way, the performance of the RAID 5 array is much better than that of a RAID 3 array. RAID 5 is a popular solution because it offers fast and fault-tolerant storage.

RAID 6: RAID 6 is an extension to RAID 5 where an extra disk is used for parity. Because this extra disk is used, in a RAID 6 array you can lose up to two disks without losing productivity.

RAID 10: RAID 10 is a combination of RAID 1 and RAID 0. For better performance, two disks are configured in a stripe set, and these two disks are mirrored for better fault tolerance.

Different solutions are available to configure a server with RAID. A popular solution is the solution where a RAID 5 array is used for storing user data. To add fault tolerance to the system data, you can store the system data on a RAID 1 mirror set. If you need to combine mirroring with better performance, you can use RAID 10 instead. The following section discusses how to set up RAID 0 in SUSE Linux Enterprise Server 10. After that, you can read how to use YaST to set up RAID 5.

Setting Up RAID 0 from the Command Line

In this section, you learn how to set up a RAID 0 from the command line. As its first step, you install the partitions of the Linux RAID type. Then you use the /etc/raidtab configuration file to configure the software RAID.

1. In fdisk, create two partitions of the same size. After creating the partitions, use the t command from within the fdisk interface to set the partition type to Linux RAID. If you want to be able to boot from the software RAID, you need to set both partitions to the type fd. If you are not planning to use the RAID to boot from, you can omit changing the partition type.

2. Now create the /etc/raidtab file. This file must contain the complete definition of the RAID array. For a RAID 0 array, this would include the RAID level, the number of RAID disks and other parameters, and an indication of the devices that need to be added to the array. Listing 8-1 shows what this should look like in a RAID 0 configuration.

Listing 8-1. *Example of* /etc/raidtab

```
raiddev /dev/md0
  raid-level 0
  nr-raid-disks 2
  persistent superblock 1
  chunk-size 4

  device /dev/sdb1
  raid-disk 0
  device /dev/sdc1
  raid-disk 1
```

3. After specifying the array in the raidtab, you need to create it. You can do this with the command mkraid /dev/md0, which will create the RAID according to the specifications you have made in /etc/raidtab.

4. When the device has been created, you can see its parameters in /proc/mdstat. This file always displays the current status of the array and therefore is an excellent method to monitor if everything goes well. When the RAID device has been added, you can treat it like an ordinary storage device and create a file system on it. Next you can mount it and work on it.

Creating a RAID 5 Array Using YaST

SUSE's YaST ensures an easy method to create a RAID array. The following steps describe how to set up a RAID 5 array using YaST. Before you start, you need to prepare the RAID devices. Software RAID needs partitions to configure the RAID, and these partitions must be of the type 0xFD or 0x83 and must not be formatted. If you intend to boot from the RAID array, use partition type 0xFD; if you are not intending to boot from the RAID array, you can use 0x83 as well. To set up a RAID 5, you need at least three of these partitions since RAID 5 works on at least three devices. Use YaST or fdisk to create these partitions before you start.

1. Start YaST, and select System ➤ Partitioner. Then from the Expert Partitioner main screen, click RAID ➤ Create RAID. The RAID Wizard now opens.

2. Now you have to select the RAID type you want to create. YaST offers the choice between RAID 0, 1, and 5. Also, you can choose to use Multipath. This is a method where two controllers are connected to the same device. If your hardware supports multipath, click Autodetect Multipath to detect all the required drivers automatically. To create a RAID 5 array, select RAID 5 (see Figure 8-12). Then click Next to continue.

3. In the next step of the RAID Wizard, you need to add partitions to your RAID. An overview of all available partitions is provided. Select each partition you want to add, and then click Add. After adding all partitions you want to use, click Next to continue.

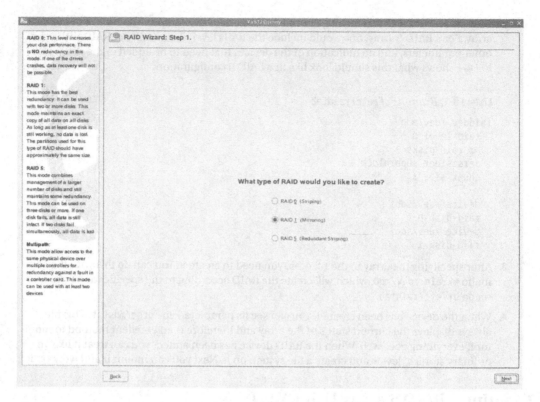

Figure 8-12. *YaST offers three different RAIDs and multipath.*

4. Now you need to finalize creating the RAID device. For a RAID 5 array, you need to select the chunk size and the parity algorithm. The chunk size is the smallest data allocation unit that you can use; 128KB is a good choice for a RAID 5 array. You can select the parity algorithm as well. The default choice of Left-Asymmetric is a good choice. After selecting the RAID properties (see Figure 8-13), choose the file system and mount point you want to use for the RAID device. Then click Finish to finalize the procedure. This will create the device and mount it at the specified mount point.

After creating the RAID 5 array, you can work on it like you can work on any other device. The essence of working with RAID, however, is the built-in fault tolerance; if one of the devices fails, you can just replace it by some other device. This procedure is not hard. After the failure of a device in the RAID array, its status will become degraded. When this happens, you will see alerts occurring in the log files of your server. Next, you can start YaST to manage the array. Just remove the failing device from the array, and replace it with a new device. Then, the software needs to build the array again; this can take some time since in a busy array much data must be swapped over. After rebuilding the array, however, you can use it again like you did before the failure occurred. And the good thing is that if you have created a RAID solution that allows for fault tolerance, you can continue working on the device, even after a failure.

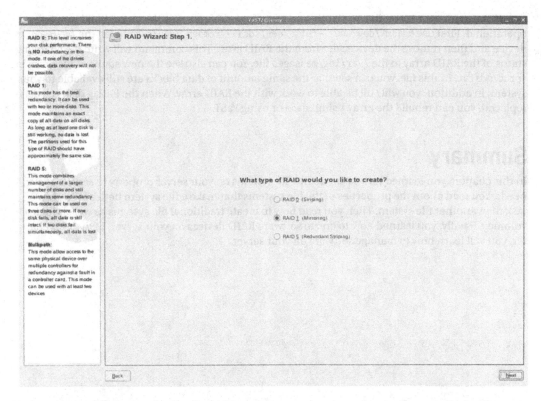

Figure 8-13. *In addition to selecting the RAID options you want to use, you need to specify the file system and mount point of the RAID array.*

Managing the RAID Array

Managing the RAID array is possible from the command line as well as from YaST. If you want to manage the array from the command line, you need the mdadm command. This command offers many options to handle the RAID array. One of the most important options is the --monitor option. If you are using this option on an existing RAID device, the software will check the consistency of the RAID array, and if necessary when the array is in a degraded state, it will automatically start rebuilding the array. Usually, however, you wouldn't even need to do this, since the RAID drivers will rebuild a degraded RAID array automatically. If you are not sure, you can monitor the array from the /proc/mdstat file. In this file, you will always find the current status of an array. Listing 8-2 shows an example of this file.

Listing 8-2. *Example of* /proc/mdstat

```
Personalities : [raid5] [raid4]
md0 : active raid5 sdd1[2] dsc1[1] dsb1[0]
     16771584 blocks level 5, 128 k chunk, algorithm 2 [3/3] [UUU]

unused devices: <none>
```

If you want to, it is possible to test that an array is working and see the autorebuild process operational. First use `mdadm /dev/md0 --fail /dev/sdc1 --remove /dev/sdc1` to fail the `/dev/sdc1` device and then remove the device `sdc1` from the RAID array. This command will write the changing status of the RAID array to the `/var/log/messages` file. You can also see the new status of the array in `/proc/mdstat`. In this file, you can see that the same amount of data blocks are still available to your system; in addition, you will still be able to work with the RAID array. When the failing disk has been replaced, you can rebuild the array using `mdadm` or using YaST.

Summary

In this chapter, you learned how to set up the file systems on your server properly to serve all your needs. You read about the properties of the file systems that make a file system better for a given task than another file system. Then you read how to create traditional file systems as well as logical volumes. Finally, you learned how to create software RAID devices on your server. In the next chapter, you will learn how to manage software on your server.

CHAPTER 9

■ ■ ■

Managing Software

SUSE Linux Enterprise Server 10 supports innumerable software packages, with many of the most popular included on the installation CDs or DVD. Sometimes, however, you'll need to download installable software packages from the Internet or even compile the software you've just downloaded. In this chapter, you will learn about everything you need to install and manage software on your server. This includes installing software from the installation media, compiling software from sources, and managing libraries.

Installing Software with YaST

The easiest way to install software is straight from the installation media using the YaST utility. YaST offers an easy interface where you can browse for and select available software. Also with YaST, you can easily install software that isn't included with SUSE Linux Enterprise Server 10. In the following sections, you will learn how to perform both tasks.

Caution Although it is possible to install everything you want on your SUSE Linux Enterprise Server, you should use extreme caution in doing so. If the software isn't furnished on the installation media, Novell does not support it. As a result, you may lose support on your entire system. Usually this will not be true for "regular" programs, but be careful when installing drivers, libraries, and kernel modules.

Installing from the Installation Media

Installing software from the installation media is a pretty straightforward process. Follow these steps:

1. From YaST, select Software ➤ Software Management. This will start the module that allows you to install new software packages.

2. You will see the software management utility, as shown in Figure 9-1. By default, it will open the Search utility from the drop-down list in the upper-left corner. This option allows you to search for a software package in the list of available software. For example, if you want to install the kernel sources to your system, use kernel, and next click Search. This will list all the software that has the word *kernel* in its description. The search option offers many possibilities. Ordinarily, YaST will search for software that contains the keyword you have entered in either its name or its summary. If this doesn't provide the result you want, select the Description option as well. This will force the utility to search in the description of the package as well. Because this is more extensive, you will have a better chance of succeeding in your search.

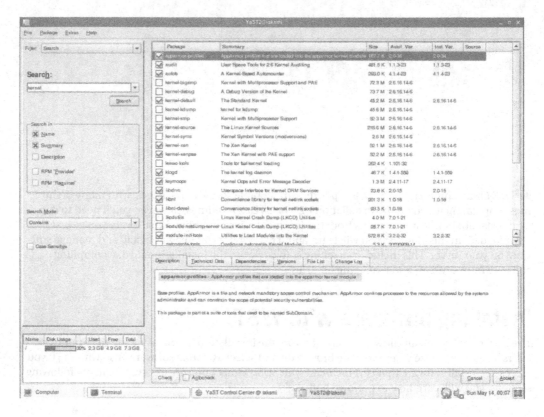

Figure 9-1. *YaST offers an extensive interface to manage software.*

3. In the list of software presented by YaST, click the software you'd like to install. You can also click software that has already been installed. Clicking it once will force the module to update the software, and if you click it again, the selected software package will be removed when you apply all changes.

4. If you are not sure about the package you need to install, you can see a description of the selected software package in the lower-right corner. This description works because SUSE Linux Enterprise Server uses the Red Hat Package Manager (RPM) standard for software installation, and in RPM packages, you can always find a description of the software. The following descriptive fields are available:

   - *Description*: This tab provides a short description of the software package. Usually it explains what the package will do.

   - *Technical Data*: On this tab you can see information about the package, such as its author(s), the time it was built, and so on.

   - *Provides*: This is an important field, because you can see what exactly is installed with this software package. In the Installed Version column, the field Provides shows exactly what files are installed by this package. Also, in the Prerequisites and Requires fields, you can see the dependency information for this package. In these fields, you can see what software needs to be present on your system in order to install this package properly.

Note Most software packages have dependencies. These are software packages that need to be present on your system in order to install the selected package. YaST will always do an automatic dependency check. If there are missing dependencies, these will be installed as well.

- *Versions*: This tab shows you which versions of the software package are currently installed.
- *File List*: For debugging purposes, this is also a pretty important tab; you can see a list of all the individual files that were installed with this software package.
- *Change Log*: This log file shows you some history about the package. This is development-related history where the programmer has noted what changes have been applied. You will notice that some of the changes for older packages are in German.

5. After selecting one software package, you can enter the name of some other packages you want to install and repeat the previous procedure. Always keep an eye on the lower-left corner of the software installation screen; there you can see an overview of the amount of disk space that is required on your server and the amount of disk space that is still available. Keeping an eye on this option makes sure you don't select more packages than can be contained by your server's hard drive.

6. When finished making your selections, click Accept. This will start the installation of the software you have selected and copy the files contained by the packages to your server. If so required, the installer will ask you to insert the installation media it inserts, and then it will start copying files.

In the previous procedure, you learned how to search for software packages. The software installation program in YaST offers some other options as well. You can select them from the drop-down box in the upper-left corner of the screen. The following options are available:

Patterns: Select this option to find the installation patterns that you have also used when initially installing your server. On this screen (see Figure 9-2), you can easily select a complete product group and packages from this product group. Use this option to install, for example, a type of server, such as a file server, XEN virtual host, and so on.

Package Groups: The Package Groups option provides an overview of software, categorized by the type of software it is. For example, you can find the option Amusement, the option Toys that shows all toys that have been installed, and the option Documentation that shows generic information. The option Man will provide an overview of all the man pages that are currently installed.

Languages: Although not recommended for support reasons, SUSE Linux Enterprise Server does offer you different languages to work with. From the Languages interface, you can see which languages are currently installed and add languages if so required.

Installation Sources: SUSE Linux Enterprise Server can work with different installation sources. For example, you can install software from the DVD but also from the network. On the Installation Sources screen, you can see the software that was installed from a certain installation source.

Tip Want to know exactly what packages are on what installation sources? In the installation source, you will always find a file with the name ARCHIVES.gz. This is a gzip-compressed file with a complete list of all the software packages on the media. To view its contents, execute zcat ARCHIVES.gz, and you can see exactly what software is on the installation source and from where the software is installed.

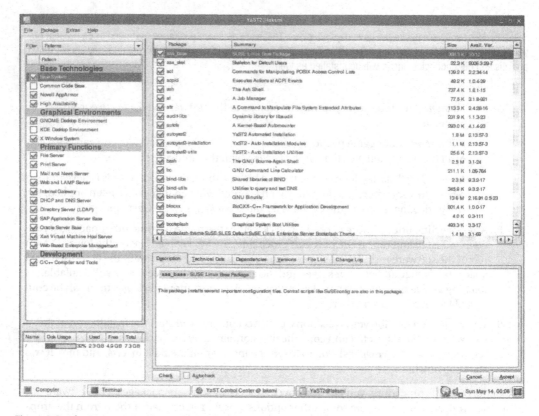

Figure 9-2. *The Patterns option in the software installer makes it easy to install a certain type of service.*

Installation Summary: This gives an overview of all the packages that currently are installed. This is useful because you can also see the current status of the packages. For example, on this screen, you can find all the packages that are marked for deletion. This is a useful option to make sure the right thing is happening before you click the OK button.

Selecting the Installation Source

By default, when you select some software for installation, SUSE Linux Enterprise Server will always first look on the media from which you installed the server. This is not always good; imagine that your server has been installed over the network from an NFS server that is no longer available. As a result, YaST will be incapable of installing any additional components. Therefore, as an administrator, it is useful if you can change the installation sources to tell YaST it has to look in other locations as well. Many installation sources are supported, such as the local hard drive of your server, an FTP server on the Internet, or a CD. The following steps explain how to change the installation source:

1. In YaST, select Software ➤ Installation Source. This will show a screen with all the media on which the installer is currently looking for new software (see Figure 9-3).

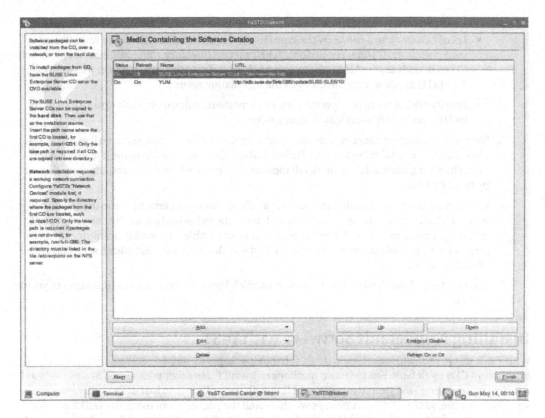

Figure 9-3. *This screen lists all the media on which the installer will look for new packages.*

2. To add a new installation source, click the Add button. This will list the installation sources you can use:

   - *Scan Using SLP*: If an installation server is available on your local network, you can scan for this server automatically. Select the Scan Using SLP option to find and use installation servers without administrator intervention.

   - *FTP*: Use this option to install from an FTP server that contains all the software packages. This requires you to set up an FTP installation server. See Chapter 35 for more information about this.

   - *HTTP*: Use this option to contact an HTTP installation server. Check Chapter 35 for more details about how to set up such a server.

   - *HTTPS*: Use this option if you have an installation server that works over HTTPS.

   - *SMB/CIFS*: If your installation server is using SMB/CIFS to make files accessible, select this option, and next specify the path where the installation server can be reached.

   - *NFS*: NFS is still the fastest network protocol you can use to do a network-based installation. If there is an NFS installation server available in your environment, use this option to select it.

   - *CD*: In addition to different network-based installation types, you can install from CDs as well. Use this option to locate additional software packages on CDs.

- *DVD*: Check this option to specify that a DVD should be used for installation.

- *Local Directory*: You can copy the contents of the installation CDs to the hard disk of your computer. If you want to do this, just make a directory with a subdirectory for each CD in it, such as /install/cd1, and so on. Next, refer to the base path (in this example, /install) to add a local directory as the installation source.

- *Specify URL*: If there is a specific location anywhere, you can use this option to specify its URL and add it as an installation source.

3. For most installation sources, you can select a path to all the packages, as well as an ISO file. This allows you to perform the installation without first creating the complete installation tree. Therefore, when adding an installation source, choose between installing from files or from an ISO file.

4. When more than one installation source is available, you can perform some management on that. First, you can move sources up and down the list to make sure they are processed at the right moment. Next, it is possible to enable or disable an installation source on a temporary basis. Just select the source you want to enable or disable, and click the Enable or Disable button.

5. After adding all required installation sources, click Finish to write the configuration to your system.

Installing Nondefault Software with YaST

With YaST, it is possible to install nondefault software packages as well as packages that are on the installation CDs by default. You have two methods to install these other packages. The easy method consists of executing YaST from the command line with the option -i to install the software package. For example, yast2 -i tool.i386.rpm would install the package tool using the YaST2 graphical interface. The advantage of using this method over invoking the rpm command from the command line is that the administrator can choose to check and resolve dependencies automatically.

An alternative for installing nondefault software packages consists of copying the packages to a given directory first and to specify this directory as an installation source next. If you are installing packages from the same directory often, this might be a useful way of working. However, if you want to install one single package occasionally, you will do so much faster using the command yast2 -i.

Updating Software

A commercial Linux server such as SUSE Linux Enterprise Server offers the ability to subscribe to updates. To be safe from all possible threats to your server, it is mandatory to have a server that is consistently running the latest stable software. To use the update mechanism available in SUSE Linux Enterprise Server 10, you must be registered with Novell. This requires you to purchase the SUSE Linux Enterprise Server product.

Tip If you want to test SUSE Linux Enterprise Server, you can get a 30-day trial subscription from the Novell website. If you have the Novell Software Evaluation Library (SEL), you are entitled to a free registration. With this registration, you are allowed to run SUSE Linux Enterprise Server in a test environment.

Setting up the online update environment is a procedure that consists of three parts. First you need to activate the Novell Customer Center in which you can prove you are a paying customer.

Next you need to set up automatic update defaults. Then you can configure your system for software updates. The following steps show how to set up the Novell Customer Center:

1. From YaST, select Software ➤ Novell Customer Center Configuration (see Figure 9-4). This screen allows you to manage all your subscriptions to Novell software.

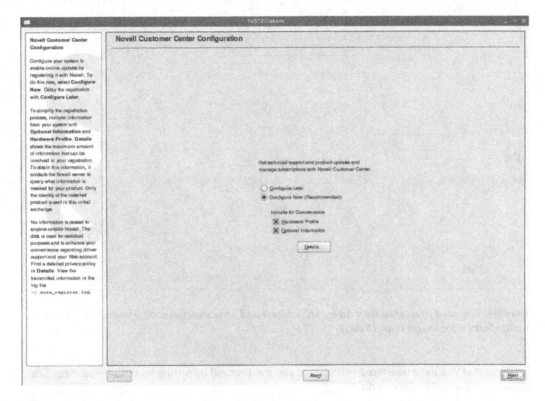

Figure 9-4. *On the Novell Customer Center Configuration screen, you can manage all your subscriptions to Novell software.*

2. Make sure the Configure Now option is selected. Next, on the same screen, you can select the amount of information that is exchanged with the Novell registration server. By default, your hardware profile is sent to the Novell server. Some optional information is sent as well. If you want to see exactly what information is sent to the Novell server, click the Details button; this will list all the information that is sent to the Novell registration servers.

3. Click the Next button. This will open a browser that will bring you to the Novell registration website. On the screen displayed by this browser (see Figure 9-5), you need to enter your e-mail address and an activation code. The e-mail address is mandatory; without a proper activation code, you can use the update service for 15 days. You also need a valid Novell account (visit http://www.novell.com for more details) to proceed. Make sure the e-mail address you enter here is the same as the e-mail address you are using in your Novell account.

4. After entering the e-mail address, click Submit. This will enter your data in the database on the Novell web server and entitle you to allow the online update feature.

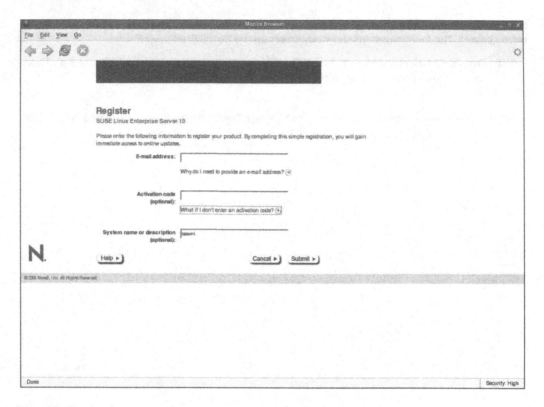

Figure 9-5. *You need to enter at least an e-mail address and an activation code if you want to use the update feature for longer than 15 days.*

Now that you have registered your server, you can proceed by setting up online updating. The following steps explain how to do this:

1. Using the YaST Software Options screen, select Online Update Setup.

2. On the screen shown in Figure 9-6, check the Enable Automatic Update box to enable automatic online updates. Next, specify whether you want the updates to occur on a daily or on a weekly basis, and specify the time of day you want the updates to occur. Next, you can select two options; use Only Download Patches if you just want to download the patches without automatic installation. If this option is enabled, you can choose which patches you want to install and which patches you don't want to install. Select Skip Interactive Patches if you want the update to occur completely automatic. With this option enabled, only patches that can be installed automatically are downloaded and installed. Be aware that you do need to perform a manual update from time to time to ensure that the patches that can't be installed automatically are installed as well.

3. Now click Finish to complete the procedure. You will see a message that indicates that an update server was added successfully to your configuration. In this message, click Details for more details about this server, or click OK to complete the procedure.

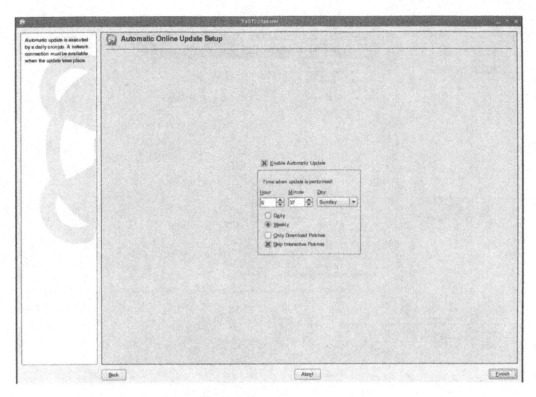

Figure 9-6. *Use the Automatic Online Update Setup screen to specify when and how updates should occur.*

Now that the online update service has been set up successfully, you still need to explore the options of the manual update option. This is because it is not recommended that you install all patches in all situations automatically.

1. On the YaST ➤ Software screen, select the Automatic Update option, and click Next on the opening screen.

2. You will see the YaST software installation screen, as shown in Figure 9-7. This screen lists all the available patches that haven't been installed yet. Choose which patches you want to install and which patches you don't want, and then click Accept to install the selected patches.

■**Caution** Be careful applying updates to the kernel. Installing a new kernel version (even if it is offered by the update software) can cause software or drivers to stop working, so make sure you have tested a new kernel version on an isolated server before applying it to your live servers.

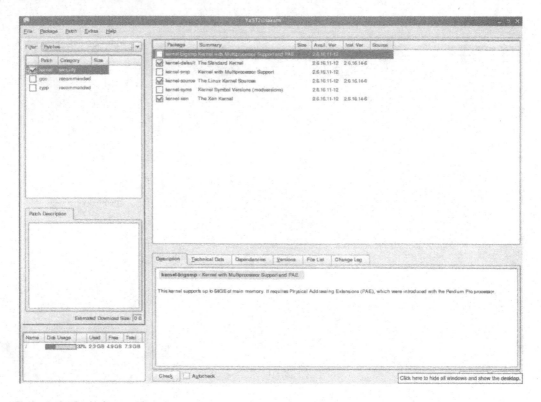

Figure 9-7. *The online update feature gives you access to all the patches that you can install.*

3. After clicking Accept, all selected patches are downloaded and installed. Notice the messages on the installation screen, because in some situations your input is needed to install the patch. Then click Finish. This will complete the procedure and write all changes you have made to your server. After installation, the patches are in general available immediately.

■**Tip** Make sure you run the online update feature after installing new software from the installation media. Installing software will, in all cases, install the original software as it is on the installation CDs, without any patches applied.

Compiling Software from Source

Most software comes in the form of RPM packages, which are easy to install. In some scenarios, however, it will be necessary to install software from source files because no RPMs or other easy-to-install formats are available. This software has to be compiled first. Fortunately, most programmers that deliver software in source packages use a uniform installation procedure. The software is distributed in a tar archive that is often zipped.

Caution Be careful with what you install. Installing source files may cause you to lose your support on SUSE Linux Enterprise Server.

Follow the next steps to install and compile the software. In the example, you will learn how to install the tool.tgz software:

1. To install software from the sources, you need a C compiler. Make sure this compiler is installed before proceeding.

2. Download the distribution of the source file packages to your home directory.

3. Use tar to extract and unzip the packaged software. Assuming that the name of the package is tool.tgz, you would do this with the command tar zxvf tool.tgz. In most cases, this will create a subdirectory with the name of the package (tools/ in this case) in your current directory. Activate this directory with the cd command.

Tip You don't want to end up with hundreds of source files after extracting the .tgz file that contains the software you want to install. Before extracting, it is always a good idea to use tar with the t option (tar tzvf tool.tgz, for example) to see what is inside. If you see only filenames without a directory name, put the .tgz file in a temporary directory, and extract it from there.

---

4. In the directory where your software has been installed, you will almost certainly see a file with the name configure. If you see it, execute it with ./configure (don't forget the ./ before configure!). If you don't see it, check whether there's a document called README, INSTALL, or something similar, and read it for specific instructions before proceeding. If the ./configure command did work, your system will be preconfigured to perform a successful installation of the source files.

5. Now you need to compile the software. Fortunately, you can use the make command. This command executes the Makefile, which you will normally find in the directory containing the source files. In this Makefile, all instructions are listed that have to be executed in order to compile the software. The alternative would be that you have to enter all the gcc compiler commands yourself, and as you can see, although the make command does its job, this can be quite a challenge.

6. Working as the root user, you need to make sure that all the software components that have just been compiled are copied to the right location on your server. To do this, use the make install command. This is the only command in this procedure that you really must issue as root.

Working with RPM

All software that is installed on your server after a default installation is installed from RPM packages. As an administrator of SUSE Linux Enterprise Server, it is useful to know how to handle these RPM packages. The RPM standard was developed by Red Hat in the mid-1990s and has become the de facto standard for managing and installing software on most Linux distributions.

The core of the RPM-based installation is the RPM database, which by default is in the directory /var/lib/rpm. This database is the complete archive of everything that is installed on your server, as long as it comes from RPM packages. YaST and other management utilities are working on this database directly. In the following sections, I'll spend a few words on working with RPM from the command line. For this purpose, you can use the powerful command `rpm`.

Following the RPM Naming Convention

The first characteristic you encounter when working with RPMs directly is the long name of most RPM packages. Typically, they have a structure like `tool-2-0.i386.rpm`. The name is so long because virtually everything an administrator needs to know before installing the package is included in the name. In this example, you can see the following components:

Name: Every RPM package first starts with the name of the package. In this case, the name `tool` is used.

Version: After the name of the package, you can see the major version of the package, which is followed immediately by its release. In this example, a simple version/release name is used; these names, however, can be more complex than that. It is not uncommon to see names like `tool-2-0.1.963b`.

Architecture: The architecture part provides information about the hardware platform for which the package is written. It will often start with `i` to indicate that the package is written for the Intel platform. You may, however, also see `noarch` for packages that don't contain binary code or `src` for packages that contain source code files.

Rebuilding the RPM Database

The second important part you need to be aware of when working with RPMs is the RPM database. This file, which is in `/var/lib/rpm`, can bécome rather big. You should expect it to be about 30MB in size, although larger as well as smaller is possible as well. If the file is much larger, you will probably need to do some maintenance of the database with the `rpm --rebuilddb` command; this will reconstruct the complete RPM database.

Working with the rpm Command

Because it is so easy to use, you will probably work with YaST in most situations for installing and managing packages. It can, however, be useful to work directly from the command line with the `rpm` command to install, update, and query packages. Next, I'll discuss some of the most popular tasks you can perform with this command.

Before installing an RPM package, you probably want to make sure the package is all right and has not been tampered with. To check this, all packages on SUSE Linux are signed with a GnuPG key. Other trustworthy sources of RPM packages will add their own key to an RPM package as well. To check the authenticity of an RPM package, you can use the `--checksig` option. For example, if you need to check where `tool-2-0.i386.rpm` comes from, use `rpm --checksig tool-2.0.i386.rpm`.

Installing, Updating, and Removing Packages

Another common task when working with the `rpm` command is installing packages. You can use this command to update and remove packages as well. This section presents some examples of how to use the `rpm` command.

First, the following is the most common use of the `rpm` command. Use the `-i` option to install new packages to your system:

```
rpm -i package.rpm
```

Second, if a package is already installed, you cannot install it again. In that case, you need to perform an update of the package. That is what the -U option is meant for:

```
rpm -U package.rpm
```

The -U option will remove existing files from a package and immediately replace them with the new version of the file. If the file has been changed since installing the original package, the rpm command will make sure the changes are stored in a temporary file and are applied to the new configuration file after the update has been completed. When applying updates to files, the rpm command creates temporary files with the extensions .rpmsave and .rpmnew. Make sure these are removed every now and then; otherwise, they could interfere the next time you are updating software.

Finally, the -e option removes an RPM package from your system. This will work only if there are no dependencies on the package. If the package is needed by some other package, you cannot remove it this way.

```
rpm -e package.rpm
```

Querying Packages

Apart from installing, removing, and updating packages with the rpm command, you can use it to perform some extensive querying options. The generic option to perform a query is -q, but this option always needs a second option to determine how the query should be performed. This section presents some examples of how to perform a query on RPM packages.

First, to perform maintenance on individual files, it can be useful to find out from where the file comes. For this purpose, use the -f option. When used on any file on your system, it will display the RPM package from which the file is installed. Be careful, the option works only if you enter the complete path of the file.

```
rpm -qf /usr/bin/passwd
```

Second, the following command lists all the RPM packages installed on your server:

```
rpm -qa
```

This doesn't seem like a useful option, but it may make some sense to use it anyway. For example, if you need to know whether the usbutils package is installed on your server, you can run rpm -qa and pipe the output of the command through grep to check whether the given package is present on your server. This would look like rpm -qa | grep usbutils.

The rpm command has many other uses as well. In fact, if you know exactly how it works, it is even possible to build your own RPM archives. For more information, consult the man page of the RPM command, which covers all its options. Be warned, however; only a few commands have as many options available as the rpm command!

Managing Libraries

You will normally not run into this too often, but you should be aware of the role of libraries on your SUSE Linux Enterprise Server. On Linux, a *library* is a file that contains common code. This is code that is used by more than one program on your server. These libraries are essential for programming an efficient operating system; they allow programmers to focus on the exact work they want to do and not to implement common functionality that is needed by other programs. Sometimes it may happen that your server is not configured the right way to access these libraries. Normally the installation procedure of your software will handle library access as well; sometimes, however, it is necessary to do some manual tuning.

Almost all the programs on your system are using libraries. You can use the `ldd` command to display the libraries that are used by a given program. Listing 9-1 shows you how this works.

Listing 9-1. *Displaying Library Usage with* ldd

```
# ldd /usr/bin/passwd
        linux-gate.so.1 =>  (0xffffe000)
        libpam_misc.so.0 => /lib/libpam_misc.so.0 (0x40034000)
        libpam.so.0 => /lib/libpam.so.0 (0x40037000)
        libldap-2.2.so.7 => /usr/lib/libldap-2.2.so.7 (0x40040000)
        liblber-2.2.so.7 => /usr/lib/liblber-2.2.so.7 (0x4006e000)
        libnsl.so.1 => /lib/libnsl.so.1 (0x4007a000)
        libselinux.so.1 => /lib/libselinux.so.1 (0x40090000)
        libnscd.so.1 => /lib/libnscd.so.1 (0x400a1000)
        libc.so.6 => /lib/tls/libc.so.6 (0x400a3000)
        libdl.so.2 => /lib/libdl.so.2 (0x401c2000)
        libresolv.so.2 => /lib/libresolv.so.2 (0x401c6000)
        libsasl2.so.2 => /usr/lib/libsasl2.so.2 (0x401d9000)
        libssl.so.0.9.7 => /usr/lib/libssl.so.0.9.7 (0x401ef000)
        libcrypto.so.0.9.7 => /usr/lib/libcrypto.so.0.9.7 (0x40220000)
        /lib/ld-linux.so.2 (0x40000000)
```

When accessing library files, you use the file `/etc/ld.so.conf`. This file provides a list of paths. These are the directories that your system uses when looking for libraries. Sometimes installing a program fails to update this list to include all required paths. In that case, you need to update it manually. To do so, you must be root. Then you can use an editor to include any path you need.

■**Tip** If a library is not listed in the `ld.so.conf` file, you can include it by using the `LD_LIBRARY_PATH` variable. To add a directory to the current library path, use the command `export LD_LIBRARY_PATH=$PATH:/some/new/dir`.

When a program starts, the program `ld.so` (the runtime linker) makes sure all the required libraries can be found. If you modify the library cache files, you need to update the library linker cache that is consulted by `ld.so`; otherwise, the new library paths cannot be found. This is always required if you change the `ld.so.conf` file by hand. To update the linker cache, you need to run the `ldconfig` command as root. As a result, the cache file that is in `/etc/ld.so.cache` is updated, and all the programs can find their required libraries again.

Summary

In this chapter, you learned everything you need to know about software installation. You read about the software installation options for YaST, as well as the other options that exist to get the software you need on your server. In the next chapter, you will learn how to manage the system initialization procedure.

CHAPTER 10

■ ■ ■

Managing the Boot Procedure

A lot of things are happening when your system boots up. When started up, the Power On Self Test (POST) causes the computer to look for a bootable device. On this device, it will look for a valid boot record, usually written to the master boot record of the device. From there, it will start the boot loader, which on Linux by default is the Grand Unified Boot Loader (GRUB). The boot loader will in turn activate the kernel, which is helped by some drivers in its initial RAM drive (initrd, explained later in this chapter). From there, init, the mother of all processes, is loaded. This process reads its configuration file, inittab, to see what happens next. Usually this involves executing some boot scripts that always need to be executed and then activating the runlevel in which all services needed by your server are started. Once that is completed, your server generates a login prompt where the user can authenticate to the system.

This chapter discusses in detail all these phases of the boot procedure. This is important information, because it may help you troubleshoot your server when you find it's not booting properly. Also, it helps you activate services automatically when booting.

Using GRUB and Its Configuration

The BIOS of every computer has a setting for the device that should boot by default. Often, the server will look on its hard drive from which to initiate the boot procedure. On there, it reads the first sector of 512 bytes, which is called the *master boot record* (MBR). If your server has SUSE Linux Enterprise Server installed, it will find the GRUB primary boot loader in its first 446 bytes. After that, the partition table is stored in 64 bytes, and a *magic code* is written in the last two bytes of the 512 bytes. Upon installation of your server, the installation program writes the GRUB boot code automatically. This code makes sure your server displays a boot screen, as shown in Figure 10-1. In the following sections, you will learn how you can modify this code if so required.

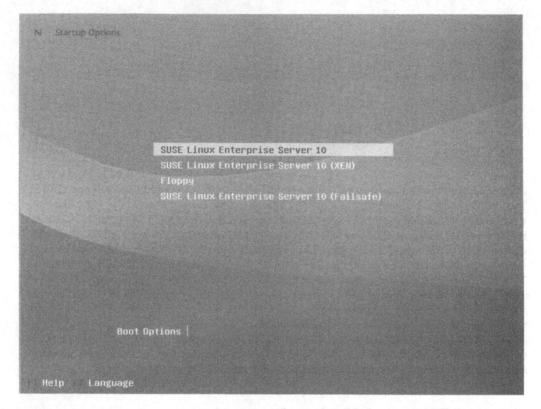

Figure 10-1. *GRUB offers you a boot screen where you can specify what you want to start.*

Working with the GRUB Configuration File

GRUB has a configuration file that defines all the options from the boot menu. This text file is /boot/grub/menu.lst. In this file, you can specify the different boot options on your server. Listing 10-1 shows the code that usually appears in the GRUB configuration file. This code comes from an installation where Xen (see Chapter 31) was also installed.

Listing 10-1. *Example GRUB* menu.lst *File*

```
color white/blue black/light-gray
default 0
timeout 8
gfxmenu (hd0,1)/boot/message

###Don't change this comment - YaST2 identifier: Original name: linux###
title SUSE Linux Enterprise Server 10
    root (hd0,1)
    kernel /boot/vmlinuz root=/dev/sda2 vga=0x314 resume=/dev/sda1 splash=silent
showopts
    initrd /boot/initrd
```

```
###Don't change this comment - YaST2 identifier: Original name: xen###
title XEN
    root (hd0,1)
    kernel /boot/xen.gz
    module /boot/vmlinuz-xen root=/dev/sda2 vga=0x314 resume =/dev/sda1
splash=silent showopts
    module /boot/initrd-xen

###Don't change this comment - YaST2 identifier: Original name: floppy###
title Floppy
    chainloader (fd0)+1

###Don't change this comment - YaST2 identifier: Original name: failsafe###
title Failsafe -- SUSE Linux Enterprise Server 10
    root (hd0,1)
    kernel /boot/vmlinuz root=/dev/sda2 vga=normal showopts ide=nodma apm=off
noresume maxcpus=0 edd=off 3
    initrd /boot/initrd
```

The GRUB configuration file in Listing 10-1 consists of several parts. First, the general section defines some options that determine how the menu is used. Next, four sections specify the different boot menu options. Each of these menu items has its own section. Listing 10-1 will eventually produce the boot menu shown in Figure 10-1.

The first part of the GRUB boot menu consists of the four lines that determine how the boot menu should be handled. The first line defines the color scheme that is to be used in this menu. Then the line default 0 specifies that the first menu item should start by default; this is what you see without user intervention. Then the timeout 8 line sets an eight-second pause in which the user can interact with the boot menu. If in this eight seconds the user doesn't do anything, the default menu item starts with its default settings. Next, the graphics of the boot menu are defined with the gfxmenu (hd0,1)/boot/message line. This specifies that the boot menu is read from the first hard drive (hd0) and then from the second partition, which makes it hd0,1. (The first item is always item number 0, which is why it's hd0. To refer to the second item, a 1 is used; to refer to the third item, a 2 is used, and so on.) On this partition, GRUB will find the file /boot/message, which is a binary file that contains the exact layout of the boot menu.

The second part specifies the first item in the boot menu. This item has the title SUSE Linux Enterprise Server 10, as is defined with the title option. Next, everything that is needed to start the server is defined for this item. First, this is the name of the root device that should be read. This line is needed for GRUB to know where it can find the kernel that it should load. In this example, this is the device root (hd0,1), which equals /dev/sda2 or /dev/hda2. However, because no device has been loaded at this stage in the boot procedure, it is not possible to refer to these device names, and that's why hd0,1, an internal GRUB reference, is used. (I'll explain the mapping of a real device to this reference later in this section.) After the specification of the root device, the kernel itself is referred to in the line that starts with kernel /boot/vmlinuz. On this same line, a lot of kernel options are specified as well; later in this section you can find an overview of the most common kernel options that are referred to here. The first line in this item specifies what to load as the initial RAM drive (initrd). Using initrd is important on modern Linux systems; initrd provides the kernel modules that are needed to boot the system.

The other menu items that are defined in this boot menu work in roughly the same fashion. The boot menu starts with a specification of the root device and then refers to the kernel that should be loaded. You can use some other options as well; for example, in the menu item for Xen, you can see the option module occurring. This option specifies what modules should be loaded as options to the Xen kernel that is loaded to start the Xen virtualization environment.

While loading a kernel, you can use some options, which are the options you see on the kernel lines. You will often see the following options:

root=: This option specifies what device to load as the root device. This is the device where the system can find the root file system.

vga=: Use this option to specify the VGA mode as a hexadecimal argument when booting. This line determines the number of columns and lines used when starting your system. As an alternative to a value such as 0x314, you can use the option ask. In that case, you can enter the mode you want to use yourself when booting.

resume=: When entering hibernation mode, the data in RAM must be stored on the hard drive. Normally, the swap partition is used for this purpose. The option resume=/dev/sda1 specifies where the kernel can find the swap partition. When restarting your system, the boot procedure will look in this partition to see whether anything is available that can be resumed.

splash=: While booting the server, you see the splash screen. This screen prevents you from seeing what is happening on your server; you see the SUSE Linux Enterprise Server 10 welcome screen instead because the option splash=silent is included in this example. If you want to see how your system is initializing all its components when starting, just remove this line.

■Tip Don't like the default splash screen? You can configure your own. Everything needed for that is in the directory /etc/bootsplash/. Consult the documentation in /usr/share/doc/splash for more details on how to do this.

---

showtops: This option just indicates that all the options that are added to the menu.lst file appear in the boot menu options list when the option is selected. This is a useful option that you should always use so you know exactly what your system is doing.

ide=: With this option, you can specify the mode that should be used for starting the IDE device. Use ide=nodma if you suspect that your server might have problems initializing IDE in DMA mode.

acpi=: ACPI stands for *advanced configuration and power interface*. This option allows you to specify what to do with this technique that can cause problems in some situations. By default, ACPI is on. Use acpi=off if you suspect that some problems are caused by this technique.

noresume: If your system was suspended, this option will just ignore it and start a new system. While starting this new system, the suspended system is terminated.

nosmp: Use this option if symmetric multiprocessing (SMP) is causing you any trouble. Be aware, however, that you will be using one CPU only if this option is used.

noapic: The advanced programmable interrupt controller (APIC) allows you to use interrupts with more outputs and options than when using normal interrupts. However, this option can cause problems; therefore, you should use noapic if you think your system can't handle working with APICs properly.

maxcpus=: This option tells your kernel how many CPUs to work with. Use maxcpus=0 to force all except the primary processor off.

edd=: This option specifies whether enhanced disk drive (EDD) support should be used. If you suspect it is causing you problems, switch it off here.

One of the nice features of GRUB is that is reads its configuration dynamically. This means if you modify the options used in menu.lst, it is not necessary to recompile or reinstall GRUB. This is a huge advantage compared to the legacy boot loader LILO, where you had to run the lilo command after all the changes or modifications to the configuration. Any changes you make to menu.lst will show immediately the next time you restart your server.

Installing GRUB

You have two ways of installing GRUB: manually and from YaST. If you are not afraid of editing the /boot/grub/menu.lst file by hand, you don't need to use YaST. Just edit it, and the changes will be applied automatically. If GRUB hasn't been written to the master boot sector of your system before, you can install it by using the grub-install command, followed by the device on which you want to install it. For example, use grub-install /dev/sda to install it on the sda device.

Tip Before starting your GRUB configuration, make a backup of the MBR of your server's primary hard drive. To do this, use the command dd if=/dev/sda of=/boot/mbr.backup bs=512 count=1. To restore this backup if necessary, use dd if=/boot.mbr.backup of=/dev/sda bs=446 count=1. Restoring only the first 446 bytes restores the MBR; in addition, restoring the remaining 64 bytes of the backup would recover the partition table.

If you need to build a GRUB configuration from scratch, the easiest option to do so is to use YaST. YaST offers several options that make creating a boot configuration easy; use them if ever you run into trouble. From YaST, select System ➤ Boot Loader. This shows the current boot loader settings that are used on your server on the Section Management tab (see Figure 10-2). On this screen, you have different options:

- Use the Up and Down buttons to change the order in which the different sections are offered.

- Select an option, and click Set As Default to make it the default section.

- Click Add to add a new item.

- Select an item, and click Edit to edit its parameters.

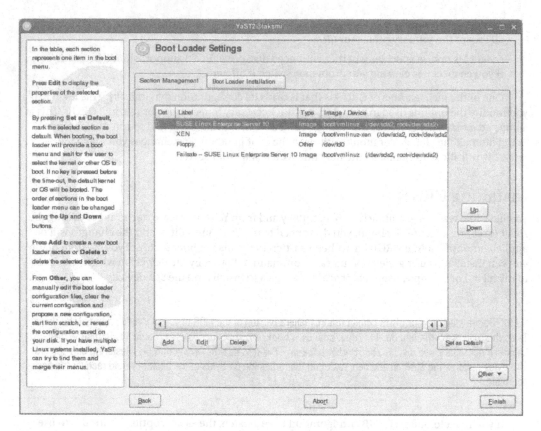

Figure 10-2. *The Section Management tab on the Boot Loader Settings screen offers some easy management options for the GRUB configuration.*

Some powerful options are available when you click the Other button. This button gives you access to six advanced management options:

Edit Configuration Files: Click this to get access to the configuration files directly. This opens an interface where you can access three configuration files:

- /boot/grub/device.map: This file lists all the devices that exist on your system and a translation of the name GRUB uses internally for the device to the Linux device name (see Figure 10-3). This file should always include all the devices that you refer to from the menu.lst file.

- /boot/grub/menu.lst: This is the file that contains the GRUB configuration. See the previous section for more details.

- /etc/grub.conf: This file contains some settings that are needed when installing GRUB with the grub-install command. Usually, you don't need to change anything in this file.

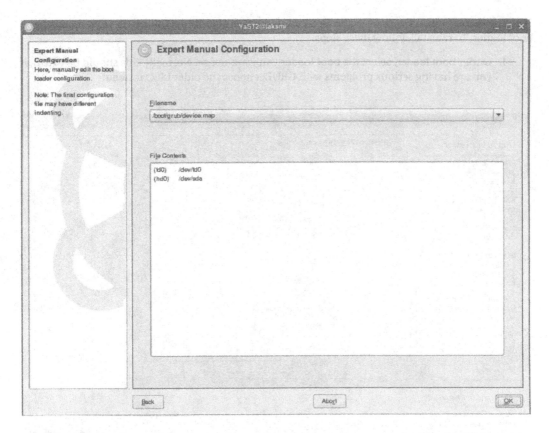

Figure 10-3. *The* device.map *file has a list where Linux device names are translated to GRUB device names.*

Propose New Configuration: This option scans your hard drive to propose a new configuration. Use this option if you are missing one or more options that should exist from the GRUB interface menu.

Start from Scratch: This option wipes your complete GRUB configuration, which allows you to start from scratch. Use this option if you have serious problems with your configuration.

Reread Configuration from Disk: Use this option to synchronize the options in the graphical menu with the configuration in your configuration files.

Propose and Merge with Existing GRUB Menus: With this option, you can scan your disk for options that could be included in the GRUB menu. The difference between this and Propose New Configuration is that this option will merge the newly found information with any existing GRUB menus.

Restore MBR of Hard Disk: Use this option if you have serious problems on your system. This option replaces the current MBR with the MBR as it was before you started installing Linux. Use this option if you want to wipe everything before reinstalling GRUB.

The second tab in the Boot Loader Settings menu (see Figure 10-4) allows you to reinstall the boot loader. To reinstall, follow these steps:

1. Under boot loader, select the boot loader you want to use. Normally, this should be GRUB; if you are having serious problems with GRUB, choose the older LILO instead.

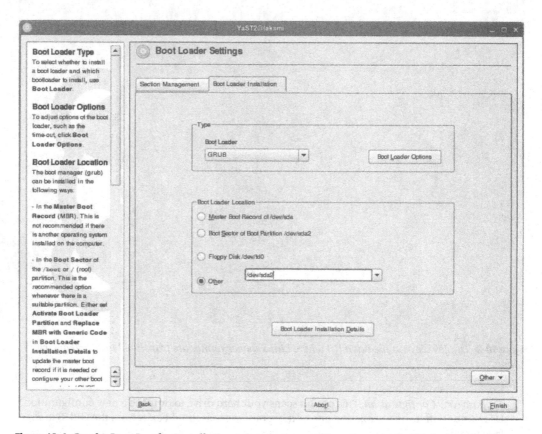

Figure 10-4. *On the Boot Loader Installation tab, you can specify options to rebuild the boot loader configuration.*

2. Click Boot Loader Options to show the window with advanced boot loader options (see Figure 10-5). From this window, the following options are available:

   - *Show Boot Menu:* By default, this option is selected. If you want to eliminate the possibility to interfere in the boot process from the GRUB boot menu, deselect this option.

   - *Continue Booting After a Time-Out:* Select this option if you want the system to continue booting automatically after a timeout. The timeout you want to use is specified with the Boot Menu Time-Out option. If you display a boot menu, it makes sense to select this option. If you don't, GRUB will just wait until you tell it what to do when booting your server.

- *Protect Boot Loader with Password*: Use this option to protect the boot loader with a password. Without this password, no one can enter options at the boot loader prompt. Although this sounds like good security, you should realize that it is a useless option if a user can still boot your server from a boot CD. So for maximal security, also configure the BIOS to boot from the hard disk only and protect the BIOS with a password.

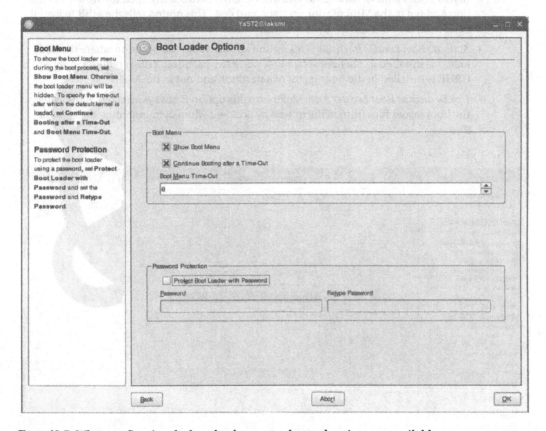

Figure 10-5. *When configuring the boot loader, some advanced options are available.*

3. As the next important part of the GRUB installation, you should specify where you want to install it. The configuration menu shows you all the available options. Ordinarily, you would install it on the master boot record of your primary disk in your system; it may, however, also make sense to install it, for example, in the boot sector of a floppy disk. If you don't want to overwrite the MBR of your server's primary disk, you can specify that you want to install GRUB on the boot sector of a partition. In that case, take special notice of the option mentioned in step 4 of this procedure.

Note On a modern Linux system such as SUSE Linux Enterprise Server, it is not necessary to create a boot floppy as a rescue disk. A complete rescue system is available from the installation CD or DVD.

---

4. Some advanced options used when copying the boot loader to the hard disk of your server are available on the Boot Loader Installation Details screen (see Figure 10-6). On this screen, you can first select the disk order. The order listed here should always be the same as the order according to your BIOS. Then you'll see three options that determine how the boot loader is copied to the MBR of your hard drive:

- *Replace MBR with Generic Code*: Use this option if GRUB is installed on the active partition and not in the MBR of your primary hard disk. This option tells the MBR to load the code from the boot sector of the active partition.

- *Activate Boot Loader Partition*: This option specifies that the partition where the boot loader is installed in the boot sector is set as active partition. This is required only when GRUB is installed in the boot sector of a partition and not in the MBR.

- *Use Dedicated Boot Loader Area*: Make sure this option is always selected. It prevents the boot loader files from being moved by accident when defragmenting the server's disk.

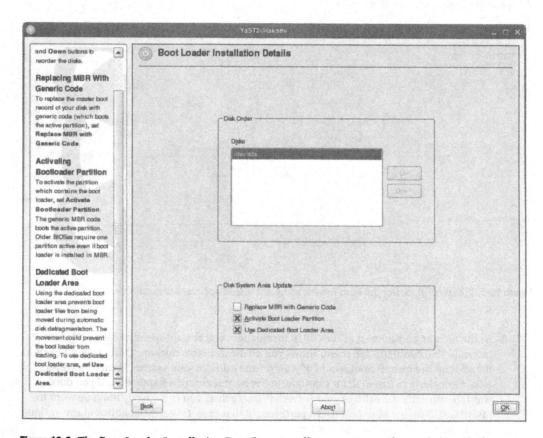

Figure 10-6. *The Boot Loader Installation Details screen allows you to specify exactly how the boot loader should be copied to the hard drive of your server.*

5. After specifying everything you need, click Finish to complete the GRUB installation procedure and write the configuration to your server's hard drive.

Working with the GRUB Boot Menu

The result of working with GRUB is a nice boot menu that is displayed when booting your server. From this menu, you will normally have a choice between four different options. Ordinarily you will select the option SUSE Linux Enterprise Server 10 to boot the server. In case you want to use your server for Xen virtualization, select the XEN option from the boot menu. (This option is available only if you have installed the Xen software.) The Floppy option is rarely used to work with a GRUB boot disk, and finally, the Failsafe option is the one you need if you run into trouble.

An option of special interest is the Boot Options prompt at the bottom of the GRUB boot menu. On this prompt, you can enter any option you need in order to determine how you want to start your server. This prompt is particularly useful when troubleshooting your server. For example, if your server refuses for some reason to come up in its default runlevel 5, you can enter a 3 here to start it in the text-only runlevel 3. Or, if you have serious problems, you can enter something like init=/bin/bash to enter the most elementary troubleshooting mode. You will learn more about troubleshooting in Chapter 34.

Understanding the Kernel and Its initrd

From a management perspective, loading the kernel and the initrd is not very interesting; if everything is in order, they will just load. The interesting part occurs when they don't load. In that case, you need to do some troubleshooting. If the kernel has always worked, it will usually work this time as well. If, however, you have recently added a new piece of hardware, this may lead to problems. Also, if some vital system component has gone mad, it may lead to the infamous *kernel panic*.

When loading the kernel, the initial RAM drive must be loaded as well. This initrd is loaded to make sure that all the drivers that are needed to complete the boot procedure are present on your system while booting the kernel. You can probably imagine what happens if the kernel tries to access the hard drive on your server but the module that allows access to this same hard drive currently is not loaded. This is why your system works with an initial RAM drive. In Chapter 26 you will learn much more about the kernel and the initrd and how you can tune them when something is wrong.

Using Init and /etc/inittab

Once the kernel has loaded and mounted the device where the root directory of your server is stored, the init process is the next to load. This process is the mother of all processes, as you will learn later in this book. init is also responsible for everything that happens in the system initialization procedure from now on. To do its work, init reads its configuration file, /etc/inittab. From there, it learns what else it needs to do. Two of the major tasks handled by init are the initial boot procedure and after that the starting of services. Because they are so important, the next two sections in this chapter are dedicated to those subjects. In this section, I'll cover everything else. In Listing 10-2, you can find the contents of /etc/inittab as it is created after a default installation of SUSE Linux Enterprise Server.

Listing 10-2. /etc/inittab

```
#
# /etc/inittab
#
# Copyright (c) 1996-2002 SuSE Linux AG, Nuernberg, Germany.  All rights reserved.
#
# Author: Florian La Roche, 1996
# Please send feedback to http://www.suse.de/feedback
#
# This is the main configuration file of /sbin/init, which
# is executed by the kernel on startup. It describes what
# scripts are used for the different run-levels.
#
# All scripts for runlevel changes are in /etc/init.d/.
#
# This file may be modified by SuSEconfig unless CHECK_INITTAB
# in /etc/sysconfig/suseconfig is set to "no"
#

# The default runlevel is defined here
id:5:initdefault:

# First script to be executed, if not booting in emergency (-b) mode
si::bootwait:/etc/init.d/boot

# /etc/init.d/rc takes care of runlevel handling
#
# runlevel 0  is  System halt   (Do not use this for initdefault!)
# runlevel 1  is  Single user mode
# runlevel 2  is  Local multiuser without remote network (e.g. NFS)
# runlevel 3  is  Full multiuser with network
# runlevel 4  is  Not used
# runlevel 5  is  Full multiuser with network and xdm
# runlevel 6  is  System reboot (Do not use this for initdefault!)
#
l0:0:wait:/etc/init.d/rc 0
l1:1:wait:/etc/init.d/rc 1
l2:2:wait:/etc/init.d/rc 2
l3:3:wait:/etc/init.d/rc 3
#l4:4:wait:/etc/init.d/rc 4
l5:5:wait:/etc/init.d/rc 5
l6:6:wait:/etc/init.d/rc 6

# what to do in single-user mode
ls:S:wait:/etc/init.d/rc S
~~:S:respawn:/sbin/sulogin

# what to do when CTRL-ALT-DEL is pressed
ca::ctrlaltdel:/sbin/shutdown -r -t 4 now

# special keyboard request (Alt-UpArrow)
# look into the kbd-0.90 docs for this
kb::kbrequest:/bin/echo "Keyboard Request -- edit /etc/inittab to let this work.
"
```

```
# what to do when power fails/returns
pf::powerwait:/etc/init.d/powerfail start
pn::powerfailnow:/etc/init.d/powerfail now
#pn::powerfail:/etc/init.d/powerfail now
po::powerokwait:/etc/init.d/powerfail stop

# for ARGO UPS
sh:12345:powerfail:/sbin/shutdown -h now THE POWER IS FAILING

# getty-programs for the normal runlevels
# <id>:<runlevels>:<action>:<process>
# The "id" field  MUST be the same as the last
# characters of the device (after "tty").
1:2345:respawn:/sbin/mingetty --noclear tty1
2:2345:respawn:/sbin/mingetty tty2
3:2345:respawn:/sbin/mingetty tty3
4:2345:respawn:/sbin/mingetty tty4
5:2345:respawn:/sbin/mingetty tty5
6:2345:respawn:/sbin/mingetty tty6
#
#S0:12345:respawn:/sbin/agetty -L 9600 ttyS0 vt102

#
#  Note: Do not use tty7 in runlevel 3, this virtual line
#  is occupied by the programm xdm.
#

#  This is for the package xdmsc, after installing and
#  and configuration you should remove the comment character
#  from the following line:
#7:3:respawn:+/etc/init.d/rx tty7

# modem getty.
# mo:235:respawn:/usr/sbin/mgetty -s 38400 modem

# fax getty (hylafax)
# mo:35:respawn:/usr/lib/fax/faxgetty /dev/modem

# vbox (voice box) getty
# I6:35:respawn:/usr/sbin/vboxgetty -d /dev/ttyI6
# I7:35:respawn:/usr/sbin/vboxgetty -d /dev/ttyI7

# end of /etc/inittab
```

As you can see, many tasks take place in /etc/inittab. The first task that really matters is
the definition of the default runlevel for your server. The runlevel is the default status in which
your server is started; it determines the number of services that start when booting the server. By
default, SUSE Linux Enterprise Server uses runlevel 5. In this runlevel you have a fully functional
server, including a graphical user interface that starts by default. Because most system administrators consider this graphical user interface unnecessary, many prefer runlevel 3 as the default.
This runlevel starts the same number of services but doesn't start the graphical user interface by
default. After all, if you do really need a graphical user interface, you can just use the startx command from the console.

When setting the default runlevel to something else, you should be careful. Runlevels 3 and 5 do fine, but other runlevels usually are not a good choice as the system default. Imagine, for example, what would happen if you set the default runlevel to runlevel 6, which is the runlevel that reboots your server!

After the definition of the default runlevel, the boot script is called from the line si:: bootwait:/etc/init.d/boot. This line calls the first boot script, which is covered in the next section. After that, the runlevels are defined, and the rc script is called. This script then activates all the services that need to be started in the runlevels. You'll learn much more about this in the later section "Managing Services Start-Up."

After the definition and calling of the runlevels, you'll see the following lines:

```
ls:S:wait:/etc/init.d/rc S
~~:S:respawn:/sbin/sulogin
```

These two lines define what should happen when entering single-user mode (let's call this the Linux *safe mode*). In this mode, the sulogin command is called. This command asks for the password of the user root. This ensures that also in single-user mode, a password has to be entered before the root prompt opens.

■Caution The sulogin program may give you a false sense of protection. When someone enters init=/ bin/bash at the boot prompt of your server, he will get a root prompt without entering the root user's password. Therefore, be sure to physically secure your server to prevent a compromise of this nature.

You may have noted that all the lines in /etc/inittab follow more or less the same structure. All the lines consist of four fields, and these four fields make sure that some command is executed. In the first field, a unique identifier is used. It doesn't really matter what you use here, as long as it is unique. Next, in the second field the runlevels where this line has to be active are defined. This field may be empty, in which case the line is used in all runlevels. Next, the third field contains a definition of the way that the command that is executed should be executed. You can use different options in this field:

respawn: The process is restarted whenever it is terminated.

wait: The process starts once when the specific runlevel is entered, and init will wait for its termination.

once: The process runs only once.

boot: The process will be executed during system boot. If this option is used, the runlevels field is ignored.

bootwait: The process is executed during system boot, and init waits for its execution before continuing.

off: The process is disabled.

ondemand: This is a rarely used option that can be used when a nondefault "on-demand" runlevel is called.

initdefault: This specific option specifies the default runlevel that should be started when booting the system.

sysinit: The process is executed during system boot, even before the lines with the boot option are executed.

powerwait: This command is executed when the power goes down. To let this work, some process must be running that talks to the UPS. init waits for the execution of this process to complete.

powerfail: Like powerwait, but init does not wait for the process to complete.

powerfailnow: This process is executed when init is told that the battery of the UPS is almost empty.

resume: This command is executed when software suspend has resumed on this machine.

ctrlaltdel: This command is executed when the Ctrl+Alt+Del key sequence has been used.

kbrequest: Use this option to activate a command when a signal is received by a special key combination from the keyboard.

Back to the important lines in /etc/inittab: the next important line after calling sulogin in single-user mode is the line where the Ctrl+Alt+Del key sequence is captured. Usually, this key sequence will have a system reboot as its result; the reboot is initiated by the shutdown command. This is all defined in the following line of code:

```
ca::ctrlaltdel:/sbin/shutdown -r -t 4 now
```

Some administrators like this feature; after all, it does help you reboot the system gracefully when problems occur. On the other hand, it may cause you some problems when someone uses the Ctrl+Alt+Del sequence by accident. Therefore, it is good to know that you can define something else to happen when Ctrl+Alt+Del is pressed. Just replace the /sbin/shutdown command with something more useful, such as with /bin/logger "someone pressed Ctrl+Alt+Del." That way, only a message is written to the log file, and nothing really happens.

Note Make sure always to use the complete command, including its path when calling a command from /etc/inittab. This is because from inittab, no search path is available yet.

The next important block of lines in /etc/inittab are the lines where the powerfail process is called. This process is called when a problem occurs with the power on your server. The only step you as an administrator need to take is to make sure the powerfail process starts. These lines will do the rest. The lines that do this are repeated in the following listing:

```
# what to do when power fails/returns
pf::powerwait:/etc/init.d/powerfail start
pn::powerfailnow:/etc/init.d/powerfail now
#pn::powerfail:/etc/init.d/powerfail now
po::powerokwait:/etc/init.d/powerfail stop

# for ARGO UPS
sh:12345:powerfail:/sbin/shutdown -h now THE POWER IS FAILING
```

The last important piece of code in /etc/inittab are the lines where the mingetty process is called:

```
1:2345:respawn:/sbin/mingetty --noclear tty1
2:2345:respawn:/sbin/mingetty tty2
3:2345:respawn:/sbin/mingetty tty3
4:2345:respawn:/sbin/mingetty tty4
5:2345:respawn:/sbin/mingetty tty5
6:2345:respawn:/sbin/mingetty tty6
```

The mingetty process is the process that creates virtual consoles on your server. It opens the virtual console and displays a login prompt on it. As the argument for mingetty, the name of the virtual console is mentioned. As you can see, by default virtual consoles are started for tty1 until tty6. From these lines, it is relatively easy to create an additional virtual console on, for example, tty8; just add the following line:

```
8:2345:respawn:/sbin/mingetty tty8
```

Caution When defining new virtual consoles, make sure you are not redefining a tty that is already in use. For example, tty7 is already used by your graphical environment, and tty10 is already used for logging purposes. Don't redefine them!

Be aware that all changes to /etc/inittab have to be activated. This is because the init process usually reads only its inittab when booting your server. To activate manual changes you have made to /etc/inittab, use the init q command.

At the end of /etc/inittab, some more lines are included, but they are all commented out. You can activate these lines when you need to make a serial connection directly to your server or when you want to use your server for dialing with a modem. Since these techniques are not used often anymore, I won't cover them in this book.

Working with the Boot Scripts

When the init process is started, two important stages in the boot process have to be executed. In the first stage, all the important services must be started. These are hardware-related services, such as the activation of the swap space, the EVMS volume manager, and more. The boot script, which is activated with the following line in /etc/inittab, starts all these services:

```
si::bootwait:/etc/init.d/boot
```

The main function of the boot script is to start a bunch of services. These services have their own start scripts in the directory /etc/init.d. The name of this script starts with boot, followed by the name of the service. For example, the boot.evms script starts on a server where EVMS is needed. To make sure the right scripts start upon system initialization, you need to activate them somehow. You can do this manually or with YaST.

Manually Tuning the Initial Boot Phase

If you want to tune the boot procedure manually, you have to work with symbolic links from the directory /etc/init.d/boot.d. In this directory, you will find a symbolic link for all services that need to be started when the system is booted and that need to be stopped when the system is halted. If the name of the link starts with an S, it makes sure the script it is linked to is started automatically, and if it starts with a K, it makes sure the script is terminated when the system shuts down as well. In Figure 10-7 you can see an example of some of these links.

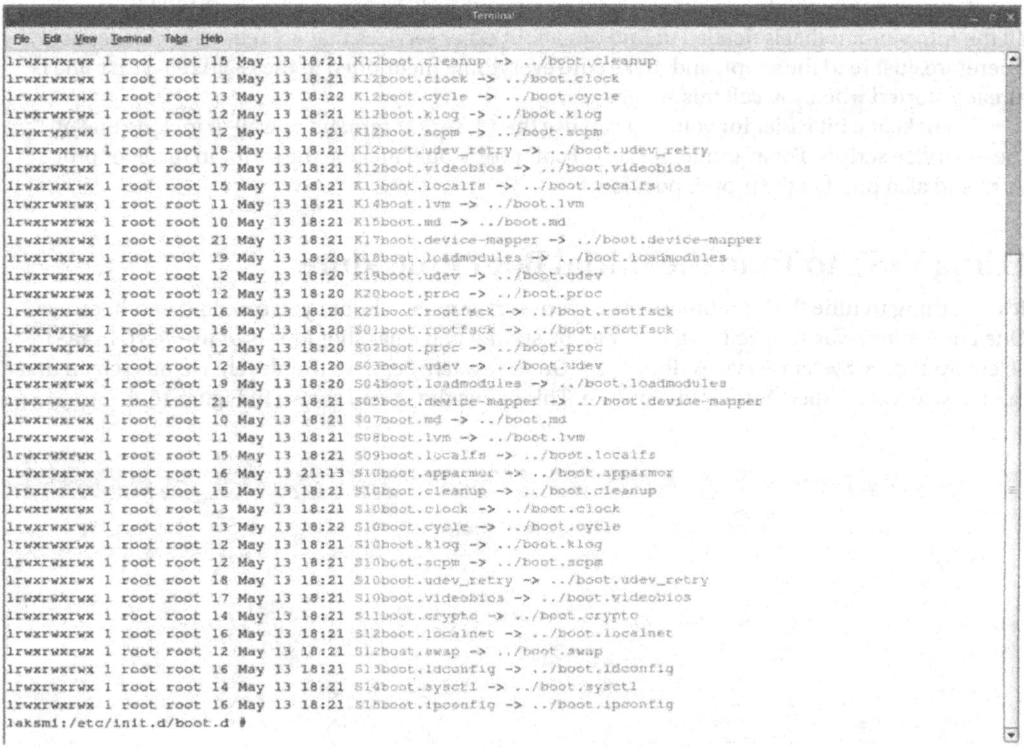

Figure 10-7. *To make sure that a boot script is executed, you just have to make a symbolic link to it.*

To tune the boot procedure manually, you need to create a symbolic link to make sure a boot script is executed automatically when booting the system. For example, to include the boot.evms script, from the /etc/init.d/boot.d directory use the ln -s ../boot.evms S08boot.evms command.

Working this way, however, has a problem. Directly after the S or K, you can see a number that determines the order in which the script is loaded. Between these scripts there are some dependencies; for example, if your swap partition is created on an EVMS volume, you have to make sure EVMS is loaded before swap. Manually this is hard to do. However, on SUSE Linux Enterprise Server, all the boot scripts in /etc/init.d start with some information that describes how the script should be used: the INIT INFO. In Listing 10-3, you can see what it looks like for the boot.evms script.

Listing 10-3. *The* INIT INFO

```
### BEGIN INIT INFO
# Provides:        boot.evms
# Required-Start   boot.proc boot.device-mapper
# X-UnitedLinux-Should-Start: boot.ibmsis
# Required-Stop:
# Default-Start:      B
# Default-Stop:
# Description:        start Enterprise Volume Management System
### END INIT INFO
```

As you can see, this information field that occurs on all the boot scripts in SUSE Linux contains all the information that is needed to find out about other services that are related to this service. Therefore, just read the script, and make sure everything mentioned in the Required-Start line is already started when you call this service.

To make it a bit easier for you, you can use the insserv command as well to include one of these service scripts. For example, insserv boot.evms would include the script in the boot procedure and also put it at the proper position.

Using YaST to Tune the Initial Boot Procedure

It's one thing to tune the boot procedure of your server manually, but you can do it in other ways. One convenient way to specify what should be started and what shouldn't is to use YaST. In YaST, select System ➤ System Services (Runlevel). On the System Services (Runlevel): Details screen that opens, select the Expert Mode radio button. This opens the screen shown in Figure 10-8.

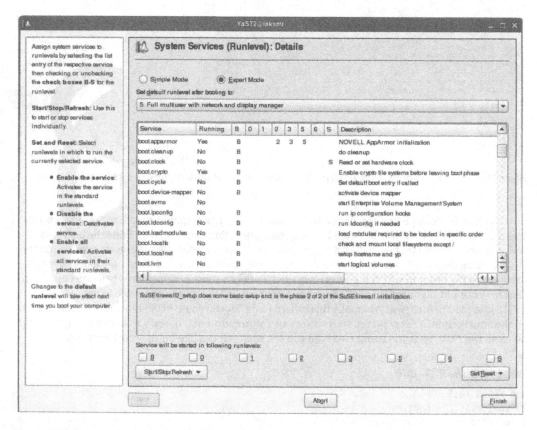

Figure 10-8. *With the Expert Mode option selected on the System Services (Runlevel): Details screen, you can see a list of all the boot services.*

Now browse to the list of services that start with boot. To enable such a service when booting, click it, and then make sure the B option that you see on the bottom of the screen is selected. This will automatically start the service the next time you boot your system. Then click Finish to save and apply your settings.

Including Your Own Services in boot.local

Sometimes, it is necessary to include services in the boot procedure that don't start automatically. If you want to do this, you should edit the /etc/init.d/boot.local script. In this script, you can include all the services you want to add to the boot procedure; that way, you can be sure they don't interfere with the services that are started from /etc/init.d/boot. Make sure that in this script, you include only those services that should be activated immediately after booting and before the first runlevel.

Note If there's a conflict between a setting in a boot script from /etc/init.d/boot.d and a setting you've created yourself in the boot.local script, your setting from boot.local will always win. This is because the system reads it last, so it is applied last as well.

Managing Services Start-Up

Now that you know how to start services in the initial boot procedure, it is easy to understand how the other services are started. The procedure to start services is virtually the same. Starting services automatically when your server boots is based on two principles:

- Each service has a script in /etc/init.d.
- To start a service automatically, it must be added to the runlevel where you want to start it. For each runlevel, a subdirectory exists in /etc/init.d where you can create a symbolic link to start or stop the service. The name of these subdirectories is rcn.d, where n is the number of the runlevel to which the directory refers.

Before I discuss how to add services to a runlevel, I'll talk about the concept of runlevels.

Understanding the Concept of Runlevels

When starting a server, you probably need the server to be fully functional. Sometimes, however, for troubleshooting a server, you need to start with only a few services loaded, instead of loading all services. Linux meets this need with *runlevels*. By default, seven runlevels determine exactly what is happening when your server boots one of them. Listing 10-4 shows how these runlevels are defined in /etc/inittab.

Listing 10-4. *Defining Runlevels in* inittab

```
# runlevel 0 is System halt (Do not use this for initdefault!)
# runlevel 1 is Single user mode
# runlevel 2 is Local multiuser without remote network (e.g. NFS)
# runlevel 3 is Full multiuser with network
# runlevel 4 is Not used
# runlevel 5 is Full multiuser with network and xdm
# runlevel 6 is System reboot (Do not use this for initdefault!)
```

As you can see, you can actually use four runlevels when booting the system. Runlevel 4 is not in use, runlevel 0 is for system halt, and runlevel 6 is for system reboot, so they are not used to determine what should happen when booting. Of these runlevels, runlevel 1 is the basic runlevel. In this runlevel, only a few services start, which ensures that a user can log in to single-user mode. This mode offers only a few more items than the items that are activated in the initial boot phase and is therefore perfect for troubleshooting. Runlevel 1 doesn't provide a normal login prompt but activates the sulogin program. This program prompts for the password of user root after starting the runlevel. You should be aware of the following characteristics when working in single-user mode:

- There are no virtual consoles, except for the first tty1.

- Just one user can be logged in at the same time.

- There is no network.

- No graphical user environment can be used.

Some more services are offered when booting in runlevel 2. This runlevel adds the option to work with multiple users and some basic networking to the items started in runlevel 1. You should, however, be aware that no network services are started in runlevel 2; just the scripts to use your server as a client to other network services are started. Because no network services are started in runlevel 2, this is not a runlevel you would like to use as an operational runlevel but rather for troubleshooting connectivity on the network. Runlevel 2 can be summarized as follows:

- Multiple users can log in.

- The system can be used as a network client.

- No network services are started.

- No graphical user environment is started automatically.

Runlevel 3 is often the default runlevel for servers, because it provides everything you need except for the graphical user environment. The most important characteristics of runlevel 3 are as follows:

- It offers a complete operational server.

- Graphical environment can be started manually.

After a default installation, your server will start runlevel 5. In this runlevel, you'll have it all—a complete graphical environment as well as all network services. Although this is a complete runlevel offering everything you need, on servers it doesn't make sense to make it your default runlevel because it loads the graphical environment by default. This graphical environment uses a lot of resources and often is not needed, especially when your server is installed in a server room without a monitor connected to it. If you want to run graphical programs on your server remotely, you don't need to run a complete graphical environment on the server. See Chapter 18 for more information.

Adding Services to a Runlevel Manually

As you learned earlier when reading about boot scripts, you can add services to a runlevel manually as well. You can use any of the following three methods to do this:

- You can create a symbolic link by hand.

- You can use the insserv command.

- You can use the chkconfig command.

In the following sections, you will learn about all three methods.

Creating Links to Add Services to the Runlevel

The basic way to add services to a runlevel is by manually creating a symbolic link. After all, this is what happens no matter what method you use. Each runlevel has its own subdirectory in /etc/init.d/rc*x*.d (where the *x* represents the number of the runlevel used by the directory). This method works for services that have a start script in /etc/init.d, which is almost all services on your computer.

■ **Tip** If you have a service that doesn't have its own start script in /etc/init.d, you can always create such a script for it. You can see an example script in /etc/init.d/skeleton. In this script, the foo service is started. Just replace the name foo with the name of the service you want to add, and you will have created your own init script for your service.

If you know the name of the service you want to create a start script for, the rest is easy; you just have to create the links. The name of the link in the runlevel directory starts with an S to make sure the service is started when the runlevel is activated, and you also need a link that starts with a K to make sure the service is stopped when you leave the runlevel. After the S or K, there is a number. Use a low number to make sure the service is started early, and use a high number to make sure that it is started late. For the numbers to be used when shutting down the service, you'll do the opposite. Therefore, if you use S99foo to start your service automatically, you will probably need K01foo to stop it early when you leave the runlevel.

Although you can use any random number you like, some risk is involved because services also have their dependencies. Imagine what would happen if you tried to start your Samba server before you have started the network; it wouldn't work. To help you choose the right number, every script in /etc/init.d has some information about how the service should be started in the beginning of the script. As an example, Listing 10-5 shows the information that is listed in /etc/init.d/smb.

Listing 10-5. *The* INIT INFO *in the Runlevel Scripts*

```
### BEGIN INIT INFO
# Provides:        smb
# Required-Start: $network $remote_fs syslog
# X-UnitedLinux-Should-Start: cupsd winbind nmb
# Required-Stop:
# Default-Start: 3 5
# Default-Stop: 0 1 2 6
# Description: Samba SMB/CIFS file and print server
### END INIT INFO
```

In Listing 10-5, you can see that some dependencies exist for the script that starts the Samba server. It needs a network, a remote file system, and the syslog service started first. You can see this in the line # Required-Start: $network $remote_fs syslog. Also, you can see that this service should start some other services as well: cupsd, winbind, and nmb. All these services typically are present in an environment where Samba is used. When you have determined where exactly the script needs to be started, all the rest is to create the link. Don't forget that you always need two scripts: one to start and one to stop the service. The following example shows how you can do this for the imaginary service foo. Note that the commands are given from the directory where you want to create the link. So if you need the links in /etc/init.d/rc5.d, don't forget to activate that directory first by using the cd command.

```
ln -s ../foo S15foo
ln -s ../foo K85foo
```

Using the insserv Command

As mentioned, you can use the insserv command to start the boot scripts automatically. You can use this command for the services you want to add to their default runlevels as well. How it works is simple: it reads the INIT INFO that occurs in the beginning of each script in /etc/init.d. From this information, it determines where exactly the service has to be inserted, and it will do that automatically in all the default runlevels in which the script needs to be started. Therefore, the insserv command works fine if you just want to add a script to its default runlevels; it isn't, however, the best way to go if you really want to tune the services that are started automatically on your server. insserv is easy to use; just supply it with the name of the service you want to start automatically; for example, use insserv foo to start the foo services automatically in all its default runlevels.

Using the chkconfig Command

Another way of adding services to a runlevel is by using the chkconfig command. You can look at this command as a front end to insserv; it has different modes available to determine how a service should be added. In its first mode, you can use the command just to display a list of the current status of all services; just type chkconfig, and the command will check each service and see whether currently it is on or off. It will do this not only for services that are in /etc/init.d but also for network services that are started from xinetd (see Chapter 19 for more details on xinetd).

Also useful is the option to display the detailed status for all the services on your server. To do this, use chkconfig -l; this command shows the status of all the services in all runlevels and also gives an overview of the services that are started from xinetd. See Listing 10-6 for a partial output of this command.

Listing 10-6. *The Command* chkconfig -l

```
SFO:~ # chkconfig -l
```

Makefile	0:off	1:off	2:off	3:off	4:off	5:off	6:off	
SuSEfirewall2_init	0:off	1:off	2:off	3:off	4:off	5:off	6:off	B:on
SuSEfirewall2_setup	0:off	1:off	2:off	3:on	4:on	5:on	6:off	
aaeventd	0:off	1:off	2:off	3:off	4:off	5:off	6:off	
acpid	0:off	1:off	2:on	3:on	4:off	5:on	6:off	
alsasound	0:off	1:off	2:on	3:on	4:off	5:on	6:off	
apache2	0:off	1:off	2:off	3:off	4:off	5:off	6:off	
atalk	0:off	1:off	2:off	3:off	4:off	5:off	6:off	
atd	0:off	1:off	2:off	3:off	4:off	5:off	6:off	
atieventsd	0:off	1:off	2:off	3:on	4:off	5:on	6:off	
auditd	0:off	1:off	2:off	3:on	4:off	5:on	6:off	
autofs	0:off	1:off	2:off	3:off	4:off	5:off	6:off	
autoyast	0:off	1:off	2:off	3:off	4:off	5:off	6:off	
avguard	0:off	1:off	2:off	3:off	4:off	5:off	6:off	
bgpd	0:off	1:off	2:off	3:off	4:off	5:off	6:off	
bluetooth	0:off	1:off	2:off	3:off	4:off	5:off	6:off	
boot.apparmor	0:off	1:off	2:on	3:on	4:off	5:on	6:off	B:on
bzflagserver	0:off	1:off	2:off	3:off	4:off	5:off	6:off	
cron	0:off	1:off	2:on	3:on	4:off	5:on	6:off	
cups	0:off	1:off	2:on	3:on	4:off	5:on	6:off	

You can use the chkconfig command to add and delete services from one or more runlevels. Use chkconfig -a foo to add foo to its default runlevels or chkconfig -d foo to remove it from all its default runlevels. With chkconfig, you can add services to a specific runlevel as well. For example, use chkconfig foo 35 to start foo only in runlevels 3 and 5.

Note You just learned how to start the services automatically when booting your server. You can start them manually as well. All services in /etc/init.d listen to a couple of arguments. To start a service from this directory, call the script followed by the start option. To stop it, just use the stop option. To restart it, use the restart option, and to force the script to reread its settings, just use the reload option. For example, the command /etc/init.d/smb restart would restart your Samba server.

Using YaST to Add Services to a Runlevel

If you don't like the command line to do it manually, you can use YaST as well to manage services on your server. The following steps describe how to do this:

1. From YaST, select System ➤ System Services (Runlevel), or use the command yast2 runlevel to start this module automatically.

2. You now see the Simple Mode in the runlevel editor (see Figure 10-9). In this mode, you can see a list of all the services that can be enabled and their current status. Select a service, and then click Enable to enable it or Disable to get rid of it. This will enable or disable the service for all its default runlevels.

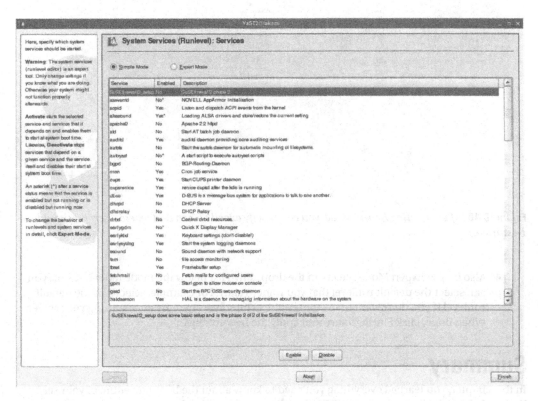

Figure 10-9. *After selecting Simple Mode, you can just enable or disable the services you want to manage.*

3. For more details, click the Expert Mode radio button. This will show the screen shown in Figure 10-10. In this mode, you can manage your runlevels. As discussed earlier in this chapter, in this mode, you can see a list of all the services that need to be activated in the initial boot phase of your server. Also, you can see all the other services, except for services that are started from xinetd. If you select any normal service, you can specify the runlevels in which you want to start it. Also, you can click the Start, Stop, or Refresh button to start, stop, or refresh the status of the selected service.

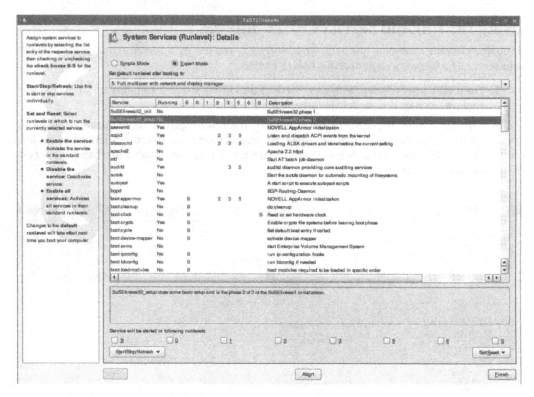

Figure 10-10. *After selecting Expert Mode, you can specify exactly when and where a service should be started.*

4. Also on the Expert Mode screen, in the drop-down list below the mode radio buttons, you can select the default runlevel that you want to start. For example, select 3 as the default runlevel if you don't want to see the graphical interface anymore after starting your server. When done, click Finish to save and apply the new settings.

Summary

In this chapter, you learned everything you need to know about the boot procedure of your server. You read about the boot manager, GRUB, that allows you to start a kernel for your server. Next you learned about the kernel and its initrd. That was followed by some in-depth information about the init process and its configuration file, /etc/inittab. Finally, you learned how to tune the services that are started automatically when your server is booted. In the next chapter, you will learn about process management.

## CHAPTER 11

Managing Processes

Everything you do on a Linux server is handled as a process by that server. Therefore, it is of the highest importance that you know how to manage processes. In this chapter, you'll learn how to start and stop processes, what different processes are available on your system, how to run and manage processes in the foreground and the background, and how to manage processes. You will also learn how to use cron and at to schedule processes for future execution.

Understanding the Different Kinds of Processes

It depends on the way you look at them, but you could say that basically on Linux there are two different kinds of processes. First, services that start automatically when you boot your server are known as *daemons*. Daemons are processes that run in the background and ordinarily do not write their output directly to the standard output. Second, *interactive processes* are the processes that users start from a shell. Any command started by a user and producing output on the standard output is an interactive process.

To start an interactive process, a user needs to type the corresponding command. The process will then run as a child process from the shell in which the user has entered the command to start the processes. The process will do its work, and when it has finished, it will terminate. While terminating, it will write its exit status to its parent, which is the shell if the process was an interactive process. Only after a child process has told its parent that it has terminated can it be closed properly. In case the parent is no longer present (which in general is considered an error condition), the child process will become a *zombie* process. In general, zombie processes are the result of bad programming.

The concept of parent and child processes is universal on your system. The init process is started as the first process, and from there, all other processes are started. You can get an overview of the hierarchical process structure by using the pstree command, which you can see in Figure 11-1.

■**Tip** Instead of pstree, you can also use ps --forest. This command doesn't show only the hierarchical relation between commands but also displays some information about the commands.

Although interactive processes are important for users working on your machine, daemon processes are more important for a server that is providing services. Daemon processes run in the background and ordinarily don't show any output to the terminal of your server. To see what they are doing, you must check the log files where the daemon processes are writing.

Ordinarily, daemon processes are started automatically from the boot procedure of your server; you can read everything about that in Chapter 10 of this book. From a management perspective, it doesn't really matter whether you are working with daemon or interactive processes, because you can handle both in the same way.

```
                                          Terminal                              _ □ x
 File  Edit  View  Terminal  Tabs  Help
laksmi:~ # pstree
init──┬─acpid
      ├─application-bro
      ├─auditd────{auditd}
      ├─bonobo-activati
      ├─cron
      ├─cupsd
      ├─2*[dbus-daemon]
      ├─dbus-launch
      ├─events/0
      ├─gconfd-2
      ├─gdm────gdm──┬─X
      │             └─gnome-session
      ├─gnome-keyring-d
      ├─gnome-panel
      ├─gnome-power-man
      ├─gnome-screensav
      ├─gnome-settings────{gnome-settings-}
      ├─gnome-terminal──┬─bash────pstree
      │                 ├─gnome-pty-helpe
      │                 └─{gnome-terminal}
      ├─gnome-vfs-daemo────{gnome-vfs-daemo}
      ├─gnome-volume-ma
      ├─gpg-agent
      ├─hald──┬─hald-addon-acpi
      │       └─hald-addon-stor
      ├─khelper
      ├─klogd
      ├─ksoftirqd/0
      ├─kswapd0
      ├─kthread──┬─aio/0
      │          ├─cqueue/0
      │          ├─kacpid
      │          ├─kauditd
      │          ├─kblockd/0
      │          ├─khubd
      │          ├─kpsmoused
      │          ├─kseriod
```

Figure 11-1. *The* pstree *command shows relations between parent and child processes.*

Running in the Foreground and Background

When working with interactive processes, it can be useful to know that processes can run in the foreground and in the background. Before talking about the way you can start and manage processes that run in the background, I'll talk about some process details so that you can understand what's happening. A process always works with three standard file handlers: the standard input, the standard output, and the standard error. Ordinarily, when a process is running in the foreground, the standard input (STDIN) is your keyboard, the standard output (STDOUT) is the terminal the process is working on, and the standard error (STDERR) also is the terminal on which the process is working.

Now, the interesting part is that these don't change when you decide to run a process in the background. When the process starts, the STDIN, STDOUT, and STDERR for a process are set, and no matter what you do to the process, once they are set, they stay like that. Therefore, you can run a long command such as find / -name "*" -exec grep -ls something {} \; as a background job, but you still will see its output and errors on your screen. If you don't want that, you should use redirection. By putting > /somewhere after the command, you are redirecting the standard output to a file called /somewhere, and by using 2> /dev/null, you can specify that all errors are redirected to the null device.

■Tip Really want to know what's happening? In the /proc file system, you can see how the STDIN, STDOUT, and STDERR are defined. To do this, check the directory with the PID of the process as its name (see the next section for more details). In this directory, activate the subdirectory fd (short for *file descriptors*). In this directory you will see a list of all the files the process currently has open, in other words the file descriptors. Specifically, 0 is STDIN, 1 is STDOUT, and 2 is STDERR. Check what they are linked to, and you know how the STDIN, STDOUT, and STDERR are set for this process.

Now that you know what to expect when working with processes in the background, it's time to learn how you can tell a process that it should be a background process. Basically, you have two ways of doing this:

- Put & after the name of the command when starting it. It will make it a background job immediately.

- Interrupt the process with the Ctrl+Z key sequence, and then use the bg command to restart it in the background.

Once the command is running as a background job, you can still control it. To get an overview of all the current background processes, use the jobs command. It will list all the interactive processes that have been started from the same shell environment. In front of each of these processes, you can see the job number they currently have. You can use this job number to manage the process with the fg and bg commands. For example, if jobs gives you a result like this:

```
laksmi:~# jobs
[1]-  Running          cat /dev/sda > /dev/null &
[2]+  Running          find / -name "*" -exec grep -ls help \; > /dev/null &
```

and you want to be able to terminate the cat command by sending it a Ctrl+C, use fg 1 to put the cat command at the foreground again.

Performing Day-to-Day Process Management

As a Linux administrator, process management is a major task. For example, if your server is reacting slowly, you can probably find a process that is responsible. If this is the case, you need to know how to terminate that process or maybe how you can reset its priority so that it can still do its work while other processes can still do what they have to do, making everyone happy. The next sections describe what you need to know to perform day-to-day process management tasks.

Tuning Process Activity

If something is not OK on your server, you want to know. So before you can do any process management, you need to tune process activity. Linux has an excellent tool that allows you to see exactly what's happening on your server: the top utility. It is easy to start the top utility: just type top. When it starts, you will see something like Figure 11-2.

```
                                      Terminal                                  - □ x
File  Edit  View  Terminal  Tabs  Help
top - 21:42:05 up  8:21,   3 users,   load average: 0.06, 0.06, 0.05
Tasks:  76 total,    1 running,   75 sleeping,    0 stopped,    0 zombie
Cpu(s):  2.3% us,   1.0% sy,   0.0% ni, 80.1% id, 16.3% wa,   0.0% hi,   0.3% si
Mem:    516400k total,   508136k used,    8264k free,    366812k buffers
Swap:   779112k total,      84k used,  779028k free,     47244k cached

  PID USER      PR  NI  VIRT  RES  SHR S %CPU %MEM    TIME+  COMMAND
 6920 root      15   0 41336  14m 6548 S  2.9  2.9  0:32.92 X
 8338 root      16   0  4736 1732 1316 R  0.3  0.3  0:00.11 top
    1 root      16   0   716  296  244 S  0.0  0.1  0:01.85 init
    2 root      34  19     0    0    0 S  0.0  0.0  0:00.00 ksoftirqd/0
    3 root      10  -5     0    0    0 S  0.0  0.0  0:00.57 events/0
    4 root      11  -5     0    0    0 S  0.0  0.0  0:00.03 khelper
    5 root      11  -5     0    0    0 S  0.0  0.0  0:00.00 kthread
    7 root      10  -5     0    0    0 S  0.0  0.0  0:00.37 kblockd/0
    8 root      20  -5     0    0    0 S  0.0  0.0  0:00.00 kacpid
   95 root      20   0     0    0    0 S  0.0  0.0  0:00.00 pdflush
   96 root      15   0     0    0    0 S  0.0  0.0  0:03.55 pdflush
   98 root      11  -5     0    0    0 S  0.0  0.0  0:00.00 aio/0
   97 root      15   0     0    0    0 S  0.0  0.0  0:00.50 kswapd0
  304 root      11  -5     0    0    0 S  0.0  0.0  0:00.00 cqueue/0
  305 root      10  -5     0    0    0 S  0.0  0.0  0:00.01 kseriod
  345 root      11  -5     0    0    0 S  0.0  0.0  0:00.00 kpsmoused
  710 root      11  -5     0    0    0 S  0.0  0.0  0:00.00 scsi_eh_0
  769 root      10  -5     0    0    0 S  0.0  0.0  0:00.03 reiserfs/0
 1309 root      10  -5     0    0    0 S  0.0  0.0  0:00.00 khubd
 1325 root      20   0     0    0    0 S  0.0  0.0  0:00.00 shpchpd_event
 2125 root      13  -4  4344  696  344 S  0.0  0.1  0:00.99 udevd
 2855 root      16   0  1524  504  428 S  0.0  0.1  0:00.00 acpid
 2870 messageb  16   0  6548 1964  972 S  0.0  0.4  0:25.42 dbus-daemon
 2917 root      17   0  4744 2324 1816 S  0.0  0.5  0:00.10 resmgrd
 2980 root      16   0  4256 2848 1440 S  0.0  0.6  0:19.43 hald
 3084 root      18   0  1820  604  524 S  0.0  0.1  0:00.00 hald-addon-acpi
 3181 root      16   0  1816  572  496 S  0.0  0.1  0:23.46 hald-addon-stor
 3339 daemon    16   0  4584 1228  912 S  0.0  0.2  0:17.41 slpd
 3364 root      13  -3  9860  612  472 S  0.0  0.1  0:00.02 auditd
 3365 nobody    16   0  1556  420  332 S  0.0  0.1  0:00.02 portmap
 3367 root      10  -5     0    0    0 S  0.0  0.0  0:00.00 kauditd
```

Figure 11-2. *The* top *utility gives you everything you need to know about the current state of your server.*

Using top to Monitor System Activity

The top window consists of two major parts. The first part is a generic overview of the current state of your system. These are the first five lines you see in Figure 11-2. In the lower part of the output, you can see a list of processes, with information about the activity of these processes.

The first line of the top output starts with the current system time. This time is followed by the up time; in the figure you can see that the system is up for 8 hours and 20 minutes. Next you see the number of users currently logged in to your server. At the end of the first line, you see some information that really counts: the load average. This line shows three numbers. The first one is the load average for the last minute, the second one is the load average for the last five minutes, and at the end you can see the load average for the last fifteen minutes.

The load average is a number that indicates the current activity of the process queue. This is the list of processes waiting to be handled by the CPU on your system. On a one-CPU system, a load average of 1.00 indicates that the CPU is completely occupied but no processes are waiting in the queue. If the value exceeds 1.00, this shows that processes are lining up, and users may experience delays while communicating with your server. It is hard to say what exactly is a critical value. On many systems, a value anywhere from 1 to 4 indicates that the system is just busy. If an intensive task such as a virus scanner becomes active, the load average can easily exceed 4. It can also happen that the load average reaches an extreme number like 254. In that scenario, it is likely that processes are waiting for their turn in the process queue for so long that they will die spontaneously. You can determine the number that indicates a healthy system only by properly baselining your server. You should note that 1.00 is the ideal number for a one-CPU system; if your server has hyperthreading, a dual core, or two CPUs, the value will be 2.00. On a 32-CPU system where hyperthreading is enabled on all CPUs, the value will be 64.

The second line of the top output shows you how many tasks currently are active on your server and also shows you the status of these tasks. The status of a process can be one of these four:

Running: In the last polling interval, the process has been active.

Sleeping: The process has been active, but it was waiting for input. This is a typical status for an inactive daemon process.

Stopped: The process is stopped. Occasionally you will see a process with the Stopped status, but that status should disappear soon. This status indicates that the process is already gone but still is not cleaned up from the kernel tables of open processes.

Zombie: The process has stopped, but it hasn't been able to send its exit status to the parent process. Typically this is an example of bad programming. Zombie processes will sometimes disappear after a while and will always disappear when you have rebooted your system.

The third row of top shows you information about the current CPU activity. This activity is separated into different statistics:

us: CPU activity in user space. Typically, these are commands that have been started by regular users.

sy: CPU activity in system space. Typically, these are kernel routines that are doing their work.

id: CPU inactivity, also known as the *idle loop*. If you see a high value here, this just indicates your system is doing nothing.

wa: Waiting. This is the percentage of time that the CPU has been waiting for new input. This should ordinarily be a low value.

hi: Hardware interrupt. This is the time the CPU has spent communicating with hardware.

si: Software interrupt. This is the time your CPU has spent communicating with software programs.

On the fourth and fifth lines of the top output, you can see memory statistics. These lines show you information about the current use of physical RAM (Mem) and swap space (Swap). The important piece of information here is that there is not much swap space in use. If all memory is in use, you should look at the balance between buffers and cache. The *cache* is memory that can be freed for processes instantaneously, and *buffer memory* is memory that is actually used by processes and that cannot be freed easily. A healthy server should have a relatively high value for the cache and a relatively low value for buffers. On a busy workstation, you should expect the opposite.

The second part of the top window gives details about the most active processes. The first process that you see here is the most active process. For each of these processes, you'll see some usage statistics:

PID: Every process has a unique PID. Many management tools need this PID for process management.

User: This is the name of the user ID the process is using. Most processes run as root, so you will see the username root often.

PRI: This is the priority indication for the process. This number indicates when the process will get some CPU cycles again.

NI: This is the nice value of the process. See "Setting Process Priority" later in this chapter for more details about prioritizing a command using the nice command.

VIRT: This is the total amount of memory that is claimed by the process.

RES: This is the resident memory size. This is the memory the process is actually using at the moment.

SHR: This is the amount of shared memory. This is the memory the process shares with other processes. You will see this quite often, because processes often share libraries with other processes.

S: This is the status of the process.

%CPU: This is the amount of CPU activity that the process has caused in the last polling cycle.

%MEM: This is the percentage of memory the process has used in the last polling cycle.

TIME+: This is the total amount of CPU time the process has used since it was first started.

Command: This is the command that was used to start the process.

As you have seen, the top command gives a lot of information about current system activity. Based upon that information, you can tune your system so it works in the most optimal way.

Using Other Tools to Monitor System Activity

Although this is not the only tool you can use for process monitoring, top is the most important tool. Some other tools are available as well. In this section, I'll give you a short overview of some of these other tools:

ps: The ps tool lists processes.

uptime: This tool shows how long the server has been up and gives details about the load average.

free: Use this tool to show information about memory usage.

From the GNOME graphical desktop, you can also start the GNOME System Monitor to display detailed information about your system, processes, resources, and devices. In Figure 11-3 you can see what this utility looks like.

In the GNOME System Monitor, four tabs show information. On the System tab, you get generic information about the status of the operating system. This tab shows you the amount of RAM that is available, and under System Status, it shows you the amount of space on your hard drive that is available. Note that the information is in MiB and GiB, which are, respectively, a million bytes and a billion bytes.

To see top-like information about the status of processes, you can go to the Processes tab. On this tab, you will see the load averages for your system, as well as detailed information per process. If you want to see more information for each process, click the More Info option in the lower part of the window. While you are working in this window, also note the options in the View menu. These options help you determine what exactly you will see. For example, by default you will see only the processes that you have started yourself. If you also want to see processes that have been started by other users, select the All Processes option from this menu.

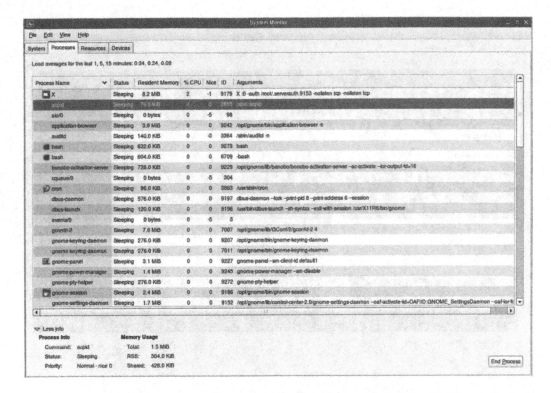

Figure 11-3. *The GNOME System Monitor can show process information in a graphical interface.*

The third tab in the GNOME System Monitor is Resources. On this tab you can see graphs that display the system resource usage for the past period on your server, as shown in Figure 11-4.

The fourth and last tab in the GNOME System Monitor, Devices, gives you information about device usage. In particular, this is about disk devices; it will show you the amount of free space on all the devices in your system.

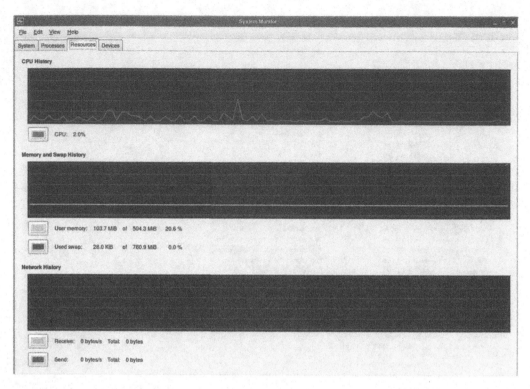

Figure 11-4. *On the Resources tab you get a graphical overview of your systems activity.*

Terminating Processes

In your work as an administrator, you will need to terminate processes occasionally because they are misbehaving. When you are terminating a process, you will send it a predefined signal. In general, the three important signals are SIGHUP, SIGKILL, and SIGTERM. If you send the first of these signals to a process, it doesn't really terminate the process but will just force it to reread its configuration files. This is a useful signal to make sure that changes you have made to configuration files are applied properly. Next, there is SIGKILL; this signal is sent to a process when someone uses the infamous command kill -9 <PID> to terminate a process. The SIGKILL signal will not terminate a process nicely; it will just cut it off. The results of such an action can be severe. This is because the process will not have an opportunity to save open files. SIGKILL will definitely damage any open files and possibly even lead to system instability. Therefore, you should use it only as a last resort. The third signal that works for almost all processes is SIGTERM. When a process receives this signal, it will shut down gracefully. This means it will close all open configuration files and also tell its parent that it has gone. Using SIGTERM is the recommended way to terminate processes you don't need anymore. The kill command uses this signal by default if no other signal is specified.

Commands for Process Termination

To terminate a process, you can use different commands. The following are the most important commands:

kill: This is one of the most used commands to terminate processes. It works with the PID of the process you need to kill. If a special signal needs to be sent to a process, the signal is referred to with its numeric argument, for example kill -9 1498. If no signal is referred to, the default SIGTERM signal (signal 15) is sent to the process.

killall: The major disadvantage of kill is that it works with a PID and therefore can be used on one process at a time only. If you need to terminate several instances of the same processes, this isn't really useful. In such cases, you can use killall, which works with the name of the process. For example, killall httpd will kill all instances of the Apache web server that currently are active on your server. By default, killall will send SIGTERM to the processes you want to kill. If you need it to do something else, add the name of the signal you want to send to the process; for example, use killall -SIGKILL httpd to kill all the instances of the Apache web server.

top: Killing a process from top is easy. From the top interface, press the K key. top will first ask you the PID of the process you want to kill. Enter it. Then top will ask you what signal to send to the process. Specify the numeric value of the signal, and hit Enter. This will terminate your process.

pkill: The pkill command is useful if you want to kill a process based on any information about the process. This command is related to the pgrep command, which allows you to find process details easily. You can use pkill, for example, to kill all the processes that are owned by a certain user; for example, pkill -U 501 will kill all the processes owned by the user with UID 501.

Using ps to Get Details About Processes

Before killing a process, you most likely want to have some more information about it. To get this information, you can use top, which was discussed earlier in this chapter. This utility, however, has the disadvantage that it will show only the most active processes. If you need to manage a process that isn't amongst the most active processes, the ps utility is useful. By using the right parameters, this command will show all the processes that are currently active on your server.

If you don't use any options with ps, it will just show you the processes that are interactive and that you own. Ordinarily, this will be a rather short list. As a system administrator, you probably want to see a complete list of all the processes. Note that you can use the ps command in the BSD-style Unix syntax, but you can also use it with the System V style syntax. You probably don't care what kind of syntax you are using, and you just want to see a list of active processes. You can do this by using the ps -ef command; alternatively, ps -aux will do just fine. Both will give you a complete list of all the processes that are running on your system. Now, ps by itself has some options to do sorting, but instead of remembering what these options do, you can use grep to do some filtering. For example, ps -ef | grep httpd will show detailed information but only for the output line where the httpd string occurred.

Setting Process Priority

Killing a process may be a solution for improving the performance of your server, but what if you just need the process? In that case, "renicing" it may be an option. To understand what the commands nice and renice are doing, you first need to look at the way the process scheduler is working. On a busy system, there is a process queue. All processes are sitting in the process queue and get some CPU cycles one by one. So if there are three processes named process-a, process-b, and process-c, they will each get an equal amount of CPU cycles. When process-a has been handled, it will reenter the process queue if it needs more cycles. Because it was the last process that was handled, it will reenter the process queue in the last position.

This sounds pretty fair to all processes, but in some cases it just doesn't work. Imagine that process-a is the company database that causes 90 percent of all workload on your server, and say that process-b and process-c are just minor processes. In that case, you would like to give a higher priority to process-a and give a lower priority to the other two processes. This is exactly what the nice command was made to do.

You can use the commands nice and renice to reset process priority. Both commands work with a numeric argument from –20 to 19. If a process has the nice value –20, it will get the most favorable scheduling, and if it has the 19 value, it will get the least favorable scheduling. This may appear to be a good solution for important processes, and you may be tempted to give your critical company database the nice value –20. But you shouldn't do that. A busy process that gets a nice value of –20 will push away all the other processes. Since, for example, kernel processes such as writing to disk also need to enter the process queue, you would give your database the highest priority, but the database wouldn't have any possibility to write its data to disk. Therefore, that wouldn't work. The –20 value is a nice value you should probably never use. If you want to use renice on a process, do it carefully, such as by increasing or decreasing the nice value of a process with increments of 5.

Several methods are available to "renice" processes:

nice: You can use the nice command to start a process with a given nice value. For example, nice 10 find / -name "*" -exec grep -ld help {} \; will start the find command with a lower priority.

renice: The renice command resets the priority of a running command. The renice command ordinarily works with the PID of the process you want to renice. For example, renice -10 1234 would increase the priority of process 1234.

top: A convenient way to renice a process is by using the top interface. From this interface, hit the N key. top will next ask you to enter the PID of the process you want to renice. After entering this PID, give the new nice value you want this process to have, and it will be reniced immediately.

Scheduling Processes

On a server system, it is often important that processes are executed at a regular predefined time. Linux offers the cron facility to do that. The cron facility works with two parts: a daemon called *crond* and some configuration files where the administrator can specify when the processes should be started. Both ensure that the command is executed at regular times. In addition to cron, there is the at command that you can use to run a command just once.

Configuring the cron Service

The cron service is activated by default. It checks its configuration files every minute to see whether something needs to be done. The cron process looks for configuration at different locations:

- The generic file /etc/crontab can contain lines that tell cron when to execute a given command. This file is not edited usually on SUSE Linux Enterprise Server.

- In the directory /etc/cron.d, an administrator can put a file that defines what should happen and when it should happen.

- Every user can have their own cron configuration file, telling the system when to execute certain tasks.

- The directories /etc/cron.hourly, cron.daily, cron.weekly, and cron.monthly activate jobs once an hour, a day, a week, or a month, respectively. These directories contain files that are activated every hour, day, week, or month. The crontab process evaluates these directories every 15 minutes, so it can take up to 15 minutes before a process is first started this way.

Working with the cron.hourly (and so on) mechanism makes it easy for an administrator to start jobs on a regular basis. The scripts in these directories are just regular shell scripts that make sure the job is done. This means all you have to do is include a shell script that activates the job you want to start. These scripts can be simple; just a line that starts the service is enough. You should be aware that the scripts in /etc/cron.hourly, cron.daily, cron.weekly, and cron.monthly are default scripts that are placed there when you install your server. When you perform an update, these directories will be overwritten. Therefore, make sure any modifications you make to these directories are put in /etc/cron.hourly.local (and so on); this ensures that your modifications will still exist after an update.

Note You need to restart some daemons to make sure the changes are activated. This is not true for cron, which will reread its configuration every minute to check whether any new jobs have been scheduled.

Configuring Cron User Jobs

You can set up your system to allow individual users to start their cron jobs. Such a configuration starts with the files /var/spool/cron/allow and /var/spool/cron/deny. A user who is listed in /var/spool/cron/allow or who is not listed in /var/pool/cron/deny is capable of adding cron jobs. If /var/spool/cron/allow exists, only this file is evaluated, and the settings in /var/spool/cron/deny are ignored. If both files don't exist, only root can create cron jobs. The cron configuration files for individual users are stored in the directory /var/spool/cron/tabs. You can use the crontab command to edit this file. Next you can see some examples of the use of the crontab command:

crontab -e: This creates or edits cron jobs for the user who executes the command. You can use the editor vi to modify these files.

crontab -l: This command lists all the jobs that are scheduled for the current user.

crontab -r: This command deletes all the jobs for the current user.

In the cron files, you use lines to define what should happen. On each line, you specify one command. Each line consists of six fields. The first five fields specify when the command should be activated, and the last field specifies what command should be activated. Next you can see an example of such a line:

```
*/5 8-18 * * 1-6 fetchmail mailserver
```

The easiest part to understand in the previous line is the command. This is the command fetchmail mailserver. This command makes sure incoming mail is fetched from the mail server. Then in the first five fields, you can see an indication of the times that should happen. These fields have the following meaning:

Minutes: This field specifies the minute when the command should be executed. This field has a range from 0 to 59. Always specify something for this field, because if you don't, the command will run every minute. In the example, the construction */5 specifies that the command should run every five minutes; specifically, * refers to every minute, and the construction /5 is used as a modifier that specifies it should run every five minutes only.

Hours: This field specifies the hour the command should run. Possible values are from 0 to 23. In the previous example, you can see that the command will run every hour from 8 to 18.

Day of the Month: Use this field to execute a command only on given days of the month. Often this field is not specified.

Month: Use this field to specify in which month of the year the command should run.

Day of Week: This field specifies on which day of the week the command should run. The range is from 0 to 7, and the values from 0 and 7 both specify that the command should run on Sunday.

Note You usually will not use it, but if you ever want to work with the /etc/crontab file, be aware that between the time setting and the command you want to execute, you enter the name of the user whose account should be used to execute the command. For example, 0 17 * * * root /sbin/shutdown -h now will make sure the system shuts down automatically every day at 5 p.m. by using the permissions of the user root.

Executing Once with at

The cron mechanism executes commands automatically at a regular basis. If you want to execute a command just once, at is the solution you need. The at mechanism consists of different parts:

- The at service atd. Make sure it is started if you want to schedule commands to run once; it is not started by default. Use insserv atd to make sure it starts the next time you reboot your server.

- The files /etc/at.allow and /etc/at.deny that can be used to specify which users can and cannot schedule commands with at.

- The at command, which can be used to schedule a command.

- The atq command, which is used to display an overview of all the commands that currently have been scheduled.

- The atrm command, which is used to delete jobs from the at execution queue.

Scheduling a job with at is not hard; just use the at command followed by the time when you want to run the command; for example, at 17:00 opens the interactive at prompt from where you can enter the commands you want to schedule for execution at the time specified. When you are finished entering the names of commands, press Ctrl+D to close the interactive at prompt, and the commands will be scheduled.

Summary

In this chapter, you learned how to manage processes. You first read how to monitor the performance of your system. After that, I discussed how to terminate processes and reset the priority of processes. Finally, you learned how to schedule processes for execution at regular intervals or just once. In the next chapter, you will learn how to manage logging on SUSE Linux Enterprise Server 10.

## CHAPTER 12

Using System Logging

Even if everything is going well on your server, you might want to know exactly what's happening. Are any critical messages being generated when booting the server? Is all the hardware being recognized properly? Do the services on your server write critical messages to the system logging functionality? In this chapter, you will learn how to find all the relevant information and how to tune it to meet all your requirements.

Reading the Boot Messages

When SUSE Linux Enterprise Server starts, you'll see a lot of messages scrolling by on the screen of your server. These messages are generated by the kernel and indicate whether everything is going well. Unfortunately, the messages scroll by way too fast for you to be able to read what's happening. Fortunately, you have two ways to monitor what has happened when your system has finished booting.

The first method to get more information about the boot procedure is to use the dmesg command on the command line. This command reads the *kernel ring buffer*, which contains all the messages that are generated by your system while it was booting. Also, you can use the dmesg command to display messages that are generated by the kernel later in the boot procedure. The dmesg command will just dump the complete contents of the kernel ring buffer on the screen, so if you use it, make sure you pipe it through less or another filtering utility for better readability. In Figure 12-1 you can see an example of what the dmesg output looks like.

■Tip When booting in a nongraphical runlevel, you can use another method to see what happened when booting your server. By pressing the Shift+Page Up key sequence, you can browse up the screen. This works the same way as when using a scroll bar in a window to scroll up to see previous messages.

```
                              Terminal                              _ □ ×
 File  Edit  View  Terminal  Tabs  Help
Linux version 2.6.16.14-6-default (geeko@buildhost) (gcc version 4.1.0 (SUSE Linux)) #1 Tue
 May 9 12:09:06 UTC 2006
BIOS-provided physical RAM map:
 BIOS-e820: 0000000000000000 - 000000000009f800 (usable)
 BIOS-e820: 000000000009f800 - 00000000000a0000 (reserved)
 BIOS-e820: 00000000000ca000 - 00000000000cc000 (reserved)
 BIOS-e820: 00000000000dc000 - 0000000000100000 (reserved)
 BIOS-e820: 0000000000100000 - 000000001fef0000 (usable)
 BIOS-e820: 000000001fef0000 - 000000001fefc000 (ACPI data)
 BIOS-e820: 000000001fefc000 - 000000001ff00000 (ACPI NVS)
 BIOS-e820: 000000001ff00000 - 0000000020000000 (usable)
 BIOS-e820: 00000000fec00000 - 00000000fec10000 (reserved)
 BIOS-e820: 00000000fee00000 - 00000000fee01000 (reserved)
 BIOS-e820: 00000000fffe0000 - 0000000100000000 (reserved)
0MB HIGHMEM available.
512MB LOWMEM available.
found SMP MP-table at 000f6ce0
On node 0 totalpages: 131072
   DMA zone: 4096 pages, LIFO batch:0
   DMA32 zone: 0 pages, LIFO batch:0
   Normal zone: 126976 pages, LIFO batch:31
   HighMem zone: 0 pages, LIFO batch:0
DMI present.
IO/L-APIC allowed because system is MP or new enough
ACPI: RSDP (v000 PTLTD                                   ) @ 0x000f6c70
ACPI: RSDT (v001 PTLTD     RSDT    0x06040000 LTP 0x00000000) @ 0x1fef7c02
ACPI: FADT (v001 INTEL  440BX      0x06040000 PTL  0x000f4240) @ 0x1fefbf14
ACPI: MADT (v001 PTLTD             APIC    0x06040000 LTP 0x00000000) @ 0x1fefbf88
ACPI: BOOT (v001 PTLTD  $SBFTBL$ 0x06040000 LTP 0x00000001) @ 0x1fefbfd8
ACPI: DSDT (v001 PTLTD  Custom     0x06040000 MSFT 0x0100000d) @ 0x00000000
ACPI: PM-Timer IO Port: 0x1008
ACPI: Local APIC address 0xfee00000
ACPI: LAPIC (acpi_id[0x00] lapic_id[0x00] enabled)
```

Figure 12-1. *To see what happened while booting your server, use the* dmesg *command.*

Besides using the dmesg command to view what happened while booting your server, you can use YaST to see exactly what happened while booting your system. From YaST, select Miscellaneous ➤ View Startup Log. This opens the file /var/log/boot.msg, which contains the entire contents of the kernel ring buffer (see Figure 12-2). Basically, it is the same information as offered when you are using the dmesg command, with the difference being that it appears in a graphical window; therefore, it is easier to browse its contents.

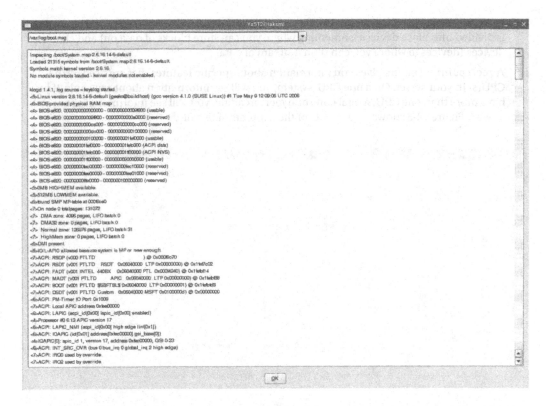

Figure 12-2. *The YaST option View Startup Log allows you to browse through the* boot.msg *log file, which contains all the boot messages.*

Getting Hardware Information

When you are troubleshooting your server, it is essential to know whether all the hardware is functioning properly. For this, you have different options. All these options use the information that is written to the /proc file system. In this virtual file system (which in fact is an interface to give you access to real-time information about what's happening in your server's memory), several files exist that give you information about the hardware in your server. From these files, you can get important information about how critical hardware devices are working. YaST offers a graphical tool to browse your hardware.

Browsing the /proc File System

If you really want to be sure you have access to real-time information about what's happening on your server, you should look at the /proc file system. This file system reads directly from memory what's happening on your server. In this directory, you'll find a lot of files that contain important information:

/proc/devices: This file gives an overview of all the devices used on your system. This overview is divided into block devices (something where you can store blocks of data on) and character devices (devices to where you can send a stream of data).

/proc/cpuinfo: This file gives you information about specific features that are used by the CPU(s) in your server. On a one CPU-system, you will see information about cpu0 only. If you have more than one CPU, a dual core, or hyperthreading, you will see information about cpu1 as well. Figure 12-3 shows an example of the contents of this file.

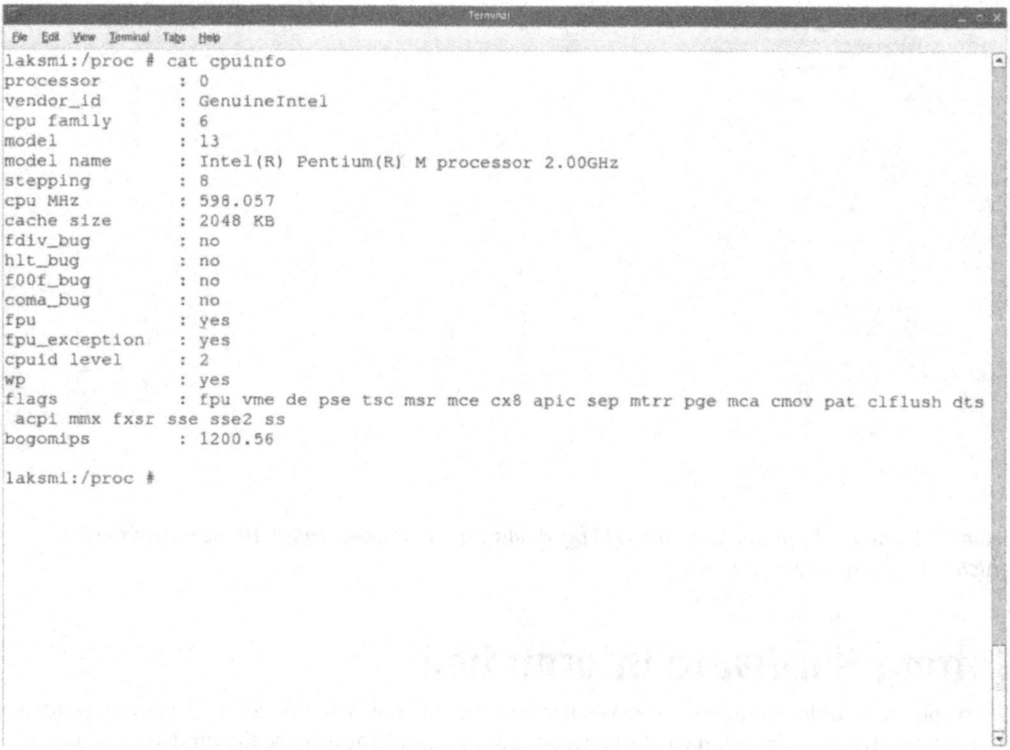

```
laksmi:/proc # cat cpuinfo
processor       : 0
vendor_id       : GenuineIntel
cpu family      : 6
model           : 13
model name      : Intel(R) Pentium(R) M processor 2.00GHz
stepping        : 8
cpu MHz         : 598.057
cache size      : 2048 KB
fdiv_bug        : no
hlt_bug         : no
f00f_bug        : no
coma_bug        : no
fpu             : yes
fpu_exception   : yes
cpuid level     : 2
wp              : yes
flags           : fpu vme de pse tsc msr mce cx8 apic sep mtrr pge mca cmov pat clflush dts
 acpi mmx fxsr sse sse2 ss
bogomips        : 1200.56

laksmi:/proc #
```

Figure 12-3. *The* /proc/cpuinfo *file gives detailed information about features supported by the CPU in your server.*

/proc/fb: In this file, you'll find information about the frame buffer device. This device is used as an abstraction of the graphics hardware in your server. In the file you will see in which mode the frame buffer device is currently used.

/proc/interrupts: In this file, you'll find an overview of interrupts that are currently in use to allow hardware to communicate with the CPU.

/proc/ioports: This file shows information about all the I/O ports in use on your server.

/proc/bus: This directory shows information about all the devices connected to the system bus of your server. For example, in /proc/bus/pci/devices you can get more information about the PCI devices in use on your server, and /proc/bus/usb gives information about the USB devices connected to your server.

/proc/scsi: In this subdirectory you can find information about the SCSI devices connected to your system. Also, information about SAN-related devices such as Fibre Channel adapters is stored in this subdirectory.

Although the information in the /proc file system is good, deep, and real time, it takes a lot of knowledge and experience to see what is really happening on your system. Therefore, it may not be the best place to start if you need more in-depth information about what's happening on your server. The next section gives information about the YaST interface, which you can use to browse this information.

Tip An easy way to get all the relevant information from the proc file system is to use the procinfo command. This command shows an overview of all the relevant information that is in /proc.

Using YaST Hardware Information

If you need access to information about the hardware in use on your server, the YaST Hardware Information utility is a good starting point. You can open this utility by selecting YaST ➤ Hardware ➤ Hardware Information. When starting this utility, you will notice that it takes some time to load. This is because the utility is probing your system to see what hardware is present at the moment you are running the utility. As a result of this probing activity, a screen opens that displays all the hardware devices that the utility found on your server. If you see a plus (+) sign in front of an item, more information is available; just click the + to open the device and see its properties. Depending on the driver used to talk to the device, the level of details displayed about the devices can be deep. In Figure 12-4 you can see an example of the information displayed with the Hardware Information utility.

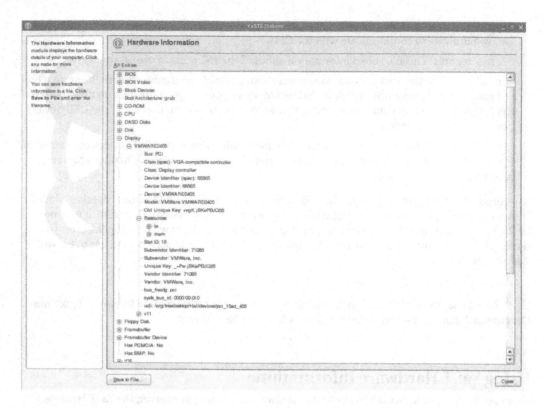

Figure 12-4. *The YaST Hardware Information utility shows a detailed level of information about the hardware devices connected to your system.*

Using the syslog-ng Service

The ability to see exactly what the processes on a Linux system are doing is important for troubleshooting your system. Some services have their own logging facility that is hard-coded in the service. Other services use the generic functionality known as syslog, which provides a generic interface for logging that all services can use. On SUSE Linux Enterprise Server 10, you can choose between two versions of syslog. By default, the syslog-ng service is installed. The syslog-ng service is backward compatible with the old syslog service, so usually you won't need it. Therefore, in the following sections, I'll just discuss how syslog-ng works.

Introducing syslog-ng

Because it offers more flexibility, SUSE Linux Enterprise Server 10 uses the syslog-ng service instead of the older syslog services. The syslog-ng service offers some important improvements over the old service. One of the most important improvements is the ability to apply filtering on messages, thus allowing the administrator to specify how a message should be handled. Also, the configuration options for use in a networked environment are greatly improved.

Messages that are generated by services on your server are sent by syslog-ng to different destinations, based on an assigned facility/priority pair. This destination can be a log file, a TTY, a user who is currently logged in, or a central log server on the network. The facility determines where a message should be sent, and the priority defines the severity level of a message that is logged. One problem in the old syslog structure was that this solution was far too generic. Some facilities, such as daemon, for example, are used by many programs that aren't even related to each other. This syslog-ng service resolves this problem. One of its major benefits is the ability to filter messages based on the contents of the messages. This ability is added to the old way of matching priorities and facilities. Another advantage of syslog-ng compared to the old syslog solution is that it makes remote logging more flexible and more secure at the same time.

The most important part of the system logging services is the daemon syslog-ng that is started by default in runlevels 2, 3, and 5. To determine what it should do, syslog-ng reads its configuration file, /etc/syslog-ng/syslog-ng-conf. You can find more details about this file in the next section. To determine how it is started, syslog-ng reads a configuration file from /etc/sysconfig with the name syslog. In this configuration file, some generic parameters are set that are used by syslog-ng when it starts; these parameters determine how the service is started. For example, if you want to enable your syslogd process to accept messages from other servers, you can add the option -r to the SYSLOGD_PARAMS line in this file.

Understanding syslog-ng.conf

To understand how syslog-ng works, you must understand the message path. In syslog-ng, this consists of one or more sources, one or more filtering rules, and one or more destinations. Typically, this definition of the source provides an interface to the legacy syslog mechanism in which a process sends its log information to the /dev/log device. By defining these source devices, syslog-ng knows where it has to look for incoming messages.

On SUSE Linux Enterprise Server, in syslog-ng.conf the sources are defined as follows:

```
source src {
    internal ();
    unix-dgram("/dev/log");
    unix-dgram("/var/lib/dhcp/dev/log");
    unix-dgram("/var/lib/named/dev/log");
```

Ordinarily, you don't need to change anything for these source definitions; for generic purposes, they work fine.

The second part of syslog-ng is its filters, which are also defined in /etc/syslog-ng/syslog-ng.conf. The filters allow syslog-ng to look in the log messages and see what is happening. In these filters, log facilities and log levels are used. A log facility usually defines the category under which the messages fall. The following facilities are available:

authpriv: This is used by all the PAM modules to log messages related to authentication.

auth: This is used by SSH to log its messages.

cron: This is for events that are related to the cron service.

daemon: This is a generic facility that relates to all daemons that don't have their own facility.

kern: This is for kernel-related events.

lpr: This is for log messages that are related to the printing subsystem.

news: This relates to messages generated by an NNTP news service.

mail: This is for messages related to the mail-handling services.

syslog: This is for internal messages generated by the syslog-related services.

user: This is for events that are related to users. This logs, for example, failed attempts of users who try to log in.

uucp: This relates to the legacy UUCP system.

local0–local7: These facilities are available for your own configuration. To use them, you should configure the services to talk to one of these local facilities. Some services allow you to do this by using a special option, other services can do that on compilation only, and still other services don't offer this option at all.

In addition to the different facilities, you can set some priorities in syslog-ng. In the syslog-ng configuration file, they are referred to as *levels*. These levels determine when exactly syslog-ng should undertake action, and they determine the severity of events. They allow you to define for each service when log messages should be generated. The following levels are available:

debug: This is the lowest level. Use it only for debugging purposes, because really everything will be logged.

info: This relates to all the messages with a purely informational purpose.

notice: This level describes normal system states that should be noted.

warning: Use this level to display warnings.

err: This level will log any errors.

crit: This level will inform you of any critical conditions.

alert: Use this if immediate action by the system administrator is required to keep a running service.

emerg: This informs you that the service is no longer available.

You can use all these facilities and levels to define filters that allow you to specify exactly what should happen when. Using filters makes it easier for you to refer to a specific event later in the configuration file. Most filters are defined on one line, such as the following, which comes from the default syslog-ng configuration file:

```
filter f_mailinfo { level(info) and facility(mail); };
```

The syslog-ng.conf file on SUSE Linux Enterprise Server has some default filters that are already present. You can see the first lines from syslog-ng.conf where these filters are defined in Listing 12-1.

Listing 12-1. *The Definition of Filters in* syslog-ng.conf

```
filter f_iptables { facility(kern) and match ("IN=") and match ("OUT="); };
filter f_console { level(warn) and facility(kern) and not filter(f_iptables)
                        or level(err) and not facility(authpriv); };
filter f_newsnotice { level(notice) and facility(news); };
filter f_newscrit   { level(crit)  and facility(news); };
...
```

As you can see, some default filters are present already. It is possible as well to define your own filters. For example, the following makes a filter statement that finds all the messages containing the word *deny* and coming from the host server1:

```
filter f_server1 { host("server1") and match("deny"); };
```

The third part in the log path is the destination. This defines where the log is sent if there is a match. Often, these destinations are followed immediately by the log event that should use this destination. Listing 12-2 shows an example of this. In this example, the following destinations are defined:

1. The first line defines the destination console. This is a console to which messages can be sent. Note that this line also defines the group and permissions used to write to that destination.

2. The second line states that everything coming from src (the default source) and matching the filter f_console (see Listing 12-1) should be logged to the destination console.

3. The third line defines another destination: the tty where root currently is logged in.

4. In the fourth line you can see that everything matching the definitions in f_alert is sent to this destination.

Listing 12-2. *Definition of Destinations and Logs That Should Go There*

```
destination console { file("/dev/tty10" group(tty) perm(0620)); };
log { source(src); filter(f_console); destination(console); };
destination root { usertty("root"); };
log { source(src); filter(f_alert); destination(root); };
```

Listing 12-2 should make clear it how the syslog-ng.conf file is organized. Have a look at the other definitions in it; these lines are pretty self-explanatory.

■**Caution** Do not modify /etc/syslog-ng/syslog-ng.conf directly. If you want to add something to the current log configuration, the file /etc/syslog-ng/syslog-ng.conf.in is the place to put these modifications. If you don't put them there, you risk losing them when YaST writes a new configuration to your server.

Monitoring Log Files

As you can see from the syslog-ng.conf file, log messages are directed to different locations. If the location is a file, you can most likely find it in the directory /var/log. In this directory you'll find files that were created by syslog-ng and usually also some log files that were created by processes and services that don't work with syslog-ng, such as the NTP services that make sure time is synchronized, the wtmp services that give information about users that have recently logged in to your server, and the zmd service that makes sure your server is updated properly. The most important file in this directory is /var/log/messages (see Figure 12-5). This is the generic log file where almost all the important messages occur. When testing some new functionality, it can be useful to keep this file open in a terminal window. You can do that by using the tail -f /var/log/messages command. Some other log files are available in this directory as well. Most of them are in clear-text format; just look at the contents to see what is happening.

As an alternative to browsing /var/log/messages with viewers such as cat, less, or tail, you can also see its contents from YaST. In YaST, select Miscellaneous, and then click View System Log. This shows you the content of the /var/log/messages file. Note the drop-down list in the upper part of the window; from this list you can select other log files as well. For example, refer to the file /var/log/YaST2/y2log to see the messages generated by YaST.

```
File  Edit  View  Terminal  Tabs  Help
May 26 11:17:05 laksmi kernel: pnp: Device 00:08 disabled.
May 26 11:17:05 laksmi kernel: parport 0x378 (WARNING): CTR: wrote 0x0c, read 0xff
May 26 11:17:05 laksmi kernel: parport 0x378 (WARNING): DATA: wrote 0xaa, read 0xff
May 26 11:17:05 laksmi kernel: parport 0x378: You gave this address, but there is probably
no parallel port there!
May 26 11:17:05 laksmi kernel: parport0: PC-style at 0x378 [PCSPP,TRISTATE]
May 26 11:17:05 laksmi kernel: ppa: Version 2.07 (for Linux 2.4.x)
May 26 11:17:05 laksmi kernel: end_request: I/O error, dev fd0, sector 0
May 26 11:17:05 laksmi kernel: end_request: I/O error, dev fd0, sector 0
May 26 11:17:11 laksmi kernel: end_request: I/O error, dev fd0, sector 0
May 26 11:17:12 laksmi kernel: end_request: I/O error, dev fd0, sector 0
May 26 11:23:04 laksmi kernel: end_request: I/O error, dev fd0, sector 0
May 26 11:23:04 laksmi kernel: end_request: I/O error, dev fd0, sector 0
May 26 11:23:11 laksmi kernel: parport 0x378 (WARNING): CTR: wrote 0x0c, read 0xff
May 26 11:23:11 laksmi kernel: parport 0x378 (WARNING): DATA: wrote 0xaa, read 0xff
May 26 11:23:11 laksmi kernel: parport 0x378: You gave this address, but there is probably
no parallel port there!
May 26 11:23:11 laksmi kernel: parport0: PC-style at 0x378 [PCSPP,TRISTATE]
May 26 11:23:11 laksmi kernel: pnp: Device 00:08 activated.
May 26 11:23:11 laksmi kernel: parport: PnPBIOS parport detected.
May 26 11:23:11 laksmi kernel: parport0: PC-style at 0x378, irq 7 [PCSPP,TRISTATE]
May 26 11:23:11 laksmi kernel: lp0: using parport0 (interrupt-driven).
May 26 11:23:12 laksmi kernel: pnp: Device 00:08 disabled.
May 26 11:23:12 laksmi kernel: parport 0x378 (WARNING): CTR: wrote 0x0c, read 0xff
May 26 11:23:12 laksmi kernel: parport 0x378 (WARNING): DATA: wrote 0xaa, read 0xff
May 26 11:23:12 laksmi kernel: parport 0x378: You gave this address, but there is probably
no parallel port there!
May 26 11:23:12 laksmi kernel: parport0: PC-style at 0x378 [PCSPP,TRISTATE]
May 26 11:23:12 laksmi kernel: ppa: Version 2.07 (for Linux 2.4.x)
May 26 11:23:12 laksmi kernel: end_request: I/O error, dev fd0, sector 0
May 26 11:23:12 laksmi kernel: end_request: I/O error, dev fd0, sector 0
May 26 11:23:18 laksmi kernel: end_request: I/O error, dev fd0, sector 0
May 26 11:23:18 laksmi kernel: end_request: I/O error, dev fd0, sector 0
laksmi:/etc/syslog-ng #
```

Figure 12-5. *The file* /var/log/messages *contains messages about all the important events that occurred on your system.*

Rotating Log Files

Logging is good, but if your system writes too many log files, this can become problematic; log files that are not controlled may fill up your server's file system completely. As a solution, you can configure the logrotate service. The logrotate service runs as a daily cron job and checks its configuration files to see whether any rotation has to occur. In these configuration files, you can configure when a new log file should be opened and, if that happens, what exactly should happen to the old log file—should it, for example, be compressed or just deleted, and if it is compressed, how many versions of the old file should be kept?

The logrotate service works with two different kinds of configuration files. The main configuration file is /etc/logrotate.conf. In this file, generic settings are defined to tune how logrotate should do its work. You can see the contents of this file in Listing 12-3.

Listing 12-3. *Contents of the* logrotate.conf *Configuration File*

```
# see "man logrotate" for details
# rotate log files weekly
weekly

# keep 4 weeks worth of backlogs
rotate 4
```

```
# create new (empty) log files after rotating old ones
create

# uncomment this if you want your log files compressed
#compress

# uncomment these to switch compression to bzip2
compresscmd /usr/bin/bzip2
uncompresscmd /usr/bin/bunzip2

# former versions had to have the compresscommand set accordingly
#compressext .bz2

# RPM packages drop log rotation information into this directory
include /etc/logrotate.d

# no packages own wtmp -- we'll rotate them here
#/var/log/wtmp {
#       monthly
#       create 0664 root utmp
#       rotate 1
#}

# system-specific logs may be also be configured here.
```

Listing 12-3 uses some important keywords. Table 12-1 defines them.

Table 12-1. *Logrotate Options*

Option	Description
weekly	This option specifies that the log files should be created on a weekly basis. If nothing is specified, the old file is removed.
rotate 4	This option makes sure that four old versions of the file are saved. If the rotate option is not used, old files are deleted.
create	The old file is saved under a new name, and a new file is created. Typically, the old file will be renamed to the same filename with the date on which it was compressed appended to it, and a new file will open.
compress	Use this option to make sure the old log files are compressed.
compresscmd	This option specifies the command that should be used for creating the compressed log files.
uncompresscmd	Use this command to specify what command to use to uncompress compressed log files.
include	This important option makes sure the content of the directory /etc/logrotate.d is included. In this directory, files exist that specify how to handle some individual log files.

As you have seen, the logrotate.conf configuration file includes some generic code to specify how log files should be handled. In addition to that, most log files have a specific logrotate configuration file in /etc/logrotate.d. Figure 12-6 shows the content of this directory.

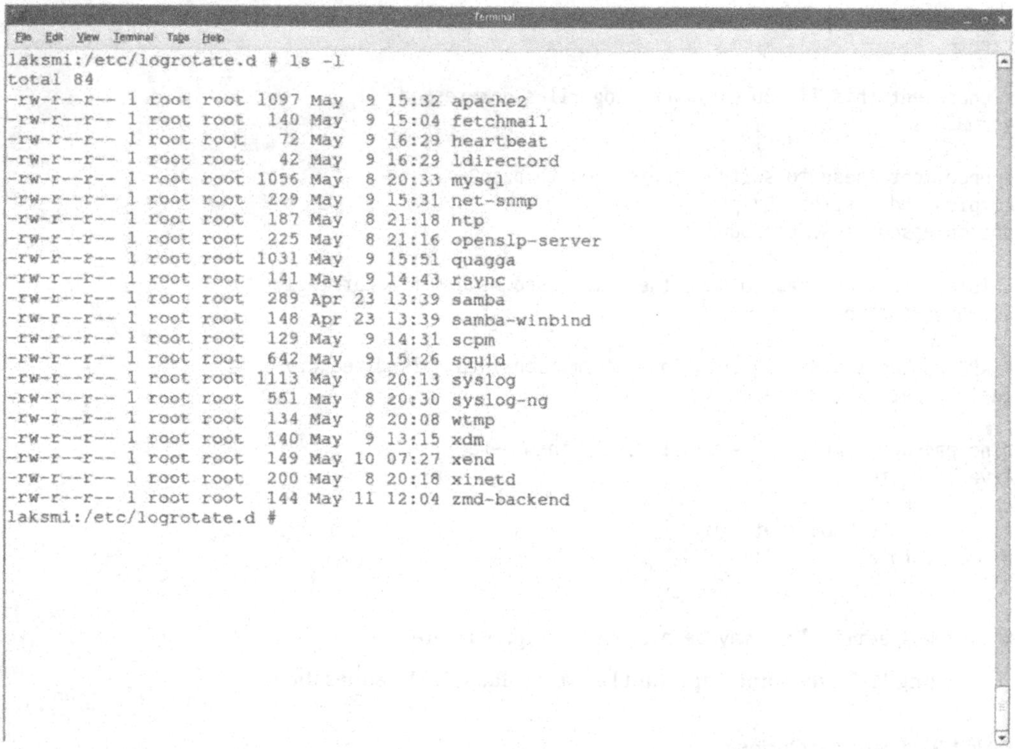
Terminal
File Edit View Terminal Tabs Help
laksmi:/etc/logrotate.d # ls -l
total 84
-rw-r--r-- 1 root root 1097 May 9 15:32 apache2
-rw-r--r-- 1 root root 140 May 9 15:04 fetchmail
-rw-r--r-- 1 root root   72 May 9 16:29 heartbeat
-rw-r--r-- 1 root root   42 May 9 16:29 ldirectord
-rw-r--r-- 1 root root 1056 May 8 20:33 mysql
-rw-r--r-- 1 root root 229 May 9 15:31 net-snmp
-rw-r--r-- 1 root root 187 May 8 21:18 ntp
-rw-r--r-- 1 root root 225 May 8 21:16 openslp-server
-rw-r--r-- 1 root root 1031 May 9 15:51 quagga
-rw-r--r-- 1 root root 141 May 9 14:43 rsync
-rw-r--r-- 1 root root 289 Apr 23 13:39 samba
-rw-r--r-- 1 root root 148 Apr 23 13:39 samba-winbind
-rw-r--r-- 1 root root 129 May 9 14:31 scpm
-rw-r--r-- 1 root root 642 May 9 15:26 squid
-rw-r--r-- 1 root root 1113 May 8 20:13 syslog
-rw-r--r-- 1 root root 551 May 8 20:30 syslog-ng
-rw-r--r-- 1 root root 134 May 8 20:08 wtmp
-rw-r--r-- 1 root root 140 May 9 13:15 xdm
-rw-r--r-- 1 root root 149 May 10 07:27 xend
-rw-r--r-- 1 root root 200 May 8 20:18 xinetd
-rw-r--r-- 1 root root 144 May 11 12:04 zmd-backend
laksmi:/etc/logrotate.d #

Figure 12-6. *In the directory* `/etc/logrotate.d`, *lots of files have their own logrotate configuration files.*

The content of the service-specific configuration files in `/etc/logrotate.d` is in general more specific than the contents of the generic `logrotate.conf`. In Listing 12-4, you can see what the configuration script for `/var/log/ntp` looks like.

Listing 12-4. *Example of the logrotate Configuration for NTP*

```
/var/log/ntp {
     compress
     dateext
     maxage 365
     rotate 99
     size=+2048k
     notifempty
     missingok
     copytruncate
     postrotate
          chmod 644 /var/log/ntp
     endscript
}
```

Listing 12-4 uses some more options. Table 12-2 gives an overview of these options and their meanings.

Table 12-2. *Options in Service-Specific logrotate Files*

Option	Description
dateext	Appends the date the file is rotated to the old name of the log files.
maxage	Specifies the number of days after which old log files should be removed.
rotate	Specifies the number of times a log file should be rotated before being removed or mailed to the address specified in the mail directive. After rotating the file, the old one is removed.
size	Rotates files that grow bigger than the size specified here.
notifempty	Does not rotate the log file when it is empty.
missingok	If the log file does not exist, go on to the next one without issuing an error message.
copytruncate	Truncates the old log file in place after creating a copy, instead of moving the old file and creating a new one. This is useful for services that cannot be told to close their log files.
postrotate	Use this option to specify some commands that should be executed after performing the logrotate on the file.
endscript	Denotes the end of the configuration file.

Like the example for the NTP log file in Listing 12-4, all other log files can have their own logrotate file. You can even create logrotate files for files that are not log files at all! Some more options are available when creating such a logrotate file; for a complete overview, check the man pages.

Summary

To see what's happening on your server, you need log files. SUSE Linux Enterprise Server 10 uses syslog-ng as its most important mechanism to create these log files. In this chapter, you learned how to configure this service. You also learned how to make sure that a log file that has gone mad is not capable of filling your system with log files completely by using the logrotate mechanism. This was the last chapter in Part 2 of this book. Part 3 is about configuring SUSE Linux Enterprise Server as a server in the network. In Chapter 13, the part's first chapter, you will learn how to set up the network connection.

Networking SUSE Linux Enterprise Server

Now that you know how to work with the SUSE Linux Enterprise Server operating system, it's time to talk about networking. In this part, you'll learn how to set up the network and how to enable the most important network services. You'll learn, for example, how to enable file sharing with popular protocols such as NFS and Samba, how to set up an LDAP server for centralized management of all kinds of information, and how to set up the most popular Internet-related services.

CHAPTER 13

■ ■ ■

Connecting to the Network

The network connection on your server is probably already operational; after all, making a network connection is easy if you are using the YaST graphical tool to configure it. However, a lot is going on behind the scenes of the YaST graphical utility. In this chapter, you will learn how to get everything out of the graphical interface that you can and how to tune the network interface from the command line and configuration files. You will also learn how to configure IPv6 and what tools are available to solve any problems that occur with the network board in your server.

Configuring the Network Interface with YaST

As with most services on SUSE Linux Enterprise Server 10, configuring the network interface starts with YaST. From YaST, you can configure different types of network cards (see Figure 13-1):

- DSL
- ISDN
- Modem
- Network card

For a server, configuring the network card is the most important task you can perform from this interface since the network card connects the server to the rest of the network. ISDN and modem connections are legacy options that are not used often anymore, and when a server is connected to a DSL connection, this happens most of the time via a specialized router. Therefore, in this chapter I'll cover only how to configure the network card.

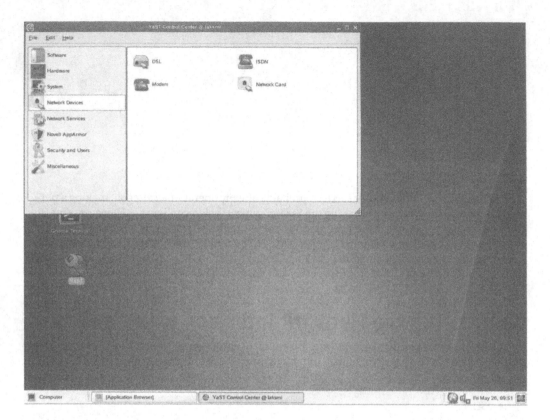

Figure 13-1. *YaST offers utilities to configure different kinds of network devices.*

To configure a network card from YaST, select Network Devices ➤ Network Card from the YaST main menu. You will be asked which method you want to use to set up the network. You can choose from two methods: using the NetworkManager or using the traditional method with ifup. The NetworkManager applet allows a user to switch quickly between different networks, either wired or wireless. This applet is useful to work with from a graphical interface on a workstation; however, on a server, it is unlikely that you'll need to switch between networks often. Besides, many servers will run without the graphical interface by default; therefore, on a server, you should always choose the Traditional Method with ifup option (see Figure 13-2).

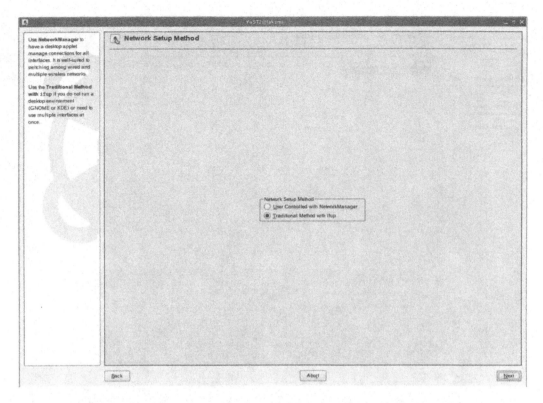

Figure 13-2. *On a server, you will usually work with the traditional network setup method.*

Next you'll see an overview of all the network cards detected on your server, as in Figure 13-3. Usually, network cards are detected automatically and without problems. However, if you have a problem connecting to a network board, you can add it manually. It is also possible to change the properties of a network card that was detected by clicking the Edit button on this screen.

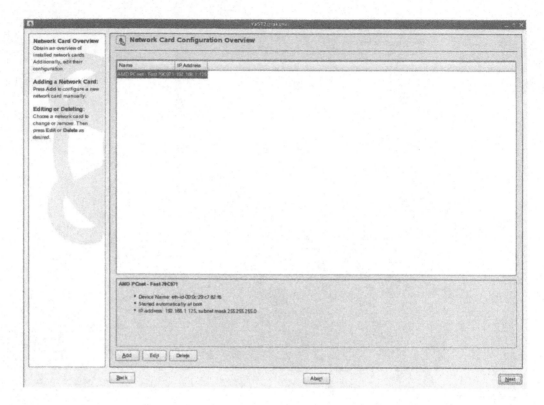

Figure 13-3. *Ordinarily, all network boards that are installed in your server are detected automatically.*

Adding a Network Card Manually

To add a network card manually, click the Add button, as shown in Figure 13-3. You can now see the Manual Network Card Configuration screen (as shown in Figure 13-4). From here, you can select all the properties of the network card. The easiest way to start is to click the Select from List button. If you click this button, a list of available network cards appears. From this list, you can select the network card that is in your server to make its configuration easier. If the network card you want to use is not in this list, you can enter its properties manually.

The following options are available:

Device Type: From this drop-down list, you need to select the type of network device you want to configure. All current network types are supported. In most cases, you will need to configure an Ethernet network card for your server, but other device types such as Token Ring and wireless are supported as well.

Configuration Name: To make it easier to work with a given network device, specify its configuration name. This configuration name basically is a number that is offered from a drop-down list. What you use here is added as the suffix for the network device; for example, Ethernet network cards use the eth device type. If you specify 0 as the configuration name here (which is a common choice if your server has just one network interface card), this device will be known as eth0. Be careful not to select a device name that is already in use, because no automatic probing takes place.

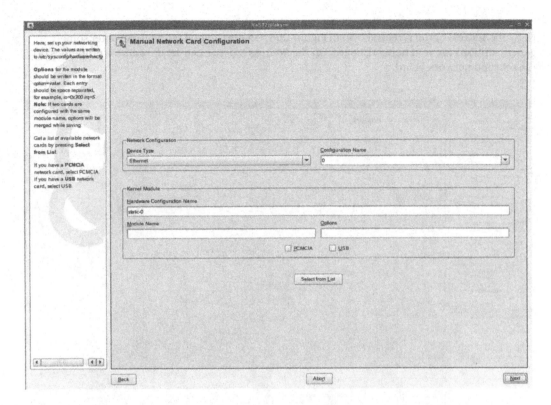

Figure 13-4. *If the network card in your server is not detected automatically, you can specify all its options manually.*

Tip From YaST it is difficult to make sure the same interface name (in other words, eth0) is always used for the same network board if more than one network board is present in your server, especially if both network boards use the same kernel module as a driver. If you want to make sure eth0 is always connected to the same network board, edit the configuration file /etc/udev/rules.d/30-net_persistent_names.rules. In this file you can add a device name such as eth0 to a specific MAC address, thus making sure the device is always using the same device name.

Hardware Configuration Name: Enter any string that makes it easier for you to recognize the network card.

Module Name: If a specific kernel module is installed on your server and you need to call that module to use your network card, refer to the name of the kernel module here. Notice that it is rare that the proper kernel module is not detected automatically and you have to specify its module by hand. See also Chapter 29 for more details about kernel configuration.

Options: For some other types of network card, it may be necessary to enter device options. If you use them, specify them in the format option=value, such as irq=5. Most modern Ethernet network cards don't need these options.

PCMCIA: Check this option if you are using a PCMCIA network card.

USB: Check this option if you are using a USB network card.

When the software recognizes all the network boards, you can enter their properties on the Network Address Setup screen shown in Figure 13-5. On the General tab, you can enter some generic options for your network board. On the Address tab, you can set the address properties of the selected network board.

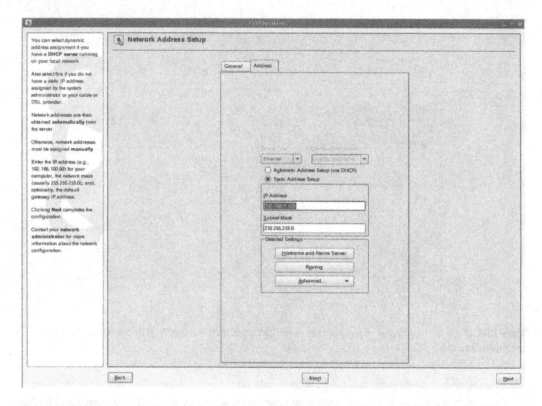

Figure 13-5. *The least you need to do for each network board is to specify how addressing should be handled.*

In addition, you can specify how the IP addressing of the device should be handled. First, you need to choose between Automatic Address Setup, in which a DHCP server delivers an IP address to your server, and Static Address Setup. Because the services offered by your server always need to be contacted on the same IP address, it is uncommon to configure a server for Automatic Address Setup (unless your DHCP server is set up to provide the IP address for the specific MAC address in use on your server using the host option). If the DHCP server determined what address the server is using, its IP address may change. Therefore, in most scenarios you should select Static Address Setup and specify an IP address that is valid for the network to which your server is connected. Together with a subnet mask, which needs to be configured on all network cards, this is enough information for your server to work with on the local network. However, if your server needs to be able to connect to computers on other networks, it needs more information. For instance, most servers need the address of a default router that they can use to connect to computers on other networks. Also, if from your server you want to be able to use computer names instead of meaningless IP addresses, you need to configure the address of a DNS name server as well.

To configure the DNS server that should be used, click the Hostname and Name Server button under Detailed Settings. This opens the Hostname and Name Server Configuration screen shown in

Figure 13-6. The first step you need to take here is to enter the name you want to use for your server. Ordinarily, you will have already specified a name during installation; if you didn't, though, you can still do it here. Also, enter the name of the DNS domain your server is in. These two pieces together make the complete DNS name of your host. Next, your server needs at least one DNS name server. Enter the IP address of at least one DNS name server that it should use. The address in the Name Server 1 box is used in all cases, except when Name Server 1 is not available. In that case, your server will try to reach the address in the Name Server 2 box, and if that also is not available, it goes to Name Server 3. If you have an internal DNS server within your company, you would use an internal DNS name server as the primary name server and external DNS name servers, such as the name servers offered by an Internet provider, as the secondary and tertiary name servers.

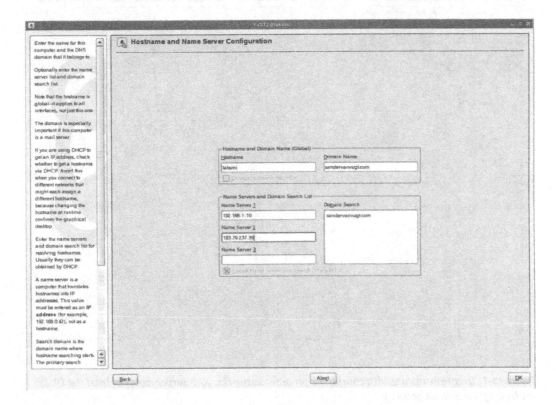

Figure 13-6. *To enable the use of DNS names instead of IP addresses, every server needs the IP address of at least one DNS name server.*

Also on this tab you'll see the Domain Search box. In this box, you can enter the names of DNS domains that should be searched if an incomplete server name is used (for example, laksmi instead of laksmi.somewhere.com). It is good practice to enter the name of your own DNS domain here.

If you have chosen to obtain an IP address from a DHCP server, you can select the option Change Hostname via DHCP. Also, if you work with an address from a DHCP server, it is possible to select the Update Name Servers and Search List via DHCP checkbox. After entering all the required information, click OK to return to the main screen where you configure the IP address of the server.

Back on the main Network Address Setup screen, you now have to enter the required routing information. The screen to enter this information appears after clicking the Routing button (see

Figure 13-7). The least that your server needs is the IP address of the default gateway; this is the address where all the packets are sent that don't have a local destination. If your server is on a LAN where more than one router is present, you can enter the address of other routers as well to reach specific destinations. These other entries will always be used before the default gateway is used. If dynamic routing is enabled on your network, these entries will be added to the network routes that your server gets from other routers. If you need to enter such information, select the Expert Configuration box, and enter the information you need. If your server is a router by itself, select the Enable IP Forwarding box.

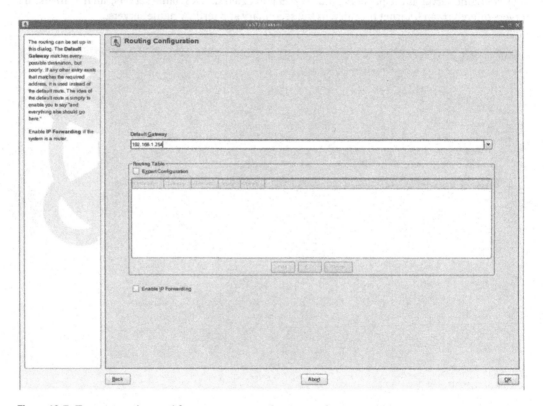

Figure 13-7. *To communicate with computers on other networks, your server needs at least the IP address of the default gateway.*

The last pieces of information that you can enter for your network card are available after you click the Advanced Configuration button (shown earlier in Figure 13-5). After clicking this button, you'll see a list of options you can use to further tune how your network card works. First, under the Hardware Details option, you can see the name of the network card as it exists internally in your server and the name of the kernel module that is used to load the network card. Also, the options for this kernel module appear.

Next, on the DHCP Client Options screen, you can specify some options that your server can use if it is configured as a DHCP client. On a server, you will rarely use these options. Last, you can use the Additional Addresses options to configure additional addresses for an interface. Using a secondary IP address can be helpful, such as when you want some specific service to be reachable on its own IP address instead of the main IP address of your server. Secondary IP addresses are also called *IP aliases*. To enter a secondary IP address, click the Add button first. Then enter the optional name you want to use for this alias, followed by the IP address and netmask you want to use for this alias. This will cause your network card to listen to packets destined for the secondary IP address as well. Note that the secondary IP address can be in the same network or in a different network.

For the properties of each network board, you also find the General tab (see Figure 13-8).

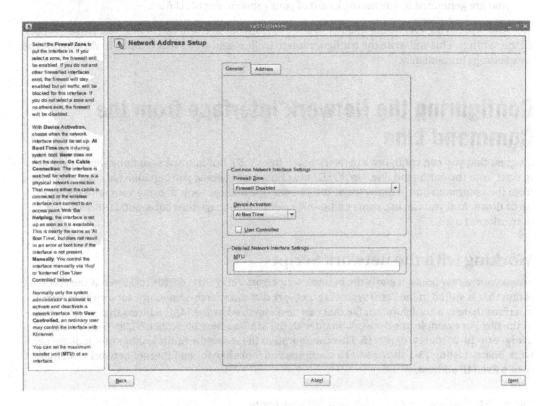

Figure 13-8. *For each network card, some general settings are available.*

The following options are available on this screen:

Firewall Zone: Use this option to specify in which zone the selected network interface is. Check Chapter 30 for more details.

Device Activation: Here you can specify when the network board should be activated. By default, it will be activated when your server boots. As an alternative, you can choose to never start the device or to start the device on a cable connection. In that case, the operating system watches whether a network cable is connected. If this is the case, the interface will be started. As an alternative, you can activate the interface on *hotplug*. This means the interface is set up at boot time normally, but it will not produce an error if this doesn't work. The last option that you can set here is Manually. In that case, the interface is controlled manually using the ifup command (see the "Using ifup, ifdown, and Related Tools" section later in this chapter) or graphical tools such as the network agent in the graphical desktop.

User Controlled: Usually, only the user root is allowed to manage a network interface. If you want to allow regular users to activate or deactivate network interfaces, make sure the User Controlled option is checked.

MTU: In some cases it is necessary to specify the maximum transfer unit (MTU), especially if large packets are used on your network. If this is the case, specify the maximum size of packets that are generated by the network card of your server in the MTU field.

After specifying everything that needs to be set for your network card, click Next twice to apply all the settings. This will write the configuration to its files, and when that is done, it will activate the new settings immediately.

Configuring the Network Interface from the Command Line

It's great that you can configure a network board from YaST, but in some situations you'll just want to do it from the command line. On SUSE Linux Enterprise Server, you can manage a network board from the command line in many ways. You can use one of three tools to bring your network board up or down. And you can use some additional options to manage the routes and DNS servers your network card uses.

Working with the network Script

When your server boots, it starts the network script from /etc/init.d. This script reads the configuration that is stored in the /etc/sysconfig/network directory. In this directory, for every network interface there is a configuration file that can be recognized by the MAC address that is in the name of the file. For example, the network board with the MAC address 00:0c:29:c7:82:f6 has the name ifcfg-eth-id-00:0c:29:c7:82:f6. This configuration file stores the entire configuration of the network board. Listing 13-1 shows what a configuration looks like for an Ethernet network card that uses a fixed IP address.

Listing 13-1. *Example Configuration for a Network Board*

```
BOOTPROTO='static'
BROADCAST=' '
ETHTOOL_OPTIONS=' '
IPADDR= '192.168.1.125'
MTU=' '
```

```
NAME='AMD PCnet - Fast 79C971'
NETMASK='255.255.255.0'
NETWORK=' '
REMOTE_IPADDR=' '
STARTMODE='auto'
UNIQUE='rBUF.weGuQ9ywYPF'
USERCONTROL='no'
_nm_name='bus-pci-0000:00:11.0'
```

Now that you know where YaST stores its configuration, you can change it directly in this file. For example, if you want to change the IP address of your network card quickly, then change it in this file and restart the network card (rcnetwork restart); it will work immediately.

■ **Tip** When duplicating virtual machines in a VMware environment, you may encounter the situation that a new MAC address is generated for the virtual machine but this configuration file still has its old name. In that case, the name of the file and the MAC address of the machine that should use it don't match, and as a result, the network card can't be initialized. You can solve this problem by renaming the file so that it reflects the new MAC address that is used by your network card. The network card that your virtual machine is using is in the readable text file with the extension .vmx for your virtual machine.

As stated, you can use the /etc/init.d/network script to bring the network up or down. However, this method has a disadvantage; it brings up or down all network interfaces, and this is not always what you want. To change the status of just one network interface and not all of them, use one of the methods described next.

Using ifup, ifdown, and Related Tools

To make managing a network board easy, the ifup and ifdown tools were created. Using these tools is simple: call the tool followed by the name of the network board you want to manage. For example, ifup eth0 will start network card eth0, and ifdown eth0 will stop it.

In addition to ifup and ifdown, you can use some useful related tools:

- ifstatus shows the state of a network interface (see Figure 13-9).

- ifrenew renews the DHCP lease on a network card.

- ifprobe checks whether the configuration for an interface has changed.

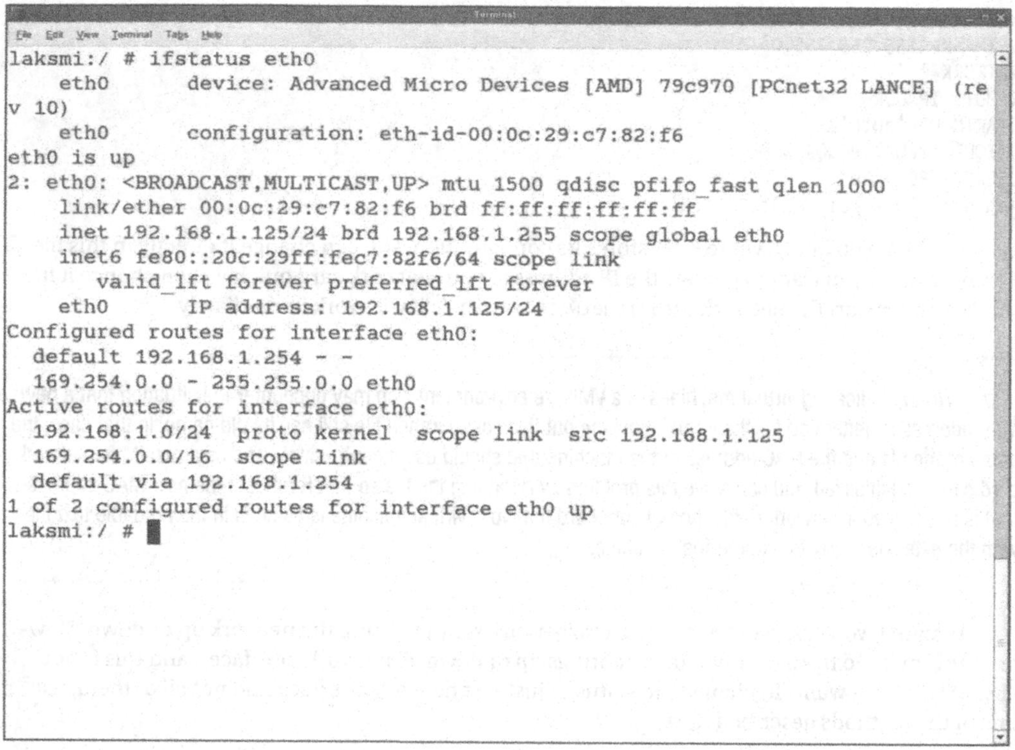

```
laksmi:/ # ifstatus eth0
    eth0        device: Advanced Micro Devices [AMD] 79c970 [PCnet32 LANCE] (re
v 10)
    eth0        configuration: eth-id-00:0c:29:c7:82:f6
eth0 is up
2: eth0: <BROADCAST,MULTICAST,UP> mtu 1500 qdisc pfifo_fast qlen 1000
    link/ether 00:0c:29:c7:82:f6 brd ff:ff:ff:ff:ff:ff
    inet 192.168.1.125/24 brd 192.168.1.255 scope global eth0
    inet6 fe80::20c:29ff:fec7:82f6/64 scope link
       valid_lft forever preferred_lft forever
    eth0        IP address: 192.168.1.125/24
Configured routes for interface eth0:
  default 192.168.1.254 - -
  169.254.0.0 - 255.255.0.0 eth0
Active routes for interface eth0:
  192.168.1.0/24  proto kernel  scope link  src 192.168.1.125
  169.254.0.0/16  scope link
  default via 192.168.1.254
1 of 2 configured routes for interface eth0 up
laksmi:/ # 
```

Figure 13-9. *To get a complete overview of the configuration of a given network interface,* ifstatus *is the most useful.*

Using ifconfig

You can use the ifconfig command to manage a network interface card. The command has been around for years now and is not the most flexible command, but it will do the job fine. If you use the ifconfig command without any parameters, it will show information about the current configuration of the network cards in your server. You can see an example of this in Figure 13-10.

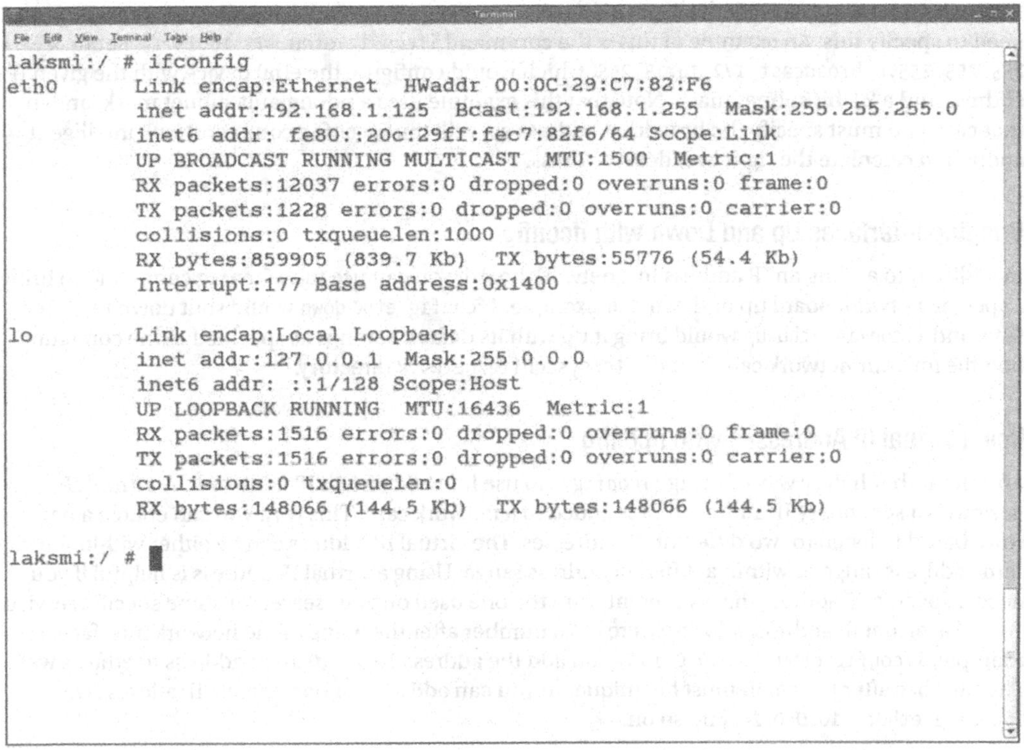

```
laksmi:/ # ifconfig
eth0      Link encap:Ethernet  HWaddr 00:0C:29:C7:82:F6
          inet addr:192.168.1.125  Bcast:192.168.1.255  Mask:255.255.255.0
          inet6 addr: fe80::20c:29ff:fec7:82f6/64 Scope:Link
          UP BROADCAST RUNNING MULTICAST  MTU:1500  Metric:1
          RX packets:12037 errors:0 dropped:0 overruns:0 frame:0
          TX packets:1228 errors:0 dropped:0 overruns:0 carrier:0
          collisions:0 txqueuelen:1000
          RX bytes:859905 (839.7 Kb)  TX bytes:55776 (54.4 Kb)
          Interrupt:177 Base address:0x1400

lo        Link encap:Local Loopback
          inet addr:127.0.0.1  Mask:255.0.0.0
          inet6 addr: ::1/128 Scope:Host
          UP LOOPBACK RUNNING  MTU:16436  Metric:1
          RX packets:1516 errors:0 dropped:0 overruns:0 frame:0
          TX packets:1516 errors:0 dropped:0 overruns:0 carrier:0
          collisions:0 txqueuelen:0
          RX bytes:148066 (144.5 Kb)  TX bytes:148066 (144.5 Kb)

laksmi:/ # 
```

Figure 13-10. *If used without any parameters,* ifconfig *shows information about the current configuration of network boards.*

Displaying Information with ifconfig

The ifconfig command gives different kinds of information about a network card. It first starts with the name of the protocol used on the network card. This is indicated with, for example, Link encap: Ethernet, which states that it is an Ethernet network board. Then, if applicable, the MAC address is mentioned as the HWaddr. This address is followed by first the IPv4-related address information and then the IPv6-related address information. Then several statistics about the network board are mentioned. Pay special attention to the RX packets (received packets) and TX packets (transmitted packets) entries; from these statistics you can see what the network board is doing and whether any errors have occurred while doing it. In addition to the information about the physical network boards that are present in your server, you will also always see information about the loopback device (lo). This is the network interface used for internal purposes on your server. You also need this loopback device because some services depend on it; for example, the graphical environment that is used on Linux is written on top of the IP stack offered by the loopback interface.

Configuring a Network Card with ifconfig

Configuring a network board with the ifconfig command is relatively easy. Just add the name of the network board you want to configure followed by the IP address you want to use on that network board; for example, use ifconfig eth0 192.168.1.125. This command will configure eth0 with a default class C subnet mask. If you need something other than a default subnet mask, you need to specify this. An example of this is the command ifconfig eth0 172.16.13.13 netmask 255.255.255.0 broadcast 172.16.13.255, which would configure the eth0 device with the given IP address and a 24-bit subnet mask. Note that this example uses a nondefault subnet mask, and in that case you must specify the broadcast address as well; the ifconfig command isn't intelligent enough to calculate the right broadcast address.

Bringing Interfaces Up and Down with ifconfig

In addition to adding an IP address to a network board, you can use the ifconfig command to bring a specific network board up or down. For example, ifconfig eth0 down would shut down the interface, and ifconfig eth0 up would bring it up with its default settings as specified in the configuration file for your network card in the /etc/sysconfig/network directory.

Using Virtual IP Addresses with ifconfig

Another rather handy way of using ifconfig is to use it to add virtual IP addresses. A *virtual IP address* is a secondary IP address that is added to a network card. This way, you can enable a network board to listen to two different IP addresses. The virtual IP address can be either within the same address range or within a different address range. Using a virtual IP address is helpful if you need a specific IP address that's different from the one used on your server for some specific service. To add a virtual IP address, add :n where n is a number after the name of the network interface. For example, ifconfig eth0:0 10.0.0.10 would add the address 10.0.0.10 as an address to eth0 as well. The number after the colon must be unique, so you can add a secondary virtual IP address with ifconfig eth0:1 10.0.0.20, and so on.

Using the ip Tool

You can use the ifconfig tool to display information about the configuration of a network card, but it is not the only tool available. A more flexible (but also more difficult to use) tool is the ip tool. This tool can work with many options to manage virtually all aspects of the network connection. What exactly you want to do with the ip tool is determined by the first option you use after the command. This first option is a reference to the *object*, and for each object there are different ways to go. You can use the following objects:

link: Use this to manage or display properties of a network device.

addr: Use this to manage or display IPv4 or IPv6 network addresses on a device.

route: Use this to manage or display entries in the routing table.

rule: Use this to manage or display rules in the routing policy database.

neigh: Use this to manage or display entries in the ARP cache.

tunnel: Use this to manage or display IP tunnels.

maddr: Use this to manage or display multicast addresses for interfaces.

mroute: Use this to manage or display multicast routing cache entries.

monitor: Use this to monitor what happens on a given device.

Each of these objects that can be used with the ip tool has options. The easiest way to find out about these options is to use the ip command followed by the object followed by the help keyword. For example, ip address help would provide information about how to use the ip address command.

Displaying IP Address Setup Information with the ip Tool

One common use of the ip tool is to display information about the use of IP addresses for a given interface. The command to use for this purpose is ip address show. Note that if it is clear what exactly you want and there can be no confusion between options, you can specify the options used with the ip command in short notation as well; for example, ip a s would perform the same task as ip address show. This command would display the information shown in Figure 13-11.

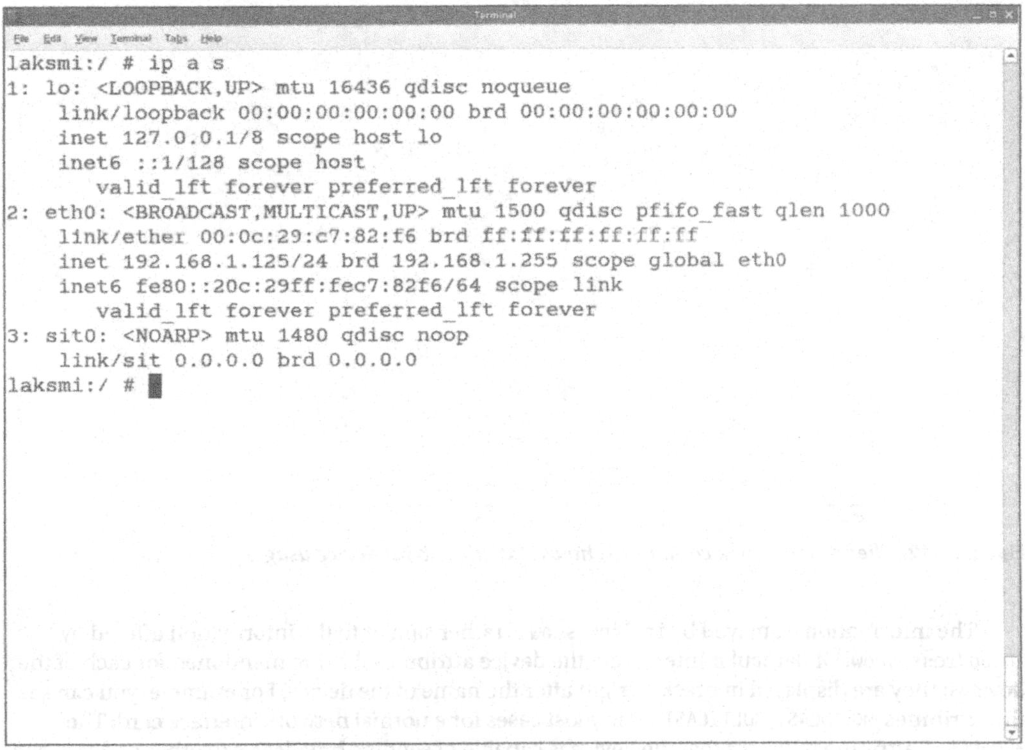

Figure 13-11. *The* ip address show *command gives complete information about the current configuration of the network interfaces in your server.*

In Figure 13-11, you can see that information for three different network interfaces appears. First you see the information for the loopback interface, and then you can see the eth0 device, which is followed by the sit0 device. The latter is a special virtual device that you can use to encapsulate IPv6 into IPv4 packets; it is needed on networks where both IPv4 and IPv6 packets are sent. Note that this sit0 device is always created automatically, even if you don't use IPv6 at all on your network.

Monitoring Device Attributes

Another use of the ip tool is to show only device attributes. You can do that with the ip link show command. This command shows only usage statistics for the device you have specified and no address information. Figure 13-12 shows an example of the output of this command.

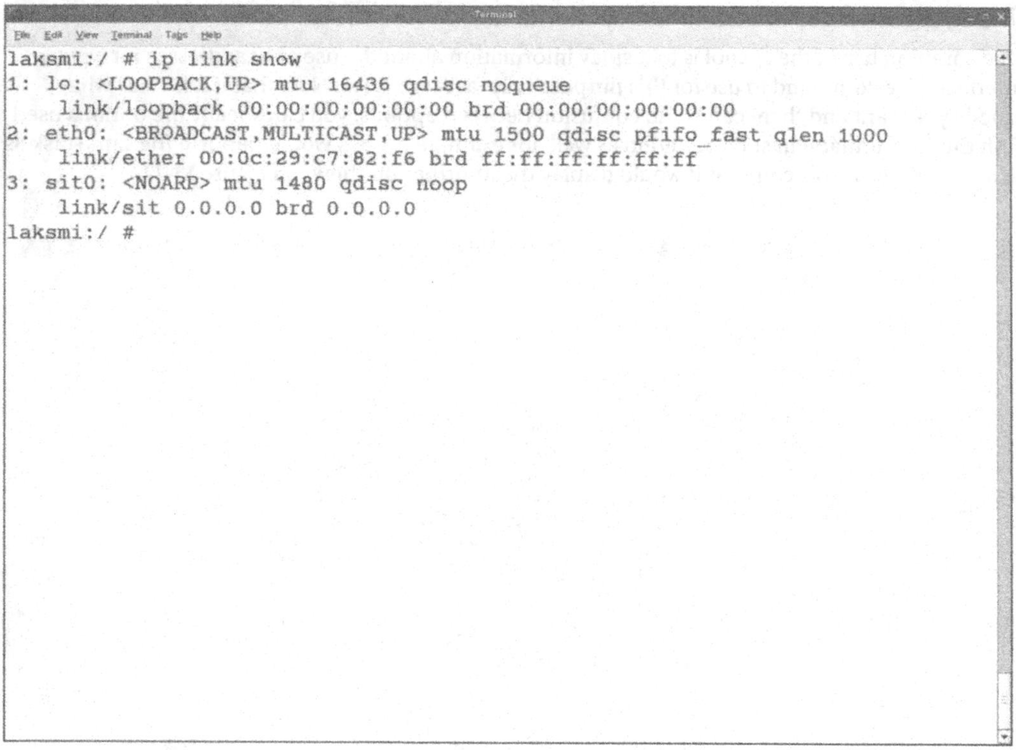

```
                                        Terminal                                    _ □ x
 File  Edit  View  Terminal  Tabs  Help
laksmi:/ # ip link show
1: lo: <LOOPBACK,UP> mtu 16436 qdisc noqueue
     link/loopback 00:00:00:00:00:00 brd 00:00:00:00:00:00
2: eth0: <BROADCAST,MULTICAST,UP> mtu 1500 qdisc pfifo_fast qlen 1000
     link/ether 00:0c:29:c7:82:f6 brd ff:ff:ff:ff:ff:ff
3: sit0: <NOARP> mtu 1480 qdisc noop
     link/sit 0.0.0.0 brd 0.0.0.0
laksmi:/ #
```

Figure 13-12. *The* ip link show *command shows statistics about device usage.*

The information displayed by ip link show is rather similar to the information offered by ip address show. Of particular interest are the device attributes that are mentioned for each of the devices; they are displayed in brackets right after the name of the device. For example, you can see the attributes BROADCAST,MULTICAST,UP in most cases for a normal network interface card. The BROADCAST attribute indicates that the device is capable of sending broadcasts to other nodes in the network. The MULTICAST attribute indicates that the device can send multicast packets as well, and finally UP indicates that the device is working.

Setting the IP Address

Like the ifconfig tool, the ip tool can assign an IP address to a device. To do this, you could use a command like ip address add 10.0.0.10/16 brd + dev eth0. This command would set the IP address to 10.0.0.10 for eth0. With this IP address, a 16-bit subnet mask is used, which is indicated by the /16 directly after the IP address that needs to be set. The broadcast address is calculated automatically, which is indicated with the brd + construction. Once you have set the IP address with the ip tool, you can use the following command to check whether it is set all right: ip address show dev eth0.

Like with the ifconfig command, you can add more than one IP address to a network interface when using the ip tool. It is not hard to do this; just use ip address add 10.0.0.20/16 brd + dev eth0, and 10.0.0.20 with its specified properties is added as a second IP address to eth0. You should, however, note that there is a difference between secondary IP addresses that are added with ifconfig and IP addresses that are added with the ip tool. An address that is added with ip will not show when you use ifconfig, and an address that is added with ifconfig will not show with ip address show. So when using secondary IP addresses, make sure you use the right tool to check their properties.

Managing IPv6

Currently, IPv4 is still the default protocol used on most servers. However, IPv4 has some serious shortcomings. The most important of these is that there just aren't enough addresses for future use. Therefore, some years ago the development of a new version of IP started. Since the draft for IP version 5 just didn't make it, this new generation of Internet Protocol is called IPv6, and you can use it on SUSE Linux Enterprise Server. In the next sections, you will learn about the properties of IPv6 and how to get it working on your server. This is not meant as an in-depth coverage of IPv6 and all its properties; it is just meant to help you configure IPv6 on a server so you can see whether it is useful for your environment.

IPv6 Addressing

Before you start the actual implementation of IPv6, you should know about its particularities. The first and most important feature is the address length. Where IPv4 has to work with 32-bit addresses, which allow for about 4 billion unique addresses theoretically, IPv6 offers a 128-bit address space. This offers more than enough IP addresses to assign an address to every square meter of Earth's surface. The IPv6 addresses are written as hexadecimal addresses, grouped in groups of 16 bits. An example of such an address is 2ba0:bfb1:5655:8812:0BFC:1234:0:1234. This is probably not the kind of address that you as an administrator want to memorize!

If in an IPv6 address more than one group of 16 bits has the value 0, you can abbreviate this with ::. For example, you can write the IPv6 address 2bad:0:0:0:0:1234:5678:90ab as 2bad::1234:5678:90ab, and 0:0:0:0:0:0:0:1 is just ::1. This makes working with IPv6 addresses a lot easier! Another nice feature of IPv6 is that an IP address can be shared amongst different network interface boards. This enables an easy-to-implement method for load balancing.

Since in an IPv6 address more than enough bits are available, there is a default division between the network part of the address and the node part of the address. The last 64 bits of an IPv6 address normally are used as the node ID. This node ID is a so-called IEEE EIA-64 ID, which on Ethernet consists of the 48-bit MAC address with FFFE added between the vendor identifier and the node identifier. If a network interface doesn't have a MAC address, the node ID is generated randomly.

By including the MAC address in the IPv6 address, the node in an IPv6 network is capable of determining its own IPv6 address! All that a node has to do is listen on the network to check for the network address that is in use. Next it can add its own MAC address and transform that to an IEEE EIA-64 ID, and it will be able to communicate with the rest of the network automatically!

Although not strictly necessary, an IPv6 address can work with a subnet mask. This subnet mask by default for all addresses is /64 (64 bits), but you can use subnet masks other than this default as well. However, the last 64 bits of an address are always reserved for the node address, so you cannot use them in the subnet mask.

Address Types

In IPv6, you can use different types of addresses. The following is a summary of these address types:

Link-local addresses: These addresses can be compared to APIPA addresses in IPv4. These addresses are used if no specific information about the network configuration could be found. You can consider them IP addresses for local use only. These addresses always start with FE80 in the first 2 bytes. They are not routable, but they are necessary for neighbor discovery (see later in this section). Link-local addresses are always created automatically if IPv6 is enabled.

Site-local addresses: You can compare these addresses with the addresses that are defined in the private address ranges for IPv4. Site-local addresses always start with FEC0 and have a default 48-bit subnet mask. You can use the last 16 bits for internal subnetting. Site-local addresses are not created automatically.

Aggregatable global unicast addresses: These are the "normal" addresses that are used on IPv6 networks. They are assigned by an administrator and always start with 2 or 3 (binary 001).

Multicast addresses: These are addresses used to address groups of nodes. They always start with FF.

Anycast addresses: These are the IPv6 alternative for a broadcast address. When using anycast, the IPv6 node gets an answer from any node that matches the anycast criterion.

In IPv6, broadcast addresses are not used.
On a single Linux host, you will always find more than one IPv6 address:

- A loopback address (::1) is used on the loopback interface.

- A link-local address is generated automatically for every interface.

- If the administrator has configured it, every interface has a unicast address. This can be a site-local address, an aggregatable global unicast address, or both.

The Neighbor Discovery Protocol

One of the design goals of IPv6 was to make configuration easier. For this purpose, RFC 2461 defines the neighbor discovery protocol. The purpose of this protocol is to provide automatic IP address assignment; neighbor discovery makes sure that a node can find routers, addresses, prefixes, and other required configuration information automatically. With this protocol, a router advertises all relevant information such as the best next hop. Individual nodes check their neighbors and keep information about the neighbors in the neighbor cache so that they always have up-to-date information about the rest of the network. In this neighbor cache, a node keeps information such as addresses of neighbors, a list of prefixes (IPv6 addresses) that are in use by the neighbors, and a list of routers that can be used as default routers.

Assigning IPv6 Addresses in SUSE Linux Enterprise Server

On SUSE Linux Enterprise Server, you can use the ip tools as well as the ifconfig tools to configure an IPv6 address. All required kernel modules are loaded by default, so with regard to that, you don't need to do any extra work. These are some examples of how to configure IPv6 on your server:

ifconfig eth0 inet6 add 2000:10:20:30:20c:29ff:fec7:82f6/64: This command configures eth0 with an IPv6 address that is an aggregatable global unicast address. Note that the second part of the address assigned here is the IEEE EIA-64 ID of the network interface card to which the address is added. You need to configure only one address per LAN in this way; all other nodes will get the aggregatable global unicast address assigned automatically by means of the neighbor discovery protocol.

ip address add 2000:10:20:30:20c:29ff:fec7:82f6/64 dev eth0: This is the same as the previous command, with the exception that here the ip tool is used instead of ifconfig.

ip address add fec0:10:20:30:29ff:fec7:82f6 dev eth0: This adds a site address to interface eth0. Note that this also has to be done on just one node per LAN. Instead of using the ip tool, you can do the same with ifconfig eth0 inet6 add fec0:10:20:30:29ff:fec7:82f6 dev eth0.

route -A inet6: This shows information about currently existing IPv6 routes.

route -A inet6 add 2000::/3 gw 3ffe:ffff:0:f101::1: This adds a route in which all addresses that start with binary 001 (decimal notes as 2) will be sent to the specified default gateway.

Once you have set up your IPv6 interface, you probably want to test that it works. From the Linux iputils package, some tools are available. For example, you can use the ping6 utility to ping other hosts to check for their availability. Note that when using ping6, you always need to specify the interface you want to send the ping packets from, such as ping6 -I eth0 fe80::2e0:18ff: fe90:9205. From the same iputils package, other tools are available, such as traceroute6, which can trace the route to a given destination, and tracepath6, which does more or less the same but without the need to use superuser privileges. You'll learn more about these tools in the "Tuning and Troubleshooting" section of this chapter.

Managing Routes

Until now, you have read about the way you can provide a network interface with an IP address. To be completely functional on the network, you have to specify some routes as well. At a minimum, you need to set the default route. This route specifies where packets need to be sent that don't have a destination on the local network. The IP address of the router used for the default route is always a router on the same network where your server resides; just consider it to be the door that helps you get out of the local network. To set the default route, you can use two tools: the ip tool and the route utility.

Setting the Default Route with route

The classical command to set the default route is the route command. If no options are used with this command, it will just show you a list of all routes that currently are defined on this host; you can see an example of this in Figure 13-13. When you use the route command without options, the command will always try to resolve the name for a given IP address. This takes some time. If you don't want any name resolving to occur, use the option -n; this will make the command a lot faster.

```
laksmi:/ # route
Kernel IP routing table
Destination      Gateway            Genmask          Flags Metric Ref    Use Iface
192.168.1.0      *                  255.255.255.0    U     0      0        0 eth0
link-local       *                  255.255.0.0      U     0      0        0 eth0
loopback         *                  255.0.0.0        U     0      0        0 lo
default          192.168.1.254      0.0.0.0          UG    0      0        0 eth0
laksmi:/ #
```

Figure 13-13. *The* route *command gives an overview of all routes that are currently defined.*

In the output of the route command, several columns are displayed, as shown in Figure 13-13. The first column mentions the destination; this is the network or host for which a route is defined. Next you can see the gateway. This is the router that needs to be contacted to reach the destination specified. If in the Gateway column you see a *, this means the local host is the gateway for that destination. For external routers that are used as the destination, you will see the IP address (or name) of that router. Next you see the Genmask, which is the subnet mask used on the specified destination. Then the Flags, Metric, Ref, and Use columns show some more detailed information. First the Flags parameter shows whether the route is up. Ordinarily, all routes should be flagged with a U, indicating the route is up. For the default gateway, you'll also see the flag G. Other flags do exist but are applied only if a dynamic routing protocol is used. Dynamic routing is outside the scope of this chapter. Next, the Metric parameter defines the distance for a given network. Since in this example all networks are connected directly, you can see the metric 0 in all columns. The Ref column isn't used in the Linux kernel. The last column is Use, which indicates the amount of lookups appearing for this route. Finally, the Iface column tells you what network interface is used to route packets.

To specify a route, the minimum you need to specify is which network you want to add an entry to and which router is used as a gateway. All the other information is added automatically. For example, if you want to specify that the router with IP address 192.168.1.254 should be used as the default gateway, use the command route add default gw 192.168.1.254.

Note In most cases, you will just use a simple static route on your Linux server. If it is a part of a complex network where several routers communicate with each other, you can also install a routing daemon. The task of such a routing daemon is to exchange information with other routers and in that way make sure routing tables are automatically filled with the right entries. To do this on SUSE Linux Enterprise Server, first install the quagga package, and next use insserc bgpd to activate dynamic routing.

If you need to change the default gateway, you should be aware that you have to remove the old route first. You can do this with the route del command. For example, to remove the current setting for the default gateway so that you can specify a new route, use route del default gw.

Using the ip Tool to Specify the Default Gateway

If you know what information has to be entered when defining a route, it is easy to do it with either the route or the ip tool. The syntax has only minor differences. To set the default gateway to 192.168.1.254 using the ip tool, use the ip route add default via 192.168.1.254 command. This command makes sure all packets sent to on-local destinations go through 192.168.1.254. Likewise, you can delete the default route with ip route del default. It doesn't really matter whether you use route or ip route add to set routing information; both tools have the same result.

Storing Routing Information

When you enter information such as the default gateway that should be used from the command line, it will be lost the next time you reboot your server. To make sure the information is persistent after a reboot, you can store it in the /etc/sysconfig/network/routes file. This file is read every time the network is activated. The entry used in this file to store the default route is not complex:

```
default 192.168.1.254 - -
```

You don't need anything else to specify the default route. The first entry in the routes file gives the network for which the route is created. Then in the second column, you see the IP address of the router that should be used. The third column can specify the subnet mask of the destination network, but you don't need a subnet mask for the default route specification. In the last column, you can specify the interface packets through which this gateway should be sent. On a server with one network card only, this column doesn't need to be specified either.

Configuring the DNS Resolver

If you want to configure a network connection manually, you also need to specify what DNS name server should be used. This is the DNS *resolver*. On Linux you do this by modifying the file /etc/resolv.conf. Typically in this file you will find the IP address of at least two DNS name servers and a search domain. The nameserver specification indicates what DNS name server should be contacted to translate DNS names to IP addresses, and vice versa. The search domain specifies what domain name should be appended if an incomplete host name is used. Listing 13-2 shows an example of the content of /etc/resolv.conf.

Listing 13-2. *Example of* /etc/resolv.conf

```
nameserver 192.168.1.10
nameserver 193.79.237.39
search sandervanvugt.com
```

In Listing 13-2, you see that name server 192.168.1.10 is used as the default name server. All DNS requests will be sent to that name server. Only if this server doesn't respond to DNS queries is the second server in the list contacted. Make sure always to specify the addresses of two name servers. You can use a third name server as well, but you probably will never use one; this is because it is contacted only if the first *and* the second name servers are unavailable. The third line of Listing 13-2 specifies the search domain. So if a user, for example, uses the command ping ftp, which uses an incomplete host name, then the name of the domain specified with the search option in resolv.conf is added automatically to it; therefore, with resolv.conf in Listing 13-2, the command ping ftp would cause the server ftp.sandervanvugt.com to answer.

The Role of nsswitch.conf

Most people consider it evident that DNS is used to resolve host names to IP addresses. This, however, is not the case. On every Linux box, the file /etc/nsswitch.conf determines what exactly should happen when translating a host name to an IP address, and vice versa. Many things are specified in this file, but for resolving host names, only the following lines are important:

```
hosts:          files dns
networks:       files dns
```

These two lines specify that for resolving host names, as well as network names, first "files" should be used. In that case, for resolving host names, the file /etc/hosts will be used, and for resolving network names, it will be the file /etc/networks. If the files don't contain more information about the given host, then the DNS subsystem will be used with that configuration. This way, an administrator can keep resolving the frequently accessed host locally and contact the DNS server only if the files don't have information about the host.

Using /etc/hosts

Using the /etc/hosts file to resolve host names to IP addresses, and the other way around, is one of the oldest ways to do it. It is rather primitive, because the file has to be maintained on every host where you need it and because no synchronization is established between hosts. However, it is a fast way to make information available locally that needs to be available locally. In fact, using the /etc/hosts file makes name resolving faster and reduces Internet traffic; in addition, you can use it to add some host names that need to be available locally only. Listing 13-3 shows the contents of this file as it is created after a default installation of SUSE Linux Enterprise Server.

Listing 13-3. *Example of* /etc/hosts

```
#
# hosts      This file describes a number of hostname-to-address
#                 mappings for the TCP/IP subsystem. It is mostly
#                 used at boot time, when no name servers are running.
#                 On small systems, this file can be used instead of a
#                 "named" name server.
# Syntax:
#
# IP-Address Full-Qualified-Hostname Short-Hostname
#
```

```
127.0.0.1          localhost

# special IPv6 addresses
::1                localhost ipv6-localhost ipv6-loopback

fe00::0            ipv6-localnet

ff00::0            ipv6-mcastprefix
ff02::1            ipv6-allnodes
ff02::2            ipv6-allrouters
ff02::3            ipv6-allhosts
127.0.0.2          laksmi.sandervanvugt.com laksmi
192.168.1.125      laksmi.sandervanvugt.com laksmi
```

As you can see, the contents of the /etc/hosts file are rather simple. First you see the IP address of the host, which can be an IPv4 as well as an IPv6 IP address. Next, you see the fully qualified host name. This is the name of the host, followed by its DNS suffix. Last, you see the short host name. It will, however, also work if you use just the IP address followed by the name of the host you want to add. For example, the following will also work:

```
192.168.1.130  damayanti
```

In most cases, it is not necessary to specify anything in /etc/hosts; if, however, you want to make sure certain information can be resolved faster or can be resolved when the records are not available in DNS, it is a good idea to use this file.

Tuning and Troubleshooting

Based on the previous information, you should now have a working network connection. Even if now it is working fine, you sometimes might need to do some tuning and troubleshooting, and that's exactly what the following sections are about. You will learn how to test that everything is working the way it should be working, and you'll learn how to monitor what is happening on the network as well as the network interface.

Testing Connectivity

After configuring a network card, you want to make sure it is working the way it should work. To do this, the ping command is one of your best options. It's easy to use; just enter the command followed by the name or address of the host you want to test connectivity to, for example ping www.novell.com. This will force ping to start uninterrupted output; you can interrupt it by using the Ctrl+C key sequence. Using ping in a clever way, you can test a lot with it. I recommend using it in a certain order:

1. Ping localhost. If you pass this test, you have verified that the IP stack on your local machine is working properly. Also ping yourself to make sure the IP address you've configured works.

2. Ping a machine on the local network by using its IP address; if this works, you have verified that IP is bound to the network board of your server properly and that it can connect to other nodes on the network. If it fails, first make sure the ping packet isn't filtered out by a firewall policy on the remote host. Next, you need to check the information you have entered with the ifconfig or ip command; it could, for example, be that you have made an error entering the subnet mask for your network interface.

3. Ping a machine on the Internet using its IP address. The address 137.65.1.1 is a good bet; it is a server at Novell that has never failed me in the past ten years. Of course, you can use any other host where you know the IP address. If you do use a server on the Internet, make sure it normally is reachable. Many servers on the Internet are firewalled against ping nowadays. If this test is successful, you have verified all the routers between the local host and the destination. If it fails, somewhere in the routing chain there is an error. Check route -n on your local host to see whether the default route is defined.

4. Ping a machine on the Internet, based on its DNS name. If this test succeeds, everything is working. If it isn't, while test 3 is successful, make sure you have entered the name of the DNS server that should be used in /etc/resolv.conf.

In many cases, you will use the ping command without options, but Table 13-1 lists a few options that can be useful.

Table 13-1. *Useful* ping *Options*

Option	Description
-c *count*	Specifies the number of packets to be sent. Ping will terminate automatically after reaching this number. Use ping -c 5 somehost to send five packets only to somehost, for example.
-l *device*	Specifies the name of the network device that should be used. This is useful on a computer with several network devices. Use ping -l eth0 somehost to make sure packets to somehost are sent out on eth0, for example.
-i *seconds*	Specifies the number of seconds to wait between individual ping packets. The default setting is one second. Use ping -i 10 somehost to send one packet to somehost every ten seconds, for example.
-f	Sends packets as fast as possible but only after a reply comes in; an example of this is ping -f somehost.
-l	Sends packets without waiting for a reply. In combination with the -f option, this can cause a Denial of Service attack on the target host; therefore, you should not usually use these two options together.
-t *ttl*	Sets the Time To Live (ttl) for packets that are sent. This indicates the maximum number of routers that may be crossed to a destination.
-b	Sends packets to the broadcast address of the network. This causes every host that is up and allowed to answer ping packets to reply. Notice that in most environments, this option is useless, because such traffic will be filtered out by the firewall.

■**Note** To protect against a Denial of Service attack, many hosts are configured not to answer a ping request. Therefore, when testing connectivity, make sure you use a host that is allowed to answer.

Testing Routability

If you can ping your default router but you cannot ping a given host on the Internet, something is wrong with one of the routers between your network and the destination host. To find out where exactly it goes wrong, you can use the traceroute command. The traceroute command uses the Time To Live value of the UDP datagrams it sends. The idea is that when the TTL reaches zero, a datagram is discarded by the router that discards the packet, and a message is sent to the sender. When starting, traceroute uses the TTL 0, which causes the packet to be discarded already by the first router. This allows traceroute to identify the first router. Next, it sends the packet to the target destination again, but with a TTL of 1. This causes the packet to be discarded by the second router. traceroute goes on this way until it reaches the final destination.

To use traceroute, you usually put the host name as the argument. For example, you'd use traceroute www.novell.com. It is, however, possible to put in the IP address of a host. The result will look like Figure 13-14.

```
Terminal                                                             _ □ ×
File  Edit  View  Terminal  Tabs  Help
laksmi:/ # traceroute www.novell.com
traceroute to www.novell.com (130.57.5.25), 30 hops max, 40 byte packets
 1   192.168.1.254 (192.168.1.254)  25.075 ms   18.738 ms    16.133 ms
 2   195.190.249.90 (195.190.249.90)  44.555 ms   46.594 ms   16.527 ms
 3   42.ge-4-0-0.xr1.3d12.xs4all.net (194.109.5.49)  25.971 ms   18.744 ms   1
8.310 ms
 4   asd-dc2-ias-ur10.nl.kpn.net (194.151.244.74)  21.964 ms   19.623 ms    15.
754 ms
 5   * * *
 6   * * *
 7   asd2-rou-1021.NL.eurorings.net (134.222.230.78)  38.238 ms   33.665 ms
30.715 ms
 8   nyk-s1-rou-1001.US.eurorings.net (134.222.231.230)  116.567 ms   107.140
ms   106.014 ms
 9   nyk-s1-rou-1003.US.eurorings.net (134.222.230.98)  116.863 ms   125.124 m
s   123.473 ms
10   mar1-pos-1-0.newyorknyd.savvis.net (208.173.134.69)  118.261 ms   115.119
 ms   112.258 ms
11   bcs2-so-3-2-0.NewYork.savvis.net (204.70.193.30)  108.618 ms   105.405 ms
   102.385 ms
12   bcs2-so-4-0-0.Washington.savvis.net (204.70.192.1)  113.547 ms   123.805
ms   115.693 ms
13   bcs1-so-7-0-0.Washington.savvis.net (204.70.192.33)  111.401 ms   106.096
 ms   101.562 ms
14   dcr1-so-3-0-0.Atlanta.savvis.net (204.70.192.53)  110.257 ms   106.234 ms
   102.050 ms
15   dcr1-so-1-3-0.dallas.savvis.net (204.70.192.78)  141.943 ms   150.728 ms
```

Figure 13-14. *The* traceroute *command shows router for router the exact route that is used to a given destination.*

In the traceroute command, you will see every router that is passed. For each router, the name of the router is displayed, followed by the IP address of that router, which is followed by the round-trip times of the three packets that were sent to that router.

Testing Availability of Services

When the ping test and the traceroute test both indicate everything is working, you are the proud owner of a working network interface. The next step you may need to take is to test the availability of services. You have two methods of testing service availability: those for services on your computer or those for services on external computers. Many tools are available to test service availability. I won't try to be exhaustive here, but I will discuss two of the most popular tools to check service availability. First, you can use the netstat tool, which can test the availability of services on the host where you run the command. Then, you will read about nmap, which you can use to test the availability of services on other hosts.

Using netstat to Check Your Server

If you want to know what services are available on your server, and what exactly these services are doing, the `netstat` command is an excellent choice. `netstat` has many options; to see the most useful information offered by it, use the `-patune` options. These options have the following meanings:

- `-p` makes sure you see information about programs connected to ports.
- `-a` will show you everything there is to show.
- `-t` looks at TCP ports.
- `-u` shows information for UDP ports.
- `-n` makes sure that IP addresses are not translated into DNS names.
- `-e` makes sure some extended information is displayed as well.

If you think `netstat -patune` offers just too much information, use `netstat -patun` instead. The amount of information offered in that case is slightly shorter, which makes it easier to get the information you really need. In Figure 13-15 you can see what the first screen of output generated by `netstat -patune` looks like.

```
Active Internet connections (servers and established)
Proto Recv-Q Send-Q Local Address           Foreign Address         State
    User       Inode       PID/Program name
tcp        0      0 0.0.0.0:5989            0.0.0.0:*               LISTEN
    0          8639        2768/owcimomd
tcp        0      0 0.0.0.0:389             0.0.0.0:*               LISTEN
    0          7057        2886/slapd
tcp        0      0 192.168.1.125:427       0.0.0.0:*               LISTEN
    0          6592        2697/slpd
tcp        0      0 127.0.0.1:427           0.0.0.0:*               LISTEN
    0          6591        2697/slpd
tcp        0      0 0.0.0.0:111             0.0.0.0:*               LISTEN
    0          6523        2655/portmap
tcp        0      0 127.0.0.1:2544          0.0.0.0:*               LISTEN
    0          6843        2785/zmd
tcp        0      0 0.0.0.0:631             0.0.0.0:*               LISTEN
    0          8812        2803/cupsd
tcp        0      0 127.0.0.1:25            0.0.0.0:*               LISTEN
    0          7705        3148/master
tcp        1      0 127.0.0.1:37652         127.0.0.1:427           CLOSE_WAI
T   0          7075        2886/slapd
tcp        0      0 :::389                  :::*                    LISTEN
    0          7056        2886/slapd
tcp        0      0 :::22                   :::*                    LISTEN
    0          7453        3044/sshd
tcp        0      0 ::1:25                  :::*                    LISTEN
lines 1-14/21 63%
```

Figure 13-15. *When used with the option* `-patune`, `netstat` *gives you everything you need to know about active network services.*

The netstat command gives a lot of information when used with the -patune options. In Figure 13-15, the information described in Table 13-2 appears.

Table 13-2. *Information Offered by* netstat -patune

Item	Explanation
Proto	The protocol that is used. This can be TCP or UDP.
Recv-Q	The number of packets waiting in the receive queue for this port at the moment netstat was used.
Send-Q	The number of packets waiting to be sent for this port at the moment netstat was used.
Local Address	The local socket address. This address includes the local IP address, followed by the port number that is used.
Foreign Address	The address of the foreign host that currently has an open connection to this host, if any.
State	The current state of the protocol connected to the mentioned port.
User	The numeric user ID of the user with whose permissions the process is started.
Inode	The inode(s) of files that currently are opened by the process.
PID/Program name	The PID and name of the program that has currently claimed the mentioned port.

As you can see, netstat gives a complete overview of what is happening on your server. It is especially useful if you get error messages such as port already in use. In combination with the grep utility, it is easy to find out what program is currently holding a port open, and if so required, you can easily terminate that program. For example, to find out what program is using port 123, use netstat -patune | grep 123.

Using nmap to Check Service Availability on Remote Servers

netstat is a cool tool, but it works only on the host where you run the command. Sometimes, to find out why you cannot connect to a given service on a given host, you would like to know whether the service you want to connect to is available at all. To do that, you can use the nmap command. nmap is an expert tool that helps you find out what services are offered by another host; if used properly, it can even do that in stealth mode so the owner of that host will never know you were there. You should be aware that running a *port scan* to monitor open ports on a given host is considered an intrusion by many administrators, so be careful what you are doing with it; you may run into trouble if you are "nmapping" a host that isn't owned by you without telling its owner.

If you really want to keep things simple, just use nmap on a given host without arguments. For example, nmap 10.0.0.10 would do a basic scan on host 10.0.0.10 to find out what common ports are open on it. For day-to-day use, this gives a good result; see Figure 13-16 for an example.

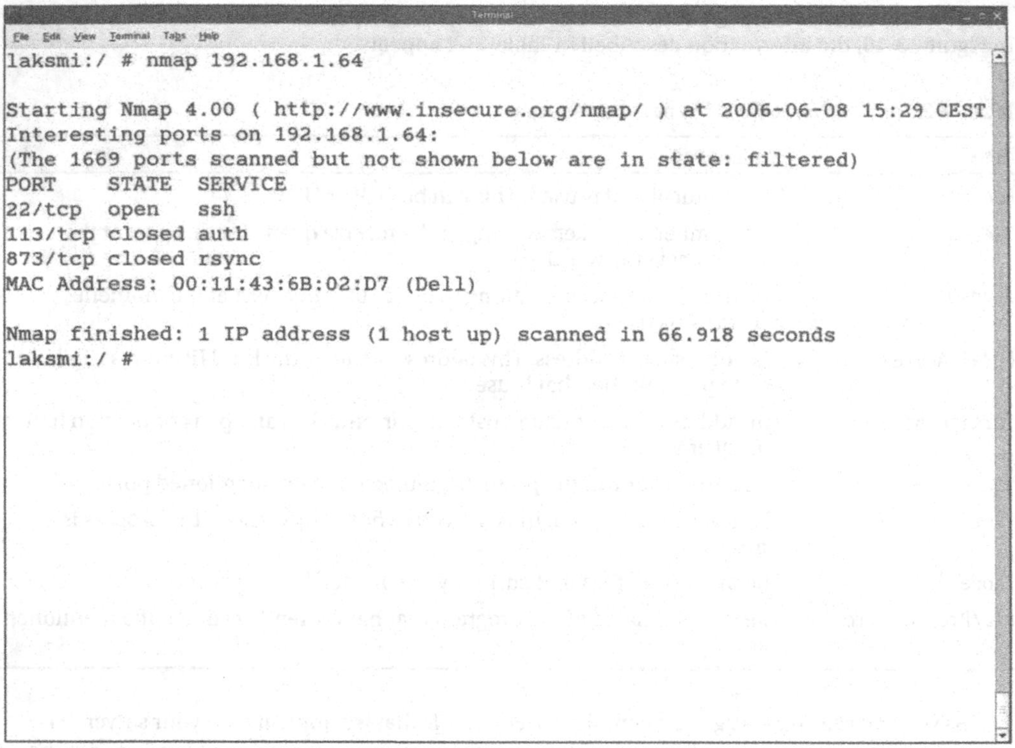

```
File Edit View Terminal Tabs Help
laksmi:/ # nmap 192.168.1.64

Starting Nmap 4.00 ( http://www.insecure.org/nmap/ ) at 2006-06-08 15:29 CEST
Interesting ports on 192.168.1.64:
(The 1669 ports scanned but not shown below are in state: filtered)
PORT     STATE  SERVICE
22/tcp   open   ssh
113/tcp  closed auth
873/tcp  closed rsync
MAC Address: 00:11:43:6B:02:D7 (Dell)

Nmap finished: 1 IP address (1 host up) scanned in 66.918 seconds
laksmi:/ #
```

Figure 13-16. *To see what ports are open on a remote host, just run* netstat *against it without any other options.*

A common reason why the previous test could fail is that nmap ordinarily tries to ping its targets first. On many hosts, ping is blocked. These hosts won't show any result when you do an nmap on them. To make sure it is working also in that case, use the -P0 option, which disables ping. Another nice option is the option -O, which tries to guess the operating system that is on the target host. And if you want to make sure both TCP and UDP ports are scanned, you should include -sT and -sU as well. So, the command becomes somewhat longer already: nmap -sT -sU -P0 -O 192.168.1.64 would scan the target host with all those options.

In the previous command, you will most likely get a better result; however, the scan is rather noisy. If you want nmap to do a stealth scan, use an option such as -sF (FIN scan), -sX (Christmas tree scan), or -sN (NULL scan). All of these will perform a stealth scan in a different way; this way, you can be certain that the target host will never know you were there. But let's be honest, why would you need that? After all, this chapter is about scanning hosts in your own network, isn't it? Table 13-3 summarizes the most useful nmap options.

Table 13-3. *Most Useful* nmap *Options*

Option	Meaning
-PO	Makes sure no ping packets are sent to the target.
-O	Tries to do an OS fingerprinting. This option is likely to reveal what operating system is used on the target.
-sT	Scans for open TCP ports.
-sU	Scans for UDP ports.
-sF	Sends an incomplete TCP packet. This packet contains just the TCP FIN bit. If a port is closed, a TCP RST (reset) is sent to indicate that the packet is erroneous. If the port is open, nothing is sent in return.
-sN	Like with -sF, sends an incomplete packet. This time, the TCP flag header is completely empty. This causes a closed port to send a TCP RST, indicating something is wrong. An open port would send nothing in return.
-sX	This is the so-called Christmas tree packet. In this packet, the TCP FIN, PSH, and URG flags are set, making it a rather unusual packet. Open ports would not reply to such a packet; closed ports reply with an RST packet.

Monitoring the Network Interface

To monitor what's happening on your server's network cards, two useful tools are available. IPTraf offers a menu-driven interface from which you can monitor protocol activity, and the iftop utility shows how much bandwidth is used by a given connection.

Monitoring Protocol Activity with IPTraf

IPTraf is not installed by default, so make sure it is installed (check Chapter 9 for more details) before you try to launch it from the command line with the iptraf command. As shown in Figure 13-17, IPTraf uses a menu interface. In this interface, several menu options are available:

IP Traffic Monitor: From this option, you can tell IPTraf to monitor what's happening on the network interfaces in your server. You can select one particular network interface, but it is possible to check all the interfaces at the same time as well. When a connection is established, you will see the connection happening in real time, indicating with what other node the connection is established and how many packets are flowing across the connection.

General Interface Statistics: From here you can see information about what's happening on a network board. This is rather generic information, such as the amount of packets sent and received by the network interface, and therefore is not the most useful information that is available.

Detailed Interface Statistics: This is the same as the previous option, but it provides more detail, such as the amount of packets sent of a specific protocol type.

Statistical breakdown: This option offers the possibility to divide the incoming information in different columns, sorted by the protocols in use.

LAN Station Monitor: This option gives you an overview of most active stations on the LAN. Be aware, however, that only packets coming in on the host where you are running IPTraf are shown by the station monitor.

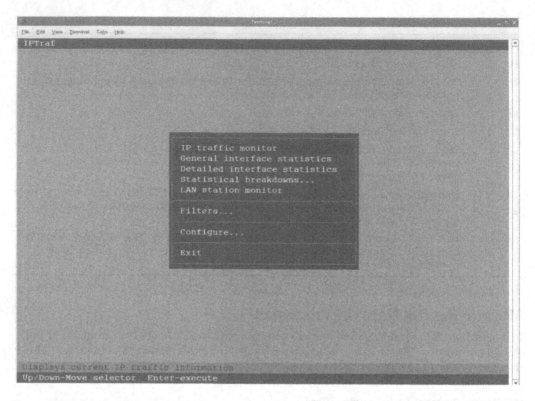

Figure 13-17. *The IPTraf tool offers different menu options to see what's happening on your server.*

In addition to these options, which you can use to specify how IPTraf should do its work, you can use a Filter option and a Configure option. The Filter option specifies what kind of packets you want to see, and the Configure option configures IPTraf itself; for example, an option allows you to specify what colors are used in the IPTraf interface.

Monitoring Bandwidth Usage with iftop

The iftop utility is simple but efficient. It shows you who has an open connection to your server and how much bandwidth is currently consumed by that connection. This overview displays the total of transmitted and received packets; by means of a black bar that moves up and down, you can also get an indication of actual bandwidth usage by a certain connection. Just run iftop from the command line, and it will display its results window, as shown in Figure 13-18.

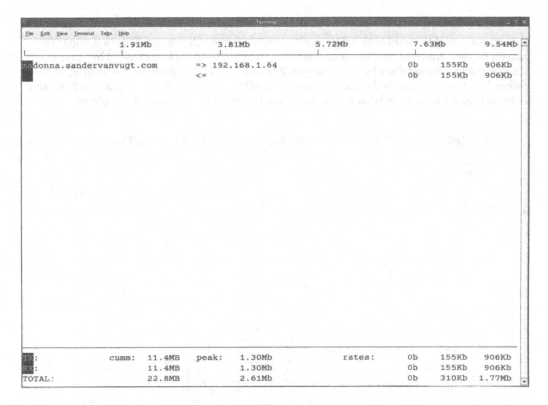

Figure 13-18. *The* iftop *utility displays actual bandwidth usage on your server.*

Monitoring Network Traffic

In addition to monitoring what is happening on the local network boards of your server, some excellent tools are available to see what is happening on the network. The mother of all of these tools is tcpdump, which just dumps IP packets on the console from where you run it. Ethereal is built on top of that and can be used to view network packets from a graphical interface. This allows you to see what protocols are used, who is sending the packets, and even what is inside them. Before starting with these tools, you should realize that they monitor only what they can see. If you are on a shared network where every node sees every packet coming by, it is easy to monitor everything sent by all hosts on the network. This is no longer the case on modern switched networks, though. If you are on a switch, you can see only those packets that are addressed to the host from where you run the monitoring software.

Other solutions can capture packets from other nodes anyway, such as the ARP poisoning tool Ettercap. This tool is not part of the SUSE Linux Enterprise Server software, though, and is therefore not covered in this book. Another option to see all the packets that are sent on the network is to connect the computer you are capturing the packets from to the management port of your switch; that way, you will see all packets sent on the network. Of course, you would use these tools only in a responsible way, because they do allow you to see exactly what a user is doing. For some protocols (Telnet, SMTP, and POP, for example), even user passwords can be snooped with these tools. Note that some companies have a clear policy against using tools like this in an unprofessional way.

Using tcpdump

`tcpdump` is a straightforward tool; it does exactly what its name indicates it will do: it dumps TCP packets on the console of your machine. That way, you can see all packets received by the network board of your server scrolling by on the screen. By default it will just show the first 96 bytes of every packet, but if you need more details, you can start it with `-v` or even with `-vv` so that it will be more verbose. Figure 13-19 shows what it looks like if you run the command with the `-v` option.

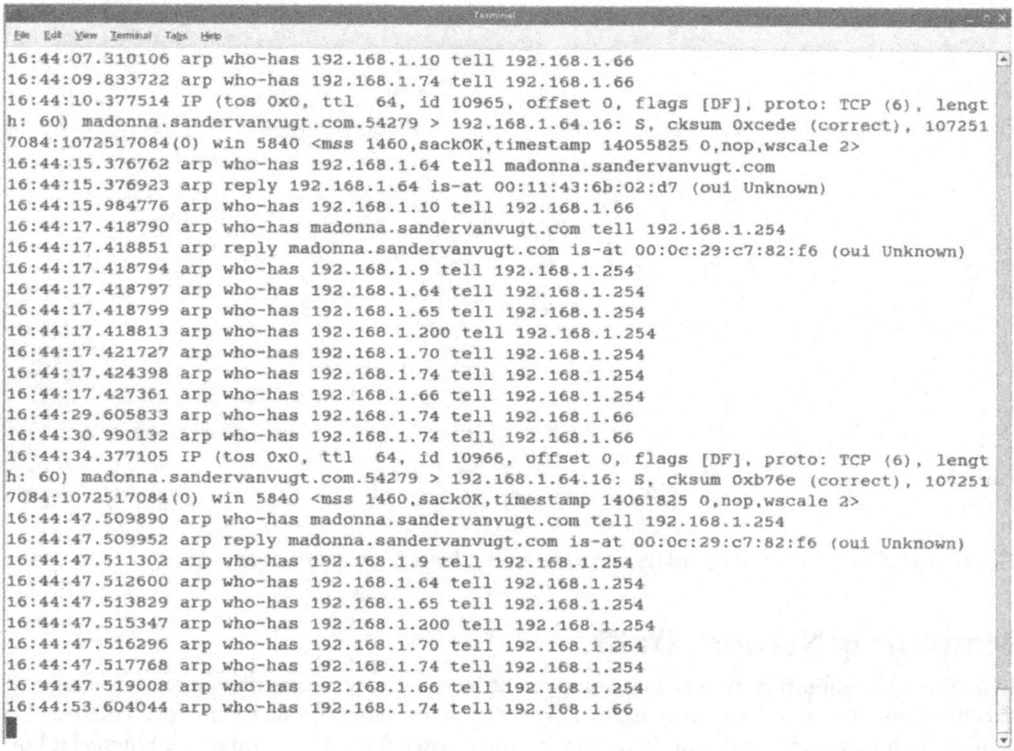

```
16:44:07.310106 arp who-has 192.168.1.10 tell 192.168.1.66
16:44:09.833722 arp who-has 192.168.1.74 tell 192.168.1.66
16:44:10.377514 IP (tos 0x0, ttl  64, id 10965, offset 0, flags [DF], proto: TCP (6), lengt
h: 60) madonna.sandervanvugt.com.54279 > 192.168.1.64.16: S, cksum 0xcede (correct), 107251
7084:1072517084(0) win 5840 <mss 1460,sackOK,timestamp 14055825 0,nop,wscale 2>
16:44:15.376762 arp who-has 192.168.1.64 tell madonna.sandervanvugt.com
16:44:15.376923 arp reply 192.168.1.64 is-at 00:11:43:6b:02:d7 (oui Unknown)
16:44:15.984776 arp who-has 192.168.1.10 tell 192.168.1.66
16:44:17.418790 arp who-has madonna.sandervanvugt.com tell 192.168.1.254
16:44:17.418851 arp reply madonna.sandervanvugt.com is-at 00:0c:29:c7:82:f6 (oui Unknown)
16:44:17.418794 arp who-has 192.168.1.9 tell 192.168.1.254
16:44:17.418797 arp who-has 192.168.1.64 tell 192.168.1.254
16:44:17.418799 arp who-has 192.168.1.65 tell 192.168.1.254
16:44:17.418813 arp who-has 192.168.1.200 tell 192.168.1.254
16:44:17.421727 arp who-has 192.168.1.70 tell 192.168.1.254
16:44:17.424398 arp who-has 192.168.1.74 tell 192.168.1.254
16:44:17.427361 arp who-has 192.168.1.66 tell 192.168.1.254
16:44:29.605833 arp who-has 192.168.1.74 tell 192.168.1.66
16:44:30.990132 arp who-has 192.168.1.74 tell 192.168.1.66
16:44:34.377105 IP (tos 0x0, ttl  64, id 10966, offset 0, flags [DF], proto: TCP (6), lengt
h: 60) madonna.sandervanvugt.com.54279 > 192.168.1.64.16: S, cksum 0xb76e (correct), 107251
7084:1072517084(0) win 5840 <mss 1460,sackOK,timestamp 14061825 0,nop,wscale 2>
16:44:47.509890 arp who-has madonna.sandervanvugt.com tell 192.168.1.254
16:44:47.509952 arp reply madonna.sandervanvugt.com is-at 00:0c:29:c7:82:f6 (oui Unknown)
16:44:47.511302 arp who-has 192.168.1.9 tell 192.168.1.254
16:44:47.512600 arp who-has 192.168.1.64 tell 192.168.1.254
16:44:47.513829 arp who-has 192.168.1.65 tell 192.168.1.254
16:44:47.515347 arp who-has 192.168.1.200 tell 192.168.1.254
16:44:47.516296 arp who-has 192.168.1.70 tell 192.168.1.254
16:44:47.517768 arp who-has 192.168.1.74 tell 192.168.1.254
16:44:47.519008 arp who-has 192.168.1.66 tell 192.168.1.254
16:44:53.604044 arp who-has 192.168.1.74 tell 192.168.1.66
```

Figure 13-19. *The purpose of* `tcpdump` *is simple; it just dumps complete TCP packets on your console!*

On a very busy server, `tcpdump` is not useful. The information passes by way too fast to see what is happening. In that case, it makes sense to pipe its output to a file and `grep` on that file for the information you really need. `tcpdump`, after all, is an excellent tool to capture packets, but it isn't the best solution available if you want to do something with the captured packets. Ethereal, on the contrary, is.

Analyzing Packets with Ethereal

Ethereal provides a graphical interface you can use to capture and analyze packets. You can start it from the application browser's System category. To start an Ethereal capture session, in Ethereal select Capture ➤ Options. In the window that pops up, make sure the interface is selected that you want to use to perform your packet capture (see Figure 13-20). Then on the same screen, click Start to start the packet capture.

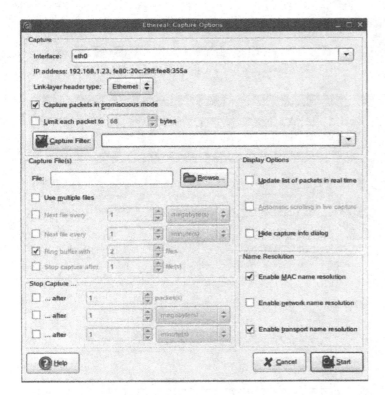

Figure 13-20. *Before starting an Ethereal packet capture, select the interface you want to perform the packet capture on, and click Start.*

Ethereal will now start filling its buffers. While this is happening, you don't see any packet contents. To see the content of the packet buffer, you need to click the Stop button. As a result, you'll see the screen shown in Figure 13-21. On this screen, you can sort packets and see packet details. To sort the packets, click one of the columns. By default, they are sorted on the number they came in with, but if you click the Source column, for example, you can sort the packets on their source addresses; when you click the Protocol column, you can sort them by the protocol that was used. You can click any of the columns in the packet results screen to filter the packet display.

When you click one of the packets, more details appear. For every packet that is captured, you can analyze all its layers. The top part of the Ethereal capture results screen just displays the list of packets; after selecting a packet in the lower part, you can see the different headers the packet contains. If for any of these parts you really need to see details, click the part you want to tune, and the contents of the selected part of the packet will appear. If available, you may even see a password that was sent in plain text over the network!

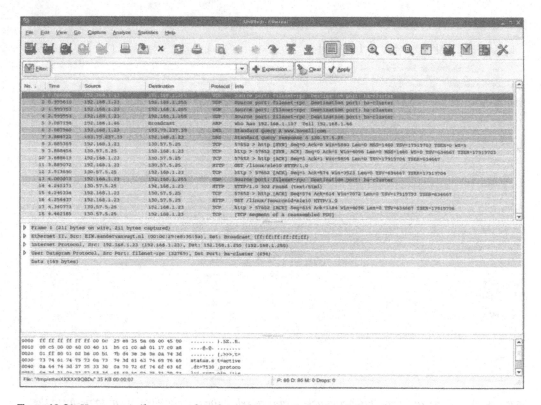

Figure 13-21. *You can easily sort packets from the packet's result window.*

Using the GNOME Network Tools

Another useful system component to analyze what's happening on your server is the GNOME Network Tools. You can start this utility from the GNOME Application Selector ➤ System section, which offers virtually all that has been discussed so far, but it is not as good as most of the individual tools. For example, a port scanner looks for open ports on a target host, but it has no options to specify how exactly the scan should be performed. It is a useful tool if you want to be able to tune and monitor what's happening on your network from one single interface, though. From the GNOME Network Tools, the following options are offered:

Devices: Use this tab to get statistics about the different network devices in your server. Per device you see an overview of protocols that are used on the selected device.

Ping: On the Ping tab, you can enter the IP address or name of a host you want to ping. By default five packets will be sent, but you can tune this value as needed.

Netstat: On this tab, you can choose to see the routing table currently in use on your server, a list of active network services, or the multicast information in use on your server.

Traceroute: Use this tab to see what route is used to connect to any host on the Internet.

Port Scan: On this tab, you can perform a simple port scan. It is, however, not as powerful as nmap because you can use it with all its options from the command line.

Lookup: On this tab, which you can see in Figure 13-22, you can access the nslookup utility to query a DNS server. For example, you can enter the name of any server on the Internet and then click the Lookup button; it will show some details about that server such as the IP address and the TTL in use for its DNS entry.

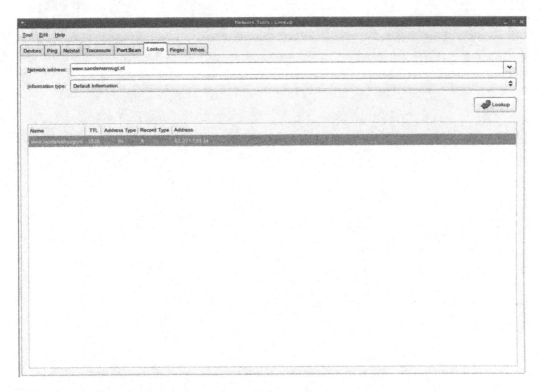

Figure 13-22. *On the Lookup tab in the GNOME Network Tools, you can query DNS for more information about any server on the Internet.*

Finger: The finger service is a legacy service that allows you to get more information about a user on a host that has the finger service enabled. You are, however, not likely to find such a host, because the finger service is unsecure.

Whois: If installed, the whois service allows you to query a DNS domain for registration information. The whois service, however, is by default not installed on SUSE Linux Enterprise Server.

Summary

In this chapter, you learned everything you need to know to configure a network interface, analyze what the network interface is doing, and troubleshoot it if you have any problems with it. I discussed different configuration methods and tools you can use for troubleshooting. In the next chapter, you will learn how to configure a print server on Linux.

■■■

## CHAPTER 14

Configuring a CUPS Print Server

Although in most organizations printers are connected to a dedicated print server, it is possible to configure SUSE Linux Enterprise Server as a print server. When choosing this option, you can choose between the two protocols that are available for printing: the traditional LPD-based printing solution and the modern Common Unix Print Server (CUPS) solution. In this chapter, I discuss the CUPS solution since it offers some significant improvements as compared to the older LPD-based system.

One of the problems with legacy Unix printing systems is that two different flavors existed to handle printers: the System V and the BSD variant. CUPS stands above both of them while at the same time offers compatibility to both systems. Another major advantage of CUPS is its support for the Internet Printing Protocol (IPP). This protocol makes it possible to select printers and print from a browser interface. Last, CUPS offers some significant improvements in the security that you can add to printers.

Installing a CUPS Printer

This section describes what you need to do to install a simple local CUPS printer; later in this chapter, you will learn about other options for configuring a printer.

Tip Installing a printer on SUSE Linux Enterprise Server can be as easy as connecting it to your machine. The hardware detection module will detect the printer and will also see what type of printer it is. All you need to do is click OK to get working. The following procedure covers how to manually install a printer because this allows you as the administrator to make more choices about how to configure the printer.

Here are the steps:

1. Start YaST. From YaST, select Hardware ➤ Printer, and click the icon to start the CUPS management interface.

2. On the Printer Configuration screen, click Add to start adding a new printer.

3. The Printer Type screen allows you to choose between two types of printers. Select Directly Connected if the printer is connected directly to your computer, or select Network Printers to use a network protocol to connect to a printer that is somewhere on the network. In these steps, you will learn how to configure a directly connected printer. After selecting the printer type, click Next to continue.

4. Now you can specify how the printer is connected to your system. All current local printer access protocols are available. Choose one of the following types, and then click Next to continue:

- *Parallel Printer.* Select this option for a printer that is connected directly to a parallel port on your server.

- *USB Printer.* Select this option to configure a printer that is connected to the USB port of your computer.

- *Serial Printer.* Some printers are connected to the computer's serial port. Check this option if you want to configure such a printer.

- *IrDA Printer.* Select this option to connect to a printer that communicates with your computer with an infrared interface.

- *Bluetooth Printer.* Select this option to configure a printer that is connected via the wireless Bluetooth protocol to your printer.

5. When configuring the printer manually, you need to specify where CUPS can find the printer. As shown in Figure 14-1, for a parallel printer, for example, this would normally be /dev/lp0, although you can use any other device, as long as the printer is connected physically to that device. After specifying the device that the printer is connected to, click Next to continue.

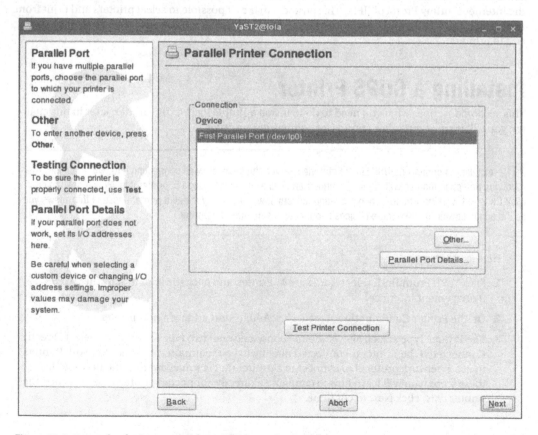

Figure 14-1. *Enter the device name where CUPS can find your printer.*

6. After identifying the way to connect to the printer, you need to configure the print queue. You must enter several properties for the queue:

   - *Name for Printing:* This is the name of the queue. I recommend using a name that is easily recognizable, especially if other printers are available on your network..

   - *Printer Description:* Here you can enter an optional description for the printer.

   - *Printer Location:* If so required, enter the name of the location of the printer in this field.

   - *Do Local Filtering:* Select this option to make sure the print job is formatted locally. This makes sense if you are installing a local printer or if you are installing a print server for clients that haven't formatted the print job yet.

7. Now you need to select the printer model. SUSE Linux Enterprise Server comes with a large database where several types of printers are available. If your printer type is not in the database and the manufacturer of your printer provides PPD files, you can select the Add PPD File to Database option to import the printer definition file in the printer database. After selecting the specific printer model you want to use, click Next to continue.

8. As you can see in Figure 14-2, the wizard now shows an overview of the options you have configured so far. On this screen, you can click the Test button to print a test page. If everything is OK, click OK. This writes the configuration to your server and will make the printer ready for use.

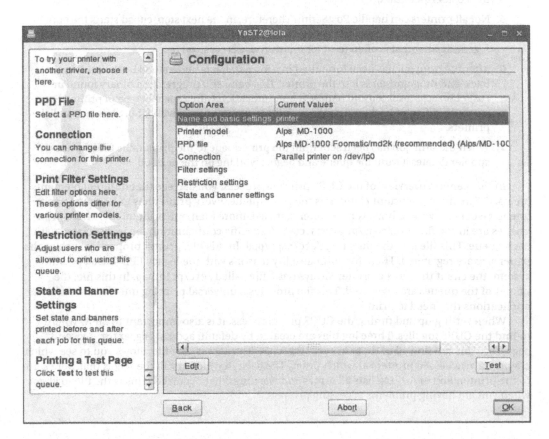

Figure 14-2. *From the configuration overview, you can use the Test button to check that everything is working correctly.*

Understanding CUPS

To manage a CUPS print environment properly, you need to understand how it works. Therefore, in this section you will learn what happens when a user sends a print job to the printer and how the CUPS print system is involved. In later sections in this chapter, I'll discuss all the different parts of the CUPS printing process in more depth.

1. Every print job starts with the user submitting a print job. If the user is a local user, this could happen by using the lpr command to submit the print job to the CUPS printer directly.

2. The printer client command (for example, lpr) determines in which queue the job needs to be placed. This queue is present as a directory in /var/spool/cups.

3. On a regular basis, the cupsd printer daemon checks the queues for changes, such as new jobs being submitted. If a print job is submitted, the CUPS daemon analyzes its data and submits it to the required filter.

4. The most important part in the CUPS printing process is the print filter. First, using the entries in /etc/cups/mime.types, CUPS determines the type of data that is submitted. Next, the data is converted to PostScript in all cases. Then the pstops program determines the number of pages the print job has. This leads to a print job that is ready but completely in the PostScript format.

5. Not all printers can handle PostScript. Therefore, in the next step, cupsd starts the appropriate filter to convert the print job to a format that is understood properly by the printer. A generic filter that is often used for this purpose is cupsomatic.

6. After the print job has been formatted in a format that is understood by the printer, the back-end program sends it to the printer. This back-end program is a binary found in /usr/lib/cups/backend and handles communication with a specific type of printer. For example, different back-end programs exist to communicate with USB, SMB, or parallel printers.

7. When the print job has been sent from the print queue to the printer, the CUPS print spooler deletes it from the queue and begins working on the next job.

In this generic overview of the CUPS printing process, you can see that different elements are used. The most important element is the print queue. Every printer has at least one print queue associated with it; however, a printer can have more than one print queue. These print queues are in the file /etc/cups/printers.conf. A specific configuration file is associated with each queue. This file is in the directory /etc/cups/ppd. In this file, printer properties such as the paper size are registered. Then, for compatibility reasons with the legacy LPD-based printing system, the client that uses a printer always has a file called /etc/printcap. In this file, the names of the queues are registered. This file provides a universal printing interface to different applications that need to print.

When setting up and tuning the CUPS print process, it is also important to know where to find the CUPS log files. Three log files are created by default: access_log, error_log, and page_log. You can find all of them in /var/log/cups. The access_log file allows you to see which clients have accessed printers at which times. The page_log file lists all the pages that were sent to the printer, and error_log lists all errors and warnings that occurred. This is the file to check when you are having problems accessing printers.

Managing CUPS

Several options are at your disposal for managing a CUPS environment. At the most fundamental level are the configuration files where you can configure the printers and can manage access restrictions. Although you can edit these with any standard editor, more accessible methods are also available:

- The lpadmin command is a flexible command-line utility that you can use for print server configuration.

- You can access CUPS's web interface at http://yourserver:631; it offers options for managing all aspects of the CUPS environment. However, before using the web interface to tune and manage CUPS, you need to set up a CUPS administrator. To add root as administrator for the CUPS environment, execute lppasswd -g sys -a root. The command will prompt for a password, and with this password, you can manage the complete CUPS environment via this web interface.

- You can use YaST for managing the CUPS environment as well. To start the YaST CUPS management interface, use the yast2 printer command.

Managing CUPS with YaST

Like for many other services, YaST is the primary program you will use for configuring the CUPS printing environment. The SUSE Hardware Plugger starts YaST automatically when a printer is attached. You have already read how to install a printer from YaST. In the following sections, you will learn how to set up your server as a print client that listens to other print servers on the network. Next, you will learn how to apply restrictions to a printer.

Installing a Print Client from YaST

One of the nice features of a CUPS print environment is the browsing feature. This allows a printer to discover for itself what other printers are present on the network. When browsing is enabled, the CUPS server uses broadcasts to send printer information to other clients on the network. When the server is configured to broadcast its information on the network, the client can discover the printers offered by the server automatically on the network. The following steps show how to set this up:

1. On the print server, start YaST. Next open the Printer Configuration dialog box, and select the printer that is already installed. Then click the Other button. From the drop-down list on this button, select CUPS Expert Settings. This opens the Expert CUPS Settings screen shown in Figure 14-3.

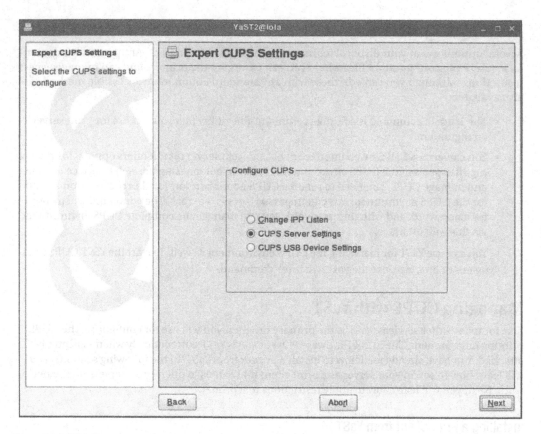

Figure 14-3. *The Expert CUPS Settings screen offers some advanced CUPS configuration options.*

2. Now select CUPS Server Settings, and click Next. This opens the CUPS Server Settings screen with some advanced server settings (see Figure 14-4).

3. To enable browsing, you need to take three steps. First, you need to enter the addresses you are allowing to browse to printers offered by this print server. Since browsing uses a broadcast mechanism, it typically makes sense to allow browsing only for the local network. Second, you need to grant permissions for these other printers in the local network to use your printer. Finally, if the firewall is activated on your server, you need to open the port in the firewall. To accomplish this, perform the following steps:

   a. In the Browse Settings area, make sure Browsing is on. Next, click Add to add the addresses you want to allow to browse, or click Propose to add the local network automatically.

   b. Under Access Settings, select / (root). There is no need to change the permissions, since by default only the addresses entered as browse addresses are allowed to print.

   c. Finally, select the Open Port in Firewall option to give other hosts access to your print server through the firewall.

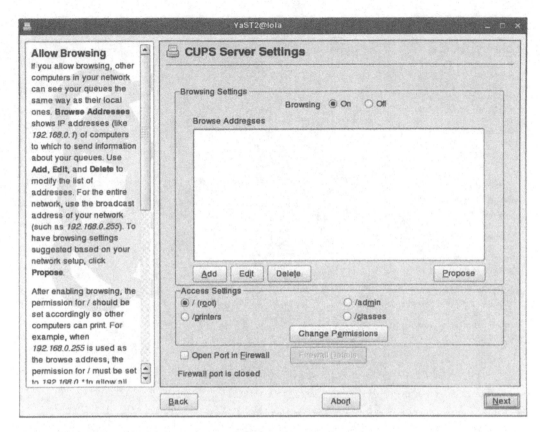

Figure 14-4. *To change the browse settings for your server, you need to open the CUPS Server Settings screen.*

4. After making the modifications to allow browsing from your server, click Next and then Finish.

5. Next, you need to set up the clients to listen to these servers. On the client, select Hardware ➤ Printer, and then click Configure.

6. Next, click Add, and then select Network Printers.

7. From the list of available network printers, select Print via CUPS Network Server, and click Next.

8. Now from the list of options shown in Figure 14-5, select CUPS Using Broadcasting, and click Next. Use CUPS Client-Only if you want to work only on network printers and disable the possibility of working with local printers. In case you want to work on one remote CUPS queue only, you can select Remote IPP Queue.

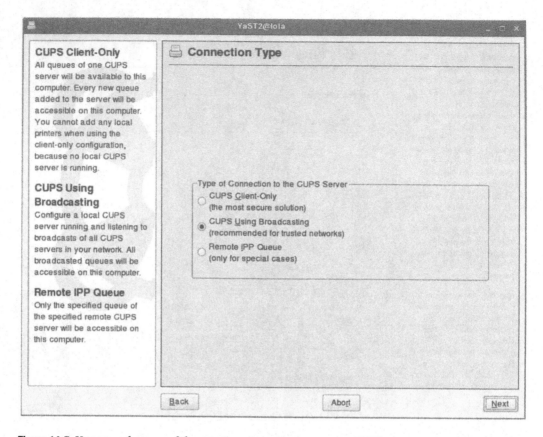

Figure 14-5. *You can select one of three options to work on a remote CUPS server.*

9. Next you need to specify how you want to listen to remote CUPS servers. Select Listen to IPP Broadcast Packets if you want to connect to servers using broadcasts, or click Select Addresses to select the address of one specific server to which you want to connect. Do not forget to check the option Open Port in Firewall, and then click OK to continue. Finally, click Finish to save and apply the settings.

You now have set up your CUPS server as well as the CUPS client. These settings are written to two different files. The /etc/cups/cupsd.conf file stores generic CUPS-related settings. Therefore, this is the file where you configure the CUPS client that listens to broadcasts from CUPS servers. On the other hand, the /etc/cups/printers.conf file stores the configuration of specific printers. Therefore, you will typically find this file only on a computer where a local printer is configured.

Applying Restrictions to Printers from YaST

CUPS provides different kinds of resources. As an administrator, it is possible to restrict access to these resources. These access restrictions are written to the cupsd.conf configuration file and have the same format as you may be used to from access restrictions on a web server. Different resources are available; each of these resources is available as a subdirectory of the CUPS root. For example, http://yourserver:631/ provides access to the CUPS server document root, and `http://yourserver:631/printers` provides direct access to the printer resources. The following is an overview of all the available resources:

`/` (`root`): This is the root directory of the CUPS server. Access restrictions that are applied here apply to all subsequent resources, unless the access restrictions are overwritten at that level.

`/printers`: These apply for all printers or queues offered by the CUPS print server.

`/classes`: On a CUPS print server, it is possible to define printer classes. You can use them as groups of printers; you could, for example, create a class "color printers" to apply special restrictions to the printers in that class.

`/jobs`: This relates to all print jobs on the CUPS server.

`/admin`: These restrictions apply to the administrative access on the server.

You can use YaST to configure restrictions for the resources:

1. From YaST, select Hardware ➤ Printer.

2. Make sure the printer you want to set restrictions to is selected, and then select Other ➤ CUPS Expert Settings. Next, select CUPS Server Settings, and click Next.

3. Choose any of the four available access settings, and then click Change Permissions to change the permissions. Note that it is not possible to change the settings for the `/jobs` resource; you need to do that from the web interface if you want to change them.

4. Now you are on the screen where you can set the access permissions for the selected resources (see Figure 14-6). First, you have to select the application order. The default order is Deny, Allow, which is the more secure application order. As an alternative, you can select Allow, Deny. In the latter case, the allow settings are evaluated before the deny settings, and this slightly increases the risk that a mistake sets your system wide open. In the permissions field, you can specify who is allowed access to the selected resources. By default, this would look like this:

```
Deny from All
Allow from 127.0.0.1
Allow from 127.0.0.2
Allow from @LOCAL
```

These default settings make sure the local host as well as all computers from the local network have access to the selected resource. The latter is realized with the `Allow from @LOCAL` line. Many other specifications are possible to allow access; for example, `@IF(eth0)` will allow all traffic coming in from eth0; `192.168.*.*` will allow access to any host whose IP address starts with 192.168; and `*.somedomain.com` will give access to all hosts from the somedomain.com domain.

■**Caution** If you want to be able to manage your CUPS print server remotely, you must set the proper access restrictions for the `/admin` resource. By default, this resource is accessible only from localhost.

You set these generic access restrictions in the generic configuration file `/etc/cups/cupsd.conf`. It is also possible to set restrictions for individual printers. These are applied from `/etc/cups/cupsd.conf` and must be edited from the configuration file or the web interface, since YaST doesn't provide an interface that can do this. Listing 14-1 shows an example of an access restriction that is set for a print queue with the name `brother1430`.

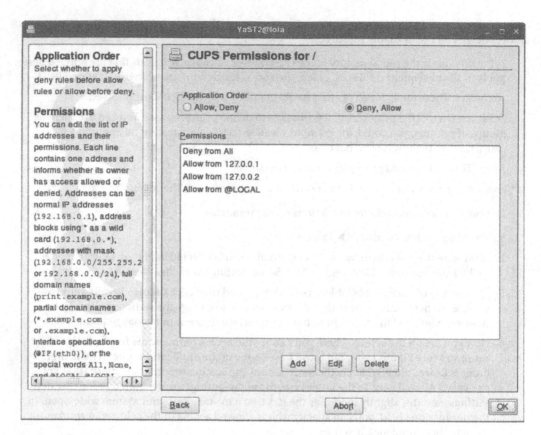

Figure 14-6. *The CUPS permissions settings look a lot like the access restrictions you can set on an Apache web server.*

Listing 14-1. *Example of an Access Restriction for a Specific Printer*

```
<Location /printers/brother1430>
Deny From All
Allow From 192.168.0.0/24
Order Allow,Deny
</Location>
```

So far, you have read about how you can restrict access based on computer names or addresses. You can also set up access restrictions for users and groups. If you need to do this, you have to deploy the lpadmin command if you want to use the full options offered by this feature. In the later section "Tuning the CUPS Environment from the Command Line," you'll learn how this works.

Using the Web Interface for CUPS Management

You have learned how to use YaST for administering your CUPS environment. CUPS also offers a browser interface at port 631, which is pretty flexible. Before you can use this interface to administer the CUPS environment, you need to set up access for the administrator account. Do this by using the command lppasswd -g sys -a root; this allows administrative access over the web interface for the root user. Enter a password, and after entering the password, you can use the web interface. As you can see from Figure 14-7, configuring a printer from the web interface is fairly intuitive. The administrative interface is divided in some main directives where you can find all the relevant tasks.

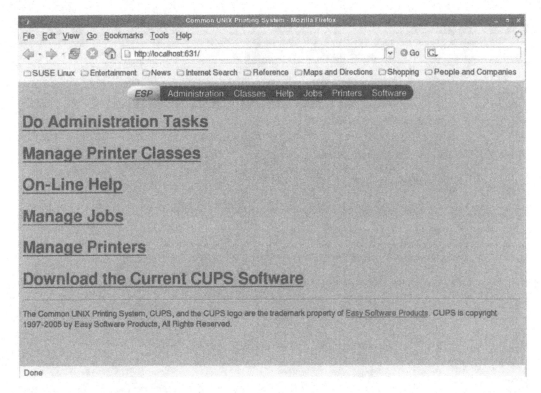

Figure 14-7. *Managing CUPS from the web interface is intuitive.*

The most useful link on the CUPS administration screen from the perspective of the network administrator is the Admin link. You can reach this link directly from http://yourserver:631/admin. On this page, you'll see three management options. You can use the Add Class option to define a group of printers. You can manage this group of printers with the Manage Classes option. Adding and managing classes is straightforward: just add printers to a class, and then specify their properties. Probably the most important link for the administrator is the Manage Jobs link. From this link, administrators can manage jobs that are currently in the queue. If jobs cannot be served and are still in the queue, you can see them from the Active Jobs overview. Also, you'll see a log of all jobs that have been completed successfully from the Show Completed Jobs overview, as shown in Figure 14-8.

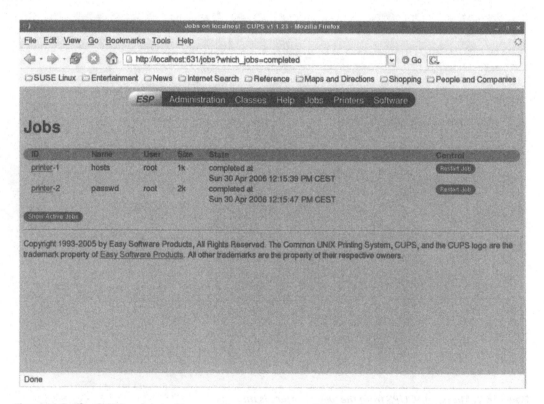

Figure 14-8. *The CUPS web interface provides an overview of both active and completed jobs.*

Another important link from the web interface is the Printer link, which takes you to the Printer screen (see Figure 14-9). On this screen, you can manage all printers on your print server and monitor their status. For an administrator, this interface is interesting in particular because you can configure and manage the printer. For example, you can tell the printer to reject jobs before you can start some scheduled maintenance on the printer.

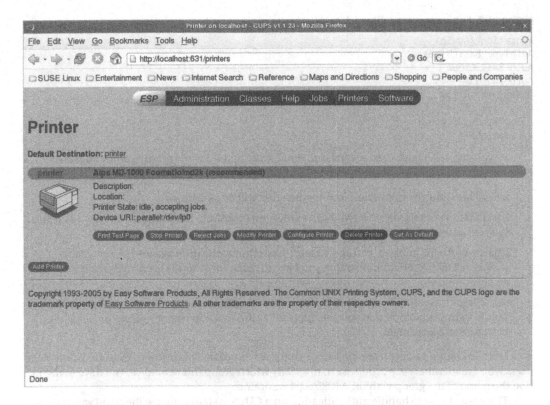

Figure 14-9. *The printer interface helps you manage and monitor printers.*

Tuning the CUPS Environment from the Command Line

You can perform many CUPS printing environment configuration tasks from the web interface or the YaST interface. Some tasks, however, just work better from the command line of your print server. To help you complete these tasks, in the following sections you'll look at two different aspects of the CUPS command line. First, you'll learn how to apply user-based security to your CUPS environment and CUPS print queues. Then, you will learn how to manage print queues.

Restricting Access to Users and Groups

CUPS allows you to set up an environment where you can manage access on specific resources for users and groups on your system. This goes for generic resources, such as the management capabilities, but also for specific printers. To set up this feature, you need to configure the access restrictions in the CUPS configuration file where you want to apply the access restriction. Next, depending on the method you are using, you need to create user and group accounts as well.

The first step for setting up the proper access restrictions happens in the CUPS configuration files. In Listing 14-2, you can see how you can apply access restrictions for the /admin resource.

Listing 14-2. *Example of User-Based Access Restrictions*

```
<Location /Admin>
AuthType BasicDigest
AuthClass Group
AuthGroupName sys
Order Deny,Allow
Deny From All
Allow From 127.0.0.1
</Location>
```

As you can see, I have used several elements in Listing 14-2 with regard to authentication. First, the AuthType option can work with four different parameters:

None: This is the default value. No authentication will be performed.

Basic: This is the simplest way you can apply authentication. Authentication is issued against the passwd and shadow files.

Digest: With this method, you apply digest-based authentication against the /etc/cups/passwd.md5 file. As an administrator, you have to make sure this file is created (see later in this section).

BasicDigest: You should apply basic authentication against the /etc/cups/passwd.md5 file. This is a simple method that you can apply for authentication where you are not using the Unix passwd mechanism.

Next, in Listing 14-2, you see the AuthClass Group directive. This restricts access to printers for users who are members of a group. Next, to specify which group this should be, you have to mention the name of the group with the AuthGroupName option.

The easiest way to handle authentication on a CUPS system is to use the AuthType Basic option. This authenticates users who exist in /etc/passwd seamlessly. If you choose to work with a separate CUPS database for authentication, however, you can use the AuthType BasicDigest option. After specifying this option, you need to create users in a separate CUPS user file. You can do this by using the lppasswd command. For example, the command lppasswd -a kylie -g sys will create a user kylie and make that user a member of the group sys. In Listing 14-2, the group sys is referred to with the option AuthGroupName. Many other options are available as well to refer to users or groups. You can, for example, also use some commands to permit printing to specific queues to specific users or groups only. The easiest way to do this is to use the lpadmin command. For example, the following command will allow printing to the queue brother1430 for users linda and rob only:

```
lpadmin -p brother1430 -u allow:linda,rob
```

Of course, you can allow access for users who are members of a specific group. The next command will allow access to all users who are members of the group users:

```
ldadmin -p brother1430 -u allow:@users
```

The interesting part of this example is where the CUPS system will look for the group users. This depends completely on the AuthType parameter, which you can set in /etc/cups/cupsd.conf. If this parameter is set to BasicDigest, you need to create a CUPS user database by using the lppasswd command as discussed earlier. If, however, the AuthType is set to Basic, the previous command will give access to users who are members of the group users as defined in /etc/passwd and /etc/group.

Tip In a complex network environment, you probably don't want to manage local user databases. As an alternative in that scenario, you can redirect CUPS authentication to LDAP. To do this, first make sure AuthType is set to Basic. Next, configure the /etc/pam.d/cups file to include a line that refers to the LDAP server. This makes sure LDAP handles all the printer-related authentication.

In the two previous examples, you saw how the lpadmin command can write user and group authentication information for specific printers to the /etc/cups/printers.conf file. The examples showed how you allow access for specific users. With the default access order allow,deny, this would make sure that all other users are denied access. If you want to deny access to some specific users, you can use lpadmin with the deny option as well. The following line shows how all members of the group account and the user harry are denied access to the printer queue brother1430:

```
lpadmin -p brother1430 -u deny:harry,@account
```

Managing CUPS Print Queues

CUPS offers a lot of tools from the command line that you can use to manage print jobs and queues. If you have worked with older Unix print systems, I have good news for you: CUPS works with tools from the Berkeley Unix dialect as well as the System V Unix dialect. Since they are more common, in the following sections I will focus on the Berkeley tools.

Creating Print Jobs

To create a print job from the command line, you need the lpr tool. With this tool, you can send a file directly to a printer. In its most basic configuration, you can issue the command lpr somefile; this command will send somefile to the default printer. If you want to specify the printer where the file is sent to, you can use the -P option followed by the name of the print queue. For example, use lpr -P hplj41 somefile to send somefile to the queue for hplj41. Want to print to a remote printer? That's also possible using lpr; use lpr -P hplj41@someserver somefile to send somefile to the queue named hplj41 at someserver.

Tuning Print Jobs

From time to time as an administrator, it is useful to display print job information. For this purpose, you can use the lpq command. To get a list of all the print jobs in the default queue, use lpq. Want to show print jobs in another queue? Just specify the name of the queue you want to monitor, such as lpq -P somequeue. This will give you a fairly high-level overview of the jobs and their properties. Want to see more detail? Use lpr -l -P somequeue. There is also an option to check just print jobs in all the queues by using lpq -a.

Removing Print Jobs

Have you ever made the error of sending a print job to a queue that wasn't supposed to be sent after all? If you are fast enough, you can remove that job using the lprm command. You can use this command in many ways. The most "brute" way of using it is with the - option and nothing else. This will remove all the jobs you have submitted to the queue; that is, if you are the root user, it will remove all the jobs from the queue. You can be more specific as well; for example, lprm -P hplj41 3 will remove job 3 from the queue hplj4. To find out what job number your queue is using, you can use the lpq command.

Tip When configuring CUPS from the command line, it can happen that changes are not automatically activated. If you've made a change but you don't see any result, use the rccups restart command to restart CUPS.

Configuring CUPS Clients

Up to now, I have assumed you want to install CUPS as a print server on your network. The fun of having a print server is that somewhere else there are print clients as well. In a CUPS environment, the CUPS client has two different configurations: the client that does print job formatting by itself and the CUPS client that doesn't. In the former scenario, you need to install printer drivers on all client computers. In the latter scenario, CUPS will use a print filter to format the print job properly. The advantage of not installing anything on the client is that you can keep the client thin and flexible. Also, it will do all the formatting work on the print server, thus offloading the client. It has one disadvantage, however; if you are working with Windows clients, the method to provide printer drivers from the print server is far from ideal. Therefore, when talking to Windows clients, it is recommended that you install drivers for your printers locally on the Windows workstation.

Installing a Linux CUPS Client

To install Linux as a CUPS client, you need to decide how you want to do that. If the Linux client doesn't have any printers it connects to locally, you can perform a CUPS client-only installation. If the CUPS client also has to connect to local printers, you can use the browsing feature, which you learned about earlier in this chapter, to connect to the CUPS print server. In the following steps, you will learn how to perform a CUPS client-only installation. Be aware that in this procedure you are configuring a client where no local CUPS processes are running.

1. On the CUPS Printer Configuration screen, click Add to add a new printer.

2. On the Printer Type screen, select Network Printers to connect to a printer that is offered by another CUPS print server.

3. In the list of available network printer types, select Print via CUPS Network Server.

4. Now on the Connection Type screen, select CUPS Client-Only. When clicking Next, you will see a warning that this option erases all locally configured printers. Click Yes to accept and continue.

5. On the CUPS Server screen, which you can see in Figure 14-10, you can enter the name or address of the remote server. To make it easy, select Use Server's Default Queue. If you want to use something other than the default print queue, select the queue you want to use from the drop-down list.

Tip You can of course enter the name of the server you want to use manually. If you have enabled IPP advertising, it is possible to use the Look Up option as an alternative. This option allows you to scan for all servers on the network that are offering CUPS print services.

---

6. Now click OK and then Finish. This will finalize the installation of the CUPS client.

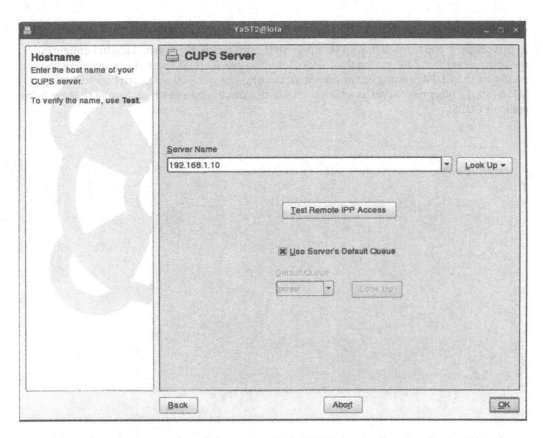

Figure 14-10. *If you want to do print job formatting on the CUPS server, all you need to specify is the name/address of the print server and the queue you want to use.*

■**Tip** Want to do some manual tuning of the CUPS client configuration? Then check the /etc/cups/ client.conf file. All configuration with regard to the CUPS client resides in this file.

Installing Windows As a Client for CUPS

If you want to make your CUPS print server available for Windows clients, you need the Samba server. I discuss this server in Chapter 15. The Samba server will make the CUPS printing environment transparently available to Windows clients. In this situation, you need a printer driver that is installed locally on the client computer. Since this is basically is a Samba configuration and not a CUPS configuration, you can find more details about this in Chapter 15.

Summary

In this chapter, you learned how to set up a CUPS print server. You learned about configuring the print server and configuring the CUPS client. You also learned about the many ways you can configure the CUPS printing environment. In the next chapter, you will learn how to configure SUSE Linux Enterprise Server as a file server. I'll also discuss how to set up Samba to share printers with CUPS.

CHAPTER 15

■ ■ ■

Sharing Files with SUSE Linux Enterprise Server

SUSE Linux Enterprise Server offers many options for being used as a file server. In this chapter, you will learn about the three most important services you can use to offer shared files to the rest of the network. First, you will learn how to use the good old Network File System (NFS) protocol to do file sharing on your network. Next, you will read about the Samba server and how you can use it to share files for Windows users. Finally, I'll discuss how to use SUSE Linux Enterprise Server as an FTP server.

Sharing Files with NFS

If you are looking for a service that can offer access to shared files in a fast way to other Linux and Unix users or servers, NFS is an excellent choice. In the next sections, I'll cover the following:

- Using the NFS server
- Configuring an NFS server
- Configuring an NFS client
- Monitoring the NFS server

Using the NFS Server

You use the NFS server to share files between Unix and Linux servers. Almost every version of Unix and Linux has native NFS support, but if it isn't present by default, it is easy to set up. Like other file-sharing protocols, NFS is particularly useful when certain directories must be stored on a central location in the network. You can, for example, use it for access to shared home directories; make sure the home directory is stored somewhere centrally on a server, and let users access it when they log in to their workstation. Note, however, that it works for Linux/Unix clients only. You can set up Windows clients to use NFS, but it's not an easy procedure. You can use other shared directories, mainly data directories, with NFS as well.

One of the most important points to remember about NFS is that its security is rather limited. The only option you have is to specify which hosts can and which hosts cannot access your NFS server. You can't limit access to an NFS share for certain remote users only. This is because NFS assumes that remote users and local users are the same. NFS is designed for an environment that has a shared mechanism for user management such as an NIS or LDAP server. If no such mechanism is present, it will just map user IDs from the NFS client computer to the NFS server. This means the user with ID 501 on the client computer will have on the server the permissions of the user who has ID 501 there. Because of this, you should make sure that, on the NFS clients and servers, users with the same name always have the same user ID; this is why using a central administration system is important when implementing this.

Currently, three versions of NFS are relevant: versions 2, 3, and 4. Of these, version 4 is a rather new addition to NFS. It allows for more advanced security than its predecessors. To use that security, your NFS client should be configured for use of version 4. To set up a secure environment where only version 4 is offered, no one should use earlier versions anymore. Since this greatly reduces the flexibility of an NFS server, SUSE Linux Enterprise Server offers version 2, 3, and 4 support by default. The information in this chapter is applicable to all these versions.

To use an NFS server, a couple of components are involved. First, the kernel of SUSE Linux Enterprise Server provides the NFS server. NFS is one of the services that works with the RPC portmapper. The RPC portmapper makes a translation between port numbers and the old RPC program numbers used by NFS (and some other services). Most modern services have their own port numbers. This is not the case by default for NFS.

NFS was created a long time ago, when the Internet port numbers in use nowadays weren't common yet. Therefore, NFS uses its own kind of port numbers, the remote procedure call (RPC) program numbers. On a modern system, these numbers must be converted to an Internet port number. This is the task of the portmapper program. When an RPC-based service, such as NFS, starts, it will tell the portmapper on which port number it is listening and which RPC program numbers it serves. When a client wants to communicate to the RPC-based service, it will first contact the portmapper on the server to find out the port number it should use. Once it knows about the port number, its requests can be tunneled over the Internet port to the correct RPC port. To find out on which RPC program numbers your server is currently listening, as root you can use the `rpcinfo -p` command. In Listing 15-1 you can see an example where this command shows its results.

Listing 15-1. *Displaying RPC Program Numbers with* `rpcinfo -p`

```
SFO:~ # rpcinfo -p
```

```
program  vers  proto  port
100000    2    tcp    111  portmapper
100000    2    udp    111  portmapper
100003    2    udp    2049 nfs
100003    3    udp    2049 nfs
100003    4    udp    2049 nfs
100003    2    tcp    2049 nfs
100003    3    tcp    2049 nfs
100003    4    tcp    2049 nfs
100024    1    udp    1147 status
100021    1    udp    1147 nlockmgr
100021    3    udp    1147 nlockmgr
100021    4    udp    1147 nlockmgr
100024    1    tcp    2357 status
100021    1    tcp    2357 nlockmgr
100021    3    tcp    2357 nlockmgr
100021    4    tcp    2357 nlockmgr
100005    1    udp    916  mountd
100005    1    tcp    917  mountd
100005    2    udp    916  mountd
100005    2    tcp    917  mountd
100005    3    udp    916  mountd
100005    3    tcp    917  mountd
```

As you can see in the Listing 15-1 output of the rpcinfo -p command, NFS is listening to Internet UDP and TCP port 2049 for version 2, 3, and 4 calls; the second column mentions the NFS version that is supported. Before the NFS server starts, you must make sure the portmapper has started. You can start it manually by using the rcportmap start command. This code will start the server once; to start it automatically when rebooting your server, issue the insserv portmap command.

After starting the portmapper, you can start the other NFS server components. First, the NFS server, implemented in the rpc.nfsd daemon, makes sure the portmapper is informed that there is an NFS server present, and it will give the proper portmapper program number to the NFS server. Next, the rpc.mountd program must be loaded. This program allows users to make NFS mounts to the NFS server. As the third component, the rpc.lockd program needs to start. This program ensures that only one user can access a file at the same time; when it is accessed, the nfs.lockd program locks access to the file for other users. You don't need to load all these programs individually; they are loaded automatically with the /etc/init.d/nfsserver script. You should add this script to the default runlevels to ensure automatic loading when the server boots; use the insserv nfsserver command to do that.

The last part of the NFS server consists of its configuration files. Two files are involved. First, the /etc/exports file specifies the NFS shares; second, the /etc/sysconfig/nfs configuration file specifies the number of NFS threads that are started.

Configuring an NFS Server

Like many tasks in SUSE Linux Enterprise Server, you have two ways to configure the NFS server: using YaST and tuning the configuration files by hand. You will read first which options are available to configure the NFS server by hand; after that, you'll learn how to do the same process with YaST.

Setting Up the NFS Server Configuration Files by Hand

If you want to manage the NFS server by hand, you use two configuration files. First, you use the /etc/exports file to configure all the NFS shares you want to offer from your NFS server. Second, you use the /etc/sysconfig/nfs file to provide a couple of parameters to the NFS server that determine the way the server offers its services.

The file /etc/exports defines the NFS shares. The generic structure of the lines where this happens is as follows:

```
directory hosts(options)
```

In this, directory is the name of the directory you would like to share, for example /share. Next, hosts refers to the hosts you want to grant access to that directory. You can use the following for the host specification:

- The name of an individual host, either its short name (such as SFO) or its fully qualified domain name (such as SFO.sandervanvugt.com)

- The IP address of an individual host

- A network referred to by its name, for example *.mydomain.com

- A network referred to by a combination of IP address and subnet mask, for example 192.168.10.0/255.255.255.0

- All networks, referred to by an asterisk

After indicating which hosts are granted access to your server, you need to specify the options with which you want to give access to the NFS share. Table 15-1 lists some of the most used options.

Table 15-1. *Commonly Used NFS Options*

Option	Meaning
ro	The file system is exported as a read-only file system. No matter what local permissions the user has, writing to the file system is denied at all times.
rw	The file system is exported as a read-write file system. Users can read and write files to the directory if they have sufficient permissions on the local file system to do that.
root_squash	The user ID of user root is mapped to the user ID 65534, which is mapped to the user nobody by default. This default behavior ensures that a user who is mounting an NFS mount as user root on the workstation does not have root access to the directory on the server.
no_root_squash	With this option, there is no limitation for the root user. He will just have root permissions on the server as well. Note that using this option may impose a security risk for your NFS server.
all_squash	Use this option if you want to limit the permissions of all users accessing the NFS share. With these options, all the users will have the permissions of user nobody on the NFS share. Use this option if you want extra security on your NFS share and the share is meant to be a read-only share anyway.
sync	This option makes sure that changes to files have been written to the file system before others are granted access to the same file. In recent versions of NFS, this option is on by default.

This is an example of how these parameters are used in /etc/exports:

```
/data    *(rw,root_squash)
```

■**Tip** After all changes to the /etc/exports file, you must restart the NFS server using the rcnfsserver restart command. NFS is one of those older Unix services that reads its configuration only on start-up.

The second file where you can tune NFS parameters is the /etc/sysconfig/nfs file. By default, this file contains four parameters that determine how your NFS server starts. Table 15-2 summarizes these parameters and their meanings.

Table 15-2. *Sysconfig Parameters for NFS*

Parameter	Meaning
USE_KERNEL_NFSD_NUMBER	The number of threads that must be started when the NFS server is started. By default four NFS servers (the so-called threads) are started; if you have a busy NFS server, consider increasing this number.
MOUNTD_PORT	By default, the NFS mountd process that makes connecting to NFS shares possible gets a random port from the portmapper process. Since that is difficult to manage in an environment where a firewall is used, you can use this parameter to specify a fixed port for the mountd process.
NFS_SECURITY_GSS	In version 4, you can secure the NFS server with RPCSEC_GSS security. This parameter specifies whether this feature is needed. By default, it is off.
NFS4_SUPPORT	Use this option to specify whether support for NFS 4 is required. By default, version 4 is supported, and it's a good idea to keep it that way.

Listing 15-2 shows how these options are applied in the /etc/sysconfig/nfs file.

Listing 15-2. *NFS Server Start-Up Parameters in* /etc/sysconfig/nfs

```
SFO:/etc/sysconfig # cat nfs

## Path:               Network/File systems/NFS server
## Description:        number of threads for kernel nfs server
## Type:               integer
## Default:            4
## ServiceRestart:     nfsserver
#
# the kernel nfs-server supports multiple server threads
#
USE_KERNEL_NFSD_NUMBER="4"

## Path:               Network/File systems/NFS server
## Description:        use fixed port number for mountd
## Type:               integer
## Default:            ""
## ServiceRestart:     nfsserver
#
#  Only set this if you want to start mountd on a fixed
#  port instead of the port assigned by rpc. Only for use
#  to export nfs-filesystems through firewalls.
#
MOUNTD_PORT=""

## Path:               Network/File systems/NFS server
## Description:        GSS security for NFS
## Type:               yesno
## Default:            yes
## ServiceRestart:     gssd
#
# Enable RPCSEC_GSS security for NFS (yes/no)
#
NFS_SECURITY_GSS="no"

## Path:               Network/File systems/NFS server
## Description:        NFSv4 protocol support
## Type:               yesno
## Default:            yes
## ServiceRestart:     idmapd
#
# Enable NFSv4 support (yes/no)
#
NFS4_SUPPORT="yes"
```

Configuring the NFS Server with YaST

Even if configuring the NFS server by hand is not hard, you can do it with YaST as well. The following steps show how:

1. From YaST, select Network Services ➤ NFS Server. This starts the NFS Server Configuration module, as shown in Figure 15-1.

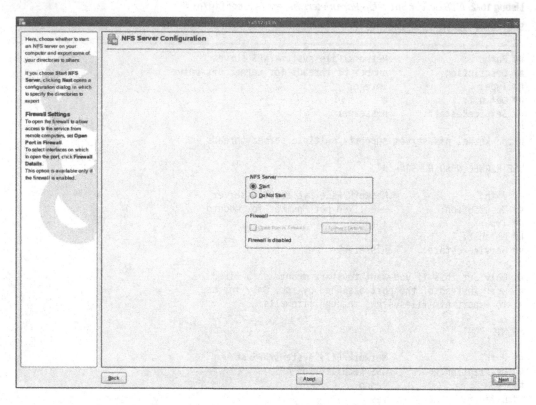

Figure 15-1. *The YaST NFS Server Configuration utility allows for the easy configuration of the NFS Server.*

2. In the NFS Server box, select the Start option to make sure the server will be started the next time your server boots. If needed, select Open Port in Firewall as well to make sure that the firewall allows NFS traffic. Then click Next to continue.

3. Now you see the Directories to Export screen, as shown in Figure 15-2. From there, click Add Directory. This opens a browser that you can use to browse to a directory in the file system. After selecting the directory you want to export, a window pops up automatically where you enter the hosts that are allowed access to this share and its security options. By default, all hosts will get read-only security to your share. Click OK to accept that or change the settings as needed.

4. Repeat this procedure to add other directories or grant access to other hosts to an existing directory. Then click Finish to complete the procedure. This starts your NFS server and makes the share accessible immediately. Also, if you would change existing exports, YaST will automatically restart the NFS server.

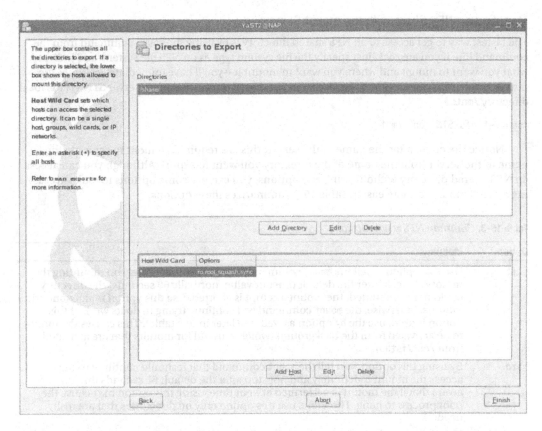

Figure 15-2. *Just add the directory you want to share, and set its permissions to make accessing the share possible.*

Exporting File Systems Temporarily

When the NFS server is activated, it keeps a list of exported file systems in the /var/lib/nfs/xtab file. This file is initialized with the list of all directories exported in the /etc/exports file by invoking the exportfs -a command when the NFS server initializes. With the exportfs command, it is possible to add a file system to this list without editing the /etc/exports file or restarting the NFS server. For example, the following exports the directory /srv to all the servers in the network 192.168.1.0:

```
exportfs 192.168.1.0/255.255.255.0:/srv
```

The exported file system will become available immediately but will be available only until the next reboot of your NFS server. If you want it to be available after a reboot as well, make sure to include it in the /etc/exports file.

Configuring an NFS Client

Now that the NFS server is operational, you can configure the clients that need to access the NFS server. On a Linux system, you can do so in three ways:

- Mount the NFS share by hand.
- Mount the NFS share automatically from fstab.
- Use YaST to mount the NFS share on SUSE.

Mounting an NFS Share with the mount Command

The fastest way to get access to an NFS shared directory is by using the mount command from the command line if you are root. Just specify the file system type as an NFS file system, and indicate what you want to mount and where you want to mount it—you'll have immediate access. In the next example, you can see how to get access to the shared directory /opt on server STN via the local directory /mnt:

```
mount -t nfs STN:/opt /mnt
```

Notice the colon after the name of the server; this is a required element to separate the name of the server from the name of the directory you want to export. Although you can access an NFS shared directory without using any options, you can use some options to make accessing an NFS mounted share easier. Table 15-3 summarizes these options.

Table 15-3. *Common NFS mount Options*

Option	Meaning
soft	Use this option to tell the mount command not to insist indefinitely on mounting the remote share. If after the default timeout value (normally 60 seconds) the directory could not be mounted, the mount attempt is aborted. Use this option for all noncritical mounts; otherwise, the mount command will continue trying to do its work. If this option is used, use the bg option as well (see later in this table). This causes the mount to be activated from the background (which is useful for mounts that are activated from /etc/fstab).
hard	By using this option, you tell the mount command that it should continue trying to access the mount indefinitely and not stop after the default 60 seconds timeout. Be aware that if the mount is performed at boot time, using this option may cause the boot process to hang. Therefore, use this option only on directories that are really needed.
fg	This default option tells the mount command that all mounts must be activated as a foreground job. The result is that you can do nothing else on that screen as long as the mount could not be completed.
bg	Perform the mount as a background job. If the first attempt is unsuccessful, all other attempts are started in the background.
rsize=n	With this option, you can specify the number of bytes that the client reads from the server at the same time. For compatibility reasons, this size is set to 1,024 bytes by default. NFS 3 (and newer) can handle much more than that. To increase the speed of your system, set it to a higher value, such as 8,192 bytes.
wsize=n	Use this option to set the maximum number of bytes that can be written simultaneously. The default is 1,024; NFS 3 (and newer) can handle much more than that, so specify 8,192 to optimize the write speed for your server.
retry=n	Use this option to specify the number of minutes a mount attempt can take. The default value is 10,000 (which is 6.94 days). Consider setting it to less to avoid waiting forever on a mount that can't be established.
nosuid	Use this option to specify that the SUID and SGID bits are ignored on the exported file system. This is a security option.
nodev	Use this option to specify that no devices can be used from the imported file system. This also is a security feature.
noexec	Use this option to avoid starting executable files from the exported file system. If you know that on a certain mount only data files should exist, always set this permission.

Mounting an NFS Share Automatically from fstab

Mounting an NFS share with the mount command will do fine for a mount you need only occasion-ally. If you need the mount more than once, it is better to automate it using /etc/fstab. If you know how to add entries to /etc/fstab, it isn't difficult to add an entry that mounts an NFS share as well. The only differences with normal mounts are that you have to specify the complete name of the NFS share instead of a device and that you must specify some NFS options. The following example code line shows what a mount line for an NFS file system in /etc/fstab would look like:

```
mysrv:/someshare      /media/mysrv/someshare   nfs rsize=8192,wsize=8192,soft  0 0
```

When mounting from fstab, you should always include the options rsize, wsize, and soft for optimal performance. To refer to the server, you can use its name as well as its IP address.

Using YaST to Configure the NFS Client

As an alternative to doing everything from the command line, you can use YaST to configure the NFS client as well:

1. From YaST, select Network Services ➤ NFS Client.

2. On the NFS Client Configuration screen (see Figure 15-3), click Add to add a new NFS share.

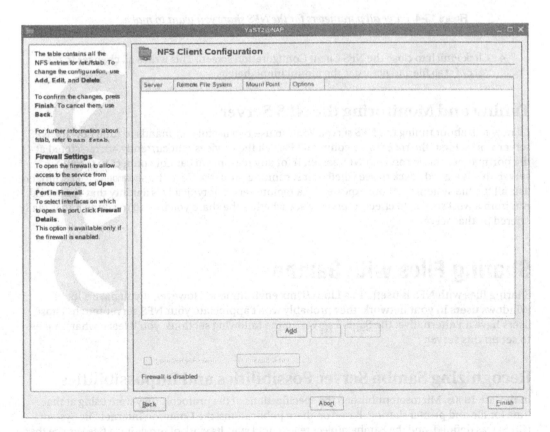

Figure 15-3. *Click Add to insert a new NFS share to your client configuration.*

3. On the screen that you see in Figure 15-4, enter the following options:

- *NFS Server Hostname*: The name or IP address of the server that offers the share. If the share is registered with SLP, you can click the Choose button to search the network for available NFS servers.

- *Remote File System*: The name of the directory that is shared on the remote server.

- *Mount Point (local)*: The name of the directory to which you want to connect the share.

- *Options*: The mount options used to connect to this share. Consider using at least the rsize=8192, wsize=8192, and soft options.

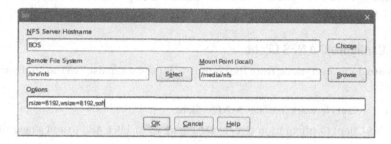

Figure 15-4. *Enter all parameters for the NFS share you want to make.*

4. Click Finish to close the NFS Client Configuration screen. This writes all changes to the /etc/fstab file and activates the mount immediately.

Tuning and Monitoring the NFS Server

I'll now talk about tuning the NFS server. You can use two useful commands to tune how the NFS server works. First, the rpcinfo -p command lists all the services that currently are registered at the portmapper service on your NFS server. If for any reason you cannot connect to the NFS server, this is a good check to see whether it is running properly. Next, the showmount -e command lists all the file systems that are exported by a remote server. It typically is a utility that you would run from a workstation to check a server to see whether the share you intend to connect to is really offered by that server.

Sharing Files with Samba

Sharing files with NFS is useful in a Linux/Unix environment. However, if you have a lot of Windows users in your network, they probably won't appreciate your NFS server much. Those users have an alternative: the Samba server. In the following sections, you'll learn what it takes to set up this server.

Recognizing Samba Server Possibilities and Impossibilities

In the late 1990s, Microsoft published the specifications of the protocols they were using at that time for file and printer sharing. Based on these publications, the Common Internet File System (CIFS) was defined, and the Samba project team could start its work of providing a free service that offers file and print services to Microsoft clients.

Since the late 1990s, many things have changed. Most important, Microsoft networking has changed a lot. Since 1998, however, Microsoft hasn't published the specifications of its networking protocols again. That is why the Samba team since then had to do its work by means of reverse engineering; in other words, the team had to analyze all the new functionality added by Microsoft networking components and then try to build something that works. Sometimes the members of the Samba team succeed quickly; at other times, the job doesn't go as quickly. For example, at the time of this writing, there still is no decent alternative for the Microsoft Active Directory Domain Controller server. The Samba server offers much functionality, though, and since it was a clean development cycle, it often is even faster than the original Microsoft protocols. Also, since it has been ported to many different operating systems, it is used in all environments. A SUSE Linux Enterprise Server with a Samba server installed is a good replacement for a Windows NT Server. In combination with an LDAP server, it can even offer a good alternative for a Windows 2000 or 2003 server with Active Directory. Be aware, however, that the options to integrate Samba in an Active Directory network are limited; as of the 3.*x* versions, Samba cannot be used as a domain controller, only as a member server in an Active Directory environment.

Configuring the Samba Server

In its most important role, Samba is a file server that offers access to shared directories and offers the option to authenticate users who access these directories. To configure a Samba server, you need several parts. Before we dive into its configuration, you should realize what elements are always needed in a Samba environment:

- A directory on the local file system
- One or more users who have local Linux permissions on that local file system
- A share that gives network access to the shared directory
- A user database on which Windows users can authenticate
- Some services that give access to the shared directory

Preparing the Local File System

The first element of a successful Samba file server is a directory configured locally to store the shared files. If the main purpose of your server is being a file server, you should consider giving this directory its own partition or logical volume to separate it from the other files on your server.

In addition to creating the directory, you shouldn't forget about the right permissions. The security for your shared directory is configured partly on the share, but the most important part is on the local Linux file system. So, create a group, grant permissions to that group, make users members of the group, and create the group owner of the shared directory to make it all work. In Chapter 6 of this book, you can read exactly how to do this. For details about setting permissions for the shared directory, you should check that chapter; here I'll just provide some tips on how to do it in the best possible way:

- Use Access control lists (ACLs) if you want to give read access to members of one group while members of another group have read/write access.

Note ACLs make it possible to give permissions to more than one user or more than one group. Read Chapter 6 for more details.

- Set the SGID permission on the shared directory to make the group that is the owner of the directory the owner of everything created in that directory and its subdirectories.

- Use sticky bit to specify that users cannot accidentally delete others' files from the shared directory.

It is a good idea to configure access on the local Linux file system first, before you do anything else on your Samba server (many people tend to forget about it otherwise).

Creating the Share

The second step in configuring a Samba server is configuring the share. For this purpose, Samba works with a configuration file with the name /etc/samba/smb.conf. In this configuration file, almost the complete Samba server is configured, including general options as well as shares. Listing 15-3 shows an example of the complete configuration file as it is used after a default installation of the Samba server on SUSE Linux Enterprise Server. I won't discuss it line by line here; the purpose is that you get a picture of how it is organized.

Listing 15-3. *Example of the* smb.conf *Configuration File*

```
# smb.conf is the main Samba configuration file. You find a full commented
# version at /usr/share/doc/packages/samba/examples/smb.conf.SUSE if the
# samba-doc package is installed.
# Date: 2006-06-16
[global]
        workgroup = TUX-NET
        printing = cups
        printcap name = cups
        printcap cache time = 750
        cups options = raw
        map to guest = Bad User
        include = /etc/samba/dhcp.conf
        logon path = \\%L\profiles\.msprofile
        logon home = \\%L\%U\.9xprofile
        logon drive = P:
[homes]
        comment = Home Directories
        valid users = %S, %D%w%S
        browseable = No
        read only = No
        inherit acls = Yes
[profiles]
        comment = Network Profiles Service
        path = %H
        read only = No
        store dos attributes = Yes
        create mask = 0600
        directory mask = 0700
[users]
        comment = All users
        path = /home
        read only = No
        inherit acls = Yes
        veto files = /aquota.user/groups/shares/
```

```
[groups]
        comment = All groups
        path = /home/groups
        read only = No
        inherit acls = Yes
[printers]
        comment = All Printers
        path = /var/tmp
        printable = Yes
        create mask = 0600
        browseable = No
[print$]
        comment = Printer Drivers
        path = /var/lib/samba/drivers
        write list = @ntadmin root
        force group = ntadmin
        create mask = 0664
        directory mask = 0775
```

The smb.conf configuration file is separated into different sections. The name of the first section is [global], which is where some settings relate to how the Samba server works overall. After that, some specific shares are created. First, the share [homes] gives access to user home directories. Then [profiles] and [users] are required to work with Windows profiles. Next, a share is created to give access to group data directories in /home/groups; note that by default these directories do not exist. Finally, the shares [printers] and [print$] are used to automatically share all printers on the network. With the installation of the Samba software on SUSE Linux Enterprise Server, you get a configuration that gives a working Samba server immediately; just start it with the rcsmb start command and access it, and you will see that it gives you access to your home directory (if your Linux user account has a home directory) and shared printers. The only thing missing is a configured user environment. Without that, Samba won't recognize the credentials of Windows users trying to access it.

Note Don't forget to open your firewall for Samba. You'll find more about how to do that in Chapter 30.

In the smb.conf configuration file in Listing 15-3, you first see the section [global]. In this section, settings are configured that apply to the complete Samba server. Some settings can be configured here only. For example, the definition of the workgroup in workgroup = TUX-NET is a setting that applies to everything that is offered by your Samba server. Apart from the global section, some shares are defined as well. Of these, the homes share gives access to the home directories of users, the profiles share allows you to work with Windows profiles that are used to store configuration information of the users' working environment on the network, and the printers and print$ shares are created to configure the printing environment completely. The users and groups shares offer nice examples of how a generic share can be configured that gives access to directories that need to be shared.

Just by following the previous example, you can create a Samba share that works pretty well to share your shared directory. In Listing 15-4, you can see an example of such a share where some additional features are used.

Listing 15-4. *Example of a Share with Some Additional Security Features Configured*

```
[sales]
    comment =  Share for the sales department
    path = /srv/samba/sales
    valid users = @ sales
    force user = dana
    force group = accounting
    read only = no
    inherit acls = yes
    veto files = *.mp3
    create mask = 660
```

The Listing 15-4 example uses some parameters that are often used on shared directories. Table 15-4 gives an overview of these parameters.

Table 15-4. *Useful Parameters for Shared Folders*

Parameter	Meaning
comment	A user querying the server for an available share will see the text that is used as the value for this parameter. Use it to explain what the share is used for.
path	This option indicates the path of the local Linux directory that is shared. In the example, the path is in /srv/samba/. It is a good idea to put all the directories shared by the Samba server under one main directory to get a better overview of what exactly is shared on your server. The /srv directory is just meant for that, so you can use it for that purpose.
valid users	Earlier in this chapter you read that Linux permissions must be configured for the file system on which you keep your shared directory. That doesn't mean that just local permission is enough security for your share. The valid users parameter is an example of some additional security. By using this parameter, you can specify a comma-separated list of users who are allowed access to the share. By default this parameter is empty, which allows anyone to log in. It is a good idea to use this parameter, followed by the name of a group, as you can see in the example to allow access only to users who are members of the group specified. If you work with group names, make sure the group name is preceded by an @ sign to indicate that it is a group. If, in addition to specifying the names of users who you do want to allow access, you want to make sure that some users absolutely don't have access, you can use the rather paranoid option invalid users to make sure some users are excluded.
force user	This parameter can be useful to force that all files created in this directory get the user specified (dana in the example in Listing 15-4) as its Linux owner. Don't use this option if you need to see which user created which file in the share.
force group	This option is the equivalent of using the SGID Linux permission on the directory that is shared; it ensures that the group that is specified becomes the owner of all files that are created in the share. Using either force user or force group makes sharing files between users in a group really easy.
read only	Without this option, users can't write to the share. By specifying read only = no, you actually say writeable = yes and thus allow users to write files to the share.
inherit acls	If ACLs are used on the Linux file system, this option makes sure they are applied to everything created under the directory with the ACL. Don't use this option if no ACLs are used on the Linux file system.

Parameter	Meaning
veto files	A veto file is a file that is always denied creation on the share. By using veto files, you can ensure that certain files just cannot be created. Like in the example, you should use patterns to indicate what files you don't want to be created. Alternatively, you can specify the names of the files you don't want to exist. For example, use veto files /*.bat/*.exe/*.mp3/ to prevent executable files as well as MP3 files to be stored on your server. Note that in this example, slashes separate the different patterns from each other.
create mask	This useful parameter specifies the default permission mode for files that are created in this directory. This parameter is not used to set default permissions to new directories; for that purpose, the parameter directory mask is used.
directory mask	Use this parameter to set default permissions for new directories.

Configuring User Access

The next important step in configuring the Samba server is to specify how user accounts should be handled. Basically, the issue is that the user connecting to a Samba share usually is a Windows user. Being a Windows user, he comes in with Windows credentials, such as a password that is encrypted with the Windows NTLM password hash. Unfortunately, this way of encrypting passwords is not compatible with the way Linux encrypts its passwords, so something must be done to allow the Windows user to log in with his Windows password. Basically, this means you need to configure some additional authentication service. In the following list, you see an overview of the available options:

- Configure an additional file in which the names of the Windows users are stored.

- Don't use user authentication at all, but work with share level security. This is an unsecure option that you should never use on a server.

- Centralize the management of Windows user credentials on one server in the network.

- Hook the Samba server up with a Windows domain to handle user authentication.

- Make the Samba server a Windows NT–style domain controller.

- Set up an LDAP directory service, and put the local Linux users as well as the Samba users in that.

I won't discuss all of these options here; that would require a book on its own. In this chapter, I'll discuss the easy method of creating an additional file in which the names of Windows users are stored. Later you'll also read how to configure your Samba server as a domain controller. In Chapter 17 of this book, you can read how to integrate Samba information in your local LDAP server.

To set up a local Samba user database, you need the command smbpasswd. With this command, you can create and later add to a Samba user database file with the name of /etc/samba/smbpasswd. For every user you want to allow access to the Samba server, you need to create an entry in this file. Before doing so, you must make sure the user already exists in the local Linux user database. If the user doesn't exist already, smbpasswd will give an error indicating that it is impossible to create the user. After verifying that the user you want to create as a Samba user already exists as a local user, use smbpasswd -a username to create the Samba user. This adds the user with its new credentials to the /etc/samba/smbpasswd file and makes sure the user can log in to your server.

Starting the Services

Three different services are involved with the Samba software on SUSE Linux Enterprise Server 10:

smbd: This process allows for the actual file sharing.

nmbd: This provides NetBIOS naming services, allowing Windows clients to work with their own naming mechanism. This service, for example, allows you to browse the network neighborhood and find all the Samba services as well.

winbind: This allows you to bind your SUSE environment to a Windows environment where Active Directory is used. With it, you can log in to Active Directory as a Linux user.

To make your Samba server fully operational, you have to make sure these services are started when booting your machine. To start them manually, you can use the /etc/init.d/smb, /etc/init.d/nmb, and /etc/init.d/winbind scripts with the start parameter; for example, use /etc/init.d/smb start to make file sharing available. To make sure these services start automatically all the time when you reboot your server, use the insserv command to add them to the default runlevels. (See Chapter 10 for more details on adding services to the start-up procedure of your server.)

Integrating CUPS with Samba

In addition to files, you can share printers with Samba. To do this, you first need to set up your Linux printing environment. In Chapter 14 you can read how to do this with CUPS. After setting up the CUPS environment, Samba will share all CUPS printers automatically. Note that this may be convenient in a home network but probably isn't a good idea to do in a professional network environment. In Listing 15-5 you can see the parameters from the default Samba configuration file that enable printer sharing with Samba.

Listing 15-5. *The Default Samba Configuration File*

```
[global]
        printing = cups
        printcap name = cups
        printcap cache time = 750
        cups options = raw
[printers]
        comment = All Printers
        path = /var/tmp
        printable = Yes
        create mask = 0600
        browseable = No
[print$]
        comment = Printer Drivers
        path = /var/lib/samba/drivers
        write list = @ntadmin root
        force group = ntadmin
        create mask = 0664
        directory mask = 0775
```

As you can see, the Samba printing environment consists of three parts. First, the section [global] uses four parameters to determine how printing should be handled:

`printing = cups`: With this option, CUPS is defined as the default printing system. Alternatively, you could use the legacy LPD print system. CUPS, however, is so much more advanced that modern Linux systems don't use LPD anymore. Therefore, `printing = cups` is a good default value.

`printcap name = cups`: This parameter indicates that the file containing printer definitions is not the legacy /etc/printcap file but the CUPS subsystem. You need this line if you are using CUPS for printing.

`printcap cache time = 750`: This option specifies the number of seconds before Samba checks the CUPS configuration again to see whether any new printers were defined. This is a reasonable setting that makes sure new printers are automatically integrated in your Samba environment every 12.5 minutes.

`cups options = raw`: With this option, you specify how print jobs offered to the CUPS server are handled. Since CUPS can't understand the data format generated by the Samba server, you should set this option to raw. Since interpreting print jobs is the job of the CUPS subsystem, you should leave this setting like this.

After the generic options in the [global] section, you must define two shares for the printers. The share [printers] sets up an environment where all printers can store their temporary print jobs. The [print$] share stores printer drivers. Just keep them at their default values; they'll work fine that way.

In the previous example, all printers on the server are shared. It is possible to share just one printer as well. Listing 15-6 shows an example of this.

Listing 15-6. *Sharing One Printer Only*

```
[laserprinter]
    printable = yes
    printer = hv1430
    path = /var/tmp
```

In this example, a share with the name laserprinter is defined. This share just needs three options. The first option, `printable = yes`, indicates that this is a printer and not a shared directory. The most important line is `printer = hv1430`; this line refers to the queue as it is defined in the CUPS subsystem. Lastly, the option `path = /var/tmp` indicates what directory should be used for the temporary spooling of printer jobs.

When sharing printers with your Samba server, you have to take care of the drivers as well. You could choose to install the drivers at the Windows workstation locally. This, however, would force you to maintain them on each individual workstation, which is not an ideal situation. Therefore, it is easier to install printer drivers on the Samba server. To do this, you need the share [print$]. Listing 15-7 shows the default values of this share.

Listing 15-7. *The* [print$] *Share Allows for Storage of Printer Drivers at the Samba Server*

```
[print$]
        comment = Printer Drivers
        path = /var/lib/samba/drivers
        write list = @ntadmin root
        force group = ntadmin
        create mask = 0664
        directory mask = 0775
```

This example uses some important options. First, this is the name of the directory where the printer drivers are stored. Next, the write list option specifies what users are allowed to write to this directory; it should be write-accessible for root and members of the group ntadmin only. With these settings in place, you can set up the printer in your Windows environment. The following steps show how to do this:

1. On Windows, start the Add Printer Wizard.

2. Indicate that you want to add a network printer and then browse to the shared printer. Tell the wizard you want to install a new printer driver.

3. Now select the printer model for which you want to install the drivers. This will install the drivers to the /var/lib/samba/drivers directory automatically.

Tip Make sure you are installing the printer drivers from your Windows workstation as a user with sufficient permissions to the printer. By default, only the user root and members of the Linux group ntadmin have permissions to write new printer drivers to the directory /var/lib/samba/drivers.

Setting Up Samba As a Domain Controller

In a Windows environment, you use a domain to manage users for a group of computers. The only way to do this in a centralized way in NT 4 is by using domains. Since Windows 2000, Active Directory has been introduced as a system that sits above that. Samba cannot be configured as an Active Directory environment yet, so the best thing you can do if you want to work with a domain-like environment is to configure Samba as an NT 4–style domain controller. The following sections give some hints on how to do that. Be aware that setting up a well-tuned scalable domain environment requires extensive knowledge of how Microsoft networks work. This goes far beyond the scope of this book; in the following sections, you'll learn just about the basic requirements needed to set up a Samba domain. Consider these sections to be an introduction to the subject matter only; for more information, consult the man pages or the documentation at http://www.samba.org.

Tuning the Samba Configuration File

The first step in setting up a domain environment is to configure the Samba configuration file properly. In Listing 15-8, you can see the settings required in the /etc/samba/smb.conf [global] section.

Listing 15-8. *Samba Domain Controller Settings*

```
[global]
    netbios name = STN
    workgroup = UK
    security = user
    passdb backend = ldapsam:ldap://HTR.mydomain.com
    logon script = %U.bat
    domain master = yes
    os level = 50
    local master = yes
    preferred master = yes
    domain logons = yes

[netlogon]
    path = /netlogin
```

Let's look at the different parameters used in this example. Table 15-5 summarizes how to use all the parameters that haven't been covered earlier.

Table 15-5. *Parameters Specific to Domain Configuration*

Parameter	Meaning
netbios name	This is the name your server will have in the Microsoft network.
security	This option specifies how security should be handled. If you want to configure your server as a domain controller, set it to security = user.
passdb backend	Use this parameter to specify in what kind of database you want to store user and group information. The most common values for this parameter are smbpasswd, tdbsam, and ldapsam. The easiest way to configure your server is to use the tdbsam option. This creates a local database on your Samba server. The most flexible way to configure it is by using the ldapsam option; this does, however, require the configuration of an LDAP server as well and makes things more complicated. If you want to set up your Samba environment with PDCs as well as backup domain controllers (BDCs), make sure to use the ldapsam option. Check Chapter 17 for more details on setting up an LDAP environment.
logon script	In a Windows environment, each user can have their own login script. This is a batch file that is executed automatically when the user logs in. In this example, the Samba server checks whether there is a script for your user that has the name of the user account, followed by .bat. This script should be placed in the directory specified with the path parameter in the [netlogon] share.
domain master	This option tells the nmbd naming process that this server must be responsible for maintaining browse lists in the complete network. These browse lists allow others in the network to view a complete list of all members of the Windows network. A domain controller should always be the domain master for your network.
local master	A domain master browser communicates with local master browsers. These are servers responsible for maintaining browse lists on local network segments. In addition to being the domain master, your Samba servers should be the local master browser as well.
os level	Even if you specify that your server should be the local master and domain master, this doesn't really guarantee that they also will be the master browser. In a Windows network, the master browser is selected by election. To increase chances that your server will be the master browser, make sure you use at least a value greater than 32 for the os level parameter. The greatest value is the most likely to win the browser elections.
preferred master	Usually, browser elections happen only occasionally. Use this option to force a new browser election immediately when the Samba server starts.
domain logins	Set this parameter to yes to make this server a domain controller.

As you can see, you need to use many options to make sure the Samba server is elected to be the master browser for your network. This requires the nmbd service to be started as well. Therefore, make sure you start this process; otherwise, your Samba server can't be a domain controller.

Creating Workstation Accounts

Now that you have your domain environment, you should add workstations to it. For every workstation that is going to be a member of a domain, you need a workstation account on the Samba server. Setting up a workstation account works like setting up a user account. First you need to add the workstation as a local account on your server, and next you have to add the workstation account as a workstation to the Samba user database. Notice that the name of the workstation should end with a $ sign to indicate it is a workstation. To create a workstation with the name ws10, first use `useradd ws10$` to create it in /etc/passwd. Next, add the workstation to the smbpasswd file by using the `smbpasswd -a -m ws10` command. Notice that in the smbpasswd command, you do not need to use $ to specify that it is a workstation; the -m option handles this. The command will add the $ to the name of the workstation automatically.

Configuring Samba with YaST

Up to now, you have read how to create a Samba server from the command line. SUSE Linux Enterprise Server does, however, also have an excellent interface in YaST that you can use to configure the Samba server. The following steps show how to use this interface:

1. From YaST, select Network Services ➤ Samba Server. This opens the screen shown in Figure 15-5. On this screen, use the drop-down box to select an existing workgroup name, or type a new workgroup name for your Samba server. Then click Next to continue.

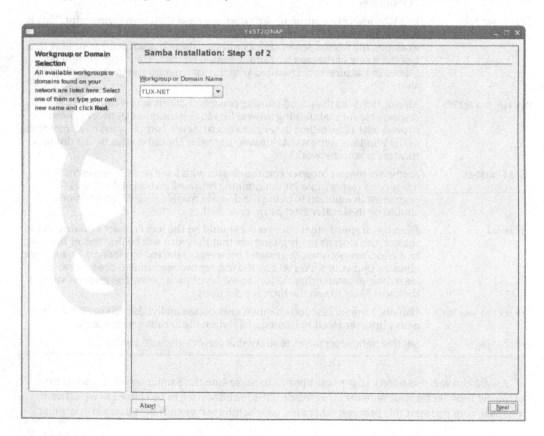

Figure 15-5. *The first step in configuring a Samba server with YaST is to enter its workgroup name.*

2. You'll now see a screen where you can decide how your Samba server should be used, as shown in Figure 15-6. Select Primary Domain Controller if this server will be the server responsible for handling all logins in the network. Check Backup Domain Controller if you already have another server in your network that is used as the Primary Domain Controller. Select Not a Domain Controller if you don't want to use any domain controller functionality at all. In this procedure, you will learn how to set up a domain controller with YaST.

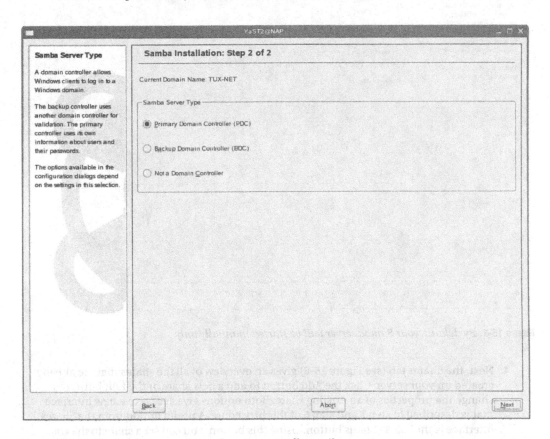

Figure 15-6. *YaST allows you to set up a domain controller easily.*

3. Now you see a multitabbed screen on which everything else can be configured for your server. First, on the Start-Up tab (see Figure 15-7), you need to specify how you want to start your server. Select During Boot to start it automatically or Manually if you want it only to be started manually. If the firewall is enabled on your server, select Open Port in Firewall as well.

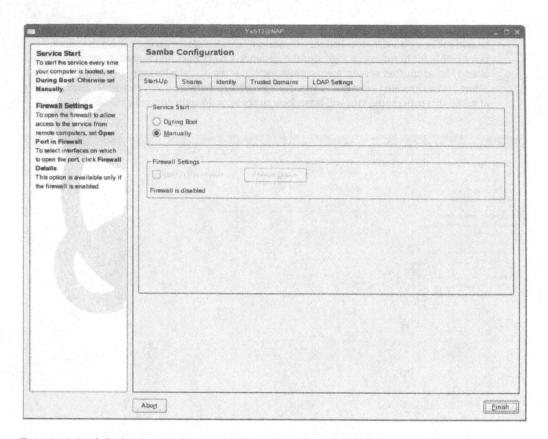

Figure 15-7. *By default, your Samba server will be started manually only.*

4. Next, the Shares tab (see Figure 15-8) gives an overview of all the shares that are already created on your server. Click the Add button to add a new share or the Edit button to change the properties of an existing share. Both options give access to a new interface that is described in step 5 and step 6 of this procedure. A useful option from the Shares interface is the Toggle Status button. Using this button, you can set a share to the Disabled status quickly so it won't be accessible anymore. Also in the Sharing by Users box, you can allow users to share their directories and, if they do, specify how these directories should be shared.

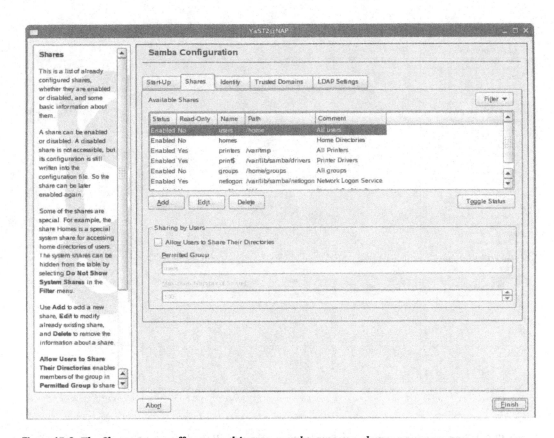

Figure 15-8. *The Shares screen offers everything you need to manage shares on your server.*

5. When clicking Add to add a new share, the New Share screen (see Figure 15-9) appears. On this screen, you can specify the name and description of the share, the path of the share, some permissions, and whether the share is a directory or a printer. After specifying all this, click OK to save the new share to your server.

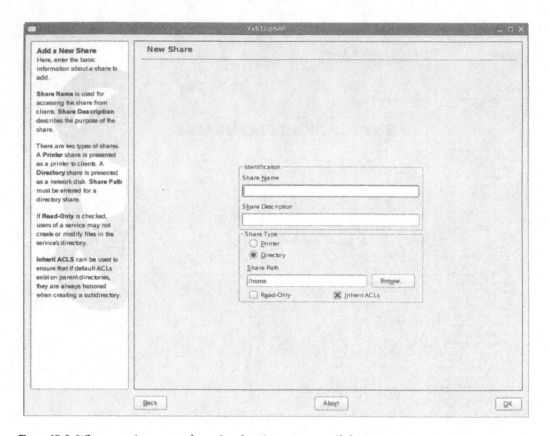

Figure 15-9. *When creating a new share, Samba gives access to all the important options.*

6. To set additional options for a new share, select the share you want to set the options for, and click Edit. This shows a screen that displays all the options that are currently set. To add new options to that, click the Add button. A new screen opens (see Figure 15-10). On this screen, you can use the drop-down list to select any of the available options for your share type and specify its value. Be aware that many options are available to set on shares. You can find a complete overview of all of these options and their meanings in the man page of smb.conf.

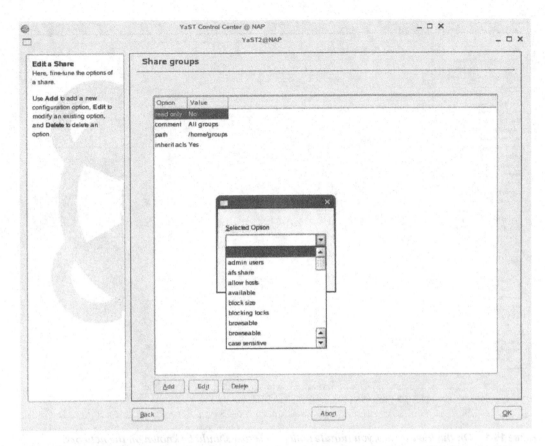

Figure 15-10. *Setting new options for a share is easy by using the drop-down box offered on the Edit Share screen.*

7. Next, on the Identity tab of the Samba configuration interface, as shown in Figure 15-11, you can control all your server's naming features. First, you'll see the base settings that you've already selected when starting this wizard. In these, you indicate the workgroup name of your server and its role (domain controller or not). Next, you can specify whether it should be used as a WINS server. In a NetBIOS network, WINS is used to translate NetBIOS names to IP addresses. If no WINS server is present in your network yet, select WINS Server Support to make your server the WINS server. Otherwise, use the Remote WINS Server option to enter the name or IP address of an existing WINS server in your network. Last, you can enter the NetBIOS host name of your server. This option determines how your server will be known in the Microsoft network. Also notice the Advanced Settings button, which gives access to advanced naming features.

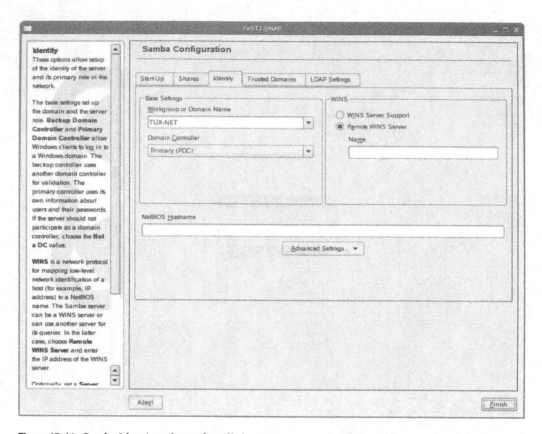

Figure 15-11. *On the Identity tab, you handle how your server should be known on the network.*

8. Next, you can use the Trusted Domains tab to establish trust relationships between Windows domains, as shown in Figure 15-12. This way you can grant access to users from other domains to resources in your domain. To do this, click the Add button, and enter the name of the domain you want to add as a trusted domain.

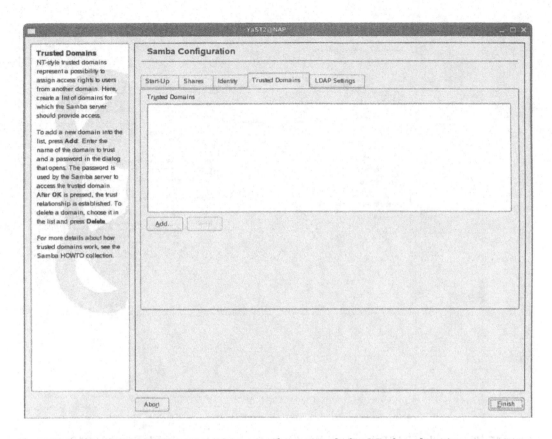

Figure 15-12. *Use the Trusted Domains tab to enter the names of other Windows domains you want to establish a trust relation with.*

9. If in a domain environment you have chosen to configure an LDAP Password back end, you need to specify how to connect to the LDAP server. To help make a connection to the LDAP server easier, use the interface that is offered from the LDAP Settings tab, as shown in Figure 15-13. This option assumes that the LDAP server is already up and running. First, select Use LDAP Password Back-End to indicate that you want to connect to an LDAP server. Then enter the LDAP Server URL that is needed to connect to the LDAP Server. Next, use the Authentication options to enter the name of the LDAP administrator and its password. The Search Base DN indicates where in the LDAP database your Samba server should look for valid user accounts. After entering these options, click the Test Connection button. This allows you to test whether the entered parameters will be working. Also, you can use the Advanced Settings button to tune some of the parameters used by your LDAP server. Check Chapter 17 for more details on the LDAP configuration.

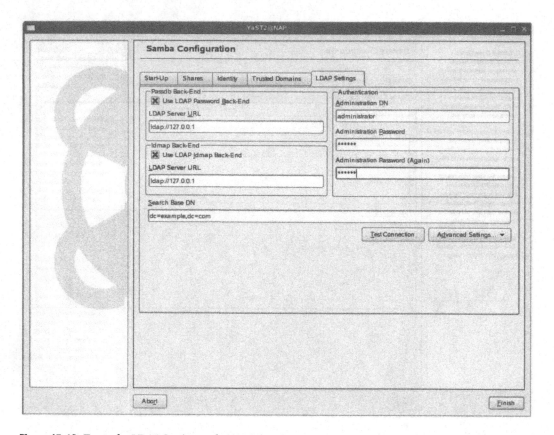

Figure 15-13. *From the LDAP Settings tab, it isn't hard to connect to an already existing LDAP server.*

10. After entering all the parameters you want to use, click Finish. This will first prompt you for the password of the Samba administrative account that is created automatically. This feature is especially useful if you don't want to give root permissions to your Samba administrator on your server. Then the configuration is saved to your server and activated. You now have a working Samba server.

Implementing Client Access to the Samba Server

Almost all operating systems can connect to your Samba server. In the next sections, you will learn how to test your Samba server from a Linux workstation. You can use three different utilities to test whether the server is working the way you were expecting it to work:

- You can use the `mount` command to make a connection to a Samba share.

- You can use the `nmblookup` utility to resolve NetBIOS names into IP addresses.

- The `smbclient` is a multipurpose utility you can use to test many aspects of your Samba server.

Mounting Shares with mount

A fast and easy way to test whether your server is providing the services you were expecting it to is to use the mount command. All you need to do is specify the smbfs file system type and the options that are required to authenticate against the Samba share. You can use the following command, for example, to test the access to a local share with the name share by connecting it to the mnt directory temporarily:

```
mount -t smbfs -o username=someone //localhost/share /mnt
```

Note that the only option that's really required is the option username. This option is necessary to tell the Samba server what user you want to authenticate. You can enter a password, but it is not a good idea to provide that at the command line since it will be stored in your local history file, which contains a history of all commands you have entered. As an alternative to the mount command followed by the -t smbfs option, you can use the smbmount command. Basically, this command offers the same options; check its man page for more details.

Like with remote NFS file systems, you can mount Samba file systems automatically as well from /etc/fstab. You should be aware of one issue: to mount the Samba share automatically, you need to enter a password. Possibly you don't want this password to be stored in the /etc/fstab file, but it is world readable. The alternative is to put the password in the smbfstab file; this file is readable by root only and therefore offers better security. Note that the syntax of the lines you need to add to this file is a little bit different from the fstab syntax:

```
//lax/data      /media/samba/lax     smbfs    username=sander,password=secret
```

In this example, the first line refers to the service that must be activated. In this case, it is a share with the name data offered by server lax. Next, the line refers to the local mount point. Then the file system type smbfs indicates that this mount should use smbfs. Finally, all required options are mentioned, in this case just the username and password. Since this line uses a server name instead of an IP address, make sure that Samba name resolving is configured as well. Do this by adding the nmb start-up script to your default runlevel with the command insserv nmb.

Using nmblookup to Test Samba Naming

To test whether Samba name services are fully operational, you can use the nmblookup command. For example, the command nmblookup lax would search the network for a host with the NetBIOS name lax and return its IP address. To return the IP address of the given host name, the utility first uses a NetBIOS broadcast on the local network. If no WINS server is configured, it wouldn't go any further. If NetBIOS nodes are present on other networks as well, a WINS server must be configured to manage the names for these hosts as well.

Testing and Accessing the Samba Server with smbclient

The smbclient utility is a versatile utility that you can use to test a Samba server. You can use it to check the availability of shares on a server, but with its FTP-like interface, you can use it to get files from and to the Samba server as well. Probably the most useful check that you can do with smbclient is to list the shares offered by a given server. Use, for example, smbclient -L //localhost to see what shares are offered by the local host. The result of this command looks like the example in Listing 15-9.

Listing 15-9. *Example of* smbclient *Output*

```
SFO:~ # smbclient -L //localhost
```

```
Password:
Domain=[SFO] OS=[Unix] Server=[Samba 3.0.22-11-SUSE-CODE10]

        Sharename       Type      Comment
        ---------       ----      -------
        profiles        Disk      Network Profiles Service
        users           Disk       All users
        share           Disk       my files
        groups          Disk      All groups
        print$          Disk       Printer Drivers
        IPC$            IPC       IPC Service (Samba 3.0.22-11-SUSE-CODE10)
        ADMIN$        IPC     IPC Service (Samba 3.0.22-11-SUSE-CODE10)
Domain=[SFO] OS=[Unix] Server=[Samba 3.0.22-11-SUSE-CODE10]

        Server          Comment
        ---------       -------

        Workgroup       Master
        ---------       -------
```

As you can see, the smbclient command first prompts for a password. This password is required for privileged options only. Since in this example only a list of available shares is requested, no password is needed. Next, a list of all available shares appears. In this list, the type of share, as well as the comment that was added to that share, appears as well.

You cannot use the smbclient utility only to query a server about the shares it offers; you can also use it to upload and download files from a share. To do that, you can use the same commands that are used from an FTP client interface. The most important of these commands are ls (list files), cd (change directory), get (download files), and put (upload files). It is not the most practical way of working, though, since the Samba file system is not integrated in the local file system at all.

Offering Files with FTP

As the third and final method to share files on your server, I'll discuss the FTP server. SUSE Linux Enterprise Server offers many different FTP servers you can use, such as the ncfrp server, the pure-ftpd server, and the vsftpd server. Since the pure-ftpd server is installed as the default choice, the next sections explain how to configure this server only.

Configuring the pure-ftpd Server

You configure the pure-ftpd server from its configuration file, /etc/pure-ftp/pure-ftpd.conf. This file contains usage options as well as start-up options. You'll learn how to set up this configuration file for using pure-ftpd as an anonymous FTP server, as well as an FTP server that can be used by authorized users.

Setting Up Anonymous FTP

If you want to set up pure-ftpd for anonymous FTP, you need an FTP user and a home directory for that user. On SUSE Linux Enterprise Server 10, both are installed by default. The name of the user is ftp, and its home directory is /srv/ftp. The basic setup that is required to support anonymous users in the /etc/pure-ftpd.conf file is as follows:

```
ChrootEveryone          yes
AnonymousOnly           yes
AnonymousCantUpload     yes
```

Of these three lines, the first makes sure users coming in as anonymous FTP users are limited (with the change root feature) to the anonymous user home directory only and cannot browse to other directories on your server because a new "fake" root directory is activated. You should always use this parameter; if you don't use it, FTP users can read all the files that are owned by others on your system. Next, the option AnonymousOnly yes makes sure access is allowed for anonymous users only. That means no authenticated users are allowed on the server. Last, the line AnonymousCantUpload yes makes the server a download server only. This always is a good option to use if you are setting up your server for anonymous users; otherwise, it possibly will be misused for sharing illegal content.

Configuring FTP for Authorized Users

For some environments, the option to configure an FTP server for authorized users is an important one; imagine, for example, that you are hosting websites for other users. In that case, your customers need to be able to upload content to their sites and FTP is the most appropriate way to do so. Setting up such an environment with pure-ftpd is really easy; just two lines are needed in the pure-ftpd.conf configuration file:

```
ChrootEveryone          yes
NoAnonymous             yes
```

Of course, this would require your users to exist on your local system already. The easiest solution is to include them in your local passwd file, but since pure-ftpd is PAM aware, you can put the users in an LDAP database as well and then modify the /etc/pam.d/pure-ftpd file to get information from the LDAP directory before trying the local files. Listing 15-10 shows how to configure the PAM file for that.

Listing 15-10. *Configuring the* pure-ftpd *PAM File for LDAP Access*

```
auth  sufficient  pam_ldap.so
auth  required  pam_listfile.so  item=user sense=deny file=/etc/ftpusers\
        onerr=succeed
auth include common-auth
auth required pam_shells.so
account include common-account
password  include  common-password
```

Starting the pure-ftpd Server

Once the pure-ftpd server is installed, you need to start it. And also don't forget to open the firewall to make it accessible; check Chapter 30 for more details on that. The handiest way to do that is from a start script in /etc/init.d or from xinetd; it works both ways. The latter method is not particularly easy. If started from xinetd, the pure-ftpd server doesn't parse its configuration file to check what options it should use. Therefore, all options you want to include must be added as server arguments in that case. Therefore, most people prefer using the start-up script. To start the server manually, use rcpure-ftpd start. To make sure it is added to all default runlevels, use insserv pure-ftpd as well.

Summary

In this chapter, you learned how to share files with SUSE Linux Enterprise Server. You read how to set up NFS to share files with Unix and Linux users, how to set up Samba for file sharing in a Windows environment, and how to configure pure-ftpd to allow for file upload and download for Internet users. In the next chapter, you'll learn how to set up SUSE Linux Enterprise Server as a mail server.

CHAPTER 16

■■■

Configuring a Mail Server

One of the most common tasks Linux is used for is as a mail server. Several programs are available to accomplish this task. In this chapter, you will learn what is necessary to build a solution to send and receive e-mail on a network. SUSE Linux Enterprise Server uses the Postfix mail server as the default mail server to send mail to other networks. Also, different solutions are available to allow users to connect to their mailboxes to fetch mail. One of the easiest to use of these solutions is Qpopper. In this chapter, you will learn everything that is necessary to build a working mail infrastructure.

Understanding How a Mail Solution Works

If you want to build a mail server that can handle e-mail for a complete network, you need to understand the three agents that process Internet e-mail:

Mail transfer agent (MTA): This is the software that sends e-mail that it receives from the client's e-mail software to the recipient's MTA. This recipient MTA will send the e-mail to an MDA (described next). Some well-known MTAs are Postfix, Sendmail, and Qmail. The Simple Mail Transfer Protocol (SMTP) is an example of a protocol that an MTA can use.

Mail delivery agent (MDA): The MDA works together with the MTA on the server that is used by the recipient. The MDA makes sure the e-mail is stored in the right location where the user can come and get it.

Mail user agent (MUA): When the MDA stores the mail in some location, the MUA is the program the user reads their mail with. The MUA can do this in several ways: using a protocol such as IMAP or POP, remotely using a file access protocol, or accessing local files. When the MUA uses IMAP or POP, there always is a server component (for example, Qpopper) and a client component.

The core component of a mail solution is the MTA. This component makes sure hosts on the Internet can exchange mail. When sending mail on the Internet, the MTA analyzes the mail address of the recipient. This mail address contains a reference to the DNS domain used by the client. The MTA then contacts the authoritative DNS server of the recipient to find out what server is used as the MTA (*mail exchanger*) in that domain. In Chapter 23, you will learn in detail how to configure a DNS server with the information it needs to find a mail exchanger for a given domain. When the MTA knows which server to contact, it sends the mail to the MTA of the recipient's domain. Once it arrives there, the MTA of the recipient checks whether the recipient is a user on the local machine. If it is, the mail is handed over to the MDA, which stores the mail in the mailbox of that user. If it is not, the MTA sends it to another MTA that helps deliver the message to the mailbox of the recipient. Figure 16-1 shows this process.

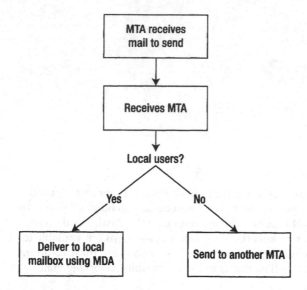

Figure 16-1. *MTAs manage the exchange of mail.*

When the mail has been stored by the MDA in the mailbox of a local user, the user can come and get it. The user can do this in several ways; amongst the most common ways are using POP and IMAP. If the user uses POP, the mail is transferred to the user, but the user can choose as well to keep the message on the server. If the user uses IMAP, all messages are stored on the server and are not transferred to the client computer. When setting up a mailbox for a user, an administrator can choose to make it either a POP mailbox or an IMAP mailbox.

Configuring the Postfix MTA

Postfix is a modular mail server in which not one huge binary is used; instead, the functionality is split amongst several little programs. This is in contrast to the other mail server that is often used in a Linux environment, Sendmail. The advantage of being a modular mail server is that it is easier for the administrator to manage all individual programs that make up the Postfix mail server. The disadvantage, however, is that as an administrator you need to know about how all these programs work. Wietse Venema originally developed the Postfix mail server with the intention of making it easier to administer and more secure than Sendmail. Because it is monolithic, Sendmail is in general much harder to secure properly. Postfix also is a rich mail server with many features; you can find a complete list of all its features and how to configure them at http://www.postfix.org/documentation.html. How Postfix works as a modular mail server will become clearer after a discussion of how Postfix handles mail traffic, which follows.

Handling Inbound and Outbound Mail

Speaking in a generic way, Postfix can handle two kinds of mail: inbound mail and outbound mail. When Postfix receives mail messages, it can be mail from a local user to another local user, and it can be e-mail that is received over the network for some local user. Also, Postfix is responsible for handling outbound mail. This outbound mail can be delivered to a local user (when the sender and recipient are on the same server) or to an e-mail user on a remote server, but it can also be an undeliverable mail.

Processing Inbound Mail

When Postfix receives a mail that is sent by another local user, it has to make sure the mail stays on the same machine. To make sure this happens, Postfix uses the postdrop command, a part of the Postfix mail solution, which places the mail in the maildrop queue before it is picked up by the pickup daemon. The pickup daemon checks the mail to see whether it matches the given rules. These rules can check the mail for content, size, and other factors. After that, the pickup daemon passes the e-mail to the cleanup daemon. The cleanup daemon has several responsibilities:

- It makes sure the mail is formatted properly.
- It will insert missing header lines if the mail program of the end user didn't do that already.
- It deletes double recipient addresses.
- It converts the e-mail header in the user@somedomain convention.
- It writes the data in the header according to the lookup tables /etc/postfix/canonical and /etc/postfix/virtual (see "Tuning Postfix with Lookup Tables" later in this chapter for a complete list of these formatting filters).

After that, the e-mail is copied to the incoming queue. Also, the queue manager will get a message that this mail has arrived. Figure 16-2 shows this process.

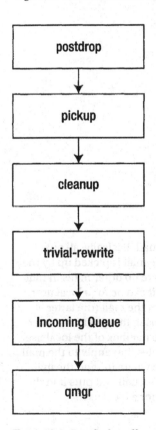

Figure 16-2. *Postfix handles mail sent by a local user to another local user.*

If an incoming mail was received over the network, the process is slightly different. This is mainly because the postdrop command doesn't need to become active to handle a mail message sent by a local user to another local user. The first part that is used to handle mail coming from the network is smtpd. This process performs some basic checks on the e-mail before handing it over to the cleanup daemon. The cleanup daemon then does its work to make sure the message is formatted properly.

Figure 16-3 summarizes this process.

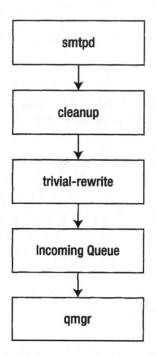

Figure 16-3. *Postfox handles inbound mail coming from the network.*

Processing Outbound Mail

Being the MTA, Postfix is responsible as well for processing outbound mail. Basically, all outbound messages are placed in the incoming queue first. From there, the mail is picked up by the queue manager (qmgr) and placed in the active queue as soon as there are no other mails in that. Next, the trivial rewrite daemon determines where the mail should go: it can be for a local user, for a user on the Internet, or for a Unix user who uses UUCP to come get the mail (the latter is somewhat primitive, so I don't discuss it here). If the mail is for a local user, the queue manager orders the local delivery service /usr/lib/postfix/local to put it in the mailbox of the local user. Before doing that, it takes into account all the aliases and forwarding rules that apply to the mail. Next, the decision is up to the local daemon; this daemon has to decide where to send the mail next. It can, for example, send it to the Procmail system that analyzes the mail and puts it in the right folder. Figure 16-4 summarizes this procedure of processing mail for a local user.

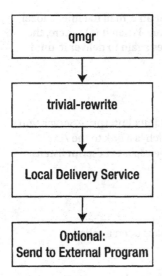

Figure 16-4. *Mail is processed for a local user.*

When the mail is for a user on a remote system, the queue manager also fetches the mail from the incoming queue and copies it to the active queue as soon as it is empty. Next, the trivial-rewrite daemon checks to see whether the mail is for a local or a remote user. By using the lookup table, it concludes the mail must be sent somewhere else, and therefore, the queue manager activates the SMTP service that delivers the e-mail on the other server. The smtpd process next uses DNS to find the MTA for the target host and delivers it there. Figure 16-5 summarizes this procedure.

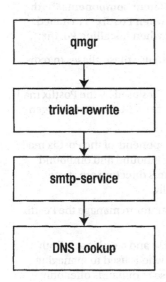

Figure 16-5. *Mail is delivered to remote users.*

Finally, the possibility exists that the queue manager cannot deliver an e-mail to either a local user or a remote user. If that's the case, it will be put in the deferred queue. When it is in there, the queue manager copies it to the active queue at regular intervals and tries again to deliver it, until a defined threshold is reached or the mail is delivered successfully.

Managing Postfix Components

The Postfix mail server consists of several components. First, on SUSE Linux Enterprise Server, you find the rc-script you can use to start it. This is the script rcpostfix, which is a link to the /etc/ init.d/postfix shell script that is used to manage the Postfix server. The rcpostfix script listens to all common arguments that can be used on most rc-scripts:

start: Starts the server

status: Displays the current status of the server

reload: Tells Postfix to reread its configuration files after changes have been applied

restart: Stops and then restarts Postfix

stop: Stops the server

On installation, by default Postfix is started in runlevels 3 and 5; to make sure this is the case for your server, use chkconfig -l postfix, which will provide an overview of all the runlevels in which the server is activated. If it is not activated in these runlevels, use insserv postfix to insert it to the proper runlevels automatically.

If you have a firewall on your server, don't forget to open the necessary ports in the firewall as well. Ordinarily, for your mail server to operate, you need to open port 25 (SNMP); ports 143, 220, 585, and 993 for all the different types of IMAP; and ports 110 and 995 for both secure and unsecure POP.

To troubleshoot a Postfix server, you must be aware of all the different components (both program files and configuration files) that are written to your server when Postfix is installed. The following are all the files and default directories that are created when installing Postfix:

/etc/aliases: This contains aliases for local mail addresses. You can use these aliases to redirect mail that comes in on a given address to some other address.

/etc/postfix/: In this directory, you can find all the configuration files used by the Postfix mail server. Some of them are the most important files: main.cf and master.cf contain all the generic settings necessary to operate the Postfix mail server.

/usr/lib/postfix/: In this directory, you can find most binary components of the Postfix mail server. Some components mentioned in the section on processing inbound and outbound mail, such as local and qmgr, are in this directory. The binaries in this directory are started when needed; an administrator doesn't need to start them manually.

/usr/sbin/: This contains all the programs needed by the administrator to manage the Postfix mail server.

/usr/bin/: In this directory, two symbolic links exist. These are mailq and newaliases. Both refer to the /sbin/sendmail program. They allow an administrator who is used to managing Sendmail to manage Postfix in a Sendmail-like style. Note that these commands offer only limited Sendmail-style management options.

/var/spool/postfix/: This directory stores and maintains all the queues used by Postfix. Also, if Postfix runs in a chroot-jail (see the following note), the subdirectories etc and lib that contain necessary configuration files are in here. SuSEconfig (see "Configuring Postfix from the /etc/sysconfig files" later in this chapter) will create these directories automatically, and in /etc/sysconfig/postfix, you set variables to specify that Postfix should run in a chroot-jail.

/usr/share/doc/packages/postfix/: This directory contains extensive documentation for Postfix.

Note A *chroot-jail* is a security feature that locks up a service in a specific directory. By using this feature, it is impossible for the service to do anything outside that directory, which adds a layer of security.

Configuring the Master Daemon

Postfix is a modular service. In this modular service, one daemon manages all other binary components (as discussed earlier in this chapter) of the Postfix server: the master daemon /usr/lib/postfix/master. This is the first process that is started when activating the rcpostfix script. To do its work, the master daemon reads its configuration file, /etc/postfix/master.cf, where all Postfix processes have an entry that specifies how they should be managed. Listing 16-1 shows an example of the top lines from this configuration file. In this section, you'll explore the settings in this file, and later in this chapter you'll learn how to manage the Postfix mail server from YaST. Since working on the configuration files offers you more possibilities, for Postfix this is the preferred way of working.

Listing 16-1. *Example Lines from* /etc/postfix/master.cf

```
#
========================================================================
# service type private unpriv chroot wakeup maxproc command+args
#               (yes)   (yes)  (yes)  (never) (100)
#
========================================================================
smtp        inet n    -       n      -       -       smtpd
#submission inet n    -       n      -       -       smtpd
#         -o smtpd_etrn_restrictions=reject
#         -o smtpd_client_restrictions=permit_sasl_authenticated
...
pickup      fifo n    -       n      60      1       qmqpd
cleanup     unix n    -       n      -       0       pickup
qmgr        fifo n    -       n      300     1       qmgr
...
rewrite     unix -    -       n      -       -       trivial-rewrite
```

In the master.cf file, at the left side of each line you can see the services that are specified by using some predefined fields. Next you can find a list of all the fields you can use and a summary of the values you can use for these fields. Note that you can't change all the field options; moreover, it is recommended that you don't change them if you are not absolutely sure what you are doing. The default values make sure the processes will usually work just fine. The following list explains what components are used in the master.cf file:

service: This is the name of the process. Ordinarily, just the name of the service is mentioned.

type: Use this field to specify the connection type. The possible values are inet if a TCP/UDP socket is used, unix if a local Unix domain socket is used for communication within the system, or fifo if it is a named pipe.

private: This field defines how the service can be accessed. Use y if the service must be accessible only from within the mail system and n if you want to allow external access as well. The latter is required if the service is of the type inet; otherwise, you wouldn't be able to access it.

unpriv: This determines whether the service will run with root privileges. Use y to tell the component it should run with the privileges of the Postfix user account and n to let the service run as root.

chroot: Use this option to determine whether the service should run in a chroot environment. If set to y, the root path is usually set to /var/spool/postfix/, but you can set an alternative root path from /etc/postfix/main.cf. I recommend always using this option because it prevents intruders from breaking through your mail server and accessing other files on your server. If this option is used, all configuration files must be copied to a subdirectory of /var/spool/postfix, since the Postfix server will see files only from that point on.

wakeup: This option is relevant for only the pickup daemon and the queue manager, because they have to become active at regular intervals. For these daemons, a number is provided. All other processes have the value 0, which disables the wakeup feature.

maxproc: This parameter gets its value from the default_process_limit value in /etc/postfix/main.cf and determines the maximum number of instances of this process that can run simultaneously. The default is usually set to 100.

command +args: This final option defines the binary name of the command and arguments that must be activated to run this component. For example, it specifies that the SMTP service is implemented by running the smtpd command. The name of this command is relative to the directory where the Postfix binaries are (/usr/lib/postfix). If you want the command to be verbose, make sure to include the -v option. Note that unlike the other options in main.cf, usually you don't need to modify this one.

Configuring Global Settings

Most of the settings that determine how Postfix does its work are set in the file /etc/postfix/main.cf. You can modify this file in two ways: directly or indirectly. SUSE Linux Enterprise Server 10 offers the option to change these files by modifying the files /etc/sysconfig/mail and /etc/sysconfig/postfix. If you want to work this way, modify these files. When ready, you need to process these settings and apply them to the main.cf configuration file by running the SuSEconfig program. If you want to modify the /etc/postfix/main.cf configuration file directly, make sure you set the variable MAIL_CREATE_CONFIG in the file /etc/sysconfig/mail to no.

Configuring Postfix from the /etc/sysconfig files

If you want to configure Postfix by modifying the /etc/sysconfig files, you must change at least two settings to /etc/sysconfig/mail:

- You must enter the DNS domain name in the variable FROM_HEADER. This is because MTAs will do a check on the DNS domain from which they are receiving mail. If the domain is not valid, the mail message will be rejected.

- Postfix must be told to listen to messages coming in from other servers. For this purpose, set the variable SMTPD_LISTEN_REMOTE to yes. If you don't do this, Postfix will accept e-mail only from the local host.

In addition to these essential parameters, the following are some other parameters that are used often:

POSTFIX_ADD_*: Several variables are available that begin with POSTFIX_ADD. These set Postfix variables. An example of such a variable is the smtpd_timeout variable, which determines how long the smtpd service keeps on trying if it has a problem establishing a connection. For a complete list of available parameters, use the postconf command; it will display all variables that are available. All these variables can be appended to POSTFIX_ADD. For example, you can set the variable trigger_timeout by using POSTFIX_ADD_TRIGGER_TIMEOUT, followed by the value you want to apply.

POSTFIX_BASIC_SPAM_PROTECTION: Use this parameter to specify how strict filter rules to protect against spam should be applied. The possible levels are off, medium, and hard. For most situations, the setting of medium is good enough.

POSTFIX_CHROOT: Set this parameter to yes if you want to run Postfix in a chroot environment. This will create a fake root directory for the Postfix service, which is used as an extra level of protection. If applied, the directory /var/lib/postfix will be set as the root directory. Make sure all configuration files are available from this directory before applying the chroot environment; for example, all files that are ordinarily in /etc/postfix should be available from /var/lib/postfix/etc/postfix instead. Otherwise, the Postfix process would not be able to work properly.

POSTFIX_DIALUP: This is a useful option if your Postfix server is connected to the Internet using a dial-up connection. In that case, you don't want the connection to be established for every single new mail message. By default, this option is set to no, which will lead to the immediate delivery of every mail message.

POSTFIX_LOCALDOMAINS: Use this variable to specify for which domains this server should accept incoming mail.

POSTFIX_MASQUERADE_DOMAIN: In some environments, a complex DNS environment is used. This may be confusing for the recipient of the mail message. If this is the case for your environment, use the variable POSTFIX_MASQUERADE_DOMAIN to specify the DNS domain name that should appear in the sender address of all the outgoing e-mail. If, for example, the user bill@software.south.somedomain.com sends a message and this variable is set to somedomain.com, the recipient will see bill@somedomain.com as the sender of the e-mail message.

POSTFIX_MDA: This specifies which MDA Postfix should cooperate with to deliver the mail locally. Throughout this chapter, you'll find more information about the choices that are available here. Possible entries are procmail, cyrus, and local. After specifying the MDA, Postfix will deliver e-mail to the MDA directly.

POSTFIX_NODNS: You can set this variable to yes to prevent your mail server from doing a DNS lookup on the sender and receiver addresses for all messages that are processed. This will make the mail server process mail faster, but it would be more vulnerable to misuse for spam purposes as well. Therefore, in general, it is better to leave this parameter to the value no.

POSTFIX_RELAYHOST: If you want your mail server to use a relay host to deliver e-mail that cannot be delivered locally, specify the name of the relay host here. You can enter a DNS name, an IP address, or the name of the relay host as the value of this parameter.

Configuring Postfix from /etc/postfix/main.cf

As an alternative to configuring the files in /etc/sysconfig related to Postfix, it is possible to edit the /etc/postfix/main.cf file directly. If you want to do this, make sure to set the variable MAIL_CREATE_CONFIG in /etc/postfix/mail to no. If you modified both the main.cf file and the files in /etc/sysconfig, when running the SuSEconfig command, it would create a file named /etc/postfix/main.cf.SuSEconfig, containing all changes that are made from the files in /etc/sysconfig and thus not affecting the settings that were made from /etc/postfix/main.cf. The Postfix main.cf file is well documented with comment lines that explain exactly what an option does. Some of the most useful settings from this file are as follows:

command_directory: Use this parameter to specify the directory where the Postfix administration tools are. The default value us /usr/sbin.

daemon_directory: Use this parameter to specify the directory where the Postfix daemon is located.

inet_interfaces: Use this parameter to specify where Postfix listens for incoming mail. The default value for this setting is the loopback UP address. If you want Postfix to listen on external interfaces as well, you must specify this by listing the IP address to listen on or by specifying all, which makes sure Postfix listens on all interfaces for incoming mail.

mail_owner: Use this parameter to specify the user who is the owner of the mail queue. By default, this is the user postfix.

mydestination: Use this parameter to specify a list of domains for which the server accepts incoming mails. If an incoming mail is sent to a domain not listed here, it will be rejected.

mynetworks: Use this parameter to specify which network is used as the local network. This setting is important, because other parameters (such as smtpd_recipient_restrictions) rely on it.

mydomain: Use this parameter to specify the domain of the computer on which Postfix is running.

myorigin: Use this parameter to specify the domain that appears as the sender for e-mails sent locally. By default, the fully qualified domain name of the host sending the mail is used.

queue_directory: Use this parameter to specify the location of the directory where the mail queues are. The default location is /var/spool/postfix.

smtpd_recipient_restrictions: Use this parameter to specify the trusted network. Ordinarily, the networks defined with the mynetworks variable are considered trusted networks. Mail clients from this network are allowed to relay mail through your Postfix mail server, whereas other clients are not.

smtpd_sender_restrictions: Use this parameter to specify which senders should always be ignored to prevent your server from accepting spam. The default value for this parameter is reject_maps_rbl.

Configuring a Simple Postfix Mail Server

Enough settings, parameters, and variables for now. The interesting question is, what work do you really need to do to enable a simple Postfix mail server? In this scenario, the simple mail server would need to send mail to the Internet for local users only. It would also be able to receive mail from the Internet, destined for users on the local domain. The following steps describe how to send mail to other servers on the Internet. To make this procedure as easy as possible, you will read next how mail can be forwarded to the mail server of the Internet provider, which is a common scenario.

1. Stop the Postfix server by using rcpostfix stop.

2. Open /etc/postfix/main.cf in an editor, and edit the following settings according to the examples. Make sure to use the settings that are appropriate for your network:

   - inet_interfaces = all: This makes Postfix listen on all interfaces.
   - mynetworks = 192.168.0.0/24: This defines the local network as 192.168.0.0.
   - smtp_recipient_restrictions = permit_mynetworks,reject: This allows users from the local network to send mail but rejects access for all others.
   - masquerade_domains = yourdomain.com: This makes sure that no matter what internal domain name is used, the sender domain is always rewritten to yourdomain.com.
   - relayhost = host.internetprovider.com: This specifies the name of a host that is used for the further handling of mail that is sent by this server.

3. Save the file, close the editor, and restart Postfix by using the rcpostfix start command.

Often, sending mail over the Internet is not the only thing your mail server needs to do. It also needs to accept mail coming from the Internet that is sent to local users on your network. In such a configuration, it is important that some basic protection is set up because you want to prevent your mail server from being misused as an open relay by spammers. Also, the worldwide DNS system must know that your mail server is the responsible mail server for your domain. You can do this by adding an MX record in the DNS database (see Chapter 23 for more on this subject). After making the required modifications to DNS, your mail server has to be configured for (at least) three extra tasks:

- Accept incoming mail that is addressed to your domain.
- Reject incoming mail that is not addressed to your domain.
- Reject mail from known spam sources.

To configure your mail server for receiving mail from the Internet, follow these steps:

1. Stop the Postfix server by using rcpostfix stop.

2. Open /etc/postfix/main.cf with your favorite editor, and edit the following settings according to the example lines. Make sure to make the proper adjustments for your environment:

   - inet_interfaces = all: This makes sure the mail server listens on all network interfaces.
   - mynetworks = 192.168.0.0/24, 127.0.0.0/8: This defines the networks for which the mail server accepts mail.
   - myhostname = myserver.mydomain.com: This specifies the host name of the mail server.
   - mydomain = mydomain.com: This specifies the name of the internal domain.

- `mydestination = $myhostname, localhost.$mydomain, $mydomain`: This specifies on which destinations the delivery of mail is allowed. This is an important parameter, because it makes sure your mail server cannot be misused as a relay host.

- `maps_rbl_domains = rbl-domains.mydomain.com`: This is a mapping to information about unallowed hosts. Postfix will use its internal list of these hosts if you let it point to your domain.

- `smtpd_sender_restrictions = reject_maps_rbl`: This checks the file with hosts that are disallowed to connect and rejects all senders coming from these hosts. This is a basic spam protection.

- `smtpd_recipient_restrictions = permit_mynetworks, reject_unauth_destination`: This indicates that for smtpd all local networks are allowed as recipient and all other destinations are not.

3. Next, save the modifications you have made to the `main.cf` file, and start the Postfix process again by using `rcpostfix start`. Your mail server is now ready to receive mail from the Internet.

Tuning Postfix with Lookup Tables

The main task of the Postfix mail server is to process mails. When processing these mails, you need to apply certain rules. For this purpose, Postfix uses lookup tables. Many lookup tables are available. They are defined as separate files in the directory `/etc/postfix` and activated from variables in the file `/etc/postfix/main.cf`. To work with lookup tables, you first need to create the file (for example, `relocated`) and then convert it to the proper database format by using the `postmap` command; this creates a file with the same name and the extension `.db` added to it. In general, applying settings from a lookup table is a two-step procedure:

1. Edit the lookup table file (for example, `/etc/postfix/sender_canonical`) with an editor, and make all the required modifications.

2. Use the `postmap` command to write the lookup table in the appropriate database format, for example `postmap hash:/etc/postfix/sender_canonical`.

As an additional step, you need to make sure that the lookup table is referred to in the right way from the `main.cf` configuration file. Usually, all required settings for that are present by default. For example, to indicate what file should be used for the `sender_canonical` lookup table, in `/etc/postfix/main.cf` you would find the following line:

```
sender_canonical_maps = hash:/etc/postfix/sender_canonical
```

All lookup tables are created according to the same syntax rules. It may not surprise you that a line starting with # is not interpreted as a command line. Less obvious is that a line that begins with a space is regarded as a continuation of the previous line. You should therefore be careful not to include any spaces in a line by accident. The following lookup tables are available:

`access`: You can use this lookup table to deny or accept mail from given hosts.

`canonical`: This lookup table specifies an address mapping (this allows addresses to be rewritten) for local and nonlocal addresses.

`recipient_canonical`: This lookup table can specify address mappings for the address of the recipient of a message.

`relocated`: You can use the information in this lookup table to provide information for a new location to which a user has moved.

`sender_canonical`: You can use this lookup table to specify address mappings for the address of the sender of an outgoing or incoming mail message.

`transport`: You can use this lookup table to specify a mapping from a mail address to a message delivery or relay host.

`virtual`: You can use this lookup table to rewrite recipient addresses for all local, virtual, and remote mail destinations. This is not like the aliases table, which is used for local destinations only.

In addition to these, there is also the aliases lookup table. This is the only lookup table that does not have a configuration file in `/etc/postfix`; it's in the `/etc` directory instead. The purpose of the aliases lookup table is to rewrite recipient addresses for local destinations. In the next sections, I'll provide more information about how to use these lookup tables.

The Access Lookup Table

You can use the access lookup table to reject or allow messages from a list of defined senders. This table is evaluated by the smtpd daemon for all incoming messages. To activate this table, make sure the line `smtpd_sender_restrictions = hash:/etc/postfix/access` is included in `main.cf`. Then in the `/etc/postfix/access` file, specify a list of mail addresses. For each mail address, define an action. The mail addresses are in the first column, and the possible actions are in the second column. You can specify the e-mail addresses as patterns. You can refer to an actual e-mail address (`someone@somewhere.com`) but also to complete or partial IP addresses or domain names. The possible actions are as follows:

`nnn message`: This rejects the e-mail with a numerical code as defined in RFC 821, followed by the text message specified here.

Note RFC 821 defines the SMTP specifications. It includes a list of error codes that make clear why a connection failed. For example, there is the error message 500, "Syntax error, command unrecognized." Using these error codes makes troubleshooting easier. For the complete text of the RFC, see `http://www.ietf.org/rfc/rfc0821.txt`.

`REJECT`: The e-mail is rejected with a generic error message.

`OK`: The message is accepted.

`DISCARD`: The message is discarded, and no information is sent to the sender.

Listing 16-2 shows some examples of the content of the access lookup table. Note that if a host, network, domain name, and so on, is not specifically mentioned in this file, it is allowed access.

Listing 16-2. *Example of the Access Lookup Table*

```
mydomain.co        OK
spam@drugs.com     550 No Spam allowed on this server
19.145.0.16        REJECT
1.2.3              REJECT
1.2.3.4            OK
```

The Canonical Lookup Table

The canonical lookup table is powerful; it rewrites the sender as well as the recipient address of incoming as well as outgoing mail. These addresses are not rewritten only in the header of your message but also in the envelope. Since it is rewritten in the envelope as well, this means no traces of the original sender are left. The canonical lookup table is processed by the cleanup daemon. To activate it, you need the following line in /etc/postfix/main.cf:

```
canonical_maps = hash:/etc/postfix/canonical
```

In the canonical table, lines specify addresses or domain names that should be rewritten. In the second column of the canonical table, the e-mail address where the mail has to be routed to is specified. Listing 16-3 shows an example of this.

Listing 16-3. *Example of the Canonical Lookup Table*

```
sales@mydomain.com      jdoe@mydomain.com
@west.mydomain.com      someone@mydomain.com
```

You should be aware that the canonical lookup table works on both e-mail recipients and on senders. If you want to rewrite only recipient addresses, or only sender addresses, use recipient_canonical or sender_canonical instead.

The Recipient Canonical Table

You use the recipient_canonical table like the canonical table to rewrite e-mail addresses. Where the canonical table works on both recipient and sender addresses, the recipient canonical table is used just on recipient addresses of incoming and outgoing mail. The syntax of this table is the same as the syntax of the canonical table. To activate it, use the following entry in /etc/postfix/main.cf:

```
recipient_canonical_maps = hash:/etc/postfix/recipient_canonical
```

The Sender Canonical Table

Where the recipient_canonical table is used to rewrite recipient addresses, you can use the sender_canonical table to rewrite sender addresses of incoming and outgoing mail. This table is read as well by the cleanup daemon, and you can activate it by including the following in main.cf:

```
sender_canonical_maps = hash:/etc/postfix/sender_canonical
```

The Relocated Table

When a user is no longer valid on your mail system, you can choose to just let the mail message bounce. As an alternative, you can send the sender of an incoming mail a message in return that informs the user where the user can be found nowadays. To activate the relocated lookup table, make sure the following is in main.cf:

```
relocated_maps = hash:/etc/postfix/relocated
```

When processing mail, the smtpd daemon checks the relocated file to see whether it has a matching line. Each line in this file contains a reference to the e-mail address of the former user in the first column. This may be the plain mail address of this user; it can, however, also be a regular expression that makes sure a series of mail addresses is matched. The second column contains an informational message. This can be just the new e-mail address, but it can also be other information about how to contact the user. Listing 16-4 shows an example of the contents of the relocated table.

Listing 16-4. *Example of the Relocated Table*

```
rmills@somewhere.com        rmills@nowhere.sh
@nowhere.com                This company doesn't exist anymore
lthomassen@somewhere.com    Doesn't work here anymore
```

The Transport Table

The main purpose of the transport table is to route e-mail messages. The main purpose of the transport lookup table is to make a decision about incoming mail: is this message going to be processed by the local mail server or by another mail server? To use this table, make sure the following is in main.cf:

```
transport_maps = hash:/etc/postfix/transport
```

The first column describes the recipient address in the message. This can be a user (someone@somedomain.com) or a domain. If a domain is used, there is a difference between somedomain and .somedomain. The former is for messages that are sent just to that domain, and the latter includes its subdomains as well. This is default behavior, however, so usually it's not necessary to include. The second column indicates how the message should be handled. This indication is in the transport:nexthop notation. For transport, you can use the values local, smtp, or uucp, specifying the method to contact the next hop. nexthop refers to the machine that should be contacted to process this message. Listing 16-5 shows an example of the transport table.

Listing 16-5. *Example of the Transport Table*

```
awesomedomain.com           smtp:mx1.awesomedomain.com
nodomain                    uucp:mx10
```

The Virtual Table

To make sending messages to the right person easier to understand, you can use virtual domains. These can be considered a subdomain of a real DNS domain. The virtual domain is a domain that doesn't really exist in DNS; it exists only on the MTA. When a mail comes in for a user in the virtual domain, the virtual table makes sure it is delivered to the correct user in the real domain. To activate the virtual domain table, make sure the following is in main.cf:

```
virtual_maps = hash:/etc/postfix/virtual
```

In the virtual domain file, first the name of the virtual domain appears. In the second column in these lines, you can put a random description. This first line is like a header for the rest of the file. In the other lines, the first column specifies users in the virtual domain. The second column mentions the name of the real user where the mail has to be forwarded. Listing 16-6 shows an example of the content of a virtual domain table.

Listing 16-6. *Example of the Virtual Table*

```
virtualdomain.com           some text
john@virtualdomain.com      john
user1@virtualdomain.com     kylie
user2@virtualdomain.com     julie
```

The Aliases Lookup Table

Finally, the aliases lookup table defines aliases in the file /etc/aliases; it is the only table that is not in /etc/postfix, probably to maintain compatibility with the Sendmail mail server, which can use the same file. To activate this table, use the following in main.cf:

```
alias_maps = hash:/etc/aliases
```

Listing 16-7 shows an example of the content of the /etc/aliases file. The \ in front of the name of the user root is to make sure the mail is delivered to a local user, whereas all other names can exist on a network system like NIS or LDAP as well. Also note the use of multiple aliases that is possible in the same alias file; this allows you to make the system more flexible.

Listing 16-7. *Example of* /etc/aliases

```
root:     \root, franck
mailer-daemon:   root
postmaster:      root
webmaster:       root
sales:           jim@somedomain.com
wwwrun:          webmaster
```

If changes are made to the aliases file, make sure these changes are processed. You can use two commands to do that; you can use postalias /etc/aliases to do it in the Postfix-style method, and you can use newaliases if you want the Sendmail style to process this file more.

Using Postfix Management Tools

Managing Postfix is not only about creating the configuration files in the correct syntax. Some management tools are available as well. These administration tools all run from the command line. Next you will find an overview of the most important tools:

newaliases: Use this tool to generate the database file /etc/aliases.db from the file /etc/ aliases.

mailq: This lists all e-mail in the mail queue that has not yet been sent.

postalias: This is the same as newaliases.

postcat: This displays the contents of a file in the queue directories in a readable form.

postconf: This tool changes the content of Postfix variables. If run without arguments, an overview is provided of the current configuration of all variables.

postfix: You can use this command as a troubleshooting command. Use postfix check to find any configuration errors. The postfix flush command forces all e-mail from the deferred queue to be sent immediately, and after making changes to the Postfix configuration files, you can use postfix reload to reload configuration files.

postmap: Use this to convert the lookup tables in the /etc/postfix directory to hash files.

postsuper: This is an important maintenance command. If used as postsuper -s, it removes all unneeded files and directories. If after a system crash old files still remain, postsuper -p cleans all unneeded old files up. You should always run postsuper -s before starting the Postfix server.

Receiving E-mail Using IMAP or POP3

Postfix is the MTA that makes sure mail is sent over the Internet. When this mail arrives, a mechanism needs to retrieve the e-mail and get it to the computer of the end user. Basically, two methods are available for this mechanism. If using IMAP, the user establishes a connection to the server and modifies mail that is on the server. This is a cool solution if the user always has a connection to the mail server. If this isn't the case, it is more useful to use POP3, which transfers all mail to the computer of the client. Be aware, however, that even if using POP3, the client has an option to keep the mail messages on the mail server.

SUSE Linux Enterprise Server offers different solutions to receive e-mail. I'll discuss the three most important solutions in the following sections:

- Use Cyrus IMAPd if you want a complete solution that allows users to access mail by either using IMAP or using POP3.

- Use Procmail to filter incoming mail (note that this uses neither IMAP nor POP3 but is meant for filtering before the mail is stored somewhere on the server).

- Use Qpopper if you want an easy solution that offers POP3 functionality only.

Fetching E-mail Using Cyrus IMAPd

Cyrus IMAPd is a flexible service that can be used to get incoming mail. In this section, you will learn what is needed to install and configure this MDA.

The first step to operate Cyrus IMAPd is to install it. For this purpose, you need the cyrus-imapd package. Once this is installed, you have to configure Postfix for providing e-mail through Cyrus IMAPd. The line that makes this possible is usually in the Postfix master.cf already:

```
cyrus unix - n n - - pipe
  user=cyrus argv=/usr/lib/cyrus/bin/deliver -e -r ${sender} -m
  ${extension} ${user}
```

From master.cf, Postfix calls the deliver program that submits all e-mail to recipients on the system. This program replaces the Postfix local program. For Cyrus IMAPd to do this, all recipients must exist as local users in /etc/passwd on the server where Postfix is used. Another task you need to perform to make Cyrus IMAPd responsible for all incoming mail is to modify /etc/postfix/transport to arrange just this. In the transport lookup table, you enter a line in which your domain is specified, and cyrus is indicated as the responsible handler for incoming mail. This line looks like this:

```
somedomain.com    cyrus:
```

Make sure that after making this modification, you generate the corresponding lookup table with the command postmap hash:/etc/postfix/transport.

Understanding Cyrus IMAPd

To implement Cyrus IMAPd successfully, you need to understand how it works. First I'll talk about all components that are written to your system when installing Cyrus IMAPd:

/etc/cyrus.conf: This is the basic configuration file Cyrus uses. The file contains generic settings that define how Cyrus will work. Ordinarily, it is not necessary to make changes to this file.

/etc/imapd.conf: This file defines how IMAP works. Some important settings are in this file, as you will read in the "Configuring /etc/impad.conf" section.

/var/lib/imap/: In this directory, you will find several important files that Cyrus uses. These include log files, database files, and information about the mailboxes of users on your system.

/var/lib/imap/mailboxes.db: This file includes all mailboxes. Make sure you back it up on a regular basis.

/var/lib/imap/log/: If you are using the Cyrus mechanism for logging, its log files are stored here. In this directory a file is created that has a name that is equivalent to the PID of the Cyrus IMAPd process.

/var/lib/imap/quota/: In here, quotas for the accounts on your server can be added.

/var/lib/imap/shutdown: If you need to shut down the system, create this file. In the file, you can include a line that will be sent to connected clients. Ordinarily, this line would be a warning telling the clients to disconnect. Also when this file exists, no new connections can be made, thus allowing you to shut down the system for maintenance.

/var/lib/imap/msg/motd: Use this file to send a message to clients when they connect. The first line in this file will be displayed to connecting clients.

/usr/lib/cyrus: This is the home directory of the user cyrus. In it you will find all the important binaries used by Cyrus IMAPd.

Configuring /etc/imapd.conf

The main configuration file for the Cyrus server is in /etc/imapd.conf. This file contains several settings that define how the server is to be used. Some of the most important settings are as follows:

configdirectory: This specifies the directory containing the working environment and important configuration files for your server. By default it is set to /var/lib/imap.

partition-default: This specifies the location where the mailboxes are stored. Set by default to /var/spool/imap.

admins: This specifies the list of users with administrative permissions for the Cyrus IMAPd server. By default, only the user cyrus has administrative permissions.

allowanonymouslogin: This specifies whether a user is allowed to log in without a username and password. Always make sure this is set to no.

autocreatequota: This specifies the maximum amount of e-mail data that can be stored in a user's mailbox. By default it is set to 10,000, which equals 10MB; you probably want to increase that. If set to 0, the user is not allowed to create new mail folders, and if set to -1, no quota is applied.

quotawarn: This specifies when the user should get a warning that he is running out of available disk space. By default, this parameter is set to 90 percent.

timeout: This specifies the amount of minutes when an inactive client is disconnected automatically.

sasl_pwcheck_method: This specifies the authentication method that should be used. By default, saslauthd is used for this purpose. This makes sure that passwords are transmitted over the network with some basic encryption applied to them.

After modifying the imapd.conf file, you should restart the IMAPd server. If saslauthd is used for the secure transmission of authentication data over the network, two processes are needed for that: first start saslauthd using rcsaslauthd start, and then use rccyrus start to start the Cyrus mail server.

Managing Users' Mailboxes

The first step in managing user mailboxes is to add users to the system. These users are regular Linux users who are added to /etc/passwd (or any other authentication mechanism; OpenLDAP would work as well, for example). These users don't need a home directory, since all they use is their mailboxes that are stored in /var/lib/imap. Also, no shell is needed. However, the users do need the ability to reset their passwords. Therefore, make sure /usr/bin/passwd is specified as the default shell.

After installing the mail server and adding users to your system, you can start administration. To perform administration tasks, you need the user account cyrus. Be aware that no default password is added for this user, so you need to set it manually. After setting it, you can use the cyradm command. This command opens an interactive shell where you can use several administration commands. To activate this shell, use the cyradm -user cyrus -auth login localhost command. Next, you can start administration tasks. The following is a summary of the most important commands you can use:

listmailbox: Lists the names of all mailboxes.

createmailbox: Creates a mailbox. The user for whom you are creating the mailbox must have a valid account in /etc/passwd.

deletemailbox: Deletes a mailbox.

renamemailbox: Renames a mailbox.

setquota: Sets quota on a mailbox.

listquota: Gives an overview of the quotas that are applied currently.

If, for example, you want to create a mailbox for user alex, perform the following steps:

1. Make sure that user alex exists in /etc/passwd.

2. Open the cyradm tool using cyradm -user cyrus -auth login localhost.

3. From the cyradm interactive shell, use createmailbox user.alex to create a mailbox for your user. Make sure the username is specified as user.alex; this will set default permissions to the mailbox.

4. Use listmailbox to check that the mailbox has been created successfully.

5. Close the interactive interface using the exit command.

Basically, this is everything you need to create a mailbox for users. Of course, many more tasks are available from the cyradm interface. You can get an overview of all options when using the help command from within the administration interface.

Filtering Incoming E-mail with Procmail

When mail is coming in to your server, you can filter this mail and determine where the mail needs to be stored. Procmail is the MDA used for this purpose. It can sort e-mail automatically, forward it to other recipients, or delete it automatically according to some criteria the user has specified. Procmail can be useful if, for example, you want to get rid of some e-mail before it even arrives in your mailbox. The last option is particularly interesting, because it helps you remove spam automatically.

To use Procmail, it has to be called from the Postfix main.cf file. This is usually done with the following line, which is added to the Postfix environment by default:

```
mailbox_command = /usr/bin/procmail
```

When it is activated, you can use Procmail to set up automatic e-mail filtering and redistribution. By default, e-mail is delivered to the user mailboxes in /var/spool/mail/. You can change this behavior by creating a .procmail file in the home directory of the individual user. Listing 16-8 shows an example of automatic mail filtering performed by Procmail.

Listing 16-8. *Example of* .procmail *Mail Filtering File*

```
PATH=/bin:/usr/bin
MAILDIR=$HOME/Mail
LOGFILE=$MAILDIR/mail.log

:0
* ^From.*somedomain
$MAILDIR/Somedomain

:0 ^Subject.*viagra
$MAILDIR/spam

:0
*
$MAILDIR/Inbox
```

In this example, you can see three rules that are applied, after some specific variables have been set that specify where mail binaries can be found. The first rule specifies that data in the From field will be compared to *somedomain. If there is a match, the mail is automatically forwarded to the Somedomain folder in the mailbox of the user. Next, you can see that all messages that have viagra in the message subject line are forwarded automatically to the spam folder. This is a primitive way of handling spam. Last, all other mail (matching the * criterion) is placed in the folder Inbox.

Getting E-mail with POP3 Using Qpopper

Especially if you want to set up a simple POP3 server, Qpopper is an excellent choice. The reason is that it is easy to set up, and it offers everything you may expect from a POP3 server. Usually, it is installed by default on your SUSE Linux Enterprise Server 10 server. Since Qpopper is ordinarily started from xinetd, you need to modify the appropriate xinetd configuration file, /etc/xinetd.d/qpopper. Listing 16-9 shows an example of its contents.

Listing 16-9. *Example of the* /etc/xinetd.d/qpopper *Configuration File*

```
#
# qpopper - pop3 mail daemon
#
service pop3
{
#
    disable         = no
    socket_type     = stream
    protocol        = tcp
    wait            = no
    user            = root
    server          = /usr/sbin/qpopper
    server_args     = -s
    flags           = IPv4
}
```

In this example, just one line is important: disable = no. This line makes sure the Qpopper service is started automatically when a POP request is incoming. After making the required modifications to this file, make sure to (re)start xinetd by using rcxinetd [re]start. Ordinarily, this service isn't activated automatically, so to make sure it is started when booting your server, use insserv xinetd, which will insert the service to the appropriate runlevels.

After making sure that Qpopper is started, just one task remains. As an end user, you have to configure your favorite POP client and connect to the POP3 server. You will see that e-mail automatically starts coming in to your mailbox.

Using YaST to Set Up an MTA

In this chapter, you have learned how to set up a mail server manually. You can also use YaST for easily configuring a mail server. You should, however, be aware that YaST offers limited options to tune your mail server. For complete control of what happens, you still need to hack the configuration files manually. If you are planning on using YaST, you have to meet one condition. You do need the OpenLDAP server to be installed and active as well. This doesn't really make sense, but if the OpenLDAP server isn't installed, you just cannot configure the mail server from YaST. You can find more information about configuring OpenLDAP in Chapter 17. The following procedure will guide you through setting up the MTA using YaST:

1. From YaST, select Network Services ➤ Mail Server. This will start the mail server program.

2. In the Connection type box you can see in Figure 16-6, select the connection type used on your server. In most cases, it will be a permanent connection. Since the AMaViS antivirus program is included with SUSE Linux Enterprise Server, I recommend always selecting the option Enable Virus Scanning as well.

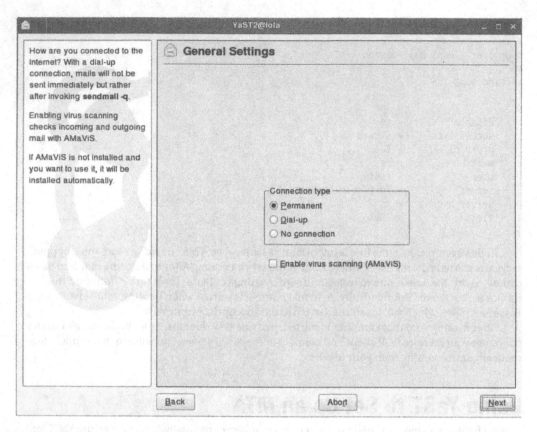

Figure 16-6. *After selecting the connection type you are using, make sure to enable virus scanning.*

3. If you are relaying e-mail to an outgoing mail server, on the screen you can see in Figure 16-7, specify what outgoing mail server to use. If you are installing a mail server that is connected to the Internet on a permanent basis, you don't need to provide anything here. If you want the canonical table to be modified automatically as well, click the Masquerading tab, and enter all e-mail addresses and how you want them to be transformed. If the outgoing mail server you want to relay to needs you to authenticate, click Authentication, and enter the credentials required to authenticate on this server.

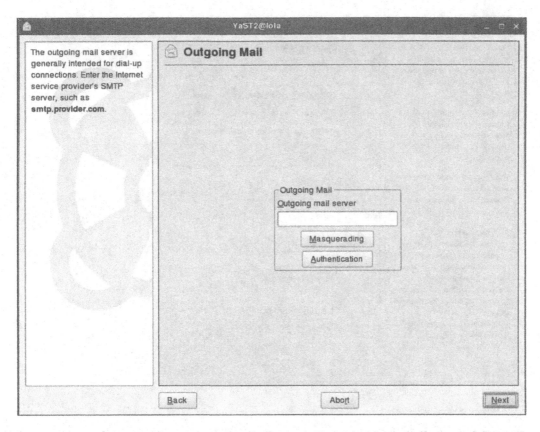

Figure 16-7. *You need to specify an outgoing mail server only if you are using a dial-up connection.*

4. In the final configuration screen, which you can see in Figure 16-8, you specify how to handle incoming mail. If you are setting up a real Internet-connected mail server, select Accept Remote SMTP Connections. If you are using a firewall, make sure the option Open Port in Firewall is selected as well. The options in the Downloading box are necessary only if you want to fetch your mail from some Internet mail server. In the Delivery Mode drop-down box, you specify how mail needs to be delivered by your MTA. The default value is Directly, which will write it to the mailboxes of local users directly; alternatives are through Procmail or Cyrus IMAPd. Select the option that applies best to your environment. Finally, on the same screen you can configure aliases as well as virtual domains. You can find more information about how to handle these in the section "Tuning Postfix with Lookup Tables" earlier in this chapter. After entering all the required settings, click Finish to finalize installation.

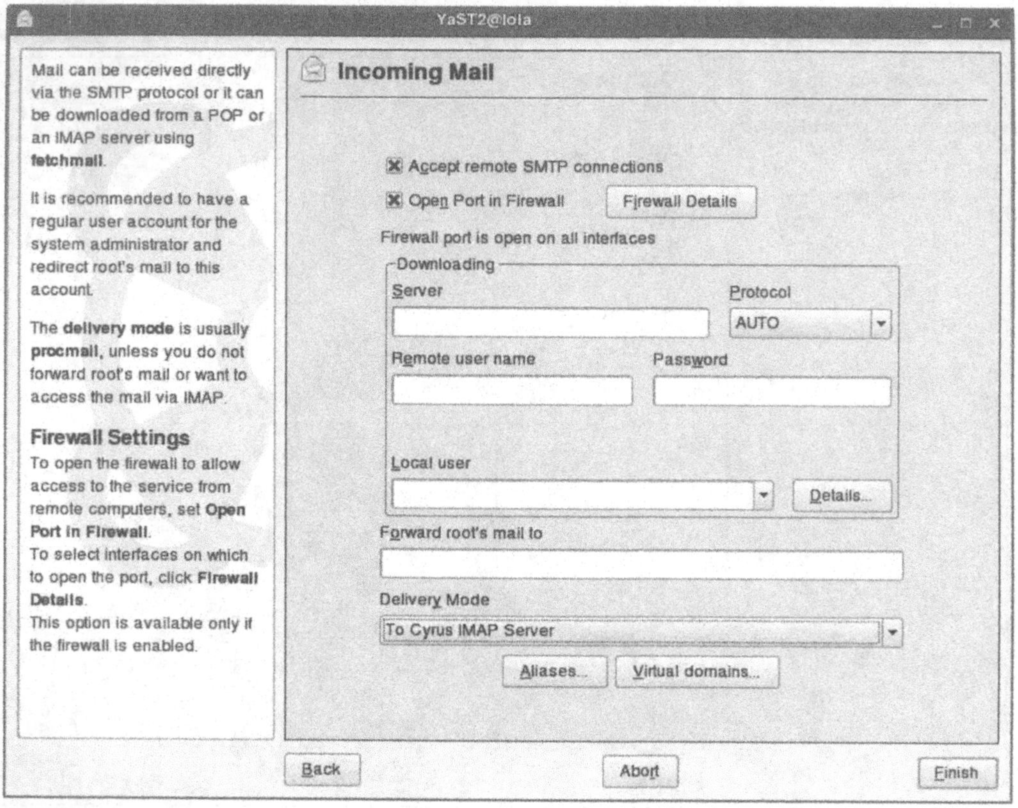

Figure 16-8. *On the Incoming Mail screen, you specify how incoming mail is handled.*

Summary

In this chapter, I introduced how to set up SUSE Linux Enterprise Server 10 as a mail server. You learned how to configure Postfix as an easy-to-maintain MTA that will exchange mail with other servers on the Internet and make sure users in your network can be reached from everywhere. Next, you learned how to set up Cyrus IMAPd as an IMAP mail server or Qpopper as an easy-to-use POP mail client. This chapter hasn't covered every aspect of setting up a successful mail server; it has just covered the basics. You should be aware that setting up a mail server involves more than just making the processes work. For example, you should configure spam and virus protection.

CHAPTER 17

■ ■ ■

Working with OpenLDAP

On a Linux system, you can configure many services. Each of these services has its own configuration files. If many Linux servers are used in a network, all these servers have many small configuration files. Therefore, you as the administrator of those servers are responsible for keeping all those configuration files up-to-date. If that sounds tedious to you, then OpenLDAP is the service for you. This directory service allows you to manage information centrally in your network, and if configured correctly, it will save you a lot of time.

Centralizing Vital Information

In the past couple of years, many attempts have been made to centralize the management of important configuration files on Linux and Unix systems. The first serious attempt was Sun's Network Information System (NIS), formerly known as Yellow Pages. In an NIS environment, based on configuration files such as /etc/passwd, NIS generated *maps*, which were stored on one or more servers. You could use the NIS master for accessing and managing that information; if it was for accessing the information only, you could use NIS slaves as well. A long time ago this model was rather popular in Unix environments; nowadays, however, it is not used often.

The modern replacement for NIS infrastructures is the Directory service. A *Directory service* allows for any kind of data to be stored centrally in a hierarchical manner. Working in a hierarchical way makes using a Directory service a lot more efficient when dealing with huge amounts of data. All major operating systems have their own Directory service. Microsoft has Active Directory, and Novell has eDirectory. On Linux, OpenLDAP is an example of such a Directory service. On SUSE Linux Enterprise Server, it is the default Directory service. If you need a more robust Directory service that has multiplatform support and is scalable for millions of objects, Novell's commercial Directory service eDirectory is a better solution.

Note To distinguish between a directory as a storage unit in the file system (like the directory /etc) and a *Directory* that is used as a centralized database to organize information in a network environment, I will use *directory* with a lowercase *d* when referring to the storage unit in the file system and *Directory* with a capital *D* to refer to the centralized database.

In addition to offering a centralized and hierarchical solution for managing important information in the network, a Directory service such as OpenLDAP is replicated according to the multimaster model. In this model, there is no clear distinction between a master copy of the database that can be written to and the slave copies of the database that cannot be written to: changes can be written on any server on the network, to any copy of the database. This is an important difference from, for example, NIS, where no modifications can be made when the NIS master is down.

The name OpenLDAP comes from the Lightweight Directory Access Protocol (LDAP), which is a standard that was developed to get data from a directory based on the X.500 Directory service. This Directory service was originally developed as a Directory for telephony services. Many Directories are based on that standard; for example, Active Directory and eDirectory are both LDAP compatible. In the Linux environment, OpenLDAP is more than just a protocol to get data out of a Directory. It is a Directory service by itself that delivers more or less the same services as other Directory services such as eDirectory and Active Directory.

Structure of an LDAP Directory

When talking about the structure of an LDAP Directory, I should make a distinction between the way the Directory is organized in a hierarchical way and the way the services are implemented in different configuration files and services. In the following sections, you will learn about both of these issues.

The LDAP Hierarchy

OpenLDAP stores its information in objects. These are, for example, the entities that use the network such as users. These objects have attributes that determine the information that can be attached to an object. For example, the full name and the password of a user are also known as the *user attributes*. The object types are also known as *object classes* (so user linda is an object, and user is the object class). The attributes that can be used by the objects, as well as the object classes themselves, are defined in the schema. You can modify the OpenLDAP schema so you can create your own object classes.

The OpenLDAP Directory contains two kinds of object classes: leaf object classes and container object classes. A *leaf object class* is the "end object," something that is really used in the network, such as a user or a printer. The *container object class* is used to organize leaf object classes in a hierarchical manner. Using container objects makes it easier to manage large amounts of leaf objects. Often the structure of the container objects follows the DNS hierarchy.

Some frequently used container object classes are as follows:

Country (c): The country object class is meant to be used on top of the LDAP hierarchy, like it is in a DNS environment.

Locality (l): The locality typically comes under the country object class. It is often used to refer to a city.

Organization (o): The organization typically comes in the locality object, if these object classes are used. It can also be used as the top of the structure, and it refers to the company where the OpenLDAP Directory is installed.

Organization unit (ou): If your organization is large, within the organization, you can use organization unit objects. These are like the divisions of your company, although you can use them to refer to geographical locations as well.

Domain component (dc): This is a generic container object type. You can use it instead of the specific object types, such as c, l, o, and ou.

Some frequently used leaf object classes are as follows:

Person: The person object class is used for the users in your environment.

Alias: An alias is not a real object by itself; it is used to point to an object elsewhere in the OpenLDAP Directory.

Based on the hierarchical structure that is used in your environment, each object has a unique name. This unique name, which is referred to as a *distinguished name* (DN), consists of the name of the leaf object, followed by a list of all the container objects the leaf object is in. In LDAP distinguished names, an abbreviation indicates what type of object it is, and the different components are separated from each other with commas. An example of such a distinguished name (DN) is as follows:

```
cn=linda, ou=mktg, o=mycomp
```

In this distinguished name, the abbreviation cn (common name) indicates that linda is a leaf object.

The ultimate purpose of a leaf object is to keep attributes together that belong together. For example, a person object class can have many attributes associated to it. What attributes those are exactly in the end is determined by the schema. Some often used attributes are as follows:

- uid stores the name a Linux user needs to log in to a server.

- uidNumber refers to the numerical user ID, as defined in the Linux /etc/passwd file.

- cn is the common name of the object as it appears in the LDAP Directory.

- sn is the surname, typically of a user object.

- objectClass indicates the object class as defined in the schema to which an object belongs.

The list of attributes you can use is virtually unlimited. It doesn't really make sense to include a complete list of them here; as long as you know what object classes and what attributes are often needed, you know enough for most situations.

Of special interest are the object classes that you need to log in to an LDAP server. These are posixAccount, which contains the properties that are ordinarily used in /etc/passwd; shadowAccount, which contains the attributes that are ordinarily defined in /etc/shadow; and posixGroup, which contains the attributes that are ordinarily defined in the /etc/groups file.

OpenLDAP Files and Directories

Before you learn about the way the OpenLDAP server is installed, I'll summarize its most important components:

- slapd is the OpenLDAP process. It runs on every OpenLDAP server.

- If OpenLDAP is configured for replication between several servers (not covered here), slurpd is the process that handles the replication.

> **Note** Replication is useful when several servers share the same OpenLDAP Directory. Replication ensures that modifications made to the Directory on one server are synchronized to the other server almost immediately.

- `slapd.conf` is the main configuration file for your OpenLDAP server. You can find it in the `/etc/openldap` directory.

- `ldap.conf` is the client configuration file for LDAP. It is needed on every workstation that needs to know how to find an LDAP server. Make sure you are using the right one, because a copy of `ldap.conf` is installed in `/etc`, and there is a copy in `/etc/openldap` as well.

- The directory `/etc/openldap/schema` contains all schema files that are installed by default. If you want to add new object classes or new attributes, you should install a schema file in this directory that defines those object classes and attributes.

- The directory `/var/lib/ldap` contains the OpenLDAP database.

- The file `/etc/sysconfig/openldap` contains start-up parameters for OpenLDAP on your server.

Installing an OpenLDAP Directory with YaST

When installing SUSE Linux Enterprise Server, an OpenLDAP server is configured automatically. As an alternative, you can choose to (re)configure the OpenLDAP server later. In the following sections, you'll learn how to change the configuration options while installing and how to change them later. First, you'll look at the available options when you are installing the server, and then you'll see what options you can modify once you have completed the installation.

Configuring the OpenLDAP Server During Installation

When you are installing your server, just after configuring the network card, a certificate authority and OpenLDAP server are automatically set up. The LDAP server is created, based on the DNS information you have entered while configuring the network board. If, for example, you have used `mydomain.com` as the DNS setting for your server, the LDAP Directory is created with the container `dc=mydomain,dc=com`. A root user with the name of `cn=Administrator,dc=mydomain,dc=com` is created, and the LDAP password is set to the password of the `root` user (see Figure 17-1). If you don't like these settings, you can change them.

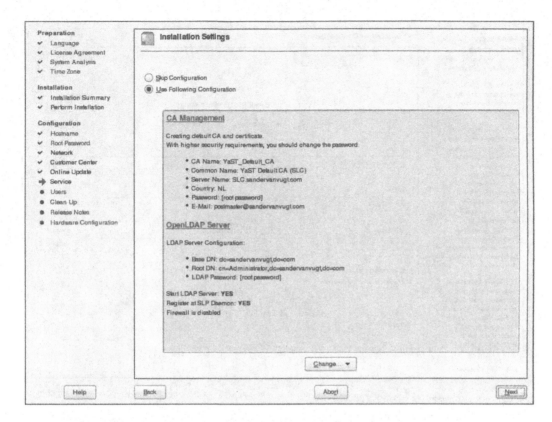

Figure 17-1. *When installing, your LDAP server is created with default settings.*

Follow these steps:

1. On the OpenLDAP server Installation Settings screen, select Change ➤ OpenLDAP Server. This opens a screen in which you can change all the settings of your server (see Figure 17-2). On the top of this screen, you'll see an error displayed, indicating that changing anything in this dialog box disables the automatic generation of the LDAP database. Click OK on that warning.

2. Now you can set all the basic settings for the OpenLDAP server. On the LDAP Server Configuration screen, the following settings are available:

   - *Enable Server/Disable Server*: Select either one of these options to start the server automatically when your server boots. In most situations, you'll probably prefer the server to be enabled by default.

   - *Base DN*: This is the container in the LDAP hierarchy where OpenLDAP will start creating its objects. By default, this container has the same name as the DNS domain you've entered while configuring the network board in your server.

   - *Root DN*: Here you enter the name of the administrator of the LDAP server. By default, the name Administrator is used, but you can change that to anything you want. Make sure the option Append Base DN is selected; this will create the administrative user in the container specified as the base DN.

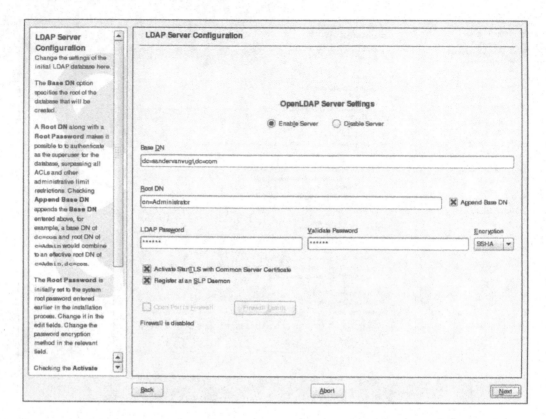

Figure 17-2. *On the LDAP Server Configuration screen, you can change all the settings used by the LDAP server.*

- *LDAP Password/Validate Password*: Here you enter the password of the root DN.

- *Encryption*: Choose between CRYPT, SMD5, SHA, SSHA, or PLAIN for the encryption of the password of the LDAP root DN. By default SSHA is selected. If some applications have a problem handling that algorithm, you can select any other algorithm, or you can select PLAIN to store the passwords in plain text in the LDAP database.

- *Activate StartTLS with Common Server Certificate*: By selecting this option, which is on by default, your LDAP server will be TLS enabled and use the default server certificate for all TLS encryption.

- *Register at an SLP Daemon*: If OpenSLP is activated (which by default is the case), selecting this option makes sure your OpenLDAP server is registered at an OpenSLP daemon. This makes searching for your LDAP server on the network a lot more convenient.

3. After making all required selections on the LDAP Server Configuration screen, click Next to proceed. This returns you to the Installation Settings screen from where you can continue the installation. When clicking Next to proceed, the OpenLDAP server is installed and its Directory is created.

4. On the next screen, you can select how you want authentication to take place on your server. If an OpenLDAP server was created, you will authenticate on the LDAP server by default. After clicking Next, you will see the LDAP Client Configuration screen. On that screen, you have to configure the LDAP client. Make sure the following options are configured in this window. You can ignore the Advanced button for now; I describe it later in this chapter:

   - *User Authentication*: Make sure Use LDAP is selected if you want to authenticate against the LDAP server.

   - *Address of LDAP Servers*: Here you need to specify where the LDAP server(s) can be found. If the LDAP server is on the same host as the LDAP client, localhost is automatically entered. To add other servers, you can enter them here as a space-separated list, or you can use the Find button to find any other OpenLDAP servers on your network using SLP.

   - *LDAP base DN*: The LDAP base DN is the container in the LDAP structure where the server will start searching for the names you enter. If, for example, the base DN is set to dc=mydomain,dc=com and a user enters the username linda in a login window, OpenLDAP will look for that username relative to the dc=mydomain,dc=com container.

   - *LDAP TLS/SLL*: Make sure this option is selected to use TLS-secured connections to the LDAP server.

   - *LDAP Version 2*: Check this option if your LDAP server doesn't understand LDAP version 3. You don't need this option for OpenLDAP because it does understand LDAP 3.

   - *Start Automounter*: If a server has been set up for storing home directories that are shared by a network protocol such as NFS, by checking this option you can make sure these home directories are mounted automatically when they are referenced.

5. After making your modifications on the LDAP Client Configuration screen, click Next to continue the installation. Check Chapter 1 for more details on the next steps.

Configuring OpenLDAP on an Operational Server

The previous section described how to install and configure OpenLDAP when installing your server. This is not the only time you can configure OpenLDAP; using YaST, you can do it anytime you want:

1. In YaST, select Network Services ➤ LDAP Server. This opens the screen you see in Figure 17-3.

2. First you need to select the radio button Yes to start the OpenLDAP server. If you want your server to be registered at an SLP daemon, select Register at an SLP Daemon as well. Then click Configure to start configuring your OpenLDAP server.

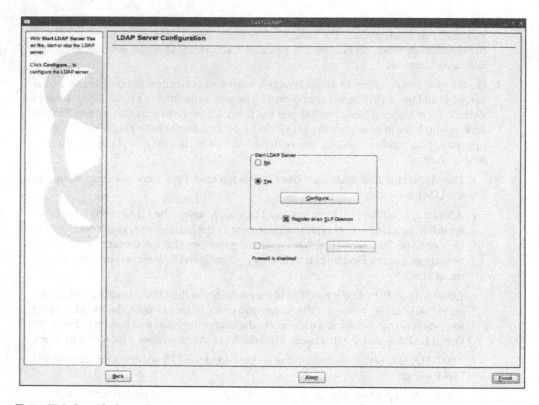

Figure 17-3. *Specify that you want to start the LDAP server, and then click Configure to continue.*

3. If an OpenLDAP Directory was already set up, you will see the screen shown in Figure 17-4. If no OpenLDAP Directory exists yet, you will see the screen in Figure 17-2. Read the section "Configuring the OpenLDAP Server During Installation" for directions on how to proceed from there. In this procedure, I assume you want to change the settings of an existing OpenLDAP server.

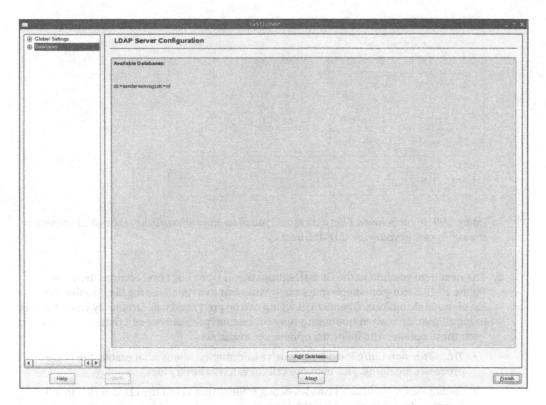

Figure 17-4. *This is the configuration screen you see if an OpenLDAP Directory already exists.*

4. On the LDAP Server Configuration screen shown in Figure 17-4, click Global Settings. This takes you to the screen where you change generic settings for your server. From there, select Schema Files. You will now see the dialog box shown in Figure 17-5. In this dialog box, you specify what schema files you want to use. Selecting the proper schema files is important, because these files determine what object classes and properties will be available for your server. The default schema files allow for user authentication; if you need to go beyond that, click Add to add schema files. Installing the Samba server installs several schema files in the directory /etc/openldap/schema. From that directory, you can select the samba3.schema file to add all the information that is needed to store Samba user information in the LDAP server. It is possible to copy third-party schema files to this directory as well and add them using the Schema Files screen.

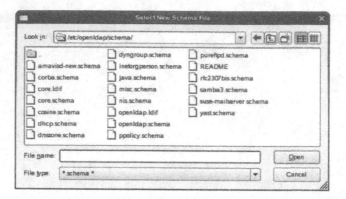

Figure 17-5. *In the Schema Files dialog box, you determine what object classes and properties are supported by your OpenLDAP Directory.*

5. The next item you find in the Global Settings menu is the Log Level Settings item (see Figure 17-6). Here, you select what exactly you want to write to the log files. As shown in the list of available options, OpenLDAP logging can be pretty verbose. Ordinarily you don't want to log all that; only when troubleshooting connection problems does it make sense to select from these options. The following options are available:

- *Trace Function Calls*: Provides extensive information about what exactly the LDAP processes are doing. This includes calls to external library files.

- *Debug Packet Handling*: Provides debug information about the LDAP traffic that is handled. This generates a lot of information.

- *Heavy Trace Debugging*: Provides detailed information about what exactly the LDAP processes are doing.

- *Connection Management*: Provides information about connections to the OpenLDAP server that are maintained and established.

- *Print Packets Sent and Received*: Prints the content of all LDAP data that is sent and received by your server.

- *Search Filter Processing*: Provides information on how information in search filters is handled by your server.

- *Access Control List Processing*: Provides information on granting or denying access based on access control lists.

- *Log Connections, Operations, and Result*: Provides useful logging options that summarize everything that happens from a given connection.

- *Log Entries Sent*: Logs what log entries have been sent.

- *Print Communication with Shell Back-ends*: Provides information about communication with external processes that are connected to the OpenLDAP server.

- *Entry Parsing*: Provides information about browsing information in the OpenLDAP Directory.

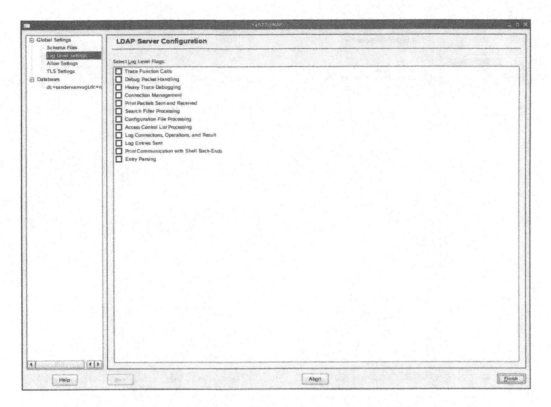

Figure 17-6. *To allow for exact tuning of what is happening on your server, different log options are available.*

6. Next, under Allow Settings (see Figure 17-7) you'll find four options to specify what exactly you want to allow on your server. If you do not have a specific reason to use one or more of these options, don't select them because they will decrease the security offered by your server. You can, for example, open your server for LDAP version 2 bind requests, but this version of the protocol is not as secure as version 3, so don't do this unless you really need it.

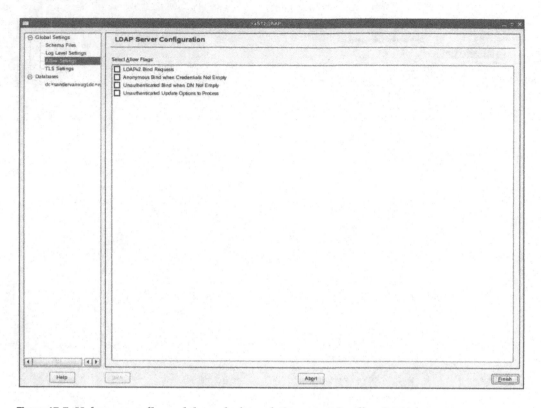

Figure 17-7. *Unless you really need them, don't touch the options in Allow Settings.*

7. On the TLS Settings screen (see Figure 17-8), you can specify whether you want to use TLS and, if you want to use it (which is a good idea; otherwise, all the information you send is readable while in transit), which certificate you want to use. Ordinarily, the default server certificate is used for TLS; if you have another certificate you want to use, you can use the Select Certificate button to browse to that certificate and install it. See Chapter 21 for more details on this.

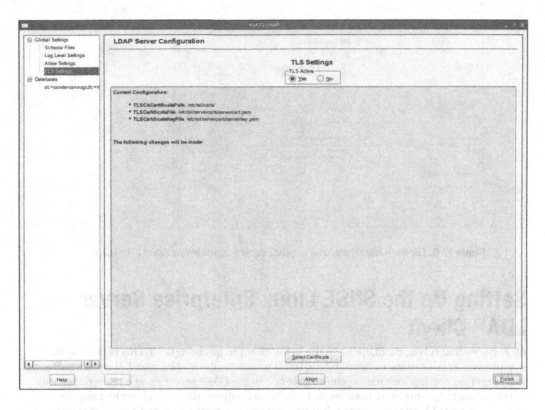

Figure 17-8. *On the TLS Settings screen, you can indicate what certificate you want to use.*

8. Finally, under the Databases option, you can manage existing databases or add new databases. To manage an existing database, select the database. This allows you to change the root DN for the selected database, its password, and the encryption algorithm that is used for the root DN password. To add a new database, click Add Database. This opens the dialog box shown in Figure 17-9. In this dialog box, you can specify the base DN used for that database and the properties for the root DN. In the Database Directory field, you can specify where you want to store the database files. By default, this will be the /var/lib/ldap directory in a subdirectory that has the name of the base DN you create for the new database.

9. After modifying your OpenLDAP environment, from the YaST interface, click Finish to save and apply your settings.

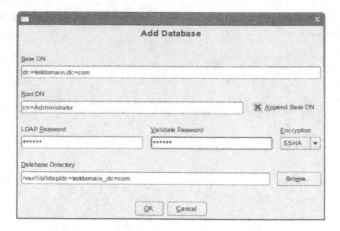

Figure 17-9. *For each new database, a subdirectory is created in* /var/lib/ldap.

Setting Up the SUSE Linux Enterprise Server LDAP Client

All services that rely upon LDAP need the LDAP client to be configured. This is true for the machines that your users are working on, but it is true for the SUSE Linux Enterprise Server as well. Services such as user management that talk to the LDAP server need a reference to this LDAP server to be able to do their work. In its basic configuration, the client just requires you to indicate what LDAP server to use, but you can also set more advanced options to tune where and how users get access to the LDAP server. In this section, you'll learn how to set up the LDAP client with YaST.

Follow these steps:

1. From YaST, select Network Services ➤ LDAP Client Configuration. On the screen shown in Figure 17-10, you can specify whether and how information must be taken from the LDAP Directory. In the User Authentication area, you specify whether LDAP must be used for user authentication. In the LDAP Client area, you specify how the LDAP server can be reached. If an LDAP server is present, you'll always need to specify the addresses of the LDAP servers and the LDAP base DN. Only if users need to authenticate to the LDAP server do you need to select the Use LDAP option. In a situation where LDAP is used as an address book for mail addresses but not for user authentication, you can set the user authentication to Do Not Use LDAP. You can learn more about this screen in the section "Configuring the LDAP Server During Installation" earlier in this chapter.

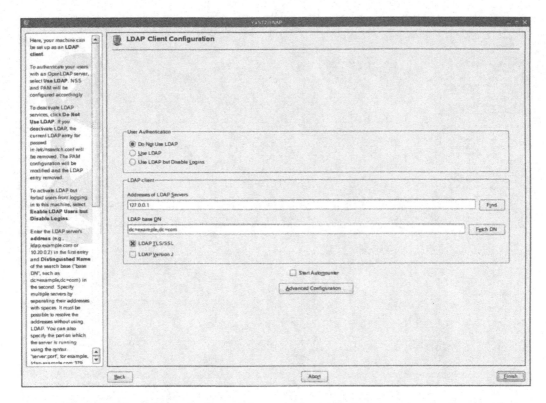

Figure 17-10. *On the LDAP Client Configuration screen, you configure user authentication as well as how you can reach the LDAP server.*

2. On the LDAP Client Configuration screen, click Advanced Configuration to get access to more advanced client settings. This opens the screen shown in Figure 17-11. Here you can specify the naming contexts. These are distinguished names of the containers where users, passwords, and groups are stored. You need to specify something here if these aren't stored in the base context; however, by default they are stored in the base context, so you don't need to change anything here. Next, use the Password Change Protocol field to indicate how the password must be changed. The default value, crypt, is fine for a Linux environment, but you may have applications that need another password change method. If this is needed, select the protocol you require from the drop-down list. Finally, the Group Member Attribute field specifies how users are added to groups. By default, the option member is used, which allows several users who are members of one group (such as the group users) by default. If you want users to be the unique member of a group with their own name, select uniquemember from the drop-down list.

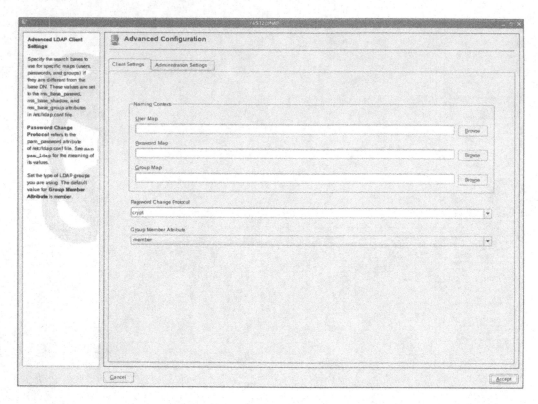

Figure 17-11. *For advanced configurations, you will often need to tune the settings on the Client Settings tab of the Advanced Configuration screen.*

3. On the Administration Settings tab (see Figure 17-12), you can specify where administrative settings need to be stored. First, the Configuration Base DN setting is the location in the LDAP Directory where configuration data is stored by default. Then, the Administrator DN option allows you to specify or change the name of the LDAP administrative account. Check the Append Base DN option to create this user in the container that is set as the base DN. The option Create Default Configuration Objects, if checked, will create objects with default settings that can be used when creating users or groups. Finally, check the Home Directories on This Machine option to inform the YaST user management module that user home directories are stored on this machine; it will not create anything.

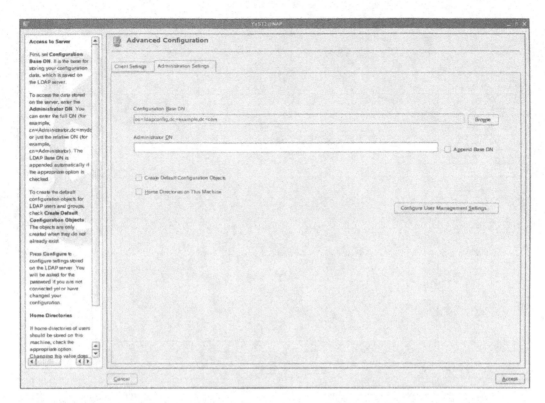

Figure 17-12. *On the Administrative Settings tab, you can specify where in the Directory administration settings should be stored.*

4. The button Configure User Management Settings provides access to a screen where you can configure defaults for user management. When you click this button, you will see a login prompt. Enter the credentials of your LDAP root account (ordinarily `administrator`) and its password. Then, if this is the first time you are using this screen and if the settings from the Administration Settings interface haven't been changed yet, you will be asked whether the container specified as the configuration base DN must be created now. Click Yes; otherwise, you cannot store the user management settings that you'll enter next. Now you will see the screen shown in Figure 17-13. On this screen, you need to create modules that contain sets of user configuration.

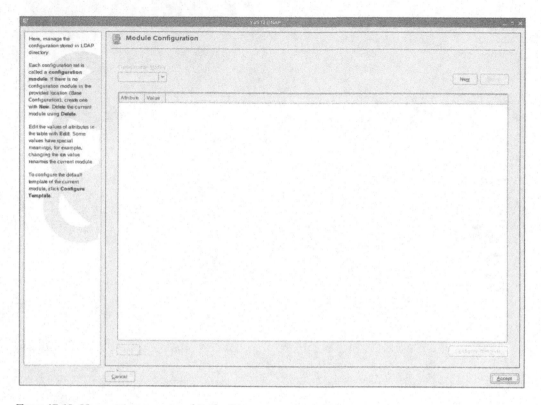

Figure 17-13. *User settings are stored in the Directory as modules.*

5. Now click New to add a new module. This opens the dialog box shown in Figure 17-14. Enter a name for the module, and then select whether you want to create a module for user configuration or for group configuration. Next click OK to continue.

Figure 17-14. *Select what kind of module you want to create, give it a name, and then click OK to continue.*

6. You now see the screen where the module you've just created is selected (see Figure 17-15). This screen displays all the properties of this module. Click any of these properties, and select Edit to change its value. Repeat this procedure for the group creation module as well to store default settings for groups, and then click Accept twice followed by Finish to store the LDAP client settings. Next time you add a new user or group, it will be added to the LDAP Directory with these settings automatically.

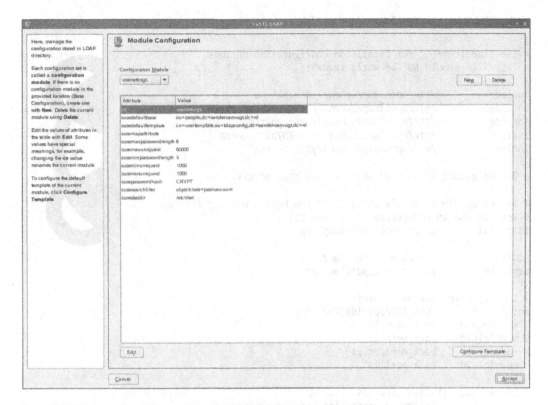

Figure 17-15. *Select any of these settings, and click Edit to change its default value.*

Tuning LDAP Configuration Files

Up to now, you have been working with YaST to configure the LDAP client and server settings. Alternatively, you can tune the LDAP configuration files directly. Three files are involved:

/etc/openldap/slapd.conf: This file contains all the settings that are used by the LDAP slapd process.

/etc/openldap/ldap.conf: This is the client configuration file that determines how your server accesses the LDAP server that's used.

/etc/ldap.conf: This file is used by all the authentication-related utilities to contact your LDAP server.

Configuring the OpenLDAP Server

The /etc/openldap/slapd.conf file is the main configuration file for your LDAP server. Because some of the more advanced settings can be configured only from this file, you should be aware of how it is organized. You can see its contents in Listing 17-1.

Listing 17-1. *The* /etc/openldap/slapd.conf *File*

```
#
# See slapd.conf(5) for details on configuration options.
# This file should NOT be world readable.
#
include         /etc/openldap/schema/core.schema
include         /etc/openldap/schema/cosine.schema
include         /etc/openldap/schema/inetorgperson.schema
include         /etc/openldap/schema/rfc2307bis.schema
include         /etc/openldap/schema/yast.schema

# Define global ACLs to disable default read access.

# Do not enable referrals until AFTER you have a working directory
# service AND an understanding of referrals.
#referral       ldap://root.openldap.org

pidfile         /var/run/slapd/slapd.pid
argsfile        /var/run/slapd/slapd.args

# Load dynamic backend modules:
modulepath      /usr/lib/openldap/modules
# moduleload    back_ldap.la
# moduleload    back_meta.la
# moduleload    back_monitor.la
# moduleload    back_perl.la

# Sample security restrictions
#       Require integrity protection (prevent hijacking)
#       Require 112-bit (3DES or better) encryption for updates
#       Require 63-bit encryption for simple bind
# security ssf=1 update_ssf=112 simple_bind=64

# Sample access control policy:
#       Root DSE: allow anyone to read it
#       Subschema (sub)entry DSE: allow anyone to read it
#       Other DSEs:
#               Allow self write access to user password
#               Allow anonymous users to authenticate
#               Allow read access to everything else
#       Directives needed to implement policy:
access to dn.base=""
        by * read

access to dn.base="cn=Subschema"
        by * read

access to attrs=userPassword,userPKCS12
        by self write
        by * auth

access to attrs=shadowLastChange
        by self write
        by * read
```

```
access to *
        by * read

# if no access controls are present, the default policy
# allows anyone and everyone to read anything but restricts
# updates to rootdn.  (e.g., "access to * by * read")
#
# rootdn can always read and write EVERYTHING!


#######################################################################
# BDB database definitions
#######################################################################

database        bdb
suffix          "dc=my-domain,dc=com"
checkpoint      1024    5
cachesize       10000
rootdn          "cn=Manager,dc=my-domain,dc=com"
# Cleartext passwords, especially for the rootdn, should
# be avoid.  See slappasswd(8) and slapd.conf(5) for details.
# Use of strong authentication encouraged.
rootpw          secret
# The database directory MUST exist prior to running slapd AND
# should only be accessible by the slapd and slap tools.
# Mode 700 recommended.
directory       /var/lib/ldap
# Indices to maintain
index   objectClass     eq
```

The first important parts in the slapd.conf file are the following lines:

```
include         /etc/openldap/schema/core.schema
include         /etc/openldap/schema/cosine.schema
include         /etc/openldap/schema/inetorgperson.schema
include         /etc/openldap/schema/rfc2307bis.schema
include         /etc/openldap/schema/yast.schema
```

With these lines, schema files are included. By default, the schema files are in /etc/openldap/ schema. You can add new schema files to that directory if necessary. To include a new schema file, add a line like in Listing 17-1; for example, include /etc/openldap/schema/samba3.schema will include the schema files that allow you to store Samba-related information in the LDAP Directory.

Following the schema files, you can use the referral option. This option refers to an external LDAP server database that is used when this LDAP server is not capable of serving the request. Using the referral option, you can connect your LDAP server to external servers running any LDAP-compatible Directory service. By default, no referrals are used. Use this option only if you really know what you are doing.

Next, the pidfile and argsfile options specify the location where the PID of the current slapd processes is kept, as well as the arguments the server used to start. Ordinarily, you are not required to change these options.

As with web servers, you can extend the functionality of OpenLDAP by using modules. These modules by default are in the directory that is specified with the modulepath option. Next, you can use the moduleload option to load any of these modules as required. By default no modules are loaded.

Next, you can include some security options. These options specify the protection level of the LDAP database, as well as how communication with the database should take place. Uncomment the line security ssf=1 update_ssf=112 simple_bind=64 for a good basic security setting.

After the security settings, some permissions are defined, as follows:

```
access to dn.base=""
        by * read

access to dn.base="cn=Subschema"
        by * read

access to attrs=userPassword,userPKCS12
        by self write
        by * auth

access to attrs=shadowLastChange
        by self write
        by * read

access to *
        by * read
```

In these options, you use the access to statement to define what you are giving access to. You can use any object class name or attribute name here. Then, the lines that start with by specify to whom access can be granted. The by option can have different parameters:

- self: The owner of the object or attribute
- dn=*somedn*: A specific user
- group=*somegroupdn*: A specific group
- *: All

Then you grant the permission level. You can set the following permissions:

- read: Allows reading
- write: Allows writing
- auth: Allows access only to authenticated users
- none: Denies all access

The default permission scheme allows anyone to read everything in the LDAP server. Users can change their passwords only, and the user specified as rootdn can read and write everything, once authenticated successfully.

After the permission settings, the database is defined. First, the database bdb line defines the LDAP database back-end type that should be used. Many database types are available, but it goes beyond the scope of this chapter to discuss all of them with all the available options. By default, the bdb (Berkeley DB) format is used, and that's fine for a small- to medium-sized LDAP server. Next the suffix option specifies what context in the Directory should be used as the base DN. After that, the checkpoint option defines when an automatic check of the database consistency should be performed. The first parameter is the amount of write actions after which it should be checked, and the second option is the maximum number of minutes between checks. Next, the cachesize option specifies the memory in kilobytes that is reserved to cache information from the database. You should consider increasing this parameter on a heavily used system because it will lead to better performance.

Next, the rootdn and root password are specified. Note that these are required only if no root user exists in the Directory already. If such a user exists, you can safely remove these lines. Also note that by default the password of the root user is stored in plain text. If you want to keep the root DN password in here, use slappasswd -s yourpassword to generate an encrypted password string. This command outputs an encrypted string that you can next copy to the slapd.conf file (see Listing 17-2).

Listing 17-2. *Generating an Encrypted Password for the* root *DN User*

```
slappasswd -s novell
{SSHA}mPDYmGGcsHriqqrvjIdJdNJpKpWZvUVh
```

Then, as the next-to-last option, the directory parameter indicates where in the file system the database should be stored. Finally, the index parameter specifies the indexes that should be created. Using a moderate amount of indexes will greatly increase the speed of your Directory. You can create an index for all attributes in the Directory. The default index is created for an exact match of all objectClass attributes and allows you to find back objects faster.

You should notice that the slapd process doesn't check for changes periodically. To activate changes you've made to the configuration, use the rcldap restart command.

Configuring the LDAP Client

Configuring the LDAP client from the command line can be confusing. This is because two LDAP client files have the name ldap.conf. The file /etc/openldap/ldap.conf is the configuration file of the LDAP client. The /etc/ldap.conf file is used by everything related to authentication; to find the LDAP server that is needed for authentication, this is the file you use.

/etc/openldap/ldap.conf

The /etc/openldap/ldap.conf file doesn't contain much information. Only three important options are set. First, the host option indicates what LDAP server to use. For example, if the LDAP server is running on the same server as the client, its setting will be host 127.0.0.1. Next, the base setting refers to the container that should be used as the default container where all searches start. Finally, the TLS_REQCERT setting specifies what to do with TLS settings. You can specify this parameter with one of the following values:

never: No TLS will be used.

allow: The client will request the server certificate. If no certificate is handed back or a bad certificate is provided, the session will continue without TLS.

try: The session is terminated when a bad certificate is received from the server. If no certificate is received, the session will continue without TLS.

demand or hard: A server certificate is requested. If no certificate could be provided or a bad certificate is received, the session will terminate immediately.

/etc/ldap.conf

The /etc/ldap.conf file, which is used for authentication, contains considerably more settings than the /etc/openldap/ldap.conf file. The good news is that most of the additional parameters don't need to be modified to perform a normal authentication session. For information about all the additional settings you'll encounter, check the man page 5 pam_ldap.

Adding, Querying, and Modifying Entries in the Directory

In some cases, you can use YaST to manage information in the LDAP Directory. In many cases, however, YaST just doesn't provide enough information. For example, YaST doesn't have a good interface to add generic information to an LDAP server, and no versatile querying tool is available either. In the following sections, you'll learn how to use command-line utilities to add, modify, and query information in the Directory.

■Tip In addition to the command-line tools, some graphical tools are available. One tool that is pretty well known is GQ. You can download this LDAP tool from `http://gq-project.org`.

Creating LDIF Files

To add, delete, or modify information in the LDAP Directory, you use the Lightweight Directory Interchange Format (LDIF). As an administrator, you need to create a file in LDIF and then add the content of the file to the Directory using the `ldapadd` command. LDIF files can contain entries for multiple objects, so you don't need to create an LDIF file for each record you want to add. It is important that in the LDIF file, you specify the distinguished name first for each entry. Listing 17-3 shows an example where some container objects are specified in an LDIF file.

Listing 17-3. *Defining New Container Objects with LDIF*

```
dn: dc=mycompany,dc=com
objectclass: organization
objectclass: dcObject
o: mycompany

dn: ou=users,dc=mycompany,dc=com
objectclass: organizationalUnit
ou: users
```

This example defines two containers. First, the top-level organization is defined as `dc=mycompany,dc=com`. Next, in that container an organizational unit is defined with the name `ou=users,dc=mycompany,dc=com`. The most difficult part of specifying how new objects should be created in the LDAP Directory is knowing what object classes are available and what attributes can be used for those object classes. To find out what you can do, you can look in the schema files where the objects are defined. Although not always easy to understand for a nonspecialist, these files contain definitions for all object classes that can be used in the Directory, as well as the attributes you can use for these object classes. To give you an idea, in Listing 17-4 you can see the definition of the `organizationalUnit` object class from the `core.schema` schema file. The most important things you can see from this example are the attributes that must be used (`MUST ou`) and the other attributes that may be used when defining this object class (`MAY ( userPassword $ ...`).

Listing 17-4. *Defining the Organizational Unit Object Class in the* core.schema *File*

```
objectclass ( 2.5.6.5 NAME 'organizationalUnit'
        DESC 'RFC2256: an organizational unit'
        SUP top STRUCTURAL
        MUST ou
        MAY ( userPassword $ searchGuide $ seeAlso $ businessCategory $
                x121Address $ registeredAddress $ destinationIndicator $
                preferredDeliveryMethod $ telexNumber $ teletexTerminalIdentifier $
                telephoneNumber $ internationaliSDNNumber $
                facsimileTelephoneNumber $ street $ postOfficeBox $ postalCode $
                postalAddress $ physicalDeliveryOfficeName $ st $ l $ description ) )
```

Once the LDIF file has been defined, you should make sure it is in the proper format. LDAP uses the Unicode format, and your editor may not use that format. To make sure the LDIF file is using the proper format, you can use the recode command. For example, the recode lat1..utf8 myldif command will make sure the file with the name myldif is recoded in the proper Unicode format. I recommend always doing this before you go on; that way, you can prevent errors that may be difficult to troubleshoot otherwise.

If you want to add users using LDIF, you must make sure all the required properties are defined. Listing 17-5 shows how to add user linda to the default user container of testdomain.com. Change the information in this example as required to add users, but make sure all properties mentioned in the example are used.

Listing 17-5. *LDIF to Add Users to Your Directory*

```
version: 1
dn: uid=linda,ou=users,dc=mydomain,dc=com
objectClass: posixAccount
objectClass: shadowAccount
objectClass: inetOrgPerson
uid: linda
uidNumber: 1000
gidNumber: 100
cn: Linda T
givenName: Linda
sn: T
homeDirectory: /home/linda
loginShell: /bin/false
shadowMax: 99999
shadowWarning: 7
shadowInactive: -1
shadowMin: 0
shadowLastChange: 13326
```

Note The syntax of LDIF files is described in RFC 2849. Every LDIF file should start with a version identifier, as shown in Listing 17-5. The current version is still version 1.

Adding Entries with ldapadd

Once you have created the LDIF file, you can add the information from the LDIF file to the Directory. You need ldapadd to do that; the following is an example of how to use this command:

```
ldapadd -x -D "cn=administrator,dc=mycompany,dc=com" -W -f myldif.ldif
```

This example uses four different options:

- -x connects to the LDAP server without using SASL authentication. You don't need it if SASL authentication has been configured already; if it isn't, use -x. This will cause passwords to be transmitted to the LDAP server in clear text, however.

- -D specifies the name of the administrative account you are using to add the information to the Directory.

- -W causes the command to prompt for a password.

- -f indicates what file should be imported. After this option, you should enter a complete name of the file you want to add.

Modifying Entries with ldapmodify

If you know how to add information to the Directory, modifying information isn't hard. To modify information, just create an LDIF file that contains the new property values for existing objects in the Directory. Next, you can use the ldapmodify command to apply the LDIF file to the Directory. This will check the existing account and make sure all new settings are applied. Like ldapadd, ldapmodify uses the options -x -D -W -f as well. So, the following command will apply modifications made in the file mychanges.ldif to the Directory:

```
ldapmodify -x -D "cn=administrator,dc=mycompany,dc=com" -W -f mychanges.ldif
```

Deleting Entries with ldapdelete

To delete information from a Directory, you need LDIF. In this case, the LDIF file just needs to list the distinguished names of objects you want to delete. After creating the LDIF file, apply it to the Directory with ldapdelete, for example:

```
ldapdelete -x -D "cn=administrator,dc=mycompany,dc=com" -W -f removeusers.ldif
```

Using ldapsearch to Query the Directory

Once your Directory has been populated with many entries, you sometimes may want to check whether a certain entry has really been created successfully. To do that, you can use the ldapsearch command. To use it with simple authentication, just use the command ldapsearch -x. This command will query your LDAP server and show what objects it finds in the container that is specified as the search base in the /etc/ldap.conf file. Note that you don't need to enter a password, because anyone (even nonauthenticated users) can have read permissions to the complete LDAP Directory.

When using ldapsearch without any further specifications, you may be overwhelmed by the amount of results that are displayed. Therefore, it is useful to tune it a little bit. For example, you may limit the output to certain object types only. You can do that with a command such as the following, where only objects that have the attribute type uid set are displayed:

```
ldapsearch -x "(uid=*)"
```

Using filter expressions, you can even filter some more. For example, the command `ldapsearch -x "(uid=l*)"` will show only those objects that use the `uid` property and have it set to something that begins with the letter *l*. To make it easy for you, `ldapsearch` displays its results in LDIF; this allows you to write the results of the command to an LDIF file and use `ldapadd` to import that file to some other Directory. That's one way of performing a fast migration!

Summary

In this chapter, you learned how to create an LDAP server on SUSE Linux Enterprise Server. A large part of this chapter was devoted to managing the OpenLDAP environment with YaST; that's because YaST offers a far easier way to manage the LDAP server than the command-line utilities, which force you to create LDIF files first. You also learned how to set up OpenLDAP for user authentication. Be aware that OpenLDAP offers much more than that. SUSE Linux by default is configured to make it easy for you to add any kind of information to the LDAP server, such as DHCP or DNS information. This flexibility really makes OpenLDAP one of the most important services to run on your server. The next chapter covers the remote management of your server with utilities such as OpenSSH.

CHAPTER 18

■ ■ ■

Enabling Remote Access

In the "old days," people used telnet to access their systems remotely. Nowadays they can't do this: telnet sends its passwords in plain text over the network, and because too often these packets are transmitted across an insecure network, this really is not an option. It is simple for someone with a packet analyzer such as Ethereal to grab packets and read your username and password from the network. Therefore, new methods of remotely accessing a server have been created. I'll discuss two of these techniques in this chapter. First you will learn how to use Secure Shell (SSH) to set up a secure (read: encrypted) connection with a server. Next, you will learn how you can use VNC to get access to the graphical display of your server remotely. VNC isn't secure by itself, but in this chapter you'll learn how to combine it with SSH to make it secure.

In this chapter, I'll cover the following subjects:

Understanding how SSH works: I'll explain how SSH uses encryption keys to establish secure remote sessions. Also, you will learn how to use SSH.

Configuring SSH: I'll explain how you can use the sshd_config and ssh_config files to tune how SSH works.

Configuring SSH key-based authentication: You will learn how to secure SSH even more by using public/private key technology for authentication.

Tunneling traffic with SSH: I'll explain how to establish a simple VPN connection between hosts using SSH.

Using VNC: You'll learn how to use VNC to get remote access to the server's graphical display.

Understanding How Secure Shell Works

The essence of SSH is its security. Public and private keys play an important role in this security. On first contact, the client and the server exchange public keys, the so-called *host key*. This host key proves the identity of the server to which a client is connecting. When connecting, the server sends its public key to the client. If this is the first time the client is connecting to this host, it replies with the message shown in Listing 18-1.

Listing 18-1. *Establishing an SSH Session with an Unknown Host*

```
The authenticity of host 'localhost' (127.0.0.1)' can't be established.
RSA key fingerprint is 79:20:76:ed:93:7e:aa:d7:01:25:e5:d7:de:0b:76:87.
Are you sure you want to continue connecting (yes/no)? yes
```

Only if the client trusts that this is really the intended host should the client answer yes to this request. As a result, the host is added to the file .ssh/known_hosts in the home directory of the user who initiated the SSH session. The next time the client connects to the same host, the client checks this known_hosts file to see whether the host is already known. This check is based on the public key fingerprint of the host, which is a unique number that is related to the public key of the host. Only if this number matches the name and public key of the server that the client is connecting to is the connection established. If both pieces of data don't match, it is likely that the host the client is connecting to is not the intended host; therefore, the connection will be refused.

Once you have established the identity of the server you want to connect to, you establish a secured channel between the client and server. To establish this secured channel, you use a session key. This is an encryption key that is the same on both the server and the client; it encrypts all the data sent between the two machines. The session key is negotiated between the client and the server based on their public keys. This negotiation, amongst others, determines the protocol that should be used. Session keys can use 3DES, Blowfish, or IDEA, for example.

After establishing this secured channel, the user on the client is asked for its credentials. If nothing is configured, this will be a prompt where the user is asked to enter a username and password. This, however, is not the only way it can be done, as you'll see in the "Using Key-Based Authentication" section. Alternatively, the user can authenticate with a public/private key pair, thus proving that the user really is the user who he says he is.

All this may sound pretty complicated. The nice part is that the user won't notice anything. The user just has to enter a username and password—that's all. If you want to go beyond simple password-based authentication, however, it is useful to understand what is happening.

Working with Public/Private Key Pairs

The essence of SSH is the public/private key pair. By default, the client tries to authenticate using RSA/DSA key pairs. To make this work, first the client gets the public key of the server to establish a secure session; this happens automatically. Next, the server must get the public key of the client, which is something that has to be configured by hand. (Later in the "Using Key-Based Authentication" section you'll find more information about this procedure.) When the client has a public/private key pair, it will generate an encrypted string with its private key. If the server is able to decrypt this string using the public key of the client, the identity of the client is proved.

When using public/private key pairs, you can configure different aspects of the encryption. First, the user needs to determine what cryptographic algorithm he wants to use. For this purpose, he can choose between RSA and DSA; the latter is considered stronger. Next, the user has to determine whether he wants to protect his private key with a passphrase. This is because the private key really is used as the identity of the user. Should anyone steal this private key, it would be possible to forge the identity of the owner; therefore, it is a good idea to secure private keys with a passphrase.

Working with Secure Shell

Basically, SSH is a suite of tools that consists of three main programs and a daemon. The name of the daemon is sshd, and it runs by default on your SUSE server. The commands are ssh, scp, and sftp. The first, ssh, establishes a secured remote session. Let's say that it is like telnet but then secured with cryptography. The second, scp, is a useful command you can use to copy files to and from another server. The third, sftp, is an FTP client interface. By using it, you can establish a secured FTP session to a server that is running the sshd. One of the best features of these tools is that you can use them without any preparation or setup, and you can set them up to work entirely according to your needs. They are easy to use and are specialized tools at the same time.

Using the ssh Command

The simplest way to work with SSH is by just entering the command ssh, followed by the name of the host to which you want to connect. For example, to connect to the host AMS.sandervanvugt.com, you would use the following:

```
ssh AMS.sandervanvugt.com
```

Depending on whether you have connected to that host before, SSH can ask you to check the credentials of the host or just ask for your password. The ssh command doesn't ask for a username, because it assumes you want to connect to the other host with the same username you are logged in with locally. You have two ways to indicate that you would rather log in with another user account. First, you can specify the username followed by the @ sign and the name of the host to which you want to connect. Alternatively, you can also use the -l option followed by the name of the user account you want to use to connect to the other host. So basically, ssh linda@AMS.sandervanvugt.com and ssh -l linda AMS.sandervanvugt.com are the same. Ready to do your work on the remote host? Enter the exit command (or press Ctrl+D) to close the session and return to your own machine.

Now, it seems like it's a lot of trouble to log in completely on a remote host if you need to enter just one or two commands. If this is a situation you face often, it is good to know you can just specify the name of the command at the end of the ssh command. So, ssh -l linda@AMS.sandervanvugt.com halt would shut down the server (if user linda is allowed to do that). Using commands as an option to SSH is especially useful in shell scripts. If you are using SSH in a shell script, it would help if the user could log in without entering a password. Later in this chapter, in the "Configuring Key-Based Authentication" section, you'll learn more about that.

Using scp to Copy Files Securely

Another part of the SSH suite you will definitely like is the scp command. You can use it to copy files securely. If you know how the cp command works, you'll also know how to handle scp. It is just the same, with the only exception that it works with a complete reference including the host name and username of the file you want to copy. Consider the following example:

```
scp /some/file linda@AMS.sandervanvugt.com:/some/file
```

This easy-to-understand command would copy /some/file to AMS.sandervanvugt.com and would place it in the directory /some/file on that host. Of course, it is possible to do the inverse: scp root@SFO.sandervanvugt.com:/some/file /some/file would copy /some/file from a remote host to the local host.

Using sftp for Secured FTP Sessions

As an alternative to copying files with scp, you can use the sftp command to connect to servers running the sshd program and establish a secured FTP session with such a server. From the sftp command, you have an interface that really looks a lot like the normal FTP client interface. All the commands you are used to working with in a classic FTP interface work here as well, with the only difference that in this case it is secured. For example, you can use the ls and cd commands to browse to a directory and see what files are available. From there, you can use the get command to copy a file to the local current directory. Figure 18-1 shows an example of this.

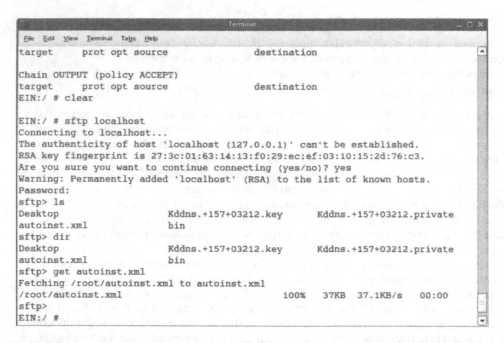

Figure 18-1. *From an* sftp *session, you can do all the things you are used to doing from a normal FTP session.*

Configuring SSH

In an SSH environment, a node can be a client and a server at the same time. So as you can imagine, both of these aspects have a configuration file. The client is configured in /etc/ssh/ssh_config, and the server has its configuration in /etc/ssh/sshd_config. Setting options for the server isn't hard to understand; just set them in /etc/ssh/sshd_config. For the client settings, however, the situation is more complicated, because you have several ways of overwriting the default client settings:

- /etc/ssh/ssh_config is a generic file that is applied to all users initiating an SSH session. The settings in this file can be overwritten by individual users who create an .ssh_config in the directory .ssh in their home directory.

- An option in /etc/ssh/ssh_config has to be supported by the sshd_config file on the server to which you are connecting. For example, if you are allowing password-based authentication from the client side but the server doesn't allow it, it will not work.

- Options in both files can be overwritten by using command-line options.

Table 18-1 gives an overview of the most useful options for ssh_config.

Table 18-1. *Most Interesting Options in* ssh_config

Option	Description
Host	This option applies the following declarations (up to the next Host keyword) to a specific host. Therefore, this option is applied on a host to which a user is connecting. The host name is taken as specified on the command line. Use this parameter to add some extra security to specific hosts. It is possible to use wildcards such as * and ? to refer to more than one host name.
CheckHostIP	If this option is set to yes (which is the default value), SSH will check the host IP address in the known_hosts file. Use this as a protection against DNS or IP address spoofing.
Ciphers	This option can have multiple values to specify the order in which the different encryption algorithms should be tried in an SSH version 2 session.
Compression	This option, which can have the values yes or no, specifies whether to use compression. The default is no.
ForwardX11	This useful option specifies whether X11 connections will be forwarded. If set to yes, graphical screens from an SSH session can be forwarded over the secure tunnel. The result is that the DISPLAY environment variable that determines where to draw graphical screens is set correctly. If you don't want to enable X-forwarding by default, you can use the option -X on the command line when establishing an SSH session.
LocalForward	Specifies that a TCP/IP port on the local machine is forwarded over SSH to the specified port on a remote machine. See the "Using Generic TCP Port Forwarding" section later in this chapter for more details.
LogLevel	Use this option to specify the verbosity level for log messages. The default value is INFO. If this doesn't go deep enough, VERBOSE, DEBUG, DEBUG1, DEBUG2, and DEBUG3 will provide more information.
PasswordAuthentication	Use this option to specify whether you want to use password authentication. By default, you can use password authentication. In a secure environment where keys are used for authentication, you can safely set this option to no to disable password authentication completely.
Protocol	This option specifies the protocol version that SSH should use. The default value is set to 2,1; version 2 is used first and if that doesn't work, version 1 is tried. It is a good idea to disable version 1 completely, because it has some known security issues.
PubkeyAuthentication	Use this option to specify whether you want to use public key–based authentication. This option should always be set to the default value yes, because public key–based authentication is the safest way of authenticating.

The counterpart of ssh_config on the client computer is the /etc/ssh/sshd_config file on the server. Many options that are used in the ssh_config file can be used in the sshd_config file as well. Some options, however, are specific for the server side of SSH. Table 18-2 gives an overview of some of these options.

Table 18-2. *Most Important Options in* sshd_config

Option	Description
AllowTcpForwarding	Use this option to specify whether you want to allow clients to do TCP port forwarding. Since this is a useful feature, you probably want to leave it to its default value, yes.
Port	Specifies the port on which the server is listening. By default, sshd is listening on port 22.
PermitRootLogin	Use this option to specify whether you want to allow root logins. To add additional security to your server, consider setting this option to no. If set to no, the root user has to establish a connection as a regular user and from there use su to become root or use sudo to perform certain tasks with root permissions.
PermitEmptyPasswords	This option specifies whether you want to accept users coming in with an empty password. From a security perspective, this might not be a good idea; therefore, the default value no suits in most cases. If you want to run SSH from a script and establish a connection without entering a password, however, it can be useful to change the value of this parameter to yes.
X11Forwarding	Use this option to specify whether you want to allow clients to use X11-forwarding. On SUSE, the default value for this parameter is yes.

Using Key-Based Authentication

Now that you know all about the basic use of SSH, it's time to look at some of the more advanced options. One of the most important of these options is key-based authentication. To use this kind of authentication, SSH uses public/private key–based authentication. Before diving into the configuration of key-based authentication, you'll learn how you can use these keys.

Introducing Cryptography

In general, you can use two methods for encryption: symmetric and asymmetric encryption. Symmetric encryption is fast, but not so secure. Asymmetric encryption is slower but more secure. In a symmetric key environment, both parties use the same key to encrypt and decrypt messages. In an asymmetric key environment, a public/private key pair is used. The latter is the important technique that is used for SSH.

If asymmetric keys are used, every user needs his own public/private key pair, and every server needs a pair of them as well. Of these keys, the private key must be protected by all means. If the private key gets compromised, the identity of the owner of the private key gets compromised as well. Therefore, a private key ordinarily is stored in a secure place where no one can access it besides the owner of the key. The public key on the contrary is available to everyone.

You can use public/private keys, generally speaking, for two purposes. The first of them is to send encrypted messages. In this scenario, the sender of the message encrypts the message with the public key of the receiver of the message, and the receiver of the message is the only one who can decrypt the message with the matching private key. This scenario requires of course that before sending an encrypted message, you need to have the public key of the person to whom you want to send the message.

The other option is to use public/private keys for authentication or to prove that a message has not changed since it was created. The latter is also known as *nonrepudiation*. In the example of authentication, the private key generates an encrypted token, the *salt*. If this salt can be decrypted with the public key of the person who wants to authenticate, then there is enough proof that a server is really dealing with the right person; therefore, access can be granted. This technique requires the public key to be copied to the server before any authentication can happen, however.

Using Public/Private Key–Based Authentication in an SSH Environment

When you use SSH key-based authentication, you have to make sure that, for all users who need to use this technology, the public key is available on the servers where they want to log in. When logging in, the user creates an authentication request that is signed with his private key. This authentication request is matched to the public key of the same user on the server where that user wants to authenticate. If it matches, the user is allowed to come in; if it doesn't, the user is denied access.

Public/private key–based authentication is enabled by default on SUSE Linux Enterprise Server; therefore, only when no keys are present will the server prompt the user for a password. The following summarizes what happens when a user tries to establish an SSH session with a server:

1. If public key authentication is enabled, which by default is the case, SSH checks the .ssh directory in the user's home directory to see whether a private key is present.

2. If a private key is found, SSH creates a packet with some data in it (the salt), encrypts that packet with the private key, and next sends it to the server. With this packet, the public key is sent as well.

3. The server now checks whether a file with the name authorized_keys exists in the home directory of the user. If it doesn't, the user cannot authenticate with his keys. If this file does exist and the public key is an allowed key and also is identical to the key that was previously stored on the server, the server uses this key to check the signature.

4. If the signature could be verified, the user is granted access. If it didn't work out, the server will prompt the user who tries to connect for his password.

All this sounds pretty complicated, but it isn't. Everything is happening transparently, if everything has been set up correctly. Also, you won't even notice a delay. All this ordinarily happens in less than a second.

Setting Up SSH for Key-Based Authentication

The best way to explain how to set up SSH for key-based authentication is by showing an example. In the following procedure, key-based authentication is enabled for the user root:

1. On the desktop where root is working from, use the command ssh-keygen -t dsa -b 1024. This generates a 1,024-bit public/private key pair. Listing 18-2 shows what happens.

Listing 18-2. *Generating a Public/Private Key Pair with* ssh-keygen

```
workstation # ssh-keygen -t dsa -b 1024
Generating public/private dsa key pair.
Enter file in which to save the key (/root/.ssh/id_dsa) :
Enter passphrase (empty for no passphrase):
Enter same passphrase again:
Your identification has been saved in /root/.ssh/id_dsa.
Your public key has been saved in /root/.ssh/id_dsa.pub.
The key fingerprint is:
59:63:b5:a0:c5:2c:b5:b8:2f:99:80:5b:43:77:3c:dd root@workstation
```

I'll explain what happens now. The user in this example uses the ssh-keygen command to generate a public key and a private key. The type encryption algorithm used to generate this key is DSA, which is considered more secure than its alternative RSA. The option -b 1024 specifies that 1,024-bit encryption should be used for this key. The longer this number, the more secure it will be. Notice, however, that a many-bits encryption algorithm will also require more system resources to use it. After generating the keys, the command asks you where to save it. By default, it will create a directory with the name .ssh in your home directory, and in this directory it creates the file id_dsa. This file contains the private key.

Next, you are prompted to enter a passphrase. This passphrase is an extra layer of protection that you can add to the key. Since anyone who has access to your private key (which isn't that easy to do) can forge your identity, your private key should always be passphrase protected. After entering the same passphrase twice, the private key is saved, and the related public key is generated and saved in the file /root/.ssh/id_dsa.pub. Also, a key fingerprint is generated. This fingerprint is a summary of your key, a checksum that is calculated on the key to see whether anything has happened with the key.

2. After creating the public/private key pair, you must transfer the public key to the server. The ultimate goal is to get the contents of the id_dsa.pub file in the file /root/.shh/authorized_keys. You can, however, not simply copy the file to the destination file authorized_keys; this is because other keys may already be stored in that file. Therefore, first use scp to copy the file to a temporary location. The command scp /root/.ssh/id_dsa.pub root@server:/root/from_workstation_key.pub will do the job.

3. Now that the public key is on the server, you have to put it in the authorized_keys file. Before doing this, make sure the directory .ssh exists on the server in the home directory of the user root, that is, has user and group root as its owner and the permission mode 700. Then, on the server with the directory /root as your current directory, use cat from_workstation_key.pub >> .ssh/authorized_keys. This appends the content of the public key file to the authorized_keys file, thus not overwriting any file that may have been there already.

4. If no errors occurred, you were successful! Return to your workstation, and start an SSH session to the server where you have just copied your public key to the authorized_keys file. You will notice that you aren't prompted for a password anymore; you are prompted for a passphrase instead. This proves you were successful. Notice, however, that you need to repeat this procedure for every server you want to be able to establish a session with that is secured with keys.

Working with keys as described is an excellent way to make SSH authentication more secure. It has a drawback, though: if from a shell script or cron job you need to establish an SSH session automatically, it is not practical to be prompted for a key first. Therefore, you need some method to execute such jobs automatically. One solution is to create a special user account with limited permissions. If you have such an account, it doesn't hurt if that user account is using a public/private key pair without a passphrase assigned to the private key. Another solution is to run ssh-agent, which caches the keys before they are used. In the next section, you will learn how that works.

Caching Keys with ssh-agent

To prevent yourself from entering private keys all the time, you can use ssh-agent. This useful program caches keys for a given shell environment. After starting ssh-agent for a given shell, you need to add the passphrase for the private key you want to use. This is something you will do for a specific shell, so after you close that specific shell or load another shell, you need to add the passphrase to that shell again.

After adding a passphrase to ssh-agent, the passphrase is stored in RAM. It is stored in a way that it cannot be accessed; only the user who added the key to RAM is able to read it from there. Also, ssh-agent listens only to the ssh and scp processes that were started locally, so you have no way to access a key that is kept by ssh-agent over the network. So, you can be sure that using ssh-agent is pretty secure. Apart from being secure, it is pretty easy to do as well. Enabling ssh-agent and adding a passphrase to it is just a simple two-step procedure:

1. From the shell prompt, use ssh-agent, followed by the name of the shell you want to use it for. For example, use ssh-agent /bin/bash to activate ssh-agent for the bash shell.

2. Now type ssh-add. This will prompt you for the passphrase of your current private key. As the result of this action, you'll see the message identity added, followed by the private key of which the passphrase is added to ssh-agent.

■**Tip** SSH is a great method to get access to other hosts. But did you know you can also use it to mount a file system on a remote system? All modern versions of SSH support this feature: just use sshfs, which gives access to all files and directories on the remote server that as a normal user on that server you can access. If you know how to mount a directory with mount, working with sshfs is easy; for example, the command sshfs linda@AMS:/ data /mnt/AMS would give access to the /data directory on the remote server and connect that directory to /mnt/AMS on the local server.

Tunneling Traffic with SSH

Apart from establishing remote login sessions, copying files, and executing commands on remote hosts, it is possible to use SSH for TCP port forwarding. This way, SSH is used as a simple VPN solution, with the capability of tunneling almost any nonsecured protocol over a secured connection. In the following sections, I'll first talk about X-forwarding and then you can read how to forward almost any protocol using SSH.

Using X-Forwarding

Wouldn't it be useful if you could start an application on a server, where all the workload is performed by the server while you can do the work itself from your client? You can with SSH X-forwarding. When using X-forwarding, you first establish an SSH session to the server to which you want to connect. Next, from this SSH session, you'll start the graphical application. This application will draw its screen on your workstation while doing all the work on the server.

Sound good? Establishing such an environment has only two requirements:

• Make sure the option X11Forwarding is set to yes in /etc/ssh/sshd_config on the server.

• Connect to the server with the ssh -X command from your client. Alternatively, you can set the option X11Forwarding in the client configuration file /etc/ssh/ssh_config, which allows you to forward graphical sessions by default. Since, however, this poses a minor security threat, this setting is not enabled by default on SUSE Linux Enterprise Server.

Now that you have established the SSH session with your server, start any command you want to use. This even allows you to run YaST from a Debian workstation!

Note Forwarding X sessions with SSH is really cool, but it has a limitation. You need an X-server on the client from which you are establishing the SSH session. On Linux, Unix, or the Mac, this is not a problem since an X-server is available for each of these operating systems. On Windows, however, this is a problem. The most-used SSH client for Windows is putty, which a useful client, but it doesn't contain an X-server. If you want to use an X-server that runs on Windows, use Cygwin/X. You can find this free X-server for Windows at http://x.cygwin.com.

Using Generic TCP Port Forwarding

X is the only service for which port forwarding is hard-coded in the SSH software. For everything else, you need to do it by hand, using the -L or the -R option. Refer to the example in Figure 18-2.

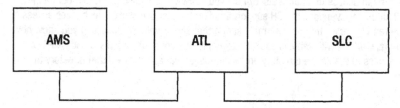

Figure 18-2. *Example network*

The example network shown in Figure 18-2 has three nodes. Node AMS is the node where the administrator is working. ATL is the node in the middle. AMS has a direct connection to ATL but not to SLC, which is behind a firewall. ATL, however, does have a direct connection, not hindered by any firewall, to SLC.

An easy example of port forwarding is the command:

```
linda@AMS:~> ssh -L 4444:ATL:110 linda@ATL
```

In this example, user linda forwards connections to port 4444 on her local host to port 110 on the host ATL as user linda on that host. This is what you would use, for example, to establish a secure session to the insecure POP service on that host. The local host first establishes a connection to the SSH server running on ATL. This SSH server connects to port 110 at ATL, whereas SSH binds to port 4444 on the local host. Now an encrypted session is established between local port 4444 and server port 110; everything sent to port 4444 on the local host would really go to port 110 at the server. For example, if you would configure your POP mail program to get its mail from local port 4444, it would really get it from port 110 at ATL. Notice this example uses a nonprivileged port. Only user root can connect to a privileged port with a port number less than 1024. No matter what port you are connecting to, you should always check in the configuration file /etc/services, where port numbers are matched to names of services if the port number is already in use by some other process, and use netstat -patune | grep <your-intended-port> to make sure the port is not already in use.

A little variation on the local port forwarding shown earlier is remote port forwarding. If you wanted to do that, you would forward all the connections to a given port on the remote port to a local port on your machine. For example, use the -R option as in the following example:

```
linda@AMS:~> ssh -R 4444:AMS:110 linda@ATL
```

In this example, user linda connects to host ATL (see the last part of the command). On this host, port 4444 is addressed by using the construction -R 4444. This remote port is redirected to port 110 on the local host. As a result, anything going to port 4444 on ATL is redirected to port 110 on AMS. This example would be useful if ATL were the client and AMS were the server running a POP mail server to which linda wants to connect.

Another useful example is when the host you want to forward to cannot be reached directly, for example because it is behind a firewall. In that case, you can establish a tunnel to another host that is reachable with SSH. Imagine that in the example in Figure 18-2, the host SLC is running a POP mail server that user linda wants to connect to; this user would use the following command:

```
linda@AMS:~> ssh -L 4444:SLC:110 linda@ATL
```

In this example, linda forwards connections to port 4444 on her local host to server ATL that is running SSH. This server would forward the connection to port 110 on server SLC. Note that in this scenario, the only requirement is that ATL has the SSH service activated; no sshd is needed on SLC for this to work. Also note that there is no need for host AMS to get in direct contact with SLC, because this would happen from host ATL.

In the previous examples, you learned how to use the SSH command to do port forwarding. This isn't your only way of doing it. If you need to establish a port-forwarding connection all the time, you can put it in the SSH configuration file on the client computer. Put it in .ssh/config in your home directory if you want it to work for your user account only or in /etc/ssh/ssh_config if you want it to apply for all users on your machine. The parameter you should use as an alternative to ssh -L 4444:ATL:110 is as follows:

```
LocalForward 4444 ATL:110
```

Using Other Methods for Remote Access

Although certainly it's the most secure and reliable method for remote access, SSH isn't the only way you can manage your server remotely. Another method that is rather popular is VNC, which allows you to take over a complete desktop remotely. In the following sections, you'll learn how to configure your server for VNC, how to use VNC remotely, and how to use screen to establish a remote session in which screens are synchronized, which is an ideal solution for helping people remotely.

Using VNC for Remote Access to Graphical Screens

Enabling VNC is easy: the YaST Remote Administration option in the Network Services section allows you to set up VNC access quickly. As shown in Figure 18-3, this module gives access to two choices: Allow Remote Administration and Do Not Allow Remote Administration. Want to enable remote administration for your server? Just click Allow Remote Administration, and you are almost there. If you have an active firewall protecting your server, don't forget to select Open Port in Firewall. This option is available only if the firewall on your server is really enabled; if it isn't, the option is disabled. Then click Finish to complete the setup for remote administration.

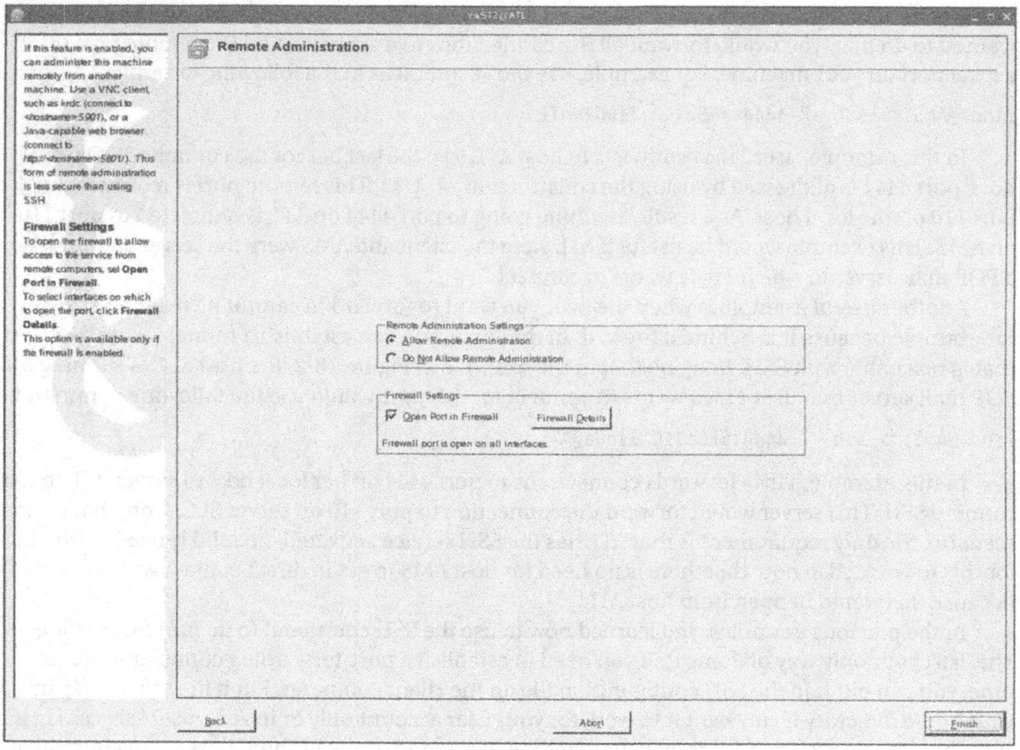

Figure 18-3. *You can easily set up VNC remote administration using YaST.*

Clicking Finish isn't the final step to make remote administration possible for your server. This is because the component that is used to log in to your server has to be enabled for remote administration as well. Depending on the graphical desktop environment you are using, this component is xdm (generic for X), kdm (for KDE), or gdm (for the GNOME desktop environment). Remote administration of your server is possible only after this component is restarted. On SUSE Linux Enterprise Server, you can accomplish this by using the command rcxdm restart from a shell command line. Next, your server is enabled for VNC remote access.

You can now connect with a Java-enabled web browser to VNC port 5801 on your server by going to http://yourserver:5801. As an alternative, you can use a dedicated VNC client from either Linux or Windows to connect to port 5901 at the remote server. As a result, you will see a login prompt that you can connect to, and that will give you access to the remote server (see Figure 18-4).

You should note that there are some small differences between the normal login interface that XDM is offering you and the interface offered when accessing a server via VNC. The latter option offers an Administration button. If you click this button, you are asked for the password of user root. After entering it, you are redirected to YaST, which is available as your only option to administer the remote system.

Figure 18-4. *VNC gives access to the graphical login of a server from a browser or a dedicated VNC client.*

Enabling VNC via xinetd

Using the remote administration option from YaST is one way to enable VNC. There is also another way that offers some more advantages, and that is to enable VNC via xinetd. Since xinetd is the subject of the next chapter; I will not cover the details of this configuration here. You should, however, know that there are some advantages when using xinetd to configure access to VNC. The most important of these is that some more access control is possible. When combining xinetd with TCP Wrapper, you can specify exactly what hosts you do want to give access to and what hosts you don't. Check Chapter 19 for more details on how this works.

Securing VNC Remote Access with SSH

Setting up your server for remote administration is one thing; making sure this remote administration happens in a secure way is another thing. By default, VNC traffic is sent over the network unencrypted. Tunneling VNC over SSH is an easy solution for that problem:

1. On your workstation, use the command `ssh -X root@yourserver -L 5901:yourserver:5901`. This makes sure that all traffic addressed to local port 5901 is forwarded to port 5901 on your server.

2. Now from your workstation, use a tool like vncviewer to connect to the local VNC port. Note that you shouldn't connect to port 5901 but to port 1, which is an internal VNC port.

You can now access VNC, just like you did when connecting to it without encryption. The only difference is that when the tool asks for passwords, they aren't sent in plain text over the network anymore.

Using screen to Synchronize Remote Sessions

Ever tried to imagine what someone is seeing while working on a remote system? Don't imagine! With screen, you can see just what happens. The idea is simple: the user on the remote server uses the screen command. Next, you use screen -x from an SSH session to attach to that screen. The next step is that everything the user in question types into his console is displayed in your SSH session as well, and everything you are typing shows up on his screen. You are in fact sharing the same screen in this scenario. The next procedure shows how to set this up. Note that this is just one of the many uses of screen. Check its man page for more information about this versatile utility:

1. On the server, just type screen in a terminal window.

2. From a client, establish an SSH session to the server. Any plain SSH session will do fine.

3. Now from the client, type screen -x. This gives a list of screens to which you can connect (see Listing 18-3).

Listing 18-3. *Example of Screen Usage*

```
AMS:~ # screen -x
There are several suitable screens on:
        7068.pts-1.AMS  (Attached)
        7188.pts-6.AMS  (Attached)
Type "screen [-d] -r [pid.]tty.host" to resume on of them.
```

4. Read the message that screen -x is giving you, and next connect to one of the screen sessions that are mentioned. In this example, you can do that by using the command screen -x -r 7068.pts-1.AMS. This command will connect you to the console window where screen is running on the server. Enjoy!

Summary

If people are talking about remote administration or remote access, they are probably talking about SSH, which is the real standard for remote administration on Linux. In this chapter, you learned everything you should know to manage your server remotely with SSH. However, SSH isn't the only option you can use to manage your server remotely. Another popular solution is VNC, which you can enable from YaST easily. You not only learned how to do this but also how to use VNC securely by tunneling it with SSH. Finally, you read about another useful tool, the screen command. In the next chapter, you will read how to enable lots of network services by using the Xinetd "superdaemon."

CHAPTER 19

■ ■ ■

Configuring xinetd

You can start services in two ways. First, you can fire up the service when your system boots. In that case, it will occupy its port and wait for incoming connections all the time. However, if you need a service only occasionally, starting it at system boot and keeping it available all the time is a waste of system resources. This is exactly what xinetd is for; the xinetd process listens on behalf of other processes to see whether a connection comes in. If it does, it starts the process, thus making optimal use of system resources. In this chapter, you'll learn how to configure xinetd.

Specifically, I'll cover the following:

- Configuring xinetd with YaST
- Tuning xinetd by hand
- Tuning access to services with TCP Wrapper, a service that you can use to restrict access to services started from xinetd

Configuring xinetd with YaST

The easiest way to configure xinetd is by using YaST. The module to configure xinetd is called Network Services, and you can find it in the YaST menu item Network Services. By default, you will find that xinetd is disabled. That's a good thing from a security perspective, so start by selecting Enable. Now, as shown in Figure 19-1, the xinetd services are no longer disabled, and you can manage each individual service.

The list of currently available services gives an overview of all the services that you can manage using xinetd. Refer to the Status column to get their current status. If set to NI, the service currently is not installed and can therefore not be configured. All the other services by default have the status —, which means they are inactive. To switch the status of an inactive protocol, you can select it and next click the Toggle Status (On or Off) button. If you do this for a service that currently isn't installed, the installer will prompt you that you need to install the RPMs for this service first.

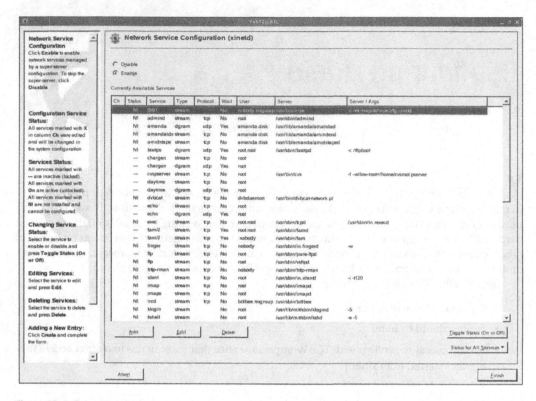

Figure 19-1. *From YaST it is easy to manage xinetd services.*

From YaST, you can set some properties of the services as well. To do this, select the service, and click the Edit button. This opens a screen showing all the options the service has to offer. Figure 19-2 shows what the service editor looks like for the telnet service.

Note After reading the previous chapter, you know that telnet is an insecure service and shouldn't be used. Still, many environments really do need telnet, so therefore you'll learn here how to enable it with xinetd.

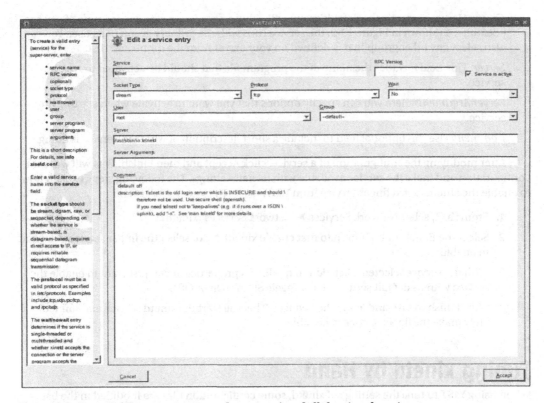

Figure 19-2. *From YaST, you can manage the properties of all the xinetd services.*

For all the services, you have to enter the same parameters. You can see these parameters in Figure 19-2. The following are the parameters you can specify:

Service: Enter the name of the service here. This name must match a service name in the /etc/services configuration file.

RPC Version: Use this optional field to enter the RPC version number that this service should use.

Socket Type: This field describes how the service should be contacted. Ordinarily, the right socket type is selected by default for services that are installed to be managed with xinetd. You can choose from the following: socket types stream, dgram, raw, and seqpacket.

Protocol: Each service can establish a connection in one of four ways. You can choose from the following: tcp, udp, RPC over TCP (rpc/tcp), and RPC over UDP (rpc/udp). Make sure this field matches the way your service works.

Wait: In the Wait field, you specify whether the service should wait for new connections after a current connection closes its session. Set this to Yes for UDP-based services, and set it to No for TCP-based services.

User: In this field, you specify which user the service should run as. Many services run as root by default, which isn't always a good idea.

Group: Here you specify the default group with whose permissions the service runs. If you see –default–, as shown in Figure 19-2, the service runs with the primary group of its user. You can also select any other group that is defined on your server from the drop-down list.

Server: This field includes the name of the program file that should be activated to run the service.

Server Arguments: Here you can specify options that you want to activate when starting the service.

Comment: Use this optional field to include a short description of what the service is doing.

After modifying the configuration of a service, click Accept and then Finish. This will write the configuration and make the service available with its new settings. The following steps explain how to enable the xinetd-based finger service from YaST:

1. From YaST, select Network Services ➤ Network Services (xinetd).

2. Select the Enable radio button to first enable xinetd. Next, select the finger service you want to enable.

3. With the service selected, click Edit to modify its properties. If you just want to enable the service with its default settings, click Toggle Status (On or Off).

4. Click Finish to save and apply the changes. This will start the xinetd service and immediately make the finger service accessible.

Tuning xinetd by Hand

When using YaST to tune the settings of xinetd, some configuration files are modified in the background. When tuning xinetd by hand, you have to modify the following components:

- The xinetd daemon
- The default configuration file /etc/xinetd.conf
- The configuration files for individual services in /etc/xinetd.d

Managing the xinetd Daemon

The xinetd service is implemented by the daemon process xinetd. This process has a script in /etc/init.d that allows you to start and stop this process automatically. Be aware that by default xinetd is not activated, so if you want to use it, enable it first with the insserv xinetd command. Using this command makes sure that xinetd starts automatically the next time you boot your server; in other words, it doesn't start it immediately after you issue insserv xinetd. To start it immediately, use the rcxinetd start command. This command reads all the services' configuration files and makes sure all the services that are enabled are reachable from that moment on.

From time to time, you'll have to restart the xinetd service. This is because it doesn't ever check its configuration files. So if you have modified the services' files, make sure to activate them by using the rcxinetd reload or rcxinetd restart command.

Setting Default Behavior

The configuration of xinetd happens in two places. First, the /etc/xinetd.conf file contains generic settings. It can, however, contain service-specific settings, but that's not the default way to go on SUSE Linux Enterprise Server. Every service has its own configuration file in /etc/xinetd.d. In this section, you'll look at the default settings you can apply in /etc/xinetd.conf. Listing 19-1 shows the default contents of this file.

Listing 19-1. *Default Settings in* /etc/xinetd.conf

```
#
# xinetd.conf
#
# Copyright (c) 1998-2001 SuSE GmbH Nuernberg, Germany.
# Copyright (c) 2002 SuSE Linux AG, Nuernberg, Germanu.
#

defaults
{
        log_type           = FILE /var/log/xinetd.log
        log_on_success     = HOST EXIT DURATION
        log_on_failure     = HOST ATTEMPT
#       only_from          ▪ localhost
        instances          = 30
        cps                = 50 10

#
# The specification of an interface is interesting, if we are on a firewall.
# For example, if you only want to provide services from an internal
# network interface, you may specify your internal interfaces IP-Address.
#
#       interface          = 127.0.0.1

}

includedir /etc/xinetd.d
```

As you can see, this example file specifies only a section with the name defaults. All the settings belonging to that section are within brackets. It is also possible to include settings for individual services. If you want to do that, you need to define the service like this:

```
service service-name
        {
                options
        }
```

In general, however, it is a good idea to leave the service definition to the configuration files in /etc/xinetd.d. Note that all the settings that are defined in /etc/xinetd.conf in the defaults section can be overwritten in the configuration files for the individual services.

The first settings defined in the example in Listing 19-1 are some log settings. The log_type option defines where log entries are sent. In the default setting, they are sent directly to the log file /var/log/xinetd.log by using the parameter FILE /var/log/xinetd.log. As an alternative, you can also redirect log messages to the syslog mechanism (see Chapter 12); you could do this by using the parameter log_type = SYSLOG local1, for example. You can use any other syslog facility as well. The next two lines define what exactly should be written to the log files. The parameter log_on_succes = HOST EXIT DURATION determines that for every successful connection, the following are written to the log files: the name of the host that a user connects from, the exit status with which the connection is terminated, and the duration of the connection is logged. The second line, log_on_failure = HOST ATTEMPT, shows the name of the host that tried to make a connection. Note that the second line causes something to be written to the log file if xinetd could not start the service, if nothing happens, or if, for example, a user connects to a service and enters an incorrect password, which causes a failure.

The default values for the log settings are fine in many scenarios; however, sometimes you might want to add something more. The options shown in Table 19-1 are available to use with the `log_on_success` and `log_on_failure` parameters.

Table 19-1. *Log Options in* `xinetd.conf`

Option	Description
PID	Logs the process ID the user connects to (`log_on_success` only).
HOST	Writes the address of the remote host that tries to establish a connection.
USERID	Tries to log the user ID of the remote user. This doesn't succeed in all cases.
EXIT	Logs the exit status of the service that a connection was established to (`log_on_success` only).
DURATION	Writes the duration of the connection (`log_on_success` only).
TRAFFIC	Records the number of bytes sent to and from the service (`log_on_success` only).
ATTEMPT	Logs that someone tried to make a connection (`log_on_failure` only).

In Listing 19-2, you can see an example of the output generated when users try to connect to the telnet service, given the default log settings.

Listing 19-2. *Example Content of* `/var/log/xinetd.log`

```
06/7/9@11:56:08: START: telnet from=192.168.1.82
06/7/9@11:56:24: EXIT: telnet status=1 duration=16(sec)
06/7/9@11:58:01: START: telnet from 192.168.1.91
06/7/9@11:59:01: EXIT: telnet status=1 duration=60(sec)
```

■**Tip** By default, xinetd logs directly to a file. In an environment where you require a higher level of security, you should log to syslog. This allows for better security settings such as logging to a remote host. You enable this type of logging by setting the `log_type` parameter in the `xinetd.log` file to `log_type = syslog <facility>` `[syslog level]`.

In addition to the log settings, the example in Listing 19-1 shows some other options. The following options are available:

`instances = 30`: This option determines the number of services that can be active for a service simultaneously. This setting limits that to a maximum of 30 instances, which should be enough in most cases. If a service requires more instances to be active at the same time, it may be a better idea to run the services with their own boot script anyway.

`cps = 50 10`:. This is the maximum number of connections per seconds. The first number indicates the maximum number of connections that can be handled per second; the second number indicates the wait time before accepting new connections after the maximum has been reached. This option has one purpose only; it protects you against Denial of Service attacks. Therefore, you should leave it as it is.

only_from: This settings determines the remote host that can connect to xinetd or to a specific service if the option is used in the service-specific configuration file. By default, any host can connect. The best way to use this option is to specify a partial or complete IP address; for example, 192.168. would allow access to any host where the IP address starts with 192.168. You can use host or domain names as well, as long as they can be resolved via DNS or /etc/hosts.

no_access: This setting can specifically deny access to one or more hosts.

access_times: This option specifies the times at which a service (or everything offered by xinetd) is available. Use, for example, access_times 07:00-18:00 to make sure a service can be reached only between 7 a.m. and 6 p.m.

interface: This option is useful if you are running xinetd on a host with more than one network card; use interface = 192.168.1.1 to bind xinetd only to the private address 192.168.1.1, or to be even more restrictive, use interface = 127.0.0.1 so that only connections from the loopback address can be established.

Be aware that I have discussed only the most interesting options you can use in /etc/xinetd.conf. Other options are available as well; check the man pages for more details about them.

Tuning the Individual Services

For generic options that you want to apply to all services, the configuration file /etc/xinetd.conf is the best place to put them. Every service needs some configuration as well. If a service has its own configuration file in /etc/xinetd.d, the settings in this file will always overwrite the settings in /etc/xinetd.conf, if there's a conflict. In addition, every service needs some specific configuration options. The most important setting in these configuration files is the option disabled = yes, which is on by default. Since it is on by default, the service will not run until you remove this option or change it to disabled = no. In Listing 19-3 you can see what the configuration file for the systat service looks like.

Listing 19-3. *Default Configuration File for the systat Service*

```
# Finger, systat and netstat give out user information which may be
# valuable to potential "system crackers." Many sites choose to disable
# some or all of these services to improve security.
# Try "telnet localhost systat" and "telnet localhost netstat" to see that
# information yourself!
#
service systat
{
        disable     = yes
        socket_type = stream
        protocol    = tcp
        wait        = no
        user        = nobody
        server      = /bin/ps
        server_args = -auwwx
}
```

Most options in this configuration file are the same as the options you've already seen for managing xinetd with YaST, so I won't go through them again. The only difference is the disable = yes option, which wasn't visible like this in YaST. I recommend keeping it that way, because systat really is something you don't want to be available on a modern network where security is a serious issue!

Tuning Access to Services with TCP Wrapper

If a service runs from xinetd, you can secure it with TCP Wrapper, which is a service that is implemented in the tcpd process and that you can use to restrict access to services. Stated in a more general way, if a service is using the libwrap.so library module, the service can be secured with TCP Wrapper. Since xinetd is using this module, you can secure it this way. You can also secure other services that aren't started with xinetd but do use this library with TCP Wrapper. To check whether a service is capable of working with TCP Wrapper, use the ldd command, followed by the complete name of the service you want to check. If libwrap.so is listed, TCP Wrapper works for this service. If it isn't, use a generic firewall such as iptables. See Listing 19-4 for an example.

Listing 19-4. *Checking Whether a Service Can Be Secured with TCP Wrapper*

```
LAX:~ # ldd /usr/sbin/xinetd
        libwrap.so.0 =>  /lib64/libwrap.so.0 (0x00002b1b3fcd0000)
        libnsl.so.1 => /lib64/libnsl.so.1 (0x00002b1b3fdd9000)
        libm.so.6 => /lib64/libm.so.6 (0x00002b1b3feef000)
        libcrypt.so.1 => /lib64/libcrypt.so.1 (0x00002b1b40045000)
        libc.so.6 => /lib64/libc.so.6 (0x0002b1b4017e000)
        /lib64/ld-linux-x86-64.so.2 (0x00002b1b3fbb3000)
```

The TCP Wrapper was developed before xinetd existed; only its predecessor inetd existed then. The inetd service didn't include any way of regulating access to services, so you can use inetd to start tcpd, the TCP Wrapper, which in turn could be configured to start the service involved. tcpd checks whether a host trying to connect to the service is allowed access. The nice feature of tcpd is that it sits between (x)inetd and the service to which a client is connecting. Therefore, from the outside, it is not possible to see whether tcpd is blocking access to a service or whether the service simply isn't there.

Working with /etc/hosts.allow and /etc/hosts.deny

TCP Wrapper works with two configuration files to determine whether access is allowed. The names of these files are /etc/hosts.allow and /etc/hosts.deny. The first lists all the hosts that can access a service; the latter lists the hosts for whom access is denied. TCP Wrapper always first reads the /etc/hosts.allow file. If the host that tries to connect is in there, access is allowed. If the name of the hosts is not in /etc/hosts.allow, the TCP Wrapper checks /etc/hosts.deny. If the host is in there, access is blocked, and if it isn't, access is allowed. Access is also allowed if one of the two configuration files is empty or does not exist.

■**Caution** Test before you trust that TCP Wrapper is really protecting your services. A small error in the configuration can result in TCP Wrapper not working anymore!

The generic syntax of the lines that you can include in the /etc/hosts.allow and /etc/hosts.deny files is not hard to understand:

```
daemon:host[:option : option ...]
```

In this example, daemon is the process involved, host is the list of hosts you want to allow or deny access to, and option is a list of options you want to include. Note that instead of referring to a specific host or daemon, you can use some generic keywords. Table 19-2 summarizes these keywords.

Table 19-2. *TCP Wrapper Keywords*

Keyword	Description
ALL	This refers to all daemons or all hosts. Note that you can define an exception to ALL by using the keyword EXCEPT.
LOCAL	You can use this option for host names only, and it refers to all host names that do not have a dot in their names. Typically, these host names must be defined in /etc/hosts.
UNKNOWN	This refers to all host names for which tcpd cannot identify the name.
KNOWN	This refers to all host names that could be identified by their name and matching IP address.
PARANOID	This refers to all hosts where the host name does not match the given IP address.

Listing 19-5 shows an example of /etc/hosts.allow and /etc/hosts.deny.

Listing 19-5. *Simple Example of* /etc/hosts.allow *and* /etc/hosts.deny

```
LAX: ~ # cat /etc/hosts.allow
ALL: LOCAL
LAX: ~ # cat /etc/hosts.deny
famd, netstatd, ps: ALL
```

In Listing 19-5, incoming hosts are first matched against the /etc/hosts.allow file. In there, access to all the services is granted for everything coming in from the local host. So, local processes look no further. For connections coming in from remote hosts, now the /etc/hosts.deny file is checked. In this file, you can see that access is denied to the famd, netstatd, and ps services for all the hosts. So, all the other services that are controlled by tcpd can be accessed by all external hosts in this example. As you notice, this example doesn't show anything very secure. It is, however, possible to create a more secure configuration, as shown in Listing 19-6.

Listing 19-6. *More Complex Example of* /etc/hosts.allow *and* /etc/hosts.deny

```
LAX: ~ # cat /etc/hosts.allow
ALL: SFO.sandervanvugt.com
in.telnetd: 192.168.1.1
ALL EXCEPT in.telnetd: 192.168.
LAX ~ # cat /etc/hosts.deny
ALL: ALL
```

In this example, you should first notice that a policy is set. In this policy, access is specifically denied for all the hosts to all the services in /etc/hosts.deny. This is good, because it creates a controlled access mechanism; if the host doesn't have an entry in /etc/hosts.allow, it doesn't get access to the services that are controlled by tcpd.

In the /etc/hosts.allow file in Listing 19-6, three different lines are specified. The first line grants access to all the services for the host SFO.sandervanvugt.com. Then you see that 192.168.1.1 gets access to only the telnet service, and in the third line, all other hosts where the IP address starts with 192.168 get access to all the services except telnet. Note that in this example, order matters. TCP Wrappers work on a "first-match" basis. If line 2 and line 3 of /etc/hosts.allow were reversed, then the host with IP address 192.168.1.1 would see a match in the ALL EXCEPT in.telnetd line and would look no further.

Why You Shouldn't Use TCP Wrapper

If a service listens to tcpd, you can build an efficient protection for it. However, this protection is far from perfect. The most important problem is that the service is used only for certain kinds of services. The line ALL:ALL in /etc/hosts.deny could, however, give you a false sense of security, letting you think everything is secure now. A much better way to implement protection for your server is by using the SUSE firewall, which is based on iptables. This is a firewall solution that works for all the services on your server. In Chapter 30, you will learn how to secure your server with this firewall.

Summary

xinetd provides access to services that are not used frequently. As such, it is an important service that you are likely to need on your server as well. In this chapter, you also learned how you can deploy tcpd to offer a limited amount of security for services that are started with xinetd. You should not rely on this, though, because the security offered by tcpd applies only to services that are started with xinetd. The iptables firewall offers much security. In the next chapter, you'll learn how to synchronize time on your network using the NTP service.

CHAPTER 20

■ ■ ■

Configuring SUSE Linux Enterprise Server As an NTP Time Server

Just as it is critical for your daily activities, time plays a crucial role in the proper operation of networked applications. For this purpose, the Network Time Protocol (NTP) is the standard for time synchronization. In this chapter, you will learn how to configure your server as an NTP time server or client. I'll cover the following subjects:

- Understanding NTP fundamentals
- Configuring a stand-alone NTP time server
- Configuring your server to fetch its time somewhere
- Tuning how NTP operates

Understanding NTP Fundamentals

NTP is responsible for ensuring that all the servers on the Internet are time synchronized; that is, they all refer to the same time. To reach this goal, all the servers communicate the same time, no matter what time zone they are in. This time is known as Universal Time Coordinated (UTC): a server receives its time in UTC and then calculates its local time from that by using the time zone setting and any daylight saving time settings. On SUSE Linux, it is easy to configure this setting from YaST:

1. Start YaST, and select System ➤ Date and Time.

2. Select the country or region you are in (see Figure 20-1), and then click OK to apply the changes. This will change the time zone setting immediately.

■Tip SUSE Linux Enterprise Server maintains its time zone setting in /etc/sysconfig/clock. You can change the current time zone setting for your server from YaST, but it is also possible to change the time zone directly by modifying this file. After making the change manually, run /etc/init.d/boot.clock to apply the changes.

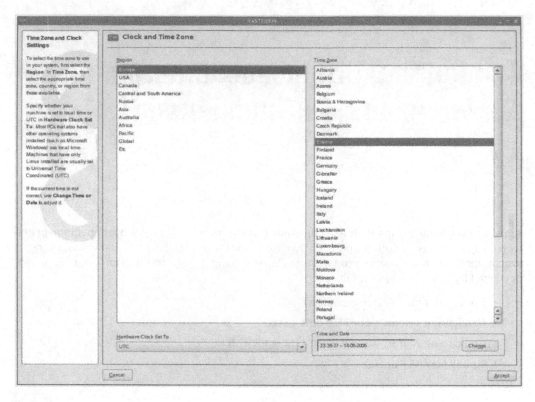

Figure 20-1. *You can easily change the current time zone using YaST.*

When synchronizing time with other servers in an NTP hierarchy, servers use a *stratum*. Every server in this hierarchy has a stratum setting from 1 to 15, with a stratum of 16 signifying a clock that is not currently synchronized. The highest stratum level that can be reached is stratum 1. Typically, this is a server that is connected directly to an atomic clock with a high accuracy. The stratum level a server will get if it is connected to an external clock directly depends on the type of external clock that is used.

A server can determine its time in two ways: by synchronizing with another NTP time server or by using a reference clock. If a server synchronizes with an NTP time server, the stratum used on that server will be determined by the server it is synchronizing with; if a server synchronizes with a stratum 3 time server, it will automatically become a stratum 4 time server by itself.

The other option is to use a reference clock. If a server uses a reference clock, the server does not get its time from a server on the Internet but will determine its own time. The default stratum used is determined by the type and brand of reference clock that is used. If it is a reliable clock such as a clock related to GPS, the default stratum setting will be high; if it is a less reliable clock (such as the local clock in a computer), the default stratum will be lower.

If a server can get its time from the Internet, it makes sense to use Internet time and use a trustworthy time server. If no Internet connection is available, use an internal clock, and set the stratum to be used accordingly. You can find more information about the different types of reference clocks that are available and their recommended settings in `/usr/share/doc/packages/xntp-doc/html/refclock.html`.

Configuring a Stand-Alone NTP Time Server

You need just two elements to configure your own NTP time server: the configuration file and the daemon process. The name of the daemon process is xntpd, and it has its configuration script in /etc/init.d/xntpd. After making all the proper settings to its configuration file, /etc/ntp.conf, you can start the daemon process manually by using rcxntpd start. Does it all work the way you want it to work? Then use insserv xntpd to add it to all the default runlevels on a permanent basis; the next time you start your servers, it will be started automatically.

Configuring ntp.conf

The content of the NTP configuration file, /etc/ntp.conf, really does not need to be complex. Basically, you just need three lines in it to create an NTP time server, as shown in Listing 20-1.

Listing 20-1. *Example* ntp.conf *Configuration*

```
server 127.127.1.0
fudge 127.127.1.0        stratum 10
server ntp.yourprovider.somewhere
```

The first line in Listing 20-1 specifies what the NTP process should use if the connection with the NTP time server is lost for a longer period; this line makes sure the local clock in your server will not drift too much. This line references a local clock. Every type of local clock has its own IP address from the range of loopback IP addresses. The format of this address is 127.127.x.x; the third byte refers to the type of local clock that is used, and the fourth byte refers to the instance of the clock to which your server is connected. The default address to use to refer to the local computer clock is 127.127.1.0. Notice that all clocks that can be used as an external reference clock have their own predefined IP address (see the refclock.html file for more on that).

Tip Even if your server is connected to an NTP server that is directly on the Internet, it makes sense to use at least one local external reference clock on your network. This way you can ensure that time synchronization will continue to work properly if the connection to the Internet fails for a longer period of time.

The second line defines what should happen when the server falls back to the local external reference clock mentioned on the first line. This line starts with the keyword fudge to indicate a situation that is not normal. In this situation, the server should use the local clock, and the server sets its stratum to 10. By using this stratum, the server indicates that it is not very trustworthy but ensures that it can be used as a time source anyway.

The last line in the previous example shows what should happen under normal circumstances. This line ordinarily refers to an IP address or server name on the network of the Internet provider. This line will always be used if nothing strange is happening.

Tip Looking for an NTP time server to use? Several are available on the Internet. At http://www.ntp.org, you'll find a list of time servers that are publicly available. You can also set pool.ntp.org as your time server. This is a publicly available time server on the Internet.

Pulling or Pushing the Time

An NTP time server can do its work in two different ways: by *pushing* (broadcasting) time across the network or by allowing other servers to come and pull the time from it. In the default setting, the NTP server that gets its time from somewhere else will ask the server once every minute what time is used. When both nodes are synchronized, this setting will be incremented to a default value of 1,024 seconds. As an administrator, you can specify how often time needs to be synchronized by using the minpoll and maxpoll arguments on the line where the NTP time server is referred to, as shown in Listing 20-2.

Listing 20-2. *Configuring the Synchronization Interval*

```
server 127.127.1.0
fudge 127.127.1.0 stratum 10
server ntp.provider.somewhere minpoll 4 maxpoll 15
```

The values for the minpoll and maxpoll parameters are kind of weird; they refer to the power of 2 that should be used. Therefore, minpoll 4 in fact is 2^4, which equals 16 seconds, and the default value of 1,024 seconds can be noted as 2^10. You can use any value from 4 to 17. The minpoll setting determines how often a client should try to synchronize its time when time currently is not synchronized properly, and the maxpoll value indicates how often synchronization should occur if time is synchronized properly.

If you are configuring an NTP node as a server, you can use the broadcast mechanism as well. This makes sense if your server is used as the NTP time server for local computers that are on the same network (since the broadcast is not forwarded by routers). If you want to do this, make sure the line broadcast 192.168.0.255 is included in the ntp.conf file on your server and that the client computer uses the broadcastclient setting.

If you want to configure a secure NTP time server, you should think twice before configuring a broadcast. Typically, a broadcast client will take its time from any server in the network, as long as it broadcasts the NTP packets on the default NTP port 123. Therefore, someone could introduce a bogus NTP time server with a high stratum configured to change time on all computers in your network.

Tuning Your NTP Server

I have explained the basic NTP time configuration so far. You can also do some tuning. First, the NTP daemon creates some files automatically. Next, you can use some security settings in ntp.conf to tune what server is allowed to get time from your server. In the following sections, you can read about the drift file, the log file, and NTP security.

Using the NTP Drift File

No matter how secure the local clock on your computer is, it always has a small defect: either the clock is running too fast or the clock is running too slow. A clock may, for example, have a difference of two seconds every hour; this difference is referred to as the *drift factor* of the clock. Since NTP is designed also to synchronize time when the connection to the NTP time server is lost, it is important that the NTP process on your local computer knows what exactly the difference is. You can calculate the drift factor by comparing the local clock with the clock on the server that provides NTP time to the local machine. To calculate the right setting for the drift factor, it is important that an accurate time is used on the other server.

When NTP time synchronization has been established, a drift file is created automatically. On SUSE Linux Enterprise Server, this file is created in /var/lib/ntp/drift/ntp.drift. From this file, the local NTP process calculates the exact drifting of your local clock, which allows it to compensate for that. The drift file is created automatically, so as an administrator, you don't need to worry about it. However, you can tune where the file is created by using the driftfile parameter in ntp.conf:

```
driftfile /var/lib/ntp/drift/ntp.drift
```

Note Remember that NTP is a daemon. Like most daemons, it reads its configuration file only when it is first started. So after all the modifications, use rcxntpd restart to make sure the modifications are applied to your current configuration.

Using the NTP Log File

Another file that is created automatically for you is the NTP log file. Like all other log files, this is an important file because it allows you to see exactly what happens. However, if time is synchronized properly, this is not the most interesting log file on your system; it will just tell you that synchronization has been established and what server is used for synchronization. Ordinarily, the NTP log file is in /var/log/ntp.log, but you can modify this if needed with the logfile option in the /etc/ntp.conf configuration file:

```
logfile  /var/log/ntp
```

Securing Your NTP Server

If your server is connected to the Internet, it may be interesting to notice that you can set some restrictions. If no restrictions are applied and port 123 is not blocked on the firewall, the entire world can access your NTP server. In case you don't like that idea, you can add some lines to the ntp.conf file, as shown in Listing 20-3.

Listing 20-3. *Applying Security Restrictions to Your NTP Time Server*

```
restrict default noquery notrustnomodify
restrict 127.0.0.1
restrict 192.168.0.0 mask 255.255.255.0
```

Note Some Linux distributions configure their NTP service in a way that no one can access it. Having problems getting time from a server? Then make sure no restrictions have been applied.

In the restrictions settings, the inappropriate conduct of clients is disallowed. In the first line in Listing 20-3 you can see what is considered inappropriate. The first line first allows the default settings for accessing the server. Then it disallows three types of packets: noquery, notrust, and nomodify. These make sure no contact whatsoever is allowed for NTP clients. Then an exception to these settings is created for the local NTP service and all the computers in the network 192.168.0.0.

Configuring an NTP Client

The first thing to do when configuring an NTP client is to make sure the time is more or less right. This is because when there is a difference of more than 1,024 seconds, NTP will consider the time source insane and will refuse to synchronize time with it. Therefore, it is recommended you synchronize time on the NTP client manually before continuing. To make a manual time synchronization, the ntpdate command is useful; you can use it to get time once only from another server offering NTP services. Use the following command to make this one time synchronization happen:

```
ntpdate ntp.yourprovider.somewhere
```

By using this command, you will make a one-time adjustment of time on the client computer. After that, you can run xntpd for automatic synchronization on the client computer.

■Caution Too often, ntpdate is used only for troubleshooting purposes when the administrator finds out that xntpd isn't synchronizing properly. In that case, the administrator is likely to see a "socket already in use" error message. This happens because xntpd has already claimed port 123 for NTP time synchronization. You can verify this with the netstat -patune | grep 123 command. This command will display all the applications currently sitting on port 123. Before you can use ntpdate successfully in this scenario, the administrator should make sure that xntpd is shut down on the client by using rcxntpd stop.

When time is more or less similar to the time used on the server you want to synchronize with, you can configure ntp.conf on the NTP client. A typical NTP client configuration can be simple; you just need to refer to the server you want to get the time from, like in the following example:

```
server 192.168.0.10
```

You may also prefer to set a backup option by using the fudge option as displayed in the previous example; this, however, is optional. Ordinarily, I recommend not setting this option on every server in the network that is using NTP. As an administrator you might prefer to set this on one server in your network only and let all other NTP clients in your network get the time from that server. In that way, you can create an NTP hierarchy where you are still in control when something goes wrong.

Checking NTP Synchronization Status

After you have started the NTP service on all the computers in your network, you probably want to know whether it is working correctly. The first tool to use is the ntptrace command, which will give you an overview of the current synchronization status. When using this command, you should be aware that it will always take some time to establish NTP time synchronization. This delay is because usually an NTP client will synchronize only every 16 seconds, and it may fail in establishing correct synchronization when it tries the first time. However, usually it should take no longer than making a cup of coffee to establish NTP time synchronization.

You can use the ntpq command to query for NTP service status. This command offers its own interactive interface from which the status of any NTP service can be requested. Like when using the FTP client, you can use a couple of commands to do "remote control" on the NTP server. In this interface, you can use the help command to see a list of available commands, as shown in Figure 20-2.

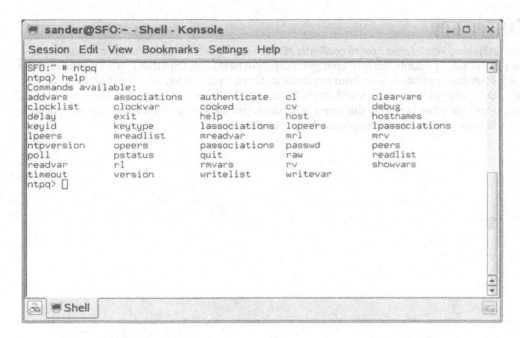

Figure 20-2. *You can use the* ntpq *interface as a remote control to your NTP server.*

As an alternative, you can run ntpq with some command-line options. For example, the command ntpq -p provides an overview of the current synchronization status. The result of this command displays several parameters:

- remote displays the name of the other server.
- refid displays the IP address of the server with which you are synchronizing.
- st displays the stratum used by the other server.
- t displays the type of clock used on the other server. L stands for local clock; if an Internet clock is used, you will find a u.
- when displays the number of seconds since the last poll.
- poll displays the number of seconds used between two polls.
- reach displays the number of times the other server has been contacted successfully.
- delay indicates the time between an NTP request issues and the answer given on that request.
- offset displays the difference in seconds between the time on your local computer and on the NTP server.
- jitter displays the error rate in your local clock, expressed in seconds.

Summary

In this chapter, you learned how to configure NTP for time synchronization in your network. You have read that, by default, the NTP configuration is not hard at all. On SUSE Linux Enterprise Server it is just usable out of the box without any modifications, if you can live with the limitation that in that case it will synchronize only with itself. To make an NTP time server more usable, you should always include a line to refer to the server with which you want to synchronize. In the next chapter, you will learn how to manage cryptography on SUSE Linux.

CHAPTER 21

■■■

Managing Cryptography

In the age of the Internet, cryptography has become increasingly important. When data is sent across insecure networks, you need to make sure that data is protected. When communicating with a host on the other side of the world, you need to make sure the host is really the host you think it is. To make sure, applied cryptography can help. In this chapter, you will learn how to use OpenSSL to implement a secure cryptographic infrastructure.

Specifically, I'll discuss the following subjects:

- Introducing SSL
- Creating a certificate authority
- Creating certificates

Introducing SSL

Before Netscape invented the Secure Sockets Layer (SSL) protocol in the mid-1990s, there was no good way to protect complete lines of communication against the eyes of interceptors when data was traveling across these lines. You could protect only specific data streams with tools such as PGP. Since the mid-1990s, you can encrypt complete data communication channels, and you can authenticate clients and servers using digital certificates. These digital certificates are based on the X.509 standard and contain not only the public key of a party on the Internet but also a digital signature that guarantees the authenticity of this public key.

Netscape wanted SSL to become an Internet standard; therefore, Netscape released enough information so that others could make SSL libraries as well. The OpenSSL suite that is used in Linux environments is a direct result of that.

Since 1994, SSL has had a successor called the Transport Layer Security (TLS) protocol. (See http://www.ietf.org/html.charters/tls-charter.html for more information about the TLS specification.) The TLS protocol does basically the same thing as SSL with one important exception: it is capable of making an existing session encrypted without changing the port number. In this chapter, I won't make a specific distinction between SSL and TLS features. This is because the OpenSSL program you will use to implement SSL/TLS doesn't make a distinction either.

Public and Private Keys

SSL is based on working with public/private key pairs. You can use this pair of keys for two purposes: to prove identity and to encrypt messages. In an SSL environment, it is necessary that every host has its own public/private key pair.

Imagine that Linda wants to send an encrypted e-mail to Kylie. For this to happen, Linda first needs to get Kylie's public key. Next she can encrypt the e-mail message to Kylie with this public key; for sending encrypted messages, users always need the public key of the user to which they want to send the encrypted message. Since the public key is directly related to the private key that Kylie has, only Kylie using her private key is able to decrypt the message. All this works because Kylie makes sure everyone has a copy of her public key. To make this as easy as possible, she can publish her public key on a website, put it on a Directory server, or attach it to every e-mail she sends.

Note To make it easier for others to work with a public key, I recommend putting it on a public service like a web server or an LDAP server. This increases the trustworthiness of the key, because before putting it there, the web or LDAP server (or its administrator) has verified that it really is the key of the intended user, whereas an e-mail message can easily be forged. If you should receive an e-mail from someone stating to be Kylie with a key attached to that e-mail message, it is hard to verify that the key really is sent by that user.

You can also use public/private key pairs to establish identity. An example of this is SSH key-based authentication. In such a scenario, the user who wants to authenticate makes sure a copy of his public key is stored on the server where he wants to authenticate. Next, on authentication, the user generates a random string and encrypts this string with his private key. The result of that is the digital signature. When this encrypted string arrives at the server, the server in turn tries to decrypt it with the public key of the same user, which is stored on the server. If it succeeds, that proves the user in question is really the user he says he is, and access is granted.

The Need for a Certificate Authority

The scenario described previously is real and works, but it has one problem. When Linda receives Kylie's public key, how can she be really sure that it is Kylie's public key and not the public key of someone pretending to be Kylie? That's where a certificate authority (CA) comes in. A *certificate authority* guarantees the public key of users and servers. It does so by signing this public key with its own private key. The result of this is a public key certificate in which the public key of the user is present along with the signature of the certificate authority. Since the user application should have a copy of the public key of the certificate authority, it can verify automatically that the signature is valid and therefore will use this guaranteed public key certificate without complaining. If, on the other hand, a certificate is signed by a CA of which the public key is unknown on the local host, the user application will complain about that; then it's up to the user to decide what to do with that certificate. Of course, the user can decide to trust that the public key in the certificate is for real, but the user has no way to guarantee that.

The main purpose of a CA is to guarantee a public key, but who in this case can guarantee the CA? This is where the trusted root comes in.

Generally speaking, two kinds of CAs exist: local CAs that run within a company and CAs that are trusted by everyone. The first type creates certificates for keys of individual servers; the latter creates keys for certificate authorities. The latter category is also referred to as the *trusted root*. It is trusted because most applications already have the public key of such a trusted root CA by default; therefore, they will automatically accept the certificate signed by such a trusted root. It is not necessary for every user to go to the trusted root directly, however; within a company, you can create your own CA. Next, you can choose whether you want to create a certificate for that CA. If you want a certificate that guarantees the authenticity of the public key in your certificate, you need to let it be signed by a trusted root instance. VeriSign (http://www.verisign.com) is a well-known example of a company that can do this for you. This way, a *chain of trusts* is created.

In a chain of trusts, the certificate of the user is signed by your own in-company CA. This CA in turn is signed by a trusted root such as VeriSign or, if the certificates are for use within your company only, by a trusted root you have created for your company. When any user receives this certificate, she will not be able to verify the certificate of the CA that signed the certificate, but since this certificate in turn is signed by a well-known trusted root, she can establish an encrypted session without problems. The bottom line is that when it is signed by a trusted root, it is good.

As a company, you can choose to sign every certificate that is used by an external CA. This will cost you a lot. To create a cheaper solution, it is recommended that you create your own CA, which signs its certificate by an external CA. This way, you will have a certificate that is trusted by all external parties. If trust with external parties is no requirement, as an alternative you can choose to create a CA with a self-signed certificate. Of course, this is not as good, but if you have the option of managing all the workstations that work with this certificate within your network, it doesn't matter. Just copy the public key certificate of your CA to all these workstations, and it will work anyway. In the next section, you will learn how to set up your own CA and how to create certificates once you have this CA set up.

Tip If someone is able to steal the private key from your certificate authority, all keys signed by that CA get compromised. Therefore, you should make sure the private key can in no way be compromised. A good method to do that is to create a dedicated CA and isolate that from the network. The CA needs to sign only public keys. To do this, no network connection is necessary anyway.

Managing Certificates

SUSE Linux Enterprise Server offers two options to create CAs and associated keys. The easiest option is to work with YaST. As an alternative, you can also use the openssl command to create it all from the command line. In the next two sections, you will learn how to do this.

Creating Certificates and a Certificate Authority with YaST

In YaST, under Security and Users, you'll find two options to manage certificates. The option CA Management helps you create your own CA. The option Common Server Certificate manages the properties of the certificate that is installed on your server by default. Note that it isn't always necessary to do something with these options; a CA and a server certificate are created automatically when installing your server. When these default objects need adjustment, then you need these YaST programs.

Managing the Certificate Authority with YaST

The YaST option CA Management gives you access to everything needed to manage your own CA environment. After a default installation, you will see the YaST default CA and its chain of trust. Since this is a CA with a self-signed certificate, it doesn't have any real chain of trust. Four options are available to manage your CA (see Figure 21-1):

Enter CA: Use this option to modify the properties of the current CA.

Delete CA: This option deletes the default CA, which allows you to create another one.

Create Root CA: Use this option if you want to create a root CA that can sign certificates for more than one CA in your network.

Import CA: Use this option to import the keys of another CA on your server. Use this option for CA consolidation on your network.

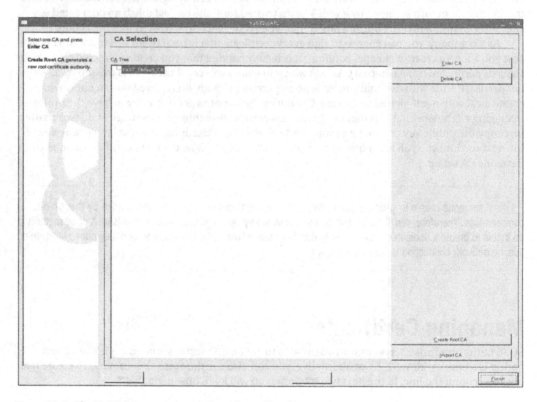

Figure 21-1. *The YaST CA management interface offers four options to manage your CA.*

Modifying Properties of Existing Certificate Authorities

Follow these steps to manage the properties of an existing CA:

1. From the YaST Certificate Authority management interface, make sure your current CA is selected, and next click Enter CA. This gives you access to the properties of the CA.

2. You now see a window with four tabs (see Figure 21-2). On these tabs, you can manage all the properties of the CA. By default, the tab Description is active. On this tab, you see the descriptive properties of the CA and their values.

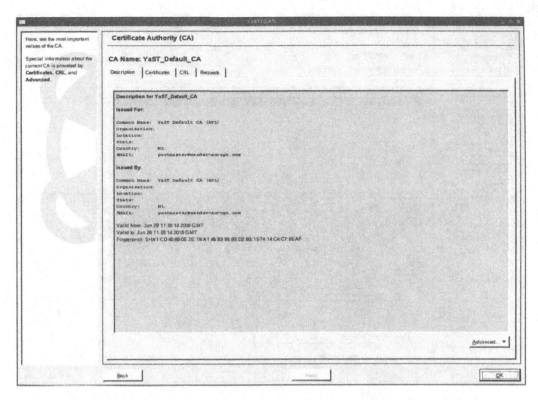

Figure 21-2. *On the tab Description, you'll find a summary of the most important properties of your CA.*

3. The tab Certificates gives you an overview of all the certificates that are signed by this CA (see Figure 21-3). By default, you will see only the server certificate that was created when installing the server. However, if you use this CA to provide certificates for all the servers in your network, you will see the other certificates as well. For each certificate, you can see the properties that are currently set. Also, if you know that the security of one of your certificates has been compromised, you can revoke it. This will create a certificate revocation list (CRL) that is published so that others using this certificate know it is not valid any longer.

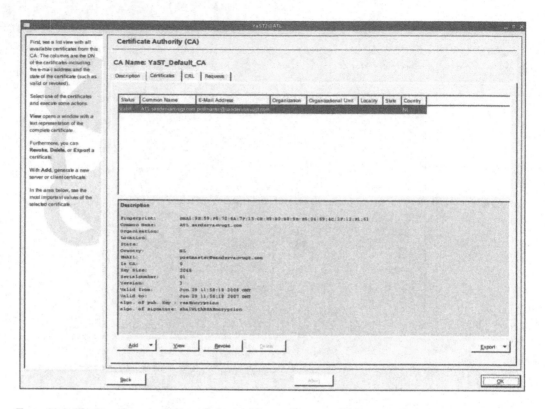

Figure 21-3. *The Certificates tab lists all the certificates that your CA is managing.*

4. On the Certificates tab, you can add new certificates by clicking the Add button. This button gives you access to two options: Add Server Certificate and Add Client Certificate. Both options do more or less the same; therefore, I'll just describe how to add a server certificate.

5. After clicking Add Server Certificate, you get access to the Create New Server Certificate Wizard (see Figure 21-4). On the first screen opened by this wizard, you need to specify the common name, e-mail address, and locality information for your certificate. Make sure these options are used as follows:

- *Common Name:* This is a complete name, including the DNS suffix for your server. The common name can be in DNS notation; RTD.sandervanvugt.nl is a good example. Make sure this is the same name as the name of the server you are using it for. If it isn't, users connecting to your server will get a warning.

- *E-mail address:* It is good practice to enter the name of one or more persons who can be contacted if something is wrong with the certificate here.

- *Organization, Organizational Unit, Locality, and State:* These are optional. Make sure, however, that the right country is selected.

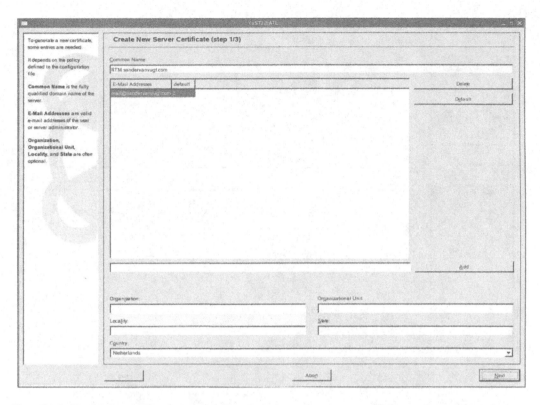

Figure 21-4. *On the Create New Server Certificate screen, you must enter all the contact information.*

6. Now you must enter the properties of the public/private key pair, as shown in Figure 21-5. The following options are available:

- *Password*: This is the passphrase that protects the private key. Every time you use the certificate, you must enter this passphrase. If you want the service to be able to start without entering a passphrase all the time, you should consider creating certificates with empty passphrases.

- *Key Length*: This is the number of bits used for the certificate's encryption. Using more bits is more secure but will also cause a heavier performance load for your server. For servers, 2,048 bits is strong enough; for user certificates, you can set this value considerably lower, such as 512 bits.

- *Valid Period*: Here you enter the number of days that the certificate is valid. By default, a certificate is valid for 365 days and has to be replaced after that.

- *Advanced Options*: You shouldn't use the Advanced Options button. Under this button you'll find a lot of options that allow you, amongst others, to modify the encryption settings that are used. Novell doesn't guarantee the working of your certificates if you use any of the advanced options, though.

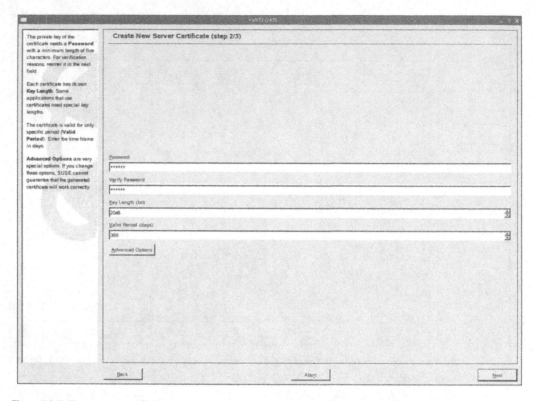

Figure 21-5. *For every certificate you create, you need to enter at least a passphrase, a key length, and a validity period.*

7. The third screen of the Create New Server Certificate Wizard just gives you an overview of what is going to be created for you. On this screen, click Create to create the certificate.

As a result of the previous procedure, you have created a new certificate and private key. All the resulting files are put in the directory /var/lib/CAM/YaST_Default_CA. The good part about using YaST is that you don't need to deal with the files stored there directly. Instead, you can use the management interface to deal with the new certificates. The important button that you have to use now is the Export button, which you can find on the Certificates tab of the Certificate Authority management interface. The options you'll find after clicking this button are as follows:

Export to File: Click this button to export the certificate to a file. This opens a new interface where you can indicate how to export the file (see Figure 21-6). On this screen, you have to make two choices. The first is whether you want to export just the certificate (which contains the public key and the signature of your CA) or the private key as well. If you have signed this certificate on behalf of another server, you probably want to export the certificate as well as the key so the other server can import it. If you have created this certificate for a service running on your server and you just want to make the public key certificate available to others, it suffices to export only the certificate. The second choice is the format you want to use. The three most often used formats are PEM, DER, and PKCS12. Basically, the format you want to use depends on the service and the client for whom you are creating the certificate. In most scenarios, PEM does fine. If PEM is not supported by your application (consult your application's documentation), however, then choose another format. After choosing what and how to export, you need to enter the password (in fact, this is the passphrase) that you used when you created the public/private key pair. Next enter a new password that protects the file you are creating, and enter a filename. Then click OK to export the certificate to a file.

Figure 21-6. *When exporting a certificate to a file, you can set different options to indicate how you want that to happen.*

Export to LDAP: Use this option if you want to publish the certificate in an LDAP Directory service. If you want to export the certificate to LDAP, enter all the required values to establish the bind to the LDAP server (see Figure 21-7). Check Chapter 17 for more information about OpenLDAP, which can be used as a Directory service for this purpose.

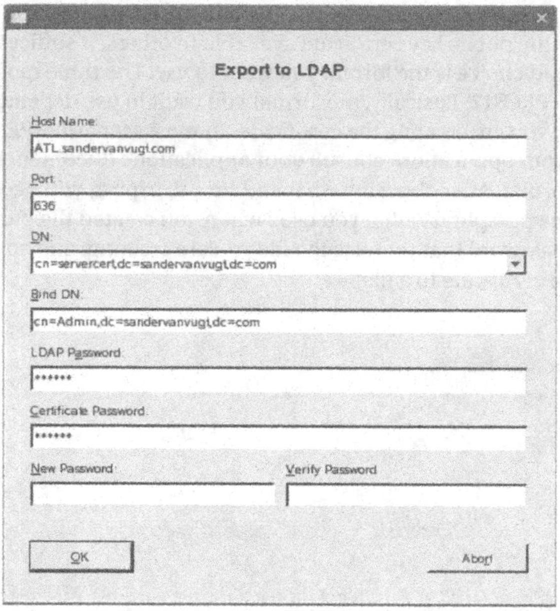

Figure 21-7. *To export to an LDAP Directory service, make sure you enter all the information to bind to the LDAP server correctly.*

Export as Common Server Certificate: This option allows you to replace the server certificate you are currently using on your server with this certificate. If you intend to do that, make sure the name of the certificate is the same as the name of your server.

Another important part of managing a CA is the CRL. You typically want to create a CRL if the security of your CA has been compromised, such as if someone has stolen the private key of your CA. To generate a CRL, on the Certificate Authority management screen, click the CRL tab, and next click Generate CRL (see Figure 21-8). This will create the CRL for you. Next, set this CRL as the default so any client coming in to check the validity of a certificate will see that it is not valid any longer.

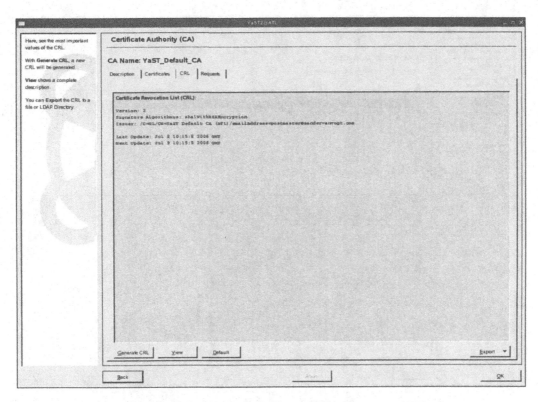

Figure 21-8. *You can create a CRL when the security of your CA has been compromised.*

The most important function of a CA is signing keys that come in from other servers and users. To do this, the other server needs to create a key-signing request and send that to your server. If the server or client that needs to sign its key is on another physical machine, you need to import the key file on the server where your CA is active. If the service that needs a signed key is on the same server, from YaST you can access the key-signing request directly. All options that are needed for signing keys are in YaST on the Requests tab of the Certificate Authority management interface (see Figure 21-9). As you can see, all certificates you have created on that server are listed automatically.

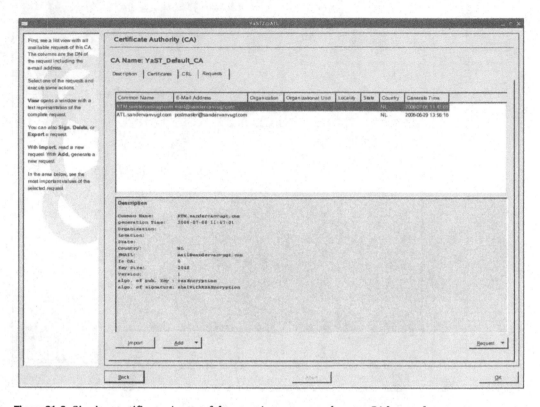

Figure 21-9. *Signing certificates is one of the most important tasks your CA has to do.*

The following steps describe how to sign one of these certificates. If the certificate that you want to sign is not on the list yet, use the Add or Import button to add it to the list.

1. From the list of certificates, select the certificate you want to sign. Then click Request ➤ Sign. From the drop-down list that appears, specify how you want to sign it. You can choose between a client certificate, a server certificate, and a CA certificate. In this example, you'll learn how to sign a server certificate.

2. As shown in Figure 21-10, you now see the properties of the certificate. Of these, you can set two properties. The first one of them is the certificate validity. By default it is set to 365 days, but you can change that to anything you want (although 365 days usually is not bad for a certificate's validity). Then you'll see a list of certificate extensions; this list is in the lower part of the window. The extensions describe what the certificate does. For example, the extension X.509v3 Basic Constraints: CA: FALSE indicates that this certificate cannot be used for a CA. When specifying the type of certificate you are signing, the correct extensions are set automatically. Make sure to select all of them, and then click Next to continue.

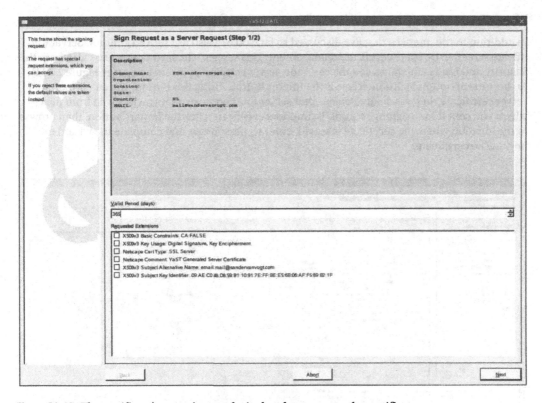

Figure 21-10. *The certificate's extensions make it clear how you use the certificate.*

3. You now see a summary of the certificate-signing request. From this summary, click Sign Request. This will generate the signed certificate. It is now added as a signed certificate to the list of certificates you find on the Certificates tab. From there, you have to export it again so that the remote machine can start using it.

Other YaST Certificate Authority Management Options

In the preceding sections, you learned how to manage the CA and its associated certificates from YaST. Other options are available in the YaST CA Management tool. They are not half as important as the options discussed in the "Modifying Properties of Existing Certificate Authorities" section, but they also don't hurt them, so here's a short description of these other options:

Delete CA: This is a rather drastic option that helps you delete your CA. Before doing this, you should realize that all the associated certificates become invalid, so be careful before clicking this option.

Create Root CA: A CA is useful only if a root CA guarantees the identity of the CA. Use this option to create your own root CA.

Import CA: A CA is just a bunch of keys and associated configurations. Since it is possible to export a complete CA, it must be possible to import a complete CA as well. In YaST, you use this option for that purpose, which is useful if you are migrating a CA from one platform to another.

The Common Server Certificate Interface

In addition to the interface that I've discussed so far, you can also use YaST's Common Server Certificate screen to do some certificate management. This screen, which you can access also from the Security and Users tab, shows you the common server certificate you are using (see Figure 21-11). An important option in this interface is the Import button. Using this button, you can import a server certificate that was created on another server or a certificate that you received from the CA where you sent it for a signing request. To import a certificate, click the Import button, then browse to the location where the certificate is stored, enter its passphrase, and complete the wizard to import the certificate.

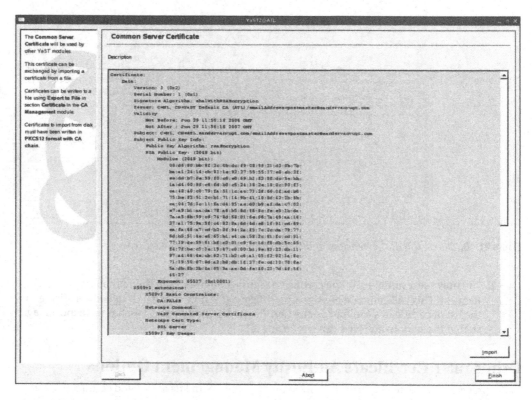

Figure 21-11. *In the Common Server Certificate screen, you can import a new signed certificate for your server.*

Managing Certificates from the Command Line

SUSE Linux Enterprise Server offers an excellent interface in YaST that helps you manage the certificates for your server. Behind YaST, however, there is a powerful command. You can use the openssl command to create and manage certificates and a certificate authority for your server. To give an impression of what's happening behind the scenes when working with YaST, in this section you'll learn how to use the openssl command to create a certificate and a self-signed CA. Since the self-signed CA in fact is the highest level in the CA hierarchy in this example, it will be a root CA.

The following steps explain how to proceed:

1. Decide where you want to create the directory structure in which you want to put the CA. This should be a directory structure that other users can't access. By default YaST puts the CA configuration in the directory /var/lib/CAM, which is readable by root only. In this directory, you must create some subdirectories. From the directory of your choice, start with mkdir root-CA to create a subdirectory in which the CA will store its files. Next, you must create some subdirectories in this root CA directory. The names of these subdirectories are fixed, so don't try anything creative. The command mkdir certs newcerts private crl will do the work for you. These subdirectories are used for the following purposes:

   - certs: This is where all signed public key certificates are stored. This directory can be publicly accessible.

   - newcerts: This directory stores all the new certificates that haven't been signed yet.

   - private: This directory stores the private key of your server. Protect it like the crown jewels! First, make sure the directory where it is stored is owned by the user root. Next, give this directory permission mode 700 (chmod 700 private), which makes sure the user root is the only one who has access to this directory.

   - crl: This directory stores CRLs, if any are needed in your environment.

2. To make creating the certificate for the root CA a bit easier, open the configuration file /etc/ssl/openssl.cnf. In this file, you will find some default settings that are used when you are creating new certificates. Read the file, and modify all the settings as required. The least you need to do is to make sure all directory paths are OK; do this by modifying the HOME and dir variables. Also, it is a good idea to set the names of the certificates to the right value. Listing 21-1 shows what this could look like. All nonessential parameters have been omitted from the list.

Listing 21-1. *Some Important Settings from the* openssl.cnf *File*

```
HOME                          = /root/root-CA
dir                           = /root/root-CA
...
certificate                   = $dir/root-CAcert.pem
...
private_key                   = $dir/root-CAkey.pem
...
```

3. Now that the configuration file has been tuned the proper way, you can create a self-signed certificate for the root CA. The following command creates the certificate with a 1,024-bit RSA key that is valid for ten years: openssl req -newkey rsa:1024 -x509 -days 3650. The main command used here is the openssl command. This command has several parameters that are used as if they were independent commands on their own. The parameter req in this example creates the self-signed certificate (check its man page to see everything you can use it for). All the other options just specify with what parameters the key must be created. Note that you can also use this command with options to specify the names of the keys you want to create. Since in step 2 of this procedure you probably have already set those names in the openssl.cnf file (see Listing 21-1), the example doesn't include these options. If you want to create key files with names other than the default names, use openssl req -newkey rsa:2048 -x509 -days 3650 -keyout private/my-CAkey.pem -out my-CAcert.pem, for

example. Creating the key will start an interface in which several questions are asked (see Figure 21-12). The most important of all these questions is the prompt for a passphrase. Especially since in this example you are creating a root CA, using a passphrase is mandatory; otherwise, it would be possible for anyone accessing your machine to create public key certificates signed by this CA, and that would make this CA absolutely worthless.

```
ATL:/etc/ssl # openssl req -newkey rsa:2048 -x509 -days 3650 -keyout private/sander-cakey.p
pem -out sander-cacert.pem
Generating a 2048 bit RSA private key
.+++
................................+++
writing new private key to 'private/sander-cakey.ppem'
Enter PEM pass phrase:
Verifying - Enter PEM pass phrase:
-----
You are about to be asked to enter information that will be incorporated
into your certificate request.
What you are about to enter is what is called a Distinguished Name or a DN.
There are quite a few fields but you can leave some blank
For some fields there will be a default value,
If you enter '.', the field will be left blank.
-----
Country Name (2 letter code) [AU]:NL
State or Province Name (full name) [Some-State]:
Locality Name (eg, city) []:
Organization Name (eg, company) [Internet Widgits Pty Ltd]:
Organizational Unit Name (eg, section) []:
Common Name (eg, YOUR name) []:myname
Email Address []:mail@sandervanvugt.nl
ATL:/etc/ssl #
```

Figure 21-12. *When creating a public/private key pair, you are prompted for the associated owner information and its passphrase.*

4. Congratulations! You now have your own root CA. This makes it possible to create your own certificates, used for any purpose. Think, for example, of server certificates that are used for secured e-mail or client certificates that are used to connect a notebook to a VPN gateway. Before you can start creating your own certificates, you need to create the OpenSSL database. This database consists of two files where OpenSSL keeps track of all the certificates that it issued; you need to create these two files by hand before you start. Change to the home directory of your root CA first, and from there, first use touch index.txt, and then use echo 01 > serial to create this simple database.

5. Now that the database index files are present as well, you need to create the key pair and the associated key-signing request. Do this by entering the command openssl req -new -keyout private/mailserverkey.pem -out certs/mailserver_req.pem -days 365. In this example, I have used the name mailserverkey, which makes it easy to identify what the key is used for; of course, you can use any name you like here.

6. If the CA that needs to sign the key won't run on your own server, you would copy it to the server that does the signing. Since in this simple setup the CA is on the same server, you can sign the CA using the following command: `openssl ca -policy policy_anything -notext -out certs/mailservercert.pem -infiles certs/mailserver_req.pem`. This command for signing the key uses the default policy. The name of this default policy is `policy_anything`, and this is defined as a bunch of settings in the `openssl.cnf` configuration file. The option `-notext` just limits the amount of output produced by this command. Then the name of the resulting certificate is given: `certs/mailservercert.pem`. You can create this certificate because only earlier you have created a signing request with the name `mailserver_req.pem`. This `mailserver_req.pem` is in the `certs` directory. If you need to sign a public key that is generated on another server, you have to make sure that only this public key is copied to this directory; the signing request would find it, and the public key certificate would be created without any problem.

You now have created the public/private key pair for your mail server, and you have signed it with your own self-signed root CA. For more details on how to use the `openssl` command, check the man page: `openssl(1)`. Also note that all the options such as `req` and `ca` have their own `man` page; check them for more details.

Summary

In this chapter, you learned how to create a CA, which is needed to secure services on your network; you can use it both to prove the identity of a user or a service and to encrypt traffic on your network. Because it is so essential, during the installation of SUSE Linux Enterprise Server, a default server CA is created automatically using either YaST or the OpenSSL utility. You can tune this as needed. In the next chapter, you'll learn how to manage the Apache web server.

CHAPTER 22

■ ■ ■

Configuring the Apache Web Server

One of the most common reasons to install Linux is to run an Apache web server on it. With a market share of nearly 70 percent, Apache is by far the most popular web server available. Therefore, in this chapter, you will read how it runs on SUSE Linux Enterprise Server. Specifically in this chapter, I'll cover the following subjects:

- Understanding how a web server works
- Installing Apache on SUSE Linux Enterprise Server
- Configuring Apache with YaST
- Configuring virtual hosts
- Managing access to the web server
- Using OpenSSL for encrypted connections

Understanding How a Web Server Works

From a technical perspective, you could say that a web server is just a special kind of file server; all a web server does is hand out files to users that are stored in a directory structure, which is called the document *root*. To offer these files, a web server uses a certain file format. This format is the Hypertext Markup Language (HTML). HTML files, however, are not the only files that a web server can offer. A web server can offer other types of files as well. Therefore, a web server is a good source for streaming audio and video, accessing databases, displaying animations, showing photos, and much more.

Originally, web content was static. Ever since a few years ago, however, web servers became a platform where people work together to create some content. One of the best examples of this is Wikipedia, the online encyclopedia where people from all over the world work together to create content. However, I won't cover interactive web pages in this chapter; in fact, this subject requires a book on its own.

The web server stores the content, but the client has to use a specific protocol to access this content. This protocol is the Hypertext Transfer Protocol (HTTP). Typically, a client uses a browser to generate HTTP commands that get content stored on a web server as HTML files. In the case of an application server, such as in the Wikipedia example or when using a Java-based service in Tomcat, it is this application that dynamically creates the content and the HTML data, but it is still the Apache web server that manages the HTTP traffic between the server and the client.

The Apache web server comes in two important versions. The most recent version is 2.*x*. This version is installed by default on SUSE Linux Enterprise Server. You may, however, encounter environments where version 1.3 is still being used. This is especially the case if the developer of some custom scripts has developed those scripts for use in a 1.3 environment. Those with urgent needs to use version 1.3 instead of 2.0, however, are increasingly rare, and therefore, I won't cover version 1.3 of the Apache web server in this chapter.

Installing Apache on SUSE Linux Enterprise Server

To manage Apache, you need to be aware of what exactly is installed on your server. Therefore, in the following sections, you'll first read about the packages that come with SUSE Linux Enterprise Server 10 and contain Apache software. Next, you will read about how to start, stop, and test the Apache web server. You will then explore the Apache configuration files to see what you need to manage.

Installing the Right Packages

Installing Apache on SUSE Linux Enterprise Server is easy; just make sure it is selected upon installation, or select the Web Server software category later (check Chapter 9 for more details on that). Its core components are in six RPM packages:

apache2-2-2*.rpm: This is the core of the Apache web server. It contains all the basic web server software you need to run Apache.

apache2-prefork-2.2*.rpm: This package offers you, as an administrator, more flexibility in using Apache in a multiprocessing environment.

apache2-example-pages*.rpm: This is where you find some HTML pages that will be offered by Apache by default. This allows you to easily test whether your web server is up and running.

apache2-doc*.rpm: This contains the Apache documentation files that are installed in /usr/share/doc/packages.

apache2-mod_php5*.rpm: This Apache module allows you to use PHP 5 scripts when working with Apache.

apache-mod_python*.rpm: This Apache module offers you the possibility of using Python scripts from the Apache web server.

As you can see in Figure 22-1, many other packages are available as well. Most of these packages allow you to add some extra functionality to your web server environment. For example, the mod_mono package allows you to run .NET applications from your Apache environment. In general, it is not the best idea to install them all by default; I recommend installing them only if you really need them. Installing unnecessary and unused modules makes your server more difficult to manage and especially more difficult to secure.

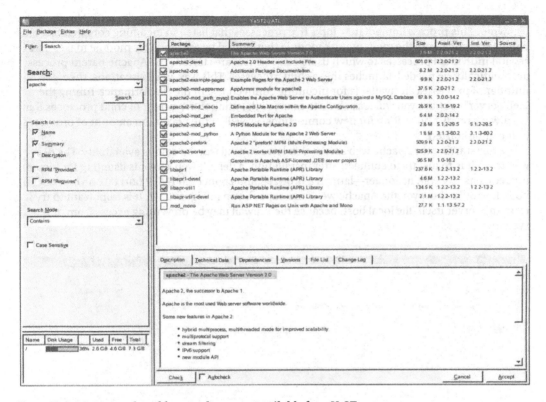

Figure 22-1. *Many Apache add-on packages are available from YaST.*

Starting, Stopping, and Testing the Apache Web Server

The core of the Apache web server is the httpd process. This process is started from the script /etc/init.d/apache2; the easiest way to activate Apache using this script from the command line is to use the rcapache2 start command. When this command finishes without errors, your web server is up and running. You can check to see whether it's running with the ps aux | grep http command; as you can see in Listing 22-1, this command shows that different instances of the Apache web server are ready and waiting for the incoming connections.

Listing 22-1. *Several Instances of the httpd Process Start Automatically*

```
ATL:~# ps aux | grep http
root      7371  1.3  1.1  45408  5852  ?       Ss    15:51     0:00  /usr/
sbin/httpd2-prefork -f /etc/apache2/httpd.conf
wwwrun    7372  0.0  0.9  45408  4800  ?       S     15:51     0:00  /usr/
sbin/httpd2-prefork -f /etc/apache2/httpd.conf
wwwrun    7373  0.0  0.9  45408  4788  ?       S     15:51     0:00  /usr/
sbin/httpd2-prefork -f /etc/apache2/httpd.conf
wwwrun    7374  0.0  0.9  45408  4788  ?       S     15:51     0:00  /usr/
sbin/httpd2-prefork -f /etc/apache2/httpd.conf
wwwrun    7371  0.0  0.9  45408  4788  ?       S     15:51     0:00  /usr/
sbin/httpd2-prefork -f /etc/apache2/httpd.conf
wwwrun    7371  0.0  0.9  45408  4788  ?       S     15:51     0:00  /usr/
sbin/httpd2-prefork -f /etc/apache2/httpd.conf
```

As you can see from the output of ps aux, the first Apache process that is started has root as its owner. This process immediately forks five processes that listen to incoming connections. This behavior comes from the mod_prefork module that is used by Apache. This module makes sure several individual processes to which users can connect are started. The Apache parent process automatically, as needed, launches these child processes. This way, in all situations, the right number of processes are available for incoming connections. In the "Performance Tuning the Web Server" section, you will learn how to manage the minimum amount of child processes that are always ready and waiting for new connections, as well as the maximum amount of processes that can be started.

After starting the Apache web server, you have several ways to test its availability. The best way to do it is to just try to connect; after installation, a default web server is listening for incoming requests. So, wait no longer—launch a browser, and connect to HTTP port 80 on your local host. It should show you the Apache welcome page shown in Figure 22-2. It is important to try it from the server itself, the local host, because the firewall may be preventing access from other systems.

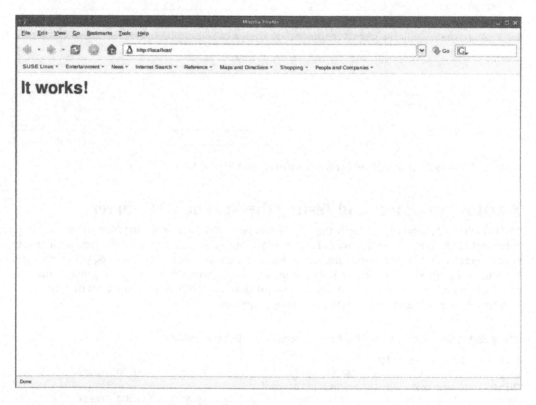

Figure 22-2. *To verify it's working, just connect to it.*

Did it work? Well, good. As the next step, you probably want to make sure it comes up automatically the next time you reboot your server. To make sure this happens, use the insserv apache2 command.

Exploring the Configuration Files

Apache once had just one relevant configuration file, which was called /etc/hpptd.conf. Those days are long gone. On SUSE Linux Enterprise Server, Apache maintains a complete structure of configuration files. The following list gives you an overview of the most important files. All the files mentioned here are in /etc/apache2 (unless specifically stated otherwise).

httpd.conf: This is the main configuration file. If you look in its contents, you will see that not much is configured here; the httpd.conf file just calls and includes other configuration files. This is, however, still the file where you should always start when analyzing a problem.

default-server.conf: This file in general contains the basic web server setup. For example, in this file, you will find the specification of the document root where the web server stores all its document files.

uid.conf: This is where you can set the default user and group ID that Apache is using.

server-tuning.conf: This file contains directives to optimize how the Apache 2 web server works.

ssl-global.conf: This is the main configuration file used to establish SSL encrypted connections.

vhosts.d: This directory contains the configuration files for virtual hosts.

listen.conf: This file contains the ports on which the Apache server is listening by default.

error.conf: This is where you specify what your server should do when a request cannot be handled correctly.

/etc/sysconfig/apache2: This file contains generic options that you want to pass to the Apache process when it is booting.

Understanding the Structure of the Apache Configuration Files

To tune the Apache web server, it is really important that you understand the structure of its configuration files. The basic element of the configuration files is a directive. *Directives* group a set of options so they apply only to a specific item. For example, in Listing 22-2, you can see the directive that is created to specify the options for the directory where the web server starts looking for its documents, the so-called document root. Note that this document root is important, because all other filenames and directory names are related to this document root. This configuration comes from the default-server.conf configuration file. Note that to increase the readability, I have removed all the comment lines from the example file.

Listing 22-2. *Specification of the Document Root in* default-server.conf

```
DocumentRoot "/srv/www/htdocs"
<Directory "/srv/www/htdocs">
        Options None
        AllowOverride None
        Order allow,deny
        Allow from all
</Directory>
```

This example first starts with the specification of DocumentRoot. Next, for this directory, a directive specifies its options. Note that the directive starts with the line <Directory "/srv/www/htdocs">, and it ends with </Directory>. This is a generic rule for creating directives; if it starts with

<Something>, it should close with </Something>. When tuning directives by hand, don't forget this closing statement! Between the start and the end of the directive, you can see its options. The first option, Options None, indicates that no specific options are applied to this directory. Next, the option AllowOverride None makes sure it is impossible to override the settings made here at a lower level in the directory structure. Without this option, a user can activate their own settings by creating a file with the name .htaccess in any subdirectory of the document root. If that file exists and AllowOverride None doesn't, the settings from that file will be applied.

Next, the Order allow,deny part indicates that allow statements must be evaluated first and only then the server should check to see whether anything is denied. This is what you would typically want for a nonsecured directory. Then the statement Allow from all confirms that this server is open to anyone; it grants access to this directory to all, which in most cases is rather reasonable for a document root. Directives for other directories look a lot like this, although some directories may have some specific options. For example, the directory cgi-bin, which refers to the location of the CGI scripts that your server can execute, may require some additional options that make sure no insecure scripts can be executed.

Checking the Configuration

After tuning configuration files, you should make sure they work. The first task you need to perform is running the apache2ctl command. This command helps you test your configuration. To do this, run apache2ctl configtest. If everything is OK, the command will tell you; if it is not, it tells you as well.

After verifying that everything is OK, you need to activate the changes. You can do this by running the rcapache2 reload command. This command will just activate the changes you've made. That is, it will not unload and reload the Apache web server. Sometimes, however, this just isn't enough, and you need to restart the Apache server anyway. In that case, use rcapache2 restart.

Configuring Apache with YaST

One of the best features of SUSE Linux Enterprise Server is YaST. YaST allows you to do a basic configuration of your Apache web server. In this section, you will read how that works. To start the Apache management module, run YaST with the module http-server by entering the yast2 http-server command (or just by clicking the HTTP Server option from the YaST Network Services interface). This will start the wizard described in the following steps:

1. On the first screen of the wizard (see Figure 22-3), you need to enter the port and interfaces on which the web server will listen. By default, after successful installation, it will listen on all the interfaces on port 80. If your server needs to be available on one specific network only, select the appropriate network interface here. If the firewall is active, don't forget to check the option Open Firewall on Selected Ports.

2. To offer interactive web pages, a modern Apache web server can offer scripts written in many languages. On the second screen of the wizard, you can specify what languages need to be supported. By default, you can choose between PHP 5, Perl, Python, and Ruby. By default, only PHP 5 is activated. If you need any other scripting language, select it here. This makes sure the module that supports that language is loaded automatically. Then click Next to continue.

Note PHP 5 is installed by default, but you can use PHP 4 as well. PHP is loaded by Apache as a module. By loading the PHP 4 module instead of PHP 5, you make sure PHP 4 is used.

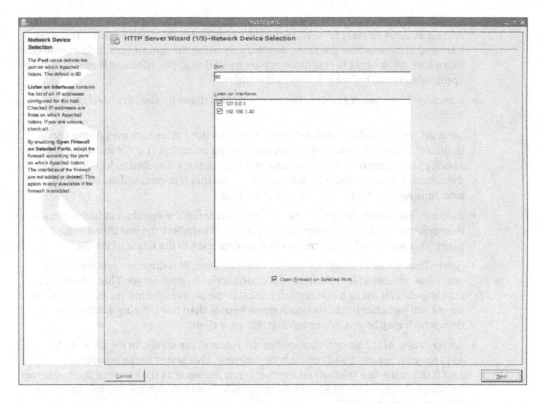

Figure 22-3. *To keep a web server private, you can limit the network interfaces on which it listens.*

3. Now, as you can see in Figure 22-4, you must specify some generic parameters for your server. You set all of these parameters in the /etc/apache2/default-server.conf configuration file. The following list describes all the default parameters and their uses; if you want to include a parameter that isn't listed by default, click the Add button to add it. To modify the value for one of the default parameters, click the parameter, and then click the Edit button. The following options are present by default (see also Figure 22-4). The list shows the options with their default value as set after installation:

- *Document Root:* "/srv/www/htdocs": This is the name of the directory where Apache looks for its files by default.

- *Directory:* "/srv/www/htdocs": This option contains all the web server settings for the /srv/www/htdocs directory. I discussed the default settings earlier in this chapter.

- *Alias:* /icons/ "/usr/share/apache2/icons/": This directive contains an alias. An *alias* is a link that indicates components would be loaded from another location. Note the / that terminates the name of the directory /icons/. This slash indicates that everything under /icons must be aliased, but not the directory /icons itself. Using this alias allows you to make the contents of the directory icons available in the document root without storing its files there.

- *Directory:* "/usr/share/apache2/icons": This directive contains all the settings for the directory /usr/share/apache2/icons. These settings determine how the contents of this directory are presented to people visiting your website.

- *ScriptAlias:* `/cgi-bin/` `"/srv/www/cgi-bin/"`: Like the alias for `/icons/`, this line creates an alias for `cgi-scripts`. Note the subtle difference between `scriptalias` used here and `alias` used for the icons directory. By using the option `scriptalias`, you can make sure documents in this directory are treated as applications; this makes sure the application is run before it is sent to the client.

- *Directory:* `"/srv/www/cgi-bin"`: Here you set the options for the `/srv/www/cgi-bin` directory.

- *Include:* `/etc/apache2/conf.d/*.conf`: This directive makes sure everything that is in the `/etc/apache2.conf.d` directory and has the extension `.conf` is included in the Apache configuration. This allows new modules that are installed to just dump their default configuration module in this directory so that it is executed automatically the next time Apache rereads its configuration files.

- *Include:* `/etc/apache2/conf.d/apache2-manual?conf`: If the Apache manual is installed, its configuration file is included this way. If it isn't installed, the installer doesn't complain. This is affected by the use of the question mark in the name of the file.

- *Server Resolution:* `Resolution via IP Address Used`: This directive sets the default graphical resolution for clients that are connecting to your server. This value makes sure the client making a connection indicates the best resolution it can use, and the server will just offer it. This is much more flexible than just offering a default resolution, which may be too low or too high for your client.

- *Server Name:* `ATL`: This option specifies the name of the server. In my case, its name is ATL; for your server, it will certainly be different. This server name is especially important if the name of a (virtual) web server is not the same as the name of the real server on which this instance of Apache is running. It should always be possible to resolve this server name by DNS.

- *Server Administrator E-mail:* `root@ATL`: This directive specifies the e-mail address of the person who manages this server.

4. One instance of the Apache web server can handle requests for more than one web server. For example, the same Apache installation can handle both the sales.yourdomain.com and the intranet.yourdomain.com web servers. This phenomenon is referred to as *virtual hosts*. In step 4 of the wizard, you can create a list of virtual hosts that your web server needs to serve. You can find more details about working with virtual hosts in the next section of this chapter.

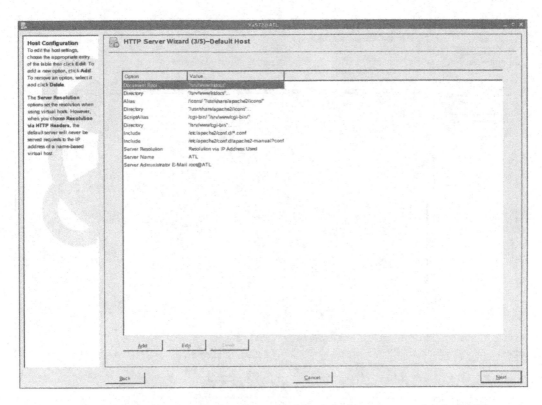

Figure 22-4. *You can set the most important parameters from* default-server.conf *using YaST.*

5. In the final part of the configuration, you will see the summary of the settings you have entered so far (see Figure 22-5). On this screen you can choose to start the Apache server manually or always when booting. Also, you will see the HTTP Server Expert Configuration button. That gives you access to some more advanced options. Before clicking Finish to close the wizard, take a moment to click this button.

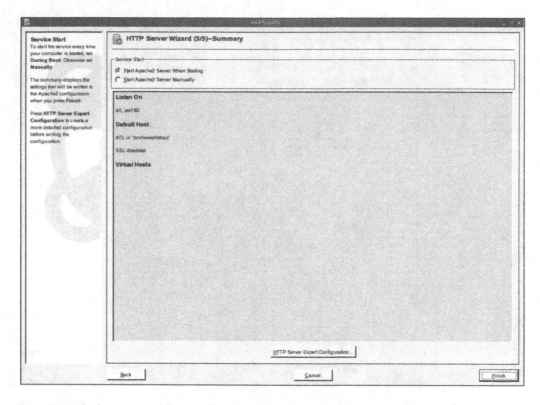

Figure 22-5. *The last screen of the wizard gives an overview of the options you have selected so far.*

6. The most interesting tab you'll see after clicking the HTTP Server Expert Configuration
    button is the Server Modules tab (see Figure 22-6). This tab gives you access to the options
    that are available from different modules that can be included on the Apache web server to
    enhance its capabilities. In this list, you can toggle the status of a given module. It is also
    possible to add new modules by clicking the Add Module button. When you are satisfied
    with the server module options, click Finish to close the Apache setup program and store
    its settings. The Apache server will automatically be started with its new settings.

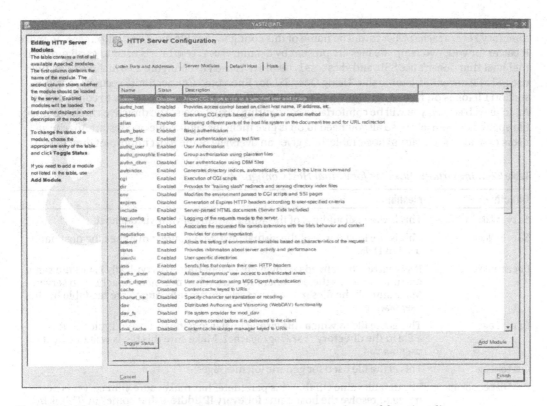

Figure 22-6. *The Apache server modules give you access to more advanced functionality.*

Working with Virtual Hosts

If you are installing the Apache web server to host several small sites, then virtual hosts will be useful. Working with virtual hosts allows you to serve several sites from one instance of the Apache web server. For example, you could host www.mydomain.com, www.yourdomain.com, and www.someoneelsesdomain.com on the same machine. To make this work, you need to set up DNS, though. You can find more details about this in Chapter 23.

When working with virtual hosts, the following process takes place when a user goes to access the virtual host:

1. The user enters the URL in the browser.

2. The DNS server redirects the user to your web server, based on the IP address that is assigned by the name of the server in the URL the user is using.

3. The request arrives at your web server, and the Apache server analyzes the request.

4. Apache matches the name that is used in the URL and forwards the packet to the right virtual host.

To configure a virtual host, you need a configuration file for every single virtual host in the directory /etc/apache2/vhosts.d. The name of this configuration file must end with .conf. To make it easier for you, two template files are present by default: vhost.template is used to configure a virtual host that doesn't use SSL, and vhost_ssl.template is used to configure a virtual host that does use SSL. I'll cover SSL later in the "Using OpenSSL for Encrypted Connections" section, so in this section I'll focus on how to configure a virtual host without SSL. If you know how to configure an Apache web server, you will be comfortable configuring virtual hosts. The directives in the template file speak for themselves, so all you need to do is give them the right value and restart Apache so users can access the virtual host. Table 22-1 gives an overview of the most important directives.

Table 22-1. *Important Directives for Virtual Host Configuration*

Directive	Meaning
ServerAdmin	This is the mail address of the administrator of your virtual host.
ServerName	This is the host name of the virtual host. Make sure it matches the host name used in DNS.
DocumentRoot	Every virtual host needs its own document root. This typically is not the same document root as the document root used by your main Apache web server. Make sure all the files in the directory you are referring to are readable by the user wwwrun.
ErrorLog	This is the file to which this virtual host is logging its errors. Typically, this is a file in the directory /var/log/apache2. Make sure this file is writable by the user wwwrun.
CustomLog	This is the file used for generic log messages.
HostnameLookups	The default value Off that this parameter has makes sure your server is not trying to resolve the host name for every IP address that comes in. This is in general useful, because this reverse name lookup usually takes a lot of time.
ScriptAlias	This sets the directory that contains the script files. If your web server doesn't need to do any scripting, make sure you disable this setting; allowing scripts to be executed by your server always imposes a certain risk.

In addition to these important directives used in the virtual host file, other directives specify the options for the directories offered by your virtual hosts. These directives do not differ from directives with the same purpose on "real" Apache web servers. Listing 22-3 shows an example.

Listing 22-3. *Example of a Directive in a Virtual Host File*

```
<Directory "/srv/www/vhosts/dummy-host.example.com/cgi-bin">
    AllowOverride None
    Options +ExecCGI -Includes
    Order allow,deny
    Allow from all
</Directory>
```

This example should be pretty clear, except maybe the line Options +ExecCGI -Includes. The purpose of this line is to allow the user to activate any script that is in the directory /srv/www/vhosts/dummy-host.example.com/cgi-bin.

Managing Access to the Web Server

In most situations, a web server is publicly available, and everyone can access all the information offered by the web server. In some situations, however, it may be necessary to add some extra layer of security and protect some directories on your web server. Without using any additional modules, Apache offers two methods of access restriction: user-based and host-based access restrictions. In the following sections, you'll learn how to configure both.

Configuring Host-Based Access Restrictions

Apache offers three directives to configure host-based access restrictions:

allow: Hosts or networks that are listed after this directive are allowed access to the web server.

deny: Hosts or networks that are listed after this directive are denied access to the web server.

order: This directive determines how the allow and deny are applied.

Listing 22-4 shows you how you can set allow and deny to protect a directory on a server. Note that the document root will always have its own settings, which can be overwritten at a lower level. In this example, you see how the default access permissions for the document root are set.

Listing 22-4. *Default Access Restrictions for the Document Root*

```
<Directory "/srv/www/htdocs">
    Order allow,deny
    Allow from all
</Directory>
```

In this example, you can see that first the order in which access restrictions are evaluated is set. In this case, Order is set to allow,deny. With this setting, the allow directives are evaluated before the deny directives. Access is denied by default. This means that all the clients that do not match an allow directive or do match a deny directive are denied access. So in Listing 22-5, access is allowed only for hosts where the IP address starts with 172.16.

Listing 22-5. *Allowing Access to Some Only*

```
<Directory "/srv/www/htdocs">
    Order allow,deny
    Allow from 172.16.0.0/16
</Directory>
```

Instead of Order allow,deny, you can also use Order deny,allow. If you see that option, access is allowed by default, and deny directives are evaluated before the allow directives. Any client that doesn't match a deny directive or does match an allow directive is therefore allowed access. The example in Listing 22-5 can be rewritten using the directives shown in Listing 22-6.

Listing 22-6. *Allowing Access to Some Only with Order* deny,allow

```
<Directory "/srv/www/htdocs">
    Order deny,allow
    Deny from all
    Allow from 192.168.0.0/8
</Directory>
```

As you can see, the effect of Listing 22-6 is the same as the result of the example in Listing 22-5; it requires only an additional code line. Also, the idea that access is allowed by default is something that doesn't please everyone. Therefore, to make your web server really secure, it is better to choose the Order allow,deny directive instead.

Note As an alternative to Order allow,deny, you may also encounter the option Order Mutual-failure. This is an old option that shouldn't be used anymore.

Note that when allowing or denying access to directives, you have different options to specify the hosts for which you want to limit access:

- You can use the all option to apply an option to all the hosts.
- You can use complete IP addresses or host names. This speaks for itself; use this to allow or deny access to one specific host only.
- You can use partial IP addresses. If you use this, the option applies to everything starting with the partial IP address. For example, 192.168.0.0/16 can be rewritten as simply 192.168 as well.
- You can use a network in CIDR notation. In a CIDR notation, you specify the number of bits that should be used in the subnet mask. For example, 172.16.0.0/16 indicates that the setting applies to everything that matches the first 2 bytes of the IP address. This can be rewritten as 172.16.0.0/255.255.0.0.
- You can use a pair of a network address and subnet mask.

Configuring User-Based Access Restrictions

Configuring access restrictions based on IP addresses may be useful if you want to grant access to an internal network and deny access to everyone else (although there may be better methods for doing that); for a more flexible access control mechanism, it may be a good idea as well to work with user-based access restrictions. Two methods are particularly interesting:

Simple authentication: When using simple authentication, you need to create a simple user file with the htpasswd2 command.

LDAP-based authentication: When using LDAP authentication, you need to include the mod_auth_ldap module to enable authentication against an LDAP back end.

Working with Simple Authentication

Working with basic authentication is the easiest solution. To use this, you need to create a simple password file with the htpasswd2 command. Basically, this file can be anywhere, but make sure it is not in a location where other users can read it. For example, storing the password file in the document root or anywhere under that is a bad idea. The default location on SUSE Linux Enterprise Server is the /etc/apache2 directory, which probably is fine. If you want to put it somewhere else, make sure it is readable by the user wwwrun.

The first time you use the htpasswd2 command, make sure you use the option -c. This option makes sure a new password file is created. For example, you can use the following command to do this:

```
htpasswd2 -c /etc/apache2/htpasswd linda
```

Next, the command will prompt you to enter the password for this user twice, and it will create an entry in the file you specified. Of course, you can use a simple hashing algorithm to encrypt this password. When you are adding more users to the Apache password file, you don't have to use the -c option anymore; the file exists, and you can just add new users to it. The htpasswd2 command also allows you to remove users from the password file; to do this, use it with the -D option. For example, htpasswd2 -D /etc/apache2/htpasswd stacey will remove user stacey from the file.

Just creating a user is not enough; you have to configure Apache to prompt for a password when a user is accessing restricted data. To do this, you need to include some code in the directory you want to protect, as shown in Listing 22-7.

Listing 22-7. *Protecting a Directory with Basic Authentication*

```
<Directory protected>
    Authtype Basic
    AuthName "Restricted directory"
    AuthUserFile /etc/apache2/htpasswd
    Require user linda
</Directory>
```

In this example, you can see that first the authentication type Basic is enabled. Next, a label is given to this directory with the AuthName "Restricted directory" directive. After that, the file containing the user information is referred to, and in the final line, one specific user is mentioned that is granted access to this directory. As an alternative, you could have used the option Require user valid-user; using this is useful if you just want to grant access to any user who is defined in the password file you are using.

Working with LDAP Authentication

Maintaining a separate password file to specify the names of users who can access certain directories on your web server is not the most practical way of implementing decent web server security. It is much more useful if you can maintain the user database somewhere external. One—but by far not the only—option you can use for this purpose is LDAP authentication. Now, Apache is not aware of any LDAP server by itself; fortunately, it isn't that hard to teach Apache that it should use LDAP for authentication purposes. To do this, you first need to make sure two modules are used with your Apache web server: mod_ldap and mod_auth_ldap.

To use mod_auth_ldap for LDAP-based authentication, you need to make sure both of the LDAP modules are loaded. On SUSE Linux Enterprise Server, you can handle this from the module's configuration file, which is /etc/apache2/sysconfig.d/loadmodule.conf. In this file, make sure the following two lines appear somewhere (of course after verifying that both modules are really present in the /usr/lib/apache2-prefork directory):

```
LoadModule mod_ldap           /usr/lib/apache2-perfork/mod_ldap.so
LoadModule mod_auth_ldap      /usr/lib/apache2-prefork/mod_auth_ldap.so
```

Once you have enabled both modules, you need to include some code that handles the proper security settings. For LDAP-based authentication, it is common to use the Location directive as an alternative to the Directory directive. The related code can look like Listing 22-8.

Listing 22-8. *Working with LDAP-Based Authentication*

```
<Location "/internal">
AuthName "confidential data"
AuthType Basic
AuthLDAPHosts "ldapserver someserver:636"
AuthLDAPBaseDN "type=user, o=somewhere,c=nl"
AuthLDAPSearchScope base
AuthLDAPUserKey webuser
AuthLDAPPassKey webpassword
require group accountants
require valid-user
</Location>
```

In the previous example, you can see that a location is defined. This is a directory that is under the document root. Next, certain sections specify where and what should be searched for in the directory. In this example, the search is for users in the container o=somewhere,c=nl. These users use the webuser property for their username and the webpassword property for the password. Of course, you can use any other valid property from the LDAP directory for this purpose as well. Check Chapter 17 for more details about LDAP.

Using OpenSSL for Encrypted Connections

By default, the Apache web server sends all its traffic unencrypted. Therefore, if someone is listening with a sniffer and you send sensitive information, they could capture and read that information. To protect against this, you can use SSL encryption. In Chapter 21 you can read all about this encryption technique; therefore, in this chapter I won't go through the entire process of creating certificates and signing them. I'll just discuss how to create a test certificate and use that with the Apache web server. The resulting communication is as follows:

1. The user connects to a web address where the URL starts with https:// and connects to the default SSL port of the web server, which is port 443.

2. The web browser requests the server for its public key, and the web server sends it.

3. The browser verifies the public key certificate with the public key of the certificate authority that has signed the certificate.

4. If the key is valid, the browser and server will exchange a session key for symmetric encryption that they will use for secure communications.

To create a self-signed key, read Chapter 21 for the detailed procedure, or follow these steps:

1. Use the command cat /dev/random > /tmp/random to create a file containing random numbers. Interrupt the creation of this file after a few seconds by using the Ctrl+C key sequence.

2. Next, enter the command openssl genrsa -des3 -out webserver.key -rand /tmp/random 1024.

3. Now make a self-signed certificate out of it by using the command openssl req -new -x509 -key webserver.key -out webserver.cert. Now you are prompted for a passphrase and all the locality information for your key. If you don't want to enter a passphrase when the private key is used (such as when starting the web server), consider creating the public/private key pair without a passphrase.

4. Now copy the two keys to their right location; both have to go to the directory /etc/apache2, where the other configuration files are. The private key must be copied to the subdirectory /etc/apache2/ssl.key, and the public key needs to be in /etc/apache2/ssl.crt.

Now that the key pair is in place (or if you already have a key pair), you need to tell Apache how to use it. First, you need to open /etc/sysconfig/apache2, which contains generic start-up options for Apache. If the private key you have created is passphrase protected, locate the variable APACHE_START_TIMEOUT and give it a value such as 5. This extends the start-up time for Apache and gives you some time to enter the passphrase. Next make the following setting in the same configuration file: APACHE_SERVER_FLAGS="SSL". This tells Apache to listen on port 443 as well as 80, and it creates some extra directives that are needed for complete SSL support.

Now that everything is in place, you need to tell Apache to use both keys. Do this by adding the code in Listing 22-9 to the /etc/apache2/default-server.conf file.

Listing 22-9. *Make Sure Apache Listens for SSL Connections*

```
SSLEngine on
SSLCipherSuite
ALL:!ADH:!EXPORT56:RC4+RSA:+HIGH:+MEDIUM:+LOW:+SSLv2:+EXP:+eNULL
SSLCertificateFile /etc/apache2/ssl.crt/webserver.crt
SSLCertificateFile /etc/apache2/ssl.key/webserver.key
```

Of these lines, the line SSLEngine on makes sure Apache is using SSL. Next, the two lines SSLCipherSuite and ALL:!ADH:!EXPORT56:RC4+RSA:+HIGH:+MEDIUM:+LOW:+SSLv2:+EXP:+eNULL make sure the proper encryption method is used. The lines in the example are the default setting for the Apache web server; don't change them unless you know exactly what you are doing. The final two lines of the example tell Apache where it can find its key files. Make sure the locations mentioned match the directories to where you have copied the files.

Everything is now in place to use SSL encryption when communicating with the Apache web server. Restart the web server using rcapache2 restart; from now on, it will listen on port 443 as well.

Though the previous example will work, it is not the best solution for making your web server secure because, in this example, users can choose for themselves how they want to connect. The server is reachable over port 80 and port 443. Ordinarily, on a web server, only some content needs to be offered encrypted, whereas other content doesn't need encryption. You can do this by adding the option SSLRequireSSL in the directive for the directory you want to protect.

As an alternative, you can also tell the entire web server that it should listen to a secure port only. To do this, edit /etc/apache2/listen.conf. By default, this file looks like the example in Listing 22-10.

Listing 22-10. *Setting of the Default Port Configuration in* listen.conf

```
Listen 80

<IfDefine SSL>
    <IfDefine !NoSSL>
        <IfModule mod_ssl.c>

                Listen 443

        </IfModule>
    </IfDefine>
</IfDefine>
```

This code is not hard to understand. By default, Apache listens on port 80. If the SSL settings are in default-server.conf or in the configuration of a virtual host, it will listen to connections coming in on port 443 as well. Disabling port 80 is not hard to do; just put a comment sign in front of it, and it won't be offered any longer.

An alternative to offering SSL on a complete server is to offer it for one or more virtual hosts only. If you want to do that, make sure the SSL port is specified as an argument in the definition of the virtual host. The line to do this would look like this: `<VirtualHost myvirtualhost:443>`.

Performance Tuning Your Web Server

If you are running a busy web server, it makes sense to do some performance tuning. The default settings are for web servers with an average workload. If you are hosting a busy web server, the performance parameters may need some tuning. The file to do this is the `/etc/apache2/server-tuning.conf` file. In this file, you can use the following options to tune the performance of your web server:

`StartServers`: This setting specifies the number of Apache processes that should always be started. The advantage of starting some processes in advance is that they are ready and listening for incoming clients and therefore are capable of replying to incoming connections quickly. By default, five servers are started. If you anticipate your web server will be heavily used, it is a good idea to set this to a greater value.

`MinSpareServers`: This is the minimal number of servers that should always be ready and waiting for new incoming connections. By default, five servers are always listening and ready for new connections.

`MaxSpareServers`: When too many server processes are waiting for new client connections that don't come, it may be reasonable to tune the `MaxSpareServers` setting. Its default value of 10 determines that if more than 10 servers are waiting for new incoming connections, they should be closed down automatically.

`ServerLimit`: This is the maximum number of clients that Apache allows at the same time. The default is set to 150, which is reasonable for many web servers.

`MaxClients`: This value does more or less the same as the `ServerLimit` setting. Make sure both have the same value.

`KeepAlive`: Use this to allow clients to open persistent connections. For performance reasons, ordinarily it is a good idea to do that, and therefore the default value for this option is `On`.

`KeepAliveTimeout`: This is the number of seconds that a keepalive connection is kept open when no new traffic comes in. The default is 15 seconds.

Summary

The information in this chapter helped you set up the Apache web server on SUSE Linux Enterprise Server. You learned how the configuration files are organized and which information should be at certain locations. Also, you were introduced to setting up SSL-secured web servers, and you read how to do some performance tuning. To make it possible to host more than one web server on the same physical machine, you also learned how to implement virtual servers. In the next chapter, you will learn how to implement DNS on SUSE Linux Enterprise Server.

## CHAPTER 23

Configuring DNS

Communications on the Internet use the Internet Protocol (IP). This protocol allows all hosts to communicate with their own unique IP addresses. This means you could contact other hosts by entering that unique number. Humans, however, are not too good at working with numbers, and that was one of the most important reasons why the Domain Name System (DNS) was developed. The purpose of DNS is to translate IP addresses to names, and vice versa. In this chapter, you'll learn how to create a DNS server on SUSE Linux Enterprise Server.

Introducing DNS

Before going into detail about the DNS server configuration on SUSE Linux Enterprise Server, I'll first explain what exactly DNS is and how it works. In the following sections, you will get to know the difference between DNS and other methods for name resolving. Also, you will find out how the DNS hierarchy is structured and what the roles of the different types of DNS servers are in this.

Methods of Name Resolving

DNS is not the only solution you can use for name resolving. Other solutions are available as well. I'll explain two of them here: the /etc/hosts file and Sun's Network Information System (NIS).

Before DNS was introduced, every host needed to keep its own file where IP addresses were mapped to names. In those days, the Internet was still a small network, so this was doable (although the administrator had to ensure these files were updated properly). Today such a mechanism still exists in the form of the /etc/hosts file. In this file, you can list commonly used names and their IP addresses. SUSE Linux Enterprise Server creates this file by default to make the resolution of localhost possible. Listing 23-1 shows an example of the file as it is created by default. Note that you can still use this file as an addition to DNS, and its contents will be checked first, before any DNS lookup is done.

Listing 23-1. *Displaying the Contents of* /etc/hosts

```
SFO:~ # cat /etc/hosts
#
# hosts         This file describes a number of hostname-to-address
#                 mappings for the TCP/IP subsystem.  It is mostly
#                 used at boot time, when no name servers are running.
#                 On small systems, this file can be used instead of a
#                 "named" name server.
# Syntax:
#
```

```
# IP-Address  Full-Qualified-Hostname  Short-Hostname
#

127.0.0.1      localhost

# special IPv6 addresses
::1            localhost ipv6-localhost ipv6-loopback

fe00::0        ipv6-localnet

ff00::0        ipv6-mcastprefix
ff02::1        ipv6-allnodes
ff02::2        ipv6-allrouters
ff02::3        ipv6-allhosts
127.0.0.2      SFO.sandervanvugt.com SFO
```

Another more advanced method you can use to keep mappings between host names and IP addresses is NIS, also known as *yellow pages*. In this system, a database was generated for important files on a server, such as the /etc/hosts file, the /etc/passwd file, and the /etc/shadow file. These files were converted to NIS *maps*, indexed files that make up the NIS database. Users could be configured as an NIS client and could get information from this database, which was offered by the NIS master server. To provide redundancy, NIS could use slave servers as well. These offered a copy of the database, which was offered by the NIS master. The master server, however, was the single point of administration.

Although NIS was a good solution to manage relevant information within a network, it never made it as a viable solution of providing name services at an Internet level. The main reason for this is that NIS does not provide a hierarchical solution; it provides flat databases only. With the large amount of data that has to be made available about Internet hosts nowadays, it would be impossible to get results from such a structure quickly. For that reason, most organizations that still use NIS for managing names within their own network are phasing it out and instead configuring DNS if it is for resolving host names to IP addresses or configuring an LDAP server if it is for managing user information.

Although DNS is the main system that is used for name resolving nowadays, it is not the only system. You can set it up in addition to an NIS system and the /etc/hosts file. If you do that, the order in which the different systems are searched is important. The /etc/nsswitch.conf file determines this search order; see Listing 23-2 for an example.

Listing 23-2. *Contents of the* /etc/nsswitch.conf *File*

```
SFO:~ # cat /etc/nsswitch.conf
#
# /etc/nsswitch.conf
#
# An example Name Service Switch config file. This file should be
# sorted with the most-used services at the beginning.
#
# The entry '[NOTFOUND=return]' means that the search for an
# entry should stop if the search in the previous entry turned
# up nothing. Note that if the search failed due to some other reason
# (like no NIS server responding) then the search continues with the
# next entry.
#
# Legal entries are:
#
#       compat                   Use compatibility setup
```

```
#       nisplus                Use NIS+ (NIS version 3)
#       nis                    Use NIS (NIS version 2), also called YP
#       dns                    Use DNS (Domain Name Service)
#       files                  Use the local files
#       [NOTFOUND=return]      Stop searching if not found so far
#
# For more information, please read the nsswitch.conf.5 manual page.
#

# passwd: files nis
# shadow: files nis
# group:  files nis

passwd: compat
group:  compat

hosts:          files dns
networks:       files dns

services:       files
protocols:      files
rpc:            files
ethers:         files
netmasks:       files
netgroup:       files nis
publickey:      files

bootparams:     files
automount:      files nis
aliases:        files
```

The nsswitch.conf file indicates, for all the important information on your server, where the NIS client should search. In the case of hosts and network information, the example file is pretty clear. It first checks local configuration files, and only after that will it check the DNS hierarchy.

Organization of the DNS Hierarchy

The most important advantage offered by DNS is that it is organized in a hierarchical way. This makes the system scalable because it can be extended by simply adding another branch to the tree-like hierarchy.

On top of the hierarchy are the root servers. These servers have one purpose only, and that's to provide information about the top-level domains (TLDs). Some fixed domain names are used for top-level domains, such as .com, .org, and .info, and top-level domains exist for all countries, such as .nl, .uk, .fr, and so on. Within these top-level domains, people and organizations can create their own domains, which can consist of subdomains. For example, the imaginary organization mydomain could create a domain called example.com, and within the structure of example.com, it could create some subdomains as well, such as east.example.com and west.example.com. It is important to understand that east and west here are not the host names. The web servers in these subdomains would be www.east.example.com and www.west.example.com. The amount of subdomains is virtually unlimited, although it seems that more than four or five levels of domains become hard to use. No one wants to type www.servers.east.nl.sandervanvugt.com all the time, do they? Figure 23-1 shows an example of the partial DNS hierarchy.

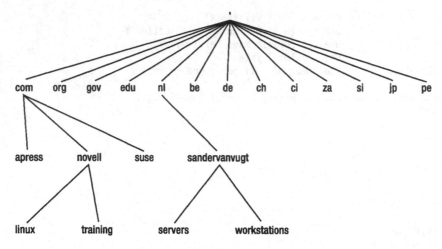

Figure 23-1. *Example of a part of the DNS hierarchy*

Master and Slave Servers

Within the DNS hierarchy, different servers are responsible for the data in a certain domain and sometimes in subdomains as well. These servers are *name servers*, and the part of the hierarchy that they are responsible for is called a *zone*. A zone can include more than just one domain. If one name server, for example, is responsible for everything in sandervanvugt.nl, including the subdomain servers and workstations, then the zone is sandervanvugt.nl. Speaking generically, a zone is just a part of the DNS hierarchy.

All zones should at least have two responsible name servers. Of these, the first is the master name server. This is the name server that in the end is responsible for the data in a zone. For fault tolerance reasons and to make the information better accessible, you can use one or more slave servers as well. These slave servers will periodically get an update of all the data on the master server by means of a *zone transfer*, which is the process the master server uses to update the database on the slave server. Note that DNS uses a single-master model; updates are performed on the master server and nowhere else. You should also know that the name servers do not need to be in the zone for which they are responsible. For example, often the name server of a given domain will be hosted by the Internet provider, which, of course, has its own domain. You can maintain your own DNS server, which is useful to do if your organization is larger than average, but you don't have to do so.

Connecting the Name Servers in the Hierarchy

DNS uses a hierarchy, so the servers in DNS need to know about each other. This is a two-directional process. First, all the servers in subordinate zones know where to find the root servers of the DNS hierarchy. Second, the servers of the upper-level zones need to know how to find the servers of lower-level zones. You can create your own DNS domain called mynicednsdomain.com and run your DNS server in it, but this doesn't make sense if the DNS server that is responsible for the .com domain doesn't know about it. This is because a client trying to find your server will first ask the name server of the domain above your zone if it knows where to find authoritative information for your domain. That's why DNS domain names need to be registered; only after that can the manager of the domain above you configure your name server as the responsible name server for your domain. This is called the *delegation of authority*.

It also helps to understand what happens when a user tries to resolve a DNS name that it doesn't know about already. The next steps describe what happens:

1. To resolve DNS names, the DNS resolver needs to be configured on the user's workstation. This is the part of the workstation where the user has configured how to find DNS servers. On a Linux system, this happens in the file /etc/resolv.conf.

2. Based on the information in the DNS resolver, the client will contact its name server and ask that server to resolve the DNS name for him, no matter what server it is and where on Earth the server is running. So if the client tries to resolve the name www.sandervanvugt.nl, it will first ask its own name server. The advantage is that the name server of the client can consult its cache to find out whether it recently already resolved that name for the client. If it knows the IP address of the requested server, the DNS name server returns that information to the client immediately.

3. If the name server of the client doesn't know the IP address of the requested server, it will check whether a forwarder is configured. A *forwarder* is a server that a name server contacts if it can't resolve a name by itself.

4. If no forwarder is configured, the DNS name server will contact a name server of the root domain and ask that name server how to contact the name server of the top-level domain it needs; in this case, this is the name server for the nl domain.

5. Once the name server of the client finds out the name server address of the top-level domain, it will contact that name server and ask for the IP address of the authoritative name server for the domain it is looking for, in this case the name server for sandervanvugt.nl.

6. Once the name server of the client finds out how to reach the authoritative name server for the domain the client asks for, it contacts that name server and asks to resolve the name for it. In return, the name server of the client will receive the IP address it needs.

7. Ultimately, the client returns the IP address of the server it wants to contact and can establish contact with that server.

DNS and Reversed DNS

Before I start talking about how to configure DNS, you need to know about reversed DNS. Translating names into IP addresses is one task of the DNS server; the other task is translating IP addresses to names. This is called *reversed DNS*, and it is necessary if you want names instead of IP addresses. This feature, for example, is useful if you want names in your log files instead of IP addresses. Although useful, you should realize that you pay a performance price if you want all IP addresses translated to names. To make this work, you need to set up reversed DNS.

To create a reversed DNS structure, you need to configure the in-addr.arpa domain. Under that domain, a structure is created that contains the inversed IP addresses for your network. For example, if you are using the class C network 201.10.19.0/24, you should create a DNS domain with the name 19.10.201.in-addr.arpa. Within that zone, you next have to create a PTR resource record for all the hosts you want to include in the DNS hierarchy.

When working with reversed DNS, you should be aware of one important limitation: it doesn't know how to handle nondefault subnet masks. This means it works only if you have the complete network and not if you have registered a couple of IP addresses only with your Internet provider.

Configuring DNS

Since DNS works with a rather complicated file structure, the best way to configure your first DNS server is by using YaST. In the following example, I'll show you how to set up a master DNS server for the domain example.com. Of course, when following this procedure, you should replace example.com with your own domain name. In the next section, you will learn what configuration files were created by DNS and how to tune these configuration files by hand.

Configuring DNS with YaST

When setting up DNS, in general you need to accomplish three things. First, you need to set up the master server for your zone. After that, in some situations you need reversed DNS. When that's in place, you basically have a working domain. As the third and last step, you should increase the availability of that domain by configuring at least one slave server. You can read how to do all this in the next three sections.

Note In some situations, reversed DNS is required. This is the case for all services that need to be able to look up the host name of a given IP address. If, however, you don't have such a service, it may be a good idea to skip reversed DNS completely. Looking up host names causes a relatively heavy performance hit.

Setting Up the Master Server with YaST

To set up the master service with YaST, follow these steps:

1. In YaST, select Network Services ➤ DNS Server. This starts the DNS server installation program.

2. On the first screen of the DNS installation program (see Figure 23-2), you can specify how to handle forwarders. Remember, a forwarder is a server that all the queries are sent to that cannot be handled by your DNS server. You might, for example, refer to the DNS server of your Internet provider as a forwarder. Be aware, however, that your server will work fine without a forwarder; in that case, the server will contact a name server of the root domain to resolve all queries that could not be resolved locally. If working with forwarders, the installer offers you two choices. You can select the option PPP Daemon Sets Forwards if your server is using PPP dial-up to connect to the rest of the Internet. In that case, you most likely want to configure forwarders on the PPP daemon. As an alternative, if you select the option Set Forwarders Manually, you can add the IP addresses of forwarders yourself. Enter the IP address you want to add in the IP Address box, and then click Add to add it to the list. Then click Next to proceed.

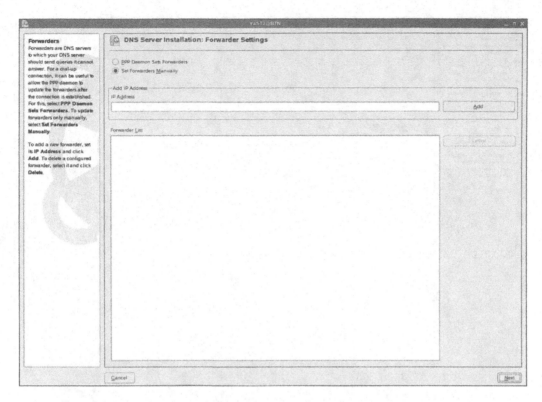

Figure 23-2. *Setting forwarders is not always required.*

3. Now you'll see the screen where you can add new DNS zones (see Figure 23-3). In this
    example, the name of the zone you are creating is example.com. Enter that name in the
    Name box. Then from the Type drop-down box, select whether you want to make this server
    a master or a slave server. Assuming that the master hasn't been set up yet, select Master,
    and then click Add. This will add the zone to the Configured DNS Zones list. Repeat this
    procedure for any other zone you'd like to add.

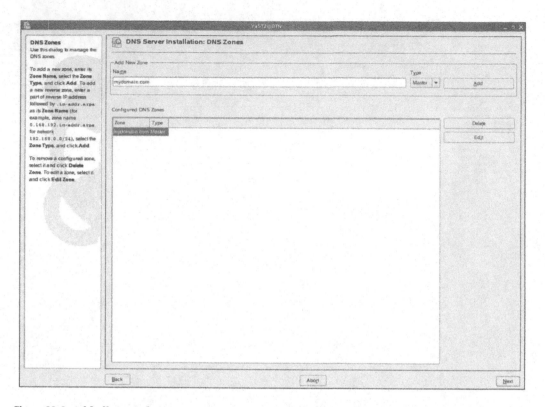

Figure 23-3. *Add all zones that your server is serving to the list of configured DNS zones.*

4. After adding the zone to the list of configured DNS zones, select it, and click Edit. This opens the screen you see in Figure 23-4. On this screen, you can enter all relevant zone settings. On the Basics tab you can configure two options. First, select the option Allow Dynamic Updates if you want your DHCP server to update your DNS server automatically. If you use this feature, specify the TSIG key, which is used to secure the dynamic updates as well. Check Chapter 24 for more details about setting up a dynamic DNS environment. Second, if this server is a master server and you want slave servers to update their database with records from the master server, select the option Enable Zone Transport option. After selecting it, you need to specify an ACL. From the list you can select between the following: any, localhost, localnets, or none. It's not possible to enter one or more IP addresses here, but you can change that later directly in the DNS configuration files. Check the next section to learn how. For now, select any to allow everyone to do a zone transfer, and remember to change it later.

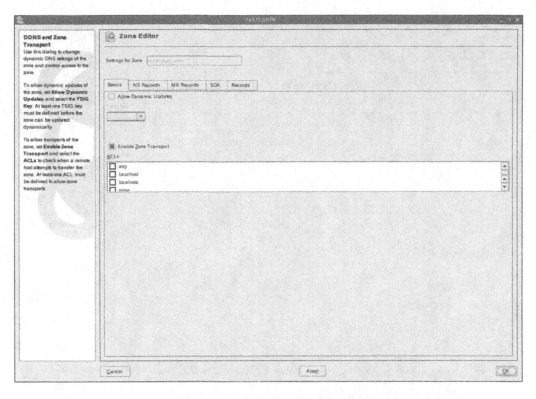

Figure 23-4. *On the tab Basics you can configure zone transfers and enable dynamic DNS.*

5. Now go to the tab NS Records. On this tab (see Figure 23-5), you need to enter a list of all the name servers that exist for this zone. Use names to add name servers. Note that the slave name servers can be in any domain on the Internet, so it doesn't have to be a server that is in your zone. If the server you are configuring now will be the only name server, you have an easy job, and you don't need to configure anything else here.

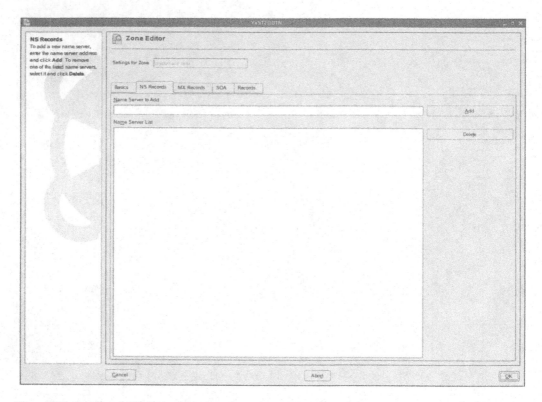

Figure 23-5. *On the tab NS Records you need to enter all the name servers that will be used for this zone.*

6. Next, on the MX Records tab, which you can see in Figure 23-6, you can enter the name of the mail servers that are used in your domain. Note that although the YaST interface tells you that you can specify names as well as IP addresses, you really do need to specify a name here. After specifying the name of your mail server, enter its priority. Remember, a lower number will lead to a higher priority. It is common to use increments of ten here, but it's not really required. Then click Add to add the mail server to the Mail Relay List area. Repeat this procedure for all the other mail servers you will be using.

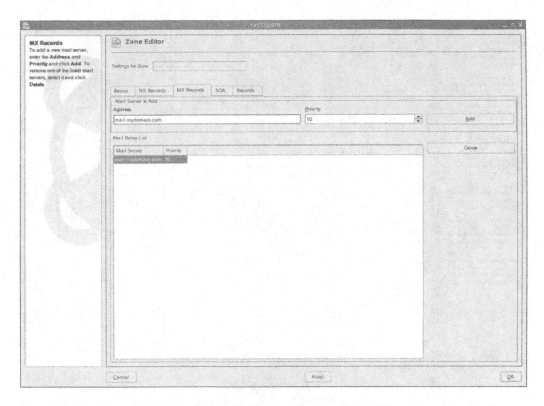

Figure 23-6. *Enter the names and priorities of all the mail servers that will be serving your zone here.*

7. On the SOA tab, shown in Figure 23-7, you can specify some generic parameters that are used by your server. The following options are available:

- *Serial*: The serial number determines whether any changes have occurred. This number starts with the current year, followed by the month and day and an event number. By updating this serial number after making changes to the database, slave servers know when changes have occurred and synchronize the zone only then.

- *TTL*: The time to live (TTL) specifies the validity of all the records in the zone. This option is relevant for slave servers that cannot contact the master server anymore. By setting the TTL of all the entries in the database, they will expire automatically when the TTL has been reached.

- *Refresh*: The Refresh option specifies how often the database should be synchronized with the database of the master server. By default, this will happen every three hours.

- *Retry*: Use this option to specify how often to retry if synchronizing the database fails. By default, the slave server will retry once only, and if that fails, it will wait for the next refresh interval.

- *Expiration*: This specifies the expiration interval set after which the zone expires on the slave server. You need this option to make sure a slave server that cannot synchronize with the master server anymore expires automatically.

- *Minimum*: This option specifies how long a slave server should cache a negative answer where resolving a name failed.

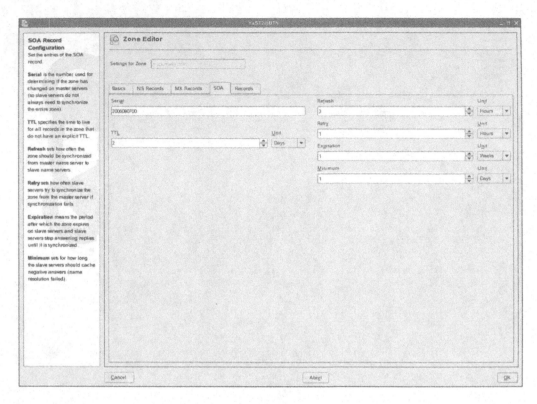

Figure 23-7. *On the SOA tab, you can specify generic parameters for your zone.*

8. On the Records tab, you enter the options you want to store in the DNS database. The most important option is the A resource record; this is used to add an IP address to a name of a host in your zone. An example is the name www for the web server or the name ftp for the FTP server. (I discuss other important resource records in the following steps of this procedure.) To add an A resource record, under Record Key you specify the name of the host you want to add. This is the host name only, without the DNS domain it is in. Next, under Value, specify the IP address of that host, and then click Add to add the resource record to the list of configured resource records (see Figure 23-8).

■**Tip** With DNS you can configure a simple network load balancer. Imagine that two servers are offering the same services, like a web server. To balance the workload between these two servers, create two A resource records, one that refers to the IP address of the first server and another that refers to the IP address of the other server. Give both resource records the same name (such as www). DNS will notice that there are two entries for www and automatically load balance packets between both servers. This is also known as the *round-robin* mechanism.

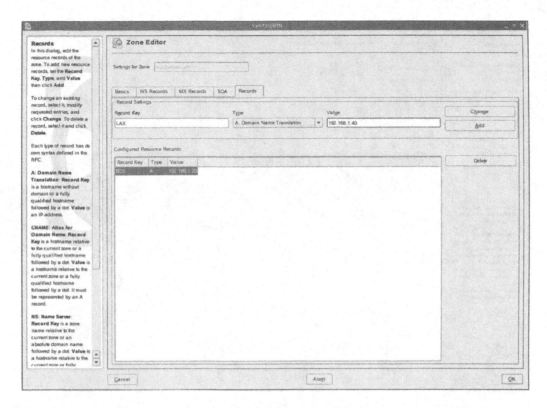

Figure 23-8. *To add an A resource record, you specify the name of the host you want to add without its DNS suffix.*

9. You can use a CNAME resource record as an alias to refer to another host. Working with aliases can be useful; if the name of the real host changes, you just need to change the name of the alias in the DNS database and do not need to inform all the users of your DNS server (which is an impossible task to do for most DNS servers anyway). To create a CNAME resource record, first from the Type drop-down list, select CNAME. Then under Record Key, specify the name of the alias, and under Value enter the name of the real host. Next click Add to add the alias to the database.

10. Next, the NS: Name Server resource record type is used to add name servers to the database. This is not the same as what you did on the NS Records tab; there you just mentioned the names of name servers without indicating the zones for which they are responsible. On this tab, you first enter the name of the zone the name server is responsible for under Record Key. This zone name can be relative to the current zone, but you can add an absolute zone name as well. In the latter case, make sure the name of the zone ends with a dot. Next, under Value, specify the name of the name server of the zone you just entered. Also, make sure an A record is available to resolve that name.

11. Finally, you can enter the MX resource record type. This option doesn't add much to the option you've already seen on the MX Records tab, so use that instead. Then click OK to return to the DNS Zones main screen. From there, click Next. This brings you to the screen shown in Figure 23-9.

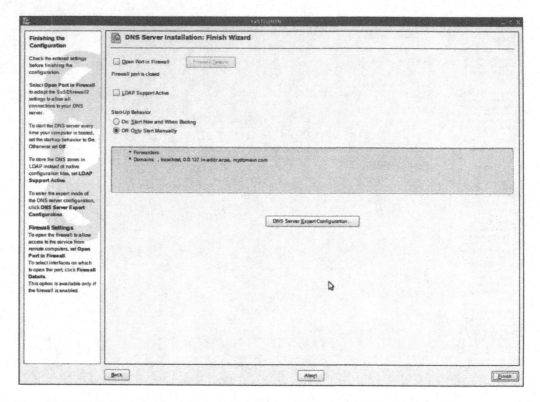

Figure 23-9. *On the final screen of the DNS installation program you can specify how the server is started.*

12. In the final screen of the DNS installation program, you can specify how the server is started. On this screen, specify how you want the DNS server to start, and then click Finish to store and activate your configuration. The following options are available:

- *Open Port in Firewall*: Select this option to make sure the DNS port is opened on the firewall.

- *LDAP Support Active*: Use this option to store the DNS zone information in an LDAP Directory server instead of the native configuration files. When selecting this option, you must realize that it makes troubleshooting errors different as well, since problems can't be fixed in the configuration files directly anymore, but you have to use LDIF to make changes to the LDAP database or use a graphical LDAP client for this. An advantage of storing the DNS information in LDAP is that it increases the availability of data since the DNS zones can be replicated with the LDAP replication process.

- *Start-Up Behavior:* Change this to On to make sure the server starts now and will be started automatically when booting.

- *DNS Server Expert Configuration:* Clicking this option opens an interface that gives access to more advanced options. Where relevant, I'll cover these options later in this chapter.

As you have seen in the procedure, resource records are a pretty important element of a DNS solution. Table 23-1 lists some of the most important types of resource records.

Table 23-1. *Some Important DNS Record Types*

Record Type	Meaning	Value
soa	Start of Authority	General parameters for the domain.
NS	Name server	The name or IP address of a name server for this domain or one of its subdomains that has its own name server.
MX	Mail exchanger	The name or IP address of a mail server for this domain. This record type also works with a priority that indicates how important this particular mail server is in case more than one mail server is available. A lower-priority number indicates a more important mail server that should be contacted first.
A	Address	The IP address of a computer. This is what DNS is all about and what helps translating DNS names in IP addresses.
PTR	Pointer	Contains the name of a computer, used by reversed DNS (see the next section).
CNAME	Canonical name	An alias for a computer.

Setting Up Reversed DNS with YaST

If you know how to set up a normal DNS zone with YaST, you can set up a zone for reversed DNS. Basically, the procedure is the same as the procedure for setting up normal DNS; just a few items need to be handled differently. In the following procedure, you'll learn how to set up reversed DNS. The procedure illustrates how to do this on a DNS server that is already configured; as you'll see, this opens a different interface than the one you saw when creating the master DNS Server for a regular zone:

1. In YaST, select Network Services ➤ DNS Server. This opens the screen shown in Figure 23-10.

2. On the left bar in the screen, select DNS Zones. Then add the name of the reversed DNS zone you need to add. This name should be the inversed bit of the network bit of your IP address, followed by in-addr.arpa. For example, for the network 193.193.100.0, it would become 100.193.193.in-addr.arpa. Specify the type Master, and then click Add to proceed. This will add the in-addr.arpa zone to the list of configured DNS zones.

3. Select the zone you've just created from the Configured DNS Zones list, and with the zone selected, click Edit. This opens the Zone Editor.

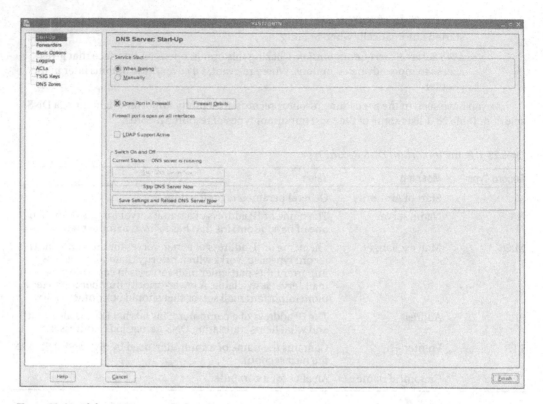

Figure 23-10. *If the DNS server is already configured, you'll do the rest of the setup work from the advanced interface.*

4. From the Zone Editor, enter all the required generic parameters as discussed earlier in this chapter. Then activate the Records tab to add some PTR records. These are the resource records that translate an IP address into a name. Under Record Key, enter the host part of the IP address (for example, if the complete IP address is 193.193.100.20, use 20 only). Next make sure the PTR record type is selected. Then under Value, enter the complete host name including the DNS zone, and make sure to put a dot at the end of that name. Then click Add to add the PTR resource record to the resource records database for your zone. See Figure 23-11 for an example of what this looks like.

5. Now click OK followed by Finish to store and apply your settings.

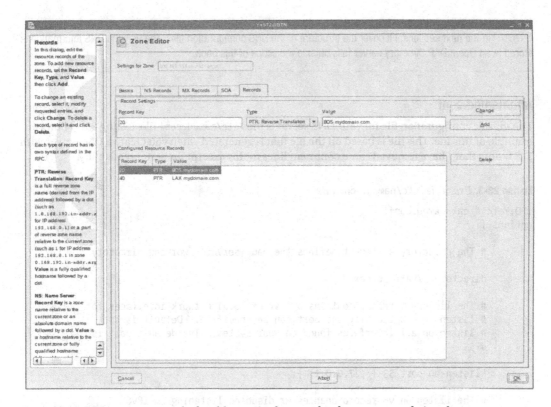

Figure 23-11. *PTR resource records should contain the complete host name as their value.*

Setting Up a Slave Server with YaST

After setting up a master server, setting up a DNS slave server with YaST is relatively easy:

1. From YaST, select Network Services ➤ DNS Server.

2. In the forwarder configuration screen, click Next without configuring anything.

3. On the Add New Zone screen, enter the name of the zone for which you want to configure the slave server. Then select Slave from the Type drop-down list, and click Add to add it.

4. Now enter the IP address of the server that holds the master zone files.

5. Complete the wizard. This will open the slave server and download the DNS zone files from the master.

Configuring DNS from Its Configuration Files

It's cool that you can create a DNS server with YaST, but if ever you need to troubleshoot it, you must at least be aware of the location and structure of its configuration files. In the next sections, you'll learn how the DNS configuration is stored on your server and how the configuration files are organized. To start the DNS server manually, you can use the rcnamed start command.

> **Note** In the next sections, I'll cover the structure of the DNS configuration files. The way the DNS information is stored in an OpenLDAP Directory server falls outside the scope of this book.

/etc/named.conf

The master configuration file for your DNS server is the /etc/named.conf file. Listing 23-3 shows an example of this file. This file is based on the file that is generated when you create a DNS server with YaST; note that I have removed some comment lines in this excerpt for better readability.

Listing 23-3. *Example* /etc/named.conf *File*

```
SFO:/etc # cat named.conf
options {

        # The directory statement defines the name server's working directory

        directory "/var/lib/named";

        # The listen-on record contains a list of local network interfaces to
        # listen on.  Optionally the port can be specified.  Default is to
        # listen on all interfaces found on your system.  The default port is
        # 53.

        #listen-on port 53 { 127.0.0.1; };

        # The listen-on-v6 record enables or disables listening on IPv6
        # interfaces.  Allowed values are 'any' and 'none' or a list of
        # addresses.

        listen-on-v6 { any; };

        notify no;
};

# The following zone definitions don't need any modification.  The first one
# is the definition of the root name servers.  The second one defines
# localhost while the third defines the reverse lookup for localhost.

zone "." in {
        type hint;
        file "root.hint";
};

zone "localhost" in {
        type master;
        file "localhost.zone";
};

zone "0.0.127.in-addr.arpa" in {
        type master;
        file "127.0.0.zone";
};
```

```
# Include the meta include file generated by createNamedConfInclude.  This
# includes all files as configured in NAMED_CONF_INCLUDE_FILES from
# /etc/sysconfig/named

include "/etc/named.conf.include";
zone "example.com" in {
        allow-transfer { any; };
        file "master/example.com";
        type master;
};
zone "0.168.192.in-addr.arpa" in {
        file "master/0.168.192.in-addr.arpa";
        type master;
};

# You can insert further zone records for your own domains below or create
# single files in /etc/named.d/ and add the file names to
# NAMED_CONF_INCLUDE_FILES.
# See /usr/share/doc/packages/bind/README.SUSE for more details.
```

As you can see, this example configuration file contains everything to create a working DNS server. Some options are defined but commented out to make sure they are not used right away. In this configuration file, the following settings are effective:

options { .... };: The named.conf file starts with a large section that has the name options. Many of the options mentioned in this list are defined within this section. Note that the section options is opened with options {, and then a list of all options that are included follows; further in the file, the section is closed by a }; construction.

directory "/var/lib/named";: This parameter defines the location where all DNS configuration files are stored. See the next section for more details. Also note the semicolon that is used at the end of the line, which is an important syntax feature.

notify no;: This option indicates that slave servers should not be notified of changes. This leaves it completely to the slave server to make sure it is up-to-date. If you want an alert to be sent to a slave server when a change occurs, change this setting to notify yes;.

include "/etc/named.conf.include";: This refers to an additional configuration file that you can use to include extra information that should be used by your DNS server.

zone ... { ...};: This structure defines the zone files. As you can see, some default zones are present to refer to the root of the DNS domain, localhost, and the reverse DNS zone for the local domain.

Amongst the most important options of the DNS server is the definition of the zones. As you can see, the first zone defined is as follows:

zone .

This refers to the root of the DNS domain. You need this definition; otherwise, your server wouldn't be able to find the name servers for the root domain. Therefore, this zone definition indicates that a list of name servers for the root domain can be found in the file root.hint. As you can see, no absolute path name is provided for this file; the path mentioned here is relative to the directory that is referred to with the directory "/var/lib/named" option. Therefore, named would expect the file root.hint to be present in that directory.

Another interesting example of the zone definition is the part where example.com is defined:

```
zone "example.com" in {
        allow-transfer { any; };
        file "master/example.com";
        type master;
};
```

As you can see, in the previous definition of example.com, all options that are valid for that zone appear between brackets. The first option you see is allow-transfer { any; };. This makes sure all hosts are allowed to do a zone transfer to your host. If you want to limit zone transfers to some hosts only, replace any with an IP address. Next, for this zone you can see the file master/ example.com is referred to, which means you can expect this file to be present in the directory /var/lib/named/master/example.com on your server. As the last definition, you can see that this server is defined as the master for the zone.

The Zone Files

The zone files of your DNS server are stored in the directory /var/lib/named. Some generic files are in /var/lib/named itself (such as the zone files for localhost and the list of name servers of the root domain in the root.hint file), the zone files of the master server are in the subdirectory master, and the zone files for the slave server are in the subdirectory slave. In Listing 23-4 you can see what the zone file for example.com looks like.

Listing 23-4. *Contents of the* example.com *Zone File*

```
SFO:/var/lib/named/master # cat example.com
$TTL 2D
@               IN SOA          SFO.example.com.  root.SFO.example.com. (
                                2006080700        ; serial
                                3H                ; refresh
                                1H                ; retry
                                1W                ; expiry
                                1D )              ; minimum

example.com.    IN MX           10 mail.example.com.
example.com.    IN NS           lax.example.com.
sfo             IN A            192.168.1.10
lax             IN A            192.168.1.40
web             IN CNAME        sfo.example.com.
```

As you can see, the zone file starts with the generic settings. First, the parameter TTL 2D specifies a validity of two days if your slave server cannot synchronize with the master. Next, the SOA settings for your server are defined. Notice the mail address for the administrator of your DNS server, which is specified as root.SFO.example.com. Following the generic information, you can see the definition of the resource records. All the settings you see here can be changed here as well, and YaST will automatically pick that up.

/etc/sysconfig/named

The last configuration file that is used by your DNS server is the sysconfig file that determines how the server should boot. Two important parameters are defined here. First, the parameter NAMED_RUN_CHROOTED indicates whether the DNS name server should run in a chroot jail. By default, it is configured to do that. This means it will run in the directory /var/lib/named and will not see anything outside that directory. Therefore, you should make sure all the configuration files are available from there. When you configure your server with YaST, YaST will take care of that automatically. If, however, you choose to configure your server by hand, make sure the configuration files are all in the chrooted environment. For security reasons, it is strongly recommended to always leave the NAMED_RUN_CHROOTED enabled.

Second, the next important parameter you'll find in the /etc/sysconfig/named file is NAMED_ARGS. If you need to start your DNS server with any specific arguments, specify them here.

Securing Zone Transfers

An important aspect of DNS server configuration is securing zone transfers. On an unsecured DNS server, anyone can do a zone transfer. To limit the hosts that can do a zone transfer, you can use the allow-transfer option in the configuration of the master zone file. This option can take two parameters: the IP address of a host that is allowed to do zone transfer and an encryption key. Since IP addresses can be forged, using encryption keys is the more secure solution. To use an encryption key, you need to generate the key first. Next, you have to copy it to the configuration file on both servers. Once copied on both, the slave server can send a signed request to do zone transfer; since signed requests have to use the proper key, only hosts that have the key can do a zone transfer from that moment. The following procedure explains how to configure this:

1. Use the ndssec-keygen command to generate the key. To do this, enter the following command on either server: dnssec-keygen -a HMAC-MD5 -b 256 -n HOST zonetransfer. In this command, the -a option specifies the type of encryption that should be used. -b 256 indicates that a 256 bits key must be created. -n HOST tells the command that the key it should create is going to be used as a host key, and dnskey is the name that is given to the file that this command will create; you can choose any name you like for the filename. As the output, the command will generate a file of which the name is echoed on the next line; see Listing 23-5.

Listing 23-5. *Creating DNS Security Keys*

```
BTN:~ # dnssec-keygen -a HMAC-MD5 -b 256 -n HOST dnskey
Kdnskey.+157+55660
```

2. As the result of the previous command, two files are created. One has the name Kdnskey.+157+55660.key; the other has the name Kzonetransfer.+157+55660.private. Of these, the .key file contains the DNS key you have to include. The private key (which is not really a private key) contains the same key and some additional information on the algorithm that has been used when creating the key. Use the cat command on either one of these files to show the contents of the key file (see Listing 23-6).

Listing 23-6. *Showing the Contents of the Key File*

```
BTN:~ # cat Kdnskey.+157+55660.key
dnskey. IN KEY 512 3 157 Cdk1If9CZnZNS9HnzDaAn+s/OPtV1AOxbXyv65Yq8H4=
```

3. Now first edit the /etc/named.conf file on the master server to add the key information. Listing 23-7 shows the relevant parts. Note that the example just adds the allow-transfer parameter for the example.com zone; make sure it is included on all domains that you want to secure with this key. Also, make sure the configuration file /etc/named.conf is readable by root only. Otherwise, unauthorized people could steal your key.

Listing 23-7. *Including Key Information in the Master's* `named.conf` *File*

```
options {
...
};

key dnskey {
    algorithm HMAC-MD5;
    secret "Cdk1If9CZnZNS9HnzDaAn+s/OPtV1AOxbXyv65Yq8H4=";
};

zone "example.com" in {
    type master;
    file "master/example.com";
    allow-transfer {
        key dnskey;
    };
};
```

4. Lastly, the `named.conf` file on the slave server needs some tuning as well. First, it needs the same section to define the key. Second, it needs a section where it specifies that if it tries to do a zone transfer with your particular master server, it should use this key. You can accomplish this by including the code shown in Listing 23-8 in the `named.conf` file for the slave server.

Listing 23-8. *Tuning* `named.conf` *on the Slave Server for Use of the Encryption Key*

```
options{
...
};

key dnskey {
    algorithm HMAC-MD5;
    secret "Cdk1If9CZnZNS9HnzDaAn+s/OPtV1AOxbXyv65Yq8H4=";
};

server 192.168.1.10 {
    keys {
        dnskey;
    };
};
```

You now can start a zone transfer from the slave server. Do this by just restarting the DNS server (`rcnamed restart`). Then check whether the zone files are created (or updated) in `/var/lib/named/slave` on the slave server, or see whether any tsig-related errors occur in `/var/log/messages`, indicating that it doesn't work.

■**Tip** Don't forget to protect your slave name servers against illegal zone transfers, because ordinarily you can do a zone transfer on a slave server as well. To do this, include the `allow-transfer {none;};` option in the options of the slave server.

Summary

In this chapter, you learned how to set up DNS. You dealt with its configuration from YaST, because YaST is a convenient tool to set up a DNS environment; it allows you to set all the relevant options. If YaST can't do it, you can still tune the configuration files mentioned in this chapter by hand to include some of the more advanced options. One of these that is particularly important is the inclusion of security keys to limit the possibility of doing a zone transfer. You learned in this chapter how to do that. In the next chapter, you will learn how to set up DHCP on SUSE Linux Enterprise Server.

CHAPTER 24

■■■

Configuring a DHCP Server

In your network, probably a lot of computers need an IP address and other IP-related information in their configuration, such as a router's IP address and the address of a DNS server. You can, of course, enter that information on all the client workstations by hand. However, it is much easier to automate this process with a Dynamic Host Configuration Protocol (DHCP) server. In this chapter, you'll learn how to configure such a server on SUSE Linux Enterprise Server.

Understanding How DHCP Works

DHCP is a broadcast-based protocol. A client is configured to obtain an IP address via DHCP and send a broadcast on start-up, trying to find one or more DHCP servers in the network. This is the DHCPDISCOVER packet. If a DHCP server sees this DHCPDISCOVER packet coming, it will answer with a DHCPOFFER packet. In that packet, it will offer an IP address and related information.

If the client receives a DHCPOFFER from more than one DHCP server, it will choose one of the offerings. It is difficult beforehand to determine with what IP configuration information the client will work; that is one of the reasons you should take care that no more than one DHCP server is available per broadcast domain to offer a configuration to the DHCP clients. To indicate that the client wants to use the IP address and related information that is offered by a DHCP server, it returns a DHCPREQUEST, thus asking to work with that information. The DHCP server then indicates that's OK by returning a DHCPACK (acknowledgment) to the client. From that moment on, the client can use the IP address.

Associated with each offering from a DHCP server is a *lease time*, which determines how long the client can use an IP address and the associated information. Before the lease ends, the client has to send a DHCPREQUEST again to renew its lease. In most cases, the server will answer to such a request by extending the lease period; in that case, the client receives a DHCPACK. If, for some reason, it is not possible to extend the lease, the client receives a DHCPNACK (negative acknowledgment). This indicates the client cannot continue its use of the IP address and associated information. If that happens, the client has to start the process all over again, beginning with the DHCPDISCOVER packet being sent over the network.

When the client machine is shut down, it lets the server know it no longer needs the IP address. In that case, it will send a DHCPRELEASE over the network. From that moment on, the IP address is available for use by other clients.

You should note that DHCP is a broadcast-based protocol. In other words, if the DHCP server is on a different subnet as the DHCP client, the client cannot reach it directly. If that's the case, a DHCP relay agent is needed, which forwards DHCP requests to a DHCP server. Later in the section "The DHCP Relay Agent," you will learn how to configure a DHCP relay agent.

Configuring a DHCP Server from YaST

As is often the case on SUSE Linux Enterprise Server, the easiest way to configure a DHCP server is from YaST. In this section, you will learn how to configure a DHCP server from YaST. Before you start, make sure no other DHCP servers are already in use on the segment where you want to configure your DHCP server; if another DHCP server is active, you'll never know with which DHCP server you are communicating. To configure a DHCP server from YaST, follow these steps:

1. In YaST, click Network Services ➤ DHCP Server. This opens the screen shown in Figure 24-1. On this screen, you need to indicate the network cards on which you want the DHCP server to listen. All network cards in your server are automatically detected and will be listed here. To enable a network card for DHCP, select it, and then click the Add button. This will add an *x* in the Active column. Also, if a firewall is active, select the Open Firewall for Selected Interface box. Then click Next.

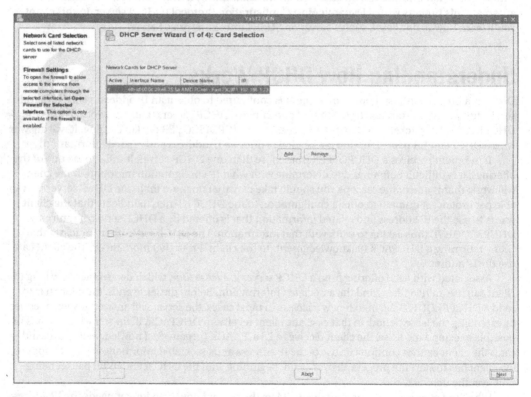

Figure 24-1. *In the first step of the DHCP Server Wizard, you have to indicate on which network card you want to enable the DHCP server.*

2. You now see the Global Settings screen (see Figure 24-2). On this screen, you can specify the global settings you want your server to use. These are settings that will be handed out to all clients. The following settings are available:

- *LDAP Support*: Select this option if you want the DHCP configuration to be stored in an LDAP database and not in the configuration file dhcpd.conf. This option requires you to set up an LDAP environment first; check Chapter 17 for more details on how to do that. Note that this is the only setting on the screen that isn't delivered to the DHCP clients.

- *Domain Name*: Use this option to specify the DNS domain name you want to deliver to the clients. Ordinarily, this would be the domain name of your own company.

- *Primary Name Server IP*: Use this option to specify the IP address of your primary DNS name server. This name server will be used in all cases, as long as it is available on your network.

- *Secondary Name Server IP:* Use this option to specify the IP address of a backup DNS name server. This server is contacted only if the primary name server is not reachable. Often, the DNS name server of the Internet provider is used here.

- *Default Gateway (Router)*: This option specifies the IP address of the default gateway. This is the IP address of the router your users need to contact in order to send packets to hosts that are not on their own subnet.

- *NTP Time Server*: Many clients support NTP to get time from a time server. Use this option to refer to the time server that should be used. See Chapter 20 for more details on how to configure an NTP time server.

- *Print Server*: Use this option to direct clients to a print server. See Chapter 14 for more information about setting up a print server.

- *WINS Server*: To resolve NetBIOS names that are used in a Windows environment, a WINS server can be a great help. If in your environment a WINS server is in use, enter its IP address here to deliver it to the clients in your network automatically.

- *Default Lease Time*: This option specifies the default lease time. This is the length of time users can utilize the IP address and associated configuration. Note that the default value is set to four hours. This is a good value for dynamic networks that don't have too many spare IP addresses. If your network is more or less static and you have enough IP addresses, you can set this value to be much greater. Three days, for example, is a reasonable setting as well.

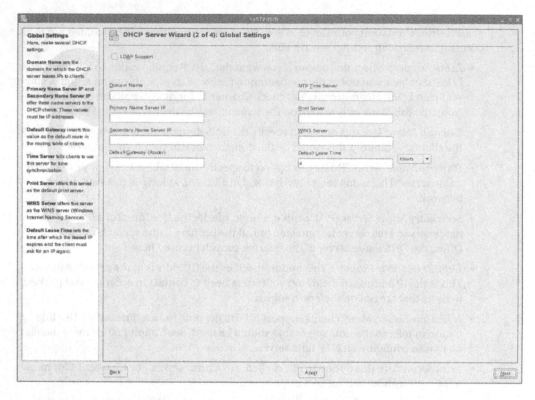

Figure 24-2. *On the Global Settings screen, you determine the settings that will be handed out to all clients that obtain address information from the DHCP server.*

3. On the next screen of the wizard (see Figure 24-3), you can set up the range of IP addresses that are handed out by your DHCP server. The IP address and network mask in use on your current network are automatically detected and appear here. All you have to do is enter the first and last IP addresses in the range of IP addresses you want to hand out. Make sure none of these IP addresses is in use already; your DHCP server doesn't check this before handing out an address. If, for this specific range, you want to use a different lease time, enter that lease time here. This is a useful feature to differentiate between, for example, the network where your servers are and the network where your clients are. As you can see in Figure 24-3, you can also specify the maximum lease time; this is the time your clients can continue using the IP address if they are not able to contact the DHCP server. It is useful to set this parameter to be much greater than the default lease time.

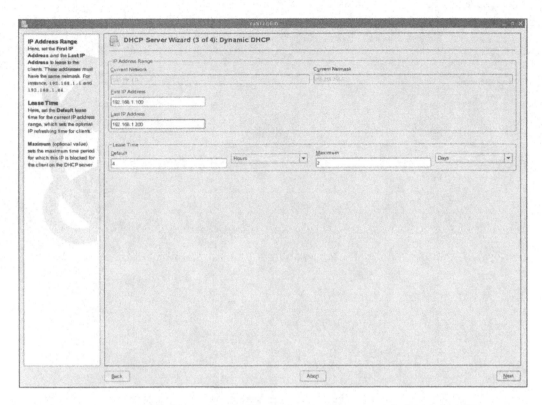

Figure 24-3. *For the range specification, you indicate what IP addresses can be handed out by your DHCP server.*

4. On the last screen of the DHCP Server Wizard (see Figure 24-4), you can specify whether you want to start the DHCP server manually or automatically when booting. Also click the DHCP Server Expert Configuration button.

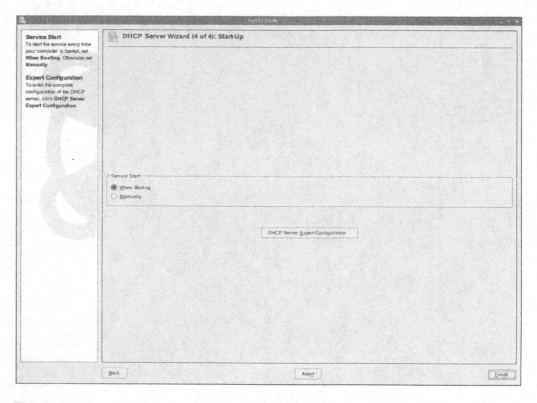

Figure 24-4. *In most cases, it makes sense to start the DHCP server automatically when your server boots.*

5. After clicking the DHCP Server Expert Configuration button, you will see the screen shown in Figure 24-5. On this screen, you have access to all the screens displayed by the DHCP Server Wizard and two new screens as well. The first of them is the Host Management screen. On this screen, you can do some host management. This is useful in case you want to assign IP addresses and names to hosts based on their hardware address. To do this, first enter the MAC address of the host you want to manage. Then enter the name and IP address you want to assign to that host. The next time your host boots, if it is configured to contact a DHCP server when booting, it will obtain the IP address as well as the name you have set up here. This option is useful if you want to make sure some hosts will always work with the same IP address and name, such as the servers on your network.

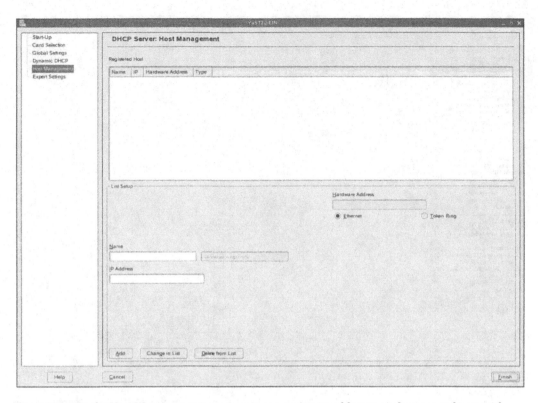

Figure 24-5. *On the Host Management screen, you can assign IP addresses and names to hosts with a specific MAC address.*

6. When clicking the Expert Settings menu item, you'll first see a warning that after displaying the expert settings, you cannot return to the settings as displayed by the wizard. To display the expert settings anyway, click Yes to continue. This opens the screen shown in Figure 24-6. This screen offers two important advantages; the configuration of these advantages is covered in steps 7 and 8:

   • You can manage more than one IP address range for your DHCP server.

   • You have access to advanced configuration options, which is useful if, for example, you need to add a specific option type to your DHCP server.

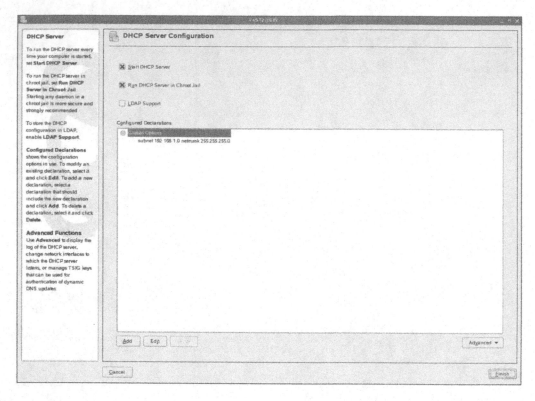

Figure 24-6. *Use the Expert Settings screen to get access to some of the more advanced configuration options.*

7. To add a new IP address range to be served by your DHCP server, click Add on the screen shown in Figure 24-6. This opens the screen shown in Figure 24-7. On this screen, you need to specify what type of information you want to add. Select the type you want to add, and then click Next to continue:

- *Subnet:* Use this to add a new IP address range for a subnet on your network.

- *Host:* Use this to add a host that has specific requirements.

- *Shared Network:* If you have one physical network on which several VLANs are defined and want to hand out IP addresses on these VLANs, check this option.

- *Group:* Use this option to add a group of declarations. This option is not used to assign new IP addresses that can be handed out by your server.

- *Pool of Addresses:* Use this to add pools of addresses that need different settings than other pools of addresses that are in use for the same subnet. This is a rather rare setting.

- *Class:* Use the Class option to define class settings and then apply them to individual hosts or subnets later.

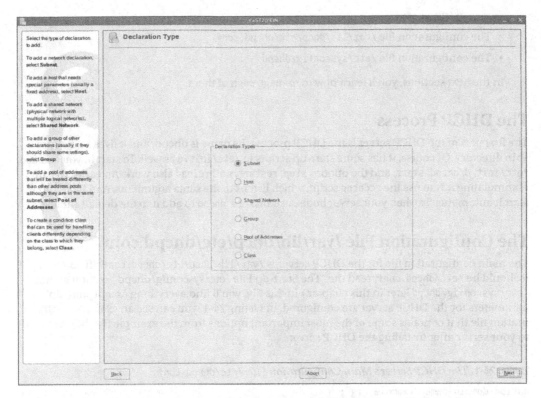

Figure 24-7. *The Declaration Type screen offers options to add different types of information to your DHCP server.*

8. On the next screen, if you click the Advanced button, you will find three options:

- *Display Log:* Select this option to display the log file. That way you can find out what your DHCP server is currently doing.

- *Interface Configuration:* Select this option to assign the DHCP server to other interfaces as well. This will make sure your server starts listening there as well.

- *Tsig Key Management:* Use this option to integrate the DHCP server with a DNS server for configuring a dynamic DNS environment.

9. When the DHCP server configuration is complete, click Finish. This will write all the settings and start the DHCP server. You can start using it immediately.

Configuring the DHCP Service Manually

You can perform all the tasks described in the previous section manually as well. When configuring DHCP manually, the following components are involved:

- The DHCP service
- The configuration file /var/lib/dhcp/etc/dhcpd.conf
- The configuration file /etc/sysconfig/dhcpd

In the next sections, you'll learn how to manage each of them.

The DHCP Process

The first part of the DHCP server is the DHCP process. Its name is dhcpd, and it lives in the /usr/sbin directory. Of course, it has some start-up scripts in /etc/init.d as well. To start it, you can use /etc/init.d/dhcpd start, and the options stop, restart, and reload also work. An easier way of manipulating it is to use the rcdhcpd script, which listens to the same arguments. And finally, to start it automatically when your server boots, use insserv dhcpd to add it to the default runlevels.

The Configuration File /var/lib/dhcp/etc/dhcpd.conf

The main configuration file for the DHCP server is /var/lib/dhcp/etc/dhcpd.conf. (If you thought it should be /etc/dhcpd.conf, read the "The Start-up File /etc/sysconfig/dhcpd" section about /etc/sysconfig/dhcpd later in this chapter.) In this file, you'll find everything except start-up parameters for the DHCP server are configured. In Listing 24-1, you can see an example configuration file that contains some of the most important options from the example file that is copied to your server after installing the DHCP server.

Listing 24-1. *The DHCP Server's Main Configuration File:* /etc/dhcpd.conf

```
option domain-name "example.org";
option domain-name-servers ns1.example.org, ns2.example.org;

default-lease-time 600;
max-lease-time 7200;

log-facility local7;

subnet 10.152.187.0 netmask 255.255.255.0 {
}

subnet 10.5.5.0 netmask 255.255.255.224 {
  range 10.5.5.26 10.5.5.30;
  option domain-name-servers ns1.internal.example.org;
  option domain-name "internal.example.org";
  option routers 10.5.5.1;
  option broadcast-address 10.5.5.31;
  default-lease-time 600;
  max-lease-time 7200;
}

host passacaglia {
  hardware ethernet 0:0:c0:5d:bd:95;
  filename "vmunix.passacaglia";
  server-name "toccata.fugue.com";
}
```

```
host fantasia {
  hardware ethernet 08:00:07:26:c0:a5;
  fixed-address fantasia.fugue.com;
}
```

As you can see, the dhcpd.conf file starts with some generic options. These options apply to all the addresses that are handed out by the DHCP server, and some apply to how the server works. The following lines are used for this purpose:

```
option domain-name "example.org";
option domain-name-servers ns1.example.org, ns2.example.org;

default-lease-time 600;
max-lease-time 7200;

log-facility local7;
```

The first two lines set the default domain name and then refer to the names of DNS servers. Notice you don't need to use an IP address here; assuming that the DNS resolver is set up as it should be, you can use names here. When editing the configuration file by hand, make sure each line ends with a semicolon. Otherwise, your server will complain. Next, you define the leases. By default, a lease is specified in minutes; therefore, the default lease time expires after 10 hours, and the maximum lease time is 120 hours. The last line specifies the log facility for syslog-ng as local7. This makes it possible to log DHCP messages to a specific location.

In the second part of the code, you'll see that two subnets are specified:

```
subnet 10.152.187.0 netmask 255.255.255.0 {
}

subnet 10.5.5.0 netmask 255.255.255.224 {
  range 10.5.5.26 10.5.5.30;
  option domain-name-servers ns1.internal.example.org;
  option domain-name "internal.example.org";
  option routers 10.5.5.1;
  option broadcast-address 10.5.5.31;
  default-lease-time 600;
  max-lease-time 7200;
}
```

The first subnet is empty. This may seem odd, but it can be useful when the DHCP server is really serving only networks that it isn't connected to directly. If no declaration is present for the subnet to which the DHCP server is connected, the DHCP process will complain. Therefore, in such cases you should just define an empty subnet.

In the second subnet definition, something real is happening. After specifying what network this definition is used for, the file defines a range of five IP addresses. Then the file defines the specific options for this subnet. Some options were defined in the global part of the configuration file already; if that's the case for your options, the subnet-specific option will just overwrite the global option. One option in this subnet is new; broadcast-address is needed in this case, because on the subnet, a nondefault address class is used. Every time you use nondefault address classes, you must specify the broadcast address for that network as well.

Next, you'll see two host definitions. These contain settings for specific hosts:

```
host passacaglia {
  hardware ethernet 0:0:c0:5d:bd:95;
  filename "vmunix.passacaglia";
  server-name "toccata.fugue.com";
}
```

```
host fantasia {
  hardware ethernet 08:00:07:26:c0:a5;
  fixed-address fantasia.fugue.com;
}
```

To make sure the setting applies to the right host, you refer to the MAC address for every host definition. This happens with the definition of the hardware ethernet address. Then you use three other options. The option filename refers to a boot file that is to be loaded by a client. A TFTP server can offer this file. Just enable the TFTP server as part of your xinetd configuration and then put the file with the name mentioned here in the directory /tftpboot (which you'll have to create manually), and the host will be capable of downloading this file. The filename option is useful for diskless workstations; it allows them to download a boot image. If a client is booting from a boot image file that has been delivered by a server, it can be useful for the client to know what server it is dealing with. To specify that, use the server-name option. It should contain the name of your DHCP server. The last new option you see here is fixed-address. This option passes a fixed IP address to the client. If DNS is set up correctly, you can use a resolvable DNS name.

The Start-up Configuration File /etc/sysconfig/dhcpd

Some more important options are in the configuration file /etc/sysconfig/dhcpd. This file defines the way the DHCP server starts. The first line you'll find here is as follows:

```
DHCPD_INTERFACE="eth-id-00:0c:29:e8:35:5a"
```

This line refers to the network interface to which the DHCP server binds. You have several ways to refer to the network interface, but the way in which the complete device name is used (like in the example line), and not just eth0, is the best. This device name is composed of the prefix eth-id, followed by the MAC address on your machine. This is because in modern Linux systems, you can't guarantee that the interface that now comes up as eth0 will be eth0 the next time and not eth1.

Tip To make sure eth0 is always referring to the same interface, you can define a rule for it. These rules are in the file /etc/udev/rules.d/30-net_persistent_names.rules. The following example makes sure a given MAC address is always assigned to eth0: SUBSYSTEM=="net", ACTION=="add", SYSFS{address}== "00:0e:35:d3:84:12", IMPORT="/lib/udev/rename_netiface %k eth0".

Next, you'll find the following line:

```
DHCPD_RUN_CHROOTED="yes"
```

This line makes sure the DHCP server runs in a *chroot jail*. This mechanism specifies a certain directory that the DHCP server runs from, which is seen by the DHCP server as the root of the file system. This is a good security setting, because if intruders broke through the DHCP server, they would see the contents of this directory only. By default, this directory is set to /var/lib/dhcp. Within this directory, you'll find all the configuration files that the DHCP server uses. For example, the file /var/lib/dhcp/etc/dhcpd.conf is the file where the configuration of the DHCP server is stored (and not the file /etc/dhcpd.conf as you might think).

The next setting lets you specify whether you want to work with include files for your DHCP server. These are files that contain additional configuration information. This may be useful if your DHCP server is handling a lot of information, such as tens of networks and hundreds of hosts that all require individual configuration. In that case, create the include files, such as in the directory /etc/dhcpd.conf.d, and use the following line to include them:

```
DHCPD_CONF_INCLUDE_FILES="/etc/dhcpd.conf.d/"
```

By default, no include files are used.

Finally, you'll see three more lines that most of the time can stay as they are. The settings are as follows:

```
DHCPD_RUN_AS="dhcpd"
DHCPD_OTHER_ARGS=""
DHCPD_BINARY=""
```

The first of these specifies the user account to run the DHCP server with. For security reasons, you should never run it as root but as the user dhcpd instead. Next, DHCPD_OTHER_ARGS specifies arguments that have to be started when starting the /usr/sbin/dhcpd process. Finally, you can use the DHCPD_BINARY statement if you don't want to run /usr/sbin/dhcpd but another binary as the default DHCP binary.

Setting Advanced Configuration Options

Based on the information in this chapter so far, you are able to set up a DHCP server that doesn't use any complicated options. Some advanced configuration options may be interesting to you. In the following sections, you'll read about three of them. You need to set all of these options using YaST. First, the section "Integrating DHCP and DNS" discusses how to set up dynamic DNS (DDNS) so the DHCP server tells the DNS server when it handed out some new configuration. Then the section "The DHCP Relay Agent" describes how you can let one DHCP server serve all the subnets in your network. Finally, I'll discuss how to configure your DHCP server for high availability using an internal feature of the DHCP server.

Integrating DHCP and DNS

If you want clients to be accessible by their names, you need to tell the DNS server when the DHCP server has handed out a new IP address to the client. To make this work, you need to configure the configuration files for both DNS and DHCP. You first need to create a cryptographic key that can be used to authorize the update. You can generate this key with the dnssec-keygen command:

```
dnssec-keygen -a HMAC-MD5 -b 128 -n HOST ddns
```

This command will generate two keys in the current directory. Part of the name of the key is a random number. The names can be as follows:

```
Kddns.+157+03212.key
Kddns.+157+03212.private
```

These two files contain the key that has to be used in clear text:

```
SFO:~ # cat Kddns.+157+03212.key
ddns. IN KEY 512 3 157 WVf7JaWqrfoIe4AtT9GGug==
```

Now edit the DNS configuration file to include this key. Listing 24-2 shows how to use the key for the zone mydomain.com and its associated reversed DNS zone.

Listing 24-2. *Securing* named.conf *with a Key for Dynamic DNS Updates*

```
key ddns {
    algorithm HMAC-MD5;
    secret WVf7JaWqrfoIe4AtT9GGug==;
};
```

```
zone "mydomain.com" in {
     type master;
     file "mydomain.zone";
     allow-update { key ddns ;};
};

zone "1.168.192.in-addr.arpa" in {
     type master;
     file "1.168.192.zone";
     allow-update { key ddns ;};
};
```

As you can see, in this example a new section is created for the key, specifying its algorithm as well as the key that is used. (Make sure the named.conf file is readable by root only if you include a key in it!) Next, you use the allow-update (key ddns ;}; statement for all zones that need this key for dynamic DNS updates. Note that ddns is just the name of the key; you can choose any name you like here.

Next, you need to modify the dhcpd.conf file.

Tip Make sure you tune the right configuration file. The DHCP server on SUSE Linux Enterprise Server runs chrooted by default, so /var/lib/dhcp/etc/dhcpd.conf is the configuration file you need!

Make sure to add the code shown Listing 24-3 in the dhcpd.conf file. The following example will work with the example DNS configuration shown previously, so you can tune it according to your own configuration.

Listing 24-3. *Including DDNS Code in* dhcpd.conf

```
ddns-update-style interim;
ddns-updates on;

key ddns {
     algorithm HMAC-MD5;
     secret WVf7JaWqrfoIe4AtT9GGug==;
}

zone 1.168.192.in-addr.arpa. {
     key ddns;
}

zone mydomain.com. {
     key ddns;
}
```

You should note a few things in this example. First, when referring to a DNS zone, make sure you put a dot after the name of the zone; it won't work without this. So, mydomain.com. is good, but mydomain.com isn't. Then, the parameter ddns-update-style specifies how the updates need to take place. You have two options: interim versus ad-hoc, but ad-hoc is deprecated, so you should use only interim here. Then the parameter ddns-updates on activates DDNS. Last, like in the named.conf configuration file, you must specify the key in this configuration file. Of course, it must be the same as the key that is specified in the named.conf file. Now fire up the DHCP server and the DNS server, and Dynamic DNS is working.

Note If the client gets its host name from the DHCP server, you have to do some more work. In that case, it is important that the client always gets the same host name. You can do this by including the option host-name in the definition of the specific host in the dhcpd.conf configuration file. In this same definition of the client, you must specify the MAC address for each client equally, using the hardware parameter. An example of this is as follows:

```
host somehost.mydomain.com {
    hardware ethernet 00:0C:29:E8:35:5A;
    ddns-hostname "somehost";
    ddns-domainname "mydomain.com";
    option host-name "somehost";
```

The DHCP Relay Agent

A DHCP broadcast is received on the local network only. DHCP broadcasts cannot cross routers. It is, however, impractical to install a DHCP server on every single network. As an alternative, you can install the DHCP server on a multihomed server so that it can serve all networks to which it is connected. An alternative is to use a DHCP relay agent.

A DHCP *relay agent* is a program that forwards packets to the DHCP server. You can run it on any server on the network or on the router. Every hardware router has embedded functionality to act as a DHCP relay agent. If you want to install a relay agent on a Linux server, you need the package dhcp-relay. After its installation, you can configure the relay agent from the /etc/sysconfig/dhcrelay file. In this file, you'll find the parameter DHCRELAY_INTERFACES. This parameter specifies on which network cards the relay agents should listen for DHCP broadcasts. You can configure it to listen on eth0 and eth1 by adding DHCRELAY_INTERFACES="eth0 eth1" to the dhcrelay file.

Next, you need to specify the IP address of the DHCP server. To do this, add it as a parameter to the DHCRELAY_SERVERS parameter. After configuring these options, use rcdhcrelay start to start the relay agent. To make sure it is started automatically the next time you restart your server, enter the insserv dhcrelay command once.

Setting Up DHCP Failover

If you need to make sure your DHCP server is always available, you can use the DHCP internal failover feature. This feature allows you to set up two (and no more than that) DHCP servers to use a shared address pool. Of these address pools, if both servers are operational, both can use about half of the available addresses. If one of the servers fails, the other server can take over immediately.

In a failover configuration, one server is primary, and the other is secondary. You also need to make sure both servers have the same configuration, with the exception for the failover code. This code is included in the dhcpd.conf configuration file. Listing 24-4 shows what this failover configuration would look like on the primary server.

Listing 24-4. *Configuring DHCP for Failover*

```
failover peer "mydomain" {
    primary;
    address 192.168.1.10;
    port 847;
    peer address 192.168.1.20;
    peer port 647;
```

```
    max-response-delay 120;
    mclt 1800;
    split 128;
    load balance max seconds 3;
}
```

This example configuration file uses the following parameters:

primary: This indicates that this server is the primary server in the pair. Use secondary on the other server.

address: This specifies the address on which this server should listen for the peer server.

port: Since DHCP failover doesn't have a fixed port assignment, you need this option to specify to which port it should listen. Usually, port 847 is used on the primary server, and port 647 is used on the secondary.

peer address: This indicates on what address the peer can be contacted.

peer port: This is the port on which the peer listens.

max-response-delay: This is the amount of seconds that the server waits before it assumes that the peer has failed.

mclt: This is the maximum client lead time. It is the length of time that can be assigned to a lease on either host if the partner is down. It is recommended that you leave this at 1800 seconds.

split: This value is defined on the primary server only and specifies where the DHCP address pool needs to be split between both servers. It is reasonable to put in the number that refers to half of the available IP addresses.

load balance max seconds: Leave this at the value of three seconds to make sure the workload is equally distributed between the servers.

The secondary server is configured slightly differently. Listing 24-5 shows an example of its configuration.

Listing 24-5. *Sample Failover Configuration for the Secondary Server*

```
failover peer "mydomain" {
    secondary;
    192.168.1.20;
    port 647;
    peer address 192.168.1.10;
    peer port 847;
    max-response-delay 120;
    load balance max seconds 3;
}
```

Next, further in the dhcpd.conf file, you must use a pool statement in which the failover configuration is included. This works in more or less the same way as a configuration in which a subnet statement is used. Listing 24-6 shows how you can modify the example file from Listing 24-1 earlier in this chapter to use a pool statement.

Listing 24-6. *Rewriting the DHCP Configuration File to Include a* pool *Statement*

```
option domain-name "example.org";
option domain-name-servers ns1.example.org, ns2.example.org;

default-lease-time 600;
max-lease-time 7200;

log-facility local7;

subnet 10.5.5.0 netmask 255.255.255.224 {
  pool {
     failover peer "mydomain";
     deny dynamic bootp clients;
     range 10.5.5.26 10.5.5.30;
     option domain-name-servers ns1.internal.example.org;
     option domain-name "internal.example.org";
     option routers 10.5.5.1;
     option broadcast-address 10.5.5.31;
     default-lease-time 600;
     max-lease-time 7200;
     }
}
```

As you can see, it isn't that hard to include a pool definition; it just adds a layer to the configuration file. Next, you add two new lines to refer to the high-availability settings. First, this is the setting failover peer mydomain. This refers to the definition of the failover settings earlier in the configuration file. Next, you must include the setting deny dynamic bootp clients. This is to disallow dynamic bootp clients to communicate to the DHCP servers that are configured for failover; this simply isn't supported. Now, open both DHCP servers, and your DHCP configuration is ready for automatic failover if one server fails.

Note Configuring DHCP for automatic failover is useful in an environment where no high-availability cluster is configured. If, however, your network has high-availability clustering configured (as described in Chapter 29 of this book), I recommend including DHCP failover in the high-availability environment. The biggest advantage of doing it that way is that you don't need to split the IP addresses that are handed out by the servers; simply one server runs the DHCP service. The other server takes over the DHCP service when the primary server fails.

Summary

In this chapter, you learned how to configure a DHCP server. As you saw, DHCP offers many options; I discussed only the most useful in this chapter. For a basic DHCP environment where only IP addresses and associated configuration have to be handed out, YaST offers enough to set up the DHCP server. However, if you need more than the basic configuration, it's a better idea to hack the configuration files manually. In the next chapter, you'll read how to configure the Squid proxy server.

■■■

## CHAPTER 25

Configuring the Squid Web
Proxy Cache

Although it's commonplace to use a firewall such as iptables to secure network access at a
packet level, you may occasionally require somewhat more sophisticated methods for managing
access, such as basing permission on usernames or the time of the day, for instance. For such purposes, the Squid web proxy cache is an excellent solution. In this chapter, you will learn how to
configure Squid.

Introducing Squid

Squid is used in network environments for three reasons:

Standard proxy server. Basically, you can use Squid as a proxy cache. This serves two goals:
it makes transmitting traffic to and from the Internet faster, and it adds security. In this role,
Squid is a proxy that sits between a user and the Internet. The user sends all HTTP requests
to the proxy and not directly to the Internet. The computers of the users do not even need a
direct connection to the Internet to generate web traffic. The proxy handles all the traffic for
the user and fetches the required data from the Internet. Then the proxy caches this data
locally. The next time another user needs the same data, they don't need to get it from the
Internet, but it can be provided from the cache that is maintained by the proxy. Used in this
way, the main advantage is that the Squid proxy increases speed for clients that need to get
data from the Internet. This chapter describes how you can use Squid in this way.

Application-level proxy. From its role as a cache, it automatically follows that rules can be
applied when retrieving data from the Internet. Used in this way, the Squid proxy also
becomes an application-level proxy that applies security rules to users transferring HTTP
traffic to and from the Internet. This chapter describes how you can use Squid proxy in
this way.

Web accelerator. You can also deploy Squid as a web accelerator, which is also known as a
reverse proxy. As a web accelerator, Squid sits between the Internet and an organization's web
server. All incoming connections to the web servers are routed via the Squid proxy in this scenario. Because the proxy handles all the connections, it can create a cache in which all the
frequently accessed web pages are stored. Therefore, they do not have to be fetched from the
hard drive of the web server, and this increases the speed at which data is transmitted to the
user. I won't cover how to configure Squid as a web accelerator in this chapter.

In large-scale environments, you can use Squid in a hierarchical configuration. In such a configuration, several Squid proxies can work together to return data to the user as quickly as possible.
Such a configuration makes sense where several locations of an office are connected but not every

location has a direct connection to the Internet. In this case, you can configure a Squid proxy on each location. On-location clients communicate with their local Squid proxy. If data cannot be fetched from the local proxy cache, the local proxy will contact the Squid proxy on the site that has the direct link to the Internet to see whether data can be delivered out of this proxy's cache. Only if this master proxy does not have the data will it go to the Internet, retrieve the data, put it in its cache, and then deliver the data to the Squid proxy on the local site. This proxy will put the data in its cache and deliver it to the user. Configuring a hierarchical proxy cache is a complex task and will not be covered in this chapter.

Before starting your work with Squid, you should be aware it is limited to working only with a few protocols. The most important of these are HTTP and FTP. For this reason, the network administrator should take measures to prevent users utilizing other protocols from going directly to the Internet. A good solution for this is to use a firewall. In Chapter 30, you can read more about how to configure a firewall on SUSE Linux Enterprise Server.

Installing Squid and Performing the Initial Configuration

Before you can use the Squid proxy, you have to install it. You can easily perform this task from the YaST utility:

1. Start YaST, enter the root password if required, and on the Software tab, select Install and Remove Software.

2. Open the drop-down list in the upper-left corner, select the Search option, and enter **Squid** as string for which to search. This will show two packages to select: Squid and Squid Guard. Select both, and then click Accept to continue. This will install all the necessary packages.

Note The YaST option Network Services ➤ Proxy is not used to configure the Squid proxy server. It is used to define client settings for your proxy.

Now that Squid is installed, you can tune the many options that are available from the main configuration file, /etc/squid/squid.conf. You will find many options in this file. Thankfully all are well documented, so you won't have a hard time finding out how to use them. If you want to configure Squid as a regular proxy server, you have to set only a limited amount of options. The following sections discuss the most important settings; in a Squid context, they are referred to as *tags*. You can group these tags into several categories:

- Network tags
- Tags that define cache settings
- Tags that specify log files and cache directories
- Optimization tags
- Tags with regard to timeout values
- Administrative tags

Note Make sure you open your firewall for Squid as well. By default, Squid works on port 3128. See Chapter 30 for more details on this.

Network Tags

The http_port tag specifies the port on which the Squid server should listen, which is by default set to 3128. If more than one network card is present in your server, you can tell Squid to listen on one interface only by specifying the IP address used on that interface as well, for example 192.168.0.1:3128.

Note It is bad practice to use the server that is offering the Squid proxy service as a router. It should be behind the firewall in the "demilitarized zone." Since it doesn't have to route packets, one network card should be enough for your Squid proxy server.

Defining Cache Settings

To cache files properly, you can use certain tags that define where and how cache files are created. To understand how this works, you should know that Squid can cache files in memory, as well as on hard disk. Memory is faster, so if speed is an issue, allocate as much memory as possible for caching files. However, always configure your file system to cache files as quickly as possible, which will lead to the maximum possible performance. Table 25-1 lists the tags that are used for this purpose.

Table 25-1. *Tags to Define Where and How Cache Is Created*

Tags	Meaning
cache_mem	This tag specifies the amount of memory Squid should use for file cache. The default value of 8MB is conservative. On a dedicated Squid server with 1GB of available memory, you won't have any problems by setting it to 512MB.
cache_swap_low and cache_swap_high	If you might run out of drive space, perhaps because of too many cache files, you can use these tags to start cleaning up files automatically. For this process, you use a least recently used algorithm; if an item is sitting in cache and hasn't been used for a long time, it will be removed first. The cache_swap_low tag, which is set to 90 percent by default, defines when the file cleanup should start, and the cache_swap_high tag defines when file cleanup should start to happen more aggressively.
maximum_object_size	This specifies the maximum size of an object to be cached. By default, this tag is set to the rather low value of 4,096KB. Therefore, an ISO file that is downloaded frequently from your network will never be cached. If you have considerable cache space, consider setting this tag much higher.
minimum_object_size	This sets the minimum size of an object that can be cached. By default, this tag is set to 0 bytes. This is a good setting because it also allows small files to be stored in cache.
maximum_object_size_in_memory	This sets the maximum size of a file that is to be cached in the memory of your server. By default, the maximum size for the object in memory is set to 8KB; consider setting it much higher.

Specifying Log Files and Cache Directories

Some tags are available to specify where logging should occur by default. Also, you can specify the structure used on the hard drive of your server to cache files. By default, in the cache directory, a subdirectory structure is used for caching files. This subdirectory structure is used like an index. The default settings are for average systems; if your Squid proxy is used frequently, you should consider configuring these tags with a value that is much higher. Table 25-2 lists the tags related to log files and cache directories.

Table 25-2. *Tags for Log Files and Cache Directories*

Tag	Meaning
cache_dir	This tag, which has a lot of options, specifies where and how the cache is stored on the file system. To specify its use, this tag has an amount of arguments that specify how it has to be used: storage-format: This specifies in what format the data has to be saved. By default, this is done in the UFS format, which is fine for most purposes. Alternatively, you can deploy the AUFS format. UFS is the Squid store type that has always been used. AUFS is meant as an improvement to UFS, but its support isn't widespread. Therefore, you would probably just want to keep it to UFS. dir: This indicates the name of the directory used for caching. By default, the directory /var/cache/squid is used for this purpose. If you expect a lot of usage, you should put this directory on a separate partition and maybe even on its own storage device for maximum performance. size: This specifies the maximum size of the cache directory. The default value is set to 100MB, which is rather limited for most purposes. L1-dir: Squid always creates two levels of subdirectories in the cache directory. Use the L1-dir tag to specify the amount of subdirectories that will be created directly under the cache directory. The default value is 16. L2-dir: This specifies how many subdirectories are to be created at the second level. By default, 256 subdirectories will be created. When all these options are applied to the cache_dir tag, this will make a definition that looks like cache_dir ufs /var/log/squid 100 16 256. You will find this line as the default setting in squid.conf.
cache_access_log	Every time a user accesses some server on the Internet, Squid will log this connection to the access log written in /var/log/squid/access.log (see Figure 25-1). On Squid servers that suffer from a heavy workload, you should consider giving this tag the argument none so that file access will never be logged. If you do want to write these logs by default, consider creating a dedicated partition or disk device for logging on your server, which allows for better performance.
cache_log	In this log, all information is logged that is not directly related to user activity. By default, this information is written to /var/log/squid/cache.log
cache_store_log	This detailed log indicates what files are put in cache, how long these files have been kept in cache, and when they were removed from cache. Although this can be useful information to tune your Squid proxy, you should consider giving this tag the argument none to disable this feature for better performance.

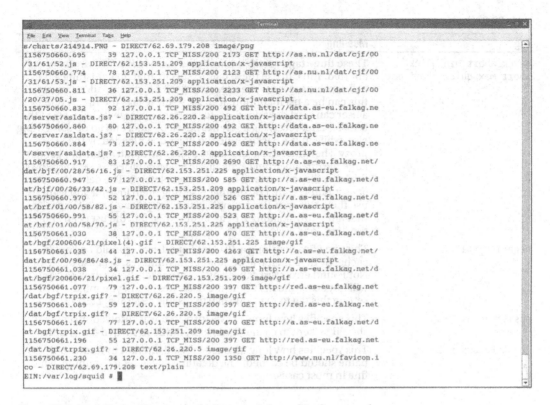

```
s/charts/214914.PNG - DIRECT/62.69.179.208 image/png
1156750660.695    39 127.0.0.1 TCP_MISS/200 2173 GET http://as.nu.nl/dat/cjf/00
/31/61/52.js - DIRECT/62.153.251.209 application/x-javascript
1156750660.774    78 127.0.0.1 TCP_MISS/200 2123 GET http://as.nu.nl/dat/cjf/00
/31/61/53.js - DIRECT/62.153.251.209 application/x-javascript
1156750660.811    36 127.0.0.1 TCP_MISS/200 2233 GET http://as.nu.nl/dat/cjf/00
/20/37/05.js - DIRECT/62.153.251.209 application/x-javascript
1156750660.832    92 127.0.0.1 TCP_MISS/200 492 GET http://data.as-eu.falkag.ne
t/server/asldata.js? - DIRECT/62.26.220.2 application/x-javascript
1156750660.860    80 127.0.0.1 TCP_MISS/200 492 GET http://data.as-eu.falkag.ne
t/server/asldata.js? - DIRECT/62.26.220.2 application/x-javascript
1156750660.884    73 127.0.0.1 TCP_MISS/200 492 GET http://data.as-eu.falkag.ne
t/server/asldata.js? - DIRECT/62.26.220.2 application/x-javascript
1156750660.917    83 127.0.0.1 TCP_MISS/200 2690 GET http://a.as-eu.falkag.net/
dat/bjf/00/28/56/16.js - DIRECT/62.153.251.225 application/x-javascript
1156750660.947    57 127.0.0.1 TCP_MISS/200 585 GET http://a.as-eu.falkag.net/d
at/bjf/00/26/33/42.js - DIRECT/62.153.251.209 application/x-javascript
1156750660.970    52 127.0.0.1 TCP_MISS/200 526 GET http://a.as-eu.falkag.net/d
at/brf/01/00/58/82.js - DIRECT/62.153.251.225 application/x-javascript
1156750660.991    55 127.0.0.1 TCP_MISS/200 523 GET http://a.as-eu.falkag.net/d
at/brf/01/00/58/70.js - DIRECT/62.153.251.225 application/x-javascript
1156750661.030    38 127.0.0.1 TCP_MISS/200 470 GET http://a.as-eu.falkag.net/d
at/bgf/200606/21/pixel(4).gif - DIRECT/62.153.251.225 image/gif
1156750661.035    44 127.0.0.1 TCP_MISS/200 4263 GET http://a.as-eu.falkag.net/
dat/brf/00/96/86/48.js - DIRECT/62.153.251.225 application/x-javascript
1156750661.038    34 127.0.0.1 TCP_MISS/200 469 GET http://a.as-eu.falkag.net/d
at/bgf/200606/21/pixel.gif - DIRECT/62.153.251.209 image/gif
1156750661.077    79 127.0.0.1 TCP_MISS/200 397 GET http://red.as-eu.falkag.net
/dat/bgf/trpix.gif? - DIRECT/62.26.220.5 image/gif
1156750661.089    59 127.0.0.1 TCP_MISS/200 397 GET http://red.as-eu.falkag.net
/dat/bgf/trpix.gif? - DIRECT/62.26.220.5 image/gif
1156750661.167    77 127.0.0.1 TCP_MISS/200 470 GET http://a.as-eu.falkag.net/d
at/bgf/trpix.gif - DIRECT/62.153.251.209 image/gif
1156750661.196    55 127.0.0.1 TCP_MISS/200 397 GET http://red.as-eu.falkag.net
/dat/bgf/trpix.gif? - DIRECT/62.26.220.5 image/gif
1156750661.230    34 127.0.0.1 TCP_MISS/200 1350 GET http://www.nu.nl/favicon.i
co - DIRECT/62.69.179.208 text/plain
EIN:/var/log/squid # ▮
```

Figure 25-1. *By default, all access to the Internet is logged in the access log.*

Optimizing Squid Performance

On a heavily used network, Squid has a lot of work to do. Therefore, it is important to use some parameters to handle web traffic in the most efficient way. Table 25-3 gives an overview of performance-related parameters.

Table 25-3. *Performance-Related Squid Tags*

Tag	Meaning
request_header_max_size	This specifies the maximum HTTP header Squid will accept. Since HTTP headers shouldn't exceed 10KB, the default value of 10KB is fine in most scenarios.
request_body_max_size	Use this tag to set a maximum size for the body of an HTTP packet. Setting this tag to a predefined maximum will prevent some traffic from being handled (think of large file uploads, for example); therefore, the default value of 0, which disables this option, is fine in most cases.

Continued

Table 25-3. *Continued*

Tag	Meaning
quick_abort_min, quick_abort_max, quick_abort_pct	These three tags specify what should happen if a file transfer is aborted. You can use these tags to specify that downloading a file will continue, even if the user aborts the file download. For users this can be a useful option; if you give these tags the right value, a user can start downloading, for example, a large ISO file, abort the transfer after receiving a given amount of data, and go do something else, while in the background the file is downloaded by the Squid proxy. Then later the user can start the download again and get the large file directly from cache (if the maximum_object_size tag allows the large file to be stored in cache completely!). The default values are set rather high; I recommend setting them lower if you want to use them this way. For example, use quick_abort_pct 2 to specify that after downloading 2 percent of a large file, the user can abort the download.
negative_ttl	This specifies how long a 404 Not Found error should be kept in cache. By default, it will be stored for 5 minutes. Because often 404 Not Found errors are caused by a few packets being dropped and will not occur the next time the user tries again, you might consider setting this tag to the value of 0 to disable negative_ttl.
positive_dns_ttl	This specifies how long a DNS entry that was resolved successfully should be kept in cache. By default, it will be cached for 6 hours.
negative_dns_ttl	This specifies how long an unsuccessful attempt to resolve a DNS name should be cached. The default value is set to 1 minute, which fine in most cases.

Timeout Settings

A busy server can maintain only a limited maximum amount of connections. If you don't want to waste the available connections, it is useful to set some connection timeouts. Table 25-4 lists the tags that allow you to do that.

Table 25-4. *Tags Related to Timeout Settings*

Tag	Meaning
connect_timeout	This tag specifies the time it takes before Squid breaks the connection. By default, connect_timeout is set to 2 minutes.
request_timeout	This tag specifies how long Squid will wait for HTTP traffic after successfully establishing a connection. By default it is set to 5 minutes, which should be enough in most cases. If, however, your proxy server is used heavily, you should consider setting this to a lower value so you don't waste available network connections.
shutdown_lifetime	Use this tag to specify how long it takes before Squid reacts to a SIGTERM or SIGHUP signal to terminate a connection. By default, this tag is set to 30 seconds.

Generic Settings

Finally, you can use some tags for generic purposes, as listed in Table 25-5.

Table 25-5. *Tags Used for Generic Administrative Purposes*

Tag	Meaning
cache_mgr	Use this tag to specify the e-mail address of the administrator of the Squid server. You can use this e-mail address to send messages to the administrator of the server if a serious error occurs.
cache_effective_user	For its normal work, the Squid server needs permissions. Therefore, the server needs a user account to which these permissions can be granted. The proxy server will use the user account specified with this parameter. By default, the user account squid is used for this purpose. This is good, and you should leave it this way; for security reasons, make sure you never run Squid as root!

Securing the Proxy with ACLs

Based on the settings specified previously, you must be able to configure a working Squid proxy cache. No security features, however, have been implemented so far. Squid offers advanced security options. Connections can be allowed or denied based on the time of day, the source address, the destination address, the requesting user, and more. For all these options, the administrator has to use access control lists (ACLs). The acl tag specifies a group to which access can be denied or allowed in an http_access tag. Therefore, you will always need both of these tags to work together. Listing 25-1 shows a simple example of how you can apply these tags.

Listing 25-1. *Example of ACL Settings*

```
acl all src 0.0.0.0/0.0.0.0
acl allowed src 10.0.0.0/24
http_acccess allow allowed
http_access deny all
```

> **Caution** Before you can use a Squid server after installation, you will need to modify the existing ACLs in the default file. By default, one ACL exists that denies access to all.

In the previous example, the ACLs define two categories of users. First is the category all, identified by the source address 0.0.0.0 with subnet mask 0.0.0.0. This notation refers to all IP addresses that exist. Then the ACLs refer to the category allowed. All nodes that have an IP address that starts with 10.0.0 belong to this category. Next, the http_access tags refer to both categories. The first rule grants access to all nodes belonging to the group of allowed hosts. For all of these hosts, the procedure ends here, because the first rule that matches will always be applied. Then for all other nodes, the policy is applied. This policy is set to deny all.

In the previous example, the ACL was based on the source IP address. However, you can use many more criteria in an ACL:

src: Refers to the source address of a node. You can use an individual IP address, a range of IP addresses, or a complete subnet mask. An example of a range specified as the source address is 192.168.1.10-192.168.1.20/32. Note the 32-bits subnet mask, which is always needed if a range is specified.

dst: Refers to the destination IP address. It is not useful to use this type to refer to addresses on the Internet, because they can change without notice. If, however, access has to be denied for users from the private network to a host in the DMZ, this type can be useful. The following is an example of this:

```
acl protected_host dst 10.0.0.10/32
acl private_network src 10.0.10.0/24
http_access deny protected_host private_network
```

srcdomain: Like src but used to refer to a DNS domain as source.

dstdomain: Like dst but based on DNS domain name.

time: Refers to the time of day and day of the week when a tag should be used. You can use the day of the week, but this is not necessary. The following are valid examples of using the time-type ACL:

```
acl toolate time 20:00-6:00
acl weekend time A-S 0:01-24:00
acl notonfriday time F 16:00-24:00
```

If referring to the days of the week, you can use the following:

- *Monday:* M
- *Tuesday:* T
- *Wednesday:* W
- *Thursday:* H
- *Friday:* F
- *Saturday:* A
- *Sunday:* S

url_regexp: Use this type to look for a regular expression in a URL. Use, for example, acl sex url_regex "sex" to deny access to all sites that have *sex* somewhere in the URL. Often this ACL has unexpected behavior, because unexpected sites can be blocked. It will just blindly deny access to all sites that have the string *sex* somewhere in the site name. For example, it will block access to a site such as http://www.essex.co.uk as well.

port: Use this type to block access on given ports.

proto: This ACL type can block access to specified protocols only.

reg_mime_type: This is a useful ACL that you can use to block access to specific file types. You can determine the type of file by looking at the MIME type. For example, think of an ACL as acl mp3 reg_mime_type "audio/mpeg".

After specifying the ACLs, it is time to define http_access tags that use the ACL. It is possible to refer to one ACL only in an http_access tag, but you can refer to more than one ACL as well; you saw an example of this in http_access deny protected_host private_network, which denied traffic coming from the private network and going to a protected host. It is possible to use exclusion in an ACL, such as in http_access deny protected_host !private_network, which denies all the hosts not coming from the private network access to the protected host.

To conclude, remember that no matter how complex the applied ACLs can be, you should always conclude the list of ACLs with a default policy. The policy defines what should happen if no specific match was found for a given package. In general, it is useful to conclude the list of http_access tags with http_access deny all to deny access to all packets that have not matched a specific http_access tag earlier in the chain.

Configuring User Authentication

In addition to analyzing the packet for where it comes from and where it goes to, it is possible to use user authentication with Squid. To make user authentication work, you just need a browser that supports user authentication, which all current browsers do. In a Squid environment, theoretically the browser and the proxy can exchange usernames and passwords in three ways:

Basic: The username and password are sent in clear text to the proxy.

Digest: When this method is used, passwords are not sent in clear text, but a digest that is derived from the password is used instead. This method is not implemented fully in the current version of Squid yet.

NTLM: This method allows for better security but isn't supported by HTTP and therefore is not a good option to use.

Since in the current version of Squid the digest method is not implemented yet, I will discuss how the Basic authentication method is used.

When authentication is used to connect to the Squid proxy, it is not the proxy itself that handles authentication but an external program. For example, you can use the Linux PAM mechanism (see Chapter 5) for proper authentication. The advantage of using PAM is that PAM can authenticate to any authentication source you can think of. By default it will try to authenticate to the local files /etc/passwd and /etc/shadow to see whether the user who authenticates exists; however, you can configure PAM to authenticate to an OpenLDAP server. Consult Chapter 17 for the gory details.

You should be aware of one fact: communication between Squid and the authentication program will be plain text. This is not an issue if the proxy server and the authentication service are used on the same server. You could, for example, put a replica of the OpenLDAP directory on the server where Squid is running. If Squid needs to communicate to the authentication service over the network, you should use digest_pw_auth. The disadvantage of this method is that on the Squid server you need to maintain a text file that contains the usernames and passwords unencrypted. Therefore, this is not considered a recommended method either. To make communications more secure, you could create an SSH tunnel between the machines that need to exchange passwords. You can learn more about this in Chapter 18 of this book.

If you want to configure Squid to authenticate to PAM, you need three tags:

auth_param: Use this tag to refer to the program used for authentication. Some other options are used as well to specify how the authentication program should be used.

acl: Use an ACL to define groups of users.

http_access: Use this tag to specify in what way users are granted access.

The following four lines specify how you can use PAM for Squid authentication:

```
auth_param basic program /usr/sbin/pam_auth
auth_param basic children 5
auth_param basic realm Squid Proxy-caching web server
auth_param basic credentialsttl 4 hours
```

The first of these lines specifies PAM as the program that should handle authentication requests. Next, you see a specification of the maximum number of authentication processes that may be started at the same time. Only on heavily used Squid servers are more than five simultaneous processes needed; if users start to complain about the time it takes to log on, consider increasing this value. Then on the third line you specify what to protect with authentication; this is the *authentication realm*. This parameter should always have the value Squid Proxy-caching web server. Finally, the last line specifies how long the credentials must be remembered. The default value is set to 2 hours. The result is that a user can connect to new resources without providing credentials for a period of 2 hours. After these 2 hours, the user has to provide the login name again. Because many companies consider this too short a period, I've set this parameter to 4 hours in the example.

After you have specified that PAM should be used as the authentication mechanism, you must create a PAM file. On SUSE Linux Enterprise Server, a default PAM file is created in /etc/pam.d/squid. This file enables authentication to the local passwd mechanism with the following two lines:

```
auth       required    pam_unix2.so
account    required    pam_unix2.so
```

If an LDAP server is available for authentication as well, you can modify this PAM configuration file easily. In the following example, you can see how the authentication process will first try to authenticate a user against an LDAP directory. If this does not work, it will authenticate against the local user database. See Chapters 5 and 17 for more information.

```
auth       sufficient  pam_ldap.so
auth       required    pam_unix2.so
account    sufficient  pam_ldap.so
account    required    pam_unix2.so
```

Now that the authentication mechanism is specified, you have to create an ACL that uses usernames, which could look like this:

```
acl allowed_users proxy_auth linda stephanie
```

In this example, only users linda and stephanie are considered allowed users, which would allow them to authenticate on the Squid server so they can use it. In many cases, you will, however, see that there is no need to limit access for a small amount of users but just to allow all authenticated users access to a resource. You can accomplish this by using REQUIRED instead of the name of one or more users, as shown here:

```
acl all_users proxy_auth REQUIRED
```

Based upon these two examples, you can create an environment where only users linda and stephanie are given access, while all other users are denied access by using the http_access tag:

```
http_access allow allowed_users
http_access deny all_users
```

While introducing user authentication, the entire list of access rules for your Squid proxy can become rather complex. This is especially the case because the first match will always be applied. Therefore, the following will not work if you want to ensure that only allowed_users and users coming from trusted_net are granted access and all others are denied access:

```
http_access allow allowed_users
http_access allow trusted_net
http_access deny all
```

The goal of these rules was to grant access only to allowed users coming from `trusted_net`; in the previous rules, however, access will be granted to a user who is not part of `allowed_user` but is on `trusted_net` as well. To solve this problem, you should make combinations in the `http_access` rules, like in the following example:

```
http_access allow allowed_users trusted_net
http_access deny all
```

Squid and URL Filtering

One of the most powerful options a well-configured proxy server has to offer is its ability to look at the URL a user wants to access. To do this in an efficient way, you should use blacklists and whitelists. A *blacklist* lists sites to which the administrator wants to deny access. A *whitelist* lists sites to which an administrator wants to allow access. Which one of these is used depends on the security policy of the company. In a restricted environment, access to everything is denied, except for sites listed in the whitelist. In most environments, however, this is not a workable scenario. Therefore, it is more useful to create a blacklist and deny access to sites that are on the blacklist. You can refer to such a blacklist by using the ACL of the type url_regex with the option -i, as in the following example:

```
acl forbidden url_regex -i "/etc/squid/blacklist"
```

To use such a blacklist, the administrator can define it. It is practically impossible, however, for one administrator to keep such a list up-to-date, without forgetting some sites that the administrator doesn't want to allow people to access. Therefore, in general it is better to download blacklists from sites such as `http://www.squidguard.org/blacklist`.

Configuring Squid for SSL Traffic

When users are sending ordinary web traffic, Squid can analyze the traffic. With SSL traffic this is much more difficult, because most of the data sent between the user and web site is encrypted. Therefore, the proxy cannot analyze the SSL traffic for forbidden content. Also, SSL-encrypted data that comes back to the proxy cannot be kept in its cache. For users, however, it is important that SSL traffic is sent through the proxy server to the Internet.

To enable the use of SSL traffic, you can use two special ACLs in combination with the http_ access tag. The following is an example of both tags:

```
acl SSL_ports port 443 8009
acl CONNECT method CONNECT
http_access deny CONNECT !SSL_ports
```

The first of these lines specifies the ports where SSL traffic can be sent. Ordinarily you would see SSL traffic just on port 443; sometimes, though, application-specific ports are listening to incoming SSL traffic. The second line is always required to send SSL traffic through the proxy. You can use different methods to send SSL traffic, but currently the CONNECT method is the only one that works, so don't bother about the rest. Last, an http_access rule denies all traffic using the CONNECT method, with the exception of SSL traffic.

However, you encounter one nasty problem when SSL traffic is sent through the proxy. This problem is that SSL traffic cannot be monitored for its contents. The only way to look at SSL traffic is to look at its port; all the rest is encrypted. Therefore, it is perfectly possible as well to tunnel other traffic through the SSL port. For this purpose, you need specialized programs such as Transconnect (http://transconnect.sourceforge.net).

If you want to try it, install the tarball to your computer. In the Transconnect software, an example configuration file with the name of tconn.conf is available. Copy this file to a hidden directory with the name .tconn in your home directory, and edit it to tunnel traffic through SSL. Have a look at the comment in tconn.conf; the file is commented well, and based upon this comment, it shouldn't be hard to create a configuration. Basically, you have to edit some settings that are specific for your network. Ready? Then start the application you want to tunnel through SSL to use a destination outside the proxy server. If, for example, you want to do this with SSH traffic, use the following command:

```
export LD_PRELOAD=/usr/lib/tconn.so ssh myserver.somewhere.com
```

To stop Transconnect from doing its work, type unset LD_PRELOAD. If no configuration is done on the SSH server, this will not work. SSH wants to make a connection on port 22, and usually, Squid doesn't allow port 22 to pass through. To make sure it works, you should configure the SSH server to listen to port 443 as well for incoming SSH traffic. Next, you can use SSH port forwarding on the SSH server to reach any web site you like:

```
LD_PRELOAD=/usr/lib/tconn.so ssh -p 443 -L 8080:forbidden.site.com:80
 myserver.somewhere.com
```

In the previous example, you saw how a user can bypass the restrictions to web sites that can be visited using the Transconnect software. Unfortunately for the administrator, you can't take many countermeasures against this possibility.

Configuring Clients for Squid Usage

Now that you have configured all the necessary settings on the proxy server, it is time to configure the clients to use the proxy. If you want to configure the proxy in a maximum restricted environment, it is a good idea to allow the proxy as the only method for the client to reach destinations on the Internet. If traffic on other ports is needed as well (for instance because clients need to use SMTP and POP mail ports to send and receive e-mail), you should configure a packet-filtering firewall to allow these needed ports and deny everything else. You can read more about the iptables firewall that can be used for this purpose in Chapter 30 of this book. Next, the user can configure his client to use the proxy. Since this procedure is different for all browsers, I will not explain how to do this here. If you don't want to configure all clients manually, then read the next section about configuring a transparent proxy.

Using Squid As a Transparent Proxy

In corporate environments, it is not a good idea to configure all the clients in the network manually to use the proxy. In these cases, you can configure a transparent proxy. With a transparent proxy, you don't need any configuration on the client, because all web traffic is sent through the proxy automatically. The best way to configure a transparent proxy is by configuring the packet filter on your router. If iptables on a Linux router is used, you can configure a transparent proxy with the following rule:

```
iptables -t nat -A PREROUTING -p TCP --dport 80 -j REDIRECT --to-port
 192.168.1.10:3128
```

In this rule, all traffic that has port 80 as its destination will be forwarded to the proxy port and IP address.

Summary

In this chapter, you learned how to use a proxy to enhance web traffic on your network. As you have seen, you can use parameters both to increase the throughput of web traffic on your network and to apply security settings for your network. In the next chapter, you will learn how to manage a kernel on your server.

CHAPTER 26

■ ■ ■

Understanding the Kernel

To communicate with hardware in your computer, you need to make sure the proper hardware is loaded. The kernel is involved heavily in this task because it loads the necessary drivers to communicate with hardware devices. The kernel is the heart of the operating system; it is the software layer that sits directly on top of the hardware in your server and makes it possible to do anything with that hardware. On SUSE Linux Enterprise Server, you are working with a default kernel in which certain functionality is enabled and other functionality isn't enabled. In this chapter, you will learn about the roles of the kernel and udev for hardware management.

Understanding Kernel Modules

To be able to work with a device, you need a driver for the device. On Linux, device drivers are implemented as part of the kernel. On all modern Linux systems, kernels are modular. This means the core of the operating system is in the kernel file itself, but lots of drivers that aren't needed by default are loaded as modules. The benefit of this modularity is increased efficiency. If a driver is needed, its module is loaded, and if it isn't needed, it isn't loaded. It's as simple as that.

For you as an administrator, module management is an important task. On SUSE Linux Enterprise Server, modules are installed in the directory /lib/modules/`uname -r`. As you can see, command substitution is used in this directory name: the command uname -r gives the correct version of the current kernel, so by using this command in the directory path, you can be sure always to refer to the right path where kernel modules can be found; for example, /lib/modules/2.6.16.13-4-default. Under this directory, you can find a directory structure where all modules are stored in an organized way, according to the type of module. You can recognize the kernel modules in this directory structure by their filenames because all kernel modules have the extension .ko.

You as an administrator should be aware of how modules are loaded. On a default installation, you don't really have to think about it. On installation, all your hardware is detected automatically, and the required modules are added to the start-up procedure of your computer automatically. So ordinarily you don't need to do anything. However, sometimes you'll need to tune the load process of modules.

In the following sections, you will learn about the most current methods to load kernel modules:

- Using initrd
- While booting
- Manually
- Automatically
- Using udev and hwup

Tuning initrd

The first moment when your system boots, it needs modules. These are the modules necessary to load the root device on your server, including the drivers that are required to get access to your storage devices. These modules are loaded by the initial RAM drive (initrd), which is loaded from GRUB. Ordinarily, this initial RAM drive is created automatically, and you don't have to worry about it. Sometimes you may need to tune your own initrd, in which case you can use the mkinitrd command.

When mkinitrd is called, it looks at the configuration file /etc/sysconfig/kernel that contains two variables relevant for creating an initrd. The first of these variables is INITRD_MODULES. This variable lists the modules that need to be added to the initrd when invoking mkinitrd. Depending on the way your system is configured, you can define the variable as INITRD_MODULES="piix processor thermal fan jbd ext3". Make sure that, at the least, this parameter contains a list of all modules needed to initialize storage on your server.

Apart from the variable INITRD_MODULES, you can also use the variable DOMU_INITRD_MODULES. This variable is required if you are using a Xen kernel, and it makes sure the drivers for the Xen virtual block and network devices are initialized at an early stage.

Loading Modules on Boot

Usually, the kernel ensures that all modules you need when booting your server are loaded automatically when the hardware they are needed for is detected on your system. In rare situations, this doesn't work properly. In that case, you can make sure the module is loaded anyway by including it in the /etc/sysconfig/kernel configuration file. In this file, you define the variable MODULES_LOADED_ON_BOOT, and its value can be a list of modules that must be loaded at all times. Using this method, you can ensure that the module is available at an early stage in the boot process but not before the kernel itself loads.

Loading Modules Manually

You can manage modules by hand as well. The following commands are involved when managing modules manually:

lsmod: This command lists all the modules that are currently loaded. In this list, it also displays the current status of the module. The output of lsmod is given in four columns (as shown in Listing 26-1). The first column mentions the name of the module. The second column shows its size. In the third column, a 1 or a 0 indicates whether the module currently is used, and the last column shows the name of other modules that require this module to be loaded.

Listing 26-1. *Output of* lsmod

```
Module                      Size   Used by
aes                         31936  1
ieee80211_crypt_ccmp        10624  1
arc4                        6400   0
fat                         51356  1     vfat
usb_storage                 74688  0
sg                          35996  0
```

modprobe: If you want to load a module by hand, the modprobe command is the way to do it. The importance of this command is that it will do a dependency check. Some modules do need another module to be present before they can do their job, and modprobe makes sure that this is the case. To load these dependent modules, it looks in the configuration file modules.dep, which is created automatically by the depmod command (discussed in a moment). Loading a module with modprobe is not hard to do; for example, if you want to load the module vfat by hand, just use the modprobe vfat command. In the early days, there was an alternative for modprobe: the lsmod command. However, lsmod doesn't look whether there are any dependencies; therefore, you shouldn't use it anymore.

rmmod: A module that isn't used takes up system resources anyway. Usually, this will not be much more than 50KB of system memory, but some heavy modules (the XFS module, for instance) can take up to 500KB. On a system that is short on memory, this is a waste of memory. If you are short in memory, use rmmod followed by the name of the module you want to remove; for example, use rmmod ext3. This will remove the module from memory and free up all the system resources it is using.

modinfo: Ever had the feeling that a module was using up precious system resources without knowing what exactly the module was doing? Then modinfo is your friend. This command will show some information that is compiled in the module itself. As an example, you can see how it works on the ext3 module in Listing 26-2. Especially for network cards, the modinfo command can be useful, because it shows you all parameters the network card is started with (for instance, its duplex settings), which can be handy for troubleshooting.

Listing 26-2. *The* modinfo *Command Showing Information About a Module*

```
myserver # modinfo ext3
filename:          /lib/modules/2.6.16.13-4-smp/kernel/fs/ext3/ext3.ko
author:            Remy Card, Stephen Tweedie, Andrew Morton, Andread Dilger,
Theodore Ts'o and others
description:       Second Extended Filesystem with journaling extensions
license:           GPL
vermagic:          2.6.16.13-4-smp SMP 586 REGPARM gcc-4.1
supported:         yes
depends:           jbd
srcversion:        FCAA51057BE1F6F27BEDBF6
```

depmod: The depmod command generates the module's dependency file in /lib/modules/ `uname -r`. The name of this file is modules.dep, and it simply contains a list of all the dependencies that are in place for modules on your system. As shown in Listing 26-2, all modules know what dependencies they have (indicated by the depends field). The depmod command just analyzes that and makes sure the dependency file is up-to-date. Usually you don't need to run this command by hand, because it is starts automatically when your system boots. However, if you have installed new kernel modules and you want to make sure the dependency file is up-to-date, run depmod manually.

Loading Modules Automatically

Many modules are loaded automatically. A nice example of this is the loading of the module for a network board. Imagine that the module for your specific network card is the pcnet32 module. Usually this module would be started automatically on system boot, so it doesn't make sense to do it manually. However, if your network card isn't initialized automatically, you would see that before configuring your network board with a command such as ifconfig, there just is no module present for it. After you have used the command ifconfig eth0 192.168.1.10 to initialize the network board, however, the module appears automatically. But how does that happen?

In the previous example, the ifconfig command tells what piece of hardware to use by specifying the eth0 argument. This argument is a generic way to refer to the kernel module, which in this case is called pcnet32. Now when you are using the eth0 argument, you are addressing the ifplugd process. This is the link detection daemon for Ethernet devices. This ifplugd process probes on what PCI hardware address it can find an Ethernet network board. This PCI hardware address is also defined in the pcnet32 module as an alias, so when ifplugd calls this specific hardware address, the pcnet32 module will reply and will load automatically.

An easier-to-understand example of how modules can be loaded automatically is for modules that use the /etc/modprobe.conf configuration file. In this configuration file, you can work with aliases, and that's the old way that the driver for your network card was loaded. In /etc/modprobe.conf, you would find the line alias eth0 pcnet32. This line would make sure when some command called for eth0, the pcnet32 module would be automatically loaded. If you browse through /etc/modprobe.conf, you can see that this alias mechanism is still used for many modules. In the modprobe.conf configuration file, you can pass options to hardware devices as well. These options can include, for example, the hardware settings required by the device or the network properties needed by a network card. Listing 26-3 shows an example of some lines in modprobe.conf.

Listing 26-3. *Loading Modules Automatically by Using* /etc/modprobe.conf

```
alias parport_lowlevel     parport_pc
options parport_pc io=0x378 irq=none,none
# If you have multiple parallel ports, specify them this way:
# options parport_pc io=0x378,0x278 irq=none,none

# Linux ACP modem (Mwave)
alias char-major-10-219  mwave
```

In Listing 26-3, you can see that first an alias is created for parport_pc. This alias accomplishes that whenever parport_pc is called, the parport_lowlevel device is loaded. The second line specifies some hardware settings for this device. Then it specifies some lines with comments in it, and finally you see that another alias is created; the name mwave is linked to the device char-major-10-219.

Using udev to Load Kernel Modules

On a SUSE Linux Enterprise Server 10 system, the udev system is the most common way of loading kernel modules. The udev system is the central point for hardware initialization on your server. It is implemented as the daemon udevd, which is started at an early stage in the boot process. When the kernel detects a device, it communicates to udev about the device. After receiving a signal from the kernel that a device has been added or removed, udev calls the hwup command to initialize the device. Then it creates the proper device files in the /dev directory. The latter is a major improvement in the way that devices are handled on a Linux system. In older Linux versions, a device file existed for all devices that could possibly exist. Nowadays, a device file is created only for devices that are really there. This is the task of udev. After initializing the device, udev informs all applications about the new device through the hardware abstraction layer (HAL).

One problem with udev is that it loads at a stage where some devices have already been initialized. Think, for example, about the hard disk from which your system is working. To initialize these devices as well in a proper way, udev parses the sysfs file system. This file system is created automatically and contains configuration parameters and other information about devices that have already been initialized.

As an administrator, it is useful to know that you can monitor udev using the udevmonitor tool. Listing 26-4 shows what happens in the udev monitor when a USB memory stick is plugged in the system.

Listing 26-4. *Udevmonitor Shows Device Activity*

```
SFO:/etc/init.d/boot.d # udevmonitor
udevmonitor prints the received event from the kernel [UEVENT]
and the event which udev sends out after rule processing [UDEV
]

UEVENT[1158665885.090105] add@/devices/pci0000:00/0000:00:1d.7
/usb4/4-6
UEVENT[1158665885.090506] add@/devices/pci0000:00/0000:00:1d.7
/usb4/4-6/4-6:1.0
UEVENT[1158665885.193049] add@/class/usb_device/usbdev4.5
UDEV  [1158665885.216195] add@/devices/pci0000:00/0000:00:1d.7
/usb4/4-6
UDEV  [1158665885.276188] add@/devices/pci0000:00/0000:00:1d.7
/usb4/4-6/4-6:1.0
UDEV  [1158665885.414101] add@/class/usb_device/usbdev4.5
UEVENT[1158665885.500944] add@/devices/pci0000:00/0000:00:1d.7
/usb4/4-6/4-6.1
UEVENT[1158665885.500968] add@/devices/pci0000:00/0000:00:1d.7
/usb4/4-6/4-6.1/4-6.1:1.0
UEVENT[1158665885.500978] add@/class/usb_device/usbdev4.6
UDEV  [1158665885.604908] add@/devices/pci0000:00/0000:00:1d.7
/usb4/4-6/4-6.1
UEVENT[1158665885.651928] add@/module/scsi_mod
UDEV  [1158665885.652919] add@/module/scsi_mod
UEVENT[1158665885.671182] add@/module/usb_storage
UDEV  [1158665885.672085] add@/module/usb_storage
UEVENT[1158665885.672652] add@/bus/usb/drivers/usb-storage
UDEV  [1158665885.673200] add@/bus/usb/drivers/usb-storage
UEVENT[1158665885.673655] add@/class/scsi_host/host0
UDEV  [1158665885.678711] add@/devices/pci0000:00/0000:00:1d.7
/usb4/4-6/4-6.1/4-6.1:1.0
UDEV  [1158665885.854067] add@/class/usb_device/usbdev4.6
UDEV  [1158665885.984639] add@/class/scsi_host/host0
UEVENT[1158665890.682084] add@/devices/pci0000:00/0000:00:1d.7/usb4/4-
 6/4-6.1/4-6.1:1.0/host0/target0:0:0/0:0:0:0
UEVENT[1158665890.682108] add@/class/scsi_device/0:0:0:0
UDEV  [1158665890.858630] add@/devices/pci0000:00/0000:00:1d.7/usb4/4-6/4
-6.1/4-6.1:1.0/host0/target0:0:0/0:0:0:0
UEVENT[1158665890.863245] add@/module/sd_mod
UEVENT[1158665890.863971] add@/bus/scsi/drivers/sd
UDEV  [1158665890.864828] add@/module/sd_mod
UDEV  [1158665890.865941] add@/bus/scsi/drivers/sd
```

```
UEVENT[1158665890.875674]  add@/block/sda
UEVENT[1158665890.875949]  add@/block/sda/sda1
UEVENT[1158665890.880180]  add@/module/sg
UDEV  [1158665890.880180]  add@/class/scsi_device/0:0:0:0
UEVENT[1158665890.880207]  add@/class/scsi_generic/sg0
UDEV  [1158665890.906347]  add@/module/sg
UDEV  [1158665890.986931]  add@/class/scsi_generic/sg0
UDEV  [1158665891.084224]  add@/block/sda
UDEV  [1158665891.187120]  add@/block/sda/sda1
UEVENT[1158665891.413225]  add@/module/fat
UDEV  [1158665891.413937]  add@/module/fat
UEVENT[1158665891.427428]  add@/module/vfat
UDEV  [1158665891.436849]  add@/module/vfat
UEVENT[1158665891.449836]  add@/module/nls_cp437
UDEV  [1158665891.451155]  add@/module/nls_cp437
UEVENT[1158665891.467257]  add@/module/nls_iso8859_1
UDEV  [1158665891.467795]  add@/module/nls_iso8859_1
UEVENT[1158665891.489400]  mount@/block/sda/sda1
UDEV  [1158665891.491809]  mount@/block/sda/sda1
```

The interesting part of the rather lengthy listing is that you can see exactly how udev interacts with the sys file system that contains information about devices. First, the kernel detects the new device. At that moment, almost nothing is known yet about the nature of the device; udev sees only the PCI ID for the device (you can show those IDs with the lspci command as well). Based on this PCI information, udev can communicate with the device, and it finds out what kernel modules need to be loaded in order to communicate with the device. You can see this in the lines that add the scsi_mod and usb_storage modules. Based on that information, udev finds out that sda and sda1 are present on the device. After finding that out, it is able to read the file system signature and load the proper modules for that as well; in this case, these are the fat and vfat modules. Once the proper file system drivers are loaded, some support modules can read the files that are on the stick, and finally, the file system on the device is mounted automatically. As you can see, working with udev makes "automagically" loading modules a lot less magical than it was.

Working with udev has one other advantage. The udev subsystem allows you to work with persistent names for an interface. Ordinarily, a device gets its device name (/dev/sda, and so on) based on the order it is plugged in to the system. In other words, the first storage device gets /dev/sda, the second storage device gets /dev/sdb, and so on. When activating a device, udev generates more than just the device name /dev/sda, and so on. For storage devices, some links are created in the directory /dev/disk. These links are in the following subdirectories:

/dev/disk/by-id: This contains information about the device based on the vendor ID and the name of the device.

/dev/disk/by-path: This contains links with a name that is based on the bus position of the device.

/dev/disk/by-uuid: In here, you can find links with a name that is based on the serial number (the UUID) of the device.

Since the information in /dev/disk will not change for a device the next time it is plugged in, you can create udev rules that work with that information and make sure the same device name is always generated. The udev rules for storage devices are in /etc/udev/rules.d/ 60-persistent-storage.rules. In this file, you can create a persistent link that makes sure a device is always initialized with the same device name. You can use this solution for disk devices and for network devices. In Listing 26-5 you find an example of the contents of the file /etc/udev/ rules.d/30-net_persistent_names.rules, where an Ethernet device ID is mapped to the MAC address of the network card.

Listing 26-5. *Matching Ethernet Device Names to a MAC Address*

```
SUBSYSTEM=="net", ACTION=="add", SYSFS{address}=="00:0e:35:d3:84:12",
 IMPORT="/lib/udev/rename_netiface %k eth1"
SUBSYSTEM=="net", ACTION=="add", SYSFS{address}=="00:11:43:6b:02:d7",
 IMPORT="/lib/udev/rename_netiface %k eth0"
```

Tuning the Kernel Source Files (or Not)

In general, it is not a good idea to tune the kernel on your system. The reason is simple: Novell provides a tuned kernel with SUSE Linux Enterprise Server. This is a working kernel, and the entire system is built around that kernel. If you are going to upgrade or modify that kernel, you may lose your support. Also, if your kernel is updated automatically, your kernel tweaks will be wiped out each time the kernel is updated. Therefore, in all situations, before you make any modifications to the kernel, make sure you can do so without losing support.

Understanding SUSE Kernel Backgrounds

The kernels that are used on SUSE Linux (no matter what version of the operating system you are using) are generated from the "vanilla" kernel sources. These are the open source kernel sources because they are produced from the kernel project. On top of these sources, a number of patches are applied. The result of this is a SUSE-specific kernel source tree that is built and compiled to the binary configuration file /boot/vmlinuz. On SUSE Linux Enterprise Server, you will always find a number of binary kernels. These are kernels that are complete for usage on specific hardware platforms, such as a 32-bit or 64-bit platform. When installing SUSE Linux Enterprise Server on a specific hardware platform, the right binary kernel is installed automatically, so for the administrator this is an entirely transparent process.

Some situations may require that the kernel sources are present. This is mainly the case if you need to be able to add new functionality to the kernel, for example to compile a module for a certain piece of hardware for which you have only the source code and no compiled version. In that situation, you need the kernel sources present on your server. When installing the kernel source's RPM package from YaST, a directory structure that contains the kernel sources is created in /usr/ src. The most important directory you'll find here is the Linux directory, which is a symbolic link pointing to the directory that contains the source files of the current kernel.

As an administrator, from the kernel sources, you can create your own binary kernel. This is referred to as *compiling* the kernel. Compiling the kernel is a five-step procedure:

1. Use YaST to install the kernel sources for your platform. For example, if you are using i386, install the kernel-source.i386.rpm package from the installation media. Next, make /usr/ src/Linux your current directory.

Caution Work with the kernel sources only as provided by Novell with SUSE Linux Enterprise Server. Downloading and installing kernel sources from ftp.kernel.org may break functionality on your server!

---

2. Configure the kernel. You can find more information about this in the next section.

3. Build the kernel and all its modules. To do this, you can use the make command. This will start the kernel compilation. Be aware that it can take a long time (from about 10 to 15 minutes on fast systems to many hours on slow systems) before this resource-intensive process completes.

4. After compiling the kernel, you must install the new kernel and its modules. Do this by first running make modules_install and next make install. Don't bother about making an initrd as well; these commands will do that for you automatically.

5. Add the new kernel to the boot manager.

Configuring the Kernel

The most important reason to compile your own kernel is that some modifications to the default kernel are required or that new functionality has to be included in your default kernel. The latter scenario is the more realistic scenario, because the default kernel on SUSE Linux Enterprise Server is flexible enough to meet most situations. Especially because of its modularity, it will do the right thing in almost any situation. Generally, you would want to recompile a kernel for four reasons:

- You need access to a new type of hardware that isn't supported by the kernel yet.
- You need some specific feature that isn't available in the default binary kernel yet.
- You really need to strip the kernel to components that are necessary, stripping everything from it that isn't.
- You are running SUSE Linux Enterprise Server on old hardware that the default binary kernel doesn't support.

To tune a kernel, you need to create a new configuration for it. After creating this configuration, you can run make as described earlier in this chapter. You use different methods for tuning what you do need and what you don't need in your kernel:

- Run make config if you want to create the .config file that is needed to compile a new kernel completely by hand. This has one drawback—if you realize that you made a mistake in the previous line after entering the next line, you have no way of going back.
- Use make oldconfig after installing patches to your kernel. This command makes sure you're prompted only for the settings for new items.
- Use make menuconfig if you want to set all kernel options from a nice menu interface. Figure 26-1 shows what this interface looks like.
- Use make xconfig to tune kernel options from a graphical interface.

If you are configuring kernel settings using make menuconfig, you work from a menu interface where kernel functionality is divided into different sections. Each of these sections handles different categories of kernel options. For example, the File Systems section handles everything related to file systems that are available, and Networking is the place to activate some obscure networking protocol.

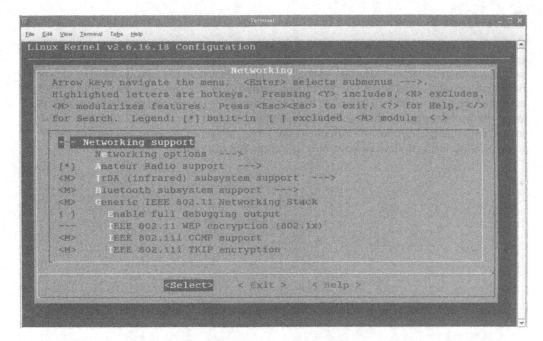

Figure 26-1. *The* make menuconfig *command offers an interface from which kernel options are easily configured.*

After opening the selection of your choice, you get access to the individual parameters. For many of these parameters, you might not immediately see what it does. If that is the case, use the Tab key to navigate to the Help button while the parameter is selected and then press Enter. You'll then see a description of the selected option, which in most cases indicates quite well whether this is a reasonable option to use. Most options have three possibilities. First, you can select it with an asterisk (*). This means the selected functionality is hard-coded in the kernel. Second, you can select it with an M (not available for all options). This means the selected component will be available as a kernel module. Third, you can, of course, choose not to select it at all.

After making your choice from the available kernel components, it is time to compile the kernel. Use the make command to do this.

Patching the Kernel

Occasionally, you will need to patch your kernel. Generally, you can do this in two ways. First, you can download a patch from anywhere and apply it to the kernel. Second, you can download patches to the kernel with ZENworks Linux Management. The latter option is the easiest, because the patches will be downloaded and installed automatically. Also, downloading patches from the Internet risks breaking the support and even the functionality of your kernel; therefore, I can be short about that option: just don't do it!

Summary

In this short chapter, you learned how to use the kernel to manage hardware on your server. The most important lesson about the kernel that you should have learned is to work with the default kernel and keep it that way! Also, you learned how the udev system uses the sys file system to communicate with the kernel and properly initialize hardware on your server. There is more to working with the kernel than what you have read here. In Chapter 31, you will learn how you can tune the kernel for optimal performance, and in Chapter 10 you learned how to make sure the kernel is loaded with the right options when booting your server. In the next chapter, you will learn how to use shell scripting to alleviate your work as a Linux administrator.

Introducing Shell Scripting

On SUSE Linux Enterprise Server, many tasks are automated with shell scripts. For example, the entire start-up procedure consists of shell scripts. For an administrator, it is useful to know how to do some shell scripting yourself. Therefore, in this chapter, you'll get an introduction to shell scripting. After a short introduction, you'll learn about the most important components you'll see in most shell scripts, such as variables and parameters, iterations, functions, and some basic calculations. This chapter is meant to give a basic overview of the way a shell script is organized and should help you write a simple shell script. But it is in no way meant to be a complete tutorial that covers all the elements you can use in a script. For that kind of information, see *From Bash to Z Shell*, by Kiddle, Peek, and Stephenson. (Apress, 2004).

Getting Started

If you know how to handle your Linux commands properly, you can do magic. Imagine the magic you can create when combining multiple Linux commands in a shell script. In this chapter, you'll get an introduction to the fine art of shell scripting. That's right: shell scripting is an art. You won't learn it by just studying the text in this chapter; instead, you need to do it, again and again. I hope you'll find the examples in this chapter inspiring enough to try modifying them to make them better and to fit them to your own situation.

To Script or Not to Script?

Before you start writing your shell scripts, you should always ask yourself whether a shell script really is the best solution. In many cases, other solutions are available. Instead of using the Bash shell as a scripting language, you can use Perl, for example, or you can write a complete program in the C programming language. Each of these solutions has its advantages and disadvantages.

The most important advantage of using Bash as your scripting language is that Bash scripts are relatively easy to understand and to make. Another advantage is that you don't have to compile them before you can start using them. Shell scripts are also easier to debug than other languages. The only piece you need on the computer where you are going to run your shell script is the shell for which the script is written. In addition, since the Bash shell is omnipresent, performing tasks with your script on other Linux computers shouldn't be a problem.

The most important disadvantage of using Bash as the solution to create your script in is that Bash is relatively slow. This is because the shell always has to interpret the commands that are in the shell. By contrast, a C program is compiled code, optimized to execute its work on the hardware of your computer directly; therefore, C is much faster.

What Shell?

Many shells are available for Linux. When writing a shell script, you should be aware of this and choose the best shell available for your script. A script written for one shell will not necessarily run on another shell well. Fortunately, the choice is relatively easy because Bash (/bin/bash) is the default shell on Linux. Bash by itself is compatible with the Unix Bourne shell (/bin/sh), which has been used on Unix since the 1970s. The good part of this compatibility is that a script that was written to run on /bin/sh will work on Bash. The opposite is, however, not necessarily true. This is because many new features have been added to Bash that don't exist in the traditional Unix Bourne shell.

In addition to Bash, you will occasionally encounter other shells on Linux. The most important of these is the Korn shell (/bin/ksh), which is the default shell on the Sun Microsystems Solaris operating system. An open source derivative of that shell is available as the Public Domain Korn Shell (/bin/pdksh). Another popular shell is the C shell, which on Linux exists as /bin/tcsh. The C shell is especially popular amongst C programmers; this is because the C shell has a scripting language that resembles the C programming language. You will sometimes encounter C-shell users in a Linux environment. The Korn shell, however, is not used often in Linux environments. The reason is that almost all its important features are offered by Bash as well.

Both the Korn shell and the C shell are not compatible with Bash (although a really simple script will run in all shells). As a result, you will not be able to run a C-shell script in a Bash environment. This has a solution, though—just include the *shebang* in your shell script. This is an indicator of the program that must be used when executing the script. The shebang is a hash, followed by an exclamation mark, which is followed by the name of the command interpreter. If the binary referred to by the shebang is present on your system, the script can run anyway, no matter what shell environment you are currently in as a user. Listing 27-1 shows an example of a script that starts with a shebang.

Listing 27-1. *Shell Scripts Should Always Start with the Shebang*

```
#!/bin/bash
#
# myscript [filename]
#
# Use this script to....
```

Basic Elements of a Shell Script

Some elements should occur in all shell scripts. I'll cover these elements in this section:

- The shebang that all shell scripts start with
- Some lines of comment to explain what you are doing
- The commands that form the body of the shell script
- An exit code to tell the shell from which the script was executed about the success or failure of the script

As you now know, every shell script should start with the shebang. After that, it is a good idea to add some lines of comment, explaining what the script does. These lines start with a hash mark (#), which makes sure the line is not interpreted by the shell. Of course, you can create your own scripts however you want, but if you start every script with some comment explaining how the script should be used, using the script later is a lot easier. Basically, at the moment you are writing the script, you probably know exactly what you are doing, but at a later stage, you might forget what your shell script does, especially if many lines of code are added to a script later.

Apart from the comment, your script includes, of course, some commands. You can use every command that runs in a Linux environment; you can refer to Bash internal commands and work with external commands. An internal command is loaded with Bash in memory and therefore can execute quickly. An external command is a command that is somewhere on disk. The disadvantage of using external commands is that they need to be loaded first, which takes extra time. In the example in Listing 27-2, you can see a rather simple shell script where all the basic elements are present.

Listing 27-2. *Example of a Simple Shell Script That Contains All the Required Elements*

```
#!/bin/bash
#
# This is just a friendly script
#
# Usage: hello
#
echo 'Hello, World!'
exit 0
```

In the example script, you can see the following happening: After the comment, the command echo greets people who run the script. Notice that the text that is echoed to the screen is between single quotes. These are also called *strong quotes*, and they make sure nothing between the single quotes is actually interpreted by the shell. In this example, it is really necessary to use them, since the exclamation mark has a special meaning for the shell. Second, after the successful termination of the script, you see the command exit 0. This command generates the *exit status* of the script; it tells the shell from which the script was executed whether the script executed successfully. Ordinarily, the exit status 0 is used to indicate that everything went OK. If some problems were encountered executing the script, you can use an exit status 1. You can use any other exit status as well; this is at the discretion of the programmer. Using more than just 0 and 1 as an exit status can make troubleshooting a lot easier. Using an exit status is important in a more complex shell script, because based on the success or failure of your script, you can decide that something else needs to happen.

■**Tip** Did you know you can request the exit status of the last command that was executed from the shell? Type echo $?, and it will display the exit status of the last command as a numerical value.

Making It Executable

Now that you have created your shell script, it is time to do something with it. Different options exist to execute your shell script:

- Activate it as an argument of your shell.
- "Source" the script.
- Make it executable, and run it.

If you just need to check that the script works, the easiest way to test it is as the argument of the shell. This means that from your shell, you start a new shell that starts the script for you. If the name of your script is hello, for example, you can start the script with the following command:

```
bash hello
```

With this method, a subshell is started, and the script is executed from there. This has one result you should understand: if you set a variable in this subshell, it is available within that subshell only and not in the parent shell. You'll learn more about variables in the "Working with Variables" section.

Tip Want a variable that is set in a script to be available in all shells? Then use the export command when defining the variable.

The second method to execute a script is to use the source method. You refer to this command by entering a dot, followed by a space and the name of the script. For example, you can start the script with the name hello as follows using the source method:

. hello

The important difference of the preceding method is that when using the source method, no subshell is started, but the script runs directly from the current shell. The result is that all variables that are defined when running the script are available after running the script as well. This can be useful but confusing at the same time. On SUSE Linux Enterprise Server, the source method is used often to include another script in a generic script, and in this other script, for example, some system variables are set. Listing 27-3 shows how this works in the runlevel script that starts the LDAP server. Notice the last line after the && part. This is the part where the /etc/sysconfig/openldap configuration file, which contains some parameters that need to be used by OpenLDAP to be sourced, will be sourced.

Listing 27-3. *Sourcing of Scripts Occurs Often in the Runlevel Script*

```
#! /bin/sh
# Copyright (c) 1997-2000 SuSE GmbH Nuernberg, Germany.
# Copyright (c) 2002 SuSE Linux AG Nuernberg, Germany.
# Copyright (c) 2006 SUSE LINUX Products GmbH, Nuernberg, Germany.
#
# Author: Carsten Hoeger
#         Ralf Haferkamp
#
# /etc/init.d/ldap
#
### BEGIN INIT INFO
# Provides:      ldap
# Required-Start: $remote_fs
# Required-Stop:
# Default-Start: 3 5
# Default-Stop:
# Description:    start the OpenLDAP2 Server
### END INIT INFO

# Determine the base and follow a runlevel link name.
base=${0##*/}
link=${base#*[SK][0-9][0-9]}

test -f /etc/sysconfig/openldap && . /etc/sysconfig/openldap
```

The last and possibly the most frequently used method to run a script is to make it executable first. You can do that by adding the execute permission to your script, like in the following command:

```
chmod +x hello
```

Note Using `chmod +x hello` may impose a security risk, since it gives the execute permission to everyone. Use `chmod u+x yourscript` if you have a more complex script that you want to allow only the owner of the script to run.

Next, you can simply run the script:

```
./hello
```

Notice that in this example, the script is executed as `./hello` and not just `hello` (assuming the script is in the current directory). This is because you need to indicate that the script must run from the current directory. No Linux shell looks for executable code in the current directory by default, which is a security feature. Without the `./`, Bash would search for `hello` in its current PATH setting and would probably not find it, unless you are creating the script in a directory that is included in your search path, in which case you could run the script by its name only, without the `./`.

Note The shell PATH variable lists the directories that should always be searched for executable files. You can see its contents by using the `echo $PATH` command.

One last remark: always be careful about how you call your script, and try avoiding names that already exist. For example, you might be tempted to use `test` as the name of your script. This would, however, conflict with the `test` command that is installed on all Linux systems by default (later in the "Using Flow Control" section you'll learn more about that command). Want to check whether the name of your script is already in use by some other command? Use the `whereis` command. This command searches all the common directories where binary files usually are for the existence of a binary with the name you've entered. In Listing 27-4 you can see the result this command gives for the `test` command.

Listing 27-4. *Checking Whether a Command Name Already Exists with* `whereis`

```
SFO:/ # whereis test
test: /usr/bin/test /usr/share/man/man1/test.1.gz /usr/share/man/man1p/test.1p.gz
```

Making a Script Interactive

It's cool if your script is capable of executing a list of commands, but it will be much better if you can make it interactive. This way, the script can ask a user for input, and the user can decide how to run the script. To make a script interactive, you can use the `read` command, followed by the name of a variable. This variable is used as a label to the input of the user; the cool part is that you can use it later in the script to check what exactly the user entered. Listing 27-5 shows an example of an interactive script. You'll also learn a new method to display script output on the screen.

Listing 27-5. *Making Your Script Interactive*

```
#!/bin/bash
#
# Send a message to the world
#
# Usage: ./hello

cat << EOF
Tell us, what message do you want to pass to the world today? Don't hesitate,
 anything is allowed, just tell me what friendly message you want to enter.
EOF

read message
echo "$message"
```

In the previous script, the first new item you can see is the *here document*, which is an alternative way to echo text to the user's screen; it is particularly useful if you want to display some lines of text on the user's screen. The advantage of using this construction is that you open it by using cat << followed by anything. In this example, I've used EOF (to refer to *end of file*), but if you want to use mydoggie instead, that's fine as well. Just make sure the opening statement for the here document is on a line by itself. Next, enter all the text you want to enter, and last, close the here document by referring to the text you've entered on a single line.

After the here document, the read command asks the user for some input. The input is placed in the temporary variable message, which is echoed in the last line of the script. Notice as well that to define the variable, no dollar sign is required, but to display the contents of the variable, you have to prepend a dollar sign. Otherwise, echo would have no way of knowing that you are referring to a variable. Listing 27-6 shows exactly what this script will do when you run it.

Listing 27-6. *Running the Interactive Script*

```
SFO:~/bin # ./hello
Tell us, what message do you want to pass to the world today? Don't hesitate,
 anything is allowed, just tell me what friendly message you want to enter
Good morning folks
Good morning folks
```

Working with Arguments

Making a script interactive is a nice solution for getting user input. It has a disadvantage, though: it requires a user to provide input to your script. This is not ideal, because many scripts run automatically. These scripts, however, also start because of some specific parameters. The way to handle the parameters is by running them as an argument on start-up. For example, you would run the hello script from the previous section as ./hello hi to let it output the text hi.

To work with arguments that are provided when activating the script, you have to refer to them in the script. You can refer to the first argument by using $1, the second argument by using $2, and so on, up to $9. ($10 would be interpreted as $1, followed by 0.) You can refer to the name of the script by using $0. In Listing 27-7 you see a simple example of a script that can work with arguments.

Listing 27-7. *Working with Arguments*

```
#!/bin/bash
#
# Script that allows you to greet someone
# Usage: ./hello [name]

echo "Hello, $1, how are you today"
```

Let's imagine you activate this script by entering ./hello, linda on the command line. This means when calling the script, $1 is filled with the value linda. When called in the actual code line, the script will therefore echo "Hello, linda, how are you today" on the screen of the user. When working with arguments, you must be aware that every word you enter is interpreted as an argument by itself. This shows when you execute the script in the previous example by entering ./hello, mister president. As the result, only the text "Hello, mister, how are you today" displays. This is because your script doesn't have any definition for $2.

Want to make sure that cases like this are handled correctly? In that case, you should use $*. The construction $* handles an unknown number of arguments that is entered. So to handle any number of arguments, without knowing beforehand how many arguments are going to be used, tune the script from Listing 27-7 as shown in Listing 27-8.

Listing 27-8. *Handling an Unknown Number of Arguments*

```
#!/bin/bash
#
# Script that allows you to greet one or more persons
# Usage: ./hello [name1] [name2] ... [namen]
echo "Hello, $1, how are you today"
```

Regular Expressions

One common task in shell scripts is working on text patterns. The easiest way to refer to a specific text pattern is by entering it literally, such as in the command grep linux *, where all files in the current directory are searched for the literal text linux. This, however, becomes somewhat more complicated if you don't know how a word is written. Many commands allow you to work with regular expressions to solve that problem. Some of the most common commands that can work with regular expressions are grep, sed, and awk.

An example of a command that uses a regular expression is grep 'lin.x' *. In this command, the pattern 'lin.x' is the regular expression. In it, the dot refers to any character. Also notice that the complete regular expression appears between single quotes; this makes sure the shell will not interpret it. I recommend always using quotes in a regular expression; this adds more clarity to what exactly should happen. Table 27-1 gives an overview of some of the most common special characters that you can use in regular expressions.

Table 27-1. *Most Common Special Characters in Regular Expressions*

Character	Meaning
^	Refers to the beginning of a line. For example, grep -ls '^hosts' * shows only files where the text *hosts* is in the beginning of the line.
$	Refers to the end of a line. For example, grep -ls 'false$' * shows only files that have the text *false* in the end of a line.
.	Refers to any character, with the exception of the newline character. An example of its use is the command grp -ls 'h.st' *.
[xy]	Refers to either *x* or *y*. For example, grep 'li[vf]e' * would find either *live* or *love*.
[^x]	Ignores the text between brackets.

Working with Variables

To create a good, working shell script, using variables is an important feature. In the previous section, you learned how to use variables to store the arguments that are entered when activating a script. You can define variables in other ways as well. In the following sections, you'll explore a few more of the possibilities when working with variables.

A variable is a reserved amount of memory with a name that you can use to store information that a script uses more than once. Using variables also makes it easier to be flexible with values that can change. A common way of defining a variable is to specify the name of the variable, followed by an = and its value; for example, today=Thursday will grant the value Thursday to today. Later in a script, it is easy to refer to the value of this variable; for example, the command echo $today will give the current value of the variable. The advantage of working with variables this way is that when the value needs to change (for example, because it is Friday), you can change this new value in one location in the script only.

Command Substitution

One way of handling variables automatically is by using *command substitution*. This is a technique that puts the result of a command in a variable that can be used in a script (or on the command line). This technique is especially useful if you need to work with information that changes often or automatically. To use command substitution, you need to put the command you want to use between backticks; for example, echo `whoami` would put the result of the whoami command in the echo command.

An example of this is a script that refers to the directory where kernel modules are installed. This directory changes with every kernel update that is installed, so it's not really a good idea to use hard references to this directory everywhere. Command substitution is an ideal solution.

You can display the name of the current kernel version with the uname -r command. So instead of referring to the directory /lib/modules/2.6.16-308a (or whatever the name of the module directory for the currently loaded kernel is), you can refer to /lib/modules/`uname -r` instead. The example script in Listing 27-9 shows how you can use command substitution.

Listing 27-9. *Example of Command Substitution*

```
#!/bin/bash
#
# Copy a kernel module to the appropriate directory
# Usage: ./modcop

echo Enter the full path name of the file that you want to copy
read file
cp $file /lib/modules/`uname -r`
```

In this example, the script first asks the user to input the complete name of the file he wants to copy. Next, it will copy the file to the directory where the current kernel stores its kernel modules.

Changing Variables

In some situations, you need to change the name of a variable. To do this, you need to define a new variable that is based on the value of an old variable. This may be useful to change the argument that a user has entered when starting the script. When changing a variable, you should be aware that you can redefine all the variables, except arguments that were entered when starting the script. So if you need to do something to the value assigned to an argument, put the current value of the argument in a new variable, and change that. The example in Listing 27-10 shows how to put the result of an existing variable in a new variable.

Listing 27-10. *Assigning the Value of Existing Variables to New Variables*

```
#!/bin/bash
#
# Greet the user in a friendly way
# Usage: ./hello, <firstname> <surname>

name="$1 $2"
echo hello, $name
```

If, for example, a user named Linda Thomson starts the script by using the ./hello, Linda Thomson command, the script will output "hello, Linda Thomson" to the screen. Now put this way, it is not extremely useful to put the current values of $1 and $2 in a new variable called name; if you want to change the value currently assigned to a variable, however, it can be useful to assign the value of old variables to a temporary used new variable. The next section makes this clear.

Substitution Operators

Within a script, it may be important to check whether a variable really has a value assigned to it before the script continues. To do this, Bash offers substitution operators. By using substitution operators, you can assign a default value if a variable doesn't have a value that is currently assigned to it, and much more. Table 27-2 gives an overview of the substitution operators and their uses.

Table 27-2. *Substitution Operators*

Operator	Use
${parameter:-value}	Shows the value if the parameter is not defined.
${parameter=value}	Assigns the value to the parameter if the parameter does not exist. This operator does nothing if the parameter exists but doesn't have a value.
${parameter:=value}	Assigns the value if the parameter currently has no value or if the parameter doesn't exist.
${parameter:?value}	Shows a message that is defined as the value if the parameter doesn't exist or is empty. Using this construction will force the shell script to be aborted immediately.
${parameter:+value}	Shows the value if the parameter does have a value. If it doesn't have a value, nothing happens.

Substitution operators can be hard to understand. To make it easier to see how they work, Listing 27-11 gives some examples. In all of these examples, something happens to the $BLAH variable. You'll see that the result of the command that is given is different depending on the substitution operator that is used. To make it easier to talk about what happens, I've added line numbers to all lines. (When trying this yourself, you should omit the line numbers.)

Listing 27-11. *Using Substitution Operators*

```
1. sander@linux %> echo $BLAH
2.
3. sander@linux %> echo ${BLAH:-variable is empty}
4 variable is empty
5. sander@linux %> echo $BLAH
6.
7. sander@linux %> echo ${BLAH=value}
8. value
9. sander@linux %> echo $BLAH
10. value
11. sander@linux %> BLAH=
12. sander@linux %> echo ${BLAH=value}
13.
14. sander@linux %> echo ${BLAH:=value}
15. value
16. sander@linux %> echo $BLAH
17. value
18. sander@linux %> echo ${BLAH:+sometext}
19. sometext
```

The previous example starts with the echo $BLAH command. This command reads the variable BLAH and shows its current value. Since BLAH doesn't have a value yet, on line 2, nothing is shown. Next, in line 3 a message is defined that should be displayed if BLAH is empty. As you can see, the message is displayed in line 4. This, however, doesn't assign a value to BLAH, which you see in lines 5 and 6 where the current value of BLAH is asked again. In line 7, BLAH finally gets a value, which is displayed in line 8. The shell remembers the new value of BLAH, which you can see in lines 9 and 10 where the value of BLAH is referred to and displayed. On line 11, BLAH is redefined but gets a null value; the variable still exists, but it just has no value here. This is proven when on line 12 echo ${BLAH=value} is used; since BLAH at that moment has a null value, no new value is assigned. Next, the construction echo ${BLAH:=value} assigns a new value to BLAH. The fact that

BLAH really gets a value from this is shown in lines 16 and 17. Finally, the construction on line 18 displays sometext if BLAH currently does have a value. Notice that this doesn't change anything in the value that is assigned to BLAH at that moment; sometext just indicates that it has a value, and that's all.

Pattern-Matching Operators

You can use substitution operators, as discussed in the preceding section, to do something if a variable does not have a value. You can use a *pattern-matching* operator to search for a pattern in a variable and, if that pattern exists, do something to the variable. This can be useful, because it allows you to tune a variable to be exactly the way you want it. Think, for example, of the situation where a user enters a complete path name of a file, but your script needs only the name of the file without the entire path. The pattern-matching operator is the way to change that; pattern-matching operators allow you to remove part of a variable automatically. In Listing 27-12 you see an example of a script that works with pattern-matching operators.

Listing 27-12. *Working with Pattern-Matching Operators*

```
#!/bin/bash
#
# script that extracts the filename from a filename that includes the complete path
# usage: stripit <complete filename>

filename=${1##*/}
echo "The name of the file is $filename"
```

When executed, the script will show the following result:

```
sander@linux %> ./stripit /bin/bash
the name of the file  is bash
```

Pattern-matching operators always try to locate a given string. In this case, the string is */. In other words, the pattern-matching operator searches for a / preceded by something. In this pattern-matching operator, ## is used to search for the longest match of the string provided, starting from the beginning of the string. In other words, the pattern-matching operator searches for the last / that occurs in the string and removes it and everything that stands before the / as well. You can prove this by running the script with /bin/bash/ as an argument; in this case, the pattern that is searched for is on the last position of the string, and the pattern-matching operator removes everything.

The previous example explains how to use the pattern-matching operator that looks for the longest match. By using a single hash sign, you can let the pattern-matching operator look for the shortest match, again starting from the beginning of the string. If, for example, the script in Listing 27-12 uses filename=${1#/}, the pattern-matching operator would look for the first / in the complete filename and remove that.

In the previous example, you saw how to use pattern-matching to start searching from the beginning of a string. You can start searching from the end of the string as well. In this case, you use % instead of #; % refers to the shortest match of the pattern, and %% refers to its longest match. The script in Listing 27-13 shows how this works.

Listing 27-13. *Using Pattern-Matching Operators to Start Searching at the End of a String*

```
#!/bin/bash
#
# script that isolates the directoryname from a complete filename
# usage: stripdir <complete filename>

dirname=${1%%/*}
echo "The directory name is $dirname"
```

While executing, you'll see that this script has a problem:

```
sander@linux %> ./stripdir /bin/bash
The directory name is
```

As you can see, the script does its work somewhat too enthusiastically and removes everything. Fortunately, you can solve this problem by first using a pattern-matching operator that removes the slash from the start of the complete filename (but only if that slash is provided) and removes everything following the first slash in the complete filename. The example in Listing 27-14 shows how this is done.

Listing 27-14. *Fixing the Example from Listing 27-13*

```
#!/bin/bash
#
# script that isolates the directoryname from a complete filename
# usage: stripdir <complete filename>

dirname=${1#/}
dirname=${1%%/*}
echo "The directory name is $dirname"
```

As you can see, the solution to the problem is to use ${#/}. This construction starts searching from the beginning of the filename to a /. Since no * is used here, it will look only for a / at the first position of the filename. If it finds one, it will remove the slash. So if a user enters usr/bin/passwd instead of /usr/bin/passwd, the ${#/} construction will do nothing. In the line after that, the variable dirname is defined again to do its work on the result of its first definition in the previous line. This line does the real job and looks for the pattern /*, starting at the end of the filename. This makes sure everything after the first slash in the filename is removed, and only the name of the top-level directory is echoed. Of course, you can tune this script easily to display the complete path where the file is in; just use dirname=${dirname%/*} instead.

Performing Calculations in Scripts

Bash offers some options that allow you to perform calculations from scripts. Of course, you are not likely to use them as a replacement for your spreadsheet program, but performing simple calculations from Bash can be useful. You can use calculation options, for example, to execute a command a number of times or to make sure a counter is used when a command executes successfully. The script in Listing 27-15 gives an example of how you can use counters.

Listing 27-15. *Using a Counter in a Script*

```
#!/bin/bash
counter=1
while true
do
    counter=$((counter + 1))
    echo counter is set to $counter
done
```

As you can see, this script uses a construction with while (which is covered in more detail in the "While" section). The construction executes a command as long as a given condition is met. In this example, the condition is simple: you must be capable of executing the true command successfully. This won't be a problem, since the name of the command is true because it always executes successfully. That is, true always gives an exit status 0, which tells the shell that it has executed with success, just like the false command always gives the exit status 1.

What has to happen if the condition is met is specified between do and done. First, the line counter=$((counter + 1)) takes the current value of the variable counter (which is set in the beginning of the script) and increments that by 1. Next, the value of the variable counter is displayed with the line echo counter is set to $counter. Once that has happened, the condition is checked again, and the command is executed again as well. The result of this script is a list of numbers on your screen that is updated quickly. Think it goes too fast? Just add a line with the command sleep 1 in the loop; that way, the calculation of the new value of counter takes place once a second only.

The previous example explains how you can perform a simple calculation from a script, but it isn't very useful. Listing 27-16 gives a more useful example. For some computer magazine, I had to test USB sticks. As you have probably heard, the life of USB storage is limited. When the media has been written to a couple of hundred or thousand times, the stick will die. To find out the exact number of times a stick of a given brand can be written to, I wrote the following shell script with the name killstick.

Listing 27-16. *Script to Test USB Sticks*

```
#!/bin/bash
#
# Script to test USB sticks
#
# usage: killstick <mountpoint of the stick>
#
counter=1
while cp /129MBfile $1
do
    sync
    rm -rf $1/129MBfile
    sync
    counter=$((counter + 1))
    echo Counter is now set to $counter
done
echo Your stick is now defunctional
```

The script again starts with a little explanation of how it works. To run this script, you first need to mount the stick on a certain mount point. You need to refer to the mount point by specifying it as an argument to the script when running the script. Next, again, a loop with while is started. The command that needs to execute successfully is cp /129MBfile $1. This script was written to test USB sticks with a capacity of 256MB. By using a 129MB file, I made sure that when copying the file, it would always write to the same location. When using small files, it will not work, because each USB stick has a built-in mechanism that makes sure data is not always written to the same physical location.

As long as copying the file is successful, the commands in the do loop are executed. First, the file is synchronized to the stick, using the sync command, to make sure it isn't just kept somewhere in memory. Next, it is immediately removed again, and this removal is synchronized to the physical storage media. Finally, the calculation is used again to increment the counter variable by 1. This continues as long as the file can be copied successfully. When copying the file fails, the while loop is terminated, and the command echo Your stick is now defunctional is displayed, thus letting you know exactly how often the file could be copied to the stick. (If you really want to know, most USB sticks get really slow when they have been written about 2,000 times and will fail at about 2,500 writes.)

Up to now, you have dealt with just one method to do script calculations. You have some other options as well. For example, you can use the expr command. You can use this external command to perform any kind of calculation; the following will give the result of the sum 1 + 2:

```
sum=`expr 1 + 2`; echo $sum
```

As you can see, a variable with the name sum is defined. This variable gets the result of the command expr 1 + 2 by using command substitution. Then a semicolon indicates that what comes next is a new command. After the semicolon, the command echo $sum shows the result of the calculation.

The expr command can work with addition (+), and other types of calculation are supported as well. Table 27-3 summarizes the options.

Table 27-3. expr *Operators*

Operator	Meaning
+	Addition (1 + 1 = 2).
−	Subtraction (10 − 2 = 8).
/	Division (10 / 2 = 5).
*	Multiplication (3 * 3 = 9).
%	Modulus. This calculates the rest value that remains after making a division. This works because expr can handle complete numbers only (11 % 3 = 2).

When working with these options, you'll see that they all work fine, with the exception of the multiplying operator, *. Using this operator will result in a syntax error:

```
linux: ~> expr 2 * 2
expr: syntax error
```

This seems curious, but * is a character that has a special meaning for the shell, such as in ls -l *. When the shell parses the command line, it will interpret the * as a wildcard, and you don't want to do that here. To indicate that the shell shouldn't touch it, you have to escape it. Therefore, change the command as follows:

```
expr 2 \* 2
```

Another way to perform some calculations is by using the internal command let. Because let is internal, it is a better solution than the external command expr, which can be loaded from memory directly and doesn't have to go all the way from your computer's hard drive. Using let, you can make your calculation and apply the result directly to a variable, as in the following example:

```
let x="1 + 2"
```

The result of the calculation in this example is stored in the variable x. The disadvantage of working this way is that let has no option for displaying the result directly as you can do when using expr. For use in a script, however, it offers excellent capabilities. In Listing 27-17 you can see a script where let performs calculations.

Listing 27-17. *Making Calculations with* let

```
#!/bin/bash
#
# usage: calc $1 $2 $3
# $1 is the first number
# $2 is the operator
# $3 is the second number
let x="$1 $2 $3"
echo $x
```

If you think that now I haven't covered all the methods to do calculations in a shell script, you're wrong. The example in Listing 27-18 shows another method you can use.

Listing 27-18. *Another Way of Making Calculations*

```
#!/bin/bash
#
# usage: calc $1 $2 $3
# $1 is the first number
# $2 is the operator
# $3 is the second number
x=(($1 $2 $3))
echo $x
```

You have seen this construction already, when you read about the script that increases the value of the variable counter. Note that you can replace the double pair of brackets with one pair of square brackets instead.

Using Flow Control

Up to now, you haven't read much about how you can make the execution of commands conditional so a command is executed only if a certain condition has been met. The technique to enable this in shell scripts is known as *flow control*. Bash offers many options to use flow control in scripts:

if: Use if to execute commands only if certain conditions are met. To tune how if works, you can use else to indicate what should happen if the condition isn't met.

case: Use case to work with options. This allows the user to specify how the command works when running the command.

for: Use this construction to run a command for a given amount of items. For example, you can use for to do something for every file in a directory that is specified.

while: Use while as long as the specified condition is met. This construction can be useful to check, for example, whether a certain host is reachable or to monitor the activity of a process.

until: This is the opposite of while. Use until to run a command until a certain condition has been met.

In the following sections, you can read about flow control in more detail. Before covering the details about flow control, I'll first cover the test command. You can use this command to perform a lot of checks to see whether a file exists, a variable has a value, and much more. Table 27-4 shows some of the more common test options. For a complete overview, consult its man page.

Table 27-4. *Common Options for the* test *Command*

Option	Use
test -e $1	Checks whether $1 is a file, without looking at what particular kind of file it is.
test -f $1	Checks whether $1 is a regular file and not a device file, a directory, or an executable file, for example.
test -d $1	Checks whether $1 is a directory.
test -x $1	Checks whether $1 is an executable file. Note that you can test for other permissions as well; for example, -g would check to see whether the SGID permission (see Chapter 6) is set.
test $1 -nt $2	Controls whether $1 is newer than $2.
test $1 -ot $2	Controls whether $1 is older than $2.
test $1 -ef $2	Checks whether $1 and $2 both refer to the same inode. This is the case if one is a hard link to the other.
test $1 -eq $2	Sees whether the integers $1 and $2 are equal to each other.
test $1 -ne $2	Checks whether the integers $1 and $2 are not equal to each other.
test $1 -gt $2	Gives true if $1 is greater than $2.
test S1 -lt $2	Gives true if $1 is less than $2.
test $1 -ge $2	Sees whether $1 is greater than or equal to $2.
test $1 -le $2	Checks whether $1 is less than or equal to $2.
test -z $1	Checks whether $1 is empty. This is a useful construction to find out whether a variable has been defined.
test $1	Gives the exit status 0 if $1 does exist.
test $1=$2	Checks whether $1 and $2 are the same. This is useful to compare the value of two variables.
test $1 != $2	Sees whether $1 and $2 are not equal to each other. You can use the exclamation mark with all other tests as well to check for the opposite.

You can use the test command in two ways. First, you can write the complete command as in test -f $1. Second, you can write this command as [-f $1]. Most of the time you'll see the latter option only; people who write shell scripts like to work as efficiently as possible.

Using if ... then ... else

Possibly the most classic example of flow control are constructions where if...then...else is used. Especially if used in conjunction with the test command, this construction offers various interesting possibilities. You can use it, for example, to find out whether a file exists, whether a variable currently has a value, and much more.

A Simple if . . . then . . . else Loop

Listing 27-19 shows an example of a construction with if...then that you can use in a shell script. In the example, else is not used, because only one condition is checked.

Listing 27-19. *Using* if...then *to Perform a Basic Check*

```
#!/bin/bash
if [ -z $1 ]
then
        echo You have to provide an argument with this command
        exit 1
fi

echo the argument is $1
```

You can use the simple check from the previous example to see whether the user who started your script has provided an argument. If the user hasn't, the code in the if loop becomes active; in this case, it will display the message that the user needs to provide an argument and then will terminate the script. If an argument has been provided, the commands within the loop aren't executed, so the script will run the line echo the argument is $1 and in this case echo the argument to the screen of the user. Also notice how the if construction works. First, you have to open it with if. Then, separated on a new line (or with a semicolon), use then. Finally, close the if loop with a fi statement. Make sure all those ingredients are used all the time, or your loop will not work.

A More Complex Example

The previous example with if is rather simple. You can make if loops more complex and test on more than one condition. To do this, use else or elif. By using else within the loop, you can make sure that something happens if the condition is not met. You can even use else in conjunction with if (elif) to open a new loop if the first condition isn't met. In Listing 27-20 you can see an example of the latter construction.

Listing 27-20. *Nesting* if *Loops*

```
if [ -f $1 ]
then
        echo "$1 is a file"
elif [ -d $1 ]
        then
        echo "$1 is a directory"
else
        echo "I don't know what \$1 is"
fi
```

In this example, the argument that was entered when running the script is checked. If it is a file (if [-f $1]), the script tells the user it is a file. If it isn't, the part after elif is executed; this basically opens a second loop. In this second loop, the first test performed is to see whether $1 is a directory. Notice that this second part of the loop becomes active only if $1 is not a file. If $1 is not a directory either, the part after else is run, and the script says that it has no idea what $1 is. Notice that for this entire construction you need only one fi to close the loop.

Using && and || As Alternatives

You should know that you can use if...then...else constructions in two different ways. You can write the complete construction as in the previous examples. Alternatively, you can use construc- tions that use && and ||. These *separators* disconnect two commands and establish a conditional relation between them. If you use &&, the second command is executed only if the first command was executed successfully, in other words, if the first command was true. If you use ||, the second command is executed only if the first command wasn't true. So in one line of code, you can check to find out whether $1 is a file:

```
[ -f $1 ] && echo $1 is a file
```

Note that you can also write this as follows:

```
[ ! -f $1 ] || echo $1 is a file
```

In case you don't exactly follow what happens in the second example, it performs a test to see whether $1 is not a file. If the test fails (which is the case if $1 is indeed a file), it will execute the part after || and echo that $1 is a file.

Up to now you have seen some pretty easy-to-understand examples. Now you'll look at some more complex examples. Consider, for example, the following line:

```
rsync -vaze ssh --delete /srv/ftp 10.0.0.20:/srv/ftp || echo "rsync failed" |
 mail admin@mydomain.com
```

In this example, the rsync command tries to synchronize the content of the directory /srv/ftp with the content of the same directory on some other machine. If this succeeds, no further evalua- tion of this line takes place. If something happens, however, the part after the || becomes active and makes sure that user admin@mydomain.com gets a message about it.

Another more complex example is the following script that monitors whether the available disk space doesn't drop below a certain threshold:

```
if [ `df -m /var | tail -n1 | awk '{print $4} '` -lt 120 ]
then
    logger running out of disk space
fi
```

The important part of this piece of code is in the first line. In this line, the result of a com- mand is specified by using backquoting, and that result is compared with the value 120. If the result is less than 120, the part after then becomes active. If it's greater than 120, nothing hap- pens. Now as for the command itself, it uses the df command to check available disk space on the volume where /var is mounted, filters out the last line of that result, and from that last line filters out the fourth column only, which is then compared to the value 120 here. And if the con- dition is true, the logger command writes a message to the system log file. Of course, this example isn't really sophisticated; to make it even better, use the following:

```
[ `df -m /var | tail -n1 | awk '{print $4}'` -lt $1 ] && logger running out of
disk space
```

This demonstrates why it is fun to write shell scripts; you can almost always make them better.

case

Let's start with an example this time, as shown in Listing 27-21. Create the script, run it, and then try to explain what it did.

Listing 27-21. *Example Script with* case

```
#!/bin/bash
# Your personal soccer expert
# usage: wm

cat << EOF
Enter the name of the country you think will be world champion soccer in 2006. Be
 aware that the name of the country you enter needs to start with an uppercase
 letter.
EOF

read COUNTRY
case $COUNTRY in
     Nederland | Holland | Netherlands)
     echo "Yes, you are an expert in soccer"
     ;;
     Deutschland | Germany | Mannschaft)
     echo "No, they are the worst team on earth"
     ;;
     England)
     echo "hahahahahahaha, you must be joking"
     ;;
     *)
     echo "Huh? Do they play also?"
     ;;
esac
```

In case you can't guess, you can use this script to analyze the next world championship games of soccer (of course you can modify it for any major sports event you like). It will first ask the person who runs the script to enter the name of the country that she thinks will be the next champion. This country is put in the $COUNTRY variable. Notice the use of uppercase for this variable; this is a nice way to identify variables easily if your script becomes rather big.

The body of this script consists of the case command. This command evaluates the input the user has entered. The generic construction used to evaluate the input is as follows:

```
alternative1 | alternative2)
command
;;
```

So, the first line evaluates everything the user can enter. Notice that most lines offer more than one alternative, which makes it easier to handle typing errors and other situations where the user hasn't typed exactly what you were expecting him to type. Then on separate lines come all the commands you want the script to execute. The example executes just one command, but you can enter 100 lines to execute commands if you like. Finally, the check is closed by using ;;. Don't forget to close all items with a ;;. Otherwise, the script doesn't understand you.

When using case, you should make it a habit to handle "all the other options." We hope your user enters something you expect her to enter. But what if she doesn't? In that case, you probably do want the user to see something. The *) at the end of the script handles this. So in this case, for everything the user enters that isn't specifically mentioned as an option in the script, the script will echo "Huh? Do they play also" to the user.

while

You use while to run a command as long as a condition is met. In Listing 27-22 you see how while can monitor the activity of an important process.

Listing 27-22. *Monitoring Process Activity with* while

```
#!/bin/bash
#
# usage: monitor <processname>

while ps aux | grep $1
do
      sleep 1
done

logger $1 is no longer present
```

The body of this script consists of the command ps aux | grep $1. This command monitors for the availability of the process of which the name was entered as an argument when starting this script. As long as the process was detected, the condition is met, and the commands in the loop are executed. In this case, the script waits just one second and then repeats its action. When the process is no longer detected, the logger command writes a message to syslog.

until

Where while does its work as long as a certain condition is met, until is used for the opposite; it runs until the condition is met. You can see this in the example in Listing 27-23 where the script monitors whether the user whose name is entered as the argument is logged in.

Listing 27-23. *Altering When a User Logs In*

```
#!/bin/bash
#
# script that alerts when a user logs in
# usage: ishere <username>

until who | grep $1 >> /dev/null
do
      echo $1 is not logged in yet
      sleep 5
done

echo $1 has just logged in
```

In this example, the command that is executed repeatedly is who | grep $1. In this command, the result of the who command that lists users currently logged in to the system is grepped for the occurrence of $1. As long as the command is not true, which is the case if the user is not logged in, the commands in the loop will be executed. At the moment the user logs in, the loop is broken, and a message is displayed indicating that the user has just logged in. Notice the use of redirection to the null device in the test; this makes sure the result of the who command is not echoed on the screen.

for

Sometimes it is necessary to execute a number of commands. The number of times can be limited; it can, however, be an unlimited amount of times. In such cases, loops with for can offer an excellent solution. Listing 27-24 shows how you can use for to run a counter.

Listing 27-24. *Using* for *to Create a Counter*

```
#!/bin/bash
#
# counter that counts from 1 to 9
for (( counter=1; counter<10; counter++ )); do
    echo "The counter is now set to $counter"
done
exit 0
```

The code used in this script is not difficult to understand. The conditional loop determines that as long as the counter has a value from 1 to 10, the variable counter must be incremented by 1 automatically. To do this, you can use the construction counter++, a technique with which a counter is incremented by 1. As long as this incrementing of the variable counter goes on, the commands between do and done are executed. In this case, it is a simple echo command; any other command will do as well. At the moment that the number that is specified has been reached, the loop is left, and the script will terminate and indicate with exit 0 to the system that it has done its work successfully.

Loops with for can be pretty versatile. For example, you can use for to do something on every line in a text file. The following illustrates how this works:

```
for i in `cat /etc/passwd`
do
    echo $i
done
```

In this example, for displays all the lines in /etc/passwd one by one. Of course, just echoing the lines is a rather silly example, but the important thing is the way that for handles this. You should notice that if you are using for in this way, it cannot handle spaces in the lines. A space would be interpreted as a field separator, and therefore after the space, a new line would begin.

Using a Stream Editor

In scripting you can use some fixed Bash functionality, such as if...then...else, for, read, and others that you have read about in this chapter. To make a script really powerful, you can use external utilities as well. One of these is the stream editor sed. In this section, I'll introduce you to some of the sed basics.

The stream editor sed can be compared to grep. Where grep is merely used to find patterns in files, sed does something to these patterns as well. To accomplish this, a sed command consists of different parts. In the first part, you indicate what exactly you want the command to do. Then you specify for what it has to search. Next, you can specify a pattern to indicate the replacement text, and finally you can specify how a replacement has to take place. You can see an example of this in the following line:

```
sed "s/english/french/g" languages.txt
```

In this example, the action that has to be performed is a substitution (s). The text that has to be located is english, and its replacement text is french. Finally, the letter g indicates that the command has to be executed as long as matches are found. Also notice that the command sed has to execute is always between quotes, which prevents the shell from interpreting the text string.

The last part you have to be aware of when working with sed is that the command will never modify the original file. It will write the modifications it makes to the original text to STDOUT. If you want these modifications to be saved somewhere, you need to write them to a new file. The most common way to do that is by redirecting to a temporary file. If so required, you can later use the temporary file to overwrite the original file. You would modify the previous example to the following to accomplish this:

```
sed "s/english/french/g" languages.txt > languages2.txt
```

Next, you can copy the new output file over the old file.

Another useful task you can accomplish with sed is removing text from a file. In that case, you just add an empty replacement text. An example of this is the following command:

```
sed "s/something//g" list.txt
```

Of course, you have to make sure the result is written to some temporary file.

Also useful is the option to remove lines that match a certain pattern from a file. For example, the following command will remove user sander from the /etc/passwd file:

```
sed "/sander/d" /etc/passwd
```

Notice that in this example no substitution is used anymore, but the d (delete) command removes the line. You can even make it somewhat more complicated by removing an empty line. In that case, you need to work with a regular expression. The next example shows how:

```
sed "/^$/d" /myfile
```

The special construction that is in use here is a regular expression that searches for the beginning of the line, indicated by $, which is followed immediately by the end of the line, which is indicated by $. Since nothing appears between the two of them, this construction helps you find empty lines.

Working with Functions

An element that can be useful in longer shell scripts is the function. A *function* is a subroutine in a script that is labeled by a name. Using functions makes it easier to refer to certain command sequences that have to be used more than once in a script. You could use it, for example, to create a generic error message if something goes wrong. You have two ways of defining functions:

```
function functionname
{
    command1
    command2
    commandn
}
```

Alternatively, you can do the same thing using the following:

```
functionname ()
{
    command1
    command2
    commandn
}
```

To increase the readability of a script, it is a good idea to use functions if you need certain code sequences more than once. Also, list all your functions at the beginning of the script to be able to easily maintain them. Listing 27-25 gives an example of a script where a function displays an error message. This script is a replacement for the file command, with the difference that this script displays a more elegant error message.

Listing 27-25. *Displaying Error Codes Using Functions*

```
#!/bin/bash
# This script shows the file type
#
# usage: filetype $1
function noarg
{
    echo "You have made an error"
    echo "When running this script, you need to specify the name of the file that
 you want to check"
    exit 1
}

if [ -z $1 ]; then
    noarg
else
    file $1
fi
exit 0
```

In the previous example, the function has the name noarg. In it, some text is specified that has to be echoed to the screen when the function is called. Since the function basically defines an error message, the function makes sure the script terminates with an exit status 1. As you can see, the function is called just once in this script, when a user forgets to enter the required argument.

Summary

In this chapter, you learned about the basic ingredients you can use in shell scripts. This chapter is meant in no way to be a complete overview of all that you can do in a shell script; it is just meant to get you familiar with the basic ingredients of scripts so you can analyze what's used on your server or write a simple script to perform repetitive tasks. In the next chapter, you will learn how to tune and optimize SUSE Linux Enterprise Server.

CHAPTER 28

■■■

Tuning and Optimizing SUSE Linux

As the administrator of a SUSE Linux Server, you are responsible for configuring this server for the best performance. Chapter 11 already covered some basics of processes and memory usage. In this chapter, I'll introduce you to the art of performance tuning and optimizing. You should consider this chapter only as an introduction to tuning and optimizing; to really get the best out of a server, you should always consider the applications that are running on that server as well. In this chapter, you'll also learn how to create kernel core dumps, which may be useful if you run into serious problems.

Managing Memory

One of the most important tasks to get an indication of the current health of your server is to monitor the usage of system memory. In Chapter 11, you learned how to interpret the statistics provided by the top command. One of the most important facts you have to remember about the usage of system memory is the difference between allocated memory and memory that is really in use. When a process loads, it will always claim more memory than the amount of memory that is really needed. This is called memory *overallocation*. Overallocation is good, because it allows the process to access more memory instantaneously when more memory is required. As a system administrator, you should monitor the relationship between memory that is allocated by a process and memory that is really used by that process. You can do this with top (see Figure 28-1).

In top, you will see two columns that are important with regard to memory management. First, the column SIZE shows the amount of memory that is claimed by the process. The size in the column RES shows what is actually used by the process in the last polling interval.

```
                                          Terminal                                    _ ◻ ✕
 File  Edit  View  Terminal  Tabs  Help
top - 18:03:16 up  1:46,  2 users,  load average: 0.01, 0.04, 0.03
Tasks: 104 total,   1 running, 103 sleeping,   0 stopped,   0 zombie
Cpu(s):  0.7%us,  0.0%sy,  0.0%ni, 99.3%id,  0.0%wa,  0.0%hi,  0.0%si,  0.0%st
Mem:    516400k total,   497132k used,    19268k free,   172488k buffers
Swap:   779112k total,       40k used,   779072k free,   216492k cached

  PID USER      PR  NI  VIRT  RES  SHR S %CPU %MEM    TIME+  COMMAND
 3137 root      15   0 39856  16m 7580 S  0.7  3.2  1:18.47 X
 6214 root      16   0  2188 1028  764 R  0.3  0.2  0:00.03 top
    1 root      16   0   720  280  244 S  0.0  0.1  0:01.42 init
    2 root      34  19     0    0    0 S  0.0  0.0  0:00.01 ksoftirqd/0
    3 root      10  -5     0    0    0 S  0.0  0.0  0:00.11 events/0
    4 root      10  -5     0    0    0 S  0.0  0.0  0:00.01 khelper
    5 root      10  -5     0    0    0 S  0.0  0.0  0:00.00 kthread
    7 root      10  -5     0    0    0 S  0.0  0.0  0:00.61 kblockd/0
    8 root      20  -5     0    0    0 S  0.0  0.0  0:00.00 kacpid
   96 root      15   0     0    0    0 S  0.0  0.0  0:00.15 pdflush
   97 root      15   0     0    0    0 S  0.0  0.0  0:03.81 pdflush
   99 root      11  -5     0    0    0 S  0.0  0.0  0:00.00 aio/0
   98 root      15   0     0    0    0 S  0.0  0.0  0:00.38 kswapd0
  305 root      11  -5     0    0    0 S  0.0  0.0  0:00.00 cqueue/0
  306 root      11  -5     0    0    0 S  0.0  0.0  0:00.01 kseriod
  346 root      11  -5     0    0    0 S  0.0  0.0  0:00.00 kpsmoused
  720 root      11  -5     0    0    0 S  0.0  0.0  0:00.00 scsi_eh_0
  825 root      10  -5     0    0    0 S  0.0  0.0  0:00.08 reiserfs/0
  893 root      11  -4  1840  656  348 S  0.0  0.1  0:01.50 udevd
 1302 root      11  -5     0    0    0 S  0.0  0.0  0:00.00 kgameportd
 1392 root      20   0     0    0    0 S  0.0  0.0  0:00.00 shpchpd_event
 1452 root      10  -5     0    0    0 S  0.0  0.0  0:00.00 khubd
 1997 messageb  16   0  3416 1016  728 S  0.0  0.2  0:04.64 dbus-daemon
 2014 root      16   0  1516  512  428 S  0.0  0.1  0:00.01 acpid
 2028 root      15   0  1892  816  576 S  0.0  0.2  0:18.30 syslog-ng
 2031 root      16   0  1656  524  324 S  0.0  0.1  0:00.04 klogd
 2094 root      17   0  2224  680  548 S  0.0  0.1  0:00.03 resmgrd
 2350 root      16   0  4272 2876 1448 S  0.0  0.6  0:06.04 hald
 2372 root      18   0  1820  600  524 S  0.0  0.1  0:00.02 hald-addon-acpi
 2413 root      15   0  1644  568  476 S  0.0  0.1  0:01.52 vmware-guestd
 2630 root      16   0  1816  728  640 S  0.0  0.1  0:04.25 hald-addon-stor
```

Figure 28-1. *Use* top *to monitor the difference between claimed memory and memory that is actually used.*

Optimizing Usage of Swap Space

One of the items that is important for memory management is swap space. The primary reason is not because swap is used if you are running out of memory but because you can use swap to park chunks of memory that aren't needed at that moment. This also makes sure that a system that is almost running out of memory will continue to function properly. In the "old days," it was a good idea to allocate twice as much swap space as the amount of physical memory. In modern days where servers can have multiple gigabytes of RAM, this doesn't make sense; a 64GB swap partition would become a large bottleneck. Therefore, you shouldn't configure more swap space than 2GB.

On Linux, swap is ordinarily configured as a partition. You can configure it as a file as well, but for performance reasons this really is not a good idea. As an administrator you don't even have to think about it; the swap partition is set up automatically when installing SUSE Linux Enterprise Server. To set up swap for optimal performance, different swap partitions can be created and load balanced on the system; this allows the swapping to take place in parallel on all those partitions at the same time, which leads to better performance. If you want to do that, you can use the pri option in /etc/fstab to indicate how the swap partition should be mounted. If the pri setting is not used, the first swap partition that is defined on your server is used first, then the second partition is used, and so on. In Listing 28-1 you can see how to set up /etc/fstab for the load balancing of swap activity.

Listing 28-1. *Configuring* /etc/fstab *for Swap Load Balancing*

```
/dev/sda2        swap        swap      pri=1      0 0
/dev/sdb2        swap        swap      pri=1      0 0
/dev/sdc2        swap        swap      pri=1      0 0
```

Monitoring Swap Activity

As an administrator, you should be able to monitor swap activity. Just using the free command and seeing that some swap space is being used is not enough, because some processes can use swap space as a parking place for data that isn't needed immediately. In that case, you can allocate a lot of swap space without causing any harm. What's important to check is the activity of your swap space. To monitor that, you can use the vmstat command. In this command, the options si and so indicate swap activity; si refers to the number of blocks that were swapped in during the last polling interval, and so refers to the number of blocks that were swapped out during the last polling interval. If you see a high number here, then something is definitely wrong with the usage of swap on your server. If you see a low number or zero, you have no problem at all. When using vmstat, you should always run it a couple of times. For example, use vmstat 5 5 to run the command five times with a polling interval of five seconds. Check Listing 28-2 for an example.

Listing 28-2. *Using* vmstat *to See Statistics About Swap Activity*

```
SFO:~ # vmstat 5 5
procs -----------memory---------- ---swap-- -----io---- --system-- ----cpu----
 r  b   swpd free    buff  cache   si  so   bi   bo    in    cs   us sy id wa
 3  0   0   52048  72888 1317852   0   0   258   40   569   877   6  2 88  4
 0  0   0   52080  72896 1317844   0   0    0    12  1044  2482   1  5 93  1
 1  0   0   52096  72904 1317836   0   0    0     3  1251  5388   3 10 86  0
 1  0   0   52096  72904 1317836   0   0    2     5  1105  5030   6  8 86  0
 0  0   0   52112  72912 1317828   0   0    0    48  1060  6619  11 1080  0
```

Adding Swap Space on the Fly

In rare situations, you may find that you are running out of swap space. If that happens, it is useful to know how to add a swap file by hand. Using swap files is not an ideal solution, because swap files are slower than swap partitions. Since it is better than running out of memory completely, though, it is better than doing nothing. To add swap space by hand, proceed as follows:

1. Use the dd command to create a file that can be used for swapping. Specify the size of the file you want to create in 1KB blocks. For example, the command dd if=/dev/zero of=/ swapfile bs=1024 count=100000 would add a 100MB empty file.

2. Mark the newly created file as a swap file using mkswap /swapfile.

3. Now as the last step in creating the swap file, use the command swapon /swapfile. This activates the swap file and will add it to your swap space immediately. Don't forget to add RAM to your system as soon as possible, because using swap space like this really is not ideal!

Using ulimit to Set Resource Limits

If you are having problems with some processes that allocate too many resources, the ulimit command may be useful. ulimit is a Bash internal that allows you to control the amount of resources that are available to the shell and processes started by it. Before starting its configuration, you should notice that ulimit is a universal setting; its limitations apply to everything that is started from the shell, and you can't limit individual processes. Therefore, you should really make sure this is what you want, so no unforeseen side effects can occur.

ulimit works with three kinds of settings. First, the *hard limit* is an absolute limit that you cannot change once it is applied. Next, the *soft limit* will be applied if set, but as root, you can change it. You can never set the soft limit above the hard limit. Last, a setting can have the unlimited value, which means there is no limitation applied to its working. Listing 28-3 gives an overview of the default settings applied by ulimit.

Listing 28-3. ulimit *Default Settings*

```
SFO:~ # ulimit -a
core file size          (blocks, -c) 0
data seg size           (kbytes, -d) unlimited
file size               (blocks, -f) unlimited
pending signals         (-i) 16381
max locked memo ry      (kbytes, -l) 32
max memory size         (kbytes, -m) unlimited
open files              (-n) 1024
pipe size               (512 bytes, -p) 8
POSIX message queues    (bytes, -q) 819200
stack size              (kbytes, -s) 8192
cpu time                (seconds, -t) unlimited
max user processes      (-u) 16381
virtual memory          (kbytes, -v) unlimited
file locks              (-x) unlimited
```

As you can see from Listing 28-3, you can use ulimit to define different settings that determine the working environment of new processes. To apply a new limitation, you must use command-line switches prepended by an S or an H, which indicate the soft or hard limit. For example, the command ulimit -Sn 2048 will set the soft limit for the number of open files to 2048, ulimit -Hn 4096 will set the hard limit, and ulimit -n will just display the current settings for open files. When applying these settings, don't forget to put them in your shell's start-up scripts such as /etc/profile; otherwise, they aren't persistent over a reboot. Table 28-1 gives an overview of all the options you can use with the ulimit command.

Table 28-1. ulimit *Options*

Option	Use
-a	Shows all current limits.
-c	Specifies the maximum size of core dump files. The default value is set to 0, which indicates no core dumps can be created.
-d	Specifies the maximum size of the process data segment. This is the section of a program that can contain variables used by the program. Don't use it, unless the person who wrote the program specifically told you that you have to use it.
-f	Specifies the maximum file size. This option limits the file size within the limits that are imposed by your file system.

Option	Use
-i	Specifies the maximum number of pending signals. These are signals that still need to be processed by the processes on your server. By default, this is set to 16,381, which is a reasonable amount.
-l	Specifies the maximum size in kilobytes that may be locked into memory. This is memory that cannot be moved dynamically anymore. You shouldn't set it to too large of a value.
-m	Specifies the maximum resident set size. This is the maximum amount of memory that a process can claim. Use no limitations, or set it to a rather large amount of memory.
-n	Specifies the maximum number of open file descriptors. This refers to the number of files that a process can have open simultaneously. By default, it is set to 1,024.
-p	Specifies the pipe size. This is the size in 512-byte blocks that is used when piping data from one command to another.
-q	Specifies the maximum number of bytes in a POSIX message queue. Processes can use these message queues to exchange data between these processes. Its default setting is 819,200 bytes, which is fine in most situations.
-s	Specifies the maximum stack size. This is the size of memory a process can use to store temporary variables. The default limitation is set to 8,192.
-t	Specifies the CPU time; use this to limit the maximum CPU time that a process can claim. This setting is useful if you have processes that have a tendency to claim all available CPU time.
-u	Specifies the maximum amount of user processes. This refers to processes that a single user can start. The default setting of 16,381 should fit in most situations.
-v	Specifies the maximum amount of virtual memory that is available to the shell. By default, no limitation is set for this parameter.
-x	Specifies the maximum number of files that can be locked simultaneously. By default, no limitation is set for this parameter.

Tuning the Kernel

Let there be no misunderstandings about it: the kernel of SUSE Linux Enterprise Server works well for most purposes. For some specific uses, however, your server may need some additional tuning. For more information, consult the documentation for the application you want to install. In tuning the kernel, the /proc directory plays an important role. The following sections will help you understand how you can use this directory.

Understanding the /proc File System

The /proc directory is an interface that a user can use to communicate to the kernel. The directory /proc is activated at an early stage in the boot procedure. To make it accessible, a special file system is used, the proc file system. In /proc, the kernel creates files that give status information about the process activity and generic kernel activity. For the overall status of the operating system, some generic files such as cpuinfo and modules are created to indicate what processes are doing; for every process, a subdirectory is created. This subdirectory has the PID of the process as its name. In Listing 28-4 you can see some of the files and directories that are created in /proc by default.

Listing 28-4. *Default Files and Directories in* /proc

```
SFO:/proc # ls
1     2490  3250  3679  4066  4185  5         driver       mtrr
1306  2512  3270  3690  4069  4190  5129      execdomains  net
1319  2546  3274  3716  4071  4194  5243      fb           partitions
1321  2555  3275  3717  4072  4218  6         filesystems  self
1343  2594  3301  3718  4081  4224  791       fs           slabinfo
135   2644  3345  3719  4084  4227  8         ide          splash
136   2702  3346  3720  4086  4255  883       interrupts   stat
137   2741  3396  3721  4088  4262  9         iomem        swaps
138   2742  3403  379   4089  4271  acpi      ioports      sys
1443  2753  344   3970  4094  4285  asound    irq          sysrq-trigger
1752  2783  3445  4     4095  4289  buddyinfo kallsyms     sysvipc
1795  2806  345   4011  4107  4456  bus       kcore        tty
1805  2822  3487  4015  4108  4804  cmdline   kmsg         uptime
1837  2824  3488  4016  4134  4806  config.gz loadavg      version
1842  3     3495  4051  4154  4871  cpuinfo   locks        vmnet
1996  3098  3526  4054  4155  4874  crypto    mdstat       vmstat
1997  3100  3546  4056  4164  4942  devices   meminfo      zoneinfo
2     3173  3551  4058  4171  4943  diskstats misc
2003  3228  3554  4063  4180  4961  dma       modules
2004  3232  3590  4065  4182  4964  dri       mounts
```

As an administrator, you can access the files and directories in /proc directly by using commands such as cat to view their contents. You should be aware, however, that many commands use the information in /proc to display it in a more accessible way. Sometimes the differences are not that big, though. You can use, for example, the cat /proc/modules command to get an overview of kernel modules that currently are loaded, or you can use the lsmod command instead. One of the most important advantages is that you can change some of the files in /proc, thus tuning the way your system works. You will see some examples of this in the "Using procinfo" section.

Some interesting features you can find in /proc are the PID directories. These are the directories that have the PID of a currently active process as their name. Listing 28-5 gives an example of the files that you can find in such a directory.

Listing 28-5. *Default Files in a* /proc *PID Directory*

```
SFO:/proc/5129 # ls
attr     cpuset   exe       mapped_base  mounts     root      stat    task
auxv     cwd      fd        maps         oom_adj    seccomp   statm   wchan
cmdline  environ  loginuid  mem          oom_score  smaps     status
```

In a PID directory, some of the most interesting files include the following:

cmdline: Contains the command used to start the process. This is useful to find out what process you are dealing with.

environ: Gives information about the working environment of the process. In this file, you can find variables used by the process.

fd: A subdirectory that contains information about the file descriptors that are in use by this process. This directory gives an indication of all its open files.

mem: A list of memory addresses in use by the process.

root: A link to the root directory that is used by the process. If a process runs in a chroot jail, you can find the directory that is used as the chroot jail here.

status: Generic information about the status of the process.

Using procinfo

One option to view information in the /proc file system is to monitor the individual files in it. As an alternative, you can use procinfo. The procinfo command displays information from the /proc file system nicely. When used without options, procinfo shows you information about memory usage, CPU load, swap activity, and IRQ usage; see Listing 28-6 for an example. You can also use several options with procinfo to indicate exactly what information you'd like to see.

Listing 28-6. *Example* procinfo *Output*

```
SFO:/ # procinfo
Linux 2.6.16.13-4-smp (geeko@buildhost) (gcc 4.1.0) #1 1CPU [SFO.]

Memory:      Total        Used        Free     Shared     Buffers
Mem:         2075400    1553972      521428         0       43716
Swap:        1052216          0     1052216

Bootup: Mon Aug 21 05:58:42 2006    Load average: 0.35 0.29 0.26 1/176 6295

user :       0:19:12.64    6.9%    page in :    1105376   disk 1:    31013r    43359w
nice :       0:01:01.97    0.4%    page out:     317807
system:      0:07:39.15    2.7%    page act:     124226
IOwait:      0:04:13.12    1.5%    page dea:          0
hw irq:      0:01:58.07    0.7%    page flt:    5546608
sw irq:      0:00:23.73    0.1%    swap in :          0
idle :       4:04:43.10   87.7%    swap out:          0
uptime:      4:39:14.77           context :   34328716

irq  0:   4187692 timer              irq  8:     47303 rtc
irq  1:     62037 i8042              irq  9:      1871 acpi
irq  2:         0 cascade [4]        irq 10:         1
irq  3:         1                    irq 11:   4554524 yenta, ehci_hcd:usb1
irq  4:         1                    irq 12:     20566 i8042
irq  5:         1                    irq 14:     77226 ide0
irq  7:   1297393 Intel 82801DB-ICH4, irq 15:   136261 ide1
```

You can use the procinfo command with several options to tune the output it provides. If you think that the default output is not enough, use procinfo -a, which will add to the output of the command a list of all kernel modules, blocks, and character devices as well as file systems that are currently loaded. To refresh the output of procinfo without stopping, you can use the option -f. Table 28-2 lists all other options that you can use with the procinfo command.

Table 28-2. procinfo *Options*

Option	Meaning
-f	Runs procinfo continuously. This refreshes the procinfo output every five seconds.
-nN	Use this option to refresh the procinfo output every *n* seconds. You can use this option in conjunction with -f only.
-m	Shows information about modules and device drivers.
-a	Shows all information that procinfo can give.
-d	In conjunction with the -f option, this option makes sure that for memory, CPU times, paging, swapping, context, and interrupt statistics, values per second instead of totals are provided.

Continued

Table 28-2. *Continued*

Option	Meaning
-D	Is like -d but will show the memory statistics as totals.
-Ffile	Redirects output to a file. Specify the name of a TTY to redirect output to a TTY.
-b	Shows read and write statistics for disk I/O.
-i	Shows the statistics for all IRQs. Ordinarily you will see information for active IRQs only.
-r	Shows an extra line to the memory information that shows real free memory. This adds the +/- buffers line that is displayed by the free command as well and that indicates the memory that is immediately accessible for processes on your system.
-v	Shows the current version number of the procinfo program.
-h	Shows a help message.

Tuning the Kernel

Kernel tuning is a difficult subject to handle properly. A default SUSE Linux Enterprise Server kernel works with parameters that do well in most situations. Of the many options that are available for tuning, some are specific for a certain kind of application. If, for example, you want to install Oracle 10g on your server, the Oracle documentation comes with an entire section on kernel-tuning options that you can use. Although these may greatly enhance the performance for your Oracle server, they may decrease the performance for other services you are using. Therefore, even when applying generic parameters, I recommend testing extensively before applying kernel-tuning options to your server.

Applying Optimization Options

Many options that you can use for performance optimization are written to the /proc/sys directory. In this directory you find several subdirectories that are related to certain performance areas on your server. You'll find two methods to tune parameters in this file. One is to redirect the new value to the appropriate configuration file. For example, to set the maximum number of file handles to 40,000, you can use echo 40000 > /proc/sys/fs/file-max. An alternative is to use the sysctl command to store the new settings permanently. sysctl is a service that is activated in the initial boot phase of your server. It reads the settings from the configuration file /etc/sysctl.conf and applies them. If no settings are configured in this file, the default settings are used. You can get an overview of these settings by using the sysctl -a command; see Listing 28-7 for a partial output of this command. Using sysctl -a is a good starting point if you want to work with sysctl anyway, because it shows a list of all the available options, which helps you use the correct syntax of options that you can put in the /etc/sysctl.conf file.

Listing 28-7. sysctl *Shows All Important Kernel Settings*

```
SFO:/etc # sysctl -a
dev.parport.default.spintime = 500
dev.parport.default.timeslice = 200
dev.cdrom.check_media = 0
dev.cdrom.lock = 1
dev.cdrom.debug = 0
dev.cdrom.autoeject = 0
dev.cdrom.autoclose = 1
```

```
dev.cdrom.info = CD-ROM information, Id: cdrom.c 3.20 2003/12/17
dev.cdrom.info =
dev.cdrom.info = drive name:              hdc
dev.cdrom.info = drive speed:             24
dev.cdrom.info = drive # of slots:        1
dev.cdrom.info = Can close tray:                    1
dev.cdrom.info = Can open tray:           1
dev.cdrom.info = Can lock tray:           1
dev.cdrom.info = Can change speed:        1
dev.cdrom.info = Can select disk:         0
dev.cdrom.info = Can read multisession: 1
dev.cdrom.info = Can read MCN:            1
dev.cdrom.info = Reports media changed: 1
dev.cdrom.info = Can play audio:                    1
dev.cdrom.info = Can write CD-R:                    1
dev.cdrom.info = Can write CD-RW:         1
dev.cdrom.info = Can read DVD:            1
dev.cdrom.info = Can write DVD-R:         1
dev.cdrom.info = Can write DVD-RAM:       0
dev.cdrom.info = Can read MRW:            1
dev.cdrom.info = Can write MRW:           1
dev.cdrom.info = Can write RAM:           1
```

Applying Common Performance-Tuning Options

You can apply some performance-tuning options in all situations. To give you an idea of how it works, in this section you will read about four common options:

- Setting the maximum number of file handles
- Tuning memory overcommitment
- Tuning swap activity
- Writing data from cache to hard disk

The first important performance-related parameter specifies the number of file handles. This specifies the amount of files that can be opened simultaneously. You can find the value that is currently in use in the file /proc/sys/fs/file-max.

Before tuning the value you see in this file, it is useful to be aware of the way the kernel works with file handles. Before doing anything to the maximum setting, refer to /proc/sys/fs/file-nr. This file gives information about the current amount of file handles in use. Listing 28-8 shows the content of this file.

Listing 28-8. *Showing the Current Settings for File Handles*

```
SFO:/proc/sys/fs # cat file-nr
4352      0       205911
```

In this file, the first number is the amount of file handles currently allocated. The second number indicates the amount of file handles allocated but not currently in use, and the third number indicates the maximum amount of file handles currently available. As you can see, the system monitored in Listing 28-8 is far from having a shortage of file handles because there is a large difference between the maximum amount of file handles and the amount of file handles currently in use. If the number of allocated file handles approaches the number of available file handles, it makes sense to raise the number of file handles that can be used concurrently. If, for example, you want to make 300,000 file handles available to your server, write the new setting to sysctl.conf by adding the line fs.file-max=300000.

Another parameter that can seriously affect the performance of your server is the memory overcommitment setting. Before explaining how to optimize it, I'll first discuss how memory overcommitment works. When processes are started, they request a certain amount of memory. By default, a process will always claim more memory than the amount of memory it really needs. This feature is called *memory overcommitment* and is in general considered to be good; it allows your process to reply promptly to a service request for which some more memory needs to be allocated. The disadvantage, however, is that when using memory overcommitment, you will run out of available memory faster. But the disadvantage of switching off memory overcommitment is that the process will need to issue a new request for memory if it needs more memory. In case the system is out of memory at that moment, this request may not be honored, which can lead to a crash of the process. If you are considering switching memory overcommitment off, always make sure you have a lot of swap space available, which will guarantee that a request for more memory can always be served. To switch using memory overcommitment on or off, you should tune the parameter vm.overcommit_memory. By default, this parameter has the value 0, which allows memory overcommitment. Switch it off by giving it the value 2. The parameter can have the value 1 as well, but this value currently is for experimental purposes only and should not be used.

The third kernel parameter that may be useful defines when the kernel should start swapping data out of real memory to your swap space. You can tune this by modifying the /proc/sys/vm/swapiness file. This file has a value from 0 to 100. If you want to use your swap file as late as possible, make sure this file has a low value. If, on the other hand, you want to use the swap file sooner, write a high value to this file. The default value for swapiness is set to 60. Tune the parameter as needed, but if you tune it, always use vmstat to monitor whether the new value is really good for the overall performance of your server. If, for example, it would lead to much higher values for swap in and swap out, it is probably not a good idea to tune this option, and you should set it to its original value.

The last generic parameters you can use to improve the performance of your server are related to writing data to the server's hard drive. When a process writes data, it has to wait for a signal given by the kernel that indicates that the data is really written. During that period, the process can't do anything else. Working with dirty cache provides a solution to this problem. This means the process doesn't write its data immediately to the hard drive but to an area in your server's RAM. This area is referred to as *cache*. Since RAM is about 1,000 times faster than a hard drive, this leads to a huge performance gain.

Using this cache in RAM does have a drawback. When RAM space is used for caching data that still needs to be written to the hard drive, it cannot be used for anything else. Therefore, you can use the dirty cache ratio parameter to indicate when the system should start writing this cache to the hard drive. The default value is set to 40 percent, which means that if 40 percent of your server's RAM is used for caching data that has to be written to the hard drive, it will start writing this data. If you have a server that is used mainly for read operations, you can set this parameter considerably lower, such as to 20 percent. If your server is mainly used for write operations, you can set the parameter higher, such as to 60 percent. To tune this parameter, tune /proc/sys/vm/dirty_ratio or the sysctl parameter vm.dirty_ratio.

In this section, you read about system tuning using the parameters in the /proc file system. I mentioned just a few examples here. More options are available; for an overview of much more kernel-tuning information, look at the files in the directory /usr/src/linux/Documentation/sysctl. Note that this directory is created only when you choose to install kernel sources to your server.

Using the Powertweak Utility

To make tuning your system a little easier, SUSE Linux Enterprise Server comes with the Powertweak utility (see Figure 28-2). For example, some of the tweaks I described earlier can be performed from Powertweak as well. You can start this utility from the YaST ➤ System interface.

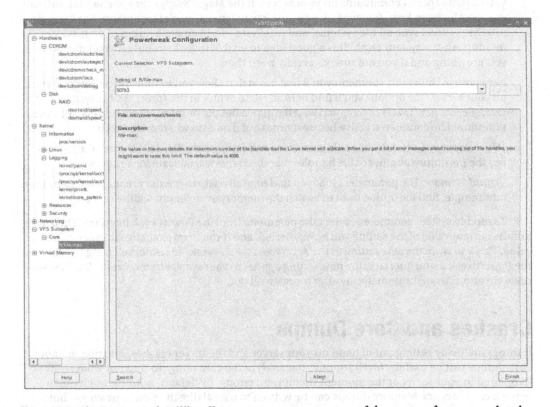

Figure 28-2. *The Powertweak utililty allows you to access some powerful system performance-related settings from a graphical menu interface.*

In the Powertweak utility, you get access to a lot of options you can use for tweaking and optimizing your server. Note that although Powertweak offers a graphical interface, it is a highly specialized tool, and you should use it only if you know what you're doing. In the worst case, applying the wrong setting in Powertweak may destroy your complete system.

Powertweak works with five main menu items:

Hardware: Here you'll find settings related to CD and disk devices. An example is the setting dev/cdrom/autoclose. This setting has the default value 1, which causes the kernel to close the door of the optical device when a mount is attempted. The settings in this menu are written to the /sys configuration tree.

Kernel: Under this item you'll find a variety of kernel-related options that are all written to the `/proc` file system. An example is the Ctrl+Alt+Del option, which specifies what should happen if the Ctrl+Alt+Del key sequence is used. Another interesting option that you'll find here is the `Magic Sysrq` setting. By changing this setting to the value 1, you enable Magic Sysrq keys. These keys can be useful for troubleshooting and debugging purposes and allow you to issue special commands on your server. If the Magic Sysrq keys are enabled, you can use the Alt+Sysrq keys, followed by a special key to issue a special command. For example, Alt+Sysrq+s will sync all file systems, and Alt+Sysrq+d will create a dump of your system memory after a system crash. It is a good idea to enable these keys only if you know what you are doing and if you are sure you really need them.

Networking: Under this submenu you'll find items that allow you to tune the networking stack on your server. The options you'll find here all relate to files in the `/proc/sys` file system. For example, the `net/ipv4/tcp_keep_alive` setting specifies the number of seconds that a connection should be considered active before it times out if no data was received on it.

VFS Subsystem: Currently, this menu contains one setting only. The `fs/file-max` setting specifies the maximum number of file handles that the kernel will allocate for a process.

Virtual Memory: The parameters that you find here all relate to memory management. You can, for example, find the option used to switch the memory overcommit feature on or off.

To modify system parameters, select the parameter from the Powertweak interface. Then monitor the current value of the setting you have selected, and if you need to change it, enter its new value. This will write the new setting to the `/etc/powertweak/tweaks` file. After selecting Finish from the Powertweak menu interface, the new setting applies to your system immediately. The new settings are also activated automatically after a system reboot.

Crashes and Core Dumps

If things are really getting out of hand on your server and the server crashes, creating memory core dumps can be useful. Novell support can analyze the core dump to find out what really happened to your server at the moment that it went wrong. By default, nothing will happen when a crash occurs. Memory dumps can be written to a local directory on your server, but alternatively they can be written to a server on the network as well. Be aware that if you choose the latter option, it may take a really long time to write the dump file to a server! If you want to use a kernel core dump server, you must have the netdump-server installed on that server. You can run the netdump-server service with its start script from `/etc/init.d`.

Tip A core dump is not the only way to provide information about your system when something goes wrong. At `http://support.novell.com`, you can download the `config.sh` script. Run this script, and it will analyze all the important configuration files on your server and put the results in a tar archive. You can then send this archive to Novell support for analysis.

To enable your system to make core dumps, you have to define what should happen when your system crashes. The following steps describe how you can do this from YaST. I recommend enabling this from YaST instead of directly tuning the appropriate configuration files, because using YaST makes sure that all the necessary kernel modules are loaded as well:

1. Make sure that the following packages are installed:

   - crash
   - lkcdutils
   - lkcdutils-netdump-server

2. Start YaST, and then select System ➤ /etc/sysconfig Editor. Then select System ➤ Kernel ➤ LKCD. This option gives access to all the parameters that are related to creating core dumps on your server (see Figure 28-3).

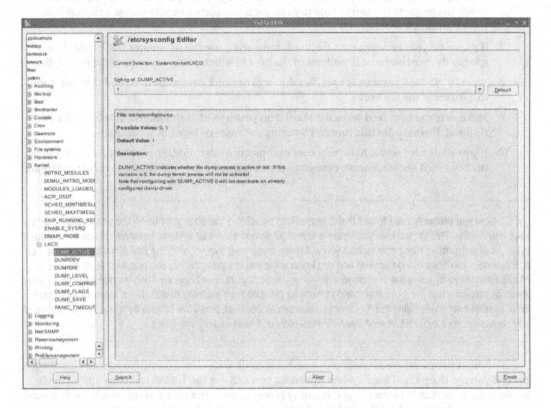

Figure 28-3. *From YaST, you can use the* /etc/sysconfig *editor to tune parameters in the* /etc/sysconfig/LKCD *file.*

3. First, turn on kernel core dumps by giving the parameter DUMP_ACTIVE the value 1.

4. Then specify in what directory a dump should be created. By default, it will be written to /var/log/dump. Make sure the file system this directory is on contains enough free space to create the dump file.

5. Use the DUMP_LEVEL parameter to specify what exactly should be dumped. Choose from the following values:

   - *0*: Nothing is dumped.
   - *1*: The dump header and the first 128 KB are dumped.

- *2*: The header and kernel pages are dumped.
- *4*: Everything is dumped, with the exception of memory pages that currently are free.
- *8*: Everything is dumped, including free memory pages. If you want to use this option, make sure that in the dump file destination directory you have an amount of free disk space that is equal to the amount of memory in your server.

6. Tune the PANIC_TIMEOUT value to specify how long after a kernel panic the system will reboot. The default value for this parameter is five seconds, which is too short if you want to dump complete kernel core files. Make sure you give this process at least the time it needs to complete the kernel core dumps; for a complete memory dump, this may take several minutes.

7. If a host on your network runs the netdump-server, use the parameter TARGET_HOST to specify the host name or IP address of the host to which you want to send the dump file.

8. The ETH_ADDRESS parameter specifies the local network device used to send the core dump to a server in the network.

9. Make sure the boot.lkcd service is started on your server. It should run at least in the boot runlevel. Enable it for this runlevel by using the inserv boot.lkcd command.

10. If you want your server to receive core dumps from other machines as well, after enabling the boot.lkcd service, enable netdump-server using the inserv netdump-server command.

Tip Now you probably want to see that it works, don't you? You can do that by using the proper Magic Sysrq keys commands. This tip will help you cause a kernel panic and stop your system; however, realize the consequences of performing these commands: you will really crash your system, with the risk of losing everything on it. Make sure you have a good backup and you know what you are doing before you proceed! First, enable the Magic Sysrq keys by using the command echo 1 > /proc/sys/kernel/sysrq. Then (to make the damage as small as possible) use the sync command to write all the data from memory to disk. Next, remount all file systems in read-only mode using the Alt+Sysrq+u key sequence. Next, crash the system by using the Als+Sysrq+d key sequence. Your system will now freeze immediately and start making the dump.

For most people, there is really only one thing to do with a core dump: send it to Novell support. If you are deep into Linux system internals, you can use the lcrash utility to interactively analyze the core dump. Since using this utility is way beyond the scope of this book, I will not discuss it any further here. Just check that a dump was created in /var/log/dump/0, and if it was, send it to Novell support.

Summary

In this chapter, you were introduced to Linux optimization. I provided some generic hints about how to make your server work more efficiently. The tips in this chapter are only an introduction to the science of optimization. To really get the most from your server, you should analyze what the server is doing and how the most important applications on your server are using system resources. When you know how that works, you can develop a good plan for performance optimization on your server. In the next chapter, you will read about how to configure Heartbeat on your server to provide high-availability clustering with SUSE Linux Enterprise Server.

PART 4

◼◼◼

Advanced SUSE Linux Enterprise Server Configuration

In the preceding three parts of this book, you learned all the basic skills necessary for administering SUSE Linux Enterprise Server. In this part, I'll cover some of the more advanced topics. These topics should especially please you if you're an advanced user, although anyone who has mastered the content of the first three parts will understand the information. Some of the subjects covered in this part are the hardware and kernel management. You will also learn how to optimize the performance of SUSE Linux Enterprise Server, create a cluster, and include shared storage with Heartbeat and iSCSI.

■ ■ ■

## CHAPTER 29

Configuring SUSE Linux Enterprise Server 10 for High-Availability Clustering

You have several options for using clustering in a Linux environment. One of the most popular is the Linux-HA project. The software from this project, also known as Heartbeat, allows administrators to configure a high-availability cluster solution in which vital applications can fail over to another node when the node currently hosting them goes down. In this chapter, you will learn what high-availability clustering is. I'll cover the following topics:

- Introducing Linux clustering
- Designing a high-availability (HA) cluster
- Configuring shared storage for the clustered environment
- Configuring failover clustering with Heartbeat
- Shooting the other node in the head and the meatware device
- Configuring a Heartbeat 2–style cluster with YaST

Introducing Linux Clustering

Definitions seem to abound regarding the term *cluster*; therefore, before discussing the Linux-HA cluster solution, it makes sense to define what exactly I'm talking about. In its broadest meaning, the word *cluster* is a group of computers working together. In a more specific way, clusters of computers are installed for three reasons:

- To increase computing power
- To distribute workload between computers
- To increase the availability of applications

The first definition refers to a *high-performance* cluster, which is also referred to as a *computational* cluster. In such a cluster solution, different computers are working together on the same task. The essence of such a cluster is that nodes are capable of sharing resources with each other. This is because computers in a high-performance cluster need to know about each other when another node has idle CPU cycles. In such a clustered environment, memory, CPUs, and storage can be shared in the most complex applications. As an alternative, however, you can also use application-level high-performance clustering. In such a solution, not the entire node is part of the cluster—just an application that is used on the node. Such a solution can work perfectly across the Internet. An example of an application-level high-performance cluster is the SETI@home project (`http://setiathome.berkeley.edu/`), where an application on a computer is activated whenever idle CPU cycles are available.

The second type of cluster, a *load-balancing* cluster, has as its goal distributing the workload between computers. In a load-balanced solution, different nodes host the same application, such as a web server. Some intelligence needs to be added to these nodes that are working together to distribute incoming requests between all hosting nodes. This intelligence is the load balancing. In its simplest form, a DNS server can perform the tasks of a load balancer and distribute tasks between different servers by using a technique known as *round-robin*. The idea is that two or more resource records are created in the DNS database, all referring to the same name, but to different IP addresses:

```
webserver.somewhere.com            a          192.168.0.10
webserver.somewhere.com            a          192.168.0.20
webserver.somewhere.com            a          192.168.0.30
```

The round-robin technique evenly distributes requests between all nodes in the network but has some disadvantages. The most important disadvantage is known as *black holing*. When one of the servers goes offline, ordinarily the DNS server has no way of knowing that the server is down and continues sending requests to the downed server. Another disadvantage is that the DNS server has no way of knowing how many spare CPU cycles the recipient server can offer; in other words, it cannot differentiate between a heavily loaded server and one with relatively little to do. Also, if a cache-only DNS server is used, round-robin will not work for that site, because a cache-only DNS server will always send packets addressed to a given name to the same IP address.

Because of the drawbacks of DNS round-robin as a load-balancing solution, other, more specialized software is available. The most used of all open source software packages is the Linux Virtual Server software; see `http://www.linux-vs.org` for more information. Also, many companies prefer not to use an open source solution for load balancing and instead use specialized hardware. The advantage is that this specialized hardware can perform tasks that are rather difficult to do with just software, such as properly terminating SSL connections or just increasing the throughput to a maximum by using chips that are programmed uniquely for that purpose.

The third type of cluster is the high-availability cluster. The most important goal of a high-availability cluster is—as the name implies—to increase the availability of important services. High availability has become important in today's marketplace where people want to purchase goods or services on a 24/7 basis, because the high-availability cluster makes sure that when an important server in the cluster goes down, another server can take over the services in a matter of seconds. This high availability is exactly what the Linux Heartbeat project addresses. In a well-configured Heartbeat cluster, the nodes involved will monitor each other, and a signal will be generated when one of the nodes in the cluster goes down so that another node can take over the work. The result is that the user will notice no important downtime and can just continue working with the application involved.

Designing an HA Cluster Solution

To create a properly functioning HA cluster solution, you should first be aware of the way this type of cluster works. In this section, I'll answer the following questions:

- What exactly can you fail over?
- How many hosts can be configured in an HA cluster?

- How are these hosts monitoring each other?
- What happens when a node fails?

The Linux-HA suite works with software resources. Basically, a resource is some service managed by the Heartbeat daemons. To configure a resource, the first element needed is a load script that is used to control the resource. This is a load script similar to the role of /etc/init.d, which is used to start various Linux services. Typically, these load scripts are in /etc/init.d or in /etc/ha.d/resource.d. Next, you need a generic file that refers to these resource load scripts. This file is /etc/ha.d/haresources in Heartbeat 1 and the Cluster Information Base (CIB) in Heartbeat 2. In these, first the primary node where the resource is used is referred to, and next the name of the resource is referred to, followed by some options if they are required. In a two-node cluster, the other node in the cluster will automatically become the backup server. Heartbeat 1 supported only two cluster nodes, whereas in Heartbeat 2 a maximum of 16 nodes is supported.

In addition to the cluster resources, you'll need a configuration file where the Heartbeat protocol settings are configured. These settings determine how often Heartbeat packages are sent over the network to see whether the other nodes are still alive. In a Heartbeat cluster, packages are sent periodically because the cluster nodes depend on them to determine whether the other nodes are still alive. These Heartbeat packages typically are not sent over the network the users are using to connect to the services offered; this is because in that scenario a faulty configured switch may lead to a node being cast off the cluster because it is not reachable anymore. In a two-node cluster, you can use a dedicated serial connection, whereas in a multinode cluster that can be used in a Heartbeat 2 environment, you should configure a dedicated network for higher fault tolerance. If you use a dedicated Ethernet network, it serves multiple purposes, because at the same time you can use it for synchronizing shared file systems as well.

You must also be cautious to prevent what's known as a *split-brain condition* from occurring. A split brain arises when more than one node in the cluster thinks it owns the clustered resources. For example, such a situation can become critical if two nodes try to modify the same database at the same time, because this may eventually corrupt the database. To prevent this, one must provide for a solution to forcibly shut down a failing node in the cluster when a split brain is detected. In Heartbeat, for this purpose a Stonith ("shoot the other node in the head") device is used.

In summary, you should dedicate at least two physical network paths in the cluster. First, there is the network used to access the cluster. Then there is the network used to send Heartbeat messages and to synchronize shared storage. Optionally, there may even be a third physical path configured, which is for users to obtain administrative access to nodes in your cluster. Whatever solution you are using for the Heartbeat network, make sure no routing occurs between the user access network and the Heartbeat network to prevent unwanted paths.

Using Shared Storage

In a clustered environment, a service can run on all nodes in the cluster. If this happens, you often need to guarantee continuous access to the data used by that application. Imagine a situation where a Samba server is active on node1, providing access to shared directories that are on a local volume. After a failure, not only the Samba service needs to fail over to another node in the cluster but also the shared files still must be accessible. To guarantee this, you need some kind of shared storage. Not only is the shared storage needed for access to shared data, offered by the clustered application, but it is also needed for access to the shared configuration files that are used in the cluster. If, for example, this Samba server fails over from node1 to node2, the configuration file /etc/samba/smb.conf on both servers should be the same to ensure the Samba server works the same after it has migrated to another server. You can, of course, make sure these configuration files are copied manually; however, it is more workable to use some kind of shared storage solution.

Overview of Shared Storage Solutions

You can implement shared storage in different ways:

- Rsync file synchronization
- The Distributed Replicated Block Device (DRBD)
- iSCSI
- A storage area network (SAN)

The simplest way to make sure that files are the same on all nodes in the cluster is by using file-level synchronization with rsync. This software solution is configured to monitor some specific files in the clustered environment and synchronize any changes occurring to these files. Rsync is a usable solution to synchronize some individual files; however, if lots of data is involved, it is not the best solution that is available. The most important disadvantage of using rsync is that there is always some delay while synchronizing the files.

In a two-node cluster, you can use DRBD to provide a shared storage solution. Using DRBD, an entire partition is synchronized over the network. This way, DRBD implements a RAID 1 solution across the network. Such a solution guarantees that data blocks are synchronized across the network whenever a change occurs, thus ensuring that there is always a complete up-to-date backup on one other node. The drawback of this solution is that it is usable in a two-node cluster only. In a two-node cluster, however, it is by far the easiest solution that can be implemented; therefore, in the next section, you will read how to configure this environment.

The third common solution for shared storage is iSCSI. In iSCSI, a local disk on a server that is configured as an iSCSI target is made accessible to other servers in the network. Note that the iSCSI target ordinarily is not part of the cluster itself. On the servers that want to access the storage that is made available by the iSCSI target, you must use iSCSI initiator software. The nodes in this environment use the SCSI protocol packages sent across the network encapsulated in IP packages.

On the storage device on the server that is configured as an iSCSI target, partitions, complete disks, or volumes are created that can be shared across the network. In such a configuration, it is common to provide one shared storage device for each service that is configured in the cluster. If a service goes down on one server, the service itself and the associated shared storage device will fail over to another server—as long as the server that is used as the iSCSI target remains available. iSCSI is a good solution to give access to data in a clustered environment.

Finally, you can use SAN for shared storage. This is the most robust solution, but it is also a solution that has a disadvantage: cost. Of course, if a SAN has already been deployed for other purposes, by all means consider using it for these purposes. Otherwise, you might consider some of the aforementioned solutions. If you want the best, most reliable, and most flexible solution for centralized storage in your network, however, use a SAN.

The Role of Cluster-Aware File Systems

Apart from the issue of the shared storage device, a cluster-aware file system might also be necessary. Whether you need such a solution depends on the kind of cluster you are using—an active-active or active-passive cluster solution.

In an *active-active* cluster, different nodes in the cluster provide redundancy to each other for a given service, where the given service is already active on those servers. For instance, this is a common situation for web servers hosting several virtual servers. If the HTTP process on one of the nodes in the cluster goes down, the virtual servers running on that server can just be migrated to another node in the cluster on which an HTTP server is already active. Of course, the other node would need to have enough available system resources to host these new virtual servers.

In an *active-passive* cluster environment, the resource is running on just one node in the cluster. If this node should go down, the resources need to be started on another node in the cluster, which of course would take some time to complete. If in an active-active cluster a resource running on two different nodes needs to write to the shared storage device, on that shared storage device a file system would need to be used that allows more than one node to simultaneously write to it. By default, a Reiser or ext3 file system does not allow that. To make it possible anyway, you need to use a specialized cluster-aware file system that allows access to more than one node at the same time. The OCFS2 file system that was originally released by Oracle for use in an active-active cluster environment can do that for you. Other file systems are available as well, but on SUSE Linux Enterprise Server 10, OCFS2 is preferred for these purposes.

Configuring Shared Storage with the Distributed Replicated Block Device

A simple and stable shared storage solution for the Heartbeat cluster is the Distributed Replicated Block Device (DRBD). The advantage is that you don't need to purchase an external storage device because you can use a local partition or existing disk on the cluster nodes. This section will discuss how to configure a shared storage device using DRBD. The setup discussed in this section assumes a two-node cluster where DRBD is used. One of these servers is configured as the master node that has access to the shared storage device; the other node is configured as the slave node. This node gets access to the shared storage device only when Heartbeat grants access to it. You should be aware that for a complete solution, the DRBD device needs to be managed by Heartbeat, which in turn makes sure the device is always accessible via one of the nodes in the cluster.

Note Remember, DRBD is good for a two-node cluster. Multinode clusters require another solution, such as iSCSI or a SAN for shared storage.

Basically, the DRBD is a RAID 1 solution running over the network. In this configuration, one node has read-write access to the DRBD device, and the other node has no access at all—it just functions as a backup. For sure, it makes sense to give read-write access to the node that currently has the clustered service running. To use the DRBD device, you have to create a specific device in the Linux device tree in /dev. Ordinarily, the device is created automatically when all required components are present on your server, but in some rare cases, you need to use the mknod command to create the device. Apart from that, you need to create the DRBD configuration files. Finally, the DRBD service that gives access to the device has to be started, and one of the nodes needs to be assigned as the primary device. The complete procedure to do this is as follows:

1. Install the DRBD software from YaST (see Chapter 9 for more about that). For a working DRBD environment, you require two packages. First, you always need the DRBD packages. You also need the package that contains the modules for the kernel you are running. The name of this package is drbd-kmp-*XXXX*, where *XXXX* refers to the kernel that you are running; replace it, for example, with *default* if you are running the default kernel or with *smp* if you are running an SMP kernel.

Tip Not sure what kernel you are currently running? In the directory /boot, you will find a file whose name starts with vmlinux. The name of this file can be vmlinux-2.6.16.21-0.8-default.gz, for example. From this filename you can see what DRBD kernel module package you need; the default in the example filename is used in the name of the kernel package you need.

---

2. After installing the DRBD software, it is a good idea to copy the example DRBD configuration file in /usr/share/doc/packages/drbd/drbd.conf to /etc/drbd.conf and edit this file. Comments in this file explain perfectly how to configure the DRBD device. Make sure the configuration file has the same contents on both servers; otherwise, the DRBD device would be available from just one server.

3. For a simple setup to provide the DRBD device, you can use the parameters shown in Listing 29-1. Note that this is just a workable example; your environment may require a different setup. Consult the drbd.conf man page for more information on how to set up the DRBD device.

Listing 29-1. *DRBD Configuration Example*

```
resource rdrbd0 {
    protocol C;
        startup {
        wfc-timeout 0;
        degr-wfc-timeout 120;
    disk {
        on-io-error detach;
    }
        syncer {
        rate 100M;
        group 1;
        al-extents 257;
}

    on node1 {
        device      /dev/drbd0;
        disk        /dev/sdb1;
        address     192.168.1.210:7788;
        meta-disk   internal;
    }

    on node2 {
        device      /dev/drbd0;
        disk        /dev/sdb1;
        address 192.168.1.220:7788;
        meta-disk   internal;
    }
}
```

This example consists of two parts. In the first part, some generic DRBD settings are configured. These settings are applied to the device drbd0, which is specified from the resource drbd0 setting. Next, the protocol that has to be used is defined. You have three possible choices: protocol A, B, and C. Protocol A is the fastest, but protocol C is the most secure, so make your own choice about which is more important to you: speed or security. If you are using DRBD to create a device in a trusted LAN environment, protocol A is recommended.

Next, you must configure some timeout values. The first parameter, wfc-timeout 0, specifies the amount of time that the init script blocks the boot process until the resources are connected. By default this value is set to 0, in which case the init script doesn't care about the actual state of the DRBD device. This ordinarily is a good setting to ensure that the boot process on your server is running smoothly. Next, the degr-wfc-timeout parameter specifies how long to wait for the connection timeout if this node is a degraded cluster. The default value specifies that it has to wait for two minutes. This allows the other node in the cluster to come back and hand over control to the device.

Be aware that this value may result in a situation where clients cannot connect to required services for this entire period.

Next the disk parameter on-io-error detach specifies what has to happen if the drbd0 device reports an error. The option detach specifies that the node drops the storage device and continues in diskless mode.

The syncer parameters are the last set of generic parameters but not the least important; they specify how synchronization between the disk devices should occur. If you forget them, the performance of synchronization between nodes is worse than lousy, so you should tune these parameters. The parameter rate 100M in the example sets the maximum amount of bandwidth for synchronizing the device to 100MB. If you do have a 100MB network and you want other traffic to happen as well, this is not a good choice, and you should set it lower so that other processes have some bandwidth as well. Since, however, in a properly designed cluster you do have a dedicated LAN for DRBD anyway, you might as well set it to 100MB. The parameters group and al-extents define the amount of physical extents that can be synchronized at the same time. Each physical extent is 4MB, so a total of 257 will allow synchronization of about 1GB at the same time. Basically, the value for the all parameters should reflect the amount of 4MB blocks needed to synchronize the DRBD device properly; for 4GB a value of 1024 is a good value, for example, as long as the available bandwidth on your network supports this. If it doesn't, I recommend setting a lower value, such as the default value of 257.

Next, some sections define how both DRBD nodes should be configured. The first parameter specifies the name of the DRBD device. Then the next parameter specifies the name of the internal device on the server that should be used as a DRBD device; this is the disk or partition that is used by the DRBD device. It makes life easier if the device names are similar on both nodes, but this is no requirement. Next, the address and port numbers need to be specified so that both nodes can find each other. Last, the meta-disk parameter specifies where metadata should be written. Ordinarily, the device specified with the disk parameter is used for this purpose. Be careful that nothing else is stored on the device mentioned, because it will all be gone once the DRBD device starts writing metadata to this device.

Now that the drbd.conf file has been created, you need to copy it to the other server that is involved in the DRBD setup. If you are currently on the server with the name node1 and you want to copy the configuration to node2, use the following command:

```
scp /etc/drbd.conf node2:/etc/drbd.conf
```

When the configuration files have been created on both servers, use the rcdrbd start command on both servers to start the DRBD services. If this happens without any obvious error messages, use the command cat /proc/drbd to monitor that the DRBD device was successfully created on both devices. Sometimes there may be an error message when loading the DRBD device, stating that the device is currently busy. If that happens, I recommend trying again in a few moments, which helps most of the time. For serious troubleshooting, use tail /var/log/messages for error messages that may indicate why the DRBD device cannot be started.

Now that you have verified that the service has started successfully, you need to make sure it starts automatically the next time you boot your servers. To insert the service to all relevant runlevels on your servers so that it will be booted automatically, use the command insserv drbd on both servers. The state of the DRBD service is currently that it will be started on both servers automatically. At this stage, however, it is not usable because it is waiting on information from the Heartbeat software to get activated. To make it usable, you need to configure the Heartbeat software in a way that one of the servers is configured as the primary server and the other is used as the secondary.

Before you configure DRBD with Heartbeat, you can dry-test it by making one of the nodes the primary node. To do that, use the following command on one of the nodes:

```
drbdsetup /dev/drbd0 primary --do-what-I-say
```

The result of this command is that one of the nodes has become the primary node. From this node, the DRBD device is writable, so you can create a file system on it and mount it on that node. Before doing that, you should use the rcdrbd status command to make sure your node has been set successfully as the primary node. This command reads the contents of the /proc/drbd file and returns a result, as shown in Listing 29-2.

Listing 29-2. *Monitoring DRBD with the* rcdrbd status *Command*

```
node1:~# rcdrbd status
drbd driver loaded OK; device status:
version: 0.7.18 (api:78/proto:74)
SVN Revision: 2186 build by lmb@chip, 2006-05-04 17:08:27
 0:  cs:Connected st:Primary/Secondary ld:Consistent
        ns:1442772 nr:0 dw:265588 dr:1177569 al:74 bm:216 lo:0 pe:0 ua:0 ap:0
```

In this information, the most important part is the line where you can see that the device is connected and this device is configured as the primary server.

Configuring iSCSI

DRBD is one solution to create a shared storage device on SUSE Linux Enterprise Server. Another solution that doesn't involve expensive hardware is iSCSI. iSCSI support is included in SUSE Linux Enterprise Server as well. In this section, you'll learn how to set it up with YaST.

In an iSCSI configuration, the system has two vital parts. First, the iSCSI target software is a service that needs to be activated and gives access to a shared disk device on the machine where it runs. This can, for example, be a hard drive you've added to your server for this purpose. You can use any server in your network for this purpose, but typically it is recommended not to run it on a server that is a member of the cluster. Alternatively, many SANs offer iSCSI access as well.

The second part of an iSCSI configuration is the iSCSI initiator. This is a service that runs on the nodes in the cluster that need to access the shared storage. You can configure both the iSCSI initiator and the iSCSI target with YaST. The following steps explain how to do this. You'll first read how to install the iSCSI target on the server that offers the shared storage and then how to configure the iSCSI initiator on the servers that need to access the shared storage.

1. From YaST, select Network Services ➤ iSCSI Target. You'll see a prompt now that you need to install the iSCSI software. After installing the software from your installation media, you'll see the screen shown in Figure 29-1.

2. First, on the Service tab, select When Booting to make sure the service starts automatically when your server boots. If a firewall is enabled on your server, don't forget to open the firewall port as well.

3. On the Global tab, you can configure authentication for the iSCSI target. This is a useful feature if you are running Heartbeat in a nonsecured network. If all nodes are in the same network segment and no others can connect anyway, you don't need either incoming or outgoing authentication. If you want to make sure that no problems can occur with illegal host authentication, use one of the authentication options.

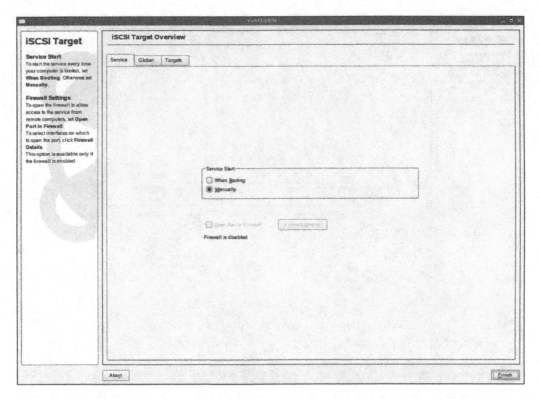

Figure 29-1. *All aspects of the iSCSI target can be configured on the iSCSI Target Overview screen.*

4. On the Targets tab (see Figure 29-2), you need to configure what you want to share and how you want to share it. You need to specify the following options here:

- *Target*: This specifies the name of the target. By default, the name is automatically generated and includes an iSCSI-qualified name (iqn), followed by a year-month specification of the date that the target was created, followed by the reversed name of the domain your server is in, such as iqn.2006-08.nl.sandervanvugt.

- *Identifier*: This is a unique identifier for the target. It is generated automatically for you, and ordinarily, you don't need to change it.

- *LUN*: This specifies the LUN used for this target. This option is relevant when configuring the iSCSI target in a SAN environment; for local disk devices, you can keep its default value 0 in almost all cases.

- *Path*: This is the most important part of the iSCSI target configuration; it specifies the path to the local disk device that is shared. Note that in the example a file is shared. This is perfectly possible but not common. In most situations, you probably want to specify the name of the real disk device you want to share with the iSCSI target.

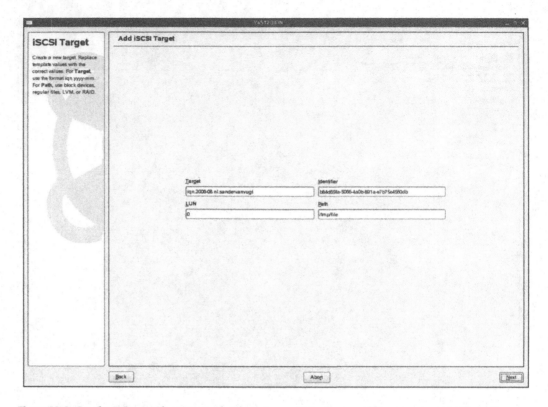

Figure 29-2. *On the Targets tab, you specify what you want to share and how you want to share it.*

5. After specifying the name of the device you want to share, click Next. This adds the target to the list of targets that are available. Then click Finish to store the configuration and start the target.

Note The iSCSI target cannot reload a new configuration without shutting down the service first. This will disconnect all current sessions and therefore is something that needs to be planned well.

---

6. After configuring the target, you need to configure the initiator as well. Remember, you have to do that on all the nodes in the cluster that you want to be able to access the storage device that is shared by the target. Also to configure the initiator, you need to install the software first. YaST will prompt you automatically for that after you have selected Network Services ➤ iSCSI Initiator to start the initiator configuration module. This opens the screen shown in Figure 29-3. On the Service tab, select When Booting first to start the iSCSI initiator service when booting.

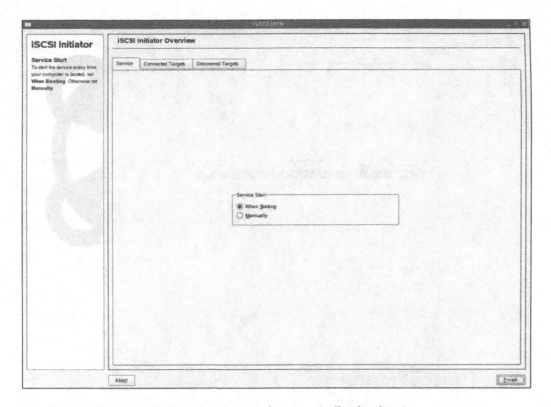

Figure 29-3. *Make sure the iSCSI initiator is started automatically when booting your server.*

7. To connect to an iSCSI target, you need to enter its details. You can specify them manually, but it's far easier to use the target discovery functionality that is offered on the Discovered Targets tab. On this tab, click Discovery, then enter the IP address of the machine that offers iSCSI target services, and finally click Discover. This ordinarily discovers the target automatically (see Figure 29-4); all you now have to do is connect to it. Do this by clicking the Log In button on the Discovered Targets tab.

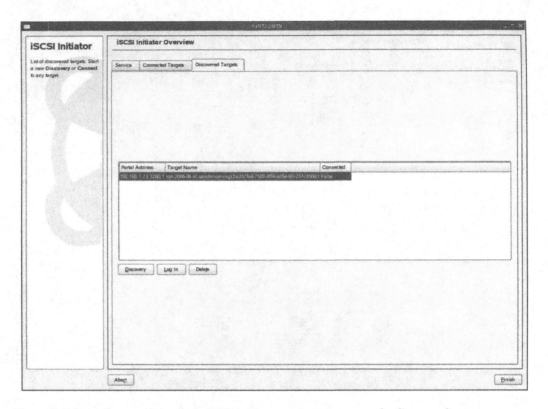

Figure 29-4. *To make connecting to an iSCSI initiator easier, you can use the discovery feature to enter its details automatically.*

8. Now check the Connected Targets tab to see that you are indeed connected to the selected iSCSI target. This will show you the iSCSI target you've just selected, with the start-up method Manual specified. To connect to the iSCSI target automatically, click the Toggle Start-Up button. This changes the start-up type to Automatic (see Figure 29-5), which makes sure the iSCSI connection is established automatically the next time your server boots.

9. Click Finish to complete the procedure. This writes the configuration information to the system. To verify that everything really works, you can start the YaST Partitioner utility. In this utility, the iSCSI device will be listed as a Type IET-VIRTUAL-DISK device. In its properties, you can see that this device really connects to the shared storage you've configured on your server.

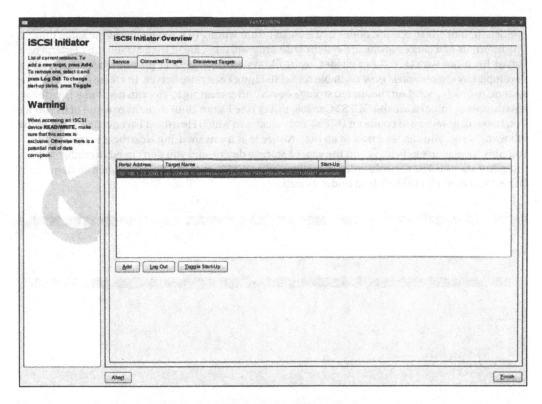

Figure 29-5. *On the Connected Targets tab, click the Toggle Start-Up button to make sure a connection to the iSCSI target is established automatically when the server boots.*

Configuring OCFS2 in an Active-Active Cluster Environment

The previous procedure taught you how to create an iSCSI device that can be shared amongst different hosts at the same time. To complete the procedure, you can now create a file system on it. You can choose from different file systems that are available in SUSE Linux Enterprise Server 10. The first choice you have to make is whether this will be a cluster file system or a nonclustered file system. If it is a nonclustered file system such as ext3 or Reiser, you should be aware that only one node can write to the file system at the same time. This usually is a perfect solution for the active-passive cluster environment that Heartbeat typically offers. If you want to configure an active-active cluster where more nodes offer a resource at the same time, it makes sense to use a cluster-aware file system. The advantage is that in such an environment, all nodes in the cluster can write to the file system at the same time. This is advantageous in the following scenarios:

- You are using an application that can work in an active-active environment, such as Oracle RAC.

- You have configured a generic Linux service for load balancing and want the servers to run multiple times on multiple nodes while always offering access to the same files.

- You are using Xen for virtualization in your network and want to use the live migration feature. (See Chapter 31 for more details about Xen.)

As you can imagine, a cluster-aware file system needs to perform some specific tasks. Most important, it needs to prevent nodes in the cluster from writing to the same file at the same time. The internals of a cluster-aware file system ordinarily will take care of that. SUSE Linux Enterprise Server 10 comes with OCFS2 as a cluster-aware file system. This general-purpose file system was developed by Oracle and is now available on SUSE Linux Enterprise Server. To create an OCFS2 file system, use `mkfs.ocfs2` on the shared storage device. After creating it, you can use it in a Heartbeat environment. You can use the OCFS2 Console utility (see Figure 29-6) to manage some of its properties. It even allows you to create an OCFS2-only cluster in which Heartbeat isn't needed at all. In the following steps, you can read how to do that. Notice that if you are using Heartbeat for clustering, you only have to use `mkfs.ocfs2` on the shared storage device, and you don't need to configure anything from the OCFS2 Console utility. Heartbeat and OCFS2 are tuned for each other, so from OCFS2 you can refer to Heartbeat nodes as well.

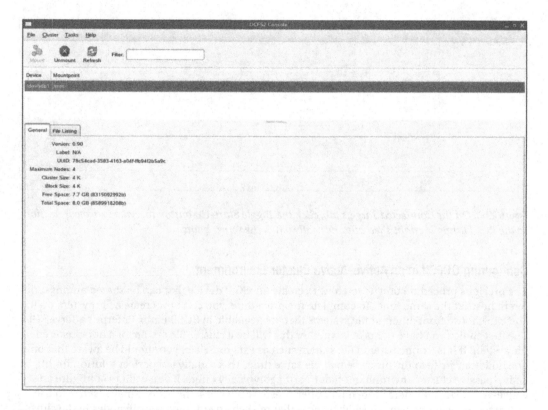

Figure 29-6. *You can use the OCFS2 Console utility to manage properties of the OCFS2 cluster-aware file system.*

The following steps show you how to configure OCFS2 to be used in an active-active cluster. The procedure explains how to install it on top of an iSCSI configuration:

1. Make sure that on all nodes in the cluster, the iSCSI initiator is operational, and the shared storage is available. You can check this with the `fdisk -l` command, which should show you a device that doesn't have a valid partition table.

2. Use a partitioning utility to create a partition on the shared device. Consult Chapter 8 for more details on how to do that.

3. On any node in the cluster, start the OCFS2 Console utility by running the ocfs2console command from a console.

4. In the OCFS2 Console utility, select Tasks ➤ Format to format it with the OCFS2 file system. Accept the default values, and click OK to continue. If more than four nodes need concurrent access to the OCFS2 file system, change the number of node slots to a value greater than its default value 4. Formatting now starts. It will take some time before it completes.

5. Still in OCFS2 Console, click Cluster ➤ Configure Nodes. You will now see a message indicating that you need to run the command /etc/init.d/o2cb enable to make sure that OCFS2 cluster services are started when your machine boots. Do this on all nodes that you want to give access to the shared storage.

6. On the Node Configuration screen, use the Add button to add all nodes that need access to the OCFS2 file system. Then click Apply. This adds both nodes to the cluster. Now click Close to close the Node Configuration screen.

7. Now select the device that the OCFS2 file system is on, and click Mount. Enter the directory you want to mount it on, and then click Mount to mount the file system. This again will take some time.

8. Next, from the OCFS2 Console, click Cluster ➤ Propagate Configuration to push the configuration to the other nodes in the cluster. To do this, use SSH. Reply to all prompts that the SSH program gives you to copy the configuration to all the other nodes. The result of the cluster configuration is written in the file /etc/ocfs2/cluster.conf. Listing 29-3 shows what it should look like at this point.

Listing 29-3. *Example of the OCFS2 Cluster Configuration File*

```
node:
        ip_port = 7777
        ip_address = 192.168.1.210
        number = 0
        name = node1
        cluster = ocfs2

node:
        ip_port = 7777
        ip_address = 192.168.1.220
        number = 1
        name = node2
        cluster = ocfs2

cluster:
        node_count = 2
        name = ocfs2
```

9. Mount the OCFS2 file system on the other nodes as well. Before doing that, make sure the Oracle 2 cluster base (o2cb) service is running by entering the command /etc/init.d/o2cb enable. Then use mount -t ocfs2 /dev/sdb1 /data to mount the device. You'll notice that it is accessible from all nodes at the same time now; try creating a file on it from all nodes, and you'll see that it works.

Tip To mount an OCFS2 file system automatically from /etc/fstab, make sure it has the option _netdev added in the Options column. This option ensures that the file system is mounted only after the network has been enabled.

---

10. To ensure that the OCFS2 file system is available after a reboot as well, you not only have to make sure that /etc/fstab is configured to do that, but you also need to make sure that both the o2cb and ocfs2 services are started automatically. To do that, use the commands insserv o2cb and insserv ocfs2 on all the servers that are involved.

Tip It can happen that you have a problem mounting the OCFS2 volume once it has been mounted on the first node in the cluster. This problem results from modules that are not initialized properly. The best way to solve this problem is by rebooting all the servers that are involved in the cluster. After that, you'll be able to mount the OCFS2 file system on all nodes. Still having problems? Use the dmesg command, which will show exactly what has happened, and may indicate what is actually wrong.

The interesting feature of OCFS2 is that you don't especially need to use Heartbeat to provide access to it. As you saw in the previous procedure, OCFS2 has its own cluster service that makes sure that several nodes can access it at the same time.

Using Heartbeat for High Availability

Configuring Heartbeat for high availability can be a daunting task. In this section, I will describe the process of creating a Heartbeat resource with the NFS server as an example. You'll learn how to do it with Heartbeat 1 in this section; I'll cover creating Heartbeat resources with version 2 in the "Configuring a Heartbeat 2–Style Cluster with YaST" section.

Note Two versions of Heartbeat show significant differences. In this chapter, I'll start explaining how to configure a cluster based on Heartbeat 1. Version 1 is still a good—and especially important—choice to set up a cluster where two nodes need to share a resource and is therefore still used a lot. With version 2, which comes with SUSE Linux Enterprise Server, you can still configure a version 1 cluster. In the "Configuring a Heartbeat 2–Style Cluster with YaST" section of this chapter, you will read how to set up resources for use in a Heartbeat 2 cluster using YaST.

Before you start with this section, make sure all the required software is installed. You can install everything that's needed with YaST; from the Software Management interface, select the installation pattern High Availability. This makes sure the Heartbeat 2 software is installed, as well as the software needed to create a DRBD environment. You can configure a Heartbeat cluster in five steps:

1. Edit the example configuration files.

2. Use the authentication keys to ensure secure communications.

3. Tune the main configuration file /etc/ha.d/ha.cf on both nodes.

4. Use the configuration file haresources to configure shared resources in the Heartbeat network.

5. Start the Heartbeat software on both nodes.

In this example, the NFS server will be configured for high availability. The server will use the DRBD device as the shared storage device.

Editing the Sample Configuration Files

To make it easier for you to configure the Heartbeat software, some example configuration files are provided when installing the software. An easy way to get started is by copying these configuration files to the directory /etc/ha.d on both servers. You can find these files in the directory /usr/share/doc/packages/heartbeat. To complete this step, you need three files:

authkeys: This file secures communications between nodes with authentication keys.

ha.cf: This is the main configuration file in which Heartbeat's default behavior is defined.

haresources: This file defines the shared resources.

Using Authentication Keys to Ensure Secure Communications

If nodal traffic must cross over an insecure network, you might consider using authentication keys to secure communication. You can do this by editing the authkeys file. The structure of this file is really simple; you need just two lines of configuration. In the first line, you specify which type of authentication needs to be used. For this purpose, you can choose between crc, sha1, and md5. crc is the ideal solution for a secure network; it doesn't offer any real security and therefore is the fastest option for use on a secure network. It just adds a cyclic redundancy check to all packets to make sure packets that are received have not been transformed while in transit. The other two options are sha1 and md5. Both are secure, so it doesn't really matter which one you use. In Listing 29-4, you see all the relevant lines that can be created in /etc/ha.d/authkeys to ensure that authentication can take place in a secure manner. Note that a long and complicated key is used in the example; the longer the key, the more difficult it is to break it using brute force.

Listing 29-4. *Example Contents of the* authkeys *File*

```
#
auth 3
#1 crc
#2 sha1 secret
3 md5 h3artb3ats3cur3k3y
```

In this example, you see that the type of authentication that has to be used is referred to on the line auth 3. The 3 refers to the third line in the configuration file (or better, to the line in the configuration file that starts with a 3), where md5 authentication is configured for the use of a shared secret. After creating this file on one of the nodes, you can copy it to the other node. You have to do this, because in a Heartbeat environment, all configuration files on all servers always must be the same. Use scp as in the following example to do this:

```
scp /etc/ha.d/authkeys othernode:/etc/ha.d
```

As a last step, you need to ensure that the permission mode for the files is set to 600 on both nodes. Use the following command to accomplish this:

```
chmod 600 /etc/ha.d/authkeys
```

Tuning the Main Configuration File ha.cf on Both Nodes

One of the major tasks in successfully configuring the Heartbeat cluster is to configure the main configuration file ha.cf. In this file, you define Heartbeat's behavior. The file should be more or less the same on both nodes, although some parameters are node specific. The first parameters you have to enable look rather trivial but will make you happy later; these are the parameters to enable logging. Use all logging mechanisms, which will make it easier for you later to troubleshoot why the software isn't acting the way you want it to act. Make sure to remove the hash sign used to comment out some of the following three lines to enable full logging:

```
debugfile /var/log/ha-debug
logfile    /var/log/ha-log
logfacility local0
```

Next, you need to specify how often Heartbeat packages are sent across the network and when the other node will be considered dead. The following lines specify this:

```
keepalive 2
deadtime 30
warntime 10
initdead 120
```

Of these parameters, the keepalive parameter specifies that a Heartbeat message should be sent every two seconds. In some environments, this will absolutely be too long, so you could consider setting it lower, such as to 500 milliseconds. To do that, add 0.5 to the configuration file. The deadtime parameter is also important, because it defines when a service will officially be considered dead and when services will start to fail over to the other node. By default this is after 30 seconds. For some environments this is definitely too long, so you should consider setting it lower. Then the warntime parameter specifies when the first warning about a service being not available is sent to the log files. You should set the warntime parameter considerably lower than the deadtime so that the administrator will have enough time to correct any problems he finds before the node is considered dead. Finally, the initdead parameter specifies the timeout value used after the services are first started. The default value will allow the other node 120 seconds to come up and activate its resources when first booting. If it hasn't come up after this period, the other node will be considered dead, and services will start on the remaining node. Because it can take some time for another node to come up, I recommend giving this parameter a rather high value.

The last options that need to be set in ha.cf are the names of the cluster nodes. The names of the nodes included here should be the same as the name of the nodes displayed when using the command uname -a on these nodes. These parameters could, for example, look like the following:

```
node server1
node server2
```

In addition to these required options, you can use many other options as well. For example, some parameters define the fail-over and fail-back behavior of resources in the network, and some parameters define how the Heartbeat packets should be sent in the network. The default behavior on fail back, for example, is that when a node originally hosting the service comes back, the service will automatically fail back to that node. This may not be what you need, because if the failing node failed for some particular reason, you may want to troubleshoot that reason first. Then you need to specify on what device and how Heartbeat packages must be sent. For this purpose, you can add the following line, ensuring the Heartbeat packages are sent as broadcast packages over network card eth0:

```
bcast eth0
```

After creating the ha.cf file on either one of the nodes in the cluster, make sure to copy it to the other node. You can do this using the scp command as follows:

```
scp /etc/ha.d/ha.cf othernode:/etc/ha.d
```

Creating Shared Resources by Editing the haresources File

Now that you have configured the generic parameters for the Heartbeat software, it is time to define the shared resources on the network. In Heartbeat 1, you can do this in the configuration file /etc/ha.d/haresources. This technique does still work in Heartbeat 2, but if using the haresources file, you can't use any advanced Heartbeat 2 options such as support for multiple nodes. To keep it simple to start, you can now read how to configure shared Heartbeat services using the Heartbeat 1 haresources file. In this file, you have to accomplish the following tasks:

- Define the name of the primary node where the resource should run.
- Define the IP address on which the shared resource can be used.
- If used, specify the name of the shared device that should be used.
- Specify which service or services should be loaded as shared resources.

Tip After creating a Heartbeat 1 environment, you can easily convert it to version 2. Heartbeat 2 comes with a Python script to do that. For example, to migrate the resources as configured in the temporary file ~/haresources.temp, use the command python /usr/lib/heartbeat/haresources2cib.py ~/haresources.temp /var/lib/heartbeat/crm/cib.xml. This creates the cib.xml file that is used to store all resource configuration in a Heartbeat 2 environment for you automatically.

The following is an example of a line used to load the NFS server as a shared resource. Take notice that this should be created as one line in the haresources configuration file:

```
server1 192.168.0.203 datadisk::drbd0 Filesystem::/dev/drbd0::/data::reiserfs
  nfsserver
```

Defining the Name of the Primary Node

Each line where a cluster resource is defined starts with the name of the primary node. The resource will always try to load on this resource. If this primary node goes down and next comes up again, the default behavior is that the resource automatically fails back to this primary node. In this example, the name of the primary node is server1.

Defining the IP Address of the Shared Resource

The only mandatory element of all shared resources is the IP address. Each resource should have its own unique IP address. The only exception to this rule is when you want to configure a group of resources that shares one IP address. The server hosting the resource will activate this IP address as one of its virtual IP addresses.

Specifying the Name of the Shared Device

If a resource uses a shared device, all information should be present in /etc/ha.d/haresources to specify how this device should be loaded. For this purpose, you can use two scripts, which are both in the subdirectory /etc/ha.d/resource.d.

Note From `haresources`, you can refer to scripts at two different locations. The scripts may be stored in `/etc/init.d` or in `/etc/ha.d/resource.d`. Both types of scripts are in a syntax that is understood by Heartbeat natively.

The first of these scripts is the script with the name `datadisk` (which actually is a link to the `drbddisk` script). This script has an important task: it activates the DRBD device on the host where the resources will be loaded. While loading the DRBD device on this host, the `datadisk` script will make it the primary device on this host. In this way, the other host cannot write to the DRBD device, and all data written to the device will be synchronized immediately to the other node. In the line where the shared resource is defined, you see that the `datadisk` script takes one argument, which is the name of the DRBD device. To separate the name of the script from the names of its arguments, use two colons.

After specifying what device is used as the shared storage, next the resource load script needs to define how that device is to be activated. Note that this task has to be connected to the loading of the resource on a server and cannot occur in `/etc/fstab`; if it were handled in `/etc/fstab`, it would be impossible to migrate the shared device from one node to the other. To mount the shared device, the `Filesystem` script (notice the capital *F*!), which is in `/etc/ha.d/resource.d`, is used. This script takes three parameters when called from `haresources`: the complete device name of the shared device, the directory on which the shared device must be loaded, and finally the name of the file system that must be used to mount the device. Here also, the script is separated from its arguments by using two colons, as shown in the previous example.

Specifying Which Services Should Be Loaded

Last, you need to specify what service should be loaded as a clustered resource. Here you can specify the name of just one service, but it is possible as well to load more than one service from one line. By default, the Heartbeat software will try to locate the name of this script from `/etc/init.d` and `/etc/ha.d/resource.d`, so make sure the script you refer to is present at one of these locations. This script will automatically be started with the `start` argument, and it will be stopped with the `stop` argument. Therefore, the script you refer to should listen to these arguments. Most, if not all, scripts that are provided with SUSE Linux Enterprise Server 10 can be executed with `start` or `stop` as a parameter.

Note You just learned how to configure a complex resource for use in the Heartbeat cluster environment. Configuring a shared resource can be much easier. It is, for example, possible to configure just a secondary IP address as the cluster resource, just the shared storage device without anything else, or just the service you want to cluster without using any shared storage. For example, the following line is a perfectly legal resource configuration that will load the IP address 192.168.0.204 on server1 by default.

`server1 192.168.0.204`

Also, you can use the following to configure a clustered resource that doesn't need any shared storage because all the configuration it requires is available on the local file system:

`server1 192.168.0.204 dhcp`

Starting the Heartbeat Software on Both Nodes

When all the configuration has been done, it is time to start the Heartbeat software on both nodes. Use the rcheartbeat command to do this. I recommend, while doing this, monitoring /var/log/ messages with the tail -f command, because it will clearly show if loading of the Heartbeat software and the shared resource is successful.

Configuring NFS for Use in the Heartbeat Cluster

The Heartbeat cluster is now configured the right way. To get the NFS server running properly, however, some minimal additional configuration is required. Most important is that the directory /var/lib/nfs, which is used by default for file locking by NFS, is replaced with a location on the shared disk. If you don't do that, file locks can't migrate when the NFS service is migrated. The best way to make information about file locks available at the other server is by making /var/lib/nfs, a symbolic link on the original file system, point to the real location of the files on the shared storage. The following procedure shows how to do this if the shared disk is mounted on the /data directory:

1. Unload the Heartbeat services on both servers by using the rcheartbeat stop command.

2. Make sure that on the server that is supposed to act as primary in the cluster, the shared storage device is accessible and mounted on its mount point. You don't need to mount it on the secondary server. (Even if you want to, you can't, because only one server at a time can access the shared device.)

3. On both servers, make a symbolic link from the location of the NFS lockfiles to the directory on the shared storage device where you want to make them accessible. If, for example, you want to store the lockfiles in /data/nfslock, use the following command on both servers to create the link:

   ln -s /var/lib/nfs /data/nfslock

4. Dismount the shared device.

5. Modify the haresources file to load the nfslock daemon as well. A line like in the following example will make sure that it is loaded properly:

   server1 192.168.0.203 datadisk::drbd0 Filesystem::/dev/drbd0::
   /data::reiserfs
   nfsserver nfslock

6. Start Heartbeat services on both servers.

Managing the Shared Resource

Now that you have the Heartbeat cluster running, it is good to know that some commands are available for managing and monitoring the cluster and its resources. In Heartbeat 1, management options are limited, and most are available as a parameter from the cl_status command. You can use this command in Heartbeat 1 and 2. The following are the most important options:

cl_status hbstatus: Shows the Heartbeat services that are running on the local computer

cl_status listnodes: Shows all the nodes currently in the cluster

cl_status rscstatus: Shows the state of clustered resources

In Heartbeat 2, you can use the apphbd process for interactive monitoring of the Heartbeat cluster. This daemon gets its configuration from apphbd.cf where basic parameters are specified to determine how the process should be used. The main purpose of apphbd is to define when and at what level logging should occur. This enables a failing node to result in a message written to any log mechanism. To make this happen, you use some parameters. In Listing 29-5, you can see all default values.

Listing 29-5. *Default Values from* apphbd.cf

```
debug_level = 3
debugfile = NULL
logfile = NULL
watchdog_device = NULL
watchdog_interval_ms = 1000
notify_plugin : no plugin
realtime = yes
```

Of these, the debug_level specifies the amount of information to log. More information will be logged if a high value is used for the debug level. The default value of 3 will make sure the log system is rather verbose. Next, the files are specified for where debug information and log information need to be redirected. As you can see, by default no files are used for this purpose, which makes sure that by default no information whatsoever is logged. The watchdog device and interval specify when monitoring should occur. One of the most interesting parts is the line where notify plug-ins are specified. For the purpose of notification when an event takes place, you can use a notify plug-in. You can find these plug-ins in /usr/lib/heartbeat/plugins/AppHBNotification, and they require a separate configuration. The purpose of these plug-ins is to redirect notification events to certain devices. Currently, not many of these plug-ins are available.

Avoiding Split Brain

One issue has not been dealt with so far. In a cluster environment, it can happen that more than one node in the cluster thinks that it has exclusive access to a cluster resource. Such a configuration is known as the *split brain*. If this resource is the shared storage device, the results can be severe; for example, if a database is stored on the shared disk device, the entire database may become corrupted. Therefore, in a serious clustered environment, you must take precautionary measures to prevent such a situation. Some nice features are available with the Heartbeat clustering software that take care that the failing node is terminated when it fails.

One solution to cast off the failing node is to use a Stonith device. Stonith stands for *shoot the other node in the head* and refers to a technique that makes sure the failing node is cast off efficiently. For Stonith configuration, you must use a smart power device connected to both servers. A serial cable or network cable running from both servers to this device allows the Heartbeat software to send commands to this device, which controls the power supply to the other server. If needed, the other node can reset a failing cluster node this way.

The Stonith device is used in the following way:

1. The remaining server doesn't hear incoming Heartbeat packages anymore and concludes that the other server fails.

2. The remaining server sends the Stonith reset command to the Stonith device.

3. The Stonith device turns off power on the failing server. This makes sure a split-brain situation is avoided.

4. All resources that were running on the other server are failed over automatically.

Because each Stonith device has its own unique set of commands, it is not possible to give a "one-size-fits-all" description of how to configure the device.

In a production environment, I recommend using a Stonith device. Your UPS manufacturer can inform you about UPS models that support Stonith. If for some reason you cannot lay your hands on such a UPS, two other methods are available. The first is the meatware device (a human being) that is alerted of a failing node in the cluster. The second is the option to use SSH to send a command to the other node in the cluster. The latter method, however, is not recommended, because there are too many situations in which it can fail. To give you an idea of how it works, the next procedure shows you how to configure a meatware device:

1. Add `stonith host * meatware` to the `/etc/ha.d/ha.cf` file, and make sure the `auto_failback` option is set. This option makes sure the same device is configured on all nodes.

2. Configure a resource, and start Heartbeat on all nodes.

3. To verify it's working, kill the Heartbeat process on the primary node to force the shared resource down. You can do this the rude way, such as by using the `killall -9 heartbeat` command.

4. Now monitor what happens in the `/var/log/messages` file on the other server. You should see a message indicating that the primary node is down and that operator intervention is required.

5. On the backup server, clear the event to allow for failover of the resource. If the name of the other server, for example, is server1, then use `meatclient -c server1` to clear the event.

6. Now restart Heartbeat on server1 to complete the test.

Configuring a Heartbeat 2–Style Cluster with YaST

Creating a Heartbeat 2–style cluster from the command line is not something that many people like to do. The most important reason is that Heartbeat 2 stores its most important configuration in an XML file, and if you don't know how to handle XML, this is difficult to tune manually. Fortunately, SUSE Linux Enterprise Server 10 comes with YaST, which provides an easy-to-use interface that allows you to set up the cluster.

Creating the Cluster

Before any resources can be added to it, you need to create the cluster with YaST. This includes setting up the network over which the Heartbeats are sent and adding nodes to the cluster. Follow these steps:

1. Make sure that the Heartbeat software is installed on all nodes in the cluster.

2. From YaST on any node in the cluster, select System ➤ High Availability. This opens the screen shown in Figure 29-7. On this screen, you need to make sure all nodes that you want to be in the cluster are added to the cluster. Don't add the node you are running this utility on; it is already there, but do add all the other nodes. Then click Next to proceed.

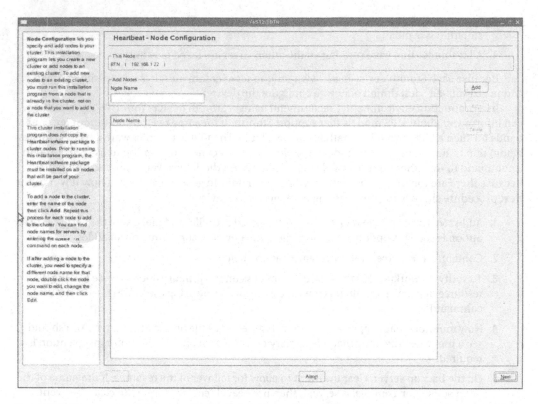

Figure 29-7. *To start the cluster, run the Node Configuration utility on one node in the cluster, and from there add the names of all the nodes you want to be in the cluster.*

3. On the Authentication Keys screen (see Figure 29-8), you specify how nodes authenticate to each other. If all nodes are in a secured data center, accept the default selection CRC (No Security). If you configure the cluster over an unsecure network, select either SHA1 or MD5, and enter a key that can be used for authentication. Then click Next to proceed.

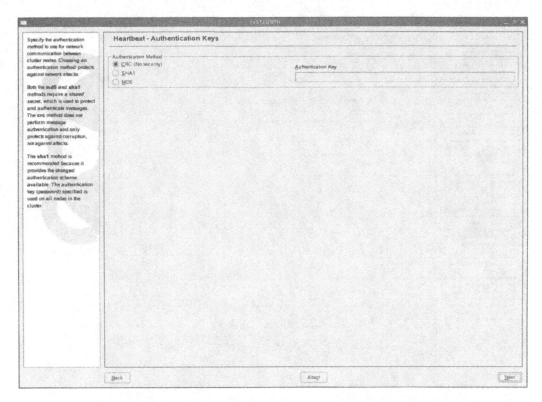

Figure 29-8. *For optimal performance on a secure network, choose CRC, which just adds a redundancy check on packets.*

4. On the screen shown in Figure 29-9, you can specify how to communicate over the Heartbeat network. This is the network that nodes use to communicate to each other and see whether the other nodes are still there. For optimal fault tolerance, you should use a dedicated network for this. By default, broadcasts will be sent. If you don't want to bother nodes that are not in the cluster with your broadcasts, select Multicast instead. Next, enter an IP address used for the multicast packets. You can use any address between 224.0.0.0 and 239.255.255.255, as long as it isn't used by something else already. After specifying how you want to communicate, click Next to proceed.

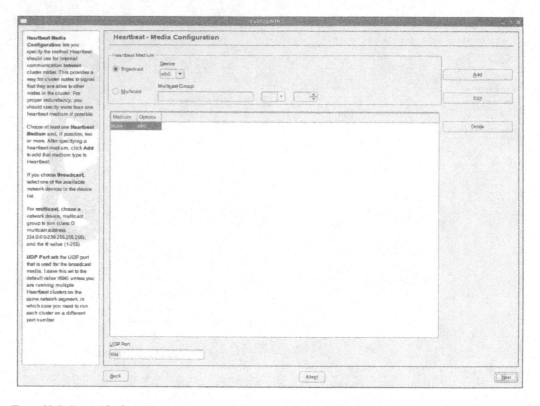

Figure 29-9. *In an ideal environment, you will have a separate network for the Heartbeat traffic.*

5. You'll now see the final screen of the YaST module that helps you in configuring Heartbeat. In here, specify that you want to start the Heartbeat software every time your server boots. Then click Finish.

6. Now from the command line on the node where you configured Heartbeat, use the /usr/lib/heartbeat/ha_propagate command. This will copy the configuration to all other nodes in the cluster if your node is able to resolve the host names of the other nodes. Notice that SSH must be available on all servers, because the configuration files are copied over an SSH connection.

7. On all other servers, use the command rcheartbeat start to start the Heartbeat service.

Creating Resources

Now that the cluster is up and running, you have to add resources to it. The best way to do that is with the graphical HA Management Client utility; as an alternative, you can use the command-line CIBAdmin tool. The next procedure describes how to add resources using the HA Management Client utility:

1. The graphical client needs the credentials of the user hacluster who has been created auto-matically when you installed the cluster. As root, use passwd hacluster to give this user a password.

2. By using the hb_gui command from a console, start the HA Management Utility. This opens the interface shown in Figure 29-10.

Figure 29-10. *Initially, the HA Management Client shows an empty interface.*

3. To do anything in the graphical utility, you need to authenticate first. Click Connection, select Login, and then enter the password of the user hacluster. The graphical utility will now connect to the cluster and show a graphical overview of it (see Figure 29-11).

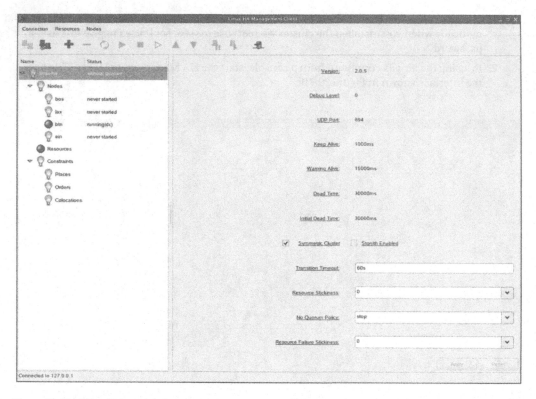

Figure 29-11. *After authenticating, you see an overview of the current status of the cluster.*

4. Now you need to add some resources. To keep it simple, click Resources ➤ Add, and then select the resource type Native. This opens the Add Native Resource screen shown in Figure 29-12. Other resource types are available as well, but it goes beyond the scope of this chapter to discuss how they work.

5. The native resource type allows you to select any service start-up script from the /etc/ init.d directory, as well as some native Heartbeat resources. From the list, select the resource you want to configure. To give a simple example, if you want to create a Heartbeat resource for an IP address, which is useful to migrate a virtual IP address across the cluster, select the resource IPaddr, which has Heartbeat as its provider and the description OCF Resource Agent Compliant IPaddr script. In Figure 29-13 you can see what the properties of this resource are.

6. In the parameters part of the Add Native Resource screen (see Figure 29-13), you can see that one of the parameters has the name *ip*. On this line, click under the Value column, and there, add the IP address you want to assign to the resource. When done, click Add to add the resource.

7. Now open the Resources item in the Heartbeat management utility. This shows the resource with the current status not running. Right-click the resource, and from the quick menu, click the Start button to start it. You will see that the resource starts running immediately on the node that was started first in the cluster. Check this node to see that the resource is really there indeed. For example, in the case of an IP address, you can use the ip address show command to see that the IP address was really added.

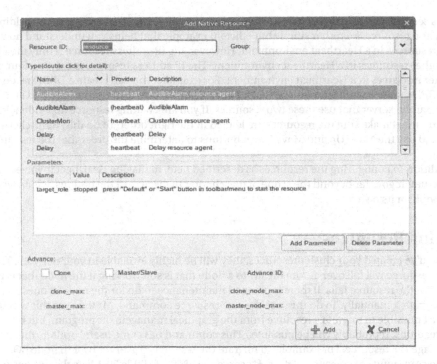

Figure 29-12. *On the Add Native Resource screen, you can specify what resource you want to configure.*

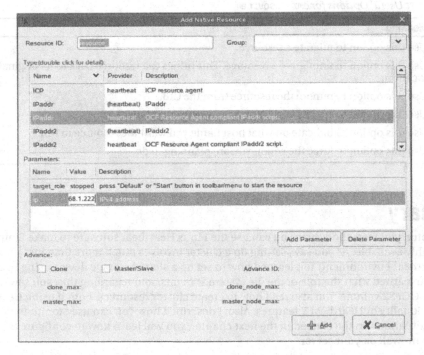

Figure 29-13. *To make sure that the resource starts successfully, you need to modify its properties.*

In this section, you read about how to create a resource in a Heartbeat environment. Adding an IP address as a resource is a rather simple but efficient example that helps you understand how to configure resources in a Heartbeat environment. However, the IP address resource is only the foundation of other resources in a Heartbeat environment. The IP address resource is only the foundation of other resources in a Heartbeat environment. For example, you can create a DRBD resource for your DRBD-based shared storage as well, and once these two are in place, you can add an NFS server or a Samba server that use these two resources. If you are creating resource dependencies this way, you must make sure the resources are loaded in the right order. To do this, right-click the resource, and use the Move Up and Move Down buttons to determine the order that the resource is loaded in.

In addition to configuring the resources as described here, managing Heartbeat involves much more than that. It goes far beyond the scope of this chapter to discuss all the options, which would require a book on its own.

Migrating Resources

Now that you've created your cluster resources, they will be highly available in your network. This means the resource will fail over automatically to a node that is still working if the node that is currently hosting the resource fails. If there is planned maintenance to do for the node in question, you can also migrate it manually. To do this, use the `crm_resource` command. (At the time this was written, it wasn't possible to migrate a resource from the graphical management program, but by the time you read this, it probably will be possible.) This command has some useful options that allow you to manage the resource. For example, to migrate the resource `ftpserver` over to node BOS, you can use the command `cmr_resource -M -r ftpserver -H BOS -f`. Table 29-1 lists the options used in this example as well as some other useful options this command offers.

Table 29-1. *Most Useful Options for* `cmr_resource`

Option	Meaning
`-M`	Use this option to migrate a resource.
`-U`	Use this option to unmigrate a resource. This brings the resource back to its original location.
`-D`	Use this option to remote the resource from the CIB.
`-r`	Use this option to specify what resource you want to manage.
`-H`	Use this option to indicate on what host name you want the resource to run.
`-f`	Use this option to force the action you are planning to do.

Summary

In this chapter, you read about how you can use the Linux Heartbeat software to make Linux services highly available. As you saw, setting up a cluster involves much more than just setting up the Heartbeat environment. You learned how to set up a shared storage device using DRBD or iSCSI. You learned what the role of the file system is in this, and regarding this, you saw how to set up an OCFS2 volume. You also read how to create cluster resources, both if using Heartbeat 1 functionality or Heartbeat 2 features. Also, I described how you can use Stonith to avoid split-brain situations on the cluster. In the next chapter, you will learn how to configure the SUSE Linux firewall on your server.

◼ ◼ ◼

## CHAPTER 30

Managing Access with the SUSE Firewall

If you run SUSE Linux Enterprise Server within a professional network, it is likely that the network is already protected by a firewall that keeps bad packets out and allows only good traffic in. Such a network firewall offers excellent protection from the outside, but it doesn't protect you from people inside your own network who might do harm to your server. To protect your server as well, you can use the SUSE firewall. In this chapter, you'll learn how to set it up.

Before Configuring the Firewall

Before even thinking about configuring a firewall on your server, you should think about the services the server offers. What sense does it make to block port 524 in your firewall if you don't need services on that port at all? Therefore, before you start, make sure all the services you don't really need are disabled (see Chapter 10 for more details on how to do that). The following is a short checklist that you can use to make sure all the services you don't really need are not available. After performing all the steps in this checklist, configure the SUSE firewall to make sure that if a rogue service is started in some way on your server, it will not be accessible from the outside.

Note Configuring the security of your server is a task that only root can do properly. Therefore, all the commands and procedures discussed in this chapter are assumed to be issued by root.

Here's the checklist:

- Check all xinetd services (see Chapter 10). By default, all services that are started from xinetd are disabled, and the xinetd service itself isn't even started automatically. In many situations, you can keep it that way. As root, use the rcxinetd status command to see whether initd is running. Next, run chkconfig --list. This lists all the xinetd services (and others as well) and their current status. In the partial output in Listing 30-1, you can see that all the xinetd-based services are disabled. If this command shows that some unexpected services are enabled anyway, tune the configuration file for that service in /etc/xinetd.d to switch it off, and don't forget to restart xinetd using rcxinetd restart after that.

Listing 30-1. *Monitoring the Current Status of Services with* chkconfig --list

```
ypserv                      0:off  1:off  2:off  3:off  4:off  5:off  6:off
ypxfrd                      0:off  1:off  2:off  3:off  4:off  5:off  6:off
zebra                       0:off  1:off  2:off  3:off  4:off  5:off  6:off
xinetd based services:
        chargen:            off
        chargen-udp:        off
        cups-lpd:           off
        cvs:                off
        daytime:            off
        daytime-udp:        off
        echo:               off
        echo-udp:           off
        fam:                off
        i4l-vbox:           off
        imap:               off
        netstat:            off
        qpopper:            off
        rsync:              off
        sane-port:          off
        servers:            off
        services:           off
        swat:               off
        systat:             off
        tftp:               off
        time:               off
        time-udp:           off
        vnc:                off
        vsftpd:             off
```

- Use the chkconfig command. This lists all the services that your server offers. For each of these services, you can see whether it is on or off. Take a critical look at the list, and check whether you really need these services for your server. If you don't need the service, use insserv -r yourservice to prevent it from being booted automatically when your server starts. Next, use rcyourservice stop to disable the service (make sure to replace yourservice with the actual name of the service).

- Look at the users who exist in /etc/passwd (see Listing 30-2). You shouldn't see any users here that you don't recognize, especially if you see an unknown user who has a shell such as /bin/bash that enables him to log in. If that's the case, find out what he needs that shell for; many service accounts don't need to do shell logins at all. A good method is to find all the files on your server that are owned by this user. To find all the files that are owned by user blah, use find / -user blah. If a user account exists but doesn't own any files, you probably don't need it. In that case, make a backup of your /etc/passwd file, and remove the line where the user is defined.

Listing 30-2. *In* /etc/passwd, *Users Are Often Created But Aren't Needed*

```
at:x:25:25:Batch jobs daemon:/var/spool/atjobs:/bin/bash
beagleindex:x:107:109:User for Beagle indexing:/var/cache/beagle:/bin/bash
bin:x:1:1:bin:/bin:/bin/bash
daemon:x:2:2:Daemon:/sbin:/bin/bash
dhcpd:x:102:65534:DHCP server daemon:/var/lib/dhcp:/bin/false
ftp:x:40:49:FTP account:/srv/ftp:/bin/bash
games:x:12:100:Games account:/var/games:/bin/bash
```

```
gdm:x:50:15:Gnome Display Manager daemon:/var/lib/gdm:/bin/bash
haldaemon:x:101:102:User for haldaemon:/var/run/hal:/bin/false
icecream:x:105:106:Icecream Daemon:/var/cache/icecream:/bin/false
irc:x:39:65534:IRC daemon:/usr/lib/ircd:/bin/bash
ldap:x:76:70:User for OpenLDAP:/var/lib/ldap:/bin/bash
lp:x:4:7:Printing daemon:/var/spool/lpd:/bin/bash
mail:x:8:12:Mailer daemon:/var/spool/clientmqueue:/bin/false
mailman:x:72:67:GNU mailing list manager:/var/lib/mailman:/bin/bash
man:x:13:62:Manual pages viewer:/var/cache/man:/bin/bash
mdnsd:x:78:65534:mDNSResponder runtime user:/var/lib/mdnsd:/bin/false
messagebus:x:100:101:User for D-BUS:/var/run/dbus:/bin/false
mysql:x:60:107:MySQL database admin:/var/lib/mysql:/bin/bash
named:x:44:44:Name server daemon:/var/lib/named:/bin/false
news:x:9:13:News system:/etc/news:/bin/bash
nobody:x:65534:65533:nobody:/var/lib/nobody:/bin/bash
ntp:x:74:105:NTP daemon:/var/lib/ntp:/bin/false
pop:x:67:100:POP admin:/var/lib/pop:/bin/false
postfix:x:51:51:Postfix Daemon:/var/spool/postfix:/bin/false
privoxy:x:104:104:Daemon user for privoxy:/var/lib/privoxy:/bin/false
quagga:x:106:108:Quagga routing daemon:/var/run/quagga:/bin/false
radiusd:x:103:103:Radius daemon:/var/lib/radiusd:/bin/false
root:x:0:0:root:/root:/bin/bash
squid:x:31:65534:WWW-proxy squid:/var/cache/squid:/bin/false
sshd:x:71:65:SSH daemon:/var/lib/sshd:/bin/false
suse-ncc:x:108:110:Novell ... :/var/lib/YaST2/suse-ncc-fakehome:/bin/bash
uucp:x:10:14:Unix-to-Unix CoPy system:/etc/uucp:/bin/bash
wwwrun:x:30:8:WWW daemon apache:/var/lib/wwwrun:/bin/false
sander:x:1000:100:sander:/home/sander:/bin/bash
```

• Use the netstat -patune command to list all the services that are listening on your server.
  If you see any services you don't need, identify the way they are started and disable them.
  If you see a service for which you don't know how it is started, use man -k to learn where
  you can find more information about that service. For example, if you have no idea what
  the portmap service is, use man -k portmap to list the man pages that describe this service.
  Next, with the help of these man pages, find out how it is started and disable it. Listing 30-3
  shows some partial output of the netstat -patune command.

Listing 30-3. netstat -patune *Shows All Open Ports*

```
SFO:/etc # netstat -patune
Active Internet connections (servers and established)
Proto Recv-Q Send-Q Local Address           Foreign Address         State
      User        Inode       PID/Program name
tcp        0        0 0.0.0.0:139             0.0.0.0:*               LISTEN
           0        10736       3718/smbd
tcp        0        0 0.0.0.0:111             0.0.0.0:*               LISTEN
           0        8723        3005/portmap
tcp        0        0 127.0.0.1:2544          0.0.0.0:*               LISTEN
           0        8632        2967/zmd
tcp        0        0 0.0.0.0:631             0.0.0.0:*               LISTEN
           0        14010       3567/cupsd
tcp        0        0 127.0.0.1:25            0.0.0.0:*               LISTEN
           0        9349        3209/master
tcp        0        0 0.0.0.0:445             0.0.0.0:*               LISTEN
           0        10735       3718/smbd
tcp        1        0 127.0.0.1:26344         127.0.0.1:631           CLOSE_WAIT
```

```
     1000      16083     4757/wine-preloader
tcp       0      0 127.0.0.1:631      127.0.0.1:6740          ESTABLISHED
     4       35170     3567/cupsd
tcp       1      0 127.0.0.1:6741     127.0.0.1:631           CLOSE_WAIT
     1000     35190     4156/evolution-2.6
```

- Scan your own server with nmap. To do a comprehensive scan on your own server, use nmap -sTUR -F -P0 -O localhost (check Listing 30-4 for an example of nmap results). This command uses the following options:

  - -sTUR: This is a concatenation of the options -sT, -sU, and -sR that scan for TCP, UDP, and RCP connections. This way, you can be sure you aren't missing any important protocols.

  - -F: This option scans all privileged ports. These are the ports 0–1023 that typically can be accessed by well-known programs only. This option also scans the most commonly used ports from 1024 to 49151, but not all ports. Without this option, nmap will take considerably longer to complete its work (but at the same time its results will be more reliable as well).

  - -P0: This option tells nmap not to ping the target host. This is an important option, because the scan will exit and fail if a ping fails, and that may lead to unreliable results on a host that has been instructed not to reply to ping packets.

  - -O: Use this option to find out what operating system the target host is using.

Listing 30-4. nmap *Finds Out What Services Are Offered by a Host*

```
SFO:/etc # nmap -sTUR -F -P0 -O localhost

Starting Nmap 4.00 ( http://www.insecure.org/nmap/ ) at 2006-08-23 11:39 CEST
Interesting ports on localhost (127.0.0.1):
(The 2231 ports scanned but not shown below are in state: closed)
PORT        STATE           SERVICE             VERSION
22/tcp      open            ssh
25/tcp      open            smtp
68/udp      open|filtered   dhcpc
111/tcp     open            rpcbind (rpcbind V2)  2 (rpc #100000)
111/udp     open            rpcbind (rpcbind V2)  2 (rpc #100000)
137/udp     open|filtered   netbios-ns
138/udp     open|filtered   netbios-dgm
139/tcp     open            netbios-ssn
445/tcp     open            microsoft-ds
631/tcp     open            ipp
32768/udp   open|filtered   omad
Device type: general purpose
Running: Linux 2.4.X|2.5.X|2.6.X
OS details: Linux 2.4.0 - 2.5.20, Linux 2.5.25 - 2.6.8 or Gentoo 1.2
    Linux 2.4.19 rc1-rc7

Nmap finished: 1 IP address (1 host up) scanned in 8.034 seconds
```

- Consider switching TCP Wrappers off. In addition to the iptables-based SUSE firewall, you can use another system to limit access to services. This system is known as TCP Wrappers. It works with two files, /etc/hosts.allow and /etc/hosts.deny, to limit access to services that can handle TCP Wrappers. I recommend not using that system at all (and this is the default on SUSE Linux Enterprise Server anyway). Use one system to limit access to services only on your server; otherwise, you may lose the overview. If TCP Wrappers currently is enabled, just remove the files /etc/hosts.allow and /etc/hosts.deny to disable it, and make sure you set up the proper firewall rules to limit access to the services that currently are limited by TCP Wrappers.

Doing all the basic checks listed here will tell you whether your server is safe. In either case, continue with the next section where you can find out how to set up the SUSE firewall.

Configuring the SUSE Firewall with YaST

On all Linux systems, firewall functionality is implemented with the netfilter package in the kernel. Since it is integrated in the Linux kernel, the netfilter firewall is fast and, if set up properly, can compete with many firewall appliances. In fact, many routers use a tuned Linux kernel to do firewalling anyway. You can manage the netfilter package with a rather complex command: iptables. Because it is complex, on many servers no firewall is active at all; many people are just not sure how to configure netfilter properly using the iptables command. To eliminate that problem, SUSE Linux Enterprise Server comes with the SUSE firewall. The SUSE firewall is a front-end interface to iptables, which makes managing security for your server a lot easier. This means the SUSE firewall writes iptables commands for you. The best way to start creating a secure server is by tuning the SUSE firewall. If later you need to tune how the SUSE firewall works and need to do things that the YaST interface doesn't allow you to do, you can use the iptables command for some additional tuning. In this section, you'll learn how to set up the SUSE firewall, and the next section discusses how to configure netfilter with the iptables command.

When installing SUSE Linux Enterprise Server, the firewall is automatically switched on and doesn't allow any traffic to come in. When configuring a service with YaST, you'll always find an option that allows you to open the port in the firewall that is necessary to access that service. If you work that way, the firewall is set up more or less automatically for you. To explain how it works, in this section I'll describe how you should enable the firewall on a system where it hasn't been enabled yet. The following steps show how to do this with YaST:

1. In YaST, select Security and Users ➤ Firewall. This opens the Firewall Configuration Start-Up screen shown in Figure 30-1.

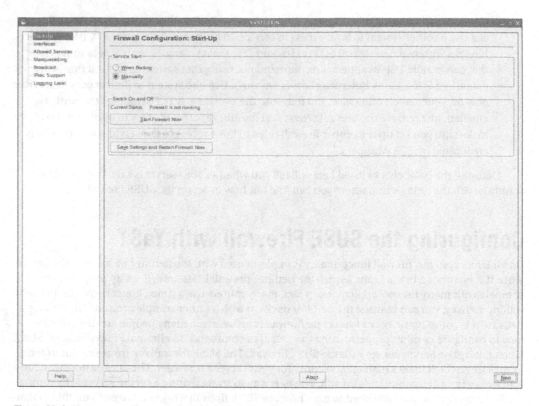

Figure 30-1. *You can easily configure the SUSE firewall from YaST.*

2. As you can see, the firewall configuration interface consists of several steps that are all listed on the left part of the screen. First, under Start-Up, you can specify how the firewall starts. Make sure under Service Start, the option When Booting is selected (see Figure 30-2). This will start the firewall as early as possible in the boot process, which is necessary for optimal protection. You should be aware that if you don't start it automatically but instead do it manually, the server is unprotected from the time the network interfaces are activated on your server to the time you start the firewall manually. Also, because you could forget to start it completely, manually enabling the firewall is a bad idea. It would leave your server unprotected if for whatever reason it reboots. On this screen, you also have options to start and stop the firewall now. If you are not working from a remote connection, it is a good idea to click Start Firewall Now. That makes sure that from this moment on, your firewall is activated, and only services that you have specifically allowed can be accessed.

Tip Instead of using the screen shown in Figure 30-2, you can use the rcSuSEfirewall start command. This will read the current firewall configuration in the files in /etc/sysconfig/scripts and activate the firewall for you. Equally, you can use rcSuSEfirewall stop to stop the firewall from the command line.

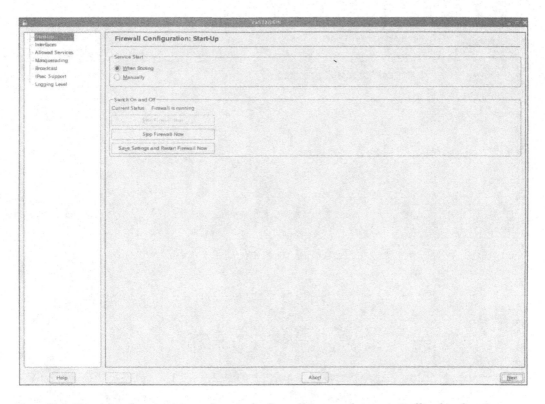

Figure 30-2. *For optimal protection, make sure the firewall is started automatically when booting the server.*

3. Now click Interfaces. This opens the screen shown in Figure 30-3. On this screen, you can specify in what zone the network interfaces in your server live. This is an important setting on a server with more than one network board; such a server will probably have a public interface and a private interface, and on the public interface more protection is required than on the private interface. Therefore, the public interface is configured as the untrusted external zone, whereas the private interface is configured as the trusted internal zone. On a server with one network board only, you don't need to assign zones to an interface. However, if more than one network board is available in your server, you need to assign a zone to each network board. Next, when specifying which services are available through your firewall, for each service you need to specify for which zones it is allowed; this is described in the following step. Even if your server has only one network board, make sure it is assigned to a zone; the external zone is a good choice in that case. You can configure the following zones:

   - *Internal:* This is the network board facing the internal network. It is the most trusted zone that is available.

   - *External:* The external zone is connected to the Internet directly. This is the least trusted zone, and most services will be denied on that interface.

   - *Demilitarized zone (DMZ):* This is a network card facing the DMZ in your network. A DMZ is the part of the network where a company's servers available for users on the Internet typically are. The DMZ is behind the external firewall but should not be considered a trusted zone.

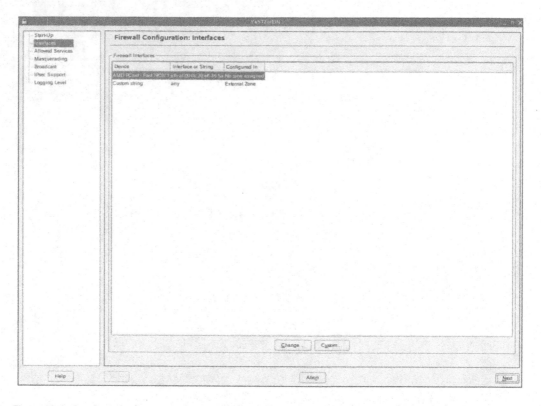

Figure 30-3. *On the Interfaces screen, you can specify in what zone a network interface lives.*

4. Now click Allowed Services. On this screen (see Figure 30-4), you can specify what services are allowed in what zones. On this tab, you must first select the zone you want to configure. For each of the three zones, you need to specify what services are available. First, start with the external zone. Then from the Service to Allow drop-down list, one by one select each service you want to allow. Next click Add to add the service to the list of allowed services. Do this for all the services you need. After doing this for the external zone, repeat this procedure for the demilitarized zone. By default, all the zones are available on the internal zone. If this is not what you want, check the Protect Firewall from Internal Zone option, and for the internal zone, specify which services you want to allow.

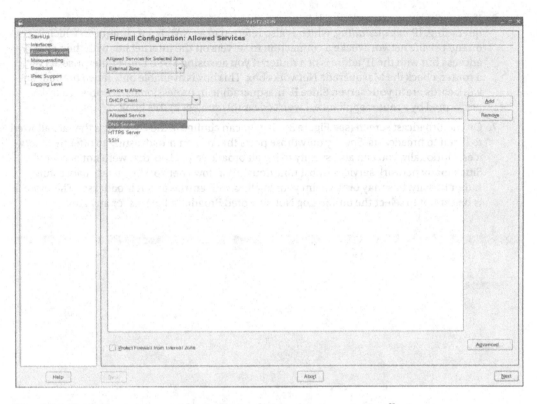

Figure 30-4. *For each zone, you need to indicate what services you want to allow.*

5. Still on the Allowed Services screen shown in Figure 30-4, click the Advanced button. This opens the screen shown in Figure 30-5. Use this screen to specify TCP, UDP, RPC, or IP ports for services that are not in the Service to Allow drop-down list. If specifying an IP protocol, make sure you use the IANA service name of the protocol. You can find a list of valid protocol names in the file /etc/protocols.

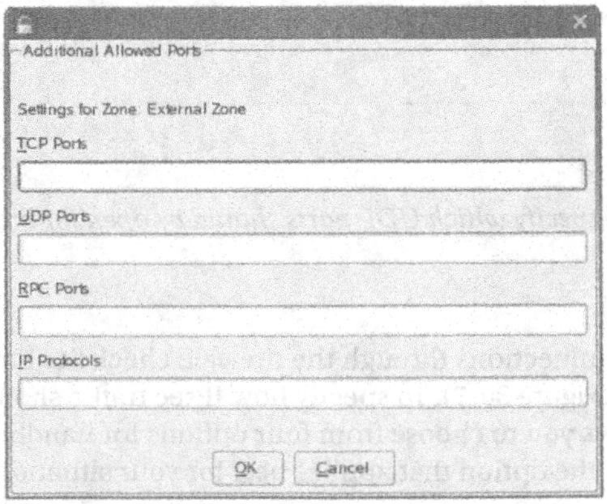

Figure 30-5. *For services that aren't in the Service to Allow drop-down list, you can use the Advanced button to enter their specific port numbers.*

6. If more than one network card is in your server, you can configure your server for masquerading. IP *masquerading*, which is also referred to as NAT, is a technique in which users on the private network make a connection to servers on the Internet not with their own IP address but with the IP address of a router. If you are using SUSE Linux Enterprise Server as a router, check the Masquerade Networks box. This box is available only if two or more network cards are in your server. Since IP masquerading in professional networks is a task performed by a router appliance, I won't cover this subject in this book.

7. On the Broadcast screen (see Figure 30-6), you can configure the UDP ports that are allowed to listen to broadcasts. Specify only those ports that rely on broadcasting to offer their services. Optionally, you can also specify to log all broadcast packets that were not accepted. Since many network services (most notoriously Windows networking) use broadcasting rather heavily, this may overwhelm your log files with entries about broadcasts. Therefore, it is better not to select the option Log Not Accepted Broadcast Packets for any zone.

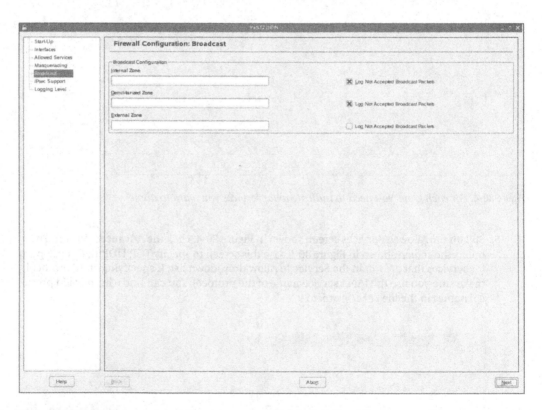

Figure 30-6. *The Broadcast screen allows you to specify which UDP ports should be open for broadcast on your server.*

8. If your server needs to accept IPsec connections through the firewall, check the Enabled box on the IPsec Support screen (see Figure 30-7). To specify how IPsec traffic should be handled, click Details next. This allows you to choose from four options for handling incoming packets. From these, select the option that applies best for your situation. You can choose from the following:

- You can trust IPsec as the same zone as the original source network.

- You can trust IPsec as a demilitarized zone.

- You can trust IPsec as an external zone.

- You can trust IPsec as an internal zone.

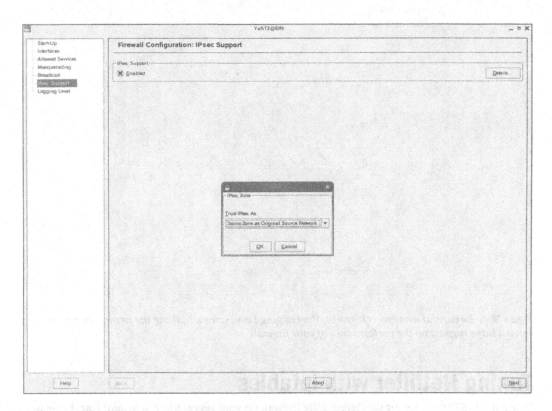

Figure 30-7. *The SUSE firewall allows you to accept incoming IPsec traffic.*

9. On the last screen in the SUSE firewall setup process, you can specify the log level you want to use (see Figure 30-8). By default, both for accepted and for not-accepted packets, only critical events are logged. If you need to troubleshoot a connection, you can specify that all packets are logged. For both, you can choose from the following:

- *Log All:* This option will cause all the packets to be logged. You usually want to do this only to troubleshoot your firewall and see what traffic is accepted or rejected. Don't leave this on by default, because it will greatly impact the performance of your firewall.

- *Log Only Critical:* This is the default selection for both incoming and outgoing traffic. Logs are written only if something abnormal occurs.

- *Do Not Log Any:* Use this option if you are confident about how your firewall works and you don't need any additional information.

10. Now that you have entered all the settings for your firewall, click Next. This will show you an overview of the current configuration you have entered so far. If you are happy with it, click Accept to write the configuration to your server, and start the firewall with these settings.

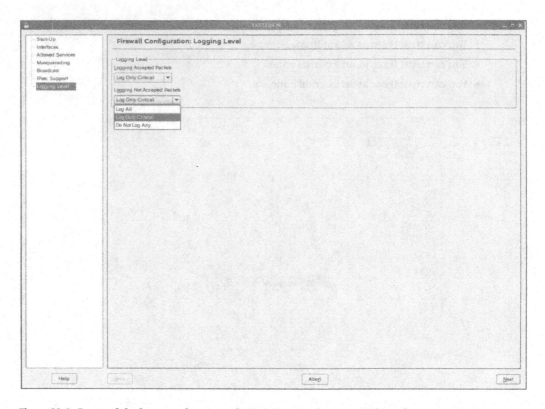

Figure 30-8. *Be careful what you choose on the Logging Level screen. Making the wrong choice can have a huge impact on the performance of your firewall.*

Tuning Netfilter with iptables

Using the YaST interface for configuring the firewall on your server offers a decent start to secure your server, but for more advanced needs it is often just not good enough. If that's the case for you, you may encounter a situation where you want to build the complete firewall by hand. To help you do that, in the following sections you'll learn how to use iptables to configure local security for your server. Note that this section does not discuss how to set up a router with iptables or how to configure NAT; it is assumed that you just want to use it as a firewall to protect your server and nothing else.

Making Proper Preparations

Configuring a firewall without the proper preparation is in general a bad idea. Before you start configuring it, you should understand what exactly it is that you need your firewall to do. For a server that has a public as well as a private network card, you could make a table like the example in Table 30-1.

Table 30-1. *Overview of Required Services for Your Firewall*

Interface	Service	Inbound/Outbound
Private	SSH	Outbound, inbound
Public	HTTP	Inbound
Public, private	Ping	Outbound
Public, private	DNS	Outbound, inbound

Once you have a simple setup matrix in place, you can start configuring the firewall. Before you start, you should know how a netfilter firewall is organized.

Netfilter Building Blocks

The most elementary building blocks for a netfilter firewall are the chains. You can consider these sets of rules that are applied to a certain traffic flow on your server. Table 30-2 describes the three default chains; Figure 30-9 shows an overview of how these chains work.

Table 30-2. *Chains, the Basic Building Blocks for a Netfilter Firewall*

Chain	Description
INPUT	This chain applies to all the incoming traffic that is destined for the server. It does not apply to traffic that needs to be routed.
OUTPUT	This chain applies to all the traffic that comes from a process on the server. It does not apply to traffic that comes from the routing process.
FORWARD	This chain applies to all the traffic that comes in on a network interface but is not destined for the local machine and has to be routed.

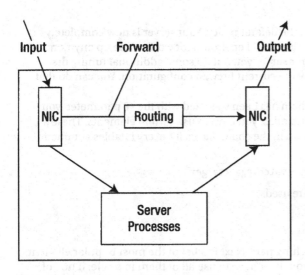

Figure 30-9. *Overview of the use of netfilter chains*

The next part that is required in a netfilter configuration is a set of rules. In these rules, different packet types are defined, and for each of them, a default action is defined. Three things may happen when a packet matches a rule: it can be accepted (ACCEPT), it can be dropped (DROP), and it can be logged (LOG). Note that instead of DROP, which silently discards a packet, you can also use REJECT. In that case, a message is sent to the source of the packet. The rules are evaluated from top to bottom, and as soon as a rule matches a packet, the rule is applied, and no other rules are evaluated. There is an exception, however, if the packet matches a LOG rule; in that case, it is logged, and it continues to the next rule. At the end of all the rule sets, a policy must be defined. You must make sure that the default policy is always set to DROP; that way, you make sure only packets that specifically match a rule are allowed, and everything else is dropped.

To define the rules, you use the `iptables` command. Be aware that nothing you configure with iptables is stored automatically, so you need to store the rules you create in a configuration file so they are executed automatically the next time your server boots. If you want to integrate your own rules with rules that are created by the SUSE firewall interface, which was discussed in the previous sections, you need to put your own rules in /etc/sysconfig/scripts/SuSEfirewall2-custom. If you want to bypass the SUSE firewall completely, create your own iptables rules, and put them in /etc/init.d/boot.local to ensure that they are activated at the earliest possible stage in the boot process.

Using iptables to Create a Firewall

When creating your own firewall with iptables, you first need to set some default policies. Do note, however, that the policy will become effective immediately, so if you are configuring your firewall from an external connection, you will be locked out immediately. In this section, I'm assuming you are configuring iptables from the machine itself (after all, you wouldn't connect an unsecured server to the network, would you?). So, start by creating some policies, entering the next commands:

```
iptables -P FORWARD DROP
iptables -P INPUT DROP
iptables -P OUTPUT DROP
```

In these commands, the option -P sets the default policy. Your server is now completely secure; in fact, it is even so secure that your graphical environment won't come up anymore, so don't save this configuration and reboot your server yet, but do some additional tuning first. Before you do that, it is a good idea to show the current firewall configuration. You can do that with the `iptables -L` command.

Now that the default policy for every chain has been specified with the -P parameter, you need to define the rules themselves. In all the rules, you have to use certain elements. These are the matching part, the target, and the position in the chain. Basically, every iptables command uses the following generic structure:

```
iptables <position in the chain> <chain> <matching> <target>
```

The next sections describe how these are used.

Defining Matching Rules

An important part of every rule is the matching part. Next is a list of the most popular elements that can be used for matching. Note that you don't have to use all of them in a rule; if one of these elements isn't specified, the rule is simply applied to all. For example, if you don't specify a source IP address but you do specify a source port number, the rule applies to the source port number, no matter where the source IP address comes from. You can use the following for matching in a rule:

Interface: Use this to specify the network interface to which the rule applies. -o refers to an output interface, and -i refers to the input interface. It may not surprise you that -o isn't used in the INPUT chain (since it refers to incoming packets only) and -i isn't used in the OUTPUT chain (which refers to outgoing packets only).

Source/destination IP address. You can use -s (source) or -d (destination) to refer to an IP address. Both are IP addresses for individual hosts, because you can use IP addresses for complete networks. For example, use -s 192.168.0.1 to refer to one host only, or use -s 192.168.0.0/16 for all hosts that have a network address starting with 192.168.

Protocol: Use this to refer to protocols as defined in the file /etc/protocols. You can use protocol numbers as well as protocol names, as used in this file. For example, -p TCP refers to all packets in which TCP is used.

Ports: A popular method to filter is based on TCP or UDP port numbers. You can use any port number; check /etc/services for a complete list of services and their default ports if you need more details. For example, use --sport 1024:65535 if you want to refer to all ports greater than port 1024, or use --dport 25 to refer to the SMTP port. Note that when using a port specification, you should always use a protocol specification. So, don't just use --dport 25, but use -p TCP --dport 25.

Specifying the Target

After specifying the matching criterion, a second part of all rules is the *target*. This is the action that has to be performed when a rule matches a packet. All rules have a target, and the following targets are available:

ACCEPT: Use this target to allow the packet.

REJECT: The packet is discarded, and a message is sent to the sender of the packet.

DROP: The packet is discarded, and no message is sent to the sender of the packet.

LOG: The packet is logged. Note that this is the only target that doesn't stop the packet from further evaluation.

Specifying the Position in the Chain

The first step you need to take is to specify where exactly in the chain you need to add a rule. Imagine, for example, that you want to disallow all traffic that has destination port 80, but you do want to allow all traffic coming from IP address 1.2.3.4. If you first create the rule that specifies the destination port and then create the rule for IP address 1.2.3.4, packets from 1.2.3.4 that have destination port 80 will be rejected as well. So, order does matter. When creating a rule, you can use the following options to specify where in the chain you want the rule to appear:

-A: Adds the rule to the end of the chain.

-D: Deletes the rule from the chain.

-R: Replaces a rule.

-I: Inserts the rule at a specific position. For example, use iptables -I INPUT 2 to place the rule on the second position in the INPUT chain.

Stateful Rules

When creating a rule to match packets that always use the same port numbers, everything is easy. Unfortunately, this isn't always the case. For example, a user who connects to a web server will always connect to that web server on port 80, but the packets that go back from the web server go out on a port number that is randomly chosen from a port number greater than 1024. You could create a rule in which outgoing packets on all ports greater than 1024 are opened, but that's not ideal for security reasons. A smart way of dealing with this problem is by using stateful packet filters. A stateful packet filter analyzes whether a packet that goes out is part of an already established connection, and if it is, it will allow the answer to go out. Stateful packet filters are useful for replies that are sent by web servers and for FTP servers as well, since in the case of an FTP server the connection is established on port 21, and once the session is established, data is sent over port 20 to the client.

By using the --state option, you can indicate at what state a rule should look. This functionality, however, is not part of the core netfilter modules; an additional module has to be loaded to allow for state checking. Therefore, in every rule that wants to look at the state that a packet is in, first the -m state option is used, followed by the state the rule is looking at; for example, -m state --state RELATED,ESTABLISHED would look at packets that are part of related packets that are already allowed or packets that are part of an established session.

The state module is not the only module you can use. Many other modules are available for more advanced configurations. There is, for example, the nth module, which allows you to look at every *n*th (every 3rd, for example) packet. Further discussion of modules is beyond the scope of this book.

Creating the Rules

Based on this information, you should be able to create some basic rules. Let's assume you have a server that has only one NIC. On this NIC, you want to allow requests to the web server to come in and replies to go out. Also, you want to allow SSH traffic. For the rest, you don't need anything else.

Like any other netfilter configuration, you would start this configuration by creating some policies. The following will make sure that no packet comes in or out of your server:

```
iptables -P FORWARD DROP
iptables -P INPUT DROP
iptables -P OUTPUT DROP
```

Now that everything is blocked, you can start allowing some packets to go in and out. First, you have to enable the loopback interface; the policies you've just defined also disable all the traffic on the loopback interface, and that's not good, since many services rely on the loopback interface. Without loopback interface, for example, you have no way to start the graphical environment on your machine, and many other services will fail as well. Imagine, for example, that the login process will query an LDAP server that runs on the localhost. Therefore, you should now open the loopback interface using the following two rules:

```
iptables -A INPUT -i lo -j ACCEPT
iptables -A OUTPUT -o lo -j ACCEPT
```

In these two rules, the -A option refers to the chain to which the rules have to be added. Since you are using -A, the rule is just appended. This would make the rule the last rule that is added to the chain, just before the policy, which is always the last rule that is evaluated. Then

-i lo and -o lo indicate that this rule matches everything that happens on the loopback interface. As the third and last part of these two rules, the target is specified by using the -j option
(which is short for "jump to target"). In this case, the target is to accept all matching packets.
So, now you have a server where nothing is allowed on the external network interfaces, but the
loopback interface is completely open.

Next, it is time to do what you want to do on your server: allow incoming SSH and HTTP traffic
and permit replies to the allowed incoming traffic to get out. Note that these two requirements consist of two parts: a part that is configured in the INPUT chain and a part that is configured in the
OUTPUT chain. Let's start with some nice rules that define the INPUT chain:

```
iptables -A INPUT -m state --state ESTABLISHED,RELATED -j ACCEPT
iptables -A INPUT -p tcp --dport 22 -m state --state NEW -j ACCEPT
iptables -A INPUT -p tcp --dport 80 -m state --state NEW -j ACCEPT
iptables -A INPUT -j LOG --log-prefix "Dropped illegal incoming packet: "
```

The first rule in this INPUT chain tells netfilter that all the packets that are part of an already
established or related session are allowed. Next, for packets coming in on SSH port 22 that have a
state NEW, the second rule indicates they are allowed. Third, packets that are sent to TCP destination port 80 (mention the combination between -p tcp and --dport 80 in this rule) and have a
state NEW are accepted. The last rule finally makes sure all the packets that didn't match any of the
earlier rules are logged before they are dropped by the policy at the end of the rule. Note that logging all the dropped packets as a default may cause you big problems!

Caution Use logging only if you need to troubleshoot your firewall. In general, it is a bad idea to switch on
logging by default, because if not done properly, it may cause huge amounts of information to be written to your
log files!

You now have defined the INPUT chain, so let's do the OUTPUT chain as well. Since no specific
services have to be allowed out, with the exception of the replies to incoming packets that were
allowed, creating the OUTPUT chain is rather simple and consists of two rules only:

```
iptables -A OUTPUT -m state RELATED,ESTABLISHED -j ACCEPT
iptables -A OUTPUT -j LOG --log-prefix "Dropped illegal outgoing packet: "
```

Using these two rules should be clear from the explanation earlier in this section. Note that
opposite to the INPUT rule, it is a good idea indeed to do logging in the OUTPUT rule. This is
because if an illegal packet goes out of your server, it would indicate that some rogue service is
active on your server, and you would absolutely need to know about that!

To make creating your own netfilter rules a little easier, Table 30-3 lists some of the most
common port numbers that are configured frequently in a netfilter firewall. For a complete list
of all the port numbers and the names of related services, check the contents of the /etc/
services file. This file lists all the known services with their default ports.

Table 30-3. *Frequently Used Port Numbers*

Port	Service
20	FTP data
21	FTP commands
22	SSH
25	SMTP
53	DNS
80	WWW
88	Kerberos authentication
110	POP3
111	RPC (used by NFS)
118	SQL databases
123	NTP Time
137–139	NetBIOS ports (used by the Samba server)
143	IMAP
161	SNMP (network management)
389	Unsecure LDAP
443	HTTPS
524	NCP (used by some native Novell services such as eDirectory)
636	Secure LDAP

For the netfilter configuration on a server that uses netfilter as a kind of personal firewall, this is probably all you need to know. Notice, however, that you can do much more with iptables, especially if your server is used as a NAT packet forwarding router. Discussing that, however, is beyond the scope of this book.

Tip Were you looking for information on how to configure your server as a NAT firewall? Although outside the scope of this book (most people use dedicated routers for this purpose), I'll share the rule to do that anyway. Use `iptables -t nat -A POSTROUTING -o eth0 -j SNAT --to-source yourserverspublicIPaddress` to make your server a NAT router. Have a lot of fun with it!

Deleting Rules

Sometimes it is necessary to delete rules from the firewall. You can do this in several ways. First, you can use the `iptables -F` command. With this command, you remove all the rules from a chain. You can use this command with the name of the chain you want to remove rules from as its argument or just as `iptables -F`. In the latter case, you remove all the rules from the chain. Be aware that in that case just the policy remains, and you may have a system that disallows connections to anything. So, don't forget to reset the policy by using the `-P` option, as discussed earlier in this chapter. It is also possible to delete individual rules from a chain by using the `-D` option. If you want to work with this option, however, you must refer to the rules by their rule number; this may be problematic if you have chains that contain a lot of rules. Of course, you can also disable the complete firewall. In that case, use the `rcSuSEfirewall stop` command.

Summary

In this chapter, you learned how to set up a firewall based on the Linux netfilter kernel-integrated firewall. Since a firewall can work well only if it is integrated in an overall server security policy, the first section of this chapter mentioned some generic security tips. After that, you learned how to use the YaST integrated program to configure the SUSE firewall, which is basically a set of scripts that allow you to create an iptables firewall easily. In the last part of this chapter, you read how to set up the netfilter firewall by hand using the `iptables` command. In the next chapter, you will read how to use Xen to implement virtualization on SUSE Linux Enterprise Server.

Summary

CHAPTER 31

■■■

Using Xen to Create a Virtual Environment

One of the hottest features in the data center nowadays is the possibility of working with virtualization. *Virtualization* allows you to run software instances of an operating system independent from the hardware. That is, different operating systems and several installations of the same operating system can run on one hardware platform at the same time. If you use the right kind of virtualization, it is even possible to migrate virtual machines to other boxes without any significant downtime. On SUSE Linux Enterprise Server, you get virtualization for free with the Xen open source hypervisor.

Working with Xen Virtualization

Before you start actually configuring virtual machines, you should have some idea of what you're doing. Virtualization is a technique where an instance of the operating system isn't necessarily attached to one physical machine but runs on a virtualized hardware layer that is separate from the actual physical hardware. The operating system doesn't access hardware directly but instead talks to the virtualization layer, which in Xen terminology is called the *hypervisor*. The hypervisor manages access to the real hardware for the virtual machines. This makes it possible to run several instances of an operating system on one physical machine. In a Xen environment, another advantage is that you can allocate hardware resources dynamically. That's to say, if one of your virtual machines is out of physical memory, you just allocate some more memory. It will depend on the operating system in your guest domain whether it will use the added memory and need to reboot.

Companies are adapting virtualization for many reasons; two of them are seen more often than others. First, by using virtualization, you can use hardware more efficiently. Instead of having a server that has a workload no higher than 20 percent of its capacity because only one instance of an operating system is used on it, virtualization allows you to run more instances of an operating system on the server, thus allowing you to use hardware more efficiently. This is especially beneficial for large data centers, since it saves expensive rack space because you just don't need as many servers if you're using virtual machines. Second, by using virtualization, you can increase availability. In a virtual environment, it is possible to replace a virtual machine from one server to another server. This allows you to do hardware maintenance on a server without it causing any downtime for your users.

Virtualization Methods

To understand how Xen works, you should know a little bit about virtualization methods. The first method is known as *full virtualization*. In a full virtualization environment, the virtualization software emulates a complete machine, including all the hardware resources. The operating system running in a full virtualization environment can communicate to the virtual hardware directly, and it isn't aware that it is running in a virtual environment. However, when working with this virtualized hardware, you have to pay a performance price. When using the proper hardware, Xen supports full virtualization. The advantage is that with full virtualization, Xen can run unmodified operating systems (although slower).

Tip Those special extensions needed to support full virtualization sound expensive, don't they? They aren't. Most recent CPUs just have them—on Intel as well as on AMD processors. The Dell laptop I bought in May 2006 is perfectly capable of running in full virtualization mode. If you can choose full virtualization when creating the virtual machine (see "Installing the First Virtual Machine" later in this chapter), your hardware supports it. You may, however, still need to activate it in your system BIOS (check for the Virtualization option).

The alternative to full virtualization is *paravirtualization*. In such an environment, the operating system in the virtual machine needs an application programming interface (API) to get access to the hardware. That is, the operating system in that case is aware that it isn't addressing hardware directly and needs to be modified. For that reason, you may have problems running most non-open source operating systems in such a virtual environment. Currently, only some Linux distributions and Novell's NetWare are modified to run in a paravirtualization environment. Xen can use paravirtualization as well.

The advantage of working with paravirtualization is that it's not necessary to create virtual drivers for all hardware; hardware can be addressed directly, and therefore paravirtualization offers a better performance than full virtualization. Also, the software in a paravirtualization environment communicates directly with the virtual hardware, which makes it possible to adjust hardware parameters without even rebooting the machine. For example, you can add or remove 128MB of memory to an operating system running in a paravirtualization environment without even rebooting it.

Xen Architecture

The most important component in a Xen environment is the virtual machine monitor, also known as the hypervisor. This is the layer between the software and the hardware. The virtual machine monitor must load before any of the virtual machines start. To make that possible, you need an adjusted version of SUSE Linux Enterprise Server that immediately loads the hypervisor. This Linux version is based on a Xen-tuned Linux kernel and will start the so-called domain-0 environment. In the "Installing the Xen Domain-0" section, you will learn how to install this special version of SUSE Linux.

Since the Xen hypervisor doesn't know anything about the hardware in your machine, you need the domain-0 environment to manage hardware access. You can consider domain-0 the host operating system; it is the only instance of your operating system that has direct access to the hardware. Because of that, it is also called the *privileged* domain. Within domain-0, the xend process starts. This process manages all the communication with the other domains. A generic term to refer to all other domains is *domain-U*. These other domains are created with their own domain number, such as domain-1, domain-2, and so on.

Installing Xen

Xen is not installed by default with SUSE Linux Enterprise Server, although you can select a certain software profile to make its installation easier. In the next sections, you'll learn how to prepare for Xen installation and how to install the software on your machine.

Note Unlike other applications, to run Xen virtualization you must not only install the software but must also boot your machine with a special Xen kernel. This kernel is installed automatically when installing the Xen software.

Preparing for Xen Installation

Before you start installing Xen, you should consider the machine you are going to run it on:

- Be aware that every virtual machine has real system requirements. So if you plan to run ten instances of SUSE Linux Enterprise Server that all require a minimum of 256MB RAM, you'll need at least 2.5GB of RAM in your server.

- To make migration easier (*migration* is basically copying a virtual machine out of the memory of one physical system to another physical system), consider installing the instances of your operating system on a SAN. Your migrated instance of the operating system is not going to work if it can't refer to its file systems on disk.

- If you want to create an environment where several physical machines are used to install Xen virtual machines on, you should make sure that all those virtual machines are installed in the same subnet.

- For best performance, each of the software instances that you are going to run needs its own disk partition. You can create these partitions in a file, but creating them on a real disk partition works much better.

Installing the Xen Domain-0

To install Xen, you need to start with the required software:

1. In YaST, open Software ➤ Software Management.

2. From the Filter drop-down list, select Patterns, and make sure that all packages in the Xen pattern are selected.

3. Click Accept to copy all the required packages to your server.

4. Open a console window, and from there use the command less /boot/grub/menu.1st to show the current contents of the GRUB boot loader's boot file. It should include the entry shown in Listing 31-1.

Listing 31-1. *Required Boot Options in* menu.1st *for the Xen Domain-0*

```
###Don't change this comment - YaST2 identifier: Original name: xen###
title XEN
     root (hd0,1)
     kernel /boot/xen.gz
     module /boot/vmlinuz-xen root=/dev/sda2 vga=0x314 resume=/dev/sda1
splash=silent showopts
     module /boot/initrd-xen
```

5. If an entry like the one shown in Listing 31-1 doesn't exist, add it with an editor. If you type it yourself, make sure you are referring to the correct hard drive partition with the root (hd0,1) and root=/dev/sda2 options. In this example, the root file system is on the second partition on the first SCSI hard drive; your system might be configured differently, so change this if needed, and then save and close the file.

6. Since the SuSE firewall cannot handle the complex network settings that are installed by Xen, you should disable SuSE firewall completely. Use the commands insserv -r SuSEfirewall2_setup and insserv -r SuSEfirewall2_init to do that. Before you reboot, make sure you have taken other measures to protect your server.

7. Now reboot your system. In the boot menu (see Figure 31-1), select the SUSE Linux Enterprise Server 10 (XEN) option, and hit Enter. This will start the domain-0 environment. While the system is starting, watch all Xen components being started automatically.

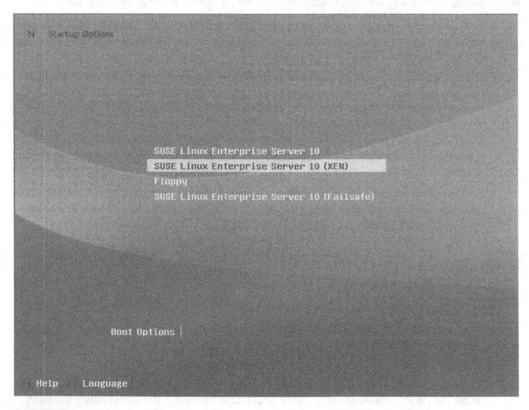

Figure 31-1. *Make sure you select the SUSE Linux Enterprise Server 10 (XEN) option when you reboot your server.*

Tip If your Xen environment has been configured, you will probably want to start it all the time from now on. To do that, open the boot loader configuration in YaST's System menu, and make it your default boot image. Check Chapter 10 for details about how to do that.

---

8. When the system is up and running again, open a terminal window, and as root, from that window, run the xm list command. This should give a result like in Listing 31-2, indicating that domain-0 is up and running.

Listing 31-2. *Use the* xm list *Command to Check That Domain-0 Is Up and Running*

```
BTN:~ # xm list
Name                     ID   Mem(MiB)   VCPUs  State    Time(s)
Domain-0                 0               463        1   r-----      441.4
```

If you've come this far, you're ready to configure the first virtual machine. In the next section you'll learn how.

Installing the First Virtual Machine

Now that the domain-0 is up and running, it's time to start installing the first virtual machine. You have two ways to do that: you can actually run the installation program, and alternatively, you can use a disk image or a physical disk that contains the operating system files.

Note At the time this was written, Xen was still a leading-edge technology. Some operating systems can have a problem when you try installing them in a Xen environment. For up-to-date status information about how to run your favorite operating system in Xen, consult http://www.novell.com/documentation/vmserver/index.html. The section "Working with Specific Operating Systems" contains valuable information.

In the following steps, you'll learn how to install another instance of SUSE Linux Enterprise Server 10:

1. From YaST, select System ➤ Virtual Machine Management (Xen). This opens the Manage Virtual Machines screen shown in Figure 31-2.

2. Make sure that the SUSE Linux installation media is present in an installation source that is registered on your domain-0 machine. Basically, if you installed from a DVD, make sure the DVD is inserted in your optical drive, and if you installed from a network server, make sure you can reach it.

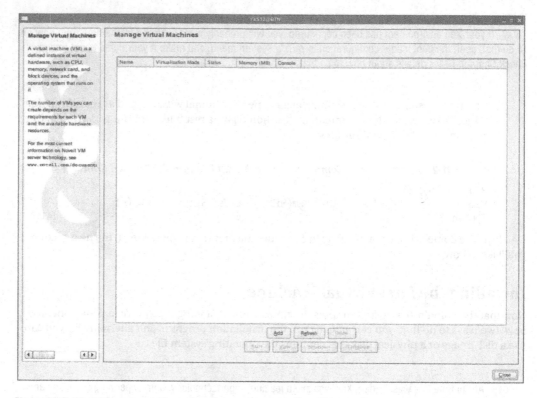

Figure 31-2. *Use this screen to install and manage virtual machines.*

3. Click Add. This opens the screen shown in Figure 31-3. On this screen, you need to specify how you want to install. Select Run an OS Installation Program to run the installer for your operating system, and select Use a Disk Image or a Physical Disk That Contains OS Boot Files if you have an image file that is prepared to run in your Xen environment.

Note To run an operating system from an image file, it must have been prepared to run in a Xen environment if you plan on using paravirtualization. If you have hardware that supports Xen, no further preparation is required.

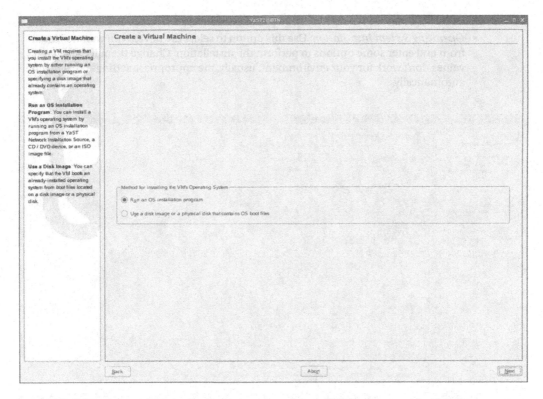

Figure 31-3. *Select Run an OS Installation Program, and then click Next to start the installation.*

4. Now you'll see the Virtual Machine (Installation Settings) screen (see Figure 31-4). On this screen, you can change the installation environment. Tune the environment as needed, and then click Next to continue and start the installation. The following options are available:

- *AutoYaST*: Use this option to specify whether an AutoYaST file is available for automatically entering all the configuration parameters. See Chapter 35 for more details about creating AutoYaST files.

- *Virtualization Mode*: Choose between paravirtualization and hardware virtualization. You can select hardware virtualization only if your hardware supports it; otherwise, the option to select it is grayed out.

- *VM Properties*: Specify properties of the virtual machine here. The most important thing you specify here is the name of the virtual machine, which by default is vm, followed by a number.

- *Hardware*: Use this option to indicate what virtual hardware to use. By default, the virtual machine gets 256MB of RAM, can access one CPU only, and will use the hardware clock with the UTC time setting.

- *Disks*: Indicate what disk devices to use. By default, the virtual machine will install to a file that is used as a partition by the virtual machine. If a free disk partition is available, you can select it here.

- *Network*: Use this option to select the number of network cards you want to use.
- *Operating System Installation*: Use this option to select the device you want to install from and enter some options to perform the installation. Change them if the default values don't work for your environment; usually, the appropriate settings are detected automatically.

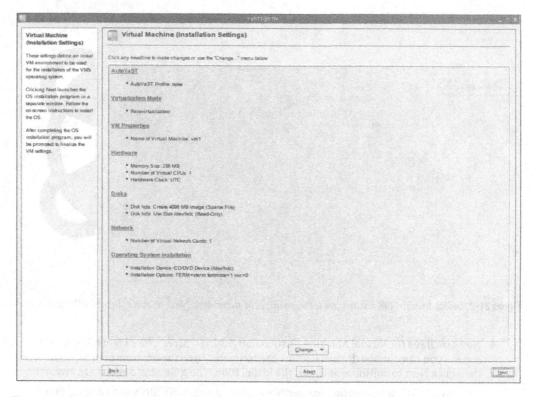

Figure 31-4. *Before you start the installation, indicate how you want to install.*

5. The virtual machine environment is now prepared. That can take a while. When this part of the installation is finished, a terminal will open (see Figure 31-5). In that terminal window, you'll see a text-based installation of SUSE Linux Enterprise Server that starts (graphical installation is not supported yet). Except that it is a text-based installation screen, it works the same way as the graphical installation; only the looks are different. So, now you'll complete the installation procedure of the new machine.

■**Tip** Don't like the text-based installation? In that case, you can use VNC installation to do a graphical installation. To enable this, make sure the following boot options are passed to the kernel when starting the installation: vnc=1 vncpassword=something dhcp=1. Of these, the option vnc=1 enables VNC for the installation program. The option vnpassword=something sets the VNC password to something, and dhcp=1 makes sure your server will ask for an IP address from a DHCP server.

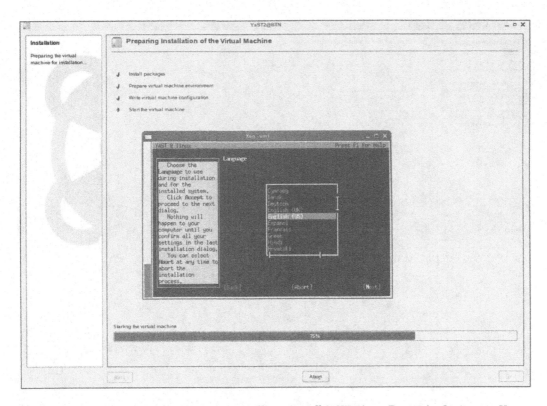

Figure 31-5. *You have to use the text-based installer to install SUSE Linux Enterprise Server as a Xen virtual machine.*

6. When the installation is finished, you'll see a message that states that virtual machine settings now need to be finalized. On this message, click Continue. This brings you to the Virtual Machine (Final Settings) screen shown in Figure 31-6. On this screen, you can see four items:

   - *VM Properties*: This specifies how the machine is activated and what should happen when power is switched off, when the domain-0 machine is rebooted, or when the domain-0 machine is restarted.

   - *Hardware*: This specifies the hardware settings of the virtual machine. From here you can, for example, change its current memory assignment.

   - *Network*: This manages your machine's network properties. Use it, for example, to add another network board to your machine.

   - *Operating System Boot*: This contains all the information that is necessary to boot the virtual machine. It contains settings that usually you would expect in a GRUB boot menu.

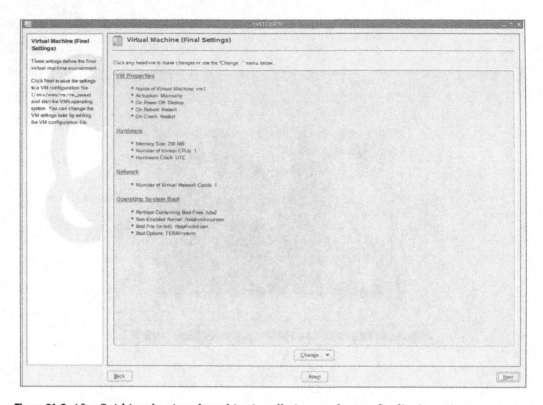

Figure 31-6. *After finishing the virtual machine installation, you have to finalize its settings.*

7. After clicking Next to write the finalized settings to your system, your virtual machine will reboot. Once it is booted, you can start using it immediately. You can follow the status of the virtual machine by using the YaST Xen management interface or by typing the xm list command on a console.

■**Tip** Depending on the installation method you are using, you may not be ready yet. If you are installing from CD, for example, the installer at this point has just installed files from CD 1, and all the other CDs still have to be inserted.

Managing Xen Domains

You can manage Xen in two ways: from the YaST interface and from the command line. To do your work from the command line, use the powerful xm command together with the Xen configuration files. From YaST, you can use the Manage Virtual Machines interface that you also used to create your virtual machine. The next sections explain both methods.

Managing Xen from the Command Line

Managing Xen from the command line involves two skills: tuning the configuration file and working with the xm tool. Both are explained in the next two sections.

Managing Xen Configuration Files

Every Xen domain has its own configuration file. Typically, you can find these configuration files in /etc/xen/vm. For this example, you'll start with the configuration file for the virtual machine that was created in Listing 31-3.

Listing 31-3. *Xen Domain Configuration File*

```
BTN:/etc/xen/vm # cat vm1
disk = [ 'file:/var/lib/xen/images/vm1/hda,hda,w', 'phy:/dev/hdc,hdb,r' ]
memory = 256
vcpus = 1
builder = 'linux'
name = 'vm1'
vif = [ 'mac=00:16:3e:66:65:5b' ]
localtime = 0
on_poweroff = 'destroy'
on_reboot = 'restart'
on_crash = 'restart'
extra = ' TERM=xterm'
bootloader = '/usr/lib/xen/boot/domUloader.py'
bootentry = 'hda2:/boot/vmlinuz-xen,/boot/initrd-xen'
```

As you will recognize, this file contains the same settings as the ones you entered on the Virtual Machine (Final Settings) screen in step 6 of the previous procedure. Nevertheless, a short explanation of the different settings used in the configuration file follows in Table 31-1.

Table 31-1. *Xen Configuration Settings*

Parameter	Explanation
disk	This parameter indicates what disk should be used. In the example, two disks are defined. First, a disk that is created in the image file /var/lib/xen/images/vm1/hda is specified. The name of this disk in the Xen virtual machine will be hda, and the w indicates that it can be written to. Next, phy specifies a physical disk. In this case, it is /dev/hdc, the CD device. The local device name of it in the Xen machine will be hdb, and it is read-only.
memory	This is the amount of memory to which the virtual machine has access. You can change this option at runtime.
vcpus	This is the number of CPUs that can be used; 1 in this case indicates that just one CPU can be used.
builder	This is the type of operating system that was used as domain-0.
name	This is the name assigned to the virtual machine.
vif	This is the MAC address of the virtual network interface.
localtime	This parameter indicates whether local time or UTC is used on the system hardware clock. The value 0 you see in the example indicates that the hardware clock is set to UTC.
on_poweroff	Use this parameter to indicate what should happen if the virtual machine powers off. The value destroy indicates it will just be stopped.
on_reboot	This parameter indicates what happens when the virtual machine is rebooted.
on_crash	This parameter specifies what happens when the virtual machine crashes.

Continued

Table 31-1. *Continued*

Parameter	Explanation
extra	Use this parameter to pass extra boot options to the kernel. In this case, the TERM variable specifies what kind of terminal to use.
bootloader	This refers to the program that is used as the boot loader. Do not change this, because domUloader.py is the only boot loader that will work.
bootentry	This option indicates which kernel and initrd should be started. In the example where the operating system in the virtual machine is the same as the domain-0 operating system, you can refer to the vmlinuz-xen en initrd-xen in the domain-0 boot directory.

In Listing 31-3, you have seen what a configuration file can look like if it has been generated with YaST. Instead of using YaST to generate the virtual machine configuration file, you can create one yourself as well. In that case, use the well-documented file /etc/xen/examples/example1. It contains all parameters that can be used for your new machine. Change them as required and next boot the virtual machine to start its installation (see the next section about how to boot the machine using the xm tool).

Working with the xm Tool

The xm tool is the universal command that you can use to configure and tune how Xen works. To do this, the xm tool communicates directly to the xend process, which is responsible for managing all Xen domains from the domain-0 environment. You can use the xm tool with different options that all behave like commands by themselves. For example, you have already seen the xm list command that lists all the virtual machines that are currently running. I'll now discuss all the other important xm commands.

First, you can use the xm create command to start a virtual machine; for example, xm create -c -f /etc/xen/vm/vm1 will start the virtual machine of which the configuration is stored in the file /etc/xen/vm/vm1. In this command, the -c option indicates that the virtual machine should run in its own console. This is not a requirement; a virtual machine can run perfectly in the background as well. If that's the case, you can easily attach it to a console with the xm console command, followed by the domain ID. To see what domain ID a virtual machine is using, use the xm list command, which will list the domain IDs of all the machines that currently are active. For example, if the ID of your virtual machine is 2, use xm console 2 to give the virtual machine its console back. To detach a machine from a console if it is actually running in a console, use the Ctrl+] key sequence.

The next interesting xm command is xm pause, followed by the domain number of your virtual machine. This command allows you to temporarily stop a virtual machine. To start it again after it has been stopped, use xm unpause followed by the domain ID. These commands are useful if you temporarily don't need a virtual machine.

The xm command also allows you to stop and restart virtual machines:

xm shutdown <domain-ID>: Use this command to shut down a domain.

xm destroy <domain-ID>: Use this to shut down a domain if it doesn't respond to the xm shutdown command.

xm save <domain-ID> <filename>: Use this to save the state of a domain. You can compare this command to the suspend command in VMware, because it allows you to restart the domain in the same status over a reboot of domain-0.

xm restore <filename>: This command restores a domain after it has been saved with the xm save command.

Another useful command you can use is the xm mem_set command. This one allows you to change the amount of RAM that is assigned to a virtual machine without even rebooting the virtual machine. To use it, specify the domain ID and the new amount of memory that it gets; for example, use xm mem_set 2 512 to assign 512MB of memory to domain 2. This command has its counterpart in the xm vcpu-set command that allows you to change the amount of CPUs that a virtual machine can use (this of course works only on a multi-CPU machine).

Another command that is useful is xentop. This command works like the regular Linux top command, but it displays the status of your virtual machines. From xentop you can, for example, get an overview of current CPU usage, memory usage, and network traffic. Check Figure 31-7 for an example.

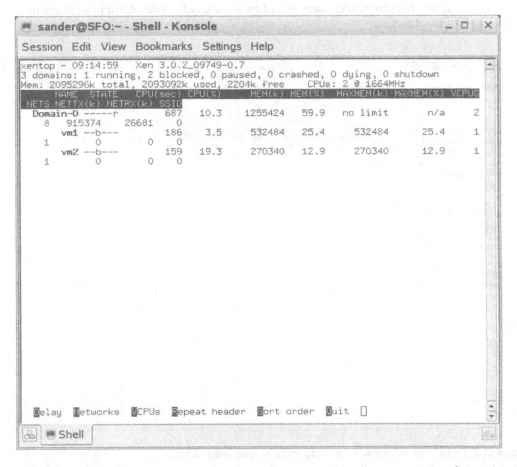

Figure 31-7. *The* xentop *command gives a performance summary for the current status of your virtual machines.*

Managing Virtual Machines from YaST

Currently, YaST offers limited functionality for virtual machine management. On the Manage Virtual Machines screen shown in Figure 31-8, seven different options are available:

Add: Use this option to define a new virtual machine.

Refresh: With this option you can refresh the status of a virtual machine.

Delete: If the selected machine currently is not active, use this option to delete it.

Start: If the selected virtual machine currently is not active, use this option to start it.

View: If the machine is not currently visible in a console, use this option to connect it to a console so that you can work in it.

Shutdown: Use this option to shut down the virtual machine.

Terminate: Use this option to terminate a virtual machine if it is no longer replying.

As you can see, the current YaST management options are rather limited. For more flexibility, use the xm command instead.

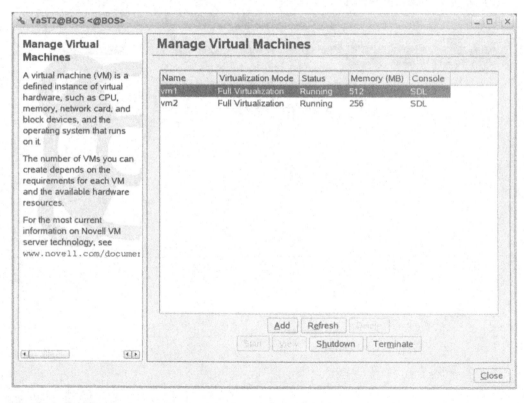

Figure 31-8. *From YaST, some limited management options are available.*

Managing Xen Networking

One of the hardest parts to understand when working with Xen is networking. The difficulty is that Xen offers so many options to connect the network card of a virtual machine to the network card of the domain-0 machine. By default, *bridging* is used. With bridging, you basically connect the virtual network adapter directly to the network. This means that the virtual machine needs an IP address in the same range as the IP address of the real network adapter in the eth0 domain.

Each network interface used by a virtual domain exists in two places: as a network interface in the domain-U and as a virtual interface in domain-0. These interfaces are connected by a point-to-point link; you can imagine this as a virtual cross-over cable. The device names for the interfaces in the virtual domains can be recognized by their names, such as vif1.0 and vif1.1. From these names, you can see that both are interfaces in domain 1; vif1.0 is the first interface that is used in that domain, and vif1.1 is its second interface. By default, the vif interfaces are bridged with the eth0 device in domain-0.

Two scripts configure Xen networking. The default scripts that are used to set up the bridge are network-bridge and vif-bridge. The scripts are in /etc/xen/scripts and are started automatically when the xend process initializes. Of these scripts, the network-bridge script creates the bridge that is used by Xen, the xen-br0 device. It also makes sure that eth0 is connected to that bridge and that routing is properly initialized. The vif-bridge script connects all interfaces to the bridge as well. The /etc/xen/xend-config.sxp script tells the xend process that it should load network bridging by default. As an alternative to that, you can use routing or NAT as well.

Tip Want to check or tune the configuration of the Ethernet bridge used by Xen? Use brctl. For example, the brctl show command displays an overview of its current configuration.

If you want to set up network routing, you need two other scripts as well. First, the network-route script must be activated to create the virtual router device. Next, the vif-route script makes sure that each of the virtual network interfaces is added to the virtual router device. If you want to use routing by default instead of bridging, change the /etc/xen/xend-config.sxp file accordingly. In this file, you'll find the following commented lines:

```
#(network-script    network-route)
#(vif-script        vif-route)
```

To activate these scripts, first remove the comment signs in the beginning of the line. Next, comment out the following lines:

```
(network-script    network-bridge)
(vif-script         vif-bridge)
```

If you don't disable these two lines by putting a comment mark in front, the xend process will try to initialize the bridge as the router and will fail in that. As an alternative to using the network-route and vif-route scripts, you can use network-nat and vif-nat to set up a NAT interface. In both cases, don't forget to set the default route in the domain-U to the eth0 device; otherwise, packets cannot be routed out of the virtual machines.

Migrating Virtual Machines

One of the coolest features of Xen is the option to move virtual machines to other hardware. This feature is extremely useful to make hardware maintenance easier: just move the virtual machines running on box A to box B (which of course needs to have xend running as well), and you can bring down box A without any problem. There is, however, one important condition to make it work that easily; after the migration, the virtual machine also needs access to its storage. So if the machine is installed on a local disk device in box A and you bring it down, there's no way it can still run. Therefore, to use this feature, you need a SAN. This can be a huge and expensive enterprise SAN; cheap shared storage based on iSCSI or even DRBD suffices; check Chapter 29 for more details about iSCSI configuration in SUSE Linux. Once the SAN is in place, you can move around virtual machines using the xm command using either the save method or the fast method.

If it doesn't matter that your users are experiencing some downtime, you can use the xm save and xm restore commands to move a virtual machine. The following steps illustrate how:

1. Use xm save <domain-id> <filename> to save the current state of a domain to a file. If you're not sure what domain ID to use, use xm list to find out.

2. Copy the file that you created with the xm save command to the other host.

3. On the other host, use xm restore <filename> to restore the virtual machine.

This method is cool but requires some downtime. Even if you do it quickly, between saving the current state of a machine on one host and restoring it on the other host, there will be at least a couple of minutes of downtime. A much faster way of doing it is by using the migrate option. If you use the --live option, this will work extremely fast. To copy the virtual machine with domain ID 2 to the host with IP address 192.168.1.30, you can use xm migrate --live 2 192.168.1.30. The --live option will tell Xen that it must try to keep the machine running while doing the migration.

Before you can use virtual machine migration, you need to tune the xend configuration file /etc/xen/xend-config.sxp on the machines that are involved. In this file, you'll find a few lines that manage whether and how relocation can happen. The following two lines are especially important:

```
(xend-relocation-server yes)
(xend-relocation-hosts-allow '^localhost$')
```

The first line indicates whether the host permits migration. Make sure this option is set to yes. The second option determines what hosts are allowed to migrate virtual machines to this host. As you can see, in this example (which contains the default setting), only localhost can do migration. To do it the easy way and allow any host to relocate virtual machines to this host, change the second line to (xend-relocation-hosts-allow ' ').

Summary

In this chapter, you learned how to work with Xen, one of the most spectacular new additions to SUSE Linux Enterprise Server. Using Xen, you can create virtual machines on your server. The paravirtualization option is the fastest method but requires some changes to the guest operating system. If your CPU supports virtualization, you can use hardware virtualization as well to run unmodified operating systems in the virtual environment. With SUSE Linux Enterprise Server, you can set up the virtual environment easily, using YaST. Also, the xm command that you can use to manage the virtual environment is not hard at all to use. In the next chapter, you will learn how to use AppArmor to provide application security.

CHAPTER 32

■ ■ ■

Using AppArmor to Secure Applications

Installing a firewall is one thing. A firewall, however, wouldn't protect you if your application had a security hole. For example, a buffer overflow problem could give an intruder root access to your system without any limitations. Therefore, you need a solution to secure applications on a per-application basis. AppArmor is such a solution, and it is integrated in SUSE Linux Enterprise Server. In this chapter, you'll learn how to configure it.

Exploring the AppArmor Components

The core component of AppArmor is the profile. You can create a profile for every application, and in these profiles, you can define exactly what an application can do and what it cannot do. How the AppArmor profiles work is based on two Linux kernel modules, apparmor and aamatch_pcre, that hook directly into the Linux Security Modules Framework of the kernel. These two working together make it possible to use POSIX capabilities to define exactly what an application can do and what an application cannot do.

Note The POSIX standard defines common standards for Linux and Unix operating systems. POSIX capabilities include all actions that can happen on a Linux system; see http://www.pasc.org for more information about this standard.

Basically, if an application is started as root and it has an AppArmor profile, the AppArmor profile determines what the application can do and doesn't care that the user is logged in as root.

An AppArmor profile contains rules, which define the capabilities that the application can have and the permissions to files for the application. Listing 32-1 gives an example of how these are applied in the default profile for xinetd. You can find this example profile in /etc/apparmor/profiles/extras/usr.sbin.xinetd.

Listing 32-1. *Example Profile for xinetd*

```
# ----------------------------------------

# include <tunables/global>

/usr/sbin/xinetd {
  #include <abstractions/base>
  #include <abstractions/nameservice>

  capability net_bind_service,
  capability setgid,
  capability setuid,

  /etc/hosts.allow           r,
  /etc/hosts.deny            r,
  /etc/xinetd.conf           r,
  /etc/xinetd.d              r,
  /etc/xinetd.d/*            r,
  /usr/sbin/xinetd           rmix,
  /var/log/xinetd.log        w,
  /var/log/xinetd.pid        rwl,

  /bin/netstat               Px,
  /bin/ps                    mix,
  /sbin/linuxconf            Px,
  ...
}
```

In this incomplete example, you see that first some additional configuration files are included. Next, the POSIX capabilities that are needed for this program are defined. If the program will run as root, it would have access to all 31 capabilities that allow for complete access to the system. In this case, you can see that the capabilities are limited to three only. For a complete list of all capabilities, consult man 7 capabilities. Following the capabilities, you'll see a list of files and directories, and for each of these files and directories, the profile defines the permissions that the process has defined. Table 32-1 gives an overview of all the permissions you can use.

Table 32-1. *Overview of AppArmor Permissions*

Permission	Use
r	Gives read access to the resource.
w	Gives write access to the file. This also allows the program to remove the file.
l	Gives link access to a file. This allows a process to create or remove links.
m	This allows for executable mapping. This permission allows executable files to be loaded in memory.
ix	Inherit Execute Mode; a program that is executed by this program inherits the current profile settings for execution.
px	Discrete Profile Execute Mode; this mode indicates that a program needs its own AppArmor profile.
Px	Like px, but the program loads without any environment variables being passed to the child process.

Permission	Use
ux	Allows the program to run without any AppArmor profile restrictions being applied to it. Don't use this permission because it is insecure.
Ux	Allows the program to run without any AppArmor profile restrictions being applied to it in its own environment, meaning that any environment variables from the parent process are not passed through to the child process. Don't use this permission because it is insecure.

To start AppArmor, you need certain services. You can start these services manually with the rcapparmor start command. To stop AppArmor, use rcapparmor stop or rcapparmor kill if you also want to unload the AppArmor kernel modules. You don't need to include AppArmor services in the start-up procedure of your server; if it is installed, it will load automatically when your server boots. Note that AppArmor has a restart/reload option; activate this with rcapparmor restart or rcapparmor reload. These two commands are the same; both will force AppArmor to reread its configuration. You should, however, be aware that if you reload the AppArmor configuration, you should reload all the applications that are confined by AppArmor as well. Therefore, it may be a better idea just to restart your complete server using the reboot command as root.

Managing AppArmor Profiles with YaST

You can manage AppArmor profiles in three ways. You can create the required configuration files by hand, you can automate the creation of these files from the command line, and you can also use YaST to perform this task. Since creating AppArmor configuration files by hand can be a daunting task (you would have to know exactly what an application is doing to do that), I recommend using YaST for this purpose. In the next sections, you'll read how to create, update, and delete profiles from YaST.

Creating a New Profile

In YaST, you'll find a dedicated menu option to manage AppArmor. Before you click the Add Profile Wizard icon on this menu, make sure the application you want to create the profile for is not currently active. Once you have disabled the application, use the following steps to create a profile for it. In these steps, you will learn how to create a profile for the Mozilla Firefox browser. I prefer covering Firefox, because profiles for most server applications are present by default. Also, many administrators use Firefox on their servers, and a misconfigured browser is a major source of infections on a server.

1. From YaST, select Novell AppArmor ➤ Add Profile Wizard. This opens the screen shown in Figure 32-1. On this screen, enter the name of the application for which you want to create the profile. You can enter a complete application name or just the name of the application you want to start. In the latter case, AppArmor will check the search path to find out where the application is installed. So to create a profile for Firefox, it suffices just to enter firefox on this screen. Then click Create to continue.

Figure 32-1. *To create a profile for an application, enter the name of the application, and then click Create to continue.*

2. You now see the start screen of the AppArmor Profile Wizard (see Figure 32-2). On this screen, you should also see the complete name of the application for which you are creating the profile. Double-check that you entered the correct name. Then start the application and perform all the tasks you usually do with your application. In the case of a web browser, make sure you access some complicated web pages, preferably some web pages that have active content. Also make sure you load and save some files from the File menu. It is important at this stage that the profiling program can get as complete an impression of what the application usually does as possible. During this learning phase of the process, a log file is created where all the activity of the application is logged. You can find this log in the file /var/log/audit/audit.log.

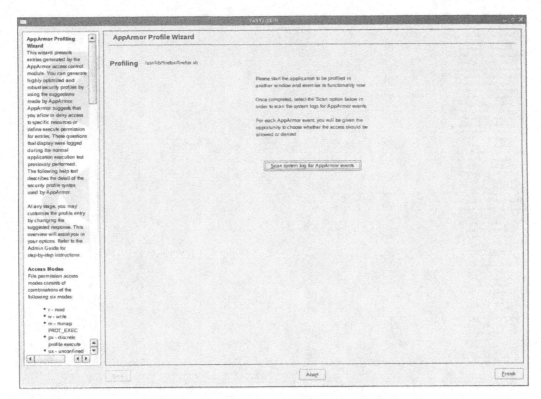

Figure 32-2. *When you see this screen, it is time to start using your application so AppArmor can analyze what exactly it is doing.*

3. Once you have done everything that is needed with your application, on the screen shown in Figure 32-2, click Scan System Log for AppArmor Events. This will display a dialog box for each event that was found. Three different types of dialog boxes can appear: one for program settings, one for capability settings, and one for file access. In Figure 32-3, you see the screen that pops up if a program file was accessed. On this screen, you need to specify what exactly you want to do for that program. You can choose from four different options:

   - *Inherit*: Choose this to let the resource inherit the current program. Use this option for programs that are started by the parent program, which really are part of the parent program and should be treated as such. It makes sure that subprocesses started by a program can all run. In most situations, this is the best choice.

   - *Profile*: Use this if you want to create a separate profile for a program. That is started from the parent program. This is a good choice for more important programs that can also run as independent programs.

   - *Unconfirmed*: This option specifies that no profile should be used for this program. Only use this option if everything else doesn't work; it will completely disable AppArmor security settings for the selected program.

   - *Deny*: Click this if you want to disallow execution of the selected program. Be aware that choosing this option will limit the usability of the program.

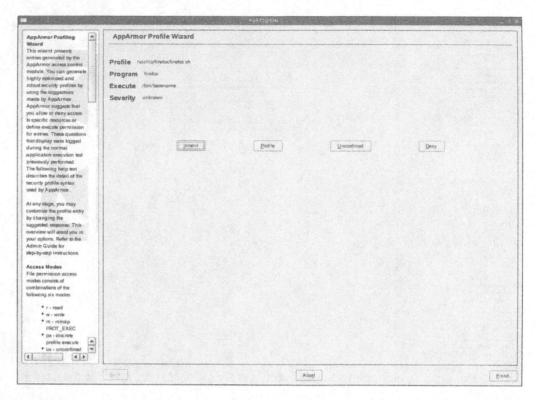

Figure 32-3. *For each program that was started by your application, you can indicate how you want AppArmor to handle the program.*

4. If you want to specify how to handle the use of one of the POSIX capabilities, the screen shown in Figure 32-4 appears. On this screen, you can indicate whether you want to allow or disallow the use of that capability. You should note that when disallowing a capability, your application can probably not do its work at all. If you want to check what exactly a certain capability is doing, check man 7 capabilities.

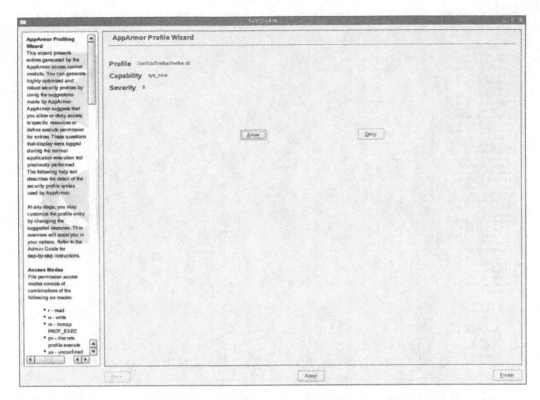

Figure 32-4. *With regard to capabilities, you can choose between allowing or denying the use of the capability.*

5. Again, you'll see a different screen when a file has been accessed (see Figure 32-5). To specify what your application can do with a file, make a choice from the following buttons:

- *Allow*: This gives the program access to the specified file or directory.

- *Deny*: This denies the program access to the specified file or directory.

- *Glob*: If you click the Glob button once, the name of the file is replaced by an asterisk (*), thus referring to all the files in the directory, but not in subdirectories. If you click the Glob button a second time, the name of the file is replaced by **, which refers to all the files in the directory where your file is, including all of its subdirectories. Every next time you click Glob, the utility walks up one level in the directory tree, thus including the parent directory of the directory that is currently selected as well.

- *Glob w/Ext*: This option is like globbing, but it keeps the extension of the selected file. So if the name of your file is blah.txt, clicking Glob w/Ext once will make sure that access is allowed to all files with the extension .txt, and clicking Glob w/Ext a second time will do the same for all of its subdirectories.

- *Edit*: Use this option to edit the highlighted filename by hand.

6. After specifying, for each file, the capabilities and processes that your application is allowed to do, click the Finish button. This exits the AppArmor Profile Wizard and writes the configuration to your system. Make sure your application is restarted now to allow complete AppArmor functionality.

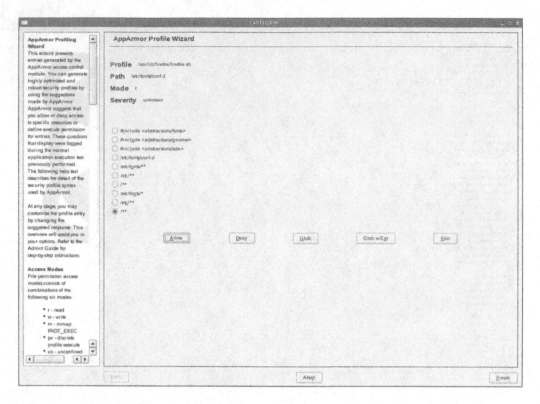

Figure 32-5. *One of the most powerful options with regard to file access is globbing. With this you can allow access to complete directory structures as well.*

You now have a profile for your application. You may, however, experience that some functionality of the application is limited. In that case, you'll need to update the profile for your application. If your program doesn't work anymore after a path or update has been applied (this can happen, such as when the name of the binary or some of the files used by the application change), you need to update the profile as well. The next section describes how you can do that.

Updating a Profile

The best method to update an existing profile is to use the YaST Update Profile Wizard. Before you can do that, though, you have to tell AppArmor that it has to be switched to learning mode. Also, after running the Update Profile Wizard, you need to tell YaST you've finished applying the updates. The following steps describe how to proceed in order to update profiles:

1. Before you start the Update Profile Wizard, issue the complain command for the application for which you want to update the profile. For example, complain firefox will activate the learning mode for Firefox.

2. Now start using the application extensively, in a way that all possible files are accessed, capabilities are used, and processes used by your application are activated.

3. Next, from YaST, run the Update Profile Wizard to start profiling the application again. This displays the same interface as the Create Profile Wizard where you have to specify the permissions you want to grant for each item.

4. When finished, use the enforce command to switch your profile from learning mode to enforce mode. For example, use enforce firefox to make sure the new profile is applied.

Deleting a Profile

In rare cases, you may encounter a situation where you want to stop AppArmor "confining" for your application completely. If that's the case, from YaST select the Delete Profile option. This opens a list where you'll see all the currently existing profiles (see Figure 32-6). From this list, select the profile you want to delete, and then click Next. Then click Yes to confirm that you really want to delete the profile, and the profile will be deleted. AppArmor will reload its profile set so that the application for which you just deleted the profile will run immediately without a profile.

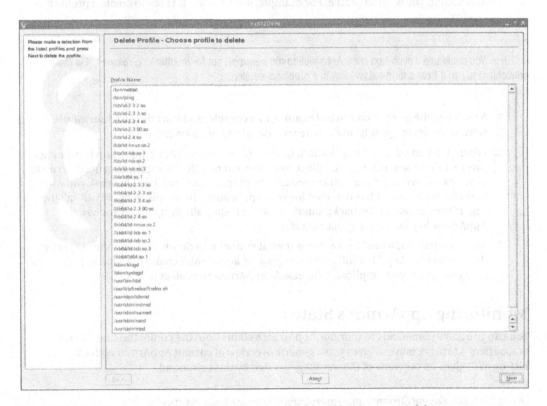

Figure 32-6. *The Delete Profile option lets you choose which profile you want to delete.*

Managing AppArmor Profiles from the Command Line

YaST is by far the easiest way to create a profile. It is, however, not the only way, and as an alternative, you can also create profiles from the command line. The most useful command to do that is genprof, which is short for *generate profile*. From the command line, you also can monitor the status of AppArmor. The following sections outline both tasks.

Creating a Profile with genprof

If working with YaST is not an option for you, you can create a profile from the command line. The following steps show you how to create a profile for Firefox with genprof:

1. From a terminal window, as root, use the genprof command followed by the name of the application you want to profile. For example, use genprof firefox to create a profile for Firefox.

Note You could use a plain-text console as well to run genprof, but for multitasking reasons, it is much more convenient to run it from a terminal window in a graphical session.

---

2. Now leave the genprof command running in a console, and start the program for which you want to create the profile. Make sure you use all its functionality.

3. When finished using the application, in the terminal where your application is running, press s to start scanning the log file to analyze what exactly the application needs to do its work. As when using the graphical wizard, the genprof command will now ask you what to do for each event it has detected for your application. To do this, genprof will call the logprof command in the background; the latter is specially designed to analyze the AppArmor log file /var/log/audit/audit.log.

4. After you have indicated for each event what you want to do with it, from the genprof window, press the f key. This will terminate genprof activity and create the profile. Now make sure you restart your application to enable AppArmor to protect it.

Monitoring AppArmor's Status

You can use a few commands to monitor AppArmor's status from the command line. First, the rcapparmor status command gives you a generic overview of current AppArmor activity. Listing 32-2 gives an overview of the output generated by this command.

Listing 32-2. *Displaying Current AppArmor Activity with* apparmor status

```
SFO:~ # rcapparmor status
apparmor module is loaded.
61 profiles are loaded.
52 profiles are in enforce mode.
9 profiles are in complain mode.
Out of 130 processes running:
6 processes have profiles defined.
6 processes have profiles in enforce mode.
0 processes have profiles in complain mode.
```

Now when you know that AppArmor is protecting some processes, you probably want to find out what processes these are. To do this, look at the `/sys/kernel/security/apparmor/profiles` file. This shows a complete list of all the process files that currently are protected by AppArmor. For an example of the output generated by this command, see Listing 32-3.

Listing 32-3. *Viewing All Process Files Currently Protected by AppArmor*

```
SFO:~ # cat /sys/kernel/security/apparmor/profiles
/usr/sbin/traceroute (enforce)
/usr/sbin/squid (enforce)
/usr/sbin/sendmail (enforce)
/usr/sbin/postqueue (enforce)
/usr/sbin/postmap (enforce)
/usr/sbin/postdrop (enforce)
/usr/sbin/postalias (enforce)
/usr/sbin/ntpd (enforce)
/usr/sbin/nscd (enforce)
/usr/sbin/named (enforce)
/usr/sbin/mdnsd (enforce)
/usr/sbin/in.identd (enforce)
/usr/sbin/identd (enforce)
/usr/lib/postfix/virtual (complain)
/usr/lib/postfix/verify (complain)
/usr/lib/postfix/trivial-rewrite (enforce)
/usr/lib/postfix/tlsmgr (enforce)
/usr/lib/postfix/spawn (complain)
/usr/lib/postfix/smtpd (enforce)
/usr/lib/postfix/smtp (enforce)
```

A third command that is pretty useful to monitor the current status of AppArmor is unconfined. This command lists all the processes that currently are active but do not have an AppArmor profile loaded. In other words, these are the unprotected commands for which you should consider creating and loading a profile as well! See Listing 32-4 for an example.

Listing 32-4. *Generating a List of All Programs Running But Not Protected by AppArmor*

```
SFO:~ # unconfined
2749 /usr/sbin/mdnsd confined by '/usr/sbin/mdnsd (enforce)'
2749 /usr/sbin/mdnsd confined by '/usr/sbin/mdnsd (enforce)'
2749 /usr/sbin/mdnsd confined by '/usr/sbin/mdnsd (enforce)'
2749 /usr/sbin/mdnsd confined by '/usr/sbin/mdnsd (enforce)'
2798 /usr/lib/zmd/zmd-bin not confined
2817 /sbin/portmap not confined
2817 /sbin/portmap not confined
3158 /usr/sbin/nmbd not confined
3158 /usr/sbin/nmbd not confined
3158 /usr/sbin/nmbd not confined
3158 /usr/sbin/nmbd not confined
3158 /usr/sbin/nmbd not confined
3158 /usr/sbin/nmbd not confined
3158 /usr/sbin/nmbd not confined
3158 /usr/sbin/nmbd not confined
3248 /usr/lib/postfix/master confined by '/usr/lib/postfix/master (enforce)'
3248 /usr/lib/postfix/master confined by '/usr/lib/postfix/master (enforce)'
3299 /usr/sbin/sshd not confined
3543 /sbin/dhclient not confined
```

```
3575 /usr/sbin/cupsd not confined
3575 /usr/sbin/cupsd not confined
3724 /usr/sbin/smbd not confined
```

Summary

In this chapter, you learned how to use AppArmor for application security. You can use AppArmor to protect applications against programming faults within the application. Such errors could give root access to your system through a misbehaving application; if, however, the application is protected by an AppArmor profile, you can indicate exactly what the application is permitted to do and what it isn't permitted to do. AppArmor, therefore, is an important part of the overall security for your SUSE Linux Enterprise Server. In the next chapter, you'll learn how to use the Service Location Protocol to make locating services on your network easier.

## CHAPTER 33

Configuring Service Location Protocol

In a TCP/IP environment, working with services happens in a static way most of the time. For example, the DNS server provides information about what IP address must be contacted as the mail server for a given domain, but it doesn't give any guarantees that this mail server is actually available when you try to contact it. A much better method to provide information about available services is to use a dynamic method. The Service Location Protocol (SLP) is an RFC standard that provides such a method. SUSE Linux Enterprise Server comes with OpenSLP, the open source implementation of that protocol. In this chapter, you'll learn how to use and configure it.

Understanding How SLP Works

The essence of how the Service Location Protocol works is that active services are registered on the network. This registration happens at the service agent (SA). Ordinarily, every server on the network has an SA that provides information about the services it is hosting. Services register only at their local SA; therefore, the SA on server 2 is ignorant of the services registered by the SA on server 1. On the computer that needs a service, SLP uses the user agent (UA). At first thought, you may think of this user agent as a typical client component, but it isn't. SLP uses user agents on servers as well. In fact, everywhere a service is needed, a UA is required. In the simplest configuration, the UA sends a broadcast over the network to all the SAs that are available. From all these SAs, it gets a list of services that are offered. A broadcast has the disadvantage that it can be used on the local LAN only; as an alternative, you can use multicast, as long as the routers are configured to forward multicast.

This basic method where a UA multicasts all SAs on the network works fine in a small-to-medium network. However, if the network grows big and thousands of SAs are available, it isn't really an option to do it that way. In that scenario, the directory agent (DA) is used. A DA functions as the central repository on the network where all services are registered. If a DA is used, SAs send an update about the services they have available to the DA on a regular basis; the essence of how SLP works, after all, is that the SAs and DAs give information about services that are really present on the network. The UA in turn has to merely contact the DA to get an overview of the available services on the network. For the UA, you can use different methods to find out what DA it should use. The UA is capable of discovering available DAs automatically, if these are configured to send heartbeats over the network regularly. As an alternative, it is possible for the UA to send multicasts over the network, thus discovering what DAs are available. A third option is that the UA is configured with the IP address of the DA so it can be contacted directly.

Now the concept of a directory agent is cool, but in a really large network, it doesn't really make sense to work with just one DA. You can use several DAs in such a scenario, where each SA is configured to contact one or more DAs directly to register its services. The same goes for UAs that are configured to contact only a limited amount of DAs on the network to find out about services that are relevant for them.

To enhance the options of the protocol, you can use scope. A *scope* is a multicast domain that can be used by UAs and SAs to share information. By default, just one scope exists, and everyone is in it. The name of that scope is DEFAULT. As an administrator, you can choose to configure other scopes as well. By using scopes, multicast packets are "labeled" so that they are sent within that scope only.

The last parts in the OpenSLP configuration are the services that need to register themselves. To make this possible, a service has to be programmed to use the SLP services. Some of the services include CUPS, NIS, Samba, OpenLDAP, Postfix SSH, NTP, and the installation server.

Configuring an SLP Server

In SUSE Linux Enterprise Server 10, the SLP configuration is integrated in YaST. From YaST, you have an easy method of setting up the SLP server. If you need more advanced options, you can tune the SLP configuration file. This is the file /etc/slp.conf. In the next sections, you will learn how to handle both.

Configuring OpenSLP from YaST

Once again, YaST offers the easiest interface to configure the OpenSLP server. To do this, you need the module slp-server, which you can start directly by using the command yast slp-server. This starts the interface shown in Figure 33-1.

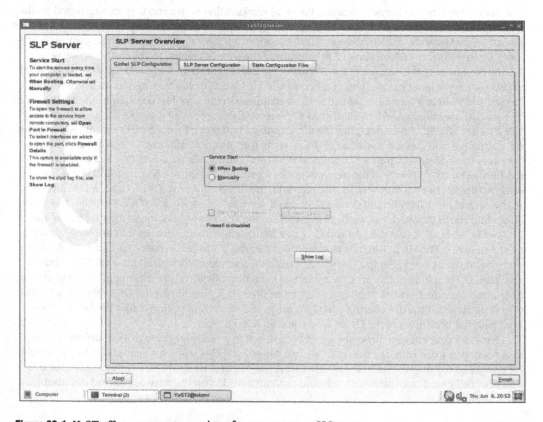

Figure 33-1. *YaST offers an easy-to-use interface to set up an SLP server.*

In the YaST interface, three different tabs are available. On the tab Global SLP Configuration, you can specify how the service starts. As shown in Figure 33-1, you have the option to start the server when booting or manually. If you are using a firewall, you must select the option Open Port in Firewall as well to allow clients to connect to this service through the firewall. To see what is happening with the SLP server, on this tab you can click the Show Log button to get access to the SLP log file in /var/log.

On the tab SLP Server Configuration (see Figure 33-2), you can configure how the SLP server is used. On this tab, you have four options to specify the way your server is working:

Broadcast: If you select this option, you are configuring an SLP SA that answers to all broadcast messages it receives. This is the default way of working, but it causes some overhead by the broadcast packets. It also has the limitation that broadcasts are often not passed through by routers; in general, this is not a good choice.

Multicast: This is the best option to use in most cases. With this option, your server answers to multicasts that are sent within the same scope. If you don't want to worry about scopes, just leave the scope called DEFAULT; every SLP SA, DA, and UA is in that scope by default. If you want to divide the SLP services into different areas, you can specify the names of other scopes that you want to use. As long as the SA and the UA are in the same scope, they can find each other.

DA Server: Use this option if you want your server to report to a DA. When selecting this option, you also need to specify the address of the DA server that should be contacted and—if used—the name of the nondefault scope that you are using for your SA to communicate with the DA.

Becomes DA Server: Use this option to make your server a DA. This means it will maintain a cache in which all services for that scope are registered.

On the SLP Server Configuration tab, you'll see an Expert Settings button. This button gives you access to all the options that are available in the slp.conf configuration file. You can read about these options in more detail in the next section of this chapter.

The third and last tab on the SLP Server screen gives you access to the SLP configuration files that you can create. Read more about these files in the section "Registering Services" later in this chapter.

Note When using SLP in a mixed environment that uses both NetWare and Linux, make sure the SLP Directory Agent is configured on a NetWare server. The SLP DA on NetWare offers features that are not offered by the SLP DA on Linux, such as integration in Novell's proprietary eDirectory. This integration doesn't work in OpenSLP.

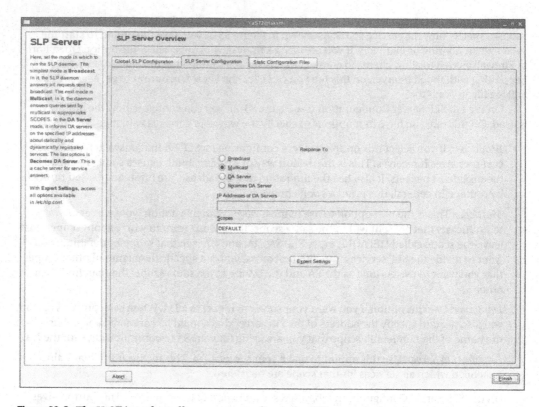

Figure 33-2. *The YaST interface allows you to configure the SLP server in four ways.*

Tweaking /etc/slp.conf

You just learned how to use YaST to configure the SLP server. Basically, YaST is just a pretty front end to the configuration file /etc/slp.conf, where the real work is happening. When the daemon slpd starts, it reads this configuration file to see what it has to do. Fortunately, this file is well documented, so you should be able to find out what the different options in this file are used for when in doubt. Table 33-1 lists some of the most relevant options. Note that the file has different sections where you completely configure how the SLP server works, without any difference between UA, SA, and DA settings. The SLP UA is implemented in the slplib library file, which can be used by client programs that need access to SLP services and not by the slpd process.

Table 33-1. slp.conf *Settings*

Setting	Explanation
net.slp.useScopes	Use this option if you want to make the SLP server a member of scopes other than the default scope DEFAULT. A server can be a member of more than one scope at the same time; in that case, use a comma-separated list to indicate what scopes should be used.
net.slp.DAAddressess	This option gets a comma-separated list of DAs that should be used.
net.slp.isDA	This option gets the value true if you want to make this server an SLP DA.

Setting	Explanation
net.slp.DAHeartBeat	If your server is a DA, it needs to send out a DA heartbeat on a regular basis to let the others know it is still there. The default value for this setting is 10,800 seconds, which is three hours.
net.slp.watchRegistrationPID	A service that registers at a local SA needs to know for sure that the slpd server is still present. You accomplish this by using this option that has the default value true. This option tells the local processes to watch the PID of the slpd service. When that PID is available no longer, the registration is automatically deregistered.
net.slp.maxResults	This is a client setting that defines the maximum number of results that can be accumulated and returned. The default value is 256, which can be problematic if large lists of services are expected as an answer.
net.slp.isBroadcastOnly	This parameter can determine that only broadcasts should be used. The parameter is in fact useless, since broadcast is used automatically if multicasts are available no longer.
net.slp.passiveDADetection	This option, which by default has the value true, makes sure the SA and UA are looking passively for DAs as well. This is a useful option to make sure you can work with new DAs when they appear to the network. On the other hand, there is a security issue because maybe you don't want your SA and UA to connect to a rogue DA by accident.
net.slp.activeDADetection	Determines whether your SAs and DAs are allowed to discover SLP DAs actively. The default value is set to yes.
net.slp.DAActiveDiscoveryInterval	Use this option to determine how often an SLP agent tries to discover DAs actively. The default value of 1 allows the agent to do DA discovery on service start-up only. To disable active discovery completely, use the value false for this option. Otherwise, you can use any value in minutes to specify the discovery frequency.
net.slp.multicastTTL	Specifies the TTL for multicast packets.
net.slp.DADiscoveryMaximumWait	The maximum amount in time in milliseconds that the SLP agent waits for a response on a DA discovery request.
net.slp.interfaces	Use this option to specify a list of interfaces on which a DA or SA should listen for SLP requests. Use this option if your server is connected to a WAN directly to restrict users from the untrusted side of the server to get information about services by accident.
net.slp.checkSourceAddr	This option, which has the default value of true, makes sure only the exact host that has made a registration is allowed to deregister a service.
net.slp.traceDATraffic	Give this option the value true if you want to be able to trace what happens on an SLP DA. By default, no tracing is active.

When modifying the contents of the slp.conf file, make sure to restart the slpd service; it doesn't check the configuration file for changes automatically.

Registering Services

For a service, you have different ways to register with an SLP SA:

- Dynamically using the `slptool` utility
- Statically via `/etc/slp.reg`
- Statically via files in `/etc/slp.reg.d`

Of these options, the most common method for registering services is to use one of the configuration files. If a service needs to be registered from a script dynamically when the service is starting, you can use the slptool utility. When registering a service with slptool, you need to provide a URL as the argument. In Listing 33-1 you can see two examples in which `smb` and `ssh` are registered.

Listing 33-1. *Registering Services with slptool*

```
slptool register service:smb://myhostname:139,en,65535
slptool register service:ssh://myhostname:22,en,65535
```

Both lines show that the slptool utility is called with the `register` argument. This is because you can use slptool with many options to specify what it has to do. Next, the URL to the service that you want to register is included. This line starts with `service` to indicate that it is a service. Next comes the name of the service. This is the *abstract type*, which is a short description of the service. The name of the service is followed by the name of the host where the service can be reached. This host name is in URL notation. After that, some options specify where the service is contacted. For both services in the example, the port and default language are mentioned. Their parameters are followed by the number 65536, which indicates the service registration should not expire.

As an alternative to registering services with the slptool utility, you can create static configuration files to register services. Ordinarily, these files are created automatically when a service is installed, but you can add these files manually as well. To do this, you can use the YaST SLP Server configuration utility; from there, select the Static Configuration Files tab (see Figure 33-3). On this tab, you can see the name of the files that currently exist in `/etc/slp.reg.d` and the service they are providing. On this screen, you can edit or delete any of these files and add new files. Deleting a file is possible only if the file currently is not owned by any package.

The YaST interface allows you to create service registration files easily from a template-like interface. This interface allows you to select from the three components that should always be present for all the services you want to register by using these files:

description: A description for the selected service

tcp-port: The TCP port on which the service is listening

service: The URL to the service

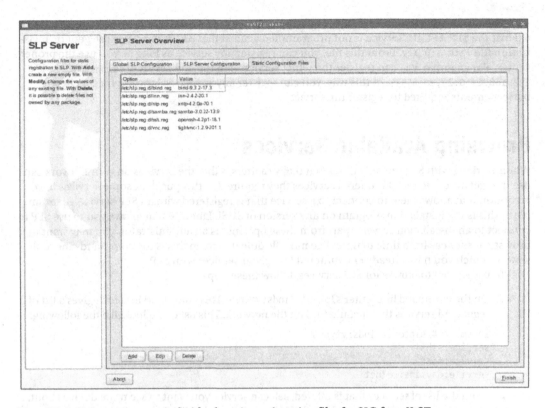

Figure 33-3. *You can manage individual service registration files for SLP from YaST.*

Instead of using the YaST interface, you can edit the files directly with any editor you like. It really makes no difference, as long as you know what you are doing. Listing 33-2 gives an example of the contents of one of the files.

Listing 33-2. *Example of an SLP Configuration File*

```
#########################################################################
#
# OpenSLP registration file
#
# register SSH daemon
#
#########################################################################

# Register the usual sshd, if it is running
service:ssh://$HOSTNAME:22,en,65535
tcp-port=22
description=Secure Shell Daemon

# ssh can get used to copy files with konqueror using the fish:/ protocol
service:fish://$HOSTNAME:22,en,65535
tcp-port=22
description=KDE file transfer via SSH
```

The registration files in /etc/slp.reg.d typically are for services that are programmed against the SLP API. If a service is not programmed against that API, it must use the generic registration file /etc/slp.reg. From this file, you can register any service as long as you use the proper syntax. For example, you can register the telnet service with the line service:telnet.myorg:// 192.168.1.10:23,en,65535. In this way, you can register any service as long as you specify the basic elements required to register the service.

Browsing Available Services

When working with SLP, the only thing that really matters is that the services on your network can use it to get access to the SLP-offered services they require. For this purpose, some services have an option that allows them to connect to a service that is registered with an SLP service. An example of this is the installation program on any version of SUSE Linux 10 that allows you to use SLP to connect to an installation server. Apart from these options, as an administrator, you may want to browse for services from time to time. The most flexible tool to do this is the command-line tool slptool, which you have already encountered to register services with SLP.

To use slptool to browse for SLP services, follow these steps:

1. On the command line, enter slptool findsrvtypes. This command in return gives a list of registered services that it could find on the network. This list could look like the following:

   ```
   laksmi:/ # slptool findsrvtypes
   service:ssh
   service:fish
   service:daytime:telnet
   ```

2. From the list of services that is offered, select a service you want to see more details about, and query that service using slptool findsrvs followed by the name of the service you want to use. For example, use slptool findsrvs service:ssh to get more information about the SSH service. This command returns a list of all the servers where the SSH service was registered. For example, a line like service:ssh://laksmi.sandervanvugt.com:22,65535 indicating where the service can be reached could be returned.

Tip Are you failing to see any SLP services on your network but are sure that everything is configured the way it should be? It probably isn't. Before doing any troubleshooting, restart the SLP service using the rcslpd restart command, and try again. If that also doesn't work, you can start troubleshooting.

As an alternative to the command-line tool slptool, you can use the YaST SLP browser. You can start it with the yast2 slp command. After connecting to an SLP server, it provides you with an overview of all the SLP-registered services that were found on the network, as shown in Figure 33-4.

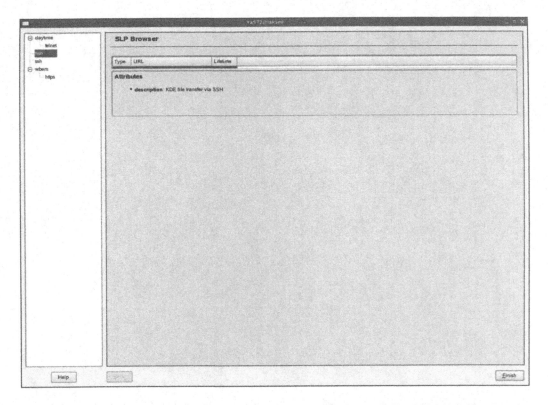

Figure 33-4. *An easier way to browse for services on your network that are offered by SLP is by using the YaST2 slp tool.*

A third option to browse for SLP-registered services is to use the SLP browser that is integrated in Konqueror. Konqueror is the default browser that is used in the KDE graphical desktop environment (not installed by default on SUSE Linux Enterprise Server 10). In this browser's URL line, enter slp:/. This offers a list of all SLP services that were found on the network. From this list, you can browse to any of the services to get more details about that service.

Summary

SLP is not the most essential service that you can have on your SUSE Linux Enterprise Server, but it is a useful service that makes locating services on large networks a lot easier. In this chapter, you learned how to enable the service, how to configure services so that it will register with the SLP server, and how to query the network for the presence of any SLP registered services. In the next chapter, you will learn about some troubleshooting techniques that you can use on SUSE Linux Enterprise Server.

■ ■ ■

## CHAPTER 34

Troubleshooting SUSE Linux Enterprise Server

Most of the time you will work happily with your SUSE Linux Enterprise Server. However, since all hardware fails sooner or later, you will one day find yourself in a situation where you need some troubleshooting skills. That's what this chapter is all about: troubleshooting. In this chapter, you'll learn about the most important tools that are available and in what situations these tools may help you. I'll cover the following topics:

- Analyzing the problem
- Troubleshooting from the GRUB boot prompt
- Using the rescue CD
- Repairing an installed system

Analyzing the Problem

Some problems are pretty evident. If the hard disk your server boots from is broken, it won't boot anymore. You'll notice that immediately. Other problems, however, are less obvious. If a user complains about your server being unreachable but you look at the console and your server still seems pretty reachable, you need to do some analysis to find out what's wrong. Although it is impossible to provide a complete list of everything you can do (such a list would be dependent on hardware and would be outdated by the time this book is in print), in the next sections you will read about the most important solutions you can use to find out what's wrong.

Analyzing the Network

Roughly half of all the problems that your server can have are network related. So if your user complains that some important application cannot be reached, you need to check the availability of the network. This check contains different steps:

1. See whether your server has an IP address.
2. Check routing and DNS information.
3. Check your firewall.

Verifying IP Configuration

The first check to do when you have a problem with network connectivity is to check the IP address configuration. You should be aware that you can use two commands for that. First, you can use the ifconfig command, but you can also use the ip command. The funny thing is that these two do not always give the same result. Both will do fine with displaying the primary (or only) IP address that is assigned to an interface. For example, use ifconfig eth0 to find out what IP address eth0 is using, or use ip address show eth0 to do the same with the ip command. Both commands will give the same result. The difference occurs when more than one IP address is added to the same interface. An address added with the ifconfig command won't show when you use the ip command to check the current configuration, and an IP address that's added with the ip command doesn't show when checking it with the ifconfig command (check Figure 34-1 to see this happening). Therefore, if you are checking IP address configuration and you really want to be sure that you see it all, use both tools.

```
                                       Terminal                              _ □ x
File  Edit  View  Terminal  Tabs  Help
SLC:~ # ip address add dev eth0 192.168.0.10
SLC:~ # ip address show
1: lo: <LOOPBACK,UP> mtu 16436 qdisc noqueue
    link/loopback 00:00:00:00:00:00 brd 00:00:00:00:00:00
    inet 127.0.0.1/8 scope host lo
    inet6 ::1/128 scope host
       valid_lft forever preferred_lft forever
2: eth0: <BROADCAST,MULTICAST,UP> mtu 1500 qdisc pfifo_fast qlen 1000
    link/ether 00:0c:29:1a:a8:ed brd ff:ff:ff:ff:ff:ff
    inet 192.168.1.18/24 brd 192.168.1.255 scope global eth0
    inet 192.168.0.10/32 scope global eth0
    inet6 fe80::20c:29ff:fe1a:a8ed/64 scope link
       valid_lft forever preferred_lft forever
3: sit0: <NOARP> mtu 1480 qdisc noop
    link/sit 0.0.0.0 brd 0.0.0.0
SLC:~ # ifconfig
eth0      Link encap:Ethernet  HWaddr 00:0C:29:1A:A8:ED
          inet addr:192.168.1.18  Bcast:192.168.1.255  Mask:255.255.255.0
          inet6 addr: fe80::20c:29ff:fe1a:a8ed/64 Scope:Link
          UP BROADCAST RUNNING MULTICAST  MTU:1500  Metric:1
          RX packets:941 errors:0 dropped:0 overruns:0 frame:0
          TX packets:12 errors:0 dropped:0 overruns:0 carrier:0
          collisions:0 txqueuelen:1000
          RX bytes:59371 (57.9 Kb)  TX bytes:956 (956.0 b)
          Interrupt:177 Base address:0x1400

lo        Link encap:Local Loopback
          inet addr:127.0.0.1  Mask:255.0.0.0
          inet6 addr: ::1/128 Scope:Host
          UP LOOPBACK RUNNING  MTU:16436  Metric:1
          RX packets:376 errors:0 dropped:0 overruns:0 frame:0
          TX packets:376 errors:0 dropped:0 overruns:0 carrier:0
          collisions:0 txqueuelen:0
          RX bytes:38669 (37.7 Kb)  TX bytes:38669 (37.7 Kb)

SLC:~ #
```

Figure 34-1. *A secondary IP address added with the* ip *command doesn't show up with the* ifconfig *command.*

■Tip Having trouble accessing a server on a newly configured machine? Double-check the subnetmask: if both machines are using different subnet masks and are on the same subnet, you will have a hard time reaching the other machine.

Checking Routing and DNS

Although it is unlikely to just change overnight, a network check should always include a check of the routing table and DNS information. You probably already know how to do it, but just to be sure, here are the instructions: check the routing table with the route -n or ip route show command, and make sure a default route is present. After that, look in the configuration file /etc/resolv.conf to verify that it is referring to the correct DNS server. Listing 34-1 shows what output you might expect from the ip route show command.

Listing 34-1. *Output of the* ip route show *Command*

```
SFO:/ # ip route show
192.168.1.0/24 dev eth1  proto kernel  scope link  src 192.168.1.69
172.16.99.0/24 dev vmnet1  proto kernel  scope link  src 172.16.99.1
192.168.217.0/24 dev vmnet8  proto kernel  scope link  src 192.168.217.1
127.0.0.0/8 dev lo  scope link
default via 192.168.1.254 dev eth1
```

■Tip Don't see an entry for default but do see an entry for network 0.0.0.0? That's OK as well; 0.0.0.0 is just the numeric notation of your default route.

Checking the Firewall

SUSE Linux Enterprise Server is protected by a firewall by default. Failure to reach a server (or an application) may be caused by a misconfigured firewall. Firewall configuration is a complex topic that's dealt with in Chapter 30 of this book, so for detailed information about how the firewall works, check that chapter. However, you can apply a quick fix: just disable the firewall completely, and see whether that changes anything.

■Caution Use this tip only if your machine is not connected to a public network directly. Disabling a firewall, even for a short while, may cause great harm on your machine!

Before you decide to flush all firewall rules, you should check whether anything is happening at all. Use the iptables -L command for that; this command gives you an overview of all the rules that are currently active on your machine. If the output looks like Listing 34-2, the problem could be firewall related.

Listing 34-2. *Partial Output of* iptables -L *on a Configured Firewall*

```
SFO:/ # iptables -L
Chain INPUT (policy DROP)
target     prot opt source              destination
ACCEPT     all  --  anywhere            anywhere
ACCEPT     all  --  anywhere            anywhere            state RELATED,ESTAB
LISHED
input_ext  all  --  anywhere            anywhere
input_ext  all  --  anywhere            anywhere
LOG        all  --  anywhere            anywhere            limit: avg 3/min bu
rst 5 LOG level warning tcp-options ip-options prefix `SFW2-IN-ILL-TARGET '
DROP       all  --  anywhere            anywhere

Chain FORWARD (policy DROP)
target     prot opt source              destination
ACCEPT     all  --  anywhere            anywhere
LOG        all  --  anywhere            anywhere            limit: avg 3/min bu
rst 5 LOG level warning tcp-options ip-options prefix `SFW2-FWD-ILL-ROUTING '

Chain OUTPUT (policy ACCEPT)
target     prot opt source              destination
ACCEPT     all  --  anywhere            anywhere
ACCEPT     all  --  anywhere            anywhere            state NEW,RELATED,E
STABLISHED
LOG        all  --  anywhere            anywhere            limit: avg 3/min bu
rst 5 LOG level warning tcp-options ip-options prefix `SFW2-OUT-ERROR '

Chain forward_ext (0 references)
target     prot opt source              destination

Chain input_ext (2 references)
target     prot opt source              destination
DROP       all  --  anywhere            anywhere            PKTTYPE = broadcast
```

However, if you see a list of only the three chains INPUT, FORWARD, and OUTPUT without any further specification, it is useless to disable your firewall. If you do see a lot of output, you can use the rcSuSEfirewall2 stop command, which brings down everything completely. Do a fast check to see whether that made a difference, and use rcSuSEfirewall2 start as fast as you can to bring the firewall up again so you are protected.

Checking Application Availability

Another hot issue is the availability of applications. You can perform certain tasks to see whether an application is offering its services; of these options, the good old ps aux (or ps -ef) commands (both do more or less the same) is the best way to start. Especially in combination with grep, they are pretty powerful. For example, ps aux | grep dhcp checks whether that DHCP server is really running. Sometimes, however, it is not that easy. For example, you might not know for sure what the exact name of the application is.

If you don't know the name of the application but you do know what port it is supposed to listen at, you can try netstat. As its name suggests, netstat displays statistics about network usage. If you use the netstat -patune command, you'll see a complete list of all open ports and sockets. In combination with grep, this is a useful command; use, for example, netstat -patune | grep 123 to see whether something is listening at port 123.

If your application is a service that should be started automatically when you boot your server but it doesn't seem to do that, the chkconfig command may prove useful. With chkconfig -l you'll get a complete overview of all the services that are started automatically when booting your server (see Figure 34-2 for a partial result of this command). If your service isn't listed there and if it does have a start-up script in /etc/init.d, you can add it with the insserv command. For example, insserv dhcpd would add your DHCP server to its default runlevels and make sure it is started automatically the next time you start your server.

```
                                       Terminal                                  _ □ ×
 File  Edit  View  Terminal  Tabs  Help
splash                         0:off  1:on   2:on   3:on   4:off  5:on   6:off  S:on
splash_early                   0:off  1:off  2:on   3:on   4:off  5:on   6:off
squid                          0:off  1:off  2:off  3:off  4:off  5:off  6:off
sshd                           0:off  1:off  2:off  3:on   4:off  5:on   6:off
svcgssd                        0:off  1:off  2:off  3:off  4:off  5:off  6:off
syslog                         0:off  1:off  2:on   3:on   4:off  5:on   6:off
sysstat                        0:off  1:off  2:off  3:off  4:off  5:off  6:off
vmware-tools                   0:off  1:off  2:on   3:on   4:off  5:on   6:off
winbind                        0:off  1:off  2:off  3:off  4:off  5:off  6:off
xdm                            0:off  1:off  2:off  3:off  4:off  5:on   6:off
xend                           0:off  1:off  2:off  3:on   4:off  5:on   6:off
xendomains                     0:off  1:off  2:off  3:on   4:off  5:on   6:off
xfs                            0:off  1:off  2:off  3:off  4:off  5:off  6:off
xinetd                         0:off  1:off  2:off  3:off  4:off  5:off  6:off
ypbind                         0:off  1:off  2:off  3:off  4:off  5:off  6:off
zebra                          0:off  1:off  2:off  3:off  4:off  5:off  6:off
xinetd based services:
        chargen:           off
        chargen-udp:       off
        cups-lpd:          off
        cvs:               off
        daytime:           off
        daytime-udp:       off
        echo:              off
        echo-udp:          off
        fam:               off
        netstat:           off
        pure-ftpd:         off
        rsync:             off
        servers:           off
        services:          off
        swat:              off
        systat:            off
        time:              off
        time-udp:          off
        vnc:               off
SLC:~ #
```

Figure 34-2. *Partial result of the* chkconfig -l *command*

Checking Logging

Something you should always do when finding out what's wrong is to perform a serious analysis of your server's logs. You probably already have your /var/log/messages open with tail -f all the time to see immediately whether something goes wrong on your server, so I won't waste any more time on that (otherwise check Chapter 12 for more details). Something else that is related to logging and that many people aren't aware of is that some events are also written to tty10 on your server. To check the really serious messages, press Ctrl+Alt+F10 to check this tty, and you will be up-to-date about everything that happened to your server recently that was really serious. Check Figure 34-3 for an example of what's happening on that tty.

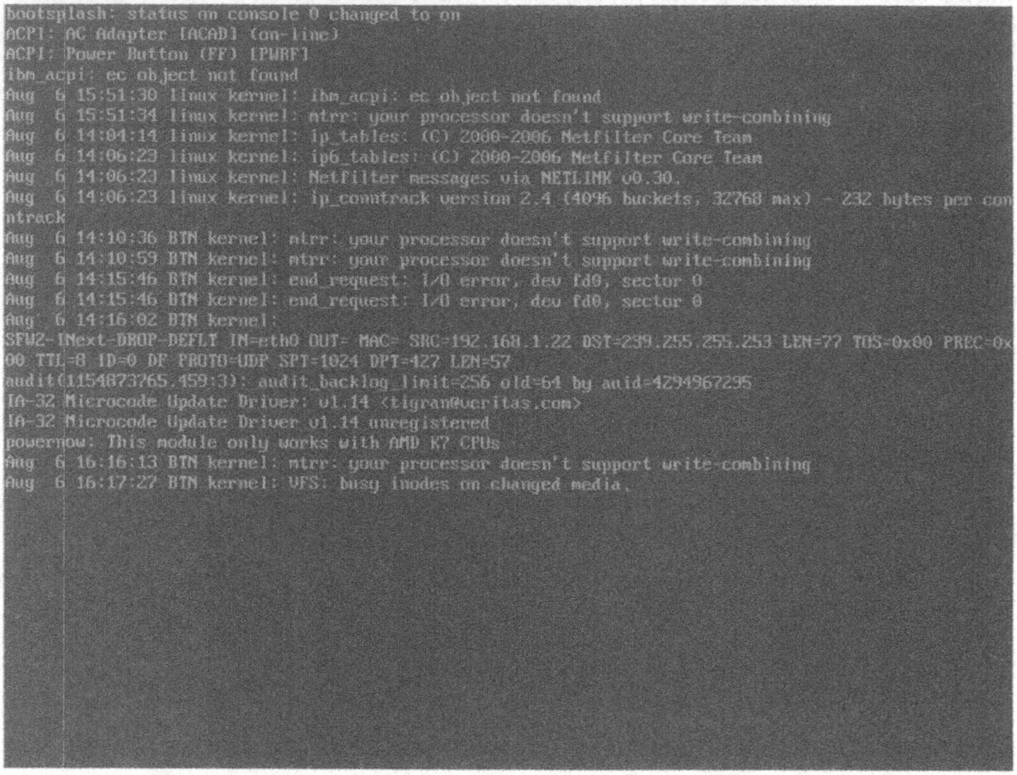

Figure 34-3. *On tty10 you'll find an overview of the most important events that really happened on your server.*

Tip If messages scroll by on a tty too quickly, you can use Ctrl+Page Up to walk back in that tty. Be aware, however, that only a small buffer is reserved in memory to keep information that has appeared on a tty, so you can't Shift+Page Up to information that happened 3,000 messages ago.

Troubleshooting from the GRUB Boot Prompt

The tips discussed so far will help you if you still have a running server. Sometimes you don't because something goes wrong in the start-up procedure. If that's the case, you need to change the way your server starts. The GRUB boot prompt (see Figure 34-4) is a helpful tool to do that.

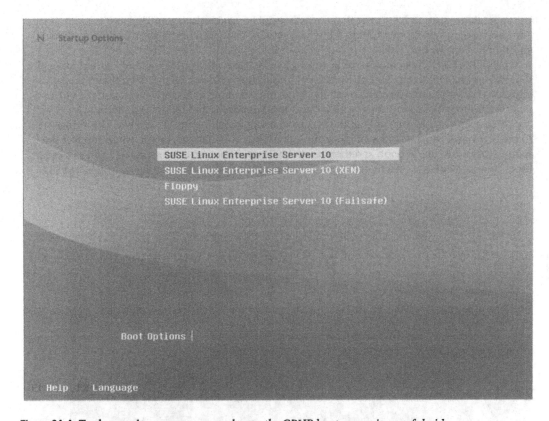

Figure 34-4. *To change the way your server boots, the GRUB boot screen is a useful aid.*

By default, your server will display the GRUB boot prompt for eight seconds and then continue booting. During these eight seconds, you can pass options that should be executed by the kernel on the Boot Options prompt. The big question, of course, is what exactly you should add there. Unfortunately, that question has no easy answer. In Chapter 10, you can find an overview of some of the most common options. Two parameters that are useful for booting are the specification of a different runlevel and the init=/bin/bash option.

Most servers boot either runlevel 3 or runlevel 5 by default. Typically, all network services are started in these runlevels. If something is wrong with any services, you can specify that a runlevel should be started that doesn't activate all of them. Typical runlevels to do that are runlevels 2 (multi-user without network) and runlevel 1 (single user). Significantly fewer services are started in runlevel 1, which may bring you to an environment where you can analyze what happens during the boot procedure and fix it.

Sometimes, even runlevel 1 is not basic enough, because the error is in an early stage of the boot procedure. In that case, it helps to replace init with bash. Ordinarily, the init process is started as the first thing by the kernel. You can use the boot parameter boot=/bin/bash to indicate that Bash should be started instead of init. This will force your server not to load anything besides Bash and your kernel. One challenge is that after loading Bash instead of init, your root file system is not mounted in read-write mode. Fix that by using the command mount -o remount,rw /. That allows you to write new files to the root file system. Also, do not forget that anything else that is usually mounted automatically from /etc/fstab is not mounted at all; you don't even have the special file systems like /proc that are so helpful in troubleshooting. The only solution is to start everything step by step to find out what's wrong. Then fix it and restart, and your server should boot properly.

From the GRUB boot menu, some other useful features are available as well. For example, the default option SUSE Linux Enterprise Server 10 (Failsafe) is particularly useful if there's a problem with some of your hardware; it skips all the items that are more or less advanced and tries to load a basic system with support for one CPU only, no DMA access, and other limitations.

Also useful is that you can quit the graphical menu by hitting the Escape key. This brings you to the text-based version of the GRUB menu (see Figure 34-5). On this menu, you can select the menu entry you'd like to boot, and then press the E key to open an editing mode. From this editing mode, you can edit the command line that is executed and thus add or omit any option you like.

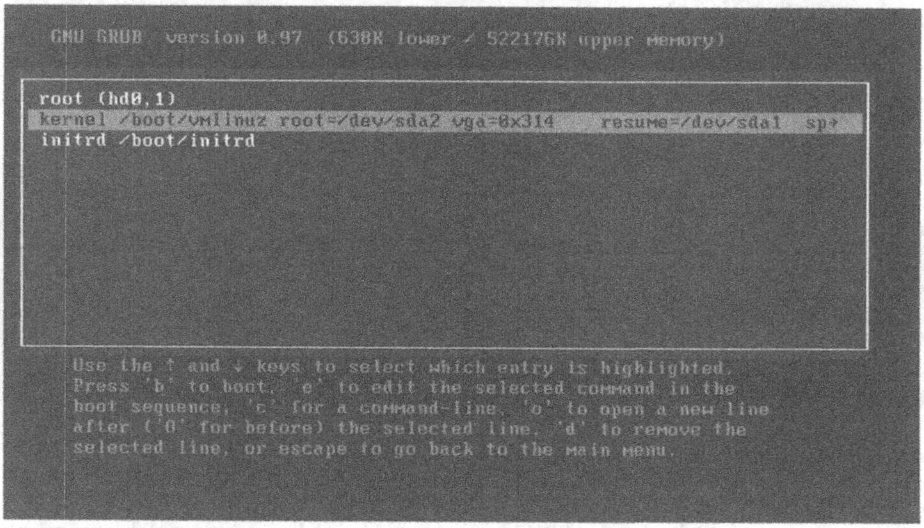

Figure 34-5. *In text mode, you can edit the GRUB menu and thus edit the lines that are executed from the* menu.lst *file.*

Booting a Rescue System

In some situations, the GRUB boot menu isn't good enough, such as when your boot loader is broken and you do not see a GRUB boot prompt at all. In that case, it is useful to know that you can start a rescue system from the installation CD or DVD of SUSE Linux Enterprise Server. One of the options in the menu that is displayed when booting from the installation media is Rescue System (see Figure 34-6). This option will boot a minimized version of SUSE Linux Enterprise Server, designed to help you repair your server in a hard-core troubleshooting session.

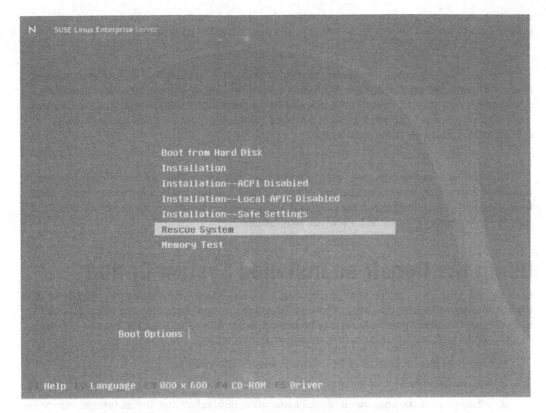

Figure 34-6. *The rescue system is designed to help you repair a broken system.*

Once the rescue system is loaded in the RAM of your machine (which may take a while), it will show you a login prompt. Enter the username root with no password to get access to the rescue system. You should be aware that on your rescue system none of the file systems usually loaded from /etc/fstab are loaded. In fact, the mount command will show you no mounted file systems at all! To repair your server, it is often required to get read-write access to your file systems. You can accomplish this by mounting the root file system on a temporary directory like /mnt. For example, if your root device is on /dev/sda1, you can mount it with mount /dev/sda1 /mnt.

Tip No clue about what partition your root device is installed on? No problem—if you do know the name of the disk device that it is on, use fdisk -l followed by the name of your disk device, for example fdisk -l /dev/sda. This lists all the partitions that are configured on your server. Look for a large partition (minimum of 4GB) that has type 83 Linux set; this could very well be the root device.

After mounting the root device on a temporary directory, it is often useful to set that directory to the new root directory by using the chroot command. This will make sure that all the paths are set the right way and are referring to files that are on your hard drive partition and not on the rescue system. If the root file system is mounted on /mnt, use chroot /mnt. From that moment on, the directory / is no longer located on the rescue system but on your own root file system. Next, you can use `fdisk -a` to automatically mount everything that is in `/etc/fstab`. You now have your original system back (provided there were no errors in mounting the file systems).

Tip Did you have errors about file systems that couldn't be mounted? Then use fsck to check the consistency of your file system. You should notice this utility comes in many versions; for example, to check a ReiserFS file system, use `fsck.reiserfs`. If you're lucky, fsck will help you repair your broken file systems, and you'll end up with a huge `/lost+found` directory that's filled with some chunks of data that once were your precious files. In the latter case, I hope you have a good backup.

Now that you have remounted your file systems as they are on disk, you can do anything that's needed to repair your server. For example, if you did have a problem loading the boot loader code from the MBR of your hard drive, use `grub-install` followed by the device name of your boot device, for example `grub-install /dev/sda`, to reinstall it.

Using the Repair an Installed System Option

Booting with `init=/bin/bash` is cool, and booting a rescue system is cool, as long as you have a clue where you should look for the cause of your problems. If you don't have any idea where to look for it, the Repair Installed System option may be helpful. In the following steps, I'll describe how you can access the well-hidden utilities that are offered by this option:

1. Insert the installation CD or DVD in your server's optical drive.

2. Restart your server, and make sure it boots from the optical drive.

3. When you see the boot menu of your installation disk, select Installation (yes, you are reading that correctly).

4. Wait until the installation code is loaded into RAM.

5. On the Language screen, select your preferred language, and click Next.

6. Click Yes, I Agree to the License Agreement, and click Next.

7. The system will now start analyzing your computer. When it has done that, it comes up with the screen shown in Figure 34-7 and asks you whether you want to perform a new installation or an update. On this screen, click the Other button.

8. On the Other Options screen, select Repair Installed System (see Figure 34-8).

Tip If you're not into command-line interfaces and you need to fix the boot loader, you can select Boot Installed System on the Other Options screen as well. This allows you to boot your server as usual and then use YaST to repair your GRUB installation. Check Chapter 10 for more details on that.

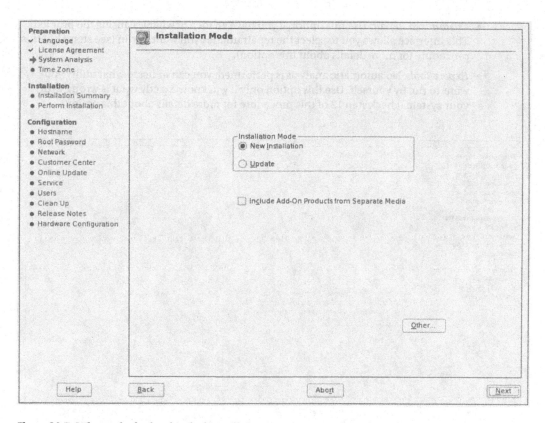

Figure 34-7. *When asked what kind of installation you want to do, click the Other button.*

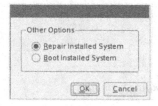

Figure 34-8. *Well-hidden in the installation menu, you can select the option to repair an installed system.*

9. After the repair options have been loaded, you see the Repair Method screen, as shown in Figure 34-9. On this screen, three options are available:

   • *Automatic Repair:* Use this option to perform a complete analysis of your system. All the critical system components are checked, and when an error is encountered, the repair utility tries to fix it automatically. Notice that it may take a long time to complete the automatic repair (see step 10 of this procedure for more details about this option).

- *Customized Repair*: Use this option if you have an idea of what is causing the problem. This interface allows you to select the repair utilities you want to run (see step 11 of this procedure for more details about this option).

- *Expert Tools*: No automatic analysis is performed; you can indicate what utility you want to run by yourself. Use this option only if you know exactly what is wrong with your system (check step 12 of this procedure for more details about this option).

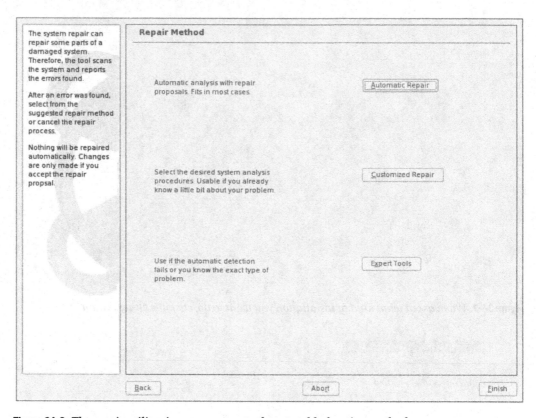

Figure 34-9. *The repair utility gives easy access to three troubleshooting methods.*

10. When you select the Automatic Repair option, the repair utility starts analyzing all system components automatically (see Figure 34-10). If a problem is encountered, it will prompt and ask you what to do. Answer all the prompts, and wait until the system check has been completed; this will probably fix your system.

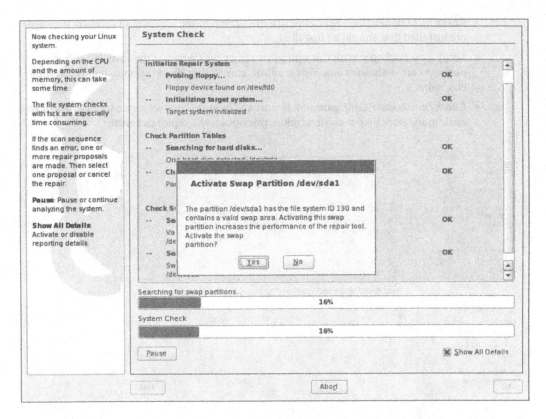

Figure 34-10. *The Automatic Repair option prompts when it needs to ask you something and otherwise just does its job.*

11. The Customized Repair option gives you access to eight options that allow you to specify what exactly you want the repair utility to do on your system. The following options are offered (see also Figure 34-11):

- *Check Partition Tables*: This option checks for errors in the partition tables and tries to fix them if they are encountered. Errors in the partition table are rather rare, so this check can safely be omitted in most cases. However, if you have deleted partitions by accident, run this utility to try to recover them.

- *Check Swap Areas*: This option sees whether swap space is available. If it is available, it will initialize it and immediately start using it so that the repair utilities can work faster. Leave it on, because it will make repairing the server faster.

- *Check File Systems*: If any of the file systems have an error, this option tries to fix that error. Often user input will be required.

- *Check fstab Entries*: This sees whether there are any errors in fstab. Not often useful.

- *Check Package Database*: This option checks the consistency of the RPM package database and, if any errors were found, will try to fix them. This is a useful option. Select it if you are not exactly sure what is wrong with your server.

- *Check Minimal Package Selection*: Use this option to see whether all software packages are installed that should be installed.

- *Verify Base Packages*: With this option you can check whether the installed software packages are without errors. This is a time-consuming check; execute it only if nothing else helps.

- *Check Boot Loader Configuration*: If you can't boot your server anymore because of an error in the boot loader configuration, this option will repair the error.

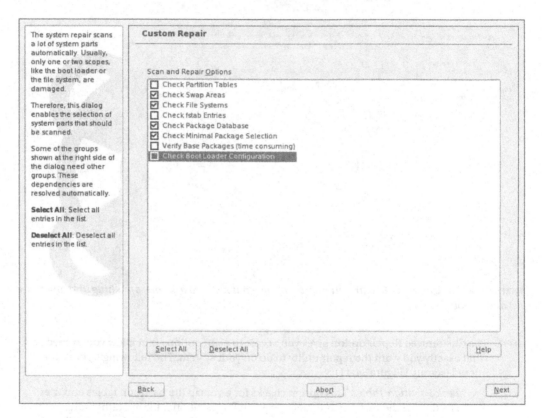

Figure 34-11. *The Custom Repair option allows you to select a number of options to run from an automated repair.*

12. The Expert Tools screen (see Figure 34-12) gives you access to some tools that you can use if you know exactly what is wrong on your server. Roughly, these are the same tools as the ones offered from the customized repair interface; you will see one option, however, and that is Save System Settings to Floppy. Use this option to create a backup of vital system parameters before trying any automated repair.

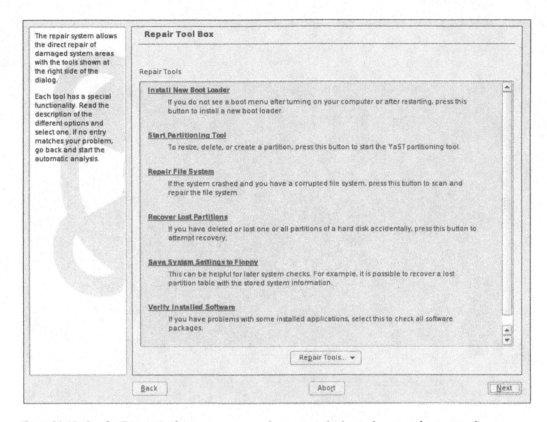

Figure 34-12. *On the Expert Tools screen, you can choose exactly the tool you need to run to fix your problem.*

Summary

In this chapter, you learned a little bit about troubleshooting. This should help you if you need to do troubleshooting when trying to fix the problem you have. I realize, however, no chapter about troubleshooting can be complete. If the solution for your problem wasn't here, try the chapter that discusses the area of your problems more specifically. In the next and last chapter of this book, you will learn how to set up an installation server, which will help you install many servers quickly.

CHAPTER 35

■ ■ ■

Creating an Installation Server

If you just have one server to install, you will install SUSE Linux Enterprise Server from the installation CDs or DVD. If you have many servers to install, it may be more practical to use an installation server to install over the network. In this chapter, you will learn how to set up such a server.

Different kinds of installation servers exist. In its most elementary form, an installation server will just offer access to installation files across the network with some network protocol. The user then needs to boot from installation CD 1, then select the network installation source, and then specify the kind of installation she wants to perform. The main disadvantage of this method is that the installer still needs to insert the first installation CD in the CD drive, and that might not be an option. What if the server does not come equipped with a CD drive, as is often the case with servers? To compensate for this, you can configure an installation server with PXE boot.

Note PXE stands for Preboot eXecution Environment. It's an IT standard to deliver a boot image to a computer. To use it, a computer needs to be able to start from the network board. In general, this is the case if there is a PXE boot ROM on the network board.

In this scenario, the server to be installed will perform a PXE boot from its network card and then download an installation image from the installation server. This requires some configuration of a DHCP server and a corresponding TFTP server to deliver the PXE boot image to the user. The installer, however, still needs to enter all required installation options manually. To remedy the tedium, you can configure an AutoYaST installation server, which will use an XML file created with AutoYaST to automatically pass along the options. The advantage of such a scenario is that the installation will be fully automatic; the installer just needs to boot the machine.

Tip An installation server is useful not just when installing servers; keeping the installation server available is also useful once the installation has been completed. The advantage is that the location of the installation server will be kept as the default installation source. Therefore, whenever you are installing an application after the initial installation, YaST will automatically look for the installation files on the installation server. Therefore, you will never again have to walk to the server room and insert a CD or DVD in the drive of your server if you have an installation server available.

Creating an Installation Server

SUSE Linux Enterprise Server 10 offers an integrated utility in YaST to create an installation server. You can access this module by selecting Miscellaneous ➤ Installation Server. The installation server will offer its services across the network using three kinds of protocols: HTTP, FTP, and NFS.

Since the NFS option offers the best performance, in this section you will learn how to create an NFS installation server. The installation procedure consists of two steps: in the first step, you add the files that must be used by the installation server from CD or ISO images, and in the second step you configure a network protocol to access these files. Once you have created an installation server in this way, you can boot a node from installation CD 1, select the network installation type, and copy files from the installation server. The following are the steps you need to accomplish:

1. From YaST, navigate to Miscellaneous ➤ Installation Server. This opens the interface to configure the installation server shown in Figure 35-1.

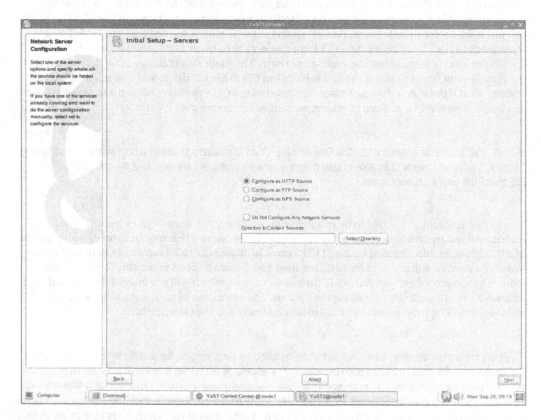

Figure 35-1. *You configure the installation server using YaST's Miscellaneous tab.*

2. On the screen shown in Figure 35-1, you need to specify several options. First, you need to tell the installation program what protocol to use. You can choose from HTTP, FTP, and NFS. If the protocol you choose as the source type is already active (for example, if you already have an NFS server that's operational), select Do Not Configure Any Network Services. Next, click Select Directory to specify where you want to put the installation source files. Choose a name that is clear and descriptive, such as SLES10. Then click Next to continue.

3. Now you need to configure the network protocol that gives access to the installation server. In Figure 35-2 you can see what it looks like for an NFS installation server. The default settings are fine; you could, however, add some security by not allowing just any host to access the installation server. For example, use 192.168.1.0/24 for the Host Wild Card setting to give access to all hosts that have an IP address that starts with 192.168.1. After entering all the configuration parameters for the network protocol, click Next to continue.

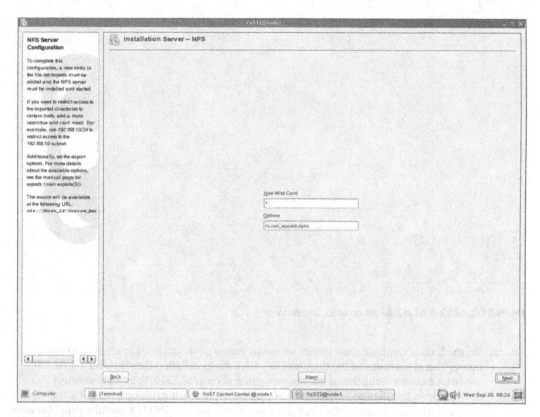

Figure 35-2. *After specifying what protocol you want to use, you need to configure the network service that gives access to that protocol.*

4. Now you'll see the Installation Server screen, as shown in Figure 35-3. On this screen, you need to add the installation sources. To do this, click Add. You don't need the Server Configuration button, which brings you back to the screen where you configured the network protocol.

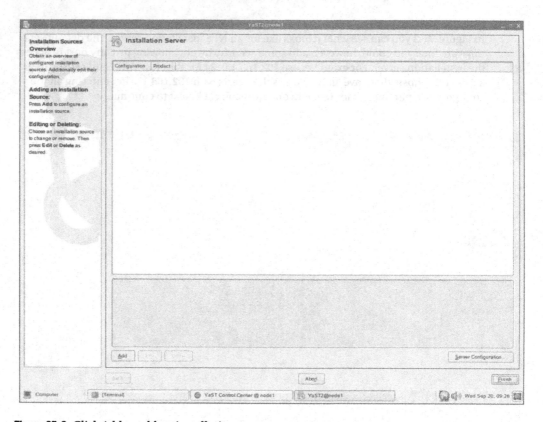

Figure 35-3. *Click Add to add an installation server.*

5. On the Source Configuration screen shown in Figure 35-4, you need to enter the source name. This is the name of the directory to where the installation files for your server are copied. Choose a name that is easy to recognize, such as SLES10. You can also select the Announce As Installation Service with SLP option. When using this option, the installation program uses SLP to locate the available installation servers. This is a useful option, because if it is used, you don't need to specify the exact location of the installation files.

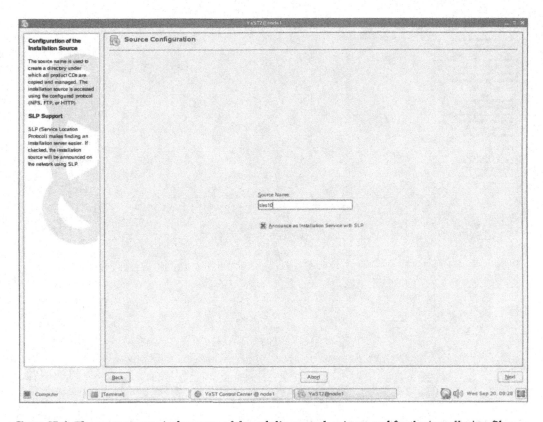

Figure 35-4. *The source name is the name of the subdirectory that is created for the installation files.*

6. Now you need to specify from where to read the installation files (see Figure 35-5). Choose Read CD or DVD Medium if you have a physical disk to install from, and select Use ISO Images if you want to copy the files from ISO images. In the latter case, you need to specify from what directory to copy the ISO files.

Note Need to copy the ISO files from one server to another? Of course you can use scp as described in Chapter 18 of this book. But you can also just tar a complete directory and use a pipe to netcat to send the output to another host. If, for example, the installation files are located on the server host1 in the directory isos and you want to copy them to the directory isos on the server labeled host2, first make sure that on both hosts /isos is your current directory. Then on host1, use tar cv . | netcat host2 2200 to start the tar command and redirect its output to netcat on port 2200. Netcat will make sure the files are sent to this host on port 2200. Next, make sure that when the files are arriving netcat is waiting on host2 by issuing the command netcat -l -p 2200 | tar xv. When the tar command has finished, all files will have been copied to your server. As an alternative, you could also create a central ISO vault on one of your servers and access that through NFS or Samba.

---

7. After selecting the installation source, click Next. You will now be prompted to provide the first installation medium. Do this, and then click OK.

8. After copying all the installation files, click Next to finalize the procedure.

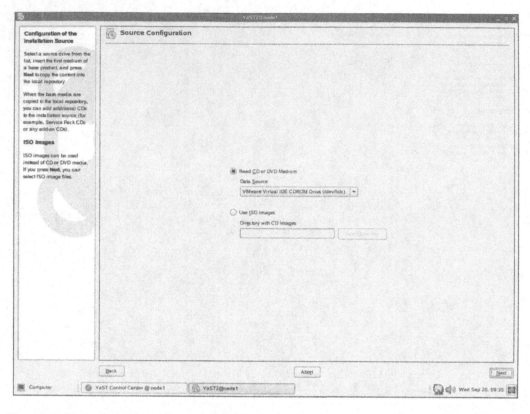

Figure 35-5. *Next select the installation medium from which you want to copy the files.*

Now that you have successfully created the NFS installation server, you can boot the server you want to install from a CD (or DVD, although in that case it doesn't make much sense to use an installation server).

Now press the F4 key, and choose NFS for the installation source (see Figure 35-6). Then enter the IP address of the NFS server and the name of the shared directory on that server, and click OK. If your installation server is SLP enabled, you can select SLP as well. After the initial installation program loads from the CD you have mounted, you will contact the NFS server to load all the other installation files. Proceed with the normal installation procedure.

Tip To start the installation from the installation server, make sure that a DHCP server is available on the network to hand out an IP address to the server that you want to install.

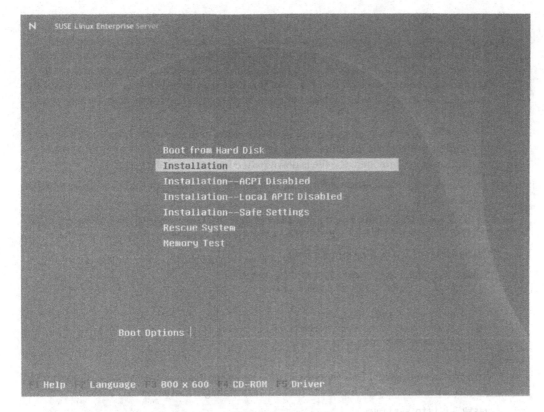

Figure 35-6. *On the boot menu offered by the installation media, press F4 to change the installation source.*

Configuring TFTP for PXE Boot

Most modern network cards have an option to boot from the network. This feature is also known as the PXE boot, where PXE stands for Preboot eXecution Environment. In this scenario, a boot image is delivered across the network. For this to work, you need to provide two elements: a DHCP server that is configured to hand out IP addresses to clients booting from the network board and a TFTP server that is configured to hand out the boot image. In the following steps, you will learn how to create this environment with SUSE Linux Enterprise Server 10. In the first steps, you will set up the DHCP server, and then you will configure the TFTP server to hand out the proper boot image. Make sure that the DHCP server packages are installed before continuing in this procedure.

Note In this section, I'll explain how to set up DHCP to support a PXE environment. Read Chapter 23 for more generic information about how to set up a DHCP server.

Here are the steps:

1. With your editor, open the configuration file /etc/dhcpd.conf, and add the three lines shown in Listing 35-1 to your existing configuration. Make sure you add them to the right position in the /etc/dhcpd.conf configuration file; you may, for example, add this to the network declaration on your DHCP server. Use the example code lines in Listing 35-1, but make sure to modify them to reflect your network settings. The listing uses the following options:

   - next-server: This is an important option; it refers to the server that the DHCP client should contact to upload the configuration file that is needed for PXE boot. If this option is not provided, the file is downloaded from the DHCP server.

   - server-name: This option informs the client about the name of the server from which it is booting.

   - filename: This option refers to the file that the TFTP server has to offer to the client.

Listing 35-1. *DHCP Options for PXE Boot*

```
subnet 192.168.1.0 netmask 255.255.255.0 {
    range 192.168.1.230 192.168.1.240;
    option routers 192.168.1.254;
    next-server 192.168.1.210;
    server-name "some.server.com";
    filename "pxelinux.0";
}
```

2. Now you need to install TFTP and the syslinux package. Execute the following command to do this (or use the Search feature in the software management program in YaST):

```
yast2 -i tftp syslinux
```

3. Next, you need to create the directory structure needed for the TFTP server:

```
mkdir -p /tftpboot/pxelinux.cfg
cp /usr/share/syslinux/pxelinux.0 /tftpboot/
```

4. Then you need to copy the Linux kernel and its initrd from the first installation CD to the data directory used by the TFTP server (which is /tftpboot). In the directory that is created when installing the NFS installation server, you will find these files in the directory boot/ *platform*/loader. (Make sure to replace *platform* with the hardware platform you are using.) The complete name of this directory can, for example, be /srv/nfs/sles10/boot/i386/ loader. With this directory as your present working directory, use the following command:

```
cp linux initrd /tftpboot
```

5. Next, create the file /tftpboot/pxelinux.cfg/default, and give it the following content. Modify the IP address, the name of the directory shared by your NFS server, and the name of the kernel module used for your network board to match your environment; also, make sure everything starting with append initrd is on one line only:

```
default SLES10
label SLES10
  kernel linux
  append initrd=initrd ramdisk_size=65536\
install=nfs://192.168.1.210/srv/nfs/sles10
```

6. Next, from YaST ➤ Network Services, activate the TFTP server (or edit /etc/xinet.d/tftp, and change the line disable = yes to disable = no). If you choose the latter method, don't forget to restart xinetd by using rcxinetd restart. If you are activating TFTP from YaST, next select Enable to enable the TFTP server, and refer to the location of the boot image directory (typically this is /tftpboot). Then click Finish to start the TFTP server.

7. Finally, make sure that the TFTP server is active. The netstat command is a valuable aid in determining that; execute netstat -patune | grep xinetd, and check that xinetd is listed as active and offers UDP port 69 to the network.

You now have the TFTP boot server available as well. Test how it works by performing a PXE boot on one of the servers; it should hand out the boot image to that server automatically and activate the installation program.

Installing a Server Automatically with AutoYaST

If you just need to install a few servers, it will be no problem to go through the installation procedure manually for each of the servers. However, if you need to configure many servers, it can be rather cumbersome to do so by hand, and the server configurations may not be consistent throughout the organization. In that case, AutoYaST can be a good option. With AutoYaST, it is possible to clone all the current settings of a system and write them to a configuration file. This configuration file can be called from the initial configuration screen, and all the settings from the file will be applied automatically. This way, it is possible to install a server without any interaction, as long as the AutoYaST configuration has been set up properly. To make it easier for you, an AutoYaST configuration file is created automatically at the end of each installation of a SUSE Linux Enterprise 10 server. It is also possible to create a tuned AutoYaST configuration file later on a running server. The next section discusses how.

Here are the steps to create an AutoYaST file:

1. From YaST, select Miscellaneous ➤ AutoInstallation. This starts the AutoYaST configuration tool. The tool provides an overview to all the settings in the installation that can be tuned from this interface. Before you make an AutoYaST reference file, however, you will not see anything. The easiest way to create a reference control file that can help you perform an installation automatically is by selecting Tools ➤ Create Reference Profile (see Figure 35-7). This opens a dialog box where you can specify all the settings you need. For example, in the System option, you can select Boot Loader and then click Configure to enter all the parameters you want to use for the boot loader. After repeating this for all required configuration parameters, your AutoYaST installation file is ready to use.

2. After installing a server, an AutoYaST reference profile is created automatically (if you didn't deselect the option, see Chapter 2 for more details). Its name is autoinst.xml, and it is saved to the /root directory. You can also select File ➤ Open from the AutoYaST configuration menu and then browse to this file to open it. The advantage is that in the reference file all the required settings already have a value, and you need to merely change the values to a value you want to use on all servers that will be using this reference file. In the next step, you can read how to create a flexible partitioning scheme in the AutoYaST partitioner utility.

Figure 35-7. *When creating an AutoYaST reference profile, you can select every single option you want to be installed.*

3. Select Hardware ➤ Partitioning, and then click Configure to configure the current partition-ing scheme on your server. This opens the partitioning plan that will be used or shows an empty partition overview if you aren't working from an existing autoyast.xml file. In this partitioning plan, you will see a partition that will be mounted as the root partition. Select this partition, and then click Edit.

4. You will see the selected partition configured with a fixed size. Since you might be installing on a server with a smaller hard drive, you need to modify this. Therefore, select the Fill to maximum allowable space option, and click OK (see Figure 35-8). You now have modified the partitioning scheme in your AutoYaST installation file to allow for more flexibility.

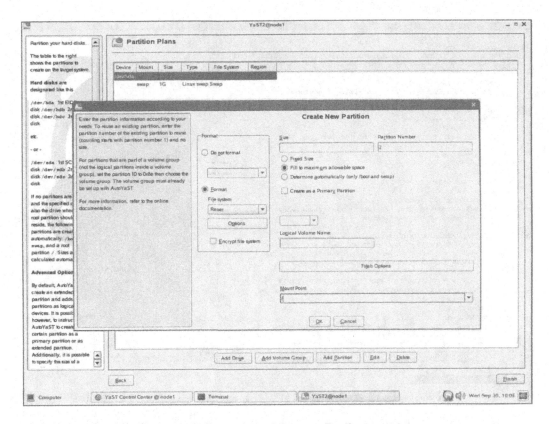

Figure 35-8. *The AutoYaST program allows you to define exactly what partitions you want to use.*

5. Now carefully look at all the other available options in the AutoYaST installation tree, and make modifications where needed. You might, for example, need to adjust the current software selection or the configuration of your network card. This is because you don't want all the servers installed based on this reference profile to be created with the same IP address as your reference server.

6. After making all the required changes, select File ➤ Save As, and save the new reference profile to a location where it can be accessed easily when installing the new server. If you are using your reference server as a network installation server, it makes sense to save the reference file to the shared network directory. Otherwise, you may have to add it to a removable medium such as a USB drive or floppy disk. The name of the file does not really matter. Since XML code is used in the file, as shown in Figure 35-9, it makes sense to give the file the .XML extension. Now the file will be generated and written to the selected directory.

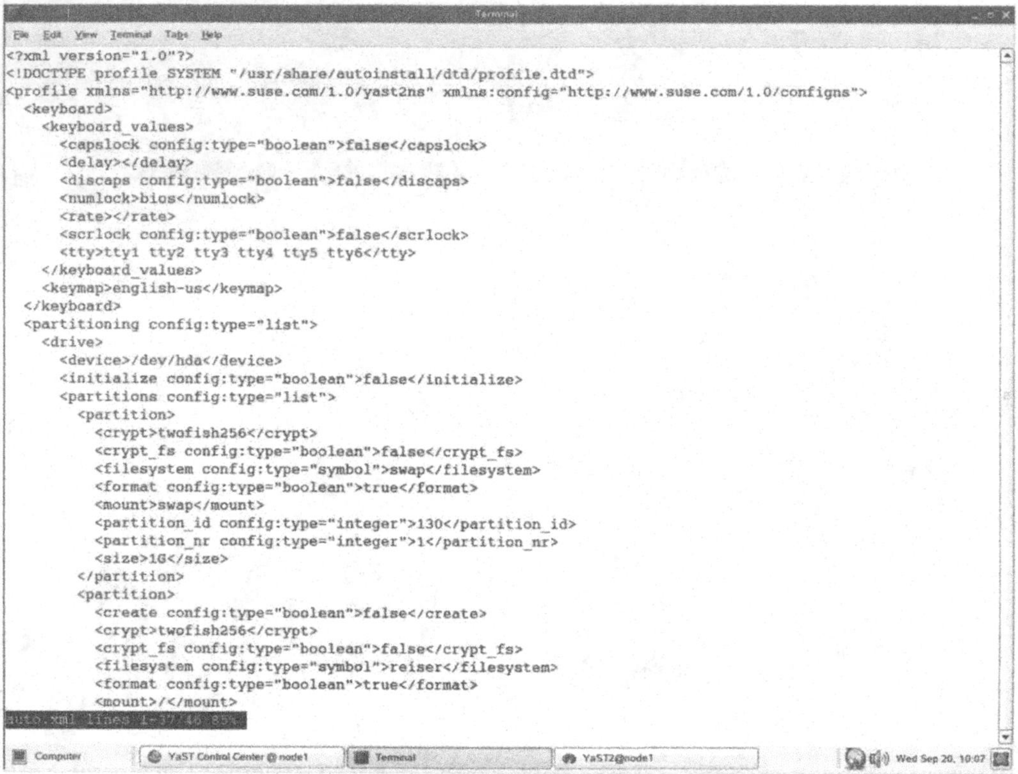

```
<?xml version="1.0"?>
<!DOCTYPE profile SYSTEM "/usr/share/autoinstall/dtd/profile.dtd">
<profile xmlns="http://www.suse.com/1.0/yast2ns" xmlns:config="http://www.suse.com/1.0/configns">
  <keyboard>
    <keyboard_values>
      <capslock config:type="boolean">false</capslock>
      <delay></delay>
      <discaps config:type="boolean">false</discaps>
      <numlock>bios</numlock>
      <rate></rate>
      <scrlock config:type="boolean">false</scrlock>
      <tty>tty1 tty2 tty3 tty4 tty5 tty6</tty>
    </keyboard_values>
    <keymap>english-us</keymap>
  </keyboard>
  <partitioning config:type="list">
    <drive>
      <device>/dev/hda</device>
      <initialize config:type="boolean">false</initialize>
      <partitions config:type="list">
        <partition>
          <crypt>twofish256</crypt>
          <crypt_fs config:type="boolean">false</crypt_fs>
          <filesystem config:type="symbol">swap</filesystem>
          <format config:type="boolean">true</format>
          <mount>swap</mount>
          <partition_id config:type="integer">130</partition_id>
          <partition_nr config:type="integer">1</partition_nr>
          <size>1G</size>
        </partition>
        <partition>
          <create config:type="boolean">false</create>
          <crypt>twofish256</crypt>
          <crypt_fs config:type="boolean">false</crypt_fs>
          <filesystem config:type="symbol">reiser</filesystem>
          <format config:type="boolean">true</format>
          <mount>/</mount>
auto.xml lines 1-37/46 85%
```

Figure 35-9. *In the autoinstallation file, XML code is used to define all required settings.*

You have just created an AutoYaST installation file. You have different options for using this file when installing a new server. First, you may refer to the file when installing from a CD. Alternatively, if you want to use the file when performing an installation using PXE boot and connecting to an NFS installation server, you need to make sure that you modify the default file on the PXE boot server properly. The next steps describe how to perform this task:

1. On the installation server, open the file `/tftpboot/pxelinux.cfg/default` with an editor.
2. Make sure that in the append line a reference to the XML file you have just created is added. This may result in a file with the following content:

```
default SLES10
label SLES10
    kernel linux
    append initrd=initrd ramdisk_size=65536\
install=nfs://192.168.1.210/srv/nfs/sles10\
autoyast=nfs://192.168.1.210/srv/nfs/sles10/autoyast.xml
```

Performing Remote Installations Using SSH or VNC

Up to now, I have discussed automatic installations. In some situations, however, you may prefer not to perform all the settings automatically but to instead have some control over the installation procedure. To do this, you may choose the option to perform an SSH or VNC installation. These installation types allow you to take over control to an installation session that is currently operational.

Performing a Remote Installation with SSH

Your first option to perform a remote installation is to use SSH to perform an installation. When booting an SSH installation server starting from CD1, you need to add some options to the boot options. As an alternative, you can also add these boot options to the defaults file on the TFTP PXE boot server, but to keep things simple, in the following steps I will discuss how to add the SSH installation options when starting to install from a CD:

1. Boot the server you want to use from its installation CD. From the boot menu on the CD, select Installation. Then on the Boot Options prompt, enter the following:

```
insmod=pcnet32 usessh=1 sshpassword=novell dhcp=1\
 install=nfs://192.168.1.210/srv/nfs/sles10
```

   These options will make sure that an SSH daemon is started on the server you want to install. The option insmod=pcnet32 loads the required driver for your network card before SSH is initialized. In this case, you really need this option, because otherwise the kernel boot option usessh=1 would be executed before the network card is loaded by the kernel. Make sure that the module you load with insmod matches the network board used on your server. Also, the installation will use an NFS server to provide access to the installation files automatically.

2. Now wait a few moments until the screen appears that the SSH daemon has started. On this screen (see Figure 35-10), you will see the instructions on how to connect to this server from another machine in your network.

3. You can now leave your installation server and move to the machine where you want to complete the installation. On this machine, type ssh -X root@yourserver, replacing yourserver with your server's hostname.

4. On the remark about the host key, click Yes. Next, type the SSH password you have used, and press Enter.

5. You will now enter a shell prompt on the remote machine. From this shell prompt, start YaST to complete the installation of the remote machine by typing yast. Next, complete the installation from the graphical YaST interface that is started on your workstation.

In the previous procedure, you have learned how to perform a remote installation using SSH. As an alternative, you can use a VNC connection. The procedure to do a VNC remote installation is pretty similar. First, on the Boot Options screen from the server you want to install, enter the following options:

```
insmod=pcnet32 vnc=1 vncpassword=novell dhcp=1\
 install=nfs://192.168.1.210/srv/nfs/exports
```

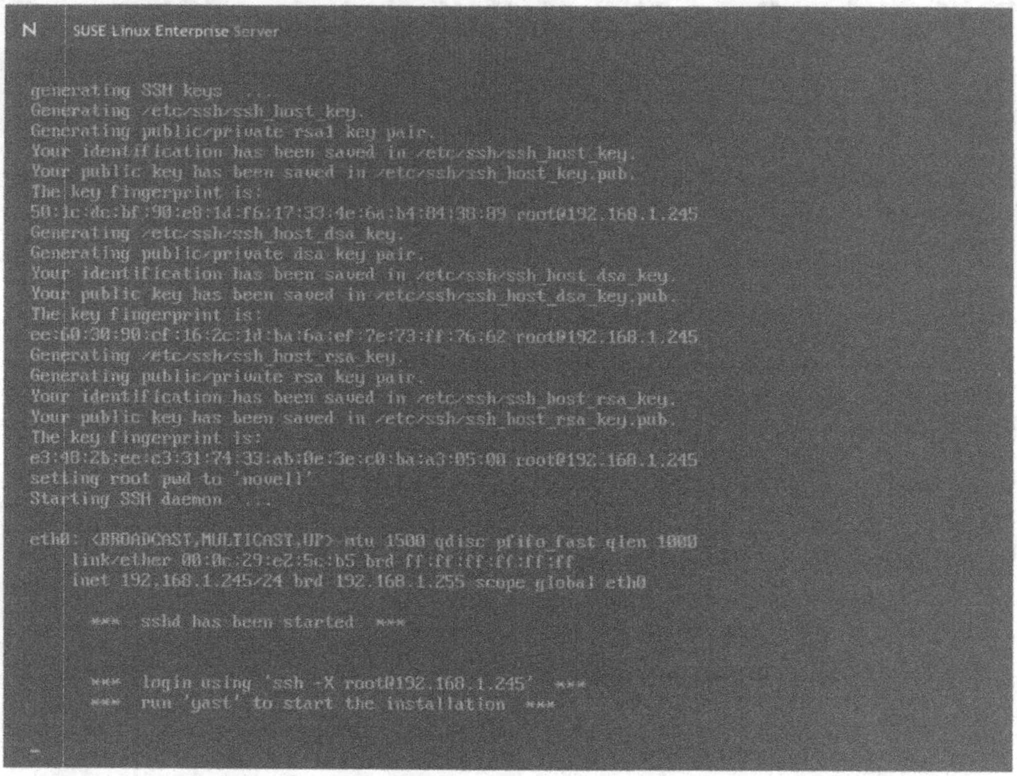

Figure 35-10. *When the SSH installation service has started, you are prompted on the server you are installing that you can make a connection from another machine.*

Then press Enter to start the installation. Wait a few minutes until you see a screen indicating that the VNC service has started. Note the IP address of this server so that you can continue the installation from the other server.

Next, from the other server, start a remote desktop connection by selecting Start ➤ System ➤ Remote Access ➤ Remote Desktop Connection. In the remote desktop text box, enter vnc:// 192.168.1.210:1. Alternatively, you can use any Java-enabled browser and enter the URL http:// 192.168.1.210:5801. This will give you a dialog box that asks how you want to access the remote server. Complete all required data. This connects you to the installation server so that you can complete the installation.

Combining SSH with VNC

In the previous section, you learned how to install over SSH or VNC. It is also possible to combine the two of them. In this section, you will learn how to use a VNC session over SSH. The advantage? By default, VNC does not use any encryption. By combining VNC technology with SSH, you can perform a safe remote installation over VNC. Then use VNC over SSH, and apply the following steps:

1. Boot the machine you want to install from its installation CD.

2. On the boot prompt of the machine you want to install, enter the following with all the other boot parameters you need:

   ```
   usessh=1 sshpassword=novell vnc=1 vncpassword=novell
   ```

3. On the workstation where you want to complete the installation, make an SSH connection. If it is a Linux workstation, use the following command. This command will redirect port 5901 to port 5901 on your local machine:

   ```
   ssh -X root@192.168.1.219 -L 5901:192.168.1.210:5901
   ```

4. Open a Java-enabled browser on your workstation, and enter the URL vnc://localhost:1. This will connect you to the VNC session that is available on your local server.

You now have access to the graphical installation program exactly as it runs on your server. In fact, VNC is just duplicating this program to your workstation. From there, complete the installation.

Summary

In this final chapter, you learned all about remote installation. You read about how to create a network installation server, as well as how to perform a boot from this server after it has been configured as a PXE boot server with DHCP and TFTP. Finally, you read how to control an installation remotely via SSH and VNC. You know have acquired the most important skills to manage a SUSE Linux Enterprise Server. Have a lot of fun!

Index

You Need the Companion eBook

Your purchase of this book entitles you to buy the companion PDF-version eBook for only $10. Take the weightless companion with you anywhere.

We believe this Apress title will prove so indispensable that you'll want to carry it with you everywhere, which is why we are offering the companion eBook (in PDF format) for $10 to customers who purchase this book now. Convenient and fully searchable, the PDF version of any content-rich, page-heavy Apress book makes a valuable addition to your programming library. You can easily find and copy code—or perform examples by quickly toggling between instructions and the application. Even simultaneously tackling a donut, diet soda, and complex code becomes simplified with hands-free eBooks!

Once you purchase your book, getting the $10 companion eBook is simple:

❶ Visit **www.apress.com/promo/tendollars/**.

❷ Complete a basic registration form to receive a randomly generated question about this title.

❸ Answer the question correctly in 60 seconds, and you will receive a promotional code to redeem for the $10.00 eBook.

2560 Ninth Street • Suite 219 • Berkeley, CA 94710

eBookshop

ASP **Today**

A**p**ress®
THE EXPERT'S VOICE™

Offer valid through 6/07.